THE PICTURE OF DORIAN GRAY

AUTHORITATIVE TEXTS
BACKGROUNDS
REVIEWS AND REACTIONS
CRITICISM

A NORTON CRITICAL EDITION

Oscar Wilde

THE PICTURE OF DORIAN GRAY

AUTHORITATIVE TEXTS
BACKGROUNDS
REVIEWS AND REACTIONS
CRITICISM

Edited by

DONALD L. LAWLER

EAST CAROLINA UNIVERSITY

California Baptist University
Annie Gabriel Library
8432 Magnolia Avenue
Riverside, CA 92504

W · W · NORTON & COMPANY · *New York* · *London*

This edition is dedicated to the memory of my mother and father: Anne Baumann Lawler and Lester Vincent Lawler.

FACSIMILE CREDITS
Page 5: PML 23513, title page The Pierpont Morgan Library
Page 171: PML 35789, title page The Pierpont Morgan Library

Printed in the United States of America.

First Edition

Library of Congress Cataloging-in-Publication Data

Wilde, Oscar, 1854–1900.
   The picture of Dorian Gray.
   (Norton critical edition)
   Bibliography: p. 461
   1. Wilde, Oscar, 1854–1900.   Picture of Dorian Gray.
I. Lawler, Donald L. II. Title.
PR5819.A1   1987   823'.8   86-12330

ISBN 0-393-95568-0

W. W. Norton & Company, Inc., 500 Fifth Avenue, New York, N. Y. 10110
W. W. Norton & Company Ltd., 37 Great Russell Street, London WC1B 3NU

4 5 6 7 8 9 0

Contents

Preface

In writing *The Picture of Dorian Gray*, his only novel, Oscar Wilde produced a work whose own history was to become tangled in the life of the author and remain for succeeding generations, as it was for his contemporaries, a sign of contradiction. This edition with its critical backgrounds attempts to represent the literary and cultural life of a work that in its own time was the subject of perhaps the most celebrated debate over art and morality and then subsequently went on to figure prominently in two of the three trials that finally led Oscar Wilde to prison, bankruptcy, disgrace, and a kind of secular martyrdom.

The history of *Dorian Gray* is woven from diverse strands of biography, popular and press reaction, literary criticism, and courtroom trial. It begins in 1883, the year of Oscar Wilde's first visit to the United States, for a lecture tour sponsored by the D'Oyly Carte opera company as a publicity stunt to promote the tour of Gilbert and Sullivan's *Patience*. The operetta burlesqued what established opinion regarded as the foolish affectations of the aesthetes. Although it is probable that Gilbert and Sullivan had William Morris, Dante Gabriel Rossetti, and Algernon C. Swinburne in mind when the libretto was written, by the time it was produced, Oscar Wilde's brand of dandyism had preempted the field. First the lily (in honor of Lillie Langtry), then the sunflower (by virtue of its gigantic uselessness) became Wilde's chosen weapons to do battle with British philistia. *Punch* and other periodicals were eager to cooperate in making a young Oscar Wilde the living symbol of youthful insolence and folly. And so it came to pass that he was taken for the aesthetic poet Bunthorne (has anyone noticed the scatology of that name?) when *Patience* first appeared.

Wilde's lecture tour proved an unexpected success, and he remained in the United States and Canada for a year. As a consequence of Wilde's instinct for the modern, what began as a Victorian freak show became the first essay of camp culture. While in Philadelphia, he met John Marshall Stoddart, then a private publisher. Seven years later, Stoddart visited England as an agent for *Lippincott's Monthly Magazine* and arranged for Wilde and Arthur Conan Doyle each to contribute a short novel. Doyle produced *The Sign of Four*, the second Sherlock Holmes novel. Wilde offered "The Fisherman and His Soul," a fairy tale about a fisherman who casts away his human soul in order to marry a mermaid but who is tricked out of immortal happiness by his vengeful soul. Stoddart rejected the tale as both too short and unsuited to an adult audience. Wilde was anxious not to let the opportunity pass, and he produced *Dorian Gray* in a few months' time, circumstances that contributed to the oft-repeated legend that the author was forced to write hastily to satisfy a venal publisher. Wilde was paid £200 for the serial rights.

The typescript that arrived at Stoddart's Philadelphia *Lippincott's* office had to be edited to conform to American spelling and punctuation. The first printed version of the novel ran over fifty thousand words and appeared in *Lippincott's Monthly Magazine* for July 1890 (vol. 46, no. 271). Stoddart had gauged his American audience well. The edition sold out, and *Dorian Gray* was well received critically as a modern morality tale. Stoddart must have been stunned by its reception in England, however. This version of *Dorian Gray* produced such critical storms in the London press for months after its appearance that Ward, Lock and Company, who produced the British edition, felt obliged to withdraw the remaining copies from the newsstands. Curiously, although there were favorable reviews in the Christian press and from clergymen who stressed the strong moral lesson of Dorian Gray's rise and fall, Wilde was accused in the popular press of having written a novel of such vicious depravity that the public prosecutor should be alerted to suppress it!

Following the debate over art and morality in the press, Wilde then set to work revising his novel with the intention of publishing a longer version as a separate volume. Although he removed further vestiges of the homoerotic innuendo found in the manuscripts, he also did what he could to suppress the "too obvious" moral, as he called it. He did so in part by adding six new chapters, further developing the social criticism, introducing the revenge motif of James Vane, and placing greater emphasis upon Dorian's increasingly gothic consciousness. The formula worked so well that the revised version did not produce anything like the sensation of the serial text, although it did receive a far greater measure of critical acclaim. As a consequence, the novel enjoyed a steady but not spectacular sale, somewhat to Wilde's chagrin. He had, after all, published a series of aphorisms earlier in the year in Frank Harris's *Fortnightly Review* as his Preface to *Dorian Gray*. Wilde obviously expected another public debate on the art and morality issue, and he was determined to launch an attack upon his critics and to fortify his positions in advance of publication.

However, the battle was not rejoined at this time, and Wilde turned his attention from criticism and fiction to drama, where he was to score his greatest success. One can see in Lord Henry's table talk in the new chapter 3 (1891) and in the Selby Royal scenes (chapter 17, added in 1891) Wilde's astonishing new mastery of melodramatic and comic pacing. Wilde simply dominated the London stage with three hit plays running in London theaters early in 1895, including the incomparable *Importance of Being Earnest*.

It was at the point of greatest success that ruin overtook him in the form of an ill-advised suit for libel brought against the marquess of Queensberry. In the course of Queensberry's justifying his having accused Wilde of "posing as a somdomite" [sic] (the accusation was made on the back of a card delivered to Wilde's club), the *Lippincott's* version of *Dorian Gray* was used as evidence of Wilde's corrupting influence on the nation's youth and on Queensberry's son in particular. Wilde won the battle of the book in the popular mind but lost the war in the court-room when he was forced to withdraw in hopes of averting criminal prosecution by the Crown. Court costs ruined Wilde, leading to bank-ruptcy, and after two subsequent trials, he was sentenced to two years in prison at hard labor and in virtual solitary confinement.

He was never to see any of his family again. His mother died during the first year of confinement. His wife, Constance, changed her name and that of the two sons to Holland, a name the family has retained ever since. Constance died shortly after his release from prison in 1897, and his brother Willie died the year before Oscar. Wilde was not permitted to visit his sons. Following his release from prison, Wilde lived and traveled restlessly, mostly in France and Italy, until his death in Paris on November 30, 1900, from meningitis, the result of an ear infection he developed after a fall in prison.

This edition could not have been completed without the cooperation and generous assistance of the following libraries and their staffs: the Berg Collection of the New York City Public Library, the William Andrews Clark Memorial Library, the J. Pierpont Morgan Library, and the libraries of Duke University, the University of North Carolina at Chapel Hill, the University of South Carolina, and East Carolina University.

I am pleased also to acknowledge with gratitude support from both the East Carolina University Research Council, which gave me grant aid, and my English Department, which gave me time to work on this project.

My wife, Therese, and our children have helped humor and support me through the long process of bringing this edition before a readership. Personal thanks are extended to Cecil Y. Lang and Violette Lang of the University of Virginia for needed help and encouragement along the way. Sincere thanks also go to Mary Hyde and Four Oaks Library, Somerville, New Jersey; to H. Montgomery Hyde for expert advice; and to Merlin Holland for his generous cooperation. Belated thanks to Arthur Norman, who introduced me to Wilde studies, and to Daniel Hall, former research assistant.

A Note on the Texts

This edition of *The Picture of Dorian Gray* reprints together for the first time the texts of the original, 1890 *Lippincott's* version of the novel and the revised, expanded version published by Ward, Lock and Company in 1891. These were the only two versions prepared for and seen through publication by the author.[1]

The Preface made its debut in the March 1891 edition of Frank Harris's *Fortnightly Review* (ns 49 [1891] 291: 480–81) as "A Preface to 'Dorian Gray,'" approximately one month before the printing of the revised version of the novel. The preface consisted of twenty-three aphorisms written by Wilde in response to the criticisms made of the *Lippincott's Dorian Gray* (see Reviews and Reactions, pp. 329–33). When the revised version was printed, Wilde had added a new aphorism to the Preface ("No artist is ever morbid. The artist can express everything"). The original ninth aphorism, beginning "The nineteenth century dislike of Realism . . ." was divided to make the final total of twenty-five aphorisms in the revised edition of *Dorian Gray*, published by Ward, Lock and Company in April 1891.

I have elected to print the revised version of 1891 ahead of the *Lippincott's* text of 1890. There are several reasons for doing so: the first is to emphasize the primacy of the revised edition of the novel as the more complete and more mature expression of the author's intentions for his novel. Because the revised version represents Wilde's final intentions, it has become the primary reading text, and I have appended to it the customary historical and biographical annotations, as well as references to significant differences between the revised and original versions of the novel.

The *Lippincott's* version (1890) is used as the reference for nearly all the textual notes and annotations that record important revisions, changes, and variants from the manuscript and typescript against this first printed

1. The first printed version of the novel ran over fifty thousand words and appeared in *Lippincott's Monthly Magazine* for July 1890 (46 [1890] 271: 3–100). The revised version was printed in crown octavo by Ward, Lock and Company in April 1891 and sold for six shillings. This was the same company that bound the British edition of *Lippincott's* magazine. A new printing was called for in October 1895, by which time the publisher had become Ward, Lock and Bowden. The novel was not reprinted again until 1901, the year following Wilde's death, by Charles Carrington, a slightly disreputable English publisher of pornographic literature in Paris, who had acquired the rights following Wilde's bankruptcy in expectation that profit was to be made from the scandal surrounding the author and his novel, which figured prominently in Wilde's famous trials in 1895. Robert Ross, as executor of the Wilde estate, eventually reacquired the rights to the novel. Since that time, the novel has never been out of print.

The Clark TS shows none of the revisions Wilde made in the text of the *Lippincott's* version, suggesting that he did his work for the revised edition on tearsheets. If this is so, none has turned up. However, some of the MSS of the six added chapters have. Chapter 3 (1891), in twenty-three leaves, is in the Clark Memorial Library. A single leaf from chapter 5 (1891) was discovered bound into a copy of the *Lippincott's* issue, also in the Clark Library. Chapter 15 (1891), in seventeen pages, is in the Berg Collection of the New York Public Library. The eighteen-page MS for chapter 16, advertised in Sotheby's sale catalog for July 27, 1911, is in a private collection.

version of the novel. I have not attempted to record all the minor acci-
dentals and variants that inevitably accumulated during the process of
proofing, revising, and rewriting as Wilde moved from manuscript to
printed text. The standard I have applied for including changes was
whether such variants revealed something potentially valuable either about
Wilde's performance as a writer or about the production process of the
novel.

It would be well beyond the scope of this edition to record all the
variants and revisions that occurred in the transmission of this text from
manuscript (hereafter MS) through typescript (hereafter TS) and thereafter into the first and then revised printed versions. However, since the
texts are reprinted together for the first time, the curious reader has the
opportunity of comparing at least the two published versions at leisure.
In the annotations to the revised (1891) version, I have highlighted
important variants in the two printed versions, while silently passing over
most of the minor stylistic changes introduced by Wilde into his final
revision. I have recorded, however, a few representative examples of
these cosmetic changes to make a point: Wilde proofed and revised with
far more care than critics in the past have acknowledged. The author's
attention to small details belies that impudent pose of careless genius
with which Wilde incited his self-righteous critics.

The two principal manuscripts that support the annotations to the
Lippincott's text have been preserved. The first is the holograph, written
by Wilde in ink on 264 folio sheets of blue lined paper, now in the
manuscript collection of the Morgan Library in New York.[2] Wilde made
numerous corrections in the holograph and sent it to Miss Dickens's
Type Writer Office, one of London's commercial agencies. The TS was
again revised by Wilde with many additions, deletions, and alterations
in his hand. This TS, consisting of 231 leaves of text, now in the collection of the William Andrews Clark Memorial Library, Los Angeles, was
used as the printer's copy text by *Lippincott's*. John Marshall Stoddart,
the editor, then made his own series of emendations and deletions, which
have become the subject of debate among textual scholars, raising the
obvious question of whether an editor should permit Stoddart's changes
to stand.[3] Indeed, it has been argued that the only version of the text
with unadulterated authorial sanction is the TS version sent to Stod-

---

2. The Morgan holograph is actually a copy of a
still earlier proto-manuscript, probably discarded
by the author. We may infer from the evidence of
the Morgan holograph that the proto-manuscript
was a working version of the entire story and was
probably heavily corrected and reworked by the
author. A complete discussion is given in my "Oscar
Wilde's First Manuscript of *The Picture of Dorian
Gray*," in *Studies in Bibliography* 25 (1972): 125–
35.

3. A balanced summary of the dispute may be read
in John Espey's "Resources for Wilde Studies at

the Clark Library," *Oscar Wilde, Two Approaches:
Papers Read at a Clark Library Seminar, April 17,
1976*, ed. Richard Ellmann and John Espey (Los
Angeles: William Andrews Clark Memorial Library,
1977) 27–30. Another approach to the theoretical
issues involved in editing nineteenth-century texts
is developed by Jerome J. McGann in *A Critique
of Modern Textual Criticism* (Chicago: U of Chicago P, 1983), although without reference to Wilde.
My own views are closer to McGann's, although
they antedate his *Critique* by seven years.

dart.[4] Still others may argue that only the holograph expresses the original intention of the author.

As this editor sees it, the question is which version or versions of the text of *Dorian Gray* are to be privileged. Should it be the earliest version, the most complete unadulterated version, one or both of the two printed versions, or possibly a composit or constructed text? I have opted for reprinting the two versions that were originally published, augmented by an array of notes and cross-references designed to reveal the hidden foundations of the two texts in the MSS. To do more would be to create texts of the novel that never appeared in print, that never inspired critical and scholarly response, and that had no influence on subsequent literary and cultural history. Given the importance of *Dorian Gray* for the literary and cultural history of the times, a critically generated text seems historically irrelevant. In the case of *Dorian Gray*, the traditional ideal of a copy text violates the developmental history of the work. It makes better sense to think of a "final intention" for *Dorian Gray* as the last stage of an evolved intention, one that required at least three manuscript versions and two printed versions to be realized. Moreover, along the way, that development involved solicited advice from consulted readers like Walter Pater, the editorial intervention of J. Marshall Stoddart (for *Lippincott's*) and Koulson Kernahan (for Ward, Lock and Company), as well as reviewers and critics both hostile and approving.

Another reason for retaining the printed texts in their original condition depends on the inference that Wilde accepted and even relied upon the editorial and review process to produce the best version of his work. After all, Wilde gave his tacit approval to most, although not all, of Stoddart's alterations by allowing them to stand when he prepared the enlarged, revised version of the novel for publication in 1891. Some of Stoddart's alterations he removed, and others he changed. Wilde exercised the same options in reacting to Kernahan's alterations to his draft of the revised version. In addition, an editor must also decide whether one version of the novel is better for his readers to know than another. The printed versions of *Dorian Gray* are clearly superior as fiction in almost every way to the MSS versions. The revised version of 1891 is more subtle, complex, and artistic, while the *Lippincott's* version has its own character and integrity, as readers will be happy to discover. The *Lippincott's* version is also the text that precipitated one of the most famous public debates in literary history over art and morality.

Let us keep in mind, then, that the last phase of the revision process before the publication of each version involved a collaboration of the author with his editors. This is a common enough situation in the production of modern texts and creates new kinds of problems for analytic bibliography to solve. It appears that an editorial answer to the issues raised in the transmission of the text of *Dorian Gray* from MS to the

4. See Espey's essay (35) for this argument.

final, revised printed version depends on issues that are more philosophical than scholarly. If the literary text is viewed from the romantic perspective as practically sacred and absolute, then editors will find the editorial intrusions of Stoddart and Kernahan inadmissible. If, however, an editor regards the text of *Dorian Gray* as contingent, having its extensions into the history of ideas and culture as well as into autobiography and reader performance, then the privileged aspects of the text become different. The choices are difficult and uncertain either way, and perhaps the best a modern editor can expect is to present a text that is authoritative within the defined limits of its methodology and the tolerance of publishers.

In one sense, of course, this Norton Critical Edition presents texts that have never been brought together before in a relationary context that is both historical and constructed. History gives us an advantage that we would be unwise to forego. We can see what no contemporary except the author could have seen—namely, how the various stages in the composition of a work evolve their meanings through the published versions. As a master of improvisation, perhaps Wilde formed a more lively appreciation of the process than most authors, although he sometimes complained when he thought an editor had gone too far and resisted those changes he did not like. We may view in a privileged perspective, in other words, the evolution of authorial intention and performance as they shaped the text of a classic story and as they were, in turn, responsive to friendly and hostile criticism at various stages of composition.

Throughout this Norton Critical Edition, all textual information given in parentheses refers you to the Selected Bibliography at the back of the volume.

Somehow the grace, the bloom of things has flown,
    And of all men we are most wretched who
Must live each other's lives and not our own
    For very pity's sake and then undo
All that we lived for—it was otherwise
When the soul and body seemed to blend in mystic symphonies.
                              —Oscar Wilde, "Humanitad"

I have finished the book, one of the few which can move one. Its deep
fantasy and very strange atmosphere took me by storm. To make it so
poignant and human with such astonishing intellectual refinement, and at
the same time to keep the perverse beauty is a miracle that you have
worked through the use of all the arts of the writer. . . . This disturbing,
full-length portrait of Dorian Gray will haunt me, as writing, having become
the book itself.
                    —Stéphane Mallarmé in a letter to Wilde

. . . nothing he ever wrote had strength to endure.
              —*Pall Mall Gazette* obituary notice, 1 December 1900

The Texts of
THE PICTURE OF
DORIAN GRAY

The Preface †

The artist is the creator of beautiful things.

To reveal art and conceal the artist is art's aim.

The critic is he who can translate into another manner or a new material his impression of beautiful things.

The highest as the lowest form of criticism is a mode of autobiography.

Those who find ugly meanings in beautiful things are corrupt without being charming. This is a fault.

Those who find beautiful meanings in beautiful things are the cultivated. For these there is hope.

They are the elect to whom beautiful things mean only Beauty.

There is no such thing as a moral or an immoral book. Books are well written, or badly written. That is all.

The nineteenth century dislike of Realism is the rage of Caliban seeing his own face in a glass.

The nineteenth century dislike of Romanticism is the rage of Caliban not seeing his own face in a glass.

The moral life of man forms part of the subject-matter of the artist, but the morality of art consists in the perfect use of an imperfect medium.

No artist desires to prove anything. Even things that are true can be proved.

No artist has ethical sympathies. An ethical sympathy in an artist is an unpardonable mannerism of style.

No artist is ever morbid. The artist can express everything.

Thought and language are to the artist instruments of an art.

Vice and virtue are to the artist materials for an art.

From the point of view of form, the type of all the arts is the art of the musician. From the point of view of feeling, the actor's craft is the type.

All art is at once surface and symbol.

Those who go beneath the surface do so at their peril.

Those who read the symbol do so at their peril.

It is the spectator, and not life, that art really mirrors.

---

† Wilde's preface to *Dorian Gray* appeared in Frank Harris's *Fortnightly Review* several months before the second edition of the novel. It seems to have three aims. The first is to take weapons out of the hands of the critics who had attacked the *Lippincott's* edition of *Dorian Gray* by anticipating some of the charges likely to be made against it. The second intent is to respond to some of the criticism made of the magazine edition. In so doing, Wilde was to repeat rather sententiously the major points of his aesthetic creed at the time (and to anticipate the main line of his defense of *Dorian Gray* at the trials). The third intention is expressed in the tone and manner of the epigrams, which anticipate those Wilde published in 1894 under the title "Phrases and Philosophies for the Use of the Young" in *The Chameleon*, an Oxford undergraduate journal. The paradoxes are not so plentiful in the former as in the latter, and the manner is less insolent, but the intent is to be provocative. It was this adopted manner that revealed Wilde could be every bit as pompous as those he ridiculed and that earned him the title "sovereign of insufferables" from Ambrose Bierce.

Diversity of opinion about a work of art shows that the work is new, complex, and vital.

When critics disagree the artist is in accord with himself.

We can forgive a man for making a useful thing as long as he does not admire it. The only excuse for making a useless thing is that one admires it intensely.

All art is quite useless.

OSCAR WILDE.

THE PICTVRE OF DORIAN. GRAY.

BY

OSCAR WILDE

WARD LOCK & AND & CO
LONDON & NEW YORK
& MELBOVRNE.

1891

The Picture of Dorian Gray (1891)

Chapter I.

The studio[1] was filled with the rich odour of roses, and when the light summer wind stirred amidst the trees of the garden there came through the open door the heavy scent of the lilac, or the more delicate perfume of the pink-flowering thorn.

From the corner of the divan of Persian saddlebags on which he was lying, smoking, as was his custom, innumerable cigarettes, Lord Henry Wotton could just catch the gleam of the honey-sweet and honey-coloured blossoms of a laburnum,[2] whose tremulous branches seemed hardly able to bear the burden of a beauty so flame-like as theirs; and now and then the fantastic shadows of birds in flight flitted across the long tussore-silk[3] curtains that were stretched in front of the huge window, producing a kind of momentary Japanese effect, and making him think of those pallid jade-faced painters of Tokio[4] who, through the medium of an art that is necessarily immobile, seek to convey the sense of swiftness and motion. The sullen murmur of the bees shouldering their way through the long unmown grass, or circling with monotonous insistence round the dusty gilt horns of the straggling woodbine, seemed to make the stillness more oppressive. The dim roar of London was like the bourdon[5] note of a distant organ.

In the centre of the room, clamped to an upright easel, stood the full-length portrait of a young man of extraordinary personal beauty, and in front of it, some little distance away, was sitting the artist himself, Basil Hallward, whose sudden disappearance some years ago caused, at the time, such public excitement, and gave rise to so many strange conjectures.

1. The exotic decor is a reproduction of Charles Ricketts's studio in London, where Wilde was a frequent visitor. Ricketts (1866–1931) may have been the original for Basil Hallward. He designed the title page and binding for *Dorian Gray* and for many other Wilde volumes.
2. A small tree or shrub bearing clusters of yellow flowers.
3. A coarse brown silk from India.
4. In Wilde's "Decay of Lying," Vivian's prescription for anyone desiring a true Japanese effect is not to go to Tokyo but to "stay at home and steep yourself in the work of certain Japanese artists, and then when you have absorbed the spirit of their style, and caught their imaginative manner of vision, you will go some afternoon and sit in the park . . . and if you cannot see an absolutely Japanese effect there, you will not see it anywhere."
5. A low, reverberating sound, as the bass stop of an organ.

As the painter looked at the gracious and comely form he had so skilfully mirrored in his art, a smile of pleasure passed across his face, and seemed about to linger there. But he suddenly started up, and, closing his eyes, placed his fingers upon the lids, as though he sought to imprison within his brain some curious dream from which he feared he might awake.

"It is your best work, Basil, the best thing you have ever done," said Lord Henry, languidly. "You must certainly send it next year to the Grosvenor.[6] The Academy[7] is too large and too vulgar. Whenever I have gone there, there have been either so many people that I have not been able to see the pictures, which was dreadful, or so many pictures that I have not been able to see the people, which was worse. The Grosvenor is really the only place."

"I don't think I shall send it anywhere," he answered, tossing his head back in that odd way that used to make his friends laugh at him at Oxford. "No: I won't send it anywhere."

Lord Henry elevated his eyebrows, and looked at him in amazement through the thin blue wreaths of smoke that curled up in such fanciful whorls from his heavy opium-tainted cigarette.[8] "Not send it anywhere? My dear fellow, why? Have you any reason? What odd chaps you painters are! You do anything in the world to gain a reputation. As soon as you have one, you seem to want to throw it away. It is silly of you, for there is only one thing in the world worse than being talked about, and that is not being talked about.[9] A portrait like this would set you far above all the young men in England, and make the old men quite jealous, if old men are ever capable of any emotion."[1]

"I know you will laugh at me," he replied, "but I really can't exhibit it. I have put too much of myself into it."

Lord Henry stretched himself out on the divan and laughed.

"Yes, I knew you would; but it is quite true, all the same."

"Too much of yourself in it! Upon my word, Basil, I didn't know you were so vain; and I really can't see any resemblance between you, with

---

6. A Bond Street art gallery established by the painter Sir Coutts Lindsay in May 1877 as an alternative to the galleries of the Royal Academy. It came to be known as the "Temple of the Aesthetic" and was parodied by Gilbert and Sullivan in *Patience* as the "greenery-yallery, Grosvenor Gallery" because of its dominant color keys. Wilde had done reviews of exhibits there in the late 1870's and early 1880's and shared Lord Henry's opinion of its worth.

7. The Royal Academy of Arts (an honorary society of painters, architects, and sculptors founded in 1768) represented the art establishment of the day.

8. Wilde gave many of his own habits and much of his own background to the three main characters, each of whom represents, alternately, idealized, true-to-life, and extreme views of their creator. (see p. 431–57). Thus, Wilde attended Oxford as

did Basil and smoked Egyptian, opium-tainted cigarettes as did Henry. However, there is little doubt that Wilde drew his characters from others as well. Basil combines qualities of Ricketts and his friend Charles H. Shannon (1863–1937), who shared lodgings with him in Chelsea. Shannon designed the bindings for Wilde's plays. He and Ricketts edited the *Dial* from 1889–97. Lord Henry may have a touch of Whistler in him but much of Wilde, but critical consensus makes Lord Ronald Sutherland-Gower (1845–1916) the leading candidate as the inspiration for Lord Henry. Gower knew Wilde at Oxford, and the two were intimates in the 1870's and 1880's.

9. A favorite, oft-repeated epigram of Wilde.

1. Wilde's insistence on the superiority of youth went against the grain of Victorian authoritarianism. It is a motif in the novel, and it anticipates the twentieth-century cult of youth worship.

your rugged strong face and your   l-black hair, and this young Adonis,[2] who looks as if he was made out ⸤ ivory and rose-leaves. Why, my dear Basil, he is a Narcissus,[3] and you—well, of course you have an intellectual expression, and all that. But beauty, real beauty, ends where an intellectual expression begins. Intellect is in itself a mode of exaggeration, and destroys the harmony of any face. The moment one sits down to think, one becomes all nose, or all forehead, or something horrid. Look at the successful men in any of the learned professions. How perfectly hideous they are! Except, of course, in the Church. But then in the Church they don't think. A bishop keeps on saying at the age of eighty what he was told to say when he was a boy of eighteen, and as a natural consequence he always looks absolutely delightful. Your mysterious young friend, whose name you have never told me, but whose picture really fascinates me, never thinks. I feel quite sure of that. He is some brainless, beautiful creature, who should be always here in winter when we have no flowers to look at, and always here in summer when we want something to chill our intelligence. Don't flatter yourself, Basil: you are not in the least like him."

"You don't understand me, Harry," answered the artist. "Of course I am not like him. I know that perfectly well. Indeed, I should be sorry to look like him. You shrug your shoulders? I am telling you the truth. There is a fatality about all physical and intellectual distinction, the sort of fatality that seems to dog through history the faltering steps of kings. It is better not to be different from one's fellows. The ugly and the stupid have the best of it in this world. They can sit at their ease and gape at the play. If they know nothing of victory, they are at least spared the knowledge of defeat. They live as we all should live, undisturbed, indifferent, and without disquiet. They neither bring ruin upon others, nor ever receive it from alien hands. Your rank and wealth, Harry; my brains, such as they are—my art, whatever it may be worth; Dorian Gray's good looks—we shall all suffer for what the gods have given us, suffer terribly."

"Dorian Gray? Is that his name?" asked Lord Henry, walking across the studio towards Basil Hallward.

"Yes, that is his name. I didn't intend to tell it to you."

"But why not?"

"Oh, I can't explain. When I like people immensely I never tell their names to any one. It is like surrendering a part of them. I have grown to love secrecy. It seems to be the one thing that can make modern life mysterious or marvellous to us. The commonest thing is delightful if one only hides it. When I leave town now I never tell my people where I am going. If I did, I would lose all my pleasure. It is a silly habit, I

2. In Greek mythology, a youth of extraordinary good looks, beloved of Aphrodite, killed by a wild boar.
3. In mythology, the youth who spurned the love of the nymph Echo, causing her death. His punishment was to fall in love with his own reflected image and pine away till death, at which moment he was transformed into the flower.

dare say, but somehow it seems to bring a great deal of romance into one's life. I suppose you think me awfully foolish about it?"

"Not at all," answered Lord Henry, "not at all, my dear Basil. You seem to forget that I am married, and the one charm of marriage is that it makes a life of deception absolutely necessary for both parties. I never know where my wife is, and my wife never knows what I am doing. When we meet—we do meet occasionally, when we dine out together, or go down to the Duke's—we tell each other the most absurd stories with the most serious faces. My wife is very good at it—much better, in fact, than I am. She never gets confused over her dates, and I always do. But when she does find me out, she makes no row at all. I sometimes wish she would; but she merely laughs at me."

"I hate the way you talk about your married life, Harry," said Basil Hallward, strolling towards the door that led into the garden. "I believe that you are really a very good husband, but that you are thoroughly ashamed of your own virtues. You are an extraordinary fellow. You never say a moral thing, and you never do a wrong thing.[4] Your cynicism is simply a pose."

"Being natural is simply a pose, and the most irritating pose I know," cried Lord Henry, laughing; and the two young men went out into the garden together, and ensconced themselves on a long bamboo seat that stood in the shade of a tall laurel bush. The sunlight slipped over the polished leaves. In the grass, white daisies were tremulous.

After a pause, Lord Henry pulled out his watch. "I am afraid I must be going, Basil," he murmured, "and before I go, I insist on your answering a question I put to you some time ago."

"What is that?" said the painter, keeping his eyes fixed on the ground.

"You know quite well."

"I do not, Harry."

"Well, I will tell you what it is. I want you to explain to me why you won't exhibit Dorian Gray's picture. I want the real reason."

"I told you the real reason."

"No, you did not. You said it was because there was too much of yourself in it. Now, that is childish."

"Harry," said Basil Hallward, looking him straight in the face, "every portrait that is painted with feeling is a portrait of the artist, not of the sitter. The sitter is merely the accident, the occasion. It is not he who is revealed by the painter; it is rather the painter who, on the coloured canvas, reveals himself. The reason I will not exhibit this picture is that I am afraid that I have shown in it the secret of my own soul."

Lord Henry laughed. "And what is that?" he asked.

"I will tell you," said Hallward; but an expression of perplexity came over his face.

4. This may be an echo of John Wilmot's (earl of Rochester) epitaph for Charles II: "Here lies a Great and Mighty King / Whose Promise none rely'd on; / He never said a Foolish Thing? / Nor ever did a Wise One" (*Dorian Gray*, Murray 239).

"I am all expectation, Basil," continued his companion, glancing at him.

"Oh, there is really very little to tell, Harry," answered the painter; "and I am afraid you will hardly understand it. Perhaps you will hardly believe it."

Lord Henry smiled, and leaning down, plucked a pink-petalled daisy from the grass, and examined it. "I am quite sure I shall understand it," he replied, gazing intently at the little golden white-feathered disk, "and as for believing things, I can believe anything, provided that it is quite incredible."

The wind shook some blossoms from the trees, and the heavy lilac-blooms, with their clustering stars, moved to and fro in the languid air. A grasshopper began to chirrup by the wall, and like a blue thread a long thin dragon-fly floated past on its brown gauze wings. Lord Henry felt as if he could hear Basil Hallward's heart beating, and wondered what was coming.

"The story is simply this," said the painter after some time. "Two months ago I went to a crush at Lady Brandon's. You know we poor artists have to show ourselves in society from time to time, just to remind the public that we are not savages. With an evening coat and a white tie, as you told me once, anybody, even a stock-broker, can gain a reputation for being civilized. Well, after I had been in the room about ten minutes, talking to huge overdressed dowagers and tedious Academicians, I suddenly became conscious that some one was looking at me. I turned half-way round, and saw Dorian Gray for the first time. When our eyes met, I felt that I was growing pale. A curious sensation of terror came over me. I knew that I had come face to face with some one whose mere personality was so fascinating that, if I allowed it to do so, it would absorb my whole nature, my whole soul, my very art itself. I did not want any external influence in my life. You know yourself, Harry, how independent I am by nature. I have always been my own master; had at least always been so, till I met Dorian Gray. Then—but I don't know how to explain it to you. Something seemed to tell me that I was on the verge of a terrible crisis in my life. I had a strange feeling that Fate had in store for me exquisite joys and exquisite sorrows. I grew afraid, and turned to quit the room. It was not conscience that made me do so: it was a sort of cowardice.[5] I take no credit to myself for trying to escape."

"Conscience and cowardice are really the same things, Basil. Conscience is the trade-name of the firm.[6] That is all."

"I don't believe that, Harry, and I don't believe you do either. However, whatever was my motive—and it may have been pride, for I used to be very proud—I certainly struggled to the door. There, of course, I

---

5. A variation on *Hamlet* 3.1.82.
6. An epigram revised from its earlier form in Wilde's 1883 play, *The Duchess of Padua*, act 1:

"Conscience is but the name which cowardice / Fleeing from battle scrawls upon its shield" (*Complete Works* 569).

stumbled against Lady Brandon. 'You are not going to run away so soon, Mr. Hallward?' she screamed out. You know her curiously shrill voice?"[7]

"Yes; she is a peacock in everything but beauty," said Lord Henry, pulling the daisy to bits with his long, nervous fingers.

"I could not get rid of her. She brought me up to Royalties, and people with Stars and Garters,[8] and elderly ladies with gigantic tiaras and parrot noses. She spoke of me as her dearest friend. I had only met her once before, but she took it into her head to lionize me. I believe some picture of mine had made a great success at the time, at least had been chattered about in the penny newspapers, which is the nineteenth-century standard of immortality. Suddenly I found myself face to face with the young man whose personality had so strangely stirred me. We were quite close, almost touching. Our eyes met again. It was reckless of me, but I asked Lady Brandon to introduce me to him. Perhaps it was not so reckless, after all. It was simply inevitable. We would have spoken to each other without any introduction. I am sure of that. Dorian told me so afterwards. He, too, felt that we were destined to know each other."

"And how did Lady Brandon describe this wonderful young man?" asked his companion. "I know she goes in for giving a rapid précis[9] of all her guests. I remember her bringing me up to a truculent and red-faced old gentleman covered all over with orders and ribbons, and hissing into my ear, in a tragic whisper which must have been perfectly audible to everybody in the room, the most astounding details. I simply fled. I like to find out people for myself. But Lady Brandon treats her guests exactly as an auctioneer treats his goods. She either explains them entirely away, or tells one everything about them except what one wants to know."

"Poor Lady Brandon! You are hard on her, Harry!" said Hallward, listlessly.

"My dear fellow, she tried to found a *salon*, and only succeeded in opening a restaurant. How could I admire her?[1] But tell me, what did she say about Mr. Dorian Gray?"

"Oh, something like, 'Charming boy—poor dear mother and I absolutely inseparable. Quite forget what he does—afraid he—doesn't do anything—oh, yes, plays the piano—or is it the violin, dear Mr. Gray?' Neither of us could help laughing, and we became friends at once."

"Laughter is not at all a bad beginning for a friendship, and it is far the best ending for one," said the young lord, plucking another daisy.

7. The cameo of Lady Brandon is said to be based in part on Wilde's mother, Lady Jane Wilde, a writer and supporter of Irish revolution in her youth. She was known for her salons in Dublin and later, in reduced circumstances, in London.

8. The Order of the Garter was the highest of all English knightly orders. Stars and "orders and ribbons" (below) refer to insignia of English orders of knighthood.

9. A summary.

1. A quip Wilde had once directed at Marc-André Raffalovich (1865–1934), thereby inciting the latter's enmity.

Hallward shook his head, "You don't understand what friendship is, Harry," he murmured—"or what enmity is, for that matter. You like every one; that is to say, you are indifferent to every one."

"How horribly unjust of you!" cried Lord Henry, tilting his hat back, and looking up at the little clouds that, like ravelled skeins of glossy white silk, were drifting across the hollowed turquoise of the summer sky. "Yes; horribly unjust of you. I make a great difference between people. I choose my friends for their good looks, my acquaintances for their good characters, and my enemies for their good intellects. A man cannot be too careful in the choice of his enemies. I have not got one who is a fool. They are all men of some intellectual power, and consequently they all appreciate me. Is that very vain of me? I think it is rather vain."

"I should think it was, Harry. But according to your category I must be merely an acquaintance."

"My dear old Basil, you are much more than an acquaintance."

"And much less than a friend. A sort of brother, I suppose?"

"Oh, brothers! I don't care for brothers. My elder brother won't die, and my younger brothers seem never to do anything else."

"Harry!" exclaimed Hallward, frowning.

"My dear fellow, I am not quite serious. But I can't help detesting my relations. I suppose it comes from the fact that none of us can stand other people having the same faults as ourselves. I quite sympathize with the rage of the English democracy against what they call the vices of the upper orders. The masses feel that drunkenness, stupidity, and immorality should be their own special property, and that if any one of us makes an ass of himself he is poaching on their preserves. When poor Southwark got into the Divorce Court, their indignation was quite magnificent. And yet I don't suppose that ten percent of the proletariat live correctly."

"I don't agree with a single word that you have said, and, what is more, Harry, I feel sure you don't either."

Lord Henry stroked his pointed brown beard, and tapped the toe of his patent-leather boot with a tasselled ebony cane. "How English you are Basil! That is the second time you have made that observation. If one puts forward an idea to a true Englishman—always a rash thing to do—he never dreams of considering whether the idea is right or wrong. The only thing he considers of any importance is whether one believes it oneself. Now, the value of an idea has nothing whatsoever to do with the sincerity of the man who expresses it. Indeed, the probabilities are that the more insincere the man is, the more purely intellectual will the idea be, as in that case it will not be coloured by either his wants, his desires, or his prejudices. However, I don't propose to discuss politics, sociology, or metaphysics with you. I like persons better than principles, and I like persons with no principles better than anything else in the world.[2] Tell me more about Mr. Dorian Gray. How often do you see him?"

"Every day. I couldn't be happy if I didn't see him every day. He is absolutely necessary to me."

"How extraordinary! I thought you would never care for anything but your art."

"He is all my art to me now," said the painter, gravely. "I sometimes think, Harry, that there are only two eras of any importance in the world's history. The first is the appearance of a new medium for art, and the second is the appearance of a new personality for art also. What the invention of oil-painting was to the Venetians, the face of Antinoüs[3] was to late Greek sculpture, and the face of Dorian Gray will some day be to me. It is not merely that I paint from him, draw from him, sketch from him. Of course I have done all that. But he is much more to me than a model or a sitter. I won't tell you that I am dissatisfied with what I have done of him, or that his beauty is such that Art cannot express it. There is nothing that Art cannot express, and I know that the work I have done, since I met Dorian Gray, is good work, is the best work of my life. But in some curious way—I wonder will you understand me?—his personality has suggested to me an entirely new manner in art, an entirely new mode of style. I see things differently, I think of them differently. I can now recreate life in a way that was hidden from me before. 'A dream of form in days of thought:'—who is it who says that? I forget; but it is what Dorian Gray has been to me. The merely visible presence of this lad—for he seems to me little more than a lad, though he is really over twenty—his merely visible presence—ah! I wonder can you realize all that that means? Unconsciously he defines for me the lines of a fresh school, a school that is to have in it all the passion of the romantic spirit, all the perfection of the spirit that is Greek.[4] The harmony of soul and body—how much that is! We in our madness have separated the two, and have invented a realism that is vulgar, an ideality that is void. Harry! if you only knew what Dorian Gray is to me! You remember that landscape of mine, for which Agnew[5] offered me such a huge price, but which I would not part with? It is one of the best things I have ever done. And why is it so? Because, while I was painting it, Dorian Gray sat beside me. Some subtle influence passed from him to me, and for the first time in my life I saw in the plain woodland the wonder I had always looked for, and always missed."

"Basil, this is extraordinary! I must see Dorian Gray."

---

2. "and I like . . . world" added in this edition. See notes to the *Lippincott's* edition.

3. A companion of the Roman emperor Hadrian, by whom he was thought an ideal of manly grace and beauty. He is the first of a series of male homosexual pinups out of history alluded to in the text.

4. Basil's aestheticism is an ideal combination of the teaching of John Ruskin ("all the passion of the romantic spirit") and Walter Pater ("all the perfection of the spirit that is Greek"). Both taught Wilde at Oxford in the 1870's.

5. Thomas Agnew & Sons are to this day art dealers in London's Old Bond Street.

Hallward got up from the seat, and walked up and down the garden. After some time he came back. "Harry," he said, "Dorian Gray is to me simply a motive in art. You might see nothing in him. I see everything in him. He is never more present in my work than when no image of him is there. He is a suggestion, as I have said, of a new manner. I find him in the curves of certain lines, in the loveliness and subtleties of certain colours. That is all."

"Then why won't you exhibit his portrait?" asked Lord Henry.

"Because, without intending it, I have put into it some expression of all this curious artistic idolatry, of which, of course, I have never cared to speak to him. He knows nothing about it. He shall never know anything about it. But the world might guess it; and I will not bare my soul to their shallow, prying eyes. My heart shall never be put under their microscope.[6] There is too much of myself in the thing, Harry—too much of myself!"

"Poets are not so scrupulous as you are. They know how useful passion is for publication. Nowadays a broken heart will run to many editions."

"I hate them for it," cried Hallward. "An artist should create beautiful things, but should put nothing of his own life into them. We live in an age when men treat art as if it were meant to be a form of autobiography. We have lost the abstract sense of beauty. Some day I will show the world what it is; and for that reason the world shall never see my portrait of Dorian Gray."

"I think you are wrong, Basil, but I won't argue with you. It is only the intellectually lost who ever argue. Tell me, is Dorian Gray very fond of you?"

The painter considered for a few moments. "He likes me," he answered after a pause; "I know he likes me. Of course I flatter him dreadfully. I find a strange pleasure in saying things to him that I know I shall be sorry for having said. As a rule, he is charming to me, and we sit in the studio and talk of a thousand things. Now and then, however, he is horribly thoughtless, and seems to take a real delight in giving me pain. Then I feel, Harry, that I have given away my whole soul to some one who treats it as if it were a flower to put in his coat, a bit of decoration to charm his vanity, an ornament for a summer's day."

"Days in summer, Basil, are apt to linger," murmured Lord Henry. "Perhaps you will tire sooner than he will. It is a sad thing to think of, but there is no doubt that Genius lasts longer than Beauty. That accounts for the fact that we all take such pains to over-educate ourselves. In the wild struggle for existence, we want to have something that endures, and so we fill our minds with rubbish and facts, in the silly hope of keeping our place. The thoroughly well-informed man—that is the modern ideal.

6. An echo of Swinburne's satirical rebuttal to his critics, titled "Under the Microscope" (1872), in which he also defended Dante Gabriel Rossetti and other Pre-Raphaelites from charges of excessive sensuality and immorality.

And the mind of the thoroughly well-informed man is a dreadful thing. It is like a bric-à-brac shop, all monsters and dust, with everything priced above its proper value. I think you will tire first, all the same. Some day you will look at your friend, and he will seem to you to be a little out of drawing, or you won't like his tone of colour, or something. You will bitterly reproach him in your own heart, and seriously think that he has behaved very badly to you. The next time he calls, you will be perfectly cold and indifferent. It will be a great pity, for it will alter you. What you have told me is quite a romance, a romance of art one might call it, and the worst of having a romance of any kind is that it leaves one so unromantic."

"Harry, don't talk like that. As long as I live, the personality of Dorian Gray will dominate me. You can't feel what I feel. You change too often."

"Ah, my dear Basil, that is exactly why I can feel it. Those who are faithful know only the trivial side of love: it is the faithless who know love's tragedies." And Lord Henry struck a light on a dainty silver case, and began to smoke a cigarette with a self-conscious and satisfied air, as if he had summed up the world in a phrase.[7] There was a rustle of chirruping sparrows in the green lacquer leaves of the ivy, and the blue cloud-shadows chased themselves across the grass like swallows. How pleasant it was in the garden! And how delightful other people's emotions were!—much more delightful than their ideas, it seemed to him. One's own soul, and the passions of one's friends—those were the fascinating things in life. He pictured to himself with silent amusement the tedious luncheon that he had missed by staying so long with Basil Hallward. Had he gone to his aunt's, he would have been sure to have met Lord Goodbody there, and the whole conversation would have been about the feeding of the poor, and the necessity for model lodging-houses. Each class would have preached the importance of those virtues, for whose exercise there was no necessity in their own lives. The rich would have spoken on the value of thrift, and the idle grown eloquent over the dignity of labour. It was charming to have escaped all that! As he thought of his aunt, an idea seemed to strike him. He turned to Hallward, and said, "My dear fellow, I have just remembered."

"Remembered what, Harry?"

"Where I heard the name of Dorian Gray."

"Where was it?" asked Hallward, with a slight frown.

"Don't look so angry, Basil. It was at my aunt, Lady Agatha's. She told me she had discovered a wonderful young man, who was going to help her in the East End,[8] and that his name was Dorian Gray. I am bound to state that she never told me he was good-looking. Women have

7. A statement Wilde was later to apply to himself in *De Profundis* (*Letters* 466).
8. A notorious slum section of London containing the dock district. It was the scene of many chari- table enterprises, often mentioned in connection with the work of the Christian Socialists and the Salvation Army.

no appreciation of good looks; at least, good women have not. She said that he was very earnest, and had a beautiful nature. I at once pictured to myself a creature with spectacles and lank hair, horribly freckled, and tramping about on huge feet. I wish I had known it was your friend."

"I am very glad you didn't, Harry."

"Why?"

"I don't want you to meet him."

"You don't want me to meet him?"

"No."

"Mr. Dorian Gray is in the studio, sir," said the butler, coming into the garden.

"You must introduce me now," cried Lord Henry, laughing.

The painter turned to his servant, who stood blinking in the sunlight. "Ask Mr. Gray to wait, Parker: I shall be in in a few moments." The man bowed, and went up the walk.

Then he looked at Lord Henry. "Dorian Gray is my dearest friend," he said. "He has a simple and beautiful nature. Your aunt was quite right in what she said of him. Don't spoil him. Don't try to influence him. Your influence would be bad. The world is wide, and has many marvellous people in it. Don't take away from me the one person who gives to my art whatever charm it possesses: my life as an artist depends on him. Mind, Harry, I trust you." He spoke very slowly, and the words seemed wrung out of him almost against his will.

"What nonsense you talk!" said Lord Henry, smiling, and, taking Hallward by the arm, he almost led him into the house.

Chapter II.

As they entered they saw Dorian Gray.[1] He was seated at the piano, with his back to them, turning over the pages of a volume of Schumann's "Forest Scenes."[2] "You must lend me these, Basil," he cried. "I want to learn them. They are perfectly charming."

"That entirely depends on how you sit to-day, Dorian."

"Oh, I am tired of sitting, and I don't want a life-sized portrait of myself," answered the lad, swinging round on the music-stool, in a wilful, petulant manner. When he caught sight of Lord Henry, a faint blush coloured his cheeks for a moment, and he started up. "I beg your pardon, Basil, but I didn't know you had any one with you."

"This is Lord Henry Wotton, Dorian, an old Oxford friend of mine. I have just been telling him what a capital sitter you were, and now you have spoiled everything."

---

1. John Espey proposes an etymology for "Dorian" from "Doric," with the implied association to "Greek or masculine love" (38). See John Espey, "Resources for Wilde Studies at the Clark Library," *Oscar Wilde, Two Approaches: Papers Read at a Clark Library Seminar, April 17, 1976*, ed. Rich-

ard Ellmann and John Espey (Los Angeles: William Andrew Clark Memorial Library, 1977).
2. Pastoral piano music by Robert Schumann (1810–56), whose melodic, romantic, and intricate compositions were highly esteemed by aesthetes.

"You have not spoiled my pleasure in meeting you, Mr. Gray," said Lord Henry, stepping forward and extending his hand. "My aunt has often spoken to me about you. You are one of her favourites, and, I am afraid, one of her victims also."

"I am in Lady Agatha's black books at present," answered Dorian, with a funny look of penitence. "I promised to go to a club in Whitechapel[3] with her last Tuesday, and I really forgot all about it. We were to have played a duet together—three duets, I believe. I don't know what she will say to me. I am far too frightened to call,"

"Oh, I will make your peace with my aunt. She is quite devoted to you. And I don't think it really matters about your not being there. The audience probably thought it was a duet. When Aunt Agatha sits down to the piano she makes quite enough noise for two people."

"That is very horrid to her, and not very nice to me," answered Dorian, laughing.

Lord Henry looked at him. Yes, he was certainly wonderfully handsome, with his finely-curved scarlet lips, his frank blue eyes, his crisp gold hair. There was something in his face that made one trust him at once. All the candour of youth was there, as well as all youth's passionate purity. One felt that he had kept himself unspotted from the world.[4] No wonder Basil Hallward worshipped him.

"You are too charming to go in for philanthropy, Mr. Gray—far too charming." And Lord Henry flung himself down on the divan, and opened his cigarette-case.

The painter had been busy mixing his colours and getting his brushes ready. He was looking worried, and when he heard Lord Henry's last remark he glanced at him, hesitated for a moment, and then said, "Harry, I want to finish this picture to-day. Would you think it awfully rude of me if I asked you to go away?"

Lord Henry smiled, and looked at Dorian Gray. "Am I to go, Mr. Gray?" he asked.

"Oh, please don't, Lord Henry. I see that Basil is in one of his sulky moods; and I can't bear him when he sulks. Besides, I want you to tell me why I should not go in for philanthropy."

"I don't know that I shall tell you that, Mr. Gray. It is so tedious a subject that one would have to talk seriously about it. But I certainly shall not run away, now that you have asked me to stop. You don't really mind, Basil, do you? You have often told me that you liked your sitters to have some one to chat to."

---

3. A district of London bordering on the East End, where service and volunteer clubs served the poor. Whitechapel contained the Jewish ghetto, especially Polish and European Jews, and Chinatown. It was described at the time as "grubby but not unprosperous." General Booth began the Salvation Army in Whitechapel in 1865.

4. James 1.27. This idealized male image exactly corresponds to the forged painting in "The Picture of Mr. W. H." and to the appearance of many of Wilde's friends and intimates, most notably R. H. Sherard, a friend and future biographer; John Gray, the poet; and Lord Alfred Douglas. The portrait painted by Ivan Albright for the MGM film of *Dorian Gray* (1944) may be seen at the Kennedy Galleries, N.Y.

Hallward bit his lip. "If Dorian wishes it, of course you must stay. Dorian's whims are laws to everybody, except himself."

Lord Henry took up his hat and gloves. "You are very pressing, Basil, but I am afraid I must go. I have promised to meet a man at the Orleans.[5] Good-bye, Mr. Gray. Come and see me some afternoon in Curzon Street.[6] I am nearly always at home at five o'clock. Write to me when you are coming. I should be sorry to miss you."

"Basil," cried Dorian Gray, "if Lord Henry Wotton goes I shall go too. You never open your lips while you are painting, and it is horribly dull standing on a platform and trying to look pleasant. Ask him to stay. I insist upon it."

"Stay, Harry, to oblige Dorian, and to oblige me," said Hallward, gazing intently at his picture. "It is quite true, I never talk when I am working, and never listen either, and it must be dreadfully tedious for my unfortunate sitters. I beg you to stay."

"But what about my man at the Orleans?"

The painter laughed. "I don't think there will be any difficulty about that. Sit down again, Harry. And now, Dorian, get up on the platform, and don't move about too much, or pay any attention to what Lord Henry says. He has a very bad influence over all his friends, with the single exception of myself."

Dorian Gray stepped up on the dais, with the air of a young Greek martyr, and made a little *moue*[7] of discontent to Lord Henry, to whom he had rather taken a fancy. He was so unlike Basil. They made a delightful contrast. And he had such a beautiful voice. After a few moments he said to him, "Have you really a very bad influence, Lord Henry? As bad as Basil says?"

"There is no such thing as a good influence, Mr. Gray. All influence is immoral—immoral from the scientific point of view."[8]

"Why?"

"Because to influence a person is to give him one's own soul. He does not think his natural thoughts, or burn with his natural passions. His virtues are not real to him. His sins, if there are such things as sins, are borrowed. He becomes an echo of some one else's music, an actor of a part that has not been written for him. The aim of life is self-development. To realize one's nature perfectly—that is what each of us is here for. People are afraid of themselves, nowadays. They have forgotten the highest of all duties, the duty that one owes to one's self. Of course they are charitable. They feed the hungry, and clothe the beggar. But their

---

5. A London club on King Street decorated with sporting scenes. The marquess of Queensberry, Wilde's nemesis, was a member.
6. In Mayfair, east of Hyde Park, south of Berkeley Square, and north of Green Park. All the London Streets mentioned in *Dorian Gray* may be found on a surveyor's map of London. Basil, Lord Henry, and Dorian all live in or near Mayfair, which remains a fashionable district of London.

7. A pouting grimace.
8. This scientific view combines Darwinism, especially Darwin's theories about child development, and the psychology of William James and the new psychoanalytic schools in Germany and Austria, all of which are bound together in this novel, in Wilde's speculative thinking at the time, and in the Decadent Movement.

own souls starve, and are naked. Courage has gone out of our race. Perhaps we never really had it. The terror of society, which is the basis of morals, the terror of God, which is the secret of religion—these are the two things that govern us. And yet—"

"Just turn your head a little more to the right, Dorian, like a good boy," said the painter, deep in his work, and conscious only that a look had come into the lad's face that he had never seen there before.

"And yet," continued Lord Henry, in his low, musical voice, and with that graceful wave of the hand that was always so characteristic of him, and that he had even in his Eton[9] days, "I believe that if one man were to live out his life fully and completely, were to give form to every feeling, expression to every thought, reality to every dream—I believe that the world would gain such a fresh impulse of joy that we would forget all the maladies of mediævalism, and return to the Hellenic ideal —[1] to something finer, richer, than the Hellenic ideal, it may be. But the bravest man amongst us is afraid of himself. The mutilation of the savage has its tragic survival in the self-denial that mars our lives. We are punished for our refusals. Every impulse that we strive to strangle broods in the mind, and poisons us. The body sins once, and has done with its sin, for action is a mode of purification. Nothing remains then but the recollection of a pleasure, or the luxury of a regret. The only way to get rid of a temptation is to yield to it. Resist it, and your soul grows sick with longing for the things it has forbidden to itself, with desire for what its monstrous laws have made monstrous and unlawful. It has been said that the great events of the world take place in the brain. It is in the brain, and the brain only, that the great sins of the world take place also. You, Mr. Gray, you yourself, with your rose-red youth and your rose-white boyhood, you have had passions that have made you afraid, thoughts that have filled you with terror, day-dreams and sleeping dreams whose mere memory might stain your cheek with shame—"

"Stop!" faltered Dorian Gray, "stop! you bewilder me. I don't know what to say. There is some answer to you, but I cannot find it. Don't speak. Let me think. Or, rather, let me try not to think."

For nearly ten minutes he stood there, motionless, with parted lips, and eyes strangely bright. He was dimly conscious that entirely fresh influences were at work within him. Yet they seemed to him to have come really from himself. The few words that Basil's friend had said to him—words spoken by chance, no doubt, and with wilful paradox in them—had touched some secret chord that had never been touched

9. The most prestigious public school in England. English public schools are equivalent to U.S. private schools.
1. In this *raisonneur* speech, Henry outlines a philosophy remarkably similar to that expressed by Wilde as his own in *De Profundis*. Some of it, at least, is based upon Wilde's interpretation of Pater, especially two chapters from *The Renaissance* (see below, pp. 296–312). The tradition in art that Pater called the "Hellenic Ideal" reached from Classical antiquity to the present. It was the ideal of beauty of form combined with sensuous appeal of both subject and treatment. Henry's version of the ideal is Wilde's variation, emphasizing Aestheticism and hedonism.

before, but that he felt was now vibrating and throbbing to curious pulses.

Music had stirred him like that. Music had troubled him many times. But music was not articulate. It was not a new world, but rather another chaos, that it created in us. Words! Mere words! How terrible they were! How clear, and vivid, and cruel! One could not escape from them. And yet what a subtle magic there was in them! They seemed to be able to give a plastic form to formless things, and to have a music of their own as sweet as that of viol or of lute. Mere words! Was there anything so real as words?[2]

Yes; there had been things in his boyhood that he had not understood. He understood them now. Life suddenly became fiery-coloured to him. It seemed to him that he had been walking in fire. Why had he not known it?

With his subtle smile, Lord Henry watched him. He knew the precise psychological moment when to say nothing. He felt intensely interested. He was amazed at the sudden impression that his words had produced, and, remembering a book that he had read when he was sixteen, a book which had revealed to him much that he had not known before, he wondered whether Dorian Gray was passing through a similar experience.[3] He had merely shot an arrow into the air. Had it hit the mark? How fascinating the lad was!

Hallward painted away with that marvellous bold touch of his, that had the true refinement and perfect delicacy that in art, at any rate comes only from strength. He was unconscious of the silence.

"Basil, I am tired of standing," cried Dorian Gray, suddenly. "I must go out and sit in the garden. The air is stifling here."

"My dear fellow, I am so sorry. When I am painting, I can't think of anything else. But you never sat better. You were perfectly still. And I have caught the effect I wanted—the half-parted lips, and the bright look in the eyes. I don't know what Harry has been saying to you, but he has certainly made you have the most wonderful expression. I suppose he has been paying you compliments. You mustn't believe a word that he says."

"He has certainly not been paying me compliments. Perhaps that is the reason that I don't believe anything he has told me."

"You know you believe it all," said Lord Henry, looking at him with his dreamy, languorous eyes. "I will go out to the garden with you. It is horribly hot in the studio. Basil, let us have something iced to drink, something with strawberries in it."

"Certainly, Harry. Just touch the bell, and when Parker comes I will tell him what you want. I have got to work up this background, so I will join you later on. Don't keep Dorian too long. I have never been in

2. Another Pater echo, this time from *Gaston de Latour*. Lord Henry's remark on p. 22, "Nothing can cure the soul but the senses, just as nothing can cure the senses but the soul," recalls a doc-trine expounded by Pater in *Marius the Epicurean* (1885) and earlier by William Blake.

3. Wilde often spoke of such an influence in his own life but never revealed the book in question.

better form for painting than I am to-day. This is going to be my masterpiece. It is my masterpiece as it stands."

Lord Henry went out to the garden, and found Dorian Gray burying his face in the great cool lilac-blossoms, feverishly drinking in their perfume as if it had been wine.[4] He came close to him, and put his hand upon his shoulder. "You are quite right to do that," he murmured. "Nothing can cure the soul but the senses, just as nothing can cure the senses but the soul."

The lad started and drew back. He was bare-headed, and the leaves had tossed his rebellious curls and tangled all their gilded threads. There was a look of fear in his eyes, such as people have when they are suddenly awakened. His finely-chiselled nostrils quivered, and some hidden nerve shook the scarlet of his lips and left them trembling.

"Yes," continued Lord Henry, "that is one of the great secrets of life—to cure the soul by means of the senses, and the senses by means of the soul. You are a wonderful creation. You know more than you think you know, just as you know less than you want to know."

Dorian Gray frowned and turned his head away. He could not help liking the tall, graceful young man who was standing by him. His romantic olive-coloured face and worn expression interested him. There was something in his low, languid voice that was absolutely fascinating. His cool, white, flower-like hands, even, had a curious charm. They moved, as he spoke, like music, and seemed to have a language of their own. But he felt afraid of him, and ashamed of being afraid. Why had it been left for a stranger to reveal him to himself? He had known Basil Hallward for months, but the friendship between them had never altered him. Suddenly there had come some one across his life who seemed to have disclosed to him life's mystery. And, yet, what was there to be afraid of? He was not a schoolboy or a girl. It was absurd to be frightened.

"Let us go and sit in the shade," said Lord Henry. "Parker has brought out the drinks, and if you stay any longer in this glare you will be quite spoiled, and Basil will never paint you again. You really must not allow. yourself to become sunburnt. It would be unbecoming."[5]

"What can it matter?" cried Dorian Gray, laughing, as he sat down on the seat at the end of the garden.

"It should matter everything to you, Mr. Gray."

"Why?"

"Because you have the most marvellous youth, and youth is the one thing worth having."

"I don't feel that, Lord Henry."

"No, you don't feel it now. Some day, when you are old and wrinkled

4. Wilde described a similar action of his own in a letter written some years before *Dorian Gray*.
5. How fashions change! Suntans were not at all fashionable among the upper class at the time. They were considered marks of the laboring class. Nowadays dermatologists warn the suntanned of the health hazards of overexposure to the sun.

and ugly, when thought has seared your forehead with its lines, and passion branded your lips with its hideous fires, you will feel it, you will feel it terribly. Now, wherever you go, you charm the world. Will it always be so? . . . You have a wonderfully beautiful face, Mr. Gray. Don't frown. You have. And Beauty is a form of Genius—is higher, indeed, than Genius as it needs no explanation. It is of the great facts of the world, like sunlight, or spring-time, or the reflection in dark waters of that silver shell we call the moon. It cannot be questioned. It has its divine right of sovereignty. It makes princes of those who have it. You smile? Ah! when you have lost it you won't smile. . . . People say sometimes that Beauty is only superficial. That may be so. But at least it is not so superficial as Thought is. To me, Beauty is the wonder of wonders. It is only shallow people who do not judge by appearances. The true mystery of the world is the visible, not the invisible. . . . Yes, Mr. Gray, the gods have been good to you. But what the gods give they quickly take away. You have only a few years in which to live really, perfectly, and fully. When your youth goes, your beauty will go with it, and then you will suddenly discover that there are no triumphs left for you, or have to content yourself with those mean triumphs that the memory of your past will make more bitter than defeats. Every month as it wanes brings you nearer to something dreadful. Time is jealous of you, and wars against your lilies and your roses. You will become sallow, and hollow-cheeked, and dull-eyed. You will suffer horribly. . . . Ah! realize your youth while you have it. Don't squander the gold of your days, listening to the tedious, trying to improve the hopeless failure, or giving away your life to the ignorant, the common, and the vulgar. These are the sickly aims, the false ideals, of our age. Live! Live the wonderful life that is in you! Let nothing be lost upon you. Be always searching for new sensations. Be afraid of nothing. . . . A new Hedonism—[6] that is what our century wants. You might be its visible symbol. With your personality there is nothing you could not do. The world belongs to you for a season. . . . The moment I met you I saw that you were quite unconscious of what you really are, of what you really might be. There was so much in you that charmed me that I felt I must tell you something about yourself. I thought how tragic it would be if you were wasted. For there is such a little time that your youth will last—such a little time. The common hill-flowers wither, but they blossom again. The laburnum will be as yellow next June as it is now. In a month there will be purple stars on the clematis, and year after year the green night of its leaves will hold its purple stars. But we never get back our

6. Old hedonism grew from the teaching of Aristippus that pleasure is the chief end of human action. Lord Henry's new hedonism is an aesthetic refinement of the old with a dash of modern science, selectively interpreted to reinforce the acquisition of new sensations. The philosophy as practiced by Dorian Gray might have been described better as a new antinomianism. Dorian sees himself absolved by the portrait from the effects of a life of self-indulgence. His sins are obvious, but his error was to try to realize an aesthetic ideal in his life and thus to make life into an art form of self-gratification.

youth. The pulse of joy that beats in us at twenty, becomes sluggish. Our limbs fail, our senses rot. We degenerate into hideous puppets, haunted by the memory of the passions of which we were too much afraid, and the exquisite temptations that we had not the courage to yield to. Youth! Youth! There is absolutely nothing in the world but youth!"[7]

Dorian Gray listened, open-eyed and wondering. The spray of lilac fell from his hand upon the gravel. A furry bee came and buzzed round it for a moment. Then it began to scramble all over the oval stellated globe of the tiny blossoms. He watched it with that strange interest in trivial things that we try to develop when things of high import make us afraid, or when we are stirred by some new emotion for which we cannot find expression, or when some thought that terrifies us lays sudden siege to the brain and calls on us to yield. After a time the bee flew away. He saw it creeping into the stained trumpet of a Tyrian convolvulus. The flower seemed to quiver, and then swayed gently to and fro.

Suddenly the painter appeared at the door of the studio, and made staccato signs for them to come in. They turned to each other, and smiled.

"I am waiting," he cried. "Do come in. The light is quite perfect, and you can bring your drinks."

They rose up, and sauntered down the walk together. Two green-and-white butterflies fluttered past them, and in the pear-tree at the corner of the garden a thrush began to sing.

"You are glad you have met me, Mr. Gray," said Lord Henry, looking at him.

"Yes, I am glad now. I wonder shall I always be glad?"

"Always! That is a dreadful word. It makes me shudder when I hear it. Women are so fond of using it. They spoil every romance by trying to make it last for ever. It is a meaningless word, too. The only difference between a caprice and a life-long passion is that the caprice lasts a little longer."

As they entered the studio, Dorian Gray put his hand upon Lord Henry's arm. "In that case, let our friendship be a caprice," he murmured, flushing at his own boldness, then stepped up on the platform and resumed his pose.

Lord Henry flung himself into a large wicker arm-chair, and watched him. The sweep and dash of the brush on the canvas made the only sound that broke the stillness, except when, now and then, Hallward stepped back to look at his work from a distance. In the slanting beams that streamed through the open doorway the dust danced and was golden. The heavy scent of the roses seemed to brood over everything.

After about a quarter of an hour Hallward stopped painting, looked for a long time at Dorian Gray, and then for a long time at the picture,

7. Henry's speech reflects Wilde's own synthesis of Pater (see, especially, p. 311), Arnold (worship of youth and fear of declining powers), Whistler (superiority of art to nature), Blake, and assorted French geniuses from Gautier to Huysmans.

biting the end of one of his huge brushes, and frowning. "It is quite finished," he cried at last, and stooping down he wrote his name in long vermilion letters on the left-hand corner of the canvas.

Lord Henry came over and examined the picture. It was certainly a wonderful work of art, and a wonderful likeness as well.

"My dear fellow, I congratulate you most warmly," he said. "It is the finest portrait of modern times. Mr. Gray, come over and look at yourself."

The lad started, as if awakened from some dream. "Is it really finished?" he murmured, stepping down from the platform.

"Quite finished," said the painter. "And you have sat splendidly today. I am awfully obliged to you."

"That is entirely due to me," broke in Lord Henry. "Isn't it, Mr. Gray?"

Dorian made no answer, but passed listlessly in front of his picture and turned towards it. When he saw it he drew back, and his cheeks flushed for a moment with pleasure. A look of joy came into his eyes, as if he had recognized himself for the first time. He stood there motionless and in wonder, dimly conscious that Hallward was speaking to him, but not catching the meaning of his words. The sense of his own beauty came on him like a revelation. He had never felt it before. Basil Hallward's compliments had seemed to him to be merely the charming exaggerations of friendship. He had listened to them, laughed at them, forgotten them. They had not influenced his nature. Then had come Lord Henry Wotton with his strange panegyric on youth, his terrible warning of its brevity. That had stirred him at the time, and now, as he stood gazing at the shadow of his own loveliness, the full reality of the description flashed across him. Yes, there would be a day when his face would be wrinkled and wizen, his eyes dim and colourless, the grace of his figure broken and deformed. The scarlet would pass away from his lips, and the gold steal from his hair. The life that was to make his soul would mar his body. He would become dreadful, hideous, and uncouth.

As he thought of it, a sharp pang of pain struck through him like a knife, and made each delicate fibre of his nature quiver. His eyes deepened into amethyst, and across them came a mist of tears. He felt as if a hand of ice had been laid upon his heart.

"Don't you like it?" cried Hallward at last, stung a little by the lad's silence, not understanding what it meant.

"Of course he likes it," said Lord Henry. "Who wouldn't like it? It is one of the greatest things in modern art. I will give you anything you like to ask for it. I must have it."

"It is not my property, Harry."

"Whose property is it?"

"Dorian's, of course," answered the painter.

"He is a very lucky fellow."

"How sad it is!" murmured Dorian Gray, with his eyes still fixed upon his own portrait. "How sad it is! I shall grow old, and horrible, and dreadful. But this picture will remain always young. It will never be older than this particular day of June. . . . If it were only the other way! If it were I who was to be always young, and the picture that was to grow old! For that—for that—I would give everything! Yes, there is nothing in the whole world I would not give! I would give my soul for that!"

"You would hardly care for such an arrangement, Basil," cried Lord Henry, laughing. "It would be rather hard lines on your work."

"I should object very strongly, Harry," said Hallward.

Dorian Gray turned and looked at him. "I believe you would, Basil. You like your art better than your friends. I am no more to you than a green bronze figure. Hardly as much, I dare say."

The painter stared in amazement. It was so unlike Dorian to speak like that. What had happened? He seemed quite angry. His face was flushed and his cheeks burning.

"Yes," he continued, "I am less to you than your ivory Hermes or your silver Faun.[8] You will like them always. How long will you like me? Till I have my first wrinkle, I suppose. I know, now, that when one loses one's good looks, whatever they may be, one loses everything. Your picture has taught me that. Lord Henry Wotton is perfectly right. Youth is the only thing worth having. When I find that I am growing old, I shall kill myself."

Hallward turned pale, and caught his hand. "Dorian! Dorian!" he cried, "don't talk like that. I have never had such a friend as you, and I shall never have such another. You are not jealous of material things, are you?—you who are finer than any of them!"

"I am jealous of everything whose beauty does not die. I am jealous of the portrait you have painted of me. Why should it keep what I must lose? Every moment that passes takes something from me, and gives something to it. Oh, if it were only the other way! If the picture could change, and I could be always what I am now! Why did you paint it? It will mock me some day—mock me horribly!" The hot tears welled into his eyes; he tore his hand away, and, flinging himself on the divan, he buried his face in the cushions, as though he was praying.

"This is your doing, Harry," said the painter, bitterly.

Lord Henry shrugged his shoulders. "It is the real Dorian Gray—that is all."

"It is not."

"If it is not, what have I to do with it?"

"You should have gone away when I asked you," he muttered.

"I stayed when you asked me," was Lord Henry's answer.

"Harry, I can't quarrel with my two best friends at once, but between

8. Son of Zeus, wing-footed messenger of the gods, and inventor of the lyre. Mercury is his Latin name. A faun was a rural demigod of lustful disposition, portrayed as half-human with goat's legs. Fauns were deities of farmers and shepherds.

you both you have made me hate the finest piece of work I have ever done, and I will destroy it. What is it but canvas and colour? I will not let it come across our three lives and mar them."

Dorian Gray lifted his golden head from the pillow, and with pallid face and tear-stained eyes looked at him, as he walked over to the deal painting-table that was set beneath the high curtained window. What was he doing there? His fingers were straying about among the litter of tin tubes and dry brushes, seeking for something. Yes, it was for the long palette-knife, with its thin blade of lithe steel. He had found it at last. He was going to rip up the canvas.

With a stifled sob the lad leaped from the couch, and, rushing over to Hallward, tore the knife out of his hand, and flung it to the end of the studio. "Don't, Basil, don't!" he cried. "It would be murder!"

"I am glad you appreciate my work at last, Dorian," said the painter, coldly, when he had recovered from his surprise. "I never thought you would."

"Appreciate it? I am in love with it, Basil. It is part of myself. I feel that."

"Well, as soon as you are dry, you shall be varnished, and framed, and sent home. Then you can do what you like with yourself." And he walked across the room and rang the bell for tea. "You will have tea, of course, Dorian? And so will you, Harry? Or do you object to such simple pleasures?"

"I adore simple pleasures," said Lord Henry. "They are the last refuge of the complex. But I don't like scenes, except on the stage. What absurd fellows you are, both of you! I wonder who it was defined man as a rational animal.[9] It was the most premature definition ever given. Man is many things, but he is not rational. I am glad he is not, after all: though I wish you chaps would not squabble over the picture. You had much better let me have it, Basil. This silly boy doesn't really want it, and I really do."

"If you let any one have it but me, Basil, I shall never forgive you!" cried Dorian Gray; "and I don't allow people to call me a silly boy."

"You know the picture is yours, Dorian. I gave it to you before it existed."

"And you know you have been a little silly, Mr. Gray, and that you don't really object to being reminded that you are extremely young."

"I should have objected very strongly this morning, Lord Henry."

"Ah! this morning! You have lived since then."

There came a knock at the door, and the butler entered with a laden tea-tray and set it down upon a small Japanese table. There was a rattle of cups and saucers and the hissing of a fluted Georgian urn. Two globe-

9. This definition of man, which predates Plato, was best known in the Latin formula *ratio animalis*. Although discredited in nearly every age, it has perversely survived to the present on the strength of tradition and style. Lord Henry's critique echoes that of Swift in *Gulliver's Travels*.

shaped china dishes were brought in by a page. Dorian Gray went over and poured out the tea. The two men sauntered languidly to the table, and examined what was under the covers.

"Let us go to the theatre to-night," said Lord Henry. "There is sure to be something on, somewhere. I have promised to dine at White's,[1] but it is only with an old friend, so I can send him a wire to say that I am ill, or that I am prevented from coming in consequence of a subsequent engagement. I think that would be a rather nice excuse: it would have all the surprise of candour."

"It is such a bore putting on one's dress-clothes," muttered Hallward. "And, when one has them on, they are so horrid."

"Yes," answered Lord Henry, dreamily, "the costume of the nineteenth century is detestable. It is so sombre, so depressing. Sin is the only real colour-element left in modern life."

"You really must not say things like that before Dorian, Harry."

"Before which Dorian? The one who is pouring out tea for us, or the one in the picture?"

"Before either."

"I should like to come to the theatre with you, Lord Henry," said the lad.

"Then you shall come; and you will come too, Basil, won't you?"

"I can't, really. I would sooner not. I have a lot of work to do."

"Well, then, you and I will go alone, Mr. Gray."

"I should like that awfully."

The painter bit his lip and walked over, cup in hand, to the picture. "I shall stay with the real Dorian," he said, sadly.

"Is it the real Dorian?" cried the original of the portrait, strolling across to him. "Am I really like that?"

"Yes; you are just like that."

"How wonderful, Basil!"

"At least you are like it in appearance. But it will never alter," sighed Hallward. "That is something."

"What a fuss people make about fidelity!" exclaimed Lord Henry. "Why, even in love it is purely a question for physiology. It has nothing to do with our own will. Young men want to be faithful, and are not; old men want to be faithless, and cannot: that is all one can say."[2]

"Don't go to the theatre to-night, Dorian," said Hallward. "Stop and dine with me."

"I can't, Basil."

"Why?"

"Because I have promised Lord Henry Wotton to go with him."

---

1. On St. James's Street, one of the older, established London clubs, known as a sporting and gambling club for the gentry. The then Prince of Wales, later King Edward VII, was a member.
2. Lord Henry underlines his view of the irreconcilable conflict of the will allied with conscience against the appetites and instincts perceived as forces of necessity. At least that is the way it appeared manifested in Darwinism and its corollaries to contemporary observers like Wilde.

"He won't like you the better for keeping your promises. He always breaks his own. I beg you not to go."

Dorian Gray laughed and shook his head.

"I entreat you."

The lad hesitated, and looked over at Lord Henry, who was watching them from the tea-table with an amused smile.

"I must go, Basil," he answered.

"Very well," said Hallward; and he went over and laid down his cup on the tray. "It is rather late, and, as you have to dress, you had better lose no time. Good-bye, Harry. Good-bye, Dorian. Come and see me soon. Come to-morrow."

"Certainly."

"You won't forget?"

"No, of course not," cried Dorian.

"And . . . Harry!"

"Yes, Basil?"

"Remember what I asked you, when we were in the garden this morning."

"I have forgotten it."

"I trust you."

"I wish I could trust myself," said Lord Henry, laughing. "Come, Mr. Gray, my hansom[3] is outside, and I can drop you at your own place. Good-bye, Basil. It has been a most interesting afternoon."

As the door closed behind them, the painter flung himself down on a sofa, and a look of pain came into his face.

Chapter III.[1]

At half-past twelve next day Lord Henry Wotton strolled from Curzon Street over to the Albany[2] to call on his uncle, Lord Fermor, a genial if somewhat rough-mannered old bachelor, whom the outside world called selfish because it derived no particular benefit from him, but who was considered generous by Society as he fed the people who amused him. His father had been our ambassador at Madrid when Isabella was young, and Prim[3] unthought of, but had retired from the Diplomatic Service in a capricious moment of annoyance on not being offered the Embassy at Paris, a post to which he considered that he was fully entitled by reason of his birth, his indolence, the good English of his despatches,

3. A hired, horse-drawn cab.
1. Chapter 3 here was the first of six new chapters added in the revised edition.
2. The former Piccadilly residence of the duke of York, second son of George III. It was converted into elegant private apartments in 1802 and is still regarded as one of the most exclusive addresses in London. Among its distinguished residents have been Lord Byron, Thomas Babington Macaulay, and Matthew G. ("Monk") Lewis. Earnest Wor-

thing of *The Importance of Being Earnest* has his London residence there in apartment B.4.
3. Isabella and Prim were two figures in nineteenth-century Spanish politics. Isabella II (1830–1904) reigned from 1843 to 1868. Both her accession to the throne and her abdication were engineered by soldier-statesman, Juan Prim (1814–70), whose career included military honors, titles, imprisonment, exile in England, and finally assassination.

and his inordinate passion for pleasure. The son, who had been his father's secretary, had resigned along with his chief, somewhat foolishly as was thought at the time, and on succeeding some months later to the title, had set himself to the serious study of the great aristocratic art of doing absolutely nothing. He had two large town houses, but preferred to live in chambers as it was less trouble, and took most of his meals at his club. He paid some attention to the management of his collieries in the Midland counties,[4] excusing himself for this taint of industry on the ground that the one advantage of having coal was that it enabled a gentleman to afford the decency of burning wood on his own hearth. In politics he was a Tory, except when the Tories were in office, during which period he roundly abused them for being a pack of Radicals.[5] He was a hero to his valet, who bullied him, and a terror to most of his relations, whom he bullied in turn. Only England could have produced him, and he always said that the country was going to the dogs. His principles were out of date, but there was a good deal to be said for his prejudices.

When Lord Henry entered the room, he found his uncle sitting in a rough shooting coat, smoking a cheroot and grumbling over *The Times*. "Well, Harry," said the old gentleman, "what brings you out so early? I thought you dandies never got up till two, and were not visible till five."

"Pure family affection, I assure you, Uncle George. I want to get something out of you."

"Money, I suppose," said Lord Fermor, making a wry face. "Well, sit down and tell me all about it. Young people, nowadays, imagine that money is everything."

"Yes," murmured Lord Henry, settling his button-hole[6] in his coat; "and when they grow older they know it. But I don't want money. It is only people who pay their bills who want that, Uncle George, and I never pay mine. Credit is the capital of a younger son, and one lives charmingly upon it. Besides, I always deal with Dartmoor's tradesmen, and consequently they never bother me. What I want is information: not useful information, of course; useless information."

"Well, I can tell you anything that is in an English Blue-book,[7] Harry, although those fellows nowadays write a lot of nonsense. When I was in the Diplomatic, things were much better. But I hear they let them in now by examination. What can you expect? Examinations, sir, are pure humbug from beginning to end. If a man is a gentleman, he knows quite

---

4. The Midland counties are noted for mining and heavy industry, with Birmingham as the industrial hub. Midlands was also renowned hunt country and the site, in Nottinghamshire, of Sherwood forest.

5. Tories were more commonly referred to as conservatives in the later nineteenth century. They were led by Benjamin Disraeli and generally supported the policies of the Crown and the growth of the Empire. Radicals were associated with the Lib-eral party, led by William Gladstone, and favored social reform policies. But "Radicals" also referred to the "Philosophical Radicals" of an earlier generation, whose economic and social theories descended from Adam Smith, Jeremy Bentham, and Thomas Malthus.

6. A flower, usually a carnation, worn through the lapel buttonhole: hence the popular name.

7. Parliamentary reports: the most memorable treated social abuses in the nineteenth century.

enough, and if he is not a gentleman, whatever he knows is bad for him."

"Mr. Dorian Gray does not belong to Bluebooks, Uncle George," said Lord Henry, languidly.

"Mr. Dorian Gray? Who is he?" asked Lord Fermor, knitting his bushy white eyebrows.

"That is what I have come to learn, Uncle George. Or rather, I know who he is. He is the last Lord Kelso's grandson.[8] His mother was a Devereux, Lady Margaret Devereux. I want you to tell me about his mother. What was she like? Whom did she marry? You have known nearly everybody in your time, so you might have known her. I am very much interested in Mr. Gray at present. I have only just met him."

"Kelso's grandson!" echoed the old gentleman—"Kelso's grandson! . . . Of course. . . . I knew his mother intimately. I believe I was at her christening. She was an extraordinarily beautiful girl, Margaret Devereux, and made all the men frantic by running away with a penniless young fellow, a mere nobody, sir, a subaltern in a foot regiment, or something of that kind. Certainly. I remember the whole thing as if it happened yesterday. The poor chap was killed in a duel at Spa a few months after the marriage. There was an ugly story about it. They said Kelso got some rascally adventurer, some Belgian brute, to insult his son-in-law in public, paid him, sir, to do it, paid him, and that the fellow spitted his man as if he had been a pigeon.[9] The thing was hushed up, but, egad, Kelso ate his chop alone at the club for some time afterwards. He brought his daughter back with him, I was told, and she never spoke to him again. Oh, yes; it was a bad business. The girl died too, died within a year. So she left a son, did she? I had forgotten that. What sort of boy is he? If he is like his mother he must be a good-looking chap."

"He is very good-looking," assented Lord Henry.

"I hope he will fall into proper hands," continued the old man. "He should have a pot of money waiting for him if Kelso did the right thing by him. His mother had money too. All the Selby property came to her, through her grandfather. Her grandfather hated Kelso, thought him a mean dog. He was, too. Came to Madrid once when I was there. Egad, I was ashamed of him. The Queen used to ask me about the English noble who was always quarrelling with the cabmen about their fares. They made quite a story of it. I didn't dare show my face at Court for a month. I hope he treated his grandson better than he did the jarvies."[1]

8. Kelso is a place in Scotland and the family seat of Sir George Brisbane Scott-Douglas, whom Wilde visited and considered "a type of old fashioned propriety" (*Letters* 273n). Wilde habitually named his characters after places and his fictitious places after friends and acquaintances. Lord Henry's name comes from Wotton-under-Edge in Gloucestershire, near the home of More Adey, Wilde's friend.

9. One of Wilde's favorite romantic fictions. Dorian's ancestry is almost identical to those Wilde provided Cyril Graham in "The Portrait of Mr. W. H.," the hero in "The Young King," and the heroine in "The Birthday of the Infanta." (The latter two stories were collected in *A House of Pomegranates*.)

1. Cabdrivers.

"I don't know," answered Lord Henry. "I fancy that the boy will be well off. He is not of age yet. He has Selby, I know. He told me so. And . . . his mother was very beautiful?"

"Margaret Devereux was one of the loveliest creatures I ever saw, Harry. What on earth induced her to behave as she did, I never could understand. She could have married anybody she chose. Carlington was mad after her. She was romantic, though. All the women of that family were. The men were a poor lot, but, egad! the women were wonderful. Carlington went on his knees to her. Told me so himself. She laughed at him, and there wasn't a girl in London at the time who wasn't after him. And by the way, Harry, talking about silly marriages, what is this humbug your father tells me about Dartmoor wanting to marry an American? Ain't English girls good enough for him?"

"It is rather fashionable to marry Americans just now, Uncle George."

"I'll back English women against the world, Harry," said Lord Fermor, striking the table with his fist.

"The betting is on the Americans."

"They don't last, I am told," muttered his uncle.

"A long engagement exhausts them, but they are capital at a steeple-chase.[2] They take things flying. I don't think Dartmoor has a chance."

"Who are her people?" grumbled the old gentleman. "Has she got any?"

Lord Henry shook his head. "American girls are as clever at concealing their parents, as English women are at concealing their past," he said, rising to go.

"They are pork-packers, I suppose?"

"I hope so, Uncle George, for Dartmoor's sake. I am told that pork-packing is the most lucrative profession in America, after politics."[3]

"Is she pretty?"

"She behaves as if she was beautiful. Most American women do. It is the secret of their charm."[4]

"Why can't these American women stay in their own country? They are always telling us that it is the Paradise for women."

"It is. That is the reason why, like Eve, they are so excessively anxious to get out of it," said Lord Henry. "Good-bye, Uncle George. I shall be late for lunch, if I stop any longer. Thanks for giving me the information I wanted. I always like to know everything about my new friends, and nothing about my old ones."

"Where are you lunching, Harry?"

2. An obstacle (horse) race run over a measured course. Henry here volleys his uncle's metaphor.
3. Wilde had visited America in 1882–83 and again the following year. He knew enough about America to understand the punning connection between "pork-packing" (with the same connotations as "pork barrel") and politics suggested here, but the refer-ence is primarily aimed at nouveau riche Americans who had made their money in unheroic trades.
4. Wilde canceled the following in MS for this added chapter: " 'Clever?' / 'So clever that if Dartmoor doesn't propose to her before the end of the week, she is quite certain to propose to him.' / 'He hasn't got a chance, then?' / 'I don't think so.' "

"At Aunt Agatha's. I have asked myself and Mr. Gray. He is her latest *protégé.*"

"Humph! tell your Aunt Agatha, Harry, not to bother me any more with her charity appeals. I am sick of them. Why, the good woman thinks that I have nothing to do but to write cheques for her silly fads."

"All right, Uncle George, I'll tell her, but it won't have any effect. Philanthropic people lose all sense of humanity. It is their distinguishing characteristic."

The old gentleman growled approvingly, and rang the bell for his servant. Lord Henry passed up the low arcade into Burlington Street, and turned his steps in the direction of Berkeley Square.[5]

So that was the story of Dorian Gray's parentage. Crudely as it had been told to him, it had yet stirred him by its suggestion of a strange, almost modern romance. A beautiful woman risking everything for a mad passion. A few wild weeks of happiness cut short by a hideous, treacherous crime. Months of voiceless agony, and then a child born in pain. The mother snatched away by death, the boy left to solitude and the tyranny of an old and loveless man. Yes; it was an interesting background. It posed the lad, made him more perfect as it were. Behind every exquisite thing that existed, there was something tragic. Worlds had to be in travail, that the meanest flower might blow. . . .[6] And how charming he had been at dinner the night before, as with startled eyes and lips parted in frightened pleasure he had sat opposite to him at the club, the red candleshades staining to a richer rose the wakening wonder of his face. Talking to him was like playing upon an exquisite violin. He answered to every touch and thrill of the bow. . . . There was something terribly enthralling in the exercise of influence.[7] No other activity was like it. To project one's soul into some gracious form, and let it tarry there for a moment; to hear one's own intellectual views echoed back to one with all the added music of passion and youth: to convey one's temperament into another as though it were a subtle fluid or a strange perfume: there was a real joy in that—perhaps the most satisfying joy left to us in an age so limited and vulgar as our own, an age grossly carnal in its pleasures, and grossly common in its aims. . . . He was a marvellous type, too, this lad, whom by so curious a chance he had met in Basil's studio, or could be fashioned into a marvellous type, at any rate. Grace was his, and the white purity of boyhood, and beauty such as old

5. Regarded as the finest square in London.
6. The phrase is a variant of the famous one from Wordsworth's "Ode: Intimations of Immortality from Recollections of Early Childhood," and the allusion is especially apropos here because of the poem's theme.
7. The question of whether Henry's views here are Wilde's has been long debated. Many who knew him testify that in both tone and substance, passages such as this faithfully reproduce Wilde's speech. On the other hand, Wilde stressed repeatedly in "The Rise of Historical Criticism," "The

Critic as Artist," and "The Soul of Man under Socialism" his censure of the sort of influence exercised here by Wotton. Of course, that does not preclude such behavior by Wilde contrary to stated principles. At the conclusion of "The Truth of Masks," one of the essays in *Intentions*, Wilde wrote, "there is no such thing [in art] as universal truth. A Truth in art is that whose contradictory is also true." As readers we need to keep that dialectic in mind when trying to frame statements about the author's views.

Greek marbles kept for us. There was nothing that one could not do with him. He could be made a Titan[8] or a toy. What a pity it was that such beauty was destined to fade! . . . And Basil? From a psychological point of view, how interesting he was! The new manner in art, the fresh mode of looking at life, suggested so strangely by the merely visible presence of one who was unconscious of it all; the silent spirit that dwelt in dim woodland, and walked unseen in open field, suddenly showing herself, Dryad-like[9] and not afraid, because in his soul who sought for her there had been wakened that wonderful vision to which alone are wonderful things revealed; the mere shapes and patterns of things becoming, as it were, refined, and gaining a kind of symbolical value, as though they were themselves patterns of some other and more perfect form whose shadow they made real: how strange it all was! He remembered something like it in history. Was it not Plato, that artist in thought, who had first analyzed it? Was it not Buonarotti[1] who had carved it in the coloured marbles of a sonnet-sequence? But in our own century it was strange. . . . Yes; he would try to be to Dorian Gray what, without knowing it, the lad was to the painter who had fashioned the wonderful portrait. He would seek to dominate him—had already, indeed, half done so. He would make that wonderful spirit his own. There was something fascinating in this son of Love and Death.

Suddenly he stopped, and glanced up at the houses. He found that he had passed his aunt's some distance, and, smiling to himself, turned back.[2] When he entered the somewhat sombre hall, the butler told him that they had gone in to lunch. He gave one of the footmen his hat and stick, and passed into the dining-room.

"Late as usual, Harry," cried his aunt, shaking her head at him.[3]

He invented a facile excuse, and having taken the vacant seat next to her, looked round to see who was there. Dorian bowed to him shyly from the end of the table, a flush of pleasure stealing into his cheek. Opposite was the Duchess of Harley, a lady of admirable good-nature and good temper, much liked by every one who knew her, and of those ample architectural proportions that in women who are not Duchesses are described by contemporary historians as stoutness. Next to her sat, on her right, Sir Thomas Burdon, a Radical member of Parliament, who followed his leader in public life, and in private life followed the best cooks, dining with the Tories, and thinking with the Liberals, in accordance with a wise and well-known rule. The post on her left was

---

8. One of the twelve giant gods and goddesses of Greek mythology, children of Uranus and Gaea, and, after them, the earliest of the gods.

9. Dryads were nymphs of woods and trees in Greek mythology.

1. A typo for Michelangelo Buonarrotti (1475–1564), the Italian Renaissance master, who was a painter, sculptor, and poet.

2. Wilde canceled the MS reading: "and wondering if he, like Basil, was going to be always wrapped in dream."

3. The scene at Henry's Aunt Agatha's is one of the two social cameos Wilde added in the revised edition. The other comes late in the novel at Selby Royal. Each forms a background for another kind of dramatic action. In this scene, Henry's performance established his influence over Dorian's mind. The scene itself, however, foreshadows the success Wilde was soon to enjoy in the theater.

occupied by Mr. Erskine of Treadley,[4] an old gentleman of considerable charm and culture, who had fallen, however, into bad habits of silence, having, as he explained once to Lady Agatha, said everything that he had to say before he was thirty. His own neighbour was Mrs. Vandeleur, one of his aunt's oldest friends, a perfect saint amongst women, but so dreadfully dowdy that she reminded one of a badly bound hymn-book. Fortunately for him she had on the other side Lord Faudel, a most intelligent middle-aged mediocrity, as bald as a Ministerial statement in the House of Commons, with whom she was conversing in that intensely earnest manner which is the one unpardonable error, as he remarked once himself, that all really good people fall into, and from which none of them ever quite escape.

"We are talking about poor Dartmoor, Lord Henry," cried the Duchess, nodding pleasantly to him across the table. "Do you think he will really marry this fascinating young person?"

"I believe she had made up her mind to propose to him, Duchess."

"How dreadful!" exclaimed Lady Agatha. "Really, some one should interfere."

"I am told, on excellent authority, that her father keeps an American dry-goods store," said Sir Thomas Burdon, looking supercilious.

"My uncle has already suggested pork-packing, Sir Thomas."

"Dry-goods! What are American Dry-goods?"[5] asked the Duchess, raising her large hands in wonder, and accentuating the verb.

"American novels," answered Lord Henry, helping himself to some quail.

The Duchess looked puzzled.

"Don't mind him, my dear," whispered Lady Agatha. "He never means anything that he says."

"When America was discovered," said the Radical member, and he began to give some wearisome facts. Like all people who try to exhaust a subject, he exhausted his listeners. The Duchess sighed, and exercised her privilege of interruption. "I wish to goodness it never had been discovered at all!" she exclaimed. "Really, our girls have no chance nowadays. It is most unfair."

"Perhaps, after all, America never has been discovered," said Mr. Erskine; "I myself would say that it had merely been detected."

"Oh! but I have seen specimens of the inhabitants," answered the Duchess, vaguely. "I must confess that most of them are extremely pretty. And they dress well, too. They get all their dresses in Paris. I wish I could afford to do the same."

"They say that when good Americans die they go to Paris," chuckled Sir Thomas, who had a large wardrobe of Humour's cast-off clothes.

4. Erskine appears in Wilde's *The Portrait of Mr. W. H.* (1889) as a major character and owner of the portrait of the title.
5. American dry goods are textiles, clothes, notions, and the like. British dry goods, meaning groceries not liquid, would refer chiefly to produce, especially grains.

"Really! And where do bad Americans go to when they die?" inquired the Duchess.

"They go to America," murmured Lord Henry.

Sir Thomas frowned. "I am afraid that your nephew is prejudiced against that great country," he said to Lady Agatha. "I have travelled all over it, in cars provided by the directors, who, in such matters, are extremely civil. I assure you that it is an education to visit."

"But must we really see Chicago in order to be educated?" asked Mr. Erskine, plaintively. "I don't feel up to the journey."

Sir Thomas waved his hand. "Mr. Erskine of Treadley has the world on his shelves. We practical men like to see things, not to read about them. The Americans are an extremely interesting people. They are absolutely reasonable. I think that is their distinguishing characteristic. Yes, Mr. Erskine, an absolutely reasonable people. I assure you there is no nonsense about the Americans."

"How dreadful!" cried Lord Henry. "I can stand brute force, but brute reason is quite unbearable. There is something unfair about its use. It is hitting below the intellect."

"I do not understand you," said Sir Thomas, growing rather red.

"I do, Lord Henry," murmured Mr. Erskine, with a smile.

"Paradoxes are all very well in their way. . . ." rejoined the Baronet.

"Was that a paradox?" asked Mr. Erskine. "I did not think so. Perhaps it was. Well, the way of paradoxes is the way of truth. To test Reality we must see it on the tight-rope. When the Verities become acrobats we can judge them."[6]

"Dear me!" said Lady Agatha, "how you men argue! I am sure I never can make out what you are talking about. Oh! Harry, I am quite vexed with you. Why do you try to persuade our nice Mr. Dorian Gray to give up the East End? I assure you he would be quite invaluable. They would love his playing."

"I want him to play to me," cried Lord Henry, smiling, and he looked down the table and caught a bright answering glance.

"But they are so unhappy in Whitechapel," continued Lady Agatha.

"I can sympathize with everything, except suffering," said Lord Henry, shrugging his shoulders. "I cannot sympathize with that. It is too ugly, too horrible, too distressing. There is something terribly morbid in the modern sympathy with pain. One should sympathize with the colour, the beauty, the joy of life. The less said about life's sores the better."

"Still, the East End is a very important problem," remarked Sir Thomas, with a grave shake of the head.

"Quite so," answered the young lord. "It is the problem of slavery, and we try to solve it by amusing the slaves."

The politician looked at him keenly. "What change do you propose, then?" he asked.

---

6. Wilde added "Paradoxes are all . . . judge them" to the margin of the MS.

Lord Henry laughed. "I don't desire to change anything in England except the weather," he answered. "I am quite content with philosophic contemplation. But, as the nineteenth century has gone bankrupt through an over-expenditure of sympathy, I would suggest that we should appeal to Science to put us straight. The advantage of the emotions is that they lead us astray, and the advantage of Science is that it is not emotional."

"But we have such grave responsibilities," ventured Mrs. Vandeleur, timidly.

"Terribly grave," echoed Lady Agatha.

Lord Henry looked over at Mr. Erskine. "Humanity takes itself too seriously. It is the world's original sin. If the caveman had known how to laugh, History would have been different."

"You are really very comforting," warbled the Duchess. "I have always felt rather guilty when I came to see your dear aunt, for I take no interest at all in the East End. For the future I shall be able to look her in the face without a blush."

"A blush is very becoming, Duchess," remarked Lord Henry.

"Only when one is young," she answered. "When an old woman like myself blushes, it is a very bad sign. Ah! Lord Henry, I wished you would tell me how to become young again."

He thought for a moment. "Can you remember any great error that you committed in your early days, Duchess?" he asked, looking at her across the table.

"A great many, I fear," she cried.

"Then commit them over again," he said, gravely. "To get back one's youth, one has merely to repeat one's follies."

"A delightful theory!" she exclaimed. "I must put it into practice."

"A dangerous theory!" came from Sir Thomas's tight lips. Lady Agatha shook her head, but could not help being amused. Mr. Erskine listened.

"Yes," he continued, "that is one of the great secrets of life. Nowadays most people die of a sort of creeping common sense, and discover when it is too late that the only things one never regrets are one's mistakes."

A laugh ran round the table.

He played with the idea, and grew wilful; tossed it into the air and transformed it; let it escape and recaptured it; made it iridescent with fancy, and winged it with paradox. The praise of folly,[7] as he went on, soared into a philosophy, and Philosophy herself became young, and catching the mad music of Pleasure, wearing, one might fancy, her winestained robe and wreath of ivy, danced like a Bacchante over the hills of life, and mocked the slow Silenus[8] for being sober. Facts fled before her like frightened forest things. Her white feet trod the huge press

7. The allusion is to Erasmus's *In Praise of Folly*. This scene has been noted especially by Wilde's biographers as illustrative of Wilde's best table-talk manner.
8. A leader of the satyrs and a notoriously drunken follower of Bacchus in mythology. Bacchante, above, refer to Maenads, female worshipers of Bacchus whose orgiastic rites were performed in the wild. The comic hyperbole is intentional.

at which wise Omar[9] sits, till the seething grape-juice rose round her bare limbs in waves of purple bubbles, or crawled in red foam over the vat's black, dripping, sloping sides. It was an extraordinary improvisation. He felt that the eyes of Dorian Gray were fixed on him, and the consciousness that amongst his audience there was one whose temperament he wished to fascinate, seemed to give his wit keenness, and to lend colour to his imagination. He was brilliant, fantastic, irresponsible. He charmed his listeners out of themselves, and they followed his pipe laughing. Dorian Gray never took his gaze off him, but sat like one under a spell, smiles chasing each other over his lips, and wonder growing grave in his darkening eyes.

At last, liveried in the costume of the age, Reality entered the room in the shape of a servant to tell the Duchess that her carriage was waiting. She wrung her hands in mock despair. "How annoying!" she cried. "I must go. I have to call for my husband at the club, to take him to some absurd meeting at Willis's Rooms,[1] where he is going to be in the chair. If I am late he is sure to be furious, and I couldn't have a scene in this bonnet. It is far too fragile. A harsh word would ruin it. No, I must go, dear Agatha. Good-bye, Lord Henry, you are quite delightful, and dreadfully demoralizing. I am sure I don't know what to say about your views. You must come and dine with us some night. Tuesday? Are you disengaged Tuesday?"

"For you I would throw over anybody, Duchess," said Lord Henry, with a bow.

"Ah! that is very nice, and very wrong of you," she cried; "so mind you come;" and she swept out of the room, followed by Lady Agatha and the other ladies.

When Lord Henry had sat down again,[2] Mr. Erskine moved round, and taking a chair close to him, placed his hand upon his arm.

"You talk books away," he said; "why don't you write one?"

"I am too fond of reading books to care to write them, Mr. Erskine. I should like to write a novel certainly, a novel that would be as lovely as a Persian carpet and as unreal. But there is no literary public in England for anything except newspapers, primers, and encyclopædias. Of all people in the world the English have the least sense of the beauty of literature."

"I fear you are right," answered Mr. Erskine. "I myself used to have literary ambitions, but I gave them up long ago. And now, my dear young friend, if you will allow me to call you so, may I ask if you really meant all that you said to us at lunch?"

9. The Persian poet-astronomer whose work was immortalized in English by Edward FitzGerald's rendering of *The Rubaiyat of Omar Khayyam*, a poem much admired by the Decadents. Omar drank wine to forget the pangs of both mortality and his loss of faith in God.

1. Formerly Almack's Assembly Rooms, a club in King Street frequented by Wilde. It was in the eighteenth century one of the most fashionable clubs for ladies and gentlemen.

2. Wilde canceled the following in MS: "he poured himself a glass of green Chartreuse and asked the butler for a light."

"I quite forget what I said," smiled Lord Henry. "Was it all very bad?"

"Very bad indeed. In fact I consider you extremely dangerous, and if anything happens to our good Duchess we shall all look on you as being primarily responsible. But I should like to talk to you about life. The generation into which I was born was tedious. Some day, when you are tired of London, come down to Treadley, and expound to me your philosophy of pleasure over some admirable Burgundy I am fortunate enough to possess."

"I shall be charmed. A visit to Treadley would be a great privilege. It has a perfect host, and a perfect library."

"You will complete it," answered the old gentleman, with a courteous bow. "And now I must bid good-bye to your excellent aunt. I am due at the Athenæum.[3] It is the hour when we sleep there."

"All of you, Mr. Erskine?"

"Forty of us, in forty arm-chairs. We are practising for an English Academy of Letters."

Lord Henry laughed, and rose. "I am going to the Park," he cried.

As he was passing out of the door Dorian Gray touched him on the arm. "Let me come with you," he murmured.

"But I thought you had promised Basil Hallward to go and see him," answered Lord Henry.

"I would sooner come with you; yes, I feel I must come with you. Do let me. And you will promise to talk to me all the time? No one talks so wonderfully as you do."

"Ah! I have talked quite enough for to-day," said Lord Henry, smiling. "All I want now is to look at life. You may come and look at it with me, if you care to."

Chapter IV.[1]

One afternoon, a month later, Dorian Gray was reclining in a luxurious arm-chair, in the little library[2] of Lord Henry's house in Mayfair. It was, in its way, a very charming room, with its high panelled wainscoting of olive-stained oak, its cream-coloured frieze and ceiling of raised plaster-work, and its brickdust felt carpet strewn with silk long-fringed Persian rugs. On a tiny satin-wood table stood a statuette by Clodion,[3] and beside it lay a copy of "Les Cent Nouvelles,"[4] bound for Margaret of Valois by Clovis Eve,[5] and powdered with the gilt daisies that Queen had selected for her device. Some large blue china jars and parrot-tulips

3. The leading literary club of London, located in Pall Mall.

1. The former chapter 3 in the magazine edition.

2. Lord Henry's library bears a striking resemblance in several details to Wilde's library in his Tite Street, Chelsea, home.

3. Claude Michel Clodion (1738–1814) was specially noted for his antique subjects.

4. A collection of bawdy French tales (1462), perennially a favorite of illustrators and collectors and prized for its spirit of pleasant indecency.

5. Margaret of Valois (1553–1615), married to Henry of Navarre, was as notorious for her dissolute behavior as she was renowned for her beauty. Clovis Eve (1584–1635) was a French bookbinder and illustrator for the royal court, remembered as the designer of the "fanfare" style of bindery decoration admired by the Aesthetes.

were ranged on the mantelshelf, and through the small leaded panes of the window streamed the apricot-coloured light of a summer day in London.

Lord Henry had not yet come in. He was always late on principle, his principle being that punctuality is the thief of time. So the lad was looking rather sulky, as with listless fingers he turned over the pages of an elaborately-illustrated edition of "Manon Lescaut"[6] that he had found in one of the bookcases. The formal monotonous ticking of the Louis Quatorze[7] clock annoyed him. Once or twice he thought of going away.

At last he heard a step outside, and the door opened. "How late you are, Harry!" he murmured.

"I am afraid it is not Harry, Mr. Gray," answered a shrill voice.

He glanced quickly round, and rose to his feet. "I beg your pardon. I thought—"

"You thought it was my husband. It is only his wife. You must let me introduce myself. I know you quite well by your photographs. I think my husband has got seventeen of them."

"Not seventeen, Lady Henry?"

"Well, eighteen, then. And I saw you with him the other night at the Opera." She laughed nervously as she spoke, and watched him with her vague forget-me-not eyes. She was a curious woman, whose dresses always looked as if they had been designed in a rage and put on in a tempest. She was usually in love with somebody, and, as her passion was never returned, she had kept all her illusions. She tried to look picturesque, but only succeeded in being untidy. Her name was Victoria, and she had a perfect mania for going to church.[8]

"That was at 'Lohengrin,'[9] Lady Henry, I think?"

"Yes; it was at dear 'Lohengrin.' I like Wagner's music better than anybody's. It is so loud that one can talk the whole time without other people hearing what one says. That is a great advantage: don't you think so, Mr. Gray?"

The same nervous staccato laugh broke from her thin lips, and her fingers began to play with a long tortoise-shell paper-knife.

Dorian smiled, and shook his head: "I am afraid I don't think so, Lady Henry. I never talk during music—at least, during good music. If one hears bad music, it is one's duty to drown it in conversation."

"Ah! that is one of Harry's views, isn't it, Mr. Gray? I always hear Harry's views from his friends. It is the only way I get to know of them. But you must not think I don't like good music. I adore it, but I am afraid of it. It makes me too romantic. I have simply worshipped pia-

---

6. Novel (1731) by Abbé de Prevost, the theme of which is the struggle between romantic love and self-indulgence. It was considered scandalous by the Victorians, who judged nearly all French novels too graphic.

7. A clock designed in the baroque manner of the period of Louis XIV of France (1638–1715).

8. Victoria Wotton is said to be modeled after Constance, Wilde's wife.

9. *Lohengrin*, the Richard Wagner opera, was first performed in 1850. It was based on one of the Grail cycle stories, that of Lohengrin, Knight of the Swan. Along with *Tannhäuser*, it constitutes a recurring motif in the novel.

nists—two at a time, sometimes, Harry tells me. I don't know what it is about them. Perhaps it is that they are foreigners. They all are, ain't they? Even those that are born in England become foreigners after a time, don't they? It is so clever of them, and such a compliment to art. Makes it quite cosmopolitan, doesn't it? You have never been to any of my parties, have you, Mr. Gray? You must come. I can't afford orchids, but I spare no expense in foreigners. They make one's rooms look so picturesque. But here is Harry!—Harry, I came in to look for you, to ask you something—I forget what it was—and I found Mr. Gray here. We have had such a pleasant chat about music. We have quite the same ideas. No; I think our ideas are quite different. But he has been most pleasant. I am so glad I've seen him."

"I am charmed, my love, quite charmed," said Lord Henry, elevating his dark crescent-shaped eyebrows and looking at them both with an amused smile. "So sorry I am late, Dorian. I went to look after a piece of old brocade in Wardour Street,[1] and had to bargain for hours for it. Nowadays people know the price of everything, and the value of nothing."

"I am afraid I must be going," exclaimed Lady Henry, breaking an awkward silence with her silly sudden laugh. "I promised to drive with the Duchess. Good-bye, Mr. Gray. Good-bye Harry. You are dining out, I suppose? So am I. Perhaps I shall see you at Lady Thornbury's."

"I dare say, my dear," said Lord Henry, shutting the door behind her, as, looking like a bird of paradise that had been out all night in the rain, she flitted out of the room, leaving a faint odour of frangipanni. Then he lit a cigarette, and flung himself down on the sofa.

"Never marry a woman with straw-coloured hair, Dorian," he said, after a few puffs.

"Why, Harry?"

"Because they are so sentimental."

"But I like sentimental people."

"Never marry at all, Dorian. Men marry because they are tired; women, because they are curious: both are disappointed."

"I don't think I am likely to marry, Harry. I am too much in love. That is one of your aphorisms. I am putting it into practice, as I do everything that you say."

"Who are you in love with?" asked Lord Henry, after a pause.

"With an actress," said Dorian Gray, blushing.

Lord Henry shrugged his shoulders, "That is a rather commonplace *début*."

"You would not say so if you saw her, Harry."

"Who is she?"

"Her name is Sibyl Vane."

"Never heard of her."

1. Famous for antique shops. The epigram of the next sentence reappears in *Lady Windermere's Fan* near the end of act 3 as Lord Darlington's definition to Cecil Graham of a cynic.

"No one has. People will some day, however. She is a genius."

"My dear boy, no woman is a genius. Women are a decorative sex. They never have anything to say, but they say it charmingly. Women represent the triumph of matter over mind, just as men represent the triumph of mind over morals."

"Harry, how can you?"

"My dear Dorian, it is quite true. I am analyzing women at present, so I ought to know. The subject is not so abstruse as I thought it was. I find that, ultimately, there are only two kinds of women, plain and the coloured. The plain women are very useful. If you want to gain a reputation for respectability, you have merely to take them down to supper. The other women are very charming. They commit one mistake, however. They paint in order to try and look young. Our grandmothers painted in order to try and talk brilliantly. *Rouge* and *esprit*[2] used to go together. That is all over now. As long as a woman can look ten years younger than her own daughter, she is perfectly satisfied. As for conversation, there are only five women in London worth talking to, and two of these can't be admitted into decent society. However, tell me about your genius. How long have you known her?"

"Ah! Harry, your views terrify me."

"Never mind that. How long have you known her?"

"About three weeks."

"And where did you came across her?"

"I will tell you, Harry; but you mustn't be unsympathetic about it. After all, it never would have happened if I had not met you. You filled me with a wild desire to know everything about life. For days after I met you, something seemed to throb in my veins. As I lounged in the Park, or strolled down Piccadilly, I used to look at every one who passed me, and wonder, with a mad curiosity, what sort of lives they led. Some of them fascinated me. Others filled me with terror. There was an exquisite poison in the air. I had a passion for sensations. . . . Well, one evening about seven o'clock, I determined to go out in search of some adventure. I felt that this grey, monstrous London of ours, with its myriads of people, its sordid sinners, and its splendid sins, as you once phrased it, must have something in store for me. I fancied a thousand things. The mere danger gave me a sense of delight. I remembered what you had said to me on that wonderful evening when we first dined together, about the search for beauty being the real secret of life. I don't know what I expected, but I went out and wandered eastward, soon losing my way in a labyrinth of grimy streets and black, grassless squares. About half-past eight I passed by an absurd little theatre, with great flaring gas-jets and gaudy play-bills. A hideous Jew, in the most amazing waistcoat I ever beheld in my life, was standing at the entrance, smoking a vile cigar. He had greasy

2. A combination of beauty and wit (literally, makeup and liveliness of mind). Compare this to Max Beerbohm's argument in "A Defense of Cosmetics," in *The Yellow Book* 1 (April 1894): 65–82.

ringlets, and an enormous diamond blazed in the centre of a soiled shirt. 'Have a box, my Lord?' he said, when he saw me, and he took off his hat with an air of gorgeous servility. There was something about him Harry, that amused me. He was such a monster. You will laugh at me, I know, but I really went in and paid a whole guinea for the stage-box. To the present day I can't make out why I did so; and yet if I hadn't— my dear Harry, if I hadn't I should have missed the greatest romance of my life. I see you are laughing. It is horrid of you!"

"I am not laughing Dorian; at least I am not laughing at you. But you should not say the greatest romance of your life. Your should say the first romance of your life. You will always be loved, and you will always be in love with love. A *grande passion* is the privilege of people who have nothing to do. That is the one use of the idle classes of a country. Don't be afraid. There are exquisite things in store for you. This is merely the beginning."

"Do you think my nature so shallow?" cried Dorian Gray, angrily.

"No; I think your nature so deep."

"How do you mean?"

"My dear boy, the people who love only once in their lives are really the shallow people. What they call their loyalty, and their fidelity, I call either the lethargy of custom or their lack of imagination. Faithfulness is to the emotional life what consistency is to the life of the intellect— simply a confession of failure. Faithfulness! I must analyze it some day. The passion for property is in it. There are many things that we would throw away if we were not afraid that others might pick them up. But I don't want to interrupt you. Go on with your story."

"Well, I found myself seated in a horrid little private box, with a vulgar drop-scene [3] staring me in the face. I looked out from behind the curtain, and surveyed the house. It was a tawdry affair, all Cupids and cornucopias, like a third-rate wedding-cake. The gallery and pit were fairly full, but the two rows of dingy stalls were quite empty, and there was hardly a person in what I suppose they called the dress-circle. Women went about with oranges and ginger-beer, and there was a terrible consumption of nuts going on."

"It must have been just like the palmy days of the British Drama."

"Just like, I should fancy, and very depressing. I began to wonder what on earth I should do, when I caught sight of the play-bill. What do you think the play was, Harry?"

"I should think 'The Idiot Boy, or Dumb but Innocent.' [4] Our fathers used to like that sort of piece, I believe. The longer I live, Dorian, the more keenly I feel that whatever was good enough for our fathers is not

3. A stage curtain on which a scene or design has been painted. At the time, scenes were usually stylized landscapes or gardens.
4. The title is Wilde's parody of a type of rustic melodrama that still appealed to lower-class audiences in the 1890's but that had reached the peak of its appeal in the mid-nineteenth century, inspired, perhaps, by the novels of Walter Scott and the philosopher-rustics of William Wordsworth. There was a play, *The Idiot of the Mill*, which may have inspired the mocking title (*Dorian Gray*, Murray 241).

good enough for us. In art, as in politics, *les grandpères ont toujours tort.*" [5]

"This play was good enough for us, Harry. It was 'Romeo and Juliet.' I must admit that I was rather annoyed at the idea of seeing Shakespeare done in such a wretched hole of a place. Still, I felt interested, in a sort of way. At any rate, I determined to wait for the first act. There was a dreadful orchestra, presided over by a young Hebrew who sat at a cracked piano, that nearly drove me away, but at last the drop-scene was drawn up, and the play began. Romeo was a stout elderly gentleman, with corked eyebrows, a husky tragedy voice, and a figure like a beer-barrel. Mercutio was almost as bad. He was played by the low-comedian, who had introduced gags of his own and was on most friendly terms with the pit. They were both as grotesque as the scenery, and that looked as if it had come out of a country-booth. But Juliet! Harry, imagine a girl, hardly seventeen years of age, with a little flower-like face, a small Greek head with plaited coils of dark-brown hair, eyes that were violet wells of passion, lips that were like the petals of a rose. She was the loveliest thing I had ever seen in my life. [6] You said to me once that pathos left you unmoved, but that beauty, mere beauty, could fill your eyes with tears. I tell you, Harry, I could hardly see this girl for the mist of tears that came across me. And her voice—I never heard such a voice. It was very low at first, with deep mellow notes, that seemed to fall singly upon one's ear. Then it became a little louder, and sounded like a flute or a distant hautbois. In the garden-scene it had all the tremulous ecstasy that one hears just before dawn when nightingales are singing. There were moments, later on, when it had the wild passion of violins. You know how a voice can stir one. Your voice and the voice of Sibyl Vane are two things that I shall never forget. When I close my eyes, I hear them, and each of them says something different. I don't know which to follow. Why should I not love her? Harry, I do love her. She is everything to me in life. Night after night I go to see her play. One evening she is Rosalind, and the next evening she is Imogen. [7] I have seen her die in the gloom of a Italian tomb, sucking the poison from her lover's lips. [8] I have watched her wandering through the forest of Arden, disguised as a pretty boy in hose and doublet and dainty cap. She has been mad, and has come into the presence of a guilty king, and given him rue to wear, and bitter herbs to taste of. She has been innocent, and the black hands of jealousy have crushed her reed-like throat. I have seen her in every age and in every costume. Ordinary women never appeal to one's imagination. They are limited to their century. No glam-

---

5. "Grandfathers are always wrong": a most un-Victorian sentiment.
6. In a letter to Lillie Langtry, famous beauty and actress, (December 1883), Wilde announced his intention to marry "a beautiful girl called Constance Lloyd, a grave, slight, violet-eyed little Artemis, with great coils of heavy brown hair which make her flower-like head droop like a blossom.

. . ." (*Letters* 154). A hautbois, below, is an oboe.
7. The daughter of Cymbeline in Shakespeare's play. Rosalind, above, is the heroine of *As You Like It.*
8. Thus Juliet dies, but in *Hamlet* 3.1.155–56, Ophelia complains, "And I, of ladies most deject and wretched / That suck'd the honey of his music vows."

our even transfigures them. One knows their minds as easily as one knows their bonnets. One can always find them. There is no mystery in any of them. They ride in the Park in the morning, and chatter at tea-parties in the afternoon. They have their stereotyped smile, and their fashionable manner. They are quite obvious. But an actress! How different an actress is! Harry! why didn't you tell me that the one thing worth loving is an actress?"

"Because I have loved so many of them, Dorian."

"Oh, yes, horrid people with dyed hair and painted faces."

"Don't run down dyed hair and painted faces. There is an extraordinary charm in them, sometimes," said Lord Henry.

"I wish now I had not told you about Sibyl Vane."

"You could not have helped telling me, Dorian. All through your life you will tell me everything you do."

"Yes, Harry, I believe that is true. I cannot help telling you things. You have a curious influence over me. If I ever did a crime, I would come and confess it to you. You would understand me."

"People like you—the wilful sunbeams of life—don't commit crimes, Dorian.[9] But I am much obliged for the compliment, all the same. And now tell me—reach me the matches, like a good boy: thanks:—what are your actual relations with Sibyl Vane?"

Dorian Gray leaped to his feet, with flushed cheeks and burning eye. "Harry! Sibyl Vane is sacred!"

"It is only the sacred things that are worth touching, Dorian," said Lord Henry, with a strange touch of pathos in his voice. "But why should you be annoyed? I suppose she will belong to you some day.[1] When one is in love, one always begins by deceiving one's self, and one always ends by deceiving others. That is what the world calls a romance. You know her, at any rate, I suppose?"

"Of course I know her. On the first night I was at the theatre, the horrid old Jew came round to the box after the performance was over, and offered to take me behind the scenes and introduce me to her. I was furious with him, and told him that Juliet had been dead for hundreds of years, and that her body was lying in a marble tomb in Verona. I think, from his blank look of amazement, that he was under the impression that I had taken too much champagne, or something."

"I am not surprised."

"Then he asked me if I wrote for any of the newspapers. I told him I never even read them. He seemed terribly disappointed at that, and confided to me that all the dramatic critics were in a conspiracy against him, and that they were every one of them to be bought."

"I should not wonder if he was quite right there. But, on the other

---

9. This is one of the many instances of Wotton's self-satisfied misjudgment of Dorian's character, growing out of the mistaken belief that Dorian was a mere projection of his own egoism.

1. One of J. M. Stoddart's substitutions made in the magazine edition and retained here. The Clark TS originally read "She will be your mistress someday." For a fuller consideration of the issue of Stoddart's emendations, see the Note on the Texts, above, especially pp. xi–xiii.

hand, judging from their appearance, most of them cannot be at all expensive."

"Well, he seemed to think that they were beyond his means," laughed Dorian. "By this time, however, the lights were being put out in the theatre, and I had to go. He wanted me to try some cigars that he strongly recommended. I declined. The next night, of course, I arrived at the place again. When he saw me he made me a low bow, and assured me that I was a munificent patron of art. He was a most offensive brute, though he had an extraordinary passion for Shakespeare. He told me once, with an air of pride, that his five bankruptcies were entirely due to 'The Bard,' as he insisted on calling him. He seemed to think it a distinction."

"It was a distinction, my dear Dorian—a great distinction. Most people become bankrupt through having invested too heavily in the prose of life. To have ruined one's self over poetry is an honour. But when did you first speak to Miss Sibyl Vane?"

"The third night. She had been playing Rosalind. I could not help going round. I had thrown her some flowers, and she had looked at me; at least I fancied that she had. The old Jew was persistent. He seemed determined to take me behind, so I consented. It was curious my not wanting to know her, wasn't it?"

"No; I don't think so."

"My dear Harry, why?"

"I will tell you some other time. Now I want to know about the girl."

"Sibyl? Oh, she was so shy, and so gentle. There is something of a child about her. Her eyes opened wide in exquisite wonder when I told her what I thought of her performance, and she seemed quite unconscious of her power. I think we were both rather nervous. The old Jew stood grinning at the doorway of the dusty greenroom,[2] making elaborate speeches about us both, while we stood looking at each other like children. He would insist on calling me 'My Lord,' so I had to assure Sibyl that I was not anything of the kind. She said quite simply to me, 'You look more like a prince. I must call you Prince Charming.'"

"Upon my word, Dorian, Miss Sibyl knows how to pay compliments."

"You don't understand her, Harry. She regarded me merely as a person in a play. She knows nothing of life. She lives with her mother, a faded tired woman who played Lady Capulet[3] in a sort of magenta dressing-wrapper on the first night, and looks as if she had seen better days."

"I know the look. It depresses me," murmured Lord Henry, examining his rings.

"The Jew wanted to tell me her history, but I said it did not interest me."

2. A reception room and lounge for performers in a theater.   3. Juliet's mother in *Romeo and Juliet*.

"You were quite right. There is always something infinitely mean about other people's tragedies."

"Sibyl is the only thing I care about. What is it to me where she came from? From her little head to her little feet, she is absolutely and entirely divine. Every night of my life I go to see her act, and every night she is more marvellous."

"That is the reason, I suppose, that you never dine with me now. I thought you must have some curious romance on hand. You have; but it is not quite what I expected."

"My dear Harry, we either lunch or sup together every day, and I have been to the Opera with you several times," said Dorian, opening his blue eyes in wonder.

"You always come dreadfully late."

"Well, I can't help going to see Sibyl play," he cried, "even if it is only for a single act. I get hungry for her presence; and when I think of the wonderful soul that is hidden away in that little ivory body, I am filled with awe."

"You can dine with me to-night, Dorian, can't you?"

He shook his head. "To-night she is Imogen," he answered, "and tomorrow night she will be Juliet."

"When is she Sibyl Vane?"

"Never."

"I congratulate you."

"How horrid you are! She is all the great heroines of the world in one. She is more than an individual. You laugh, but I tell you she has genius. I love her, and I must make her love me. You, who know all the secrets of life, tell me how to charm Sibyl Vane to love me! I want to make Romeo jealous. I want the dead lovers of the world to hear our laughter, and grow sad. I want a breath of our passion to stir their dust into consciousness, to wake their ashes into pain. My God, Harry, how I worship her!" He was walking up and down the room as he spoke. Hectic spots of red burned on his cheeks. He was terribly excited.

Lord Henry watched him with a subtle sense of pleasure. How different he was now from the shy, frightened boy he had met in Basil Hallward's studio? His nature had developed like a flower, had borne blossoms of scarlet flame. Out of its secret hiding-place had crept his Soul, and Desire had come to meet it on the way.

"And what do you propose to do?" said Lord Henry, at last.

"I want you and Basil to come with me some night and see her act. I have not the slightest fear of the result. You are certain to acknowledge her genius. Then we must get her out of the Jew's hands. She is bound to him for three years—at least for two years and eight months—from the present time. I shall have to pay him something, of course. When all that is settled, I shall take a West End theatre and bring her out properly. She will make the world as mad as she had made me."

"That would be impossible, my dear boy."

"Yes she will. She has not merely art, consummate art-instinct, in her, but she has personality also; and you have often told me that it is personalities, not principles, that move the age."

"Well, what night shall we go?"

"Let me see. To-day is Tuesday. Let us fix to-morrow. She plays Juliet to-morrow."

"All right. The Bristol[4] at eight o'clock; and I will get Basil."

"Not eight, Harry, please. Half-past six. We must be there before the curtain rises. You must see in the first act, where she meets Romeo."

"Half-past six! What an hour! It will be like having a meat-tea, or reading an English novel. It must be seven. No gentleman dines before seven. Shall you see Basil between this and then? Or shall I write to him?"

"Dear Basil! I have not laid eyes on him for a week. It is rather horrid of me, as he has sent me my portrait in the most wonderful frame, specially designed by himself, and, though I am a little jealous of the picture for being a whole month younger than I am, I must admit that I delight in it. Perhaps you better write to him. I don't want to see him alone. He says things that annoy me. He gives me good advice."

Lord Henry smiled. "People are very fond of giving away what they need most themselves. It is what I call the depth of generosity."

"Oh, Basil is the best of fellows, but he seems to me to be just a bit of a Philistine. Since I have known you, Harry, I have discovered that."

"Basil, my dear boy, puts everything that is charming in him into his work. The consequence is that he has nothing left for life but his prejudices, his principles, and his common sense. The only artists I have ever known, who are personally delightful, are bad artists. Good artists exist simply in what they make, and consequently are perfectly uninteresting in what they are. A great poet, a really great poet, is the most unpoetical of all creatures.[5] But inferior poets are absolutely fascinating. The worse their rhymes are, the more picturesque they look. The mere fact of having published a book of second-rate sonnets makes a man quite irresistible. He lives the poetry that he cannot write. The others write the poetry that they dare not realize."

"I wonder is that really so, Harry?" said Dorian Gray, putting some perfume on his handkerchief out of a large gold-topped bottle that stood on the table. "It must be, if you say it. And now I am off. Imogen is waiting for me. Don't forget about to-morrow. Good-bye."

As he left the room, Lord Henry's heavy eyelids drooped, and he began to think. Certainly few people had ever interested him so much as Dorian Gray, and yet the lad's mad adoration of some one else caused him not the slightest pang of annoyance or jealousy. He was pleased by it. It made him a more interesting study. He had been always enthralled

---

4. A luxury hotel near the Ritz in Piccadilly.
5. An allusion perhaps to John Keats's letter to Richard Woodhouse of October 27, 1818.

by the methods of natural science, but the ordinary subject-matter of that science had seemed to him trivial and of no import. And so he had begun by vivisecting himself, as he had ended by vivisecting others. Human life—that appeared to him the one thing worth investigating. Compared to it there was nothing else of any value. It was true that as one watched life in its curious crucible of pain and pleasure, one could not wear over one's face a mask of glass, nor keep the sulphurous fumes from troubling the brain and making the imagination turbid with monstrous fancies and misshapen dreams. There were poisons so subtle that to know their properties one had to sicken of them. There were maladies so strange that one had to pass through them if one sought to understand their nature. And, yet, what a great reward one received! How wonderful the whole world became to one! To note the curious hard logic of passion, and the emotional coloured life of the intellect—to observe where they met, and where they separated, at what point they were in unison, and at what point they were at discord—there was a delight in that! What matter what the cost was? One could never pay too high a price for any sensation.

He was conscious—and the thought brought a gleam of pleasure into his brown agate eyes—that it was through certain words of his, musical words said with musical utterance, that Dorian Gray's soul had turned to this white girl[6] and bowed in worship before her. To a large extent the lad was his own creation. He had made him premature. That was something. Ordinary people waited till life disclosed to them its secrets, but to the few, to the elect, the mysteries of life were revealed before the veil was drawn away. Sometimes this was the effect of art, and chiefly of the art of literature, which dealt immediately with the passions and the intellect. But now and then a complex personality took the place and assumed the office of art, was indeed, in its way, a real work of art, Life having its elaborate masterpieces, just as poetry has, or sculpture, or paintings.[7]

Yes, the lad was premature. He was gathering his harvest while it was yet spring. The pulse and passion of youth were in him, but he was becoming self-conscious. It was delightful to watch him. With his beautiful face, and his beautiful soul, he was a thing to wonder at. It was no matter how it all ended, or was destined to end. He was like one of those gracious figures in a pageant or a play, whose joys seemed to be remote from one, but whose sorrows stir one's sense of beauty, and whose wounds are like red roses.

Soul and body, body and soul—how mysterious they were! There was

6. A reference to Whistler's picture of that name, on which Swinburne based his poem "Before the Mirror," in *Poems and Ballads* (1866).
7. This is an Aesthetic doctrine Wilde often espoused, and yet Wotton's influence on Dorian is pernicious according to Wilde's philosophy because it interferes with Dorian's natural devel-opment. Wotton's dream of being an artist by shaping Dorian's life is doomed. As Wilde wrote in "The Critic as Artist": "action of every kind belongs to the sphere of ethics. The aim of art is simply to create a mood": and later: "Whatever actually occurs is spoiled for art."

animalism in the soul, and the body had its moments of spirituality. The senses could refine, and the intellect could degrade. Who could say where the fleshly impulse ceased, or the psychical impulse began? How shallow were the arbitrary definitions of ordinary psychologists! And yet how difficult to decide between the claims of the various schools! Was the soul a shadow seated in the house of sin? Or was the body really in the soul, as Giordano Bruno[8] thought? The separation of spirit from matter was a mystery, and the union of spirit with matter was a mystery also.

He began to wonder whether we could ever make psychology so absolute a science that each little spring of life would be revealed to us. As it was, we always misunderstood ourselves, and rarely understood others. Experience was of no ethical value. It was merely the name men gave to their mistakes. Moralists had, as a rule, regarded it as a mode of warning, had claimed for it a certain ethical efficacy in the formation of character, had praised it as something that taught us what to follow and showed us what to avoid. But there was no motive power in experience. It was as little of an active cause as conscience itself. All that it really demonstrated was that our future would be the same as our past, and that the sin we had done once, and with loathing, we would do many times, and with joy.

It was clear to him that the experimental method was the only method by which one could arrive at any scientific analysis of the passions; and certainly Dorian Gray was a subject made to his hand, and seemed to promise rich and fruitful results. His sudden mad love for Sibyl Vane was a psychological phenomenon of no small interest. There was no doubt that curiosity had much to do with it, curiosity and the desire for new experiences; yet it was not a simple but rather a very complex passion. What there was in it of the purely sensuous instinct of boyhood had been transformed by the workings of the imagination, changed into something that seemed to the lad himself to be remote from sense, and was for that very reason all the more dangerous. It was the passions about whose origin we deceived ourselves that tyrannized most strongly over us. Our weakest motives were those of whose nature we were conscious. It often happened that when we thought we were experimenting on others we were really experimenting on ourselves.

While Lord Henry sat dreaming on these things, a knock came to the door, and his valet entered, and reminded him it was time to dress for dinner. He got up and looked out into the street. The sunset had smitten into scarlet gold the upper windows of the houses opposite. The panes glowed like plates of heated metal. The sky above was like a faded rose.

8. Proponent of the new astronomy of Copernicus and an advocate of freedom of thought. Bruno (1548–1600) was put to death by the Inquisition, largely as the result of his attacks on orthodox Aristotelianism. Pater wrote an essay on Bruno, which appeared in *The Fortnightly Review* (August 1889); Wilde would have known it. Bruno has been a cultural hero of writers and intellectuals since the mid-nineteenth century.

He thought of his friend's young fiery-coloured life, and wondered how it was all going to end.

When he arrived home, about half-past twelve o'clock, he saw a telegram lying on the hall table. He opened it, and found it was from Dorian Gray. It was to tell him that he was engaged to be married to Sibyl Vane.

Chapter V.[1]

"Mother, mother, I am so happy!" whispered the girl, burying her face in the lap of the faded, tired-looking woman who, with back turned to the shrill intrusive light, was sitting in the one arm-chair that their dingy sitting-room contained. "I am so happy!"she repeated, "and you must be happy too!"

Mrs. Vane winced, and put her thin bismuth-whitened[2] hands on her daughter's head. "Happy!" she echoed, "I am only happy, Sibyl, when I see you act. You must not think of anything but your acting. Mr. Isaacs has been very good to us, and we owe him money."

The girl looked up and pouted. "Money, mother?" she cried, "what does money matter? Love is more than money."

"Mr. Isaacs has advanced us fifty pounds to pay off our debts, and to get a proper outfit for James. You must not forget that, Sibyl. Fifty pounds is a very large sum.[3] Mr. Isaacs has been most considerate."

"He is not a gentleman, mother, and I hate the way he talks to me," said the girl, rising to her feet, and going over to the window.

"I don't know how we could manage without him," answered the elder woman, querulously.

Sibyl Vane tossed her head and laughed. "We don't want him any more, mother. Prince Charming[4] rules life for us now." Then she paused. A rose shook in her blood, and shadowed her cheeks. Quick breath parted the petals of her lips. They trembled. Some southern wind of passion swept over her, and stirred the dainty folds of her dress. "I love him," she said, simply.

"Foolish child! foolish child!" was the parrot-phrase flung in answer. The waving of crooked, false-jewelled fingers gave grotesqueness to the words.

The girl laughed again. The joy of a caged bird was in her voice. Her eyes caught the melody, and echoed it in radiance: then closed for a moment, as though to hide their secret. When they opened, the mist of a dream had passed across them.

Thin-lipped wisdom spoke at her from the worn chair, hinted at prudence, quoted from that book of cowardice whose author apes the name of common sense. She did not listen. She was free in her prison of

1. The second of the new chapters written for the revised edition.
2. Bismuth, a whitening agent in paints and cosmetics, is still used in the theater, especially by mimes and clowns.
3. Fifty pounds would have an equivalent value today of ten thousand dollars.
4. Dorian's performance as Sibyl's Prince Charming is a cruel reversal of the fairy tale prince; Sibyl's fate is similarly reversed.

passion.[5] Her prince, Prince Charming, was with her. She had called on Memory to remake him. She had sent her soul to search for him, and it had brought him back. His kiss burned again upon her mouth. Her eyelids were warm with his breath.

Then Wisdom altered its method and spoke of espial and discovery. This young man might be rich. If so, marriage should be thought of. Against the shell of her ear broke the waves of worldly cunning. The arrows of craft shot by her. She saw the thin lips moving, and smiled.

Suddenly she felt the need to speak. The wordy silence troubled her. "Mother, mother," she cried, "why does he love me so much? I know why I love him. I love him because he is like what Love himself should be. But what does he see in me? I am not worthy of him. And yet—why, I cannot tell—though I feel so much beneath him, I don't feel humble. I feel proud, terribly proud. Mother, did you love my father as I love Prince Charming?"

The elder woman grew pale beneath the coarse powder that daubed her cheeks, and her dry lips twitched with a spasm of pain. Sibyl rushed to her, flung her arms round her neck, and kissed her. "Forgive me, mother. I know it pains you to talk about our father. But it only pains you because you loved him so much. Don't look so sad. I am as happy to-day as you were twenty years ago. Ah! let me be happy for ever!"

"My child, you are far too young to think of falling in love. Besides, what do you know of this young man? You don't even know his name. The whole thing is most inconvenient, and really, when James[6] is going away to Australia, and I have so much to think of, I must say that you should have shown more consideration. However, as I said before, if he is rich . . ."

"Ah! mother, mother, let me be happy!"

Mrs. Vane glanced at her, and with one of those false theatrical gestures that so often become a mode of second nature to a stage-player, clasped her in her arms. At this moment the door opened, and a young lad with rough brown hair came into the room. He was thick-set of figure, and his hands and feet were large, and somewhat clumsy in movement. He was not so finely bred as his sister.[7] One would hardly have guessed the close relationship that existed between them. Mrs. Vane fixed her eyes on him, and intensified her smile. She mentally elevated her son to the dignity of an audience. She felt sure that the *tableau*[8] was interesting.

"You might keep some of your kisses for me, Sibyl, I think," said the lad, with a good-natured grumble.

"Ah! but you don't like being kissed, Jim," she cried. "You are a

---

5. An allusion to the theme of Richard Lovelace's "To Althea from Prison," with another reversal of roles of lover / beloved.
6. Sibyl's brother, Dorian's unsuccessful nemesis and one of Wilde's inspired additions to his text for the revised edition.

7. The physical appearance of James Vane appears to owe a good deal to the appearance of Willie, Oscar Wilde's brother.
8. A striking, theatrical arrangement of persons in a frozen dramatic pose, very popular with theater-goers of the times.

dreadful old bear." And she ran across the room and hugged him.

James Vane looked into his sister's face with tenderness. "I want you to come out with me for a walk, Sibyl. I don't suppose I shall ever see this horrid London again. I am sure I don't want to."

"My son, don't say such dreadful things," murmured Mrs. Vane, taking up a tawdry theatrical dress, with a sigh, and beginning to patch it. She felt a little disappointed that he had not joined the group. It would have increased the theatrical picturesqueness of the situation.

"Why not, mother? I mean it."

"You pain me, my son. I trust you will return from Australia in a position of affluence. I believe there is no society of any kind in the Colonies, nothing that I would call society; so when you have made your fortune you must come back and assert yourself in London."

"Society!" muttered the lad. "I don't want to know anything about that. I should like to make some money to take you and Sibyl off the stage. I hate it."

"Oh, Jim!" said Sibyl, laughing, "how unkind of you! But are you really going for a walk with me? That will be nice! I was afraid you were going to say good-bye to some of your friends—to Tom Hardy, who gave you the hideous pipe, or Ned Langton, who makes fun of you for smoking it. It is very sweet of you to let me have your last afternoon. Where shall we go? Let us go to the Park."[9]

"I am too shabby," he answered, frowning. "Only swell[1] people go to the Park."

"Nonsense, Jim," she whispered, stroking the sleeve of his coat.

He hesitated for a moment. "Very well," he said at last, "but don't be too long dressing." She danced out of the door. One could hear her singing as she ran upstairs. Her little feet pattered overhead.

He walked up and down the room two or three times. Then he turned to the still figure in the chair. "Mother, are my things ready?" he asked.

"Quite ready, James," she answered, keeping her eyes on her work. For some months past she had felt ill at ease when she was alone with this rough, stern son of hers. Her shallow secret nature was troubled when their eyes met. She used to wonder if he suspected anything. The silence, for he made no other observation, became intolerable to her. She began to complain. Women defend themselves by attacking, just as they attack by sudden and strange surrenders. "I hope you will be contented, James, with your sea-faring life," she said. 'You must remember that it is your own choice. You might have entered a solicitor's office. Solicitors are a very respectable class, and in the country often dine with the best families."

"I hate officers, and I hate clerks," he replied. "But you are quite right. I have chosen my own life. All I say is, watch over Sibyl. Don't let her come to any harm. Mother, you must watch over her."

9. Hyde Park.   1. Fashionable and wealthy.

"James, you really talk very strangely. Of course I watch over Sibyl."

"I hear a gentleman comes every night to the theatre, and goes behind to talk to her. Is that right? What about that?"

"You are speaking about things you don't understand, James. In the profession we are accustomed to receive a great deal of most gratifying attention. I myself used to receive many bouquets at one time. That was when acting was really understood. As for Sibyl, I do not know at present whether her attachment is serious or not. But there is no doubt that the young man in question is a perfect gentleman. He is always most polite to me. Besides, he has the appearance of being rich, and the flowers he sends are lovely."

"You don't know his name, though," said the lad, harshly.

"No," answered his mother, with a placid expression in her face. "He has not yet revealed his real name. I think it is quite romantic of him. He is probably a member of the aristocracy."

James Vane bit his lip. "Watch over Sibyl, mother," he cried, "watch over her."

"My son, you distress me very much. Sibyl is always under my special care. Of course, if this gentleman is wealthy, there is no reason why she should not contract an alliance with him. I trust he is one of the aristocracy. He has all the appearance of it, I must say. It might be a most brilliant marriage for Sibyl. They would make a charming couple. His good looks are really quite remarkable; everybody notices them."

The lad muttered something to himself, and drummed on the window-pane with his coarse fingers. He had just turned round to say something, when the door opened, and Sibyl ran in.

"How serious you both are!" she cried. "What is the matter?"

"Nothing," he answered. "I suppose one must be serious sometimes. Good-bye mother; I will have my dinner at five o'clock. Everything is packed, except my shirts, so you need not trouble."

"Good-bye, my son," she answered, with a bow of strained stateliness.

She was extremely annoyed at the tone he had adopted with her, and there was something in his look that had made her feel afraid.

"Kiss me, mother," said the girl. Her flower-like lips touched the withered cheek, and warmed its frost.

"My child! my child!" cried Mrs. Vane, looking up to the ceiling in search of an imaginary gallery.

"Come, Sibyl," said her brother, impatiently. He hated his mother's affections.[2]

They went out into the flickering wind-blown sunlight, and strolled down the dreary Euston Road.[3] The passers-by glanced in wonder at the sullen, heavy youth, who, in coarse, ill-fitting clothes, was in the com-

2. Many of the mannerisms of Mrs. Vane are copied from Oscar's mother, Lady Jane Wilde.
3. Three great rail terminals in Euston Road helped turn the district into the site of flophouses, pawn-shops, second-hand dealers, brothels, and cheap theaters. The giant Doric granite portal of Euston Road was symbolic of the commercial gateway to the city.

pany of such a graceful, refined-looking girl. He was like a common gardener walking with a rose.

Jim frowned from time to time when he caught the inquisitive glance of some stranger. He had that dislike of being stared at which comes on geniuses late in life, and never leaves the commonplace. Sibyl, however, was quite unconscious of the effect she was producing. Her love was trembling in laughter on her lips. She was thinking of Prince Charming, and, that she might think of him all the more, she did not talk of him, but prattled on about the ship in which Jim was going to sail, about the gold he was certain to find, about the wonderful heiress whose life he was to save from the wicked, red-shirted bushrangers. For he was not to remain a sailor, or a super-cargo, or whatever he was going to be. Oh, no! A sailor's existence was dreadful. Fancy being cooped up in a horrid ship, with the hoarse, hump-backed waves trying to get in, and a black wind blowing the masts down, and tearing the sails into long screaming ribands! He was to leave the vessel at Melbourne, bid a polite good-bye to the captain, and go off at once to the gold-fields. Before a week was over he was to come across a large nugget of pure gold, the largest nugget that had ever been discovered, and bring it down to the coast in a waggon guarded by six mounted policemen. The bushrangers were to attack them three times, and be defeated with immense slaughter. Or, no. He was not to go to the gold-fields at all. They were horrid places, where men got intoxicated, and shot each other in bar-rooms, and used bad language. He was to be a nice sheep-farmer, and one evening, as he was riding home, he was to see the beautiful heiress being carried off by a robber on a black horse, and give chase, and rescue her. Of course she would fall in love with him, and he with her, and they would get married, and come home, and live in an immense house in London. Yes, there were delightful things in store for him. But he must be very good, and not lose his temper, or spend his money foolishly. She was only a year older than he was, but she knew so much more of life. He must be sure, also, to write to her by every mail, and to say his prayers each night before he went to sleep. God was very good, and would watch over him. She would pray for him too, and in a few years he would come back quite rich and happy.[4]

The lad listened sulkily to her, and made no answer. He was heartsick at leaving home.

Yet it was not this alone that made him gloomy and morose. Inexperienced though he was, he had still a strong sense of danger of Sibyl's position. This young dandy who was making love to her could mean her no good. He was a gentleman, and he hated him for that, hated him through some curious race-instinct for which he could not account, and which for that reason was all the more dominant within him. He was conscious also of the shallowness and vanity of his mother's nature, and

4. There are echoes in Sibyl's speech, reported indirectly here, of the voice of Constance Wilde, Oscar's wife.

in that saw infinite peril for Sibyl and Sibyl's happiness. Children begin by loving their parents; as they grow older they judge them; sometimes they forgive them.

His mother! He had something on his mind to ask of her, something that he had brooded on for many months of silence. A chance phrase that he had heard at the theatre, a whispered sneer that had reached his ears one night as he waited at the stage-door, had set loose a train of horrible thoughts. He remembered it as if it had been the lash of a hunting-crop across his face. His brows knit together into a wedge-like furrow, and with a twitch of pain he bit his under-lip.

"You are not listening to a word I am saying, Jim," cried Sibyl, "and I am making the most delightful plans for your future. Do say something."

"What do you want me to say?"

"Oh! that you will be a good boy, and not forget us," she answered, smiling at him.

He shrugged his shoulders. "You are more likely to forget me, than I am to forget you, Sibyl."

She flushed. "What do you mean, Jim?" she asked.

"You have a new friend, I hear. Who is he? Why have you not told me about him? He means you no good."

"Stop, Jim!" she exclaimed. "You must not say anything against him. I love him."

"Why, you don't even know his name," answered the lad. "Who is he? I have a right to know."

"He is called Prince Charming. Don't you like the name. Oh! you silly boy! you should never forget it. If you only saw him, you would think him the most wonderful person in the world. Some day you will meet him: when you come back from Australia. You will like him so much. Everybody likes him, and I . . . love him. I wish you could come to the theatre to-night. He is going to be there, and I am to play Juliet. Oh! how I shall play it! Fancy, Jim, to be in love and play Juliet! To have him sitting there! To play for his delight! I am afraid I may frighten the company, frighten or enthrall them. To be in love is to surpass one's self. Poor dreadful Mr. Isaacs will be shouting 'genius' to his loafers at the bar. He has preached me as a dogma; to-night he will announce me as a revelation. I feel it. And it is all his, his only, Prince Charming, my wonderful lover, my god of graces. But I am poor beside him. Poor? What does that matter? When poverty creeps in at the door, love flies in through the window. Our proverbs want re-writing. They were made in winter, and it is summer now; spring-time for me, I think, a very dance of blossoms in blue skies."

"He is a gentleman," said the lad, sullenly.

"A Prince!" she cried, musically. "What more do you want?"

"He wants to enslave you."

"I shudder at the thought of being free."

"I want you to beware of him."

"To see him is to worship him, to know him is to trust him."

"Sibyl, you are mad about him."

She laughed, and took his arm. "You dear old Jim, you talk as if you were a hundred. Some day you will be in love yourself. Then you will know what it is. Don't look so sulky. Surely you should be glad to think that, though you are going away, you leave me happier than I have ever been before. Life has been hard for us both, terribly hard and difficult. But it will be different now. You are going to a new world, and I have found one. Here are two chairs; let us sit down and see the smart people go by."

They took their seats amidst a crowd of watchers. The tulip-beds across the road flamed like throbbing rings of fire. A white dust, tremulous cloud of orris-root[5] it seemed, hung in the panting air. The brightly-coloured parasols danced and dipped like monstrous butterflies.

She made her brother talk of himself, his hopes, his prospects. He spoke slowly and with effort. They passed words to each other as players at a game pass counters. Sibyl felt oppressed. She could not communicate her joy. A faint smile curving that sullen mouth was all the echo she could win. After some time she became silent. Suddenly she caught a glimpse of golden hair and laughing lips, and in an open carriage with two ladies Dorian Gray drove past.

She started to her feet. "There he is!" she cried.

"Who?" said Jim Vane.

"Prince Charming," she answered, looking after the victoria.

He jumped up, and seized her roughly by the arm. "Show him to me. Which is he? Point him out. I must see him!" he exclaimed; but at that moment the Duke of Berwick's four-in-hand came between, and when it had left the space clear, the carriage had swept out of the Park.

"He is gone," murmured Sibyl, sadly. "I wish you had seen him."

"I wish I had, for as sure as there is a God in heaven, if he ever does you any wrong, I shall kill him."

She looked at him in horror. He repeated his words. They cut the air like a dagger. The people round began to gape. A lady standing close to her tittered.

"Come away, Jim; come away," she whispered. He followed her doggedly, as she passed through the crowd. He felt glad at what he had said.

When they reached the Achilles Statue[6] she turned round. There was pity in her eyes that became laughter on her lips. She shook her head at him. "You are foolish, Jim, utterly foolish; a bad-tempered boy, that is all. How can you say such horrible things? You don't know what you

5. Used as a perfume, it has the scent of violets.
6. A giant nude bronze statue by Sir Richard Westmacott, a copy of the original in Cavallo, Italy, erected by the ladies of England in 1822 to com- memorate the duke of Wellington's victories. James and Sibyl are now near the southeast corner of Hyde Park.

are talking about. You are simply jealous and unkind. Ah! I wish you would fall in love. Love makes people good, and what you said was wicked."

"I am sixteen," he answered, "and I know what I am about. Mother is no help to you. She doesn't understand how to look after you. I wish now that I was not going to Australia at all. I have a great mind to chuck the whole thing up. I would, if my articles hadn't been signed."

"Oh, don't be so serious, Jim. You are like one of the heroes of those silly melodramas mother used to be so fond of acting in. I am not going to quarrel with you. I have seen him, and oh! to see him is perfect happiness. We won't quarrel. I know you would never harm any one I love, would you?"

"Not as long as you love him, I suppose," was the sullen answer.

"I shall love him for ever!" she cried.

"And he?"

"For ever, too!"

"He had better."

She shrank from him. Then she laughed and put her hand on his arm. He was merely a boy.

At the Marble Arch[7] they hailed an omnibus, which left them close to their shabby home in the Euston Road. It was after five o'clock, and Sibyl had to lie down for a couple of hours before acting. Jim insisted that she should do so. He said that he would sooner part with her when their mother was not present. She would be sure to make a scene, and he detested scenes of every kind.

In Sybil's own room they parted. There was jealousy in the lad's heart, and a fierce, murderous hatred of the stranger who, as it seemed to him, had come between them. Yet, when her arms were flung round his neck, and her fingers strayed through his hair, he softened, and kissed her with real affection. There were tears in his eyes as he went downstairs.

His mother was waiting for him below. She grumbled at his unpunctuality, as he entered. He made no answer, but sat down to his meagre meal. The flies buzzed round the table, and crawled over the stained cloth. Through the rumble of omnibuses, and the clatter of street-cabs, he could hear the droning voice devouring each minute that was left to him.

After some time, he thrust away his plate, and put his head in his hands. He felt that he had a right to know. It should have been told to him before, if it was as he suspected. Leaden with fear, his mother watched him. Words dropped mechanically from her lips. A tattered lace handkerchief twitched in her fingers. When the clock struck six, he got up, and went to the door. Then he turned back, and looked at her. Their eyes met. In hers he saw a wild appeal for mercy. It enraged him.

7. A triumphal single arch modeled after that of Titus at Rome and located at the northeast entrance to Hyde Park.

"Mother, I have something to ask you," he said. Her eyes wandered vaguely about the room. She made no answer. "Tell me the truth. I have a right to know. Were you married to my father?"

She heaved a deep sigh. It was a sigh of relief. The terrible moment, the moment that night and day, for weeks and months, she had dreaded, had come at last, and yet she felt no terror. Indeed in some measure it was a disappointment to her. The vulgar directness of the question called for a direct answer. The situation had not been gradually led up to. It was crude. It reminded her of a bad rehearsal.

"No," she answered, wondering at the harsh simplicity of life.

"My father was a scoundrel then!" cried the lad, clenching his fists.

She shook her head. "I knew he was not free. We loved each other very much. If he had lived, he would have made provision for us. Don't speak against him, my son. He was your father, and a gentleman. Indeed he was highly connected."

An oath broke from his lips. "I don't care for myself," he exclaimed, "but don't let Sibyl. . . . It is a gentleman, isn't it, who is in love with her, or says he is? Highly connected, too, I suppose."

For a moment a hideous sense of humiliation came over the woman. Her head drooped. She wiped her eyes with shaking hands. "Sibyl has a mother," she murmured; "I had none."

The lad was touched. He went towards her, and stooping down he kissed her. "I am sorry if I have pained you by asking about my father," he said, "but I could not help it. I must go now. Good-bye. Don't forget that you will have only one child now to look after, and believe me that if this man wrongs my sister, I will find out who he is, track him down, and kill him like a dog. I swear it."

The exaggerated folly of the threat, the passionate gesture that accompanied it, the mad melodramatic words, made life seem more vivid to her. She was familiar with the atmosphere. She breathed more freely, and for the first time for many months she really admired her son. She would have liked to have continued the scene on the same emotional scale, but he cut her short. Trunks had to be carried down, and mufflers looked for. The lodging-house drudge bustled in and out. There was the bargaining with the cab-man. The moment was lost in vulgar details. It was with a renewed feeling of disappointment that she waved the tattered lace handkerchief from the window, as her son drove away. She was conscious that a great opportunity had been wasted. She consoled herself by telling Sibyl how desolate she felt her life would be, now that she had only one child to look after. She remembered the phrase. It had pleased her. Of the threat she said nothing. It was vividly and dramatically expressed. She felt that they would all laugh at it some day.

Chapter VI.[1]

"I suppose you have heard the news, Basil?" said Lord Henry that evening, as Hallward was shown into a little private room at the Bristol where dinner had been laid for three.

"No, Harry," answered the artist, giving his hat and coat to the bowing waiter. "What is it? Nothing about politics, I hope? They don't interest me. There is hardly a single person in the House of Commons worth painting; though many of them would be the better for a little white-washing."

"Dorian Gray is engaged to be married," said Lord Henry, watching him as he spoke.

Hallward started, and then frowned. "Dorian engaged to be married!" he cried. "Impossible!"

"It is perfectly true."

"To whom?"

"To some little actress or other."

"I can't believe it. Dorian is far too sensible."

"Dorian is far too wise not to do foolish things now and then, my dear Basil."

"Marriage is hardly a thing that one can do now and then, Harry."

"Except in America," rejoined Lord Henry, languidly. "But I didn't say he was married. I said he was engaged to be married. There is a great difference. I have a distinct remembrance of being married, but I have no recollection at all of being engaged. I am inclined to think that I never was engaged."

"But think of Dorian's birth, and position, and wealth. It would be absurd for him to marry so much beneath him."

"If you want to make him marry this girl tell him that, Basil. He is sure to do it, then. Whenever a man does a thoroughly stupid thing, it is always from the noblest motives."

"I hope the girl is good, Harry. I don't want to see Dorian tied to some vile creature, who might degrade his nature and ruin his intellect."

"Oh, she is better than good—she is beautiful," murmured Lord Henry, sipping a glass of vermouth and orange-bitters. "Dorian says she is beautiful; and he is not often wrong about things of that kind. Your portrait of him has quickened his appreciation of the personal appearance of other people. It has had that excellent effect, amongst others. We are to see her to-night, if that boy doesn't forget his appointment."

"Are you serious?"

"Quite serious, Basil. I should be miserable if I thought I should ever be more serious than I am at the present moment."

"But do you approve of it, Harry?" asked the painter, walking up and

---

1. Chapter 4 in the *Lippincott's* edition.

down the room, and biting his lip. "You can't approve of it, possibly. It is some silly infatuation."

"I never approve, or disapprove, of anything now. It is an absurd attitude to take towards life. We are not sent into the world to air our moral prejudices. I never take any notice of what common people say, and I never interfere with what charming people do. If a personality fascinates me, whatever mode of expression that personality selects is absolutely delightful to me. Dorian Gray falls in love with a beautiful girl who acts Juliet, and proposes to marry her. Why not? If he wedded Messalina [2] he would be none the less interesting. You know I am not a champion of marriage. The real drawback to marriage is that it makes one unselfish. And unselfish people are colourless. They lack individuality. Still, there are certain temperaments that marriage makes more complex. They retain their egotism, and add to it many other egos. They are forced to have more than one life. They become more highly organized, and to be highly organized is, I should fancy, the object of man's existence. Besides, every experience is of value, and, whatever one may say against marriage, it is certainly an experience. I hope that Dorian Gray will make this girl his wife, passionately adore her for six months, and then suddenly become fascinated by some one else. He would be a wonderful study."

"You don't mean a single word of all that, Harry; you know you don't. If Dorian Gray's life were spoiled, no one would be sorrier than yourself. You are much better than you pretend to be."

Lord Henry laughed. "The reason we all like to think so well of others is that we are all afraid for ourselves. The basis of optimism is sheer terror. We think that we are generous because we credit our neighbour with the possession of those virtues that are likely to be a benefit to us. We praise the banker that we may overdraw our account, and find good qualities in the highwayman in the hope that he may spare our pockets. I mean everything that I have said. I have the greatest contempt for optimism. [3] As for a spoiled life, no life is spoiled but one whose growth is arrested. If you want to mar a nature, you have merely to reform it. As for marriage, of course that would be silly, but there are other and more interesting bonds between men and women. I will certainly encourage them. They have the charm of being fashionable. But here is Dorian himself. He will tell you more than I can."

"My dear Harry, my dear Basil, you must both congratulate me!" said the lad, throwing off his evening cape with its satin-lined wings, and shaking each of his friends by the hand in turn. "I have never been so happy. Of course it is sudden: all really delightful things are. And yet it seems to me to be the one thing I have been looking for all my life." He

2. Empress of Rome, wife of Claudius, put to death in A.D. 48 for gross indecency and treason.

3. In part, Decadence was a reaction against Victorian middle-class optimism.

was flushed with excitement and pleasure, and looked extraordinarily handsome.

"I hope you will always be very happy, Dorian," said Hallward, "but I don't quite forgive you for not having let me know of your engagement. You let Harry know."

"And I don't forgive you for being late for dinner," broke in Lord Henry, putting his hand on the lad's shoulder, and smiling as he spoke. "Come, let us sit down and try what the new *chef* here is like, and then you will tell us how it all came about."

"There is really not much to tell," cried Dorian, as they took their seats at the small round table. "What happened was simply this. After I left you yesterday evening, Harry, I dressed, had some dinner at that little Italian restaurant in Rupert Street, you introduced me to, and went down at eight o'clock to the theatre. Sibyl was playing Rosalind. Of course the scenery was dreadful, and the Orlando absurd. But Sibyl! You should have seen her! When she came on in her boy's clothes she was perfectly wonderful. She wore a moss-coloured velvet jerkin[4] with cinnamon sleeves, slim brown cross-gartered hose, a dainty little green cap with a hawk's feather caught in a jewel, and a hooded cloak lined with dull red. She had never seemed to me more exquisite. She had all the delicate grace of that Tanagra[5] figurine that you have in your studio, Basil. Her hair clustered round her face like dark leaves round a pale rose. As for her acting—well, you shall see her to-night. She is simply a born artist. I sat in the dingy box absolutely enthralled. I forgot that I was in London and in the nineteenth century. I was away with my love in a forest that no man had ever seen. After the performance was over I went behind, and spoke to her. As we were sitting together, suddenly there came into her eyes a look that I have never seen there before. My lips moved towards hers. We kissed each other. I can't describe to you what I felt at that moment. It seemed to me that all my life had been narrowed to one perfect point of rose-coloured joy. She trembled all over, and shook like a white narcissus. Then she flung herself on her knees and kissed my hands. I feel that I should not tell you all this, but I can't help it. Of course our engagement is a dead secret. She has not even told her own mother. I don't know what my guardians will say. Lord Radley is sure to be furious. I don't care. I shall be of age in less than a year, and then I can do what I like. I have been right, Basil, haven't I, to take my love out of poetry, and to find my wife in Shakespeare's plays? Lips that Shakespeare taught to speak have whispered their secret in my ear. I have had the arms of Rosalind around me, and kissed Juliet on the mouth."

4. A vest. Rosalind is disguised as a boy, Ganymed, for much of *As You Like It*. Many of the Shakespeare allusions are to plays in which disguises conceal the true sex of the character: in most instances, young women are disguised as young men. The charade is further complicated because boys played all the female roles in Shakespeare's theater.

5. Wilde admired Tanagra statuettes on his early trips to Greece and kept one in the library of his Tite Street house. They were molded out of red clay.

"Yes, Dorian, I suppose you were right," said Hallward, slowly.

"Have you seen her to-day?" asked Lord Henry.

Dorian Gray shook his head. "I left her in the forest of Arden, I shall find her in an orchard in Verona."

Lord Henry sipped his champagne in a meditative manner. "At what particular point did you mention the word marriage, Dorian? And what did she say in answer? Perhaps you forgot all about it."

"My dear Harry, I did not treat it as a business transaction, and I did not make any formal proposal. I told her that I loved her, and she said she was not worthy to be my wife. Not worthy! Why, the whole world is nothing to me compared with her."

"Women are wonderfully practical," murmured Lord Henry,—"much more practical than we are. In situations of that kind we often forget to say anything about marriage, and they always remind us."

Hallward laid his hand upon his arm. "Don't, Harry. You have annoyed Dorian. He is not like other men. He would never bring misery upon any one. His nature is too fine for that."

Lord Henry looked across the table. "Dorian is never annoyed with me," answered. "I asked the question for the best reason possible, for the only reason, indeed, that excuses one for asking any question—simple curiosity. I have a theory that it is always the women who propose to us, and not we who propose to the women. Except, of course, in middle-class life. But then the middle classes are not modern."

Dorian Gray laughed, and tossed his head. "You are quite incorrigible, Harry; but I don't mind. It is impossible to be angry with you. When you see Sibyl Vane you will feel that the man who could wrong her would be a beast, a beast without a heart. I cannot understand how any one can wish to shame the thing he loves. I love Sibyl Vane. I want to place her on a pedestal of gold, and to see the world worship the woman who is mine. What is marriage? An irrevocable vow. You mock at it for that. Ah! don't mock. It is an irrevocable vow that I want to take. Her trust makes me faithful, her belief makes me good. When I am with her, I regret all that you have taught me. I become different from what you have known me to be. I am changed, and the mere touch of Sibyl Vane's hand makes me forget you and all your wrong, fascinating, poisonous, delightful theories."

"And those are . . . ?" asked Lord Henry, helping himself to some salad.

"Oh, your theories about life, your theories about love, your theories about pleasure. All your theories, in fact, Harry."

"Pleasure is the only thing worth having a theory about," he answered, in his slow, melodious voice. "But I am afraid I cannot claim my theory as my own. It belongs to Nature, not to me. Pleasure is Nature's test, her sign of approval. When we are happy we are always good, but when we are good we are not always happy."

"Ah! but what do you mean by good?" cried Basil Hallward.

"Yes," echoed Dorian, leaning back in his chair, and looking at Lord Henry over the heavy clusters of purple-lipped irises that stood in the centre of the table, "what do you mean by good, Harry?"

"To be good is to be in harmony with one's self," he replied, touching the thin stem of his glass with his pale, fine-pointed fingers. "Discord is to be forced to be in harmony with others. One's own life—that is the important thing. As for the lives of one's neighbours, if one wishes to be a prig or a Puritan, one can flaunt one's moral views about them, but they are not one's concern. Besides, Individualism[6] has really the higher aim. Modern morality consists in accepting the standard of one's age. I consider that for any man of culture to accept the standard of his age is a form of the grossest immorality."

"But, surely, if one lives merely for one's self, Harry, one pays a terrible price for doing so?" suggested the painter.

"Yes, we are overcharged for everything nowadays. I should fancy that the real tragedy of the poor is that they can afford nothing but self-denial. Beautiful sins, like beautiful things, are the privilege of the rich."

"One has to pay in other ways but money."

"What sort of ways, Basil?"

"Oh! I should fancy in remorse, in suffering, in . . . well, in the consciousness of degradation."

Lord Henry shrugged his shoulders. "My dear fellow, mediæval art is charming, but mediæval emotions are out of date.[7] One can use them in fiction, of course. But then the only things that one can use in fiction are the things that one has ceased to use in fact. Believe me, no civilized man ever regrets a pleasure, and no uncivilized man ever knows what a pleasure is."

"I know what pleasure is," cried Dorian Gray. "It is to adore some one."

"That is certainly better than being adored," he answered, toying with some fruits. "Being adored is a nuisance. Women treat us just as Humanity treats its gods. They worship us, and are always bothering us to do something for them."

"I should have said that whatever they ask for they had first given to us," murmured the lad, gravely. "They create Love in our natures. They have a right to demand it back."

"That is quite true, Dorian," cried Hallward.

"Nothing is ever quite true," said Lord Henry.

"This is," interrupted Dorian. "You must admit, Harry, that women give to men the very gold of their lives."

---

6. Lord Henry is speaking here for Wilde, but contradicting his own desire to influence Dorian. Wilde developed his views of individualism in the social sphere in "The Soul of Man under Socialism" and later, while in prison, gave fullest expression of them in relation to his own life in *De Profundis*. Lord Henry's argument that it is immoral to accept an alien standard for one's personal development is another example of his application of Darwinism to the moral sphere, especially of Darwin's views on early development of individual and species.

7. A reference to the influence of Ruskin, Morris, D. G. Rossetti, and the Gothic revival of the mid-century, considered by Wilde to have been superseded by Pater, Darwin, and James.

"Possibly," he sighed, "but they invariably want it back in such very small change.[8] That is the worry. Women, as some witty Frenchman once put it, inspire us with the desire to do masterpieces, and always prevent us from carrying them out."

"Harry, you are dreadful! I don't know why I like you so much."

"You will always like me, Dorian," he replied. "Will you have some coffee, you fellows?—Waiter, bring coffee, and *fine-champagne*,[9] and some cigarettes. No: don't mind the cigarettes; I have some. Basil, I can't allow you to smoke cigars. You must have a cigarette. A cigarette is the perfect type of a perfect pleasure. It is exquisite, and it leaves one unsatisfied. What more can one want? Yes, Dorian, you will always be fond of me. I represent to you all the sins you have never had the courage to commit."

"What nonsense you talk, Harry!" cried the lad, taking a light from a fire-breathing silver dragon that the waiter had placed on the table. "Let us go down to the theatre. When Sibyl comes on the stage you will have a new ideal of life. She will represent something to you that you have never known."

"I have known everything," said Lord Henry, with a tired look in his eyes, "but I am always ready for a new emotion. I am afraid, however, that, for me at any rate, there is no such thing. Still, your wonderful girl may thrill me. I love acting. It is so much more real than life. Let us go. Dorian, you will come with me. I am so sorry, Basil, but there is only room for two in the brougham. You must follow us in a hansom."[1]

They got up and put on their coats, sipping their coffee standing. The painter was silent and preoccupied. There was a gloom over him. He could not bear this marriage, and yet it seemed to him to be better than many other things that might have happened. After a few minutes, they all passed downstairs. He drove off by himself, as had been arranged, and watched the flashing lights of the little brougham in front of him. A strange sense of loss came over him. He felt that Dorian Gray would never again be to him all that he had been in the past. Life had come between them. . . . His eyes darkened, and the crowded, flaring streets became blurred to his eyes. When the cab drew up at the theatre, it seemed to him that he had grown years older.

Chapter VII.[1]

For some reason or other, the house was crowded that night, and the fat Jew manager who met them at the door was beaming from ear to ear with an oily, tremulous smile. He escorted them to their box with a sort

8. A favorite conceit, which Wilde used in several forms. A variation appears later in this novel in chapter 15, p. 137, and in *The Importance of Being Earnest*, spoken by Algernon Moncrieff, in act 1.
9. A brandy liqueur rather than a type of champagne.
1. A two-wheel, hired cab, designed for no more than two passengers. The driver rode atop and behind the cab. A brougham was a closed, boxlike carriage with a driver's seat outside in front, synonymous with luxurious appointments. It usually held four people.
1. This was chapter 5 in the *Lippincott's* edition.

of pompous humility, waving his fat jewelled hands, and talking at the top of his voice. Dorian Gray loathed him more than ever. He felt as if he had come to look for Miranda and had been met by Caliban.[2] Lord Henry, upon the other hand, rather liked him. At least he declared he did, and insisted on shaking him by the hand, and assuring him that he was proud to meet a man who had discovered a real genius and gone bankrupt over a poet. Hallward amused himself with watching the faces in the pit. The heat was terribly oppressive, and the huge sunlight flamed like a monstrous dahlia with petals of yellow fire. The youths in the gallery had taken off their coats and waistcoats and hung them over the side. They talked to each other across the theatre, and shared their oranges with the tawdry girls who sat beside them. Some women were laughing in the pit. Their voices were horribly shrill and discordant. The sound of the popping of corks came from the bar.

"What a place to find one's divinity in!" said Lord Henry.

"Yes!" answered Dorian Gray. "It was here I found her, and she is divine beyond all living things. When she acts you will forget everything. These common, rough people, with their coarse faces and brutal gestures, become quite different when she is on the stage. They sit silently and watch her. They weep and laugh as she wills them to do. She makes them as responsive as a violin. She spiritualizes them, and one feels that they are of the same flesh and blood as one's self."

"The same flesh and blood as one's self! Oh, I hope not!" exclaimed Lord Henry,[3] who was scanning the occupants of the gallery through his opera-glass.

"Don't pay any attention to him, Dorian," said the painter. "I understand what you mean, and I believe in this girl. Any one you love must be marvellous, and any girl that has the effect you describe must be fine and noble. To spiritualize one's age—that is something worth doing.[4] If this girl can give a soul to those who have lived without one, if she can create the sense of beauty in people whose lives have been sordid and ugly, if she can strip them of their selfishness and lend them tears for sorrows that are not their own, she is worthy of all your adoration, worthy of the adoration of the world. This marriage is quite right. I did not think so at first, but I admit it now. The gods made Sibyl Vane for you. Without her you would have been incomplete."

"Thanks, Basil," answered Dorian Gray, pressing his hand. "I knew that you would understand me. Harry is so cynical, he terrifies me. But here is the orchestra. It is quite dreadful, but it only lasts for about five minutes. Then the curtain rises, and you will see the girl to whom I am

2. Miranda is the daughter of Prospero, and Caliban is their reluctant, savage servant in *The Tempest*. This reference is another instance of the beauty and the beast motif that continues through the novel.

3. Lord Henry's repetition of Basil's phrase was an added touch in the second edition and recalls one of Wilde's epigrams in "The Decay of Lying": "In

point of fact what is interesting about people in good society . . . is the mask that each of them wears, not the reality that lies behind the mask. It is a humiliating confession, but we are all of us made out of the same stuff."

4. An allusion to an important theme in *Marius the Epicurean* by Walter Pater.

going to give all my life, to whom I have given everything that is good in me."

A quarter of an hour afterwards, amidst an extraordinary turmoil of applause, Sibyl Vane stepped on to the stage. Yes, she was certainly lovely to look at—one of the loveliest creatures, Lord Henry thought, that he had ever seen. There was something of the fawn in her shy grace and startled eyes. A faint blush, like the shadow of a rose in a mirror of silver, came to her cheeks as she glanced at the crowded, enthusiastic house. She stepped back a few paces, and her lips seemed to tremble. Basil Hallward leaped to his feet and began to applaud. Motionless, and as one in a dream, sat Dorian Gray, gazing at her. Lord Henry peered through his glasses, murmuring, "Charming! charming!"

The scene was the hall of Capulet's house, and Romeo in his pilgrim's dress had entered with Mercutio and his other friends. The band, such as it was, struck up a few bars of music, and the dance began. Through the crowd of ungainly, shabbily-dressed actors, Sibyl Vane moved like a creature from a finer world. Her body swayed, while she danced, as a plant sways in the water. The curves of her throat were the curves of a white lily. Her hands seemed to be made of cool ivory.

Yet she was curiously listless. She showed no sign of joy when her eyes rested on Romeo. The few words she had to speak—

> Good pilgrim, you do wrong your hand too much,
>   Which mannerly devotion shows in this;
> For saints have hands that pilgrims' hands do touch,
>   And palm to palm is holy palmers' kiss—[5]

with the brief dialogue that follows, were spoken in a thoroughly artificial manner. The voice was exquisite, but from the point of view of tone it was absolutely false. It was wrong in colour. It took away all the life from the verse. It made the passion unreal.

Dorian Gray grew pale as he watched her. He was puzzled and anxious. Neither of his friends dared to say anything to him. She seemed to them to be absolutely incompetent. They were horribly disappointed.

Yet they felt that the true test of any Juliet is the balcony scene of the second act. They waited for that. If she failed there, there was nothing in her.

She looked charming as she came out in the moonlight. That could not be denied. But the staginess of her acting was unbearable, and grew worse as she went on. Her gestures became absurdly artificial. She over-emphasized everything that she had to say. The beautiful passage—

> Thou knowest the mask of night is on my face,
> Else would a maiden blush bepaint my cheek
> For that which thou hast heard me speak to-night—

5. *Romeo and Juliet* 1.5.97–100.

was declaimed with the painful precision of a school-girl who has been taught to recite by some second-rate professor of elocution. When she leaned over the balcony and came to those wonderful lines—

> *Although I joy in thee,*
> *I have no joy of this contract to-night:*
> *It is too rash, too unadvised, too sudden;*
> *Too like the lightning, which doth cease to be*
> *Ere one can say, "It lightens." Sweet, good-night!*
> *This bud of love by summer's ripening breath*
> *May prove a beauteous flower when next we meet—*[6]

she spoke the words as though they conveyed no meaning to her. It was not nervousness. Indeed, so far from being nervous, she was absolutely self-contained. It was simply bad art. She was a complete failure.

Even the common, uneducated audience of the pit and gallery lost their interest in the play. They got restless, and began to talk loudly and to whistle. The Jew manager, who was standing at the back of the dress-circle, stamped and swore with rage. The only person unmoved was the girl herself.

When the second act was over there came a storm of hisses, and Lord Henry got up from his chair and put on his coat. "She is quite beautiful, Dorian," he said, "but she can't act. Let us go."

"I am going to see the play through," answered the lad, in a hard, bitter voice. "I am awfully sorry that I have made you waste an evening, Harry. I apologize to you both."

"My dear Dorian, I should think Miss Vane was ill," interrupted Hallward. "We will come some other night."

"I wish she were ill," he rejoined. "But she seems to me to be simply callous and cold. She has entirely altered. Last night she was a great artist. This evening she is merely a commonplace, mediocre actress."

"Don't talk like that about any one you love, Dorian. Love is a more wonderful thing than Art."

"They are both simply forms of imitation," remarked Lord Henry. "But do let us go. Dorian, you must not stay here any longer. It is not good for one's morals to see bad acting. Besides, I don't suppose you will want your wife to act. So what does it matter if she plays Juliet like a wooden doll? She is very lovely, and if she knows as little about life as she does about acting, she will be a delightful experience. There are only two kinds of people who are really fascinating—people who know absolutely everything, and people who know absolutely nothing. Good heavens, my dear boy, don't look so tragic! The secret of remaining young is never to have an emotion that is unbecoming. Come to the club with Basil and myself. We will smoke cigarettes and drink to the beauty of Sibyl Vane. She is beautiful. What more can you want?"

"Go away, Harry," cried the lad. "I want to be alone. Basil, you must

6. *Romeo and Juliet* 2.2.116–22, and above, *Romeo and Juliet* 2.2.85–87.

go. Ah! can't you see that my heart is breaking?" The hot tears came to his eyes. His lips trembled, and, rushing to the back of the box, he leaned up against the wall, hiding his face in his hands.

"Let us go, Basil," said Lord Henry, with a strange tenderness in his voice; and the two young men passed out together.

A few moments afterwards the footlights flared up, and the curtain rose on the third act. Dorian Gray went back to his seat. He looked pale, and proud, and indifferent. The play dragged on, and seemed interminable. Half of the audience went out, tramping in heavy boots, and laughing. The whole thing was a *fiasco*. The last act was played to almost empty benches. The curtain went down on a titter, and some groans.

As soon as it was over, Dorian Gray rushed behind the scenes into the greenroom. The girl was standing there alone, with a look of triumph on her face. Her eyes were lit with an exquisite fire. There was a radiance about her. Her parted lips were smiling over some secret of their own.

When he entered, she looked at him, and an expression of infinite joy came over her. "How badly I acted to-night, Dorian!" she cried.

"Horribly!" he answered, gazing at her in amazement—"horribly! It was dreadful. Are you ill? You have no idea what it was. You have no idea what I suffered."

The girl smiled. "Dorian," she answered, lingering over his name with long-drawn music in her voice, as though it were sweeter than honey to the red petals of her mouth—"Dorian, you should have understood. But you understand now, don't you?"

"Understand what?" he asked, angrily.

"Why I was so bad to-night. Why I shall always be bad. Why I shall never act well again."

He shrugged his shoulders. "You are ill, I suppose. When you are ill you shouldn't act. You make yourself ridiculous. My friends were bored. I was bored."

She seemed not to listen to him. She was transfigured with joy. An ecstasy of happiness dominated her.

"Dorian, Dorian," she cried, "before I knew you, acting was the one reality of my life. It was only in the theatre that I lived. I thought that it was all true. I was Rosalind one night, and Portia the other. The joy of Beatrice was my joy, and the sorrows of Cordelia were mine also.[7] I believed in everything. The common people who acted with me seemed to me to be godlike. The painted scenes were my world. I knew nothing but shadows, and I thought them real. You came—oh, my beautiful love!—and you freed my soul from prison. You taught me what reality really is. To-night, for the first time in my life, I saw through the hollowness, the sham, the silliness of the empty pageant in which I had always played. To-night, for the first time, I became conscious that the

7. Portia is the heroine of *The Merchant of Venice*, Beatrice of *Much Ado about Nothing*, and Cordelia of *King Lear*. Taken together, they would represent a good test of an actress's range.

Romeo was hideous, and old, and painted, that the moonlight in the orchard was false, that the scenery was vulgar, and that the words I had to speak were unreal, were not my words, were not what I wanted to say. You had brought me something higher, something of which all art is but a reflection. You had made me understand what love really is. My love! my love! Prince Charming! Prince of life! I have grown sick of shadows.[8] You are more to me than all art can ever be. What have I to do with the puppets of a play? When I came on to-night, I could not understand how it was that everything had gone from me. I thought that I was going to be wonderful. I found that I could do nothing. Suddenly it dawned on my soul what it all meant. The knowledge was exquisite to me. I heard them hissing, and I smiled. What could they know of love such as ours? Take me away, Dorian—take me away with you, where we can be quite alone. I hate the stage. I might mimic a passion that I do not feel, but I cannot mimic one that burns me like fire.[9] Oh, Dorian, Dorian, you understand now what it signifies? Even if I could do it, it would be profanation for me to play at being in love. You have made me see that."

He flung himself down on the sofa, and turned away his face. "You have killed my love," he muttered.

She looked at him in wonder, and laughed. He made no answer. She came across to him, and with her little fingers stroked his hair. She knelt down and pressed his hands to her lips. He drew them away, and a shudder ran through him.

Then he leaped up, and went to the door. "Yes," he cried, "you have killed my love. You used to stir my imagination. Now you don't even stir my curiosity. You simply produce no effect. I loved you because you were marvellous, because you had genius and intellect, because you realized the dreams of great poets and gave shape and substance to the shadows of art. You have thrown it all away. You are shallow and stupid. My God! how mad I was to love you! What a fool I have been! You are nothing to me now. I will never see you again. I will never think of you. I will never mention your name. You don't know what you were to me, once. Why, once . . . Oh, I can't bear to think of it! I wish I had never laid eyes upon you! You have spoiled the romance of my life. How little you can know of love, if you say it mars your art! Without your art you are nothing. I would have made you famous, splendid, magnificent. The world would have worshipped you, and you would have borne my name. What are you now? A third-rate actress with a pretty face."

The girl grew white, and trembled. She clenched her hands together, and her voice seemed to catch in her throat. "You are not serious, Dorian?" she murmured. "You are acting."

8. A direct allusion to Tennyson's "The Lady of Shalott."
9. Sibyl's declaration recalls one of Wilde's doctrines of art, developed most fully in "The Decay of Lying" and "The Critic as Artist," both from *Intentions*, that art is the realization of the impossible. Hence an actual realization of a feeling or emotion in nature removes it from the sphere of art.

"Acting! I leave that to you. You do it so well," he answered, bitterly.

She rose from her knees, and, with a piteous expression of pain in her face, came across the room to him. She put her hand upon his arm, and looked into his eyes. He thrust her back. "Don't touch me!" he cried.

A low moan broke from her, and she flung herself at his feet, and lay there like a trampled flower. "Dorian, Dorian, don't leave me!" she whispered. "I am so sorry I didn't act well. I was thinking of you all the time. But I will try—indeed, I will try. It came so suddenly across me, my love for you. I think I should never have known it if you had not kissed me—if we had not kissed each other. Kiss me again, my love. Don't go away from me. I couldn't bear it. Oh! don't go away from me. My brother . . . No; never mind. He didn't mean it. He was in jest. . . . But you, oh! can't you forgive me for to-night? I will work so hard, and try to improve. Don't be cruel to me because I love you better than anything in the world. After all, it is only once that I have not pleased you. But you are quite right, Dorian. I should have shown myself more of an artist. It was foolish of me; and yet I couldn't help it. Oh, don't leave me, don't leave me." A fit of passionate sobbing choked her. She crouched on the floor like a wounded thing, and Dorian Gray, with his beautiful eyes, looked down at her, and his chiselled lips curled in exquisite disdain. There is always something ridiculous about the emotions of people whom one has ceased to love. Sibyl Vane seemed to him to be absurdly melodramatic. Her tears and sobs annoyed him.

"I am going," he said at last, in his calm, clear voice. "I don't wish to be unkind, but I can't see you again. You have disappointed me."

She wept silently, and made no answer, but crept nearer. Her little hands stretched blindly out, and appeared to be seeking for him. He turned on his heel, and left the room. In a few moments he was out of the theatre.

Where he went to he hardly knew. He remembered wandering through dimly-lit streets, past gaunt black-shadowed archways and evil-looking houses. Women with hoarse voices and harsh laughter had called after him. Drunkards had reeled by cursing, and chattering to themselves like monstrous apes. He had seen grotesque children huddled upon doorsteps, and heard shrieks and oaths from gloomy courts.

As the dawn was just breaking he found himself close to Covent Garden.[1] The darkness lifted, and, flushed with faint fires, the sky hollowed itself into a perfect pearl. Huge carts filled with nodding lilies rumbled slowly down the polished empty street. The air was heavy with the perfume of the flowers, and their beauty seemed to bring him an anodyne for his pain. He followed into the market, and watched the men unload-

1. The site of the famous theater is near Trafalgar Square, an area rich in literary and theatrical history; it was also the location of open-air markets. Wilde wrote a remarkably similar scene in "Lord Arthur Savile's Crime." Professor Henry Higgins first meets Liza Doolittle selling flowers in the market in Shaw's *Pygmalion*.

ing their waggons. A white-smocked carter offered him some cherries. He thanked him, wondered why he refused to accept any money for them, and began to eat them listlessly. They had been plucked at midnight, and the coldness of the moon had entered into them. A long line of boys carrying crates of striped tulips, and of yellow and red roses, defiled in front of him, threading their way through the huge jade-green piles of vegetables. Under the portico, with its grey sun-bleached pillars, loitered a troop of draggled bareheaded girls, waiting for the auction to be over. Others crowded round the swinging doors of the coffee-house in the Piazza. The heavy cart-horses slipped and stamped upon the rough stones, shaking their bells and trappings. Some of the drivers were lying asleep on a pile of sacks. Iris-necked, and pink-footed, the pigeons ran about picking up seeds.

After a little while, he hailed a hansom, and drove home. For a few moments he loitered upon the doorstep, looking round at the silent Square[2] with its blank close-shuttered windows, and its staring blinds. The sky was pure opal now, and the roofs of the houses glistened like silver against it. From some chimney opposite a thin wreath of smoke was rising. It curled, a violet riband, through the nacre-coloured air.[3]

In the huge gilt Venetian lantern, spoil of some Doge's[4] barge, that hung from the ceiling of the great oak-panelled hall of entrance, lights were still burning from three flickering jets: thin blue petals of flame they seemed, rimmed with white fire. He turned them out, and, having thrown his hat and cape on the table, passed through the library towards the door of his bedroom, a large octagonal chamber on the ground floor that, in his new-born feeling for luxury, he had just had decorated for himself, and hung with some curious Renaissance tapestries that had been discovered stored in a disused attic at Selby Royal.[5] As he was turning the handle of the door, his eye fell upon the portrait Basil Hallward had painted of him. He started back as if in surprise. Then he went on into his own room, looking somewhat puzzled. After he had taken the buttonhole out of his coat, he seemed to hesitate. Finally he came back, went over to the picture, and examined it. In the dim arrested light that struggled through the cream-coloured silk blinds, the face appeared to him to be a little changed. The expression looked different. One would have said that there was a touch of cruelty in the mouth. It was certainly strange.

He turned round, and, walking to the window, drew up the blind. The bright dawn flooded the room, and swept the fantastic shadows into dusky corners, where they lay shuddering. But the strange expression that he had noticed in the face of the portrait seemed to linger there, to be more intensified even. The quivering, ardent sunlight showed him

2. Grosvenor Square, where Dorian had his London residence, is located in the heart of Mayfair. Wilde once lived nearby on Charles Street prior to his marriage.

3. Nacre is mother-of-pearl.
4. The elected chief magistrate of the Venetian Republic.
5. Dorian's country estate.

the lines of cruelty round the mouth as clearly as if he had been looking into a mirror after he had done some dreadful thing.

He winced, and, taking up from the table an oval glass framed in ivory Cupids, one of Lord Henry's many presents to him, glanced hurriedly into its polished depths. No line like that warped his red lips. What did it mean?

He rubbed his eyes, and came close to the picture, and examined it again. There were no signs of any change when he looked into the actual painting, and yet there was no doubt that the whole expression had altered. It was not a mere fancy of his own. The thing was horribly apparent.

He threw himself into a chair, and began to think. Suddenly there flashed across his mind what he had said in Basil Hallward's studio the day the picture had been finished. Yes, he remembered it perfectly. He had uttered a mad wish that he himself might remain young, and the portrait grow old; that his own beauty might be untarnished, and the face on the canvas bear the burden of his passions and his sins; that the painted image might be seared with the lines of suffering and thought, and that he might keep all the delicate bloom and loveliness of his then just conscious boyhood. Surely his wish had not been fulfilled? Such things were impossible. It seemed monstrous even to think of them. And, yet, there was the picture before him, with the touch of cruelty in the mouth.

Cruelty! Had he been cruel? It was the girl's fault, not his. He had dreamed of her as a great artist, had given his love to her because he had thought her great. Then she had disappointed him. She had been shallow and unworthy. And, yet, a feeling of infinite regret came over him, as he thought of her lying at his feet sobbing like a little child. He remembered with what callousness he had watched her. Why had he been made like that? Why had such a soul been given to him? But he had suffered also. During the three terrible hours that the play had lasted, he had lived centuries of pain, æon upon æon of torture. His life was well worth hers. She had marred him for a moment, if he had wounded her for an age. Besides, women were better suited to bear sorrow than men. They lived on their emotions. They only thought of their emotions. When they took lovers, it was merely to have some one with whom they could have scenes. Lord Henry had told him that, and Lord Henry knew what women were. Why should he trouble about Sibyl Vane? She was nothing to him now.

But the picture? What was he to say of that? It held the secret of his life, and told his story. It had taught him to love his own beauty. Would it teach him to loathe his own soul? Would he ever look at it again?

No; it was merely an illusion wrought on the troubled senses. The horrible night that he had passed had left phantoms behind it. Suddenly there had fallen upon his brain that tiny scarlet speck that makes men mad. The picture had not changed. It was folly to think so.

Yet it was watching him, with its beautiful marred face and its cruel smile. Its bright hair gleamed in the early sunlight. Its blue eyes met his own. A sense of infinite pity, not for himself, but for the painted image of himself, came over him. It had altered already, and would alter more. Its gold would wither into grey. Its red and white roses would die. For every sin that he committed, a stain would fleck and wreck its fairness. But he would not sin. The picture, changed or unchanged, would be to him the visible emblem of conscience. He would resist temptation. He would not see Lord Henry any more—would not, at any rate, listen to those subtle poisonous theories that in Basil Hallward's garden had first stirred within him the passion for impossible things. He would go back to Sibyl Vane,[6] make her amends, marry her, try to love her again. Yes, it was his duty to do so. She must have suffered more than he had. Poor child! He had been selfish and cruel to her. The fascination that she had exercised over him would return. They would be happy together. His life with her would be beautiful and pure.

He got up from his chair, and drew a large screen right in front of the portrait, shuddering as he glanced at it. "How horrible!" he murmured to himself, and he walked across to the window and opened it. When he stepped out on to the grass, he drew a deep breath. The fresh morning air seemed to drive away all his sombre passions. He thought only of Sibyl. A faint echo of his love came back to him. He repeated her name over and over again. The birds that were singing in the dew-drenched garden seemed to be telling the flowers about her.

Chapter VIII.[1]

It was long past noon when he awoke. His valet had crept several times on tiptoe into the room to see if he was stirring, and had wondered what made his young master sleep so late. Finally his bell sounded, and Victor came in softly with a cup of tea, and a pile of letters, on a small tray of old Sèvres china,[2] and drew back the olive-satin curtains, with their shimmering blue lining, that hung in front of the three tall windows.

"Monsieur has well slept this morning," he said, smiling.

"What o'clock is it, Victor?" asked Dorian Gray, drowsily.

"One hour and a quarter, Monsieur."

How late it was! He sat up, and, having sipped some tea, turned over his letters. One of them was from Lord Henry, and had been brought by hand that morning. He hesitated for a moment, and then put it aside. The others he opened listlessly. They contained the usual collection of cards, invitations to dinner, tickets for private views, programmes of charity

6. In MS, Wilde wrote "Sybil Fane," the first of many such slips. Wilde was a friend of Mary Montgomerie Lamb, who wrote under the name of "Violet Fane."

1. Originally chapter 6.
2. An elegant French porcelain made in Sèvres, a Paris suburb, since the eighteenth century.

concerts, and the like, that are showered on fashionable young men every morning during the season. There was a rather heavy bill, for a chased silver Louis-Quinze [3] toilet-set, that he had not yet had the courage to send on to his guardians, who were extremely old-fashioned people and did not realize that we live in an age when unnecessary things are our only necessities; and there were several very courteously worded communications from Jermyn Street money-lenders offering to advance any sum of money at a moment's notice and at the most reasonable rates of interest.

After about ten minutes he got up, and, throwing on an elaborate dressing-gown of silk-embroidered cashmere wool, passed into the onyx-paved bathroom. The cool water refreshed him after his long sleep. He seemed to have forgotten all that he had gone through. A dim sense of having taken part in some strange tragedy came to him once or twice, but there was the unreality of a dream about it.

As soon as he was dressed, he went into the library and sat down to a light French breakfast,[4] that had been laid out for him on a small round table close to the open window. It was an exquisite day. The warm air seemed laden with spices. A bee flew in, and buzzed round the blue-dragon bowl that, filled with sulphur-yellow roses, stood before him. He felt perfectly happy.

Suddenly his eye fell on the screen that he had placed in front of the portrait, and he started.

"Too cold for Monsieur?" asked his valet, putting an omelette on the table. "I shut the window?"

Dorian shook his head. "I am not cold," he murmured.

Was it all true? Had the portrait really changed? Or had it been simply his own imagination that had made him see a look of evil where there had been a look of joy? Surely a painted canvas could not alter? The thing was absurd. It would serve as a tale to tell Basil some day. It would make him smile.

And, yet, how vivid was his recollection of the whole thing! First in the dim twilight, and then in the bright dawn, he had seen the touch of cruelty round the warped lips. He almost dreaded his valet leaving the room. He knew that when he was alone he would have to examine the portrait. He was afraid of certainty. When the coffee and cigarettes had been brought and the man turned to go, he felt a wild desire to tell him to remain. As the door was closing behind him he called him back. The man stood waiting for his orders. Dorian looked at him for a moment. "I am not at home to any one, Victor," he said, with a sigh. The man bowed and retired.

Then he rose from the table, lit a cigarette, and flung himself down on a luxuriously-cushioned couch that stood facing the screen. The screen was an old one, of gilt Spanish leather, stamped and wrought with a

3. Describes the rococo style popular in mid-eigh-teenth-century France during the reign of Louis XV, denoting elegance, fantasy, and luxury.
4. Probably coffee and a sweet roll or toast.

rather florid Louis-Quatorze[5] pattern. He scanned it curiously, wondering if ever before it had concealed the secret of a man's life.

Should he move it aside, after all? Why not let it stay there? What was the use of knowing? If the thing was true, it was terrible. If it was not true, why trouble about it? But what if, by some fate or deadlier chance, eyes other than his spied behind, and saw the horrible change? What should he do if Basil Hallward came and asked to look at his own picture? Basil would be sure to do that. No; the thing had to be examined, and at once. Anything would be better than this dreadful state of doubt.

He got up, and locked both doors. At least he would be alone when he looked upon the mask of his shame. Then he drew the screen aside, and saw himself face to face. It was perfectly true. The portrait had altered.

As he often remembered afterwards, and always with no small wonder, he found himself at first gazing at the portrait with a feeling of almost scientific interest. That such a change should have taken place was incredible to him. And yet it was a fact. Was there some subtle affinity between the chemical atoms, that shaped themselves into form and colour on the canvas, and the soul that was within him? Could it be that what that soul thought, they realized?—that what it dreamed, they made true? Or was there some other, more terrible reason? He shuddered, and felt afraid, and, going back to the couch, lay there, gazing at the picture in sickened horror.

One thing, however, he felt that it had done for him. It had made him conscious how unjust, how cruel, he had been to Sibyl Vane. It was not too late to make reparation for that. She could still be his wife. His unreal and selfish love would yield to some higher influence, would be transformed into some nobler passion, and the portrait that Basil Hallward had painted of him would be a guide to him through life, would be to him what holiness is to some, and conscience to others, and the fear of God to us all. There were opiates for remorse, drugs that could lull the moral sense to sleep. But here was a visible symbol of the degradation of sin. Here was an ever-present sign of the ruin men brought upon their souls.

Three o'clock struck, and four, and the half-hour rang its double chime, but Dorian Gray did not stir. He was trying to gather up the scarlet threads of life, and to weave them into a pattern; to find his way through the sanguine labyrinth of passion through which he was wandering. He did not know what to do, or what to think. Finally, he went over to the table and wrote a passionate letter to the girl he had loved, imploring her forgiveness, and accusing himself of madness. He covered page after page with wild words of sorrow, and wilder words of pain. There is a luxury in self-reproach. When we blame ourselves we feel that no one

---

5. Louis XIV of France (1638–1715), called "The Sun King," reigned seventy-two years.

else has a right to blame us. It is the confession, not the priest, that gives us absolution. When Dorian had finished the letter, he felt that he had been forgiven.

Suddenly there came a knock to the door, and he heard Lord Henry's voice outside. "My dear boy, I must see you. Let me in at once. I can't bear your shutting yourself up like this."

He made no answer at first, but remained quite still. The knocking still continued, and grew louder. Yes, it was better to let Lord Henry in, and to explain to him the new life he was going to lead, to quarrel with him if it became necessary to quarrel, to part if parting was inevitable. He jumped up, drew the screen hastily across the picture, and unlocked the door.

"I am so sorry for it all, Dorian," said Lord Henry, as he entered. "But you must not think too much about it."

"Do you mean about Sibyl Vane?" asked the lad.

"Yes, of course," answered Lord Henry, sinking into a chair, and slowly pulling off his yellow gloves. "It is dreadful, from one point of view, but it was not your fault. Tell me, did you go behind and see her, after the play was over?"

"Yes."

"I felt sure you had. Did you make a scene with her?"

"I was brutal, Harry—perfectly brutal. But it is all right now. I am not sorry for anything that has happened. It has taught me to know myself better."

"Ah, Dorian, I am so glad you take it in that way! I was afraid I would find you plunged in remorse, and tearing that nice curly hair of yours."

"I have got through all that," said Dorian, shaking his head, and smiling. "I am perfectly happy now. I know what conscience is, to begin with. It is not what you told me it was. It is the divinest thing in us. Don't sneer at it, Harry, any more—at least not before me. I want to be good. I can't bear the idea of my soul being hideous."

"A very charming artistic basis for ethics, Dorian! I congratulate you on it. But how are you going to begin?"

"By marrying Sibyl Vane."

"Marrying Sibyl Vane!" cried Lord Henry, standing up, and looking at him in perplexed amazement. "But, my dear Dorian—"

"Yes, Harry, I know what you are going to say. Something dreadful about marriage. Don't say it. Don't ever say things of that kind to me again. Two days ago I asked Sibyl to marry me. I am not going to break my word to her. She is to be my wife."

"Your wife! Dorian! . . . Didn't you get my letter? I wrote to you this morning, and sent the note down, by my own man."

"Your letter? Oh, yes, I remember. I have not read it yet, Harry. I was afraid there might be something in it that I wouldn't like. You cut life to pieces with your epigrams."

"You know nothing then?"

"What do you mean?"

Lord Henry walked across the room, and, sitting down by Dorian Gray, took both his hands in his own, and held them tightly. "Dorian," he said, "my letter—don't be frightened—was to tell you that Sibyl Vane is dead."

A cry of pain broke from the lad's lips, and he leaped to his feet, tearing his hands away from Lord Henry's grasp. "Dead! Sibyl dead! It is not true! It is a horrible lie! How dare you say it?"

"It is quite true, Dorian," said Lord Henry, gravely. "It is in all the morning papers. I wrote down to you to ask you not to see any one till I came. There will have to be an inquest, of course, and you must not be mixed up in it. Things like that make a man fashionable in Paris. But in London people are so prejudiced. Here, one should never make one's *début* with a scandal. One should reserve that to give an interest to one's old age. I suppose they don't know your name at the theatre? If they don't, it is all right. Did any one see you going round to her room? That is an important point."

Dorian did not answer for a few moments. He was dazed with horror. Finally he stammered, in a stifled voice, "Harry, did you say an inquest? What did you mean by that? Did Sibyl—? Oh, Harry, I can't bear it! But be quick. Tell me everything at once."

"I have no doubt it was not an accident, Dorian, though it must be put in that way to the public. It seems that as she was leaving the theatre with her mother, about half-past twelve or so, she said she had forgotten something upstairs. They waited some time for her, but she did not come down again. They ultimately found her lying dead on the floor of her dressing-room. She had swallowed something by mistake, some dreadful thing they use at theatres. I don't know what it was, but it had either prussic acid or white lead in it. I should fancy it was prussic acid, as she seems to have died instantaneously."

"Harry, Harry, it is terrible!" cried the lad.

"Yes; it is very tragic, of course, but you must not get yourself mixed up in it. I see by *The Standard*[6] that she was seventeen. I should have thought she was almost younger than that. She looked such a child, and seemed to know so little about acting. Dorian, you mustn't let this thing get on your nerves. You must come and dine with me, and afterwards we will look in at the Opera. It is a Patti[7] night, and everybody will be there. You can come to my sister's box. She has got some smart women with her."

"So I have murdered Sibyl Vane," said Dorian Gray, half to himself—"murdered her as surely as if I had cut her little throat with a knife. Yet the roses are not less lovely for all that. The birds sing just as happily in my garden. And to-night I am to dine with you, and then go on to

6. A politically conservative London morning newspaper of the time.
7. Adelina Patti (1843–1919) was one of the most popular operatic sopranos of the period. Her performances were legendary.

the Opera, and sup somewhere, I suppose, afterwards. How extraordinarily dramatic life is! If I had read all this in a book, Harry, I think I would have wept over it. Somehow, now that it has happened actually, and to me, it seems far too wonderful for tears. Here is the first passionate love-letter I have ever written in my life. Strange, that my first passionate love-letter should have been addressed to a dead girl. Can they feel, I wonder, those white silent people we call the dead? Sibyl! Can she feel, or know, or listen? Oh, Harry, how I loved her once! It seems years ago to me now. She was everything to me. Then came that dreadful night—was it really only last night?—when she played so badly, and my heart almost broke. She explained it all to me. It was terribly pathetic. But I was not moved a bit. I thought her shallow. Suddenly something happened that made me afraid. I can't tell you what it was, but it was terrible. I said I would go back to her. I felt I had done wrong. And now she is dead. My God! my God! Harry, what shall I do? You don't know the danger I am in, and there is nothing to keep me straight. She would have done that for me. She had no right to kill herself. It was selfish of her."

"My dear Dorian," answered Lord Henry, taking a cigarette from his case, and producing a gold-latten[8] matchbox, "the only way a woman can ever reform a man is by boring him so completely that he loses all possible interest in life. If you had married this girl you would have been wretched. Of course you would have treated her kindly. One can always be kind to people about whom one cares nothing. But she would have soon found out that you were absolutely indifferent to her. And when a woman finds that out about her husband, she either becomes dreadfully dowdy, or wears very smart bonnets that some other woman's husband has to pay for. I say nothing about the social mistake, which would have been abject, which, of course, I would not have allowed, but I assure you that in any case the whole thing would have been an absolute failure."

"I suppose it would," muttered the lad, walking up and down the room, and looking horribly pale. "But I thought it was my duty. It is not my fault that this terrible tragedy has prevented my doing what was right. I remember your saying once that there is a fatality about good resolutions—that they are always made too late. Mine certainly were."

"Good resolutions are useless attempts to interfere with scientific laws. Their origin is pure vanity. Their result is absolutely *nil*. They give us, now and then, some of those luxurious sterile emotions that have a certain charm for the weak. That is all that can be said for them. They are simply cheques that men draw on a bank where they have no account."

"Harry," cried Dorian Gray, coming over and sitting down beside him, "why is it that I cannot feel this tragedy as much as I want to? I don't think I am heartless. Do you?"

8. Gold-plated or -foiled.

"You have done too many foolish things during the last fortnight to be entitled to give yourself that name, Dorian," answered Lord Henry, with his sweet, melancholy smile.

The lad frowned. "I don't like that explanation, Harry," he rejoined, "but I am glad you don't think I am heartless. I am nothing of the kind. I know I am not. And yet I must admit that this thing that has happened does not affect me as it should. It seems to me to be simply like a wonderful ending to a wonderful play. It has all the terrible beauty of a Greek tragedy, a tragedy in which I took a great part, but by which I have not been wounded."

"It is an interesting question," said Lord Henry, who found an exquisite pleasure in playing on the lad's unconscious egotism—"an extremely interesting question. I fancy that the true explanation is this. It often happens that the real tragedies of life occur in such an inartistic manner that they hurt us by their crude violence, their absolute incoherence, their absurd want of meaning, their entire lack of style. They affect us just as vulgarity affects us. They give us an impression of sheer brute force, and we revolt against that. Sometimes, however, a tragedy that possesses artistic elements of beauty crosses our lives. If these elements of beauty are real, the whole thing simply appeals to our sense of dramatic effect. Suddenly we find that we are no longer the actors, but the spectators of the play. Or rather we are both. We watch ourselves, and the mere wonder of the spectacle enthralls us. In the present case, what is it that has really happened? Some one has killed herself for love of you. I wish that I had ever had such an experience. It would have made me in love with love for the rest of my life. The people who have adored me—there have not been very many, but there have been some—have always insisted on living on, long after I had ceased to care for them, or they to care for me. They have become stout and tedious, and when I meet them they go in at once for reminiscences. That awful memory of woman! What a fearful thing it is! And what an utter intellectual stagnation it reveals! One should absorb the colour of life, but one should never remember its details. Details are always vulgar."

"I must sow poppies[9] in my garden," sighed Dorian.

"There is no necessity," rejoined his companion. "Life has always poppies in her hands. Of course, now and then things linger. I once wore nothing but violets all through one season, as a form of artistic mourning for a romance that would not die. Ultimately, however, it did die. I forget what killed it. I think it was her proposing to sacrifice the whole world for me. That is always a dreadful moment. It fills one with the terror of eternity. Well—would you believe it?—a week ago, at Lady Hampshire's, I found myself seated at dinner next to the lady in question, and she insisted on going over the whole thing again, and digging

9. Poppies symbolize forgetfulness and drugged sleep. Asphodel, below, symbolizes death and the underworld. Wilde changed this from "poppy" in *Lippincott's*. Flower symbolism, a familiar language to Victorians, is known today almost exclusively by florists.

up the past, and raking up the future. I had buried my romance in a bed of asphodel. She dragged it out again, and assured me that I had spoiled her life. I am bound to state that she ate an enormous dinner, so I did not feel any anxiety. But what a lack of taste she showed! The one charm of the past is that it is the past. But women never know when the curtain has fallen. They always want a sixth act, and as soon as the interest of the play is entirely over they propose to continue it. If they were allowed their own way, every comedy would have a tragic ending, and every tragedy would culminate in a farce. They are charmingly artificial, but they have no sense of art. You are more fortunate than I am. I assure you, Dorian, that not one of the women I have known would have done for me what Sibyl Vane did for you. Ordinary women always console themselves. Some of them do it by going in for sentimental colours. Never trust a woman who wears mauve, whatever her age may be, or a woman over thirty-five who is fond of pink ribbons. It always means that they have a history. Others find a great consolation in suddenly discovering the good qualities of their husbands. They flaunt their conjugal felicity in one's face, as if it were the most fascinating of sins. Religion consoles some. Its mysteries have all the charm of a flirtation, a woman once told me; and I can quite understand it. Besides, nothing makes one so vain as being told that one is a sinner. Conscience makes egotists of us all. Yes; there is really no end to the consolations that women find in modern life. Indeed, I have not mentioned the most important one."

"What is that, Harry?" said the lad, listlessly.

"Oh, the obvious consolation. Taking some one else's admirer when one loses one's own. In good society that always whitewashes a woman. But really, Dorian, how different Sibyl Vane must have been from all the women one meets! There is something to me quite beautiful about her death. I am glad I am living in a century when such wonders happen. They make one believe in the reality of the things we all play with, such as romance, passion, and love." [1]

"I was terribly cruel to her. You forget that."

"I am afraid that women appreciate cruelty, downright cruelty, more than anything else. They have wonderfully primitive instincts. We have emancipated them, but they remain slaves looking for their masters, all the same. They love being dominated. I am sure you were splendid. I have never seen you really and absolutely angry, but I can fancy how delightful you looked. And, after all, you said something to me the day before yesterday that seemed to me at the time to be merely fanciful, but that I see now was absolutely true, and it holds the key to everything."

"What was that, Harry?"

"You said to me that Sibyl Vane represented to you all the heroines of romance—that she was Desdemona one night, and Ophelia the other;

---

1. Miss Prim develops this thought in another way in *The Importance of Being Earnest*, describing her lost novel: "the good end happily, and the bad unhappily. That is what fiction means." Both are examples of Wilde's manner of couching serious ideas in a comic style.

that if she died as Juliet, she came to life as Imogen."

"She will never come to life again now," muttered the lad, burying his face in his hands.

"No, she will never come to life. She has played her last part. But you must think of that lonely death in the tawdry dressing-room simply as a strange lurid fragment from some Jacobean tragedy, as a wonderful scene from Webster, or Ford, or Cyril Tourneur.[2] The girl never really lived, and so she has never really died. To you at least she was always a dream, a phantom that flitted through Shakespeare's plays and left them lovelier for its presence, a reed through which Shakespeare's music sounded richer and more full of joy. The moment she touched actual life, she marred it, and it marred her, and so she passed away. Mourn for Ophelia, if you like. Put ashes on your head because Cordelia was strangled. Cry out against Heaven because the daughter of Brabantio died.[3] But don't waste your tears over Sibyl Vane. She was less real than they are."

There was a silence. The evening darkened in the room. Noiselessly, and with silver feet, the shadows crept in from the garden. The colours faded wearily out of things.

After some time Dorian Gray looked up. "You have explained me to myself, Harry," he murmured, with something of a sigh of relief. "I felt all that you have said, but somehow I was afraid of it, and I could not express it to myself. How well you know me! But we will not talk again of what has happened. It has been a marvellous experience. That is all. I wonder if life has still in store for me anything as marvellous."

"Life has everything in store for you, Dorian. There is nothing that you, with your extraordinary good looks, will not be able to do."

"But suppose, Harry, I became haggard, and old, and wrinkled? What then?"

"Ah, then," said Lord Henry, rising to go—"then, my dear Dorian, you would have to fight for your victories. As it is, they are brought to you. No, you must keep your good looks. We live in an age that reads too much to be wise, and that thinks too much to be beautiful. We cannot spare you. And now you had better dress, and drive down to the club. We are rather late, as it is."

"I think I shall join you at the Opera, Harry. I feel too tired to eat anything. What is the number of your sister's box?"

"Twenty-seven, I believe. It is on the grand tier. You will see her name on the door. But I am sorry you won't come and dine."

"I don't feel up to it," said Dorian, listlessly. "But I am awfully obliged to you for all that you have said to me. You are certainly my best friend. No one has ever understood me as you have."

"We are only at the beginning of our friendship, Dorian," answered

2. Webster, Ford, and Tourneur were English playwrights whose works dramatized passion and violence. They flourished during the Jacobean period (during the reign of James I of England in the early seventeenth-century).

3. Desdemona in *Othello*.

Lord Henry, shaking him by the hand. "Good-bye. I shall see you before nine-thirty, I hope. Remember, Patti is singing."

As he closed the door behind him, Dorian Gray touched the bell, and in a few minutes Victor appeared with the lamps and drew the blinds down. He waited impatiently for him to go. The man seemed to take an interminable time over everything.

As soon as he had left, he rushed to the screen, and drew it back. No; there was no further change in the picture. It had received the news of Sibyl Vane's death before he had known of it himself. It was conscious of the events of life as they occurred. The vicious cruelty that marred the fine lines of the mouth had, no doubt, appeared at the very moment that the girl had drunk the poison, whatever it was. Or was it indifferent to results? Did it merely take cognizance of what passed within the soul? He wondered, and hoped that some day he would see the change taking place before his very eyes, shuddering as he hoped it.

Poor Sibyl! what a romance it had all been! She had often mimicked death on the stage. Then Death himself had touched her, and taken her with him. How had she played that dreadful last scene? Had she cursed him, as she died? No; she had died for love of him, and love would always be a sacrament to him now. She had atoned for everything, by the sacrifice she had made of her life. He would not think any more of what she had made him go through, on that horrible night at the theatre. When he thought of her, it would be as a wonderful tragic figure sent on to the world's stage to show the supreme reality of Love. A wonderful tragic figure? Tears came to his eyes as he remembered her childlike look and winsome fanciful ways and shy tremulous grace. He brushed them away hastily, and looked again at the picture.

He felt that the time had really come for making his choice. Or had his choice already been made? Yes, life had decided that for him—life, and his own infinite curiosity about life. Eternal youth, infinite passion, pleasures subtle and secret, wild joys and wilder sins—he was to have all these things. The portrait was to bear the burden of his shame: that was all.

A feeling of pain crept over him as he thought of the desecration that was in store for the fair face on the canvas. Once, in boyish mockery of Narcissus, he had kissed, or feigned to kiss, those painted lips that now smiled so cruelly at him. Morning after morning he had sat before the portrait wondering at its beauty, almost enamoured of it, as it seemed to him at times. Was it to alter now with every mood to which he yielded? Was it to become a monstrous and loathsome thing, to be hidden away in a locked room, to be shut out from the sunlight that had so often touched to brighter gold the waving wonder of its hair? The pity of it! the pity of it![4]

For a moment he thought of praying that the horrible sympathy that

4. Key words of Othello's remark to Iago in *Othello* 4.1.195–96.

existed between him and the picture might cease. It had changed in answer to a prayer; perhaps in answer to a prayer it might remain unchanged. And, yet, who, that knew anything about Life, would surrender the chance of remaining always young, however fantastic that chance might be, or with what fateful consequences it might be fraught? Besides, was it really under his control? Had it indeed been prayer that had produced the substitution? Might there not be some curious scientific reason for it all? If thought could exercise its influence upon a living organism, might not thought exercise an influence upon dead and inorganic things? Nay, without thought or conscious desire, might not things external to ourselves vibrate in unison with our moods and passions, atom calling to atom in secret love or strange affinity? But the reason was of no importance. He would never again tempt by a prayer any terrible power. If the picture was to alter, it was to alter. That was all. Why inquire too closely into it?

For there would be a real pleasure in watching it. He would be able to follow his mind into its secret places. This portrait would be to him the most magical of mirrors. As it had revealed to him his own body, so it would reveal to him his own soul. And when winter came upon it, he would still be standing where spring trembles on the verge of summer. When the blood crept from its face, and left behind a pallid mask of chalk with leaden eyes, he would keep the glamour of boyhood. Not one blossom of his loveliness would ever fade. Not one pulse of his life would ever weaken. Like the gods of the Greeks, he would be strong, and fleet, and joyous. What did it matter what happened to the coloured image on the canvas? He would be safe. That was everything.

He drew the screen back into its former place in front of the picture, smiling as he did so, and passed into his bedroom, where his valet was already waiting for him. An hour later he was at the Opera, and Lord Henry was leaning over his chair.

Chapter IX.[1]

As he was sitting at breakfast next morning, Basil Hallward was shown into the room.

"I am so glad I have found you, Dorian," he said, gravely. "I called last night, and they told me you were at the Opera. Of course I knew that was impossible. But I wish you had left word where you had really gone to. I passed a dreadful evening, half afraid that one tragedy might be followed by another. I think you might have telegraphed for me when you heard of it first. I read of it quite by chance in a late edition of *The Globe*,[2] that I picked up at the club. I came here at once, and was miserable at not finding you. I can't tell you how heart-broken I am

1. Originally chapter 7.
2. An evening newspaper, also read by Sherlock Holmes.

about the whole thing. I know what you must suffer. But where were you? Did you go down and see the girl's mother? For a moment I thought of following you there. They gave the address in the paper. Somewhere in the Euston Road, isn't it? But I was afraid of intruding upon a sorrow that I could not lighten. Poor woman! What a state she must be in! And her only child, too! What did she say about it all?"

"My dear Basil, how do I know?" murmured Dorian Gray, sipping some pale-yellow wine from a delicate gold-beaded bubble of Venetian glass, and looking dreadfully bored. "I was at the Opera. You should have come on there. I met Lady Gwendolen, Harry's sister, for the first time. We were in her box. She is perfectly charming; and Patti sang divinely. Don't talk about horrid subjects. If one doesn't talk about a thing, it has never happened. It is simply expression, as Harry says, that gives reality to things. I may mention that she was not the woman's only child. There is a son, a charming fellow, I believe. But he is not on the stage. He is a sailor, or something. And now, tell me about yourself and what you are painting."

"You went to the Opera?" said Hallward, speaking very slowly, and with a strained touch of pain in his voice. "You went to the Opera while Sibyl Vane was lying dead in some sordid lodging? You can talk to me of other women being charming, and of Patti singing divinely, before the girl you loved has even the quiet of a grave to sleep in? Why, man, there are horrors in store for that little white body of hers!"

"Stop, Basil! I won't hear it!" cried Dorian, leaping to his feet. "You must not tell me about things. What is done is done. What is past is past."

"You call yesterday the past?"

"What has the actual lapse of time got to do with it? It is only shallow people who require years to get rid of an emotion. A man who is master of himself can end a sorrow as easily as he can invent a pleasure. I don't want to be at the mercy of my emotions. I want to use them, to enjoy them, and to dominate them."

"Dorian, this is horrible! Something has changed you completely. You look exactly the same wonderful boy who, day after day, used to come down to my studio to sit for his picture. But you were simple, natural, and affectionate then. You were the most unspoiled creature in the whole world. Now, I don't know what has come over you. You talk as if you had no heart, no pity in you. It is all Harry's influence. I see that."

The lad flushed up, and, going to the window, looked out for a few moments on the green, flickering, sun-lashed garden. "I owe a great deal to Harry, Basil," he said, at last—"more than I owe to you. You only taught me to be vain."

"Well, I am punished for that, Dorian—or shall be some day."

"I don't know what you mean, Basil," he exclaimed, turning round.

"I don't know what you want. What do you want?"

"I want the Dorian Gray I used to paint," said the artist, sadly.

"Basil," said the lad, going over to him, and putting his hand on his shoulder, "you have come too late. Yesterday when I heard that Sibyl Vane had killed herself—"

"Killed herself! Good heavens! is there no doubt about that?" cried Hallward, looking up at him with an expression of horror.

"My dear Basil! Surely you don't think it was a vulgar accident? Of course she killed herself."

The elder man buried his face in his hands. "How fearful," he muttered, and a shudder ran through him.

"No," said Dorian Gray, "there is nothing fearful about it. It is one of the great romantic tragedies of the age. As a rule, people who act lead the most commonplace lives. They are good husbands, or faithful wives, or something tedious. You know what I mean—middle-class virtue, and all that kind of thing. How different Sibyl was! She lived her finest tragedy. She was always a heroine. The last night she played—the night you saw her—she acted badly because she had known the reality of love. When she knew its unreality, she died, as Juliet might have died. She passed again into the sphere of art. There is something of the martyr about her. Her death has all the pathetic uselessness of martyrdom, all its wasted beauty. But, as I was saying, you must not think I have not suffered. If you had come in yesterday at a particular moment—about half-past five, perhaps, or a quarter of six—you would have found me in tears. Even Harry, who was here, who brought me the news, in fact, had no idea what I was going through. I suffered immensely. Then it passed away. I cannot repeat an emotion. No one can, except sentimentalists. And you are awfully unjust, Basil. You come down here to console me. That is charming of you. You find me consoled, and you are furious. How like a sympathetic person! You remind me of a story Harry told me about a certain philanthropist who spent twenty years of his life in trying to get some grievance redressed, or some unjust law altered—I forget exactly what it was. Finally he succeeded, and nothing could exceed his disappointment. He had absolutely nothing to do, almost died of *ennui*,[3] and became a confirmed misanthrope. And besides, my dear old Basil, if you really want to console me, teach me rather to forget what has happened, or to see it from a proper artistic point of view. Was it not Gautier[4] who used to write about *la consolation des arts?* I remember picking up a little vellum-covered book in your studio one day and chancing on that delightful phrase. Well, I am not like that young man you told me of when we were down at Marlow together, the young man who used to say that yellow satin could console one for all the miseries of life. I love beautiful things that one can touch and handle. Old brocades, green bronzes, lacquer-work, carved ivories, exquisite surround-

3. Weariness of spirit.
4. Théophile Gautier (1811–72), French poet and

novelist, one of the founders of Aestheticism in Europe and creator of the legend "art for art's sake."

ings, luxury, pomp, there is much to be got from all these.[5] But the artistic temperament that they create, or at any rate reveal, is still more to me. To become the spectator of one's own life, as Harry says, is to escape the suffering of life. I know you are surprised at my talking to you like this. You have not realized how I have developed. I was a schoolboy when you knew me. I am a man now. I have new passions, new thoughts, new ideas. I am different, but you must not like me less. I am changed, but you must always be my friend. Of course I am very fond of Harry. But I know that you are better than he is. You are not stronger—you are too much afraid of life—but you are better. And how happy we used to be together! Don't leave me, Basil, and don't quarrel with me. I am what I am. There is nothing more to be said."

The painter felt strangely moved. The lad was infinitely dear to him, and his personality had been the great turning-point in his art. He could not bear the idea of reproaching him any more. After all, his indifference was probably merely a mood that would pass away. There was so much in him that was good, so much in him that was noble.

"Well, Dorian," he said, at length, with a sad smile, "I won't speak to you again about this horrible thing, after to-day. I only trust your name won't be mentioned in connection with it. The inquest is to take place this afternoon. Have they summoned you?"

Dorian shook his head, and a look of annoyance passed over his face at the mention of the word "inquest." There was something so crude and vulgar about everything of the kind. "They don't know my name," he answered.

"But surely she did?"

"Only my Christian name, and that I am quite sure she never mentioned to any one. She told me once that they were all rather curious to learn who I was, and that she invariably told them my name was Prince Charming. It was pretty of her. You must do me a drawing of Sibyl, Basil. I should like to have something more of her than the memory of a few kisses and some broken pathetic words."

"I will try and do something, Dorian, if it would please you. But you must come and sit to me yourself again. I can't get on without you."

"I can never sit to you again, Basil. It is impossible!" he exclaimed, starting back.

The painter stared at him. "My dear boy, what nonsense!" he cried. "Do you mean to say you don't like what I did of you? Where is it? Why have you pulled the screen in front of it? Let me look at it. It is the best thing I have ever done. Do take the screen away, Dorian. It is simply disgraceful of your servant hiding my work like that. I felt the room looked different as I came in."

"My servant has nothing to do with it, Basil. You don't imagine I let him arrange my room for me? He settles my flowers for me sometimes—

5. Wilde developed these views at length in *Intentions* out of his earlier lectures from the 1880's, which in turn owed much to Whistler, Pater, and ultimately also to Gautier, noted above.

that is all. No; I did it myself. The light was too strong on the portrait."

"Too strong! Surely not, my dear fellow? It is an admirable place for it. Let me see it." And Hallward walked towards the corner of the room.

A cry of terror broke from Dorian Gray's lips, and he rushed between the painter and the screen. "Basil," he said, looking very pale, "you must not look at it. I don't wish you to."

"Not look at my own work! you are not serious. Why shouldn't I look at it?" exclaimed Hallward, laughing.

"If you try to look at it, Basil, on my word of honour I will never speak to you again as long as I live. I am quite serious. I don't offer any explanation, and you are not to ask for any. But, remember, if you touch this screen, everything is over between us."

Hallward was thunderstruck. He looked at Dorian Gray in absolute amazement. He had never seen him like this before. The lad was actually pallid with rage. His hands were clenched, and the pupils of his eyes were like disks of blue fire. He was trembling all over.

"Dorian!"

"Don't speak!"

"But what is the matter? Of course I won't look at it if you don't want me to," he said, rather coldly, turning on his heel, and going over towards the window. "But, really, it seems rather absurd that I shouldn't see my own work, especially as I am going to exhibit it in Paris in the autumn. I shall probably have to give it another coat of varnish before that so I must see it some day, and why not to-day?"

"To exhibit it! You want to exhibit it?" exclaimed Dorian Gray, a strange sense of terror creeping over him. Was the world going to be shown his secret? Were people to gape at the mystery of his life? That was impossible. Something—he did not know what—had to be done at once.

"Yes; I don't suppose you will object to that. Georges Petit is going to collect all my best pictures for a special exhibition in the Rue de Sèze.[6] which will open the first week in October. The portrait will only be away a month. I should think you could easily spare it for that time. In fact, you are sure to be out of town. And if you keep it always behind a screen, you can't care much about it."

Dorian Gray passed his hand over his forehead. There were beads of perspiration there. He felt that he was on the brink of a horrible danger. "You told me a month ago that you would never exhibit it," he cried. "Why have you changed your mind? You people who go in for being consistent have just as many moods as others have. The only difference is that your moods are rather meaningless. You can't have forgotten that you assured me most solemnly that nothing in the world would induce you to send it to any exhibition. You told Harry exactly the same thing." He stopped suddenly, and a gleam of light came into his eyes. He

6. Petit founded a popular gallery there in 1882, famous for its association with the French Impressionist painters.

remembered that Lord Henry had said to him once, half seriously and half in jest, "If you want to have a strange quarter of an hour, get Basil to tell you why he won't exhibit your picture. He told me why he wouldn't, and it was a revelation to me." Yes, perhaps Basil, too, had his secret. He would ask him and try.

"Basil," he said, coming over quite close, and looking him straight in the face, "we have each of us a secret. Let me know yours, and I shall tell you mine. What was your reason for refusing to exhibit my picture?"

The painter shuddered in spite of himself. "Dorian, if I told you, you might like me less than you do, and you would certainly laugh at me. I could not bear your doing either of those two things. If you wish me never to look at your picture again, I am content. I have always you to look at. If you wish the best work I have ever done to be hidden from the world, I am satisfied. Your friendship is dearer to me than any fame or reputation.

"No, Basil, you must tell me," insisted Dorian Gray. "I think I have a right to know." His feeling of terror had passed away, and curiosity had taken its place. He was determined to find out Basil Hallward's mystery.

"Let us sit down, Dorian," said the painter, looking troubled. "Let us sit down. And just answer me one question. Have you noticed in the picture something curious?—something that probably at first did not strike you, but that revealed itself to you suddenly?"

"Basil!" cried the lad, clutching the arms of his chair with trembling hands, and gazing at him with wild, startled eyes.

"I see you did. Don't speak. Wait till you hear what I have to say. Dorian, from the moment I met you, your personality had the most extraordinary influence over me. I was dominated, soul, brain, and power by you. You became to me the visible incarnation of that unseen ideal whose memory haunts us artists like an exquisite dream. I worshipped you. I grew jealous of every one to whom you spoke. I wanted to have you all to myself. I was only happy when I was with you. When you were away from me you were still present in my art. . . . Of course I never let you know anything about this. It would have been impossible. You would not have understood it. I hardly understood it myself. I only knew that I had seen perfection face to face, and that the world had become wonderful to my eyes—too wonderful, perhaps, for in such mad worships there is peril, the peril of losing them, no less than the peril of keeping them. . . . Weeks and weeks went on, and I grew more and more absorbed in you. Then came a new development. I had drawn you as Paris in dainty armour, and as Adonis with huntsman's cloak and polished boar-spear. Crowned with heavy lotus-blossoms you had sat on the prow of Adrian's barge,[7] gazing across the green turbid Nile. You had leant over the still pool of some Greek woodland, and seen in the

---

7. Antinoüs, beloved male companion of the Emperor Hadrian (here Adrian) of Rome, drowned in the Nile in A.D. 130, presumably off one of the emperor's ornately decorated barges.

water's silent silver the marvel of your own face. And it had all been what art should be, unconscious, ideal, and remote. One day, a fatal day I sometimes think, I determined to paint a wonderful portrait of you as you actually are, not in the costume of dead ages, but in your own dress and in your own time. Whether it was the Realism of the method, or the mere wonder of your personality, thus directly presented to me without mist or veil, I cannot tell. But I know that as I worked at it, every flake and film of colour seemed to me to reveal my secret. I grew afraid that others would know of my idolatry. I felt, Dorian, that I had told too much, that I had put too much of myself into it. Then it was that I resolved never to allow the picture to be exhibited. You were a little annoyed; but then you did not realize all that it meant to me. Harry, to whom I talked about it, laughed at me. But I did not mind that. When the picture was finished, and I sat alone with it, I felt that I was right. . . . Well, after a few days the thing left my studio, and as soon as I had got rid of the intolerable fascination of its presence it seemed to me that I had been foolish in imaging that I had seen anything in it, more than that you were extremely good-looking and that I could paint. Even now I cannot help feeling that it is a mistake to think that the passion one feels in creation is ever really shown in the work one creates. Art is always more abstract than we fancy. Form and colour tell us of form and colour—that is all. It often seems to me that art conceals the artist far more completely than it ever reveals him. And so when I got this offer from Paris I determined to make your portrait the principal thing in my exhibition. It never occurred to me that you would refuse. I see now that you were right. The picture cannot be shown. You must not be angry with me, Dorian, for what I have told you. As I said to Harry, once, you are made to be worshipped."

Dorian Gray drew a long breath. The colour came back to his cheeks, and a smile played about his lips. The peril was over. He was safe for the time. Yet he could not help feeling infinite pity for the painter who had just made this strange confession to him, and wondered if he himself would ever be so dominated by the personality of a friend. Lord Henry had the charm of being very dangerous. But that was all. He was too clever and too cynical to be really fond of. Would there ever be some one who would fill him with a strange idolatry? Was that one of the things that life had in store?

"It is extraordinary to me, Dorian," said Hallward, "that you should have seen this in the portrait. Did you really see it?"

"I saw something in it," he answered, "Something that seemed to me very curious."

"Well, you don't mind my looking at the thing now?"

Dorian shook his head. "You must not ask me that, Basil. I could not possibly let you stand in front of that picture."

"You will some day, surely?"

"Never."

"Well, perhaps you are right. And now good-bye, Dorian. You have been the one person in my life who has really influenced my art. Whatever I have done that is good, I owe to you. Ah! you don't know what it cost me to tell you all that I have told you."

"My dear Basil," said Dorian, "what have you told me? Simply that you felt that you admired me too much. That is not even a compliment."

"It was not intended as a compliment. It was a confession. Now that I have made it, something seems to have gone out of me. Perhaps one should never put one's worship into words."

"It was a very disappointing confession."

"Why, what did you expect, Dorian? You didn't see anything else in the picture, did you? There was nothing else to see?"

"No; there was nothing else to see. Why do you ask? But you mustn't talk about worship. It is foolish. You and I are friends, Basil, and we must always remain so."

"You have got Harry," said the painter, sadly.

"Oh, Harry!" cried the lad, with a ripple of laughter. "Harry spends his days in saying what is incredible, and his evenings in doing what is improbable. Just the sort of life I would like to lead. But still I don't think I would go to Harry if I were in trouble. I would sooner go to you, Basil."

"You will sit to me again?"

"Impossible!"

"You spoil my life as an artist by refusing, Dorian. No man came across two ideal things. Few come across one."

"I can't explain it to you, Basil, but I must never sit to you again. There is something fatal about a portrait. It has a life of its own. I will come and have tea with you. That will be just as pleasant."

"Pleasanter for you, I am afraid," murmured Hallward, regretfully. "And now good-bye. I am sorry you won't let me look at the picture once again. But that can't be helped. I quite understand what you feel about it."

As he left the room, Dorian Gray smiled to himself. Poor Basil! how little he knew of the true reason! And how strange it was that, instead of having been forced to reveal his own secret, he had succeeded, almost by chance, in wrestling a secret from his friend! How much that strange confession explained to him! The painter's absurd fits of jealousy, his wild devotion, his extravagant panegyrics, his curious reticences—he understood them all now, and he felt sorry. There seemed to him to be something tragic in a friendship so coloured by romance.

He sighed, and touched the bell. The portrait must be hidden away at all costs. He could not run such a risk of discovery again. It had been mad of him to have allowed the thing to remain, even for an hour, in a room to which any of his friends had access.

Chapter X. [1]

When his servant entered, he looked at him steadfastly, and wondered if he had thought of peering behind the screen. The man was quite impassive, and waited for his orders. Dorian lit a cigarette, and walked over to the glass and glanced into it. He could see the reflection of Victor's face perfectly. It was like a placid mask of servility. There was nothing to be afraid of, there. Yet he thought it best to be on his guard.

Speaking very slowly, he told him to tell the housekeeper that he wanted to see her, and then to go to the frame-maker and ask him to send two of his men round at once. It seemed to him that as the man left the room his eyes wandered in the direction of the screen. Or was that merely his own fancy?

After a few moments, in her black silk dress, with old-fashioned thread mittens on her wrinkled hands, Mrs. Leaf [2] bustled into the library. He asked her for the key of the schoolroom.

"The old schoolroom, Mr. Dorian?" she exclaimed. "Why, it is full of dust. I must get it arranged, and put straight before you go into it. It is not fit for you to see, sir. It is not, indeed."

"I don't want it put straight, Leaf. I only want the key."

"Well, sir, you'll be covered with cobwebs if you go into it. Why, it hasn't been opened for nearly five years, not since his lordship died."

He winced at the mention of his grandfather. He had hateful memories of him. "That does not matter," he answered. "I simply want to see the place—that is all. Give me the key."

"And here is the key, sir," said the old lady, going over the contents of her bunch with tremulously uncertain hands. "Here is the key. I'll have it off the bunch in a moment. But you don't think of living up there, sir, and you so comfortable here?"

"No, no," he cried, petulantly. "Thank you, Leaf. That will do."

She lingered for a few moments, and was garrulous over some detail of the household. He sighed, and told her to manage things as she thought best. She left the room, wreathed in smiles.

As the door closed, Dorian put the key in his pocket, and looked around the room. His eye fell on a large purple satin coverlet heavily embroidered with gold, a splendid piece of late seventeenth-century Venetian work that his grandfather had found in a convent near Bologna. Yes, that would serve to wrap the dreadful thing in. It had perhaps served often as a pall for the dead. Now it was to hide something that had a corruption of its own, worse than the corruption of death itself—something that would breed horrors and yet would never die. What the worm was to the corpse, his sins would be to the painted image on the canvas. They would mar its beauty, and eat away its grace. They would defile

---

1. Originally chapter 8.
2. Wilde revised this and the following page heavily from the first edition, greatly reducing the

importance of "poor old Leaf" from the rich vignette of the original to a faded remnant.

it, and make it shameful. And yet the thing would still live on. It would be always alive.

He shuddered, and for a moment he regretted that he had not told Basil the true reason why he had wished to hide the picture away. Basil would have helped him to resist Lord Henry's influence, and the still more poisonous influences that came from his own temperament. The love that he bore him—for it was really love—had nothing in it that was not noble and intellectual. It was not that mere physical admiration of beauty that is born of the senses, and that dies when the senses tire. It was such love as Michael Angelo had known, and Montaigne, and Winckelmann, and Shakespeare himself.[3] Yes, Basil could have saved him. But it was too late now. The past could always be annihilated. Regret, denial, or forgetfulness could do that. But the future was inevitable. There were passions in him that would find their terrible outlet, dreams that would make the shadow of their evil real.

He took up from the couch the great purple-and-gold texture that covered it, and, holding it in his hands, passed behind the screen. Was the face on the canvas viler than before? It seemed to him that it was unchanged; and yet his loathing of it was intensified. Gold hair, blue eyes, and rose-red lips—they all were there. It was simply the expression that had altered. That was horrible in its cruelty. Compared to what he saw in it of censure or rebuke, how shallow Basil's reproaches about Sibyl Vane had been!—how shallow, and of what little account! His own soul was looking out at him from the canvas and calling him to judgment. A look of pain came across him, and he flung the rich pall over the picture. As he did so, a knock came to the door. He passed out as his servant entered.

"The persons are here, Monsieur."

He felt that the man must be got rid of at once. He must not be allowed to know where the picture was being taken to. There was something sly about him, and he had thoughtful, treacherous eyes. Sitting down at the writing-table, he scribbled a note to Lord Henry, asking him to send him round something to read, and reminding him that they were to meet at eight-fifteen that evening.

"Wait for an answer," he said, handing it to him, "and show the men in here."

In two or three minutes there was another knock, and Mr. Hubbard[4]

3. Montaigne and Winckelmann were two of Wilde's cultural heroes. Michel Montaigne (1533–92), French essayist, and Johann Winckelmann (1717–68), German archeologist and art historian, were believed to be homosexuals, as were Michelangelo and Shakespeare. Wilde wrote in nearly identical terms in "The Portrait of Mr. W. H." and gave an eloquent defense of "the love that dare not speak its name" at the second trial.
4. Hubbard was "Mr. Ashton" in the magazine edition. In *In Good Company* (London: Lane, 1917) 212–13, Coulson Kernahan, the Ward, Lock and Company editor with whom Wilde worked in preparing the revised edition, gives the following account of a hoax Wilde played on him over the name change. He reports receiving a telegram from Wilde in Paris: "Terrible blunder in book, coming back specially. Stop all proofs! Wilde." Wilde arrived at the office apparently distracted: " 'Ashton is a gentleman's name,' he spoke brokenly and wrung his hands as if in anguish, 'and I've given it—God forgive me—to a tradesman! It must be changed to Hubbard. Hubbard positively smells of the tradesman.' "

himself, the celebrated frame-maker of South Audley Street,[5] came in with a somewhat rough-looking young assistant. Mr. Hubbard was a florid, red-whiskered little man, whose admiration for art was considerably tempered by the inveterate impecuniosity of most of the artists who dealt with him. As a rule, he never left his shop. He waited for people to come to him. But he always made an exception in favour of Dorian Gray. There was something about Dorian that charmed everybody. It was a pleasure even to see him.

"What can I do for you, Mr. Gray?" he said, rubbing his fat freckled hands. "I thought I would do myself the honour of coming round in person. I have just got a beauty of a frame, sir. Picked it up at a sale. Old Florentine. Came from Fonthill,[6] I believe. Admirably suited for a religious subject, Mr. Gray."

"I am so sorry you have given yourself the trouble of coming round, Mr. Hubbard. I shall certainly drop in and look at the frame—though I don't go in much at present for religious art—but to-day I only want a picture carried to the top of the house for me. It is rather heavy, so I thought I would ask you to lend me a couple of your men."

"No trouble at all, Mr. Gray. I am delighted to be of any service to you. Which is the work of art, sir?"

"This," replied Dorian, moving the screen back. "Can you move it, covering and all, just as it is? I don't want it to get scratched going upstairs."

"There will be no difficulty, sir," said the genial frame-maker, beginning, with the aid of his assistant, to unhook the picture from the long brass chains by which it was suspended. "And, now, where shall we carry it to, Mr. Gray?"

"I will show you the way, Mr. Hubbard, if you will kindly follow me. Or perhaps you had better go in front. I am afraid it is right at the top of the house. We will go up by the front staircase, as it is wider."

He held the door open for them, and they passed out into the hall and began the ascent. The elaborate character of the frame had made the picture extremely bulky, and now and then, in spite of the obsequious protests of Mr. Hubbard, who had the true tradesman's spirited dislike of seeing a gentleman doing anything useful, Dorian put his hand to it so as to help them.

"Something of a load to carry, sir," gasped the little man, when they reached the top landing. And he wiped his shiny forehead.

"I am afraid it is rather heavy," murmured Dorian, as he unlocked the door that opened into the room that was to keep for him the curious secret of his life and hide his soul from the eyes of men.

He had not entered the place for more than four years—not, indeed,

5. A street in Mayfair near Hyde Park.
6. William Beckford, author of *Vathek*, a Gothic novel much admired by Byron, built a suitably Gothic mansion in Fonthill Wood in Wiltshire.

The frame would have come from the auction of Fonthill furnishings at Christie's Auction House in 1822.

since he had used it first as a play-room when he was a child, and then as a study when he grew somewhat older. It was a large, well-proportioned room, which had been specially built by the last Lord Kelso for the use of the little grandson whom, for his strange likeness to his mother, and also for other reasons, he had always hated and desired to keep at a distance. It appeared to Dorian to have but little changed. There was the huge Italian *cassone*[7] with its fantastically-painted panels and its tarnished gilt mouldings, in which he had so often hidden himself as a boy. There the satinwood bookcase filled with his dog-eared schoolbooks. On the wall behind it was hanging the same ragged Flemish tapestry where a faded king and queen were playing chess in a garden, while a company of hawkers rode by, carrying hooded birds on their gauntleted wrists. How well he remembered it all! Every moment of his lonely childhood came back to him as he looked round. He recalled the stainless purity of his boyish life, and it seemed horrible to him that it was here the fatal portrait was to be hidden away. How little he had thought, in those dead days, of all that was in store for him!

But there was no other place in the house so secure from prying eyes as this. He had the key, and no one else could enter it. Beneath its purple pall, the face painted on the canvas could grow bestial, sodden, and unclean. What did it matter? No one could see it. He himself would not see it. Why should he watch the hideous corruption of his soul? He kept his youth—that was enough. And, besides, might not his nature grow finer, after all? There was no reason that the future should be so full of shame. Some love might come across his life, and purify him, and shield him from those sins that seemed to be already stirring in spirit and in flesh—those curious unpictured sins whose very mystery lent them their subtlety and their charm. Perhaps, some day, the cruel look would have passed away from the scarlet sensitive mouth, and he might show to the world Basil Hallward's masterpiece.

No; that was impossible. Hour by hour, and week by week, the thing upon the canvas was growing old. It might escape the hideousness of sin, but the hideousness of age was in store for it. The cheeks would become hollow or flaccid. Yellow crow's-feet would creep round the fading eyes and make them horrible. The hair would lose its brightness, the mouth would gape or droop, would be foolish or gross, as the mouths of old men are. There would be the wrinkled throat, the cold, blue-veined hands, the twisted body, that he remembered in the grandfather who had been so stern to him in his boyhood. The picture had to be concealed. There was no help for it.

"Bring it in, Mr. Hubbard, please," he said, wearily, turning round. "I am sorry I kept you so long. I was thinking of something else."

"Always glad to have a rest, Mr. Gray," answered the frame-maker, who was still gasping for breath. "Where shall we put it, sir?"

---

7. A large, ornamented Italian chest of the Renaissance.

"Oh, anywhere. Here: this will do. I don't want to have it hung up. Just lean it against the wall. Thanks."

"Might one look at the work of art, sir?"

Dorian started. "It would not interest you, Mr. Hubbard," he said, keeping his eye on the man. He felt ready to leap upon him and fling him to the ground if he dared to lift the gorgeous hanging that concealed the secret of his life. "I sha'n't trouble you any more now. I am much obliged for your kindness in coming round."

"Not at all, not at all, Mr. Gray. Ever ready to do anything for you sir." And Mr. Hubbard tramped downstairs, followed by the assistant, who glanced back at Dorian with a look of shy wonder in his rough, uncomely face. He had never seen any one so marvellous.

When the sound of their footsteps had died away, Dorian locked the door, and put the key in his pocket. He felt safe now. No one would ever look upon the horrible thing. No eye but his would ever see his shame.

On reaching the library he found that it was just after five o'clock, and that the tea had been already brought up. On a little table of dark perfumed wood thickly incrusted with nacre,[8] a present from Lady Radley, his guardian's wife, a pretty professional invalid, who had spent the preceding winter in Cairo, was lying a note from Lord Henry, and beside it was a book bound in yellow paper,[9] the cover slightly torn and the edges soiled. A copy of the third edition of The St. James's Gazette had been placed on the tea-tray. It was evident that Victor had returned. He wondered if he had met the men in the hall as they were leaving the house, and had wormed out of them what they had been doing. He would be sure to miss the picture—had no doubt missed it already, while he had been laying the tea-things. The screen had not been set back, and a blank space was visible on the wall. Perhaps some night he might find him creeping upstairs and trying to force the door of the room. It was a horrible thing to have a spy in one's house. He had heard of rich men who had been blackmailed all their lives by some servant who had read a letter, or overheard a conversation, or picked up a card with an address, or found beneath a pillow a withered flower or a shred of crumpled lace.

He sighed, and, having poured himself out some tea, opened Lord Henry's note. It was simply to say that he sent him round the evening paper, and a book that might interest him, and that he would be at the

---

8. Mother-of-pearl.
9. Dorian's yellow book is one of the most famous puzzles in literature. The case for identifying it as J. K. Huysmans's A Rebours is weakened by the evidence of TS cancellations by Stoddart of the details of "The Secret of Raoul by Catulle Sarrazin." Details of the book make it clear that it was largely imaginary, as Wilde reported in Letters (313), although partly suggested by Huysmans's novel. The imaginary "Catulle Sarrazin" seems to have been taken from the names of two contemporary French men of letters known to Wilde: Gabriel Sarrazin, a critic, and Catulle Mendes, a poet.

The St. James's Gazette was one of the London papers read by people in Wilde's set. He wrote occasional reviews and debated the art and morality issue in its columns after the appearance of the Lippincott's edition.

club at eight-fifteen. He opened *The St. James's* languidly, and looked through it. A red pencil-mark on the fifth page caught his eye. It drew attention to the following paragraph:—

> "INQUEST ON AN ACTRESS.—An inquest was held this morning at the Bell Tavern, Hoxton Road, by Mr. Danby, the District Coroner, on the body of Sibyl Vane, a young actress recently engaged at the Royal Theatre, Holborn. A verdict of death by misadventure was returned. Considerable sympathy was expressed for the mother of the deceased, who was greatly affected during the giving of her own evidence, and that of Dr. Birrell, who had made the post-mortem examination of the deceased."

He frowned, and, tearing the paper in two went across the room and flung the pieces away. How ugly it all was! And how horribly real ugliness made things! He felt a little annoyed with Lord Henry for having sent him the report. And it was certainly stupid of him to have marked it with red pencil. Victor might have read it. The man knew more than enough English for that.

Perhaps he had read it, and had begun to suspect something. And, yet, what did it matter? What had Dorian Gray to do with Sibyl Vane's death? There was nothing to fear. Dorian Gray had not killed her.

His eye fell on the yellow book that Lord Henry had sent him. What was it, he wondered. He went towards the little pearl-coloured octagonal stand, that had always looked to him like the work of some strange Egyptian bees that wrought in silver, and taking up the volume, flung himself into an arm-chair, and began to turn over the leaves. After a few minutes he became absorbed. It was the strangest book that he had ever read. It seemed to him that in exquisite raiment, and to the delicate sound of flutes, the sins of the world were passing in dumb show before him. Things that he had dimly dreamed of were suddenly made real to him. Things of which he had never dreamed were gradually revealed.

It was a novel without a plot, and with only one character, being, indeed, simply a psychological study of a certain young Parisian, who spent his life trying to realize in the nineteenth century all the passions and modes of thought that belonged to every century except his own,[1] and to sum up, as it were, in himself the various moods through which the world-spirit had ever passed, loving for their mere artificiality those renunciations that men have unwisely called virtue, as much as those natural rebellions that wise men still call sin. The style in which it was written was that curious jewelled style, vivid and obscure at once, full of *argot*[2] and of archaisms, of technical expressions and of elaborate paraphrases, that characterizes the work of some of the finest artists of the

1. In this and the preceding paragraph, echoes are heard of the chapter on Leonardo in Pater's *The Renaissance* (see pp. 296–309).

2. The idiom or slang of a particular group or class, especially associated with lowlifes.

French school of *Symbolistes*,[3] There were in it metaphors as monstrous as orchids, and as subtle in colour. The life of the senses was described in the terms of mystical philosophy. One hardly knew at times whether one was reading the spiritual ecstasies of some mediæval saint or the morbid confessions of a modern sinner. It was a poisonous book. The heavy odour of incense seemed to cling about its pages and to trouble the brain. The mere cadence of the sentences, the subtle monotony of their music, so full as it was of complex refrains and movements elaborately repeated, produced in the mind of the lad, as he passed from chapter to chapter, a form of reverie, a malady of dreaming, that made him unconscious of the falling day and creeping shadows.

Cloudless, and pierced by one solitary star, a copper-green sky gleamed through the windows. He read on by its wan light till he could read no more. Then, after his valet had reminded him several times of the lateness of the hour, he got up, and, going into the next room, placed the book on the little Florentine table that always stood at his bedside, and began to dress for dinner.

It was almost nine o'clock before he reached the club, where he found Lord Henry sitting alone, in the morning-room, looking very much bored.

"I am so sorry, Harry," he cried, "but really it is entirely your fault. That book you sent me so fascinated me that I forgot how the time was going."

"Yes: I thought you would like it," replied his host, rising from his chair.

"I didn't say I liked it, Harry. I said it fascinated me. There is a great difference."

"Ah, you have discovered that?" murmured Lord Henry. And they passed into the dining-room.

Chapter XI.[1]

For years, Dorian Gray could not free himself from the influence of this book. Or perhaps it would be more accurate to say that he never sought to free himself from it. He procured from Paris no less than nine large-paper copies of the first edition, and had them bound in different colours, so that they might suit his various moods and the changing fancies of a nature over which he seemed, at times, to have almost entirely lost control. The hero, the wonderful young Parisian, in whom the romantic and the scientific temperaments were so strangely blended,[2] became to him a kind of prefiguring type of himself. And, indeed, the

3. Wilde changed this from *Lippincott's* "Decadents." The Symbolistes were mainly French poets like Baudelaire, Rimbaud, Mallarmé, Verlaine, and Villiers d l'Isle Adam; they also included writers like Huysmans and Pierre Louys, who combined strong romanticism with contempt for realism and middle-class values. In art, the movement led to an emphasis on elusive and subtle states of mind and feeling, conveyed by symbols as the language expressing realities hidden behind appearances. Arthur Symons helped to popularize the movement in England with *The Symbolist Movement in Literature* (1899).

1. Originally chapter 9.

2. Another allusion to the chapter on Leonardo in *The Renaissance* (see pp. 296–309).

"Satyricon"[8] once had been, yet in his inmost heart he desired to be something more than a mere *arbiter elegantiarum*, to be consulted on the wearing of a jewel, or the knotting of a necktie, or the conduct of a cane. He sought to elaborate some new scheme of life that would have its reasoned philosophy and its ordered principles, and find in the spiritualizing of the senses its highest realization.[9]

The worship of the senses has often, and with much justice, been decried, men feeling a natural instinct of terror about passions and sensations that seem stronger than themselves, and that they are conscious of sharing with the less highly organized forms of existence. But it appeared to Dorian Gray that the true nature of the senses had never been understood, and that they had remained savage and animal merely because the world had sought to starve them into submission or to kill them by pain, instead of aiming at making them elements of a new spirituality, of which a fine instinct for beauty was to be the dominant characteristic. As he looked back upon man moving through History, he was haunted by a feeling of loss. So much had been surrendered! and to such little purpose! There had been mad wilful rejections, monstrous forms of self-torture and self-denial, whose origin was fear, and whose result was a degradation infinitely more terrible than that fancied degradation from which, in their ignorance, they had sought to escape, Nature, in her wonderful irony, driving out the anchorite to feed with the wild animals of the desert and giving to the hermit the beasts of the field as his companions.

Yes: there was to be, as Lord Henry had prophesied, a new Hedonism[1] that was to recreate life, and to save it from that harsh, uncomely puritanism that is having, in our own day, its curious revival. It was to have its service of the intellect, certainly; yet, it was never to accept any theory or system that would involve the sacrifice of any mode of passionate experience. Its aim, indeed, was to be experience itself, and not the fruits of experience, sweet or bitter as they might be. Of the asceticism that deadens the senses, of the vulgar profligacy that dulls them, it was to know nothing. But it was to teach man to concentrate himself upon the moments of a life that is itself but a moment.

There are few of us who have not sometimes wakened before dawn, either after one of those dreamless nights that make us almost enamoured of death, or one of those nights of horror and misshapen joy, when through the chambers of the brain sweep phantoms more terrible than reality itself, and instinct with that vivid life that lurks in all gro-

8. Petronius, author of the *Satyricon*, which both satirized and was an instance of the decadence of Nero's Rome, was himself an intimate of the emperor. His title, "arbiter elegantiarum," was partly descriptive of his role as director of revels for the emperor and partly a pun on his name and fashion: Gaius Petronius Arbiter.
9. An expression of Wilde's synthesis of Ruskin, Pater, and *Symboliste* thinking.
1. If what came before was the new Dandyism of the nineteenth-century aesthete, what follows here is Wilde's variation on the philosophy put forward by Pater in the Conclusion to *The Renaissance* (see pp. 311–12) and as the "New Cyrenaicism" in his *Marius the Epicurean* 2.9.

tesques, and that lends to Gothic art its enduring vitality, this art being, one might fancy, especially the art of those whose minds have been troubled with the malady of reverie. Gradually white fingers creep through the curtains, and they appear to tremble. In black fantastic shapes, dumb shadows crawl into the corners of the room, and crouch there. Outside, there is the stirring of birds among the leaves, or the sound of men going forth to their work, or the sigh and sob of the wind coming down from the hills, and wandering round the silent house, as though it feared to wake the sleepers, and yet must needs call forth sleep from her purple cave. Veil after veil of thin dusky gauze is lifted, and by degrees the forms and colours of things are restored to them, and we watch the dawn remaking the world in its antique pattern. The wan mirrors get back their mimic life. The flameless tapers stand where we had left them, and beside them lies the half-cut book that we had been studying, or the wired flower that we had worn at the ball, or the letter that we had been afraid to read, or that we had read too often. Nothing seems to us changed. Out of the unreal shadows of the night comes back the real life that we had known. We have to resume it where we had left off, and there steals over us a terrible sense of the necessity for the continuance of energy in the same wearisome round of stereotyped habits, or a wild longing, it may be, that our eyelids might open some morning upon a world that had been refashioned anew in the darkness for our pleasure, a world in which things would have fresh shapes and colours, and be changed, or have other secrets, a world in which the past would have little or no place, or survive, at any rate, in no conscious form of obligation or regret, the remembrance even of joy having its bitterness, and the memories of pleasure their pain.

It was the creation of such worlds as these that seemed to Dorian Gray to be the true object, or amongst the true objects, of life; and in his search for sensations that would be at once new and delightful, and possess that element of strangeness that is so essential to romance,[2] he would often adopt certain modes of thought that he knew to be really alien to his nature, abandon himself to their subtle influences, and then, having, as it were, caught their colour and satisfied his intellectual curiosity, leave them with that curious indifference that is not incompatible with a real ardour of temperament, and that indeed, according to certain modern psychologists, is often a condition of it.[3]

It was rumoured of him once that he was about to join the Roman Catholic communion;[4] and certainly the Roman ritual had always a

2. In this paragraph and in the next two, Wilde continues a variation of the development of Pater's hero in *Marius the Epicurean*, only with a vastly different outcome.
3. The reference is possibly to Wilhelm Wundt (1832–1920), Herbert Spencer (1820–1903), and William James (1842–1910), German, English, and American psychologists, whose influence on the new science was definitive (although less well-

known than Freud's) and whose ideas are reflected in many of the meditations of Henry, Dorian, and the narrator on the relations among psychology, physiology, and morals.
4. After flirting with conversion for nearly forty years, Wilde was received into the Catholic church on his deathbed. Many Decadents were similarly attracted to Catholicism.

great attraction for him. The daily sacrifice, more awful really than all the sacrifices of the antique world, stirred him as much by its superb rejection of the evidence of the senses as by the primitive simplicity of its elements and the eternal pathos of the human tragedy that it sought to symbolize. He loved to kneel down on the cold marble pavement, and watch the priest, in his stiff flowered dalmatic, slowly and with white hands moving aside the veil of the tabernacle, or raising aloft the jewelled lantern-shaped monstrance [5] with that pallid wafer that at times, one would fain think, is indeed the *"panis cœlestis,"* the bread of angels, or, robed in the garments of the Passion of Christ, breaking the Host into the chalice, and smiting his breast for his sins. The fuming censers, that the grave boys, in their lace and scarlet, tossed into the air like great gilt flowers, had their subtle fascination for him. As he passed out, he used to look with wonder at the black confessionals, and long to sit in the dim shadow of one of them and listen to men and women whispering through the worn grating the true story of their lives.

But he never fell into the error of arresting his intellectual development by any formal acceptance of creed or system, or of mistaking, for a house in which to live, an inn that is but suitable for the sojourn of a night, or for a few hours of a night in which there are no stars and the moon is in travail. Mysticism, with its marvellous power of making common things strange to us, and the subtle antinomianism [6] that always seems to accompany it, moved him for a season; and for a season he inclined to the materialistic doctrines of the *Darwinismus* movement in Germany [7] and found a curious pleasure in tracing the thoughts and passions of men to some pearly cell in the brain, or some white nerve in the body, delighting in the conception of the absolute dependence of the spirit on certain physical conditions, morbid or healthy, normal or diseased. Yet, as has been said of him before, no theory of life seemed to him to be of any importance compared with life itself. He felt keenly conscious of how barren all intellectual speculation is when separated from action and experiment. He knew that the senses, no less than the soul, have their spiritual mysteries to reveal.

And so he would now study perfumes, [8] and the secrets of their manufacture, distilling heavily-scented oils, and burning odorous gums from

5. An ornately decorated metal display stand for the consecrated host used in Roman Catholic liturgy for benedictions, processionals, and adoration vigils. An apparent confusion between consecration of the host during Mass and benediction led Wilde to substitute a vestment appropriate to the former (dalmatic) for one proper to the later (cope). A dalmatic is an outer garment, usually embroidered, having wide sleeves, worn at Mass by a deacon, abbot, bishop, or cardinal.
6. Antinomianism is an unorthodox belief by certain Christians that they are freed from the restraints of moral law by virtue of grace. By extension, it is used to refer to those who rejected moral law and church teaching.

7. The application of Darwin's theories was especially strong in Germany, where the implications of biology, comparative anatomy, anthropology, psychology, and social theory were enthusiastically explored. Wilde thought Darwin and Renan the most influential men of the times. Ernst Renan (1823–92) was a French social philosopher and Orientalist, most noted for his application of scientific, historical methodology to Hebrew and Christian traditional belief.
8. Des Esseintes, the hero of A *Rebours*, makes an even more detailed and intense study of perfumes, their psychological effects and the associations they produce.

the East. He saw that there was no mood of the mind that had not its counterpart in the sensuous life, and set himself to discover their true relations, wondering what there was in frankincense that made one mystical, and in ambergris that stirred one's passions, and in violets that woke the memory of dead romances, and in musk that troubled the brain, and in champak that stained the imagination; and seeking often to elaborate a real psychology of perfumes, and to estimate the several influences of sweet-smelling roots, and scented pollen-laden flowers, of aromatic balms, and of dark and fragrant woods, of spikenard that sickens, of hovenia that makes men mad, and of aloes that are said to be able to expel melancholy from the soul.

At another time he devoted himself entirely to music, and in a long latticed room, with a vermilion-and-gold ceiling and walls of olive-green lacquer, he used to give curious concerts in which mad gypsies tore wild music from little zithers, or grave yellow-shawled Tunisians plucked at the strained strings of monstrous lutes, while grinning negroes beat monotonously upon copper drums, and, crouching upon scarlet mats, slim turbaned Indians blew through long pipes of reed or brass, and charmed, or feigned to charm, great hooded snakes and horrible horned adders. The harsh intervals and shrill discords of barbaric music stirred him at times when Schubert's grace, and Chopin's beautiful sorrows, and the mighty harmonies of Beethoven himself, fell unheeded on his ear. He collected together from all parts of the world the strangest instruments that could be found, either in the tombs of dead nations or among the few savage tribes that have survived contact with Western civilizations, and loved to touch and try them. He had the mysterious *juruparis* of the Rio Negro Indians,[9] that women are not allowed to look at, and that even youths may not see till they have been subjected to fasting and scourging, and the earthen jars of the Peruvians that have the shrill cries of birds, and flutes of human bones such as Alfonso de Ovalle[1] heard in Chili, and the sonorous green jaspers that are found near Cuzco and give forth a note of singular sweetness. He had painted gourds filled with pebbles that rattled when they were shaken; the long *clarin* of the Mexicans, into which the performer does not blow, but through which he inhales the air; the harsh *turc* of the Amazon tribes, that is sounded by the sentinels who sit all day long in high trees, and can be heard, it is said, at the distance of three leagues; the *teponaztli*, that has two vibrating tongues of wood, and is beaten with sticks that are smeared with an elastic gum obtained from the milky juice of plants; the *yotl*-bells of the Aztecs, that are hung in clusters like grapes; and a huge cylindrical drum, covered with the skins of great serpents, like the one that Bernal Diaz saw when he went with Cortes into the Mexican temple, and of whose

9. Wilde took details of the bizarre musical instruments from Carl Engel's handbook *Musical Instruments*, one of the series of South Kensington Museum Art Handbooks he consulted in writing this chapter. Many descriptions are taken directly out of Engel's text.

1. Alfonso de Ovalle (1601–51) was a Chilean Jesuit historian whose *Historica relacion del reino de Chile* (1646) was a classic account of colonial Chile.

doleful sound he has left us so vivid a description. The fantastic character of these instruments fascinated him, and he felt a curious delight
in the thought that Art, like Nature, has her monsters, things of bestial
shape and with hideous voices. Yet, after some time, he wearied of them,
and would sit in his box at the Opera, either alone or with Lord Henry,
listening in rapt pleasure to "Tannhäuser," and seeing in the prelude to
that great work of art a presentation of the tragedy of his own soul.[2]

On one occasion he took up the study of jewels,[3] and appeared at a
costume ball as Anne de Joyeuse, Admiral of France,[4] in a dress covered
with five hundred and sixty pearls. This taste enthralled him for years,
and, indeed, may be said never to have left him. He would often spend
a whole day settling and resettling in their cases the various stones that
he had collected, such as the olive-green chrysoberyl that turns red by
lamplight, the cymophane with its wire-like line of silver, the pistachio-
coloured peridot, rose-pink and wine-yellow topazes, carbuncles of fiery
scarlet with tremulous four-rayed stars, flame-red cinnamon-stones, orange
and violet spinels, and amethysts with their alternate layers of ruby and
sapphire. He loved the red gold of the sunstone, and the moonstone's
pearly whiteness, and the broken rainbow of the milky opal. He procured from Amsterdam three emeralds of extraordinary size and richness
of colour, and had a turquoise *de la vieille roche*[5] that was the envy of
all the connoisseurs.

He discovered wonderful stories, also, about jewels. In Alphonso's
"Clericalis Disciplina" a serpent was mentioned with eyes of real jacinth,
and in the romantic history of Alexander,[6] the Conqueror of Emathia
was said to have found in the vale of Jordan snakes "with collars of real
emeralds growing on their backs." There was a gem in the brain of the
dragon, Philostratus[7] told us, and "by the exhibition of golden letters
and a scarlet robe" the monster could be thrown into a magical sleep,

2. The legend of this historical figure tells the tale
of a poet who sought forgiveness after having
enjoyed the fleshpots of Venusberg for a year. When
Tannhäuser journeys to Rome, he is told by the
Pope that forgiveness will be granted only when
the Pope's staff blossoms. The miracle occurs on
the third day after Tannhäuser's departure, too late
to save the knight, who had returned to Venusberg
in despair. In the Richard Wagner opera (1844),
Tannhäuser is forgiven at the end. Gilbert alludes
to Tannhäuser in "The Critic as Artist," and the
story also inspired Swinburne's "Laus Veneris."
Wilde seems to have been affected by the struggle
of sacred with profane love in the legend, a frequent theme in his own poetry and stories, and the
idea of divine forgiveness through miraculous signs.
Dorian is later to search his portrait in vain for
such a sign.
3. Des Esseintes's study of jewels was more elaborate in *A Rebours*. Many of the more exotic stones
mentioned here were used in Huysmans's novel as
a covering on the shell of a giant tortoise, contrib-
uting to the creature's premature demise. Huysmans is interested in his hero's use of jewels to

create new sensations and new aesthetic effects in
his life. Wilde emphasizes equally the anecdotes
connected to the jewels to add an occult, decadent
flavor to the story. He culled his information on
stones from A. H. Church's *Precious Stones* (1882),
another of the South Kensington Museum Art
Handbooks. Many of the stories come, sometimes
verbatim, out of William Jones's *History and Mystery of Precious Stones* (1880), as cited in *Dorian
Gray*, Murray 246.
4. One of the favorites of Henry III (1551–89),
named a duke and admiral by the king. Both were
homosexuals and appeared in public dressed as
women.
5. "From an old stone."
6. Alexander the Great (356–323 B.C.), one of the
earliest Western prototypes of the idealized mon-
arch who combined the leadership and courage of
the victorious warrior with the temperance and
wisdom of the scholar.
7. A Greek Sophist and biographer (A.D. 170–245).
The story comes from *Heroicus*, a fabulous account
of the heroes of the Trojan War.

and slain. According to the great alchemist, Pierre de Boniface, the diamond rendered a man invisible, and the agate of India made him eloquent. The cornelian appeased anger, and the hyacinth provoked sleep,
and the amethyst drove away the fumes of wine. The garnet cast out
demons, and the hydropicus deprived the moon of her colour. The selenite
waxed and waned with the moon, and the meloceus, that discovers thieves,
could be affected only by the blood of kids. Leonardus Camillus had
seen a white stone taken from the brain of a newly-killed toad, that was
a certain antidote against poison. The bezoar, that was found in the
heart of the Arabian deer, was a charm that could cure the plague. In
the nests of Arabian birds was the aspilates, that, according to Democritus,[8] kept the wearer from any danger by fire.

The King of Ceilan rode through his city with a large ruby in his
hand, as the ceremony of his coronation. The gates of the palace of John
the Priest[9] were "made of sardius, with the horn of the horned snake
inwrought, so that no man might bring poison within." Over the gable
were "two golden apples, in which were two carbuncles," so that the
gold might shine by day, and the carbuncles by night. In Lodge's strange
romance "A Margarite of America"[1] it was stated that in the chamber of
the queen one could behold "all the chaste ladies of the world, inchased
out of silver, looking through fair mirrours of chrysolites, carbuncles,
sapphires, and greene emeraults." Marco Polo[2] had seen the inhabitants
of Zipangu place rose-coloured pearls in the mouths of the dead. A sea-
monster had been enamoured of the pearl that the diver brought to King
Perozes, and had slain the thief, and mourned for seven moons over its
loss. When the Huns lured the king into the great pit, he flung it away—
Procopius[3] tells the story—nor was it ever found again, though the
Emperor Anastasius offered five hundred-weight of gold pieces for it.
The King of Malabar had shown to a certain Venetian a rosary of three
hundred and four pearls, one for every god that he worshipped.

When the Duke de Valentinois, son of Alexander VI., visited Louis
XII. of France,[4] his horse was loaded with gold leaves, according to
Brantôme, and his cap had double rows of rubies that threw out a great
light. Charles of England had ridden in stirrups hung with four hundred
and twenty-one diamonds. Richard II. had a coat, valued at thirty thousand marks, which was covered with balas rubies. Hall described Henry
VIII., on his way to the Tower previous to his coronation, as wearing "a

8. Greek philosopher of Athens (460–370 B.C.).
Ceilan, below, was Ceylon, now Sri Lanka.
9. Better known as Prester John, the twelfth-cen-
tury priest and emperor of a utopian realm in Asia
or Africa who has remained a legendary figure.
1. Thomas Lodge's euphuistic romance (1569) was
based on his second voyage to South America.
2. Marco Polo (1254–1324), the famous Venetian trader and world traveler. His book of travels
introduced the West to the culture and wonders of
the Orient.

3. Sixth-century Byzantine church historian, who
recorded the wars of King Perozes (457–84) and
his death at the hands of the Ephthalites. Malabar,
on the west coast of India, was ruled by Hindu
kings but seventeenth-century Portuguese mis-
sionaries brought to Malabar a strong Christian
influence.
4. In addition to sharing a theatrical sort of
hedonism, those mentioned in this paragraph were
considered notorious homosexuals.

jacket of raised gold, the placard embroidered with diamonds and other rich stones, and a great bauderike about his neck of large balasses." The favourites of James I. wore earrings of emeralds set in gold filigrane. Edward II. gave to Piers Gaveston a suit of red-gold armour studded with jacinths, a collar of gold roses set with turquoise-stones, and a skull-cap *parsemé*[5] with pearls. Henry II. wore jewelled gloves reaching to the elbow, and had a hawk-glove sewn with twelve rubies and fifty-two great orients. The ducal hat of Charles the Rash, the last Duke of Burgudy of his race, was hung with pear-shaped pearls, and studded with sapphires.

How exquisite life had once been! How gorgeous in its pomp and decoration! Even to read of the luxury of the dead was wonderful.

Then he turned his attention to embroideries,[6] and to the tapestries that performed the office of frescoes in the chill rooms of the Northern nations of Europe. As he investigated the subject—and he always had an extraordinary faculty of becoming absolutely absorbed for the moment in whatever he took up—he was almost saddened by the reflection of the ruin that Time brought on beautiful and wonderful things. He, at any rate, had escaped that. Summer followed summer, and the yellow jonquils bloomed and died many times, and nights of horror repeated the story of their shame, but he was unchanged. No winter marred his face or stained his flower-like bloom. How different it was with material things! Where had they passed to? Where was the great crocus-coloured robe, on which the gods fought against the giants, that had been worked by brown girls for the pleasure of Athena?[7] Where, the huge velarium that Nero had stretched across the Colosseum at Rome, that Titan sail of purple on which was represented the starry sky, and Apollo driving a chariot drawn by white gilt-reined steeds? He longed to see the curious table-napkins wrought for the Priest of the Sun, on which were displayed all the dainties and viands that could be wanted for a feast; the mortuary cloth of King Chilperic,[8] with its three hundred golden bees; the fantastic robes that excited the indignation of the Bishop of Pontus, and were figured with "lions, panthers, bears, dogs, forests, rocks, hunters—all, in fact, that a painter can copy from nature;" and the coat that Charles of Orleans[9] once wore, on the sleeves of which were embroidered the verses of a song beginning *"Madame, je suis tout joyeux,"* the musical accompaniment of the words being wrought in gold thread, and each note, of square shape in those days, formed with four pearls. He read of

5. Spangled.
6. Wilde copied some of the passages in this section on embroideries from a review he once did as editor of *Woman's World* of Ernest Lefébure's *Embroidery and Lace: Their Manufacture and History from the Remotest Antiquity to the Present* (1888). The review appeared in the November 1888 issue of *Woman's World*, and Wilde referred to the work as a "fascinating book." Wilde also borrowed selectively from the text of Lefébure's work.
7. Pallas Athena was the Greek goddess of war,

peace, and wisdom. Her Roman equivalent was Minerva.
8. Sixth-century Frankish king.
9. Charles d'Orleans, French poet, duke of Orleans, and father of Louis XII, spent a third of his life as a royal captive in England after Agincourt. Finally ransomed by his future wife, Mary of Cleves, he spent the last third of his life at Blois, where he kept court for the most celebrated French writers of the time, including Villon, Chastelain, and de la Marche.

the room that was prepared at the palace at Rheims for the use of Queen Joan of Burgundy, and was decorated with "thirteen hundred and twenty-one parrots, made in broidery, and blazoned with the king's arms, and five hundred and sixty-one butterflies, whose wings were similarly ornamented with the arms of the queen, the whole worked in gold." Catherine de Médicis[1] had a mourning-bed made for her of black velvet powdered with crescents and suns. Its curtains were of damask, with leafy wreaths and garlands, figured upon a gold and silver ground, and fringed along the edges with broideries of pearls, and it stood in a room hung with rows of the queen's devices in cut black velvet upon cloth of silver. Louis XIV. had gold embroidered caryatides[2] fifteen feet high in his apartment. The state bed of Sobieski, King of Poland, was made of Smyrna gold brocade embroidered in turquoises with verses from the Koran. Its supports were of silver gilt, beautifully chased, and profusely set with enamelled and jewelled medallions. It had been taken from the Turkish camp before Vienna, and the standard of Mohammed had stood beneath the tremulous gilt of its canopy.

And so, for a whole year, he sought to accumulate the most exquisite specimens that he could find of textile and embroidered work, getting the dainty Delhi muslins, finely wrought with gold-thread palmates, and stitched over with iridescent beetles' wings; the Dacca gauzes, that from their transparency are known in the East as "woven air," and "running water," and "evening dew"; strange figured cloths from Java; elaborate yellow Chinese hangings; books bound in tawny satins or fair blue silks, and wrought with *fleurs de lys*,[3] birds, and images; veils of *lacis* worked in Hungary point; Sicilian brocades, and stiff Spanish velvets; Georgian work with its gilt coins, and Japanese *Foukousas*[4] with their green-toned golds and their marvellously-plumaged birds.

He had a special passion, also, for ecclesiastical vestments, as indeed he had for everything connected with the service of the Church. In the long cedar chests that lined the west gallery of his house he had stored away many rare and beautiful specimens of what is really the raiment of the Bride of Christ, who must wear purple and jewels and fine linen that she may hide the pallid macerated body that is worn by the suffering that she seeks for, and wounded by self-inflicted pain. He possessed a gorgeous cope of crimson silk and gold-thread damask, figured with a repeating pattern of golden pomegranates set in six-petalled formal blossoms, beyond which on either side was the pine-apple device wrought in seed-pearls. The orphreys were divided into panels representing scenes from the life of the Virgin, and the coronation of the Virgin was figured

1. Daughter of Lorenzo the Magnificent, became queen of France through marriage, bore nine children, was celebrated for her love of luxury, and was notorious for her plots and assassinations while regent.
2. Columns sculptured in the form of female figures. Sobieski ruled Poland as John III (1674–96). His greatest achievement was the heroic Polish

rescue of Vienna in 1683.
3. Symbol of the French aristocracy, it is a device of heraldry rather than a real flower, resembling banded petals of an iris.
4. Foukousas (or fukusa) were embroidered or brocaded silk square gift covers, not considered part of the gift itself and hence a separate art form.

in coloured silks upon the hood. This was Italian work of the fifteenth century. Another cope was of green velvet, embroidered with heart-shaped groups of acanthus-leaves, from which spread long-stemmed white blossoms, the details of which were picked out with silver thread and coloured crystals. The morse bore a seraph's head in gold-thread raised work. The orphreys were woven in a diaper of red and gold silk, and were starred with medallions of many saints and martyrs, among whom was St. Sebastian.[5] He had chasubles, also, of amber-coloured silk, and blue silk and gold brocade, and yellow silk damask and cloth of gold, figured with representations of the Passion and Crucifixion of Christ, and embroidered with lions and peacocks and other emblems; dalmatics of white satin and pink silk damask, decorated with tulips and dolphins and *fleurs de lys*; altar frontals of crimson velvet and blue linen; and many corporals, chalice-veils, and sudaria.[6] In the mystic offices to which such things were put, there was something that quickened his imagination.

For these treasures, and everything that he collected in his lovely house, were to be to him means of forgetfulness, modes by which he could escape, for a season, from the fear that seemed to him at times to be almost too great to be borne. Upon the walls of the lonely locked room where he had spent so much of his boyhood, he had hung with his own hands the terrible portrait whose changing features showed him the real degradation of his life, and in front of it had draped the purple-and-gold pall as a curtain. For weeks he would not go there, would forget the hideous painted thing, and get back his light heart, his wonderful joyousness, his passionate absorption in mere existence. Then, suddenly, some night he would creep out of the house, go down to dreadful places near Blue Gate Fields,[7] and stay there, day after day, until he was driven away. On his return he would sit in front of the picture, sometimes loathing it and himself, but filled, at other times, with that pride of individualism that is half the fascination of sin, and smiling, with secret pleasure, at the misshapen shadow that had to bear the burden that should have been his own.

After a few years he could not endure to be long out of England, and gave up the villa that he had shared at Trouville[8] with Lord Henry, as

5. Third-century Roman martyr, a favorite of the emperor Diocletian, who nevertheless ordered him killed by archers for his Christian faith.
6. Ecclesiastical vestments of the Catholic church, one of Dorian's interests, were also an interest of Des Esseintes of *A Rebours*. The Victoria and Albert Museum contained a fine collection, which Wilde knew. Accounts in the paragraphs below may have been taken from Reverend Daniel Rock's *Textile Fabrics* (London, 1876). Chasubles are long, sleeveless vestments, colored and usually decorated, worn outside the alb during Mass. Altar frontals were decorated altar cloths hanging down in front of the altar. A corporal is a linen cloth on

which bread and wine are placed during the consecration. Chalice veils are decorated square cloth coverings for chalices used during Mass. Sudaria are handkerchiefs or napkins used to dry perspiration. A cope, above, is a decorated hood or hooded cape worn over the chasuble.
7. In the east end near Limehouse and the London Dock, between Commercial Road and New Road.
8. A beach resort on the English Channel in France. It was a favorite vacation spa for Wilde, as was Algiers, where foreign homosexuals lived openly.

well as the little white walled-in house at Algiers where they had more than once spent the winter. He hated to be separated from the picture that was such a part of his life, and was also afraid that during his absence some one might gain access to the room, in spite of the elaborate bars that he had caused to be placed upon the door.

He was quite conscious that this would tell them nothing. It was true that the portrait still preserved, under all the foulness and ugliness of the face, its marked likeness to himself; but what could they learn from that? He would laugh at any one who tried to taunt him. He had not painted it. What was it to him how vile and full of shame it looked? Even if he told them, would they believe it?

Yet he was afraid. Sometimes when he was down at his great house in Nottinghamshire, entertaining the fashionable young men of his own rank who were his chief companions, and astounding the county by the wanton luxury and gorgeous splendour of his mode of life, he would suddenly leave his guests and rush back to town to see that the door had not been tampered with, and that the picture was still there. What if it should be stolen? The mere thought made him cold with horror. Surely the world would know his secret then. Perhaps the world already suspected it.

For, while he fascinated many, there were not a few who distrusted him.[9] He was very nearly blackballed at a West End club of which his birth and social position fully entitled him to become a member, and it was said that on one occasion, when he was brought by a friend into the smoking-room of the Churchill, the Duke of Berwick and another gentleman got up in a marked manner and went out. Curious stories became current about him after he had passed his twenty-fifth year. It was rumoured that he had been seen brawling with foreign sailors in a low den in the distant parts of Whitechapel, and that he consorted with thieves and coiners and knew the mysteries of their trade. His extraordinary absences became notorious, and, when he used to reappear again in society, men would whisper to each other in corners, or pass him with a sneer, or look at him with cold searching eyes, as though they were determined to discover his secret.

Of such insolences and attempted slights[1] he, or course, took no notice, and in the opinion of most people his frank debonnair manner, his charming boyish smile, and the infinite grace of that wonderful youth that seemed never to leave him, were in themselves a sufficient answer to the calumnies, for so they termed them, that were circulated about him. It was remarked, however, that some of those who had been most intimate with him appeared, after a time, to shun him. Women who

9. Dorian has changed clubs since the *Lippincott's* edition, which had him at the Carlton, a famous conservative political club located in Pall Mall. There was nothing to prevent Dorian from belonging to more than one club, however. Wilde was in fact barred from membership in the Savile Club shortly before writing *Dorian Gray*.

1. Thanks to his own life-style, Wilde was a man well-acquainted with both.

had wildly adored him, and for his sake had braved all social censure and set convention at defiance, were seen to grow pallid with shame or horror if Dorian Gray entered the room.

Yet these whispered scandals only increased in the eyes of many, his strange and dangerous charm. His great wealth was a certain element of security. Society, civilized society at least, is never very ready to believe anything to the detriment of those who are both rich and fascinating. It feels instinctively that manners are of more importance than morals,[2] and, in its opinion, the highest respectability is of much less value than the possession of a good *chef*. And, after all, it is a very poor consolation to be told that the man who has given one a bad dinner, or poor wine, is irreproachable in his private life. Even the cardinal virtues cannot atone for half-cold *entrées*[3] as Lord Henry remarked once, in a discussion on the subject; and there is possibly a good deal to be said for his view. For the canons of good society are, or should be, the same as the canons of art. Form is absolutely essential to it. It should have the dignity of a ceremony, as well as its unreality, and should combine the insincere character of a romantic play with the wit and beauty that make such plays delightful to us. Is insincerity such a terrible thing? I think not.[4] It is merely a method by which we can multiply our personalities.

Such, at any rate, was Dorian Gray's opinion. He used to wonder at the shallow psychology[5] of those who conceive the Ego in man as a thing simple, permanent, reliable, and of one essence. To him, man was a being with myriad lives and myriad sensations, a complex multiform creature that bore within itself strange legacies of thought and passion, and whose very flesh was tainted with the monstrous maladies of the dead. He loved to stroll through the gaunt cold picture-gallery of his country house and look at the various portraits of those whose blood flowed in his veins. Here was Philip Herbert[6] described by Francis Osborne, in his "Memoires on the Reigns of Queen Elizabeth and King James," as one who was "caressed by the Court for his handsome face, which kept him not long company." Was it young Herbert's life that he sometimes led? Had some strange poisonous germ crept from body to body till it had reached his own? Was it some dim sense of that ruined grace that had made him so suddenly, and almost without cause, give utterance, in Basil Hallward's studio, to the mad prayer that had so changed his life? Here, in gold-embroidered red doublet, jewelled sur-

---

2. A favorite epigram, which appears also in "The Critic as Artist" and once again in *Lady Windermere's Fan*.

3. Principal courses at meals.

4. This is the one place in the novel in which Wilde slips into the first person, and we hear him speaking in his own voice, one whose sentiments are repeated by Gilbert in "The Critic as Artist."

5. The deep psychology that Dorian espouses was the same that had inspired Pater's famous Conclusion to *The Renaissance*. The application to Dorian's gallery of ancestral portraits reinforces the Darwinist motif introduced early in the novel.

6. A favorite of King James I of England. The incident is described in Osborne's *Miscellaneous Works* 2 (London, 1722) 133 (*Dorian Gray*, Murray 246).

coat, and gilt-edged ruff and wrist-bands, stood Sir Anthony Sherard,[7] with his silver-and black armour piled at his feet. What had this man's legacy been? Had the lover of Giovanna of Naples bequeathed him some inheritance of sin and shame? Were his own actions merely the dreams that the dead man had not dared to realize? Here, from the fading canvas, smiled Lady Elizabeth Devereux, in her gauze hood, pearl stomacher, and pink slashed sleeves. A flower was in her right hand, and her left clasped an enamelled collar of white and damask roses. On a table by her side lay a mandolin and an apple. There were large green rosettes upon her little pointed shoes. He knew her life, and the strange stories that were told about her lovers. Had he something of her temperament in him? These oval heavy-lidded eyes seemed to look curiously at him. What of George Willoughby, with his powdered hair and fantastic patches? How evil he looked! The face was saturnine and swarthy, and the sensual lips seemed to be twisted with disdain. Delicate lace ruffles fell over the lean yellow hands that were so overladen with rings. He had been a macaroni[8] of the eighteenth century, and the friend, in his youth, of Lord Ferrars. What of the second Lord Beckenham, the companion of the Prince Regent in his wildest days, and one of the witnesses at the secret marriage with Mrs. Fitzherbert?[9] How proud and handsome he was, with his chestnut curls and insolent pose! What passions had he bequeathed? The world had looked upon him as infamous. He had led the orgies at Carlton House. The star of the Garter glittered upon his breast. Beside him hung the portrait of his wife, a pallid, thin-lipped woman in black. Her blood, also, stirred within him. How curious it all seemed! And his mother with her Lady Hamilton face,[1] and her moist wine-dashed lips—he knew what he had got from her. He had got from her his beauty, and his passion for the beauty of others. She laughed at him in her loose Bacchante dress. There were vine leaves in her hair.[2] The purple spilled from the cup she was holding. The carnations of the painting had withered, but the eyes were still wonderful in their depth

---

7. One of Wilde's practical jokes. He borrowed the name from a friend and later biographer, the naïve R. H. Sherard, who was, in temperament, not at all like the fictitious lover of Giovanna of Naples. In the magazine edition, he was described as the "companion of the Prince Regent in his wildest days." When Sherard objected because he had a living relative by that name, Wilde moved him into Dorian's ancestral gallery of rogues. Elizabeth Devereux is fictitious, but her portrait seems inspired by allegorical Flemish portraits of the sixteenth century. The flower, collar, mandolin, and fruit all symbolize her domestic attributes.

8. Named after Italian dandies of the eighteenth century, remembered in the lyric of "Yankee Doodle."

9. The regent was George, prince of Wales, later George IV, who married Mrs. FitzHerbert in 1785. The marriage thereafter was ruled invalid, although their relationship continued long after George

married Caroline of Brunswick.

1. Lady Emma Hamilton (1765–1815), wife of Sir William Hamilton, British envoy at Naples, was a village girl from Cheshire and one of the great beauties of the day. Her likeness was painted by Gainsborough (1727–88), by Richard Cosway (1742–1821), and by George Romney (1734–1802) in a series of works. She is remembered for her beautiful features, her Moll Flanders-to-Roxanna rise to fame, and her long love affair with Admiral Nelson.

2. The allusion is to Ibsen's *Hedda Gabler*. Vine leaves (sacred to Bacchus) symbolize to Hedda an uninhibited paganism. Unable to overcome her own inhibitions, she tries to live vicariously through the disreputable genius Eljert Lövborg, whose sensuality she inspires, and shares, but cannot acknowledge. A Bacchante was a female priest of Bacchus and a reveler, whose dress would have been considered scandalously brief attire at the time.

and brilliancy of colour. They seemed to follow him wherever he went.

Yet one had ancestors in literature, as well as in one's own race, nearer perhaps in type and temperament, many of them, and certainly with an influence of which one was more absolutely conscious. There were times when it appeared to Dorian Gray that the whole of history was merely the record of his own life, not as he had lived it in act and circumstance, but as his imagination had created it for him, as it had been in his brain and in his passions. He felt that he had known them all, those strange terrible figures that had passed across the stage of the world and made sin so marvellous and evil so full of subtlety. It seemed to him that in some mysterious way their lives had been his own.

The hero of the wonderful novel that had so influenced his life had himself known this curious fancy. In the seventh chapter he tells how, crowned with laurel, lest lightning might strike him, he had sat, as Tiberius[3] in a garden at Capri, reading the shameful books of Elephantis,[4] while dwarfs and peacocks strutted round him and the flute-player mocked the swinger of the censer; and, as Caligula, had caroused with the green-shirted jockeys in their stables, and supped in an ivory manger with a jewel-frontleted horse; and, as Domitian,[5] had wandered through a corridor lined with marble mirrors, looking round with haggard eyes for the reflection of the dagger that was to end his days, and sick with that ennui, that terrible *tædium vitæ*, that comes on those to whom life denies nothing; and had peered through a clear emerald at the red shambles of the Circus,[6] and then, in a litter of pearl and purple drawn by silver-shod mules, been carried through the Street of Pomegranates to a House of Gold, and heard men cry on Nero Cæsar[7] as he passed by; and, as Elagabalus,[8] had painted his face with colours, and plied the distaff among the women, and brought the Moon from Carthage, and given her in mystic marriage to the Sun.

Over and over again Dorian used to read this fantastic chapter, and the two chapters immediately following, in which, as in some curious tapestries or cunningly-wrought enamels, were pictured the awful and beautiful forms of those whom Vice and Blood and Weariness had made monstrous or mad: Fillippo, Duke of Milan, who slew his wife, and painted her lips with a scarlet poison that her lover might suck death

3. Second Roman emperor (A.D. 14–37) who succeeded Augustus Caesar. Wilde took the details of the Roman emperors from Tiberius to Nero from Suetonius's *Lives of the Caesars*. The following paragraph borrows heavily from John Addington Symonds, *Renaissance in Italy*, 7 vols. (1875–86). See *Dorian Gray*, Murray 246–47.
4. A Greek authoress of amatory works mentioned by Suetonius and Martial.
5. Caligula (A.D. 12–41) and Domitian (A.D. 56–95), despotic Roman emperors who were assassinated.
6. Of the major circuses of Rome (Maximus, Flaminius, Neronis, and Maxentius), this proba-

bly refers to Circus Neronis, built by Caligula in the gardens of Agrippina. A circus was an elliptical race course.
7. Roman emperor (A.D. 54–68.), last of the Caesar family, notorious for beginning Roman persecution of Christians and for dissolute living.
8. Also called Heliogabalus (A.D. 205–22) because of his office as boy-priest of the Syrian sun god, he became Roman emperor in 218 and set a new standard for profligate living. He was put to death by the Praetorian guard. He reigned under the name Marcus Aurelius Antoninus, but he should not be confused with the earlier, stoic philosopher-emperor of the same name (121–80 A.D.).

from the dead thing he fondled; Pietro Barbi, the Venetian,[9] known as
Paul the Second, who sought in his vanity to assume the title of Formosus, and whose tiara, valued at two hundred thousand florins, was
bought at the price of a terrible sin; Gian Maria Visconti, who used
hounds to chase living men, and whose murdered body was covered
with roses by a harlot who had loved him; the Borgia on his white horse,
with Fratricide riding beside him, and his mantle stained with the blood
of Perotto; Pietro Riario, the young Cardinal Archbishop of Florence,
child and minion of Sixtus IV., whose beauty was equalled only by his
debauchery, and who received Leonora of Aragon in a pavilion of white
and crimson silk, filled with nymphs and centaurs, and gilded a boy that
he might serve at the feast as Ganymede or Hylas; Ezzelin,[1] whose melancholy could be cured only by the spectacle of death, and who had a
passion for red blood, as other men have for red wine—the son of the
Fiend, as was reported, and one who had cheated his father at dice when
gambling with him for his own soul; Giambattista Cibo, who in mockery
took the name of Innocent, and into whose torpid veins the blood of
three lads was infused by a Jewish doctor; Sigismondo Malatesta,[2] the
lover of Isotta, and the lord of Rimini, whose effigy was burned at Rome
as the enemy of God and man, who strangled Polyssena with a napkin,
and gave poison to Ginevra d'Este in a cup of emerald, and in honour
of a shameful passion built a pagan church for Christian worship; Charles
VI., who had so wildly adored his brother's wife that a leper had warned
him of the insanity that was coming on him, and who, when his brain
had sickened and grown strange, could only be soothed by Saracen cards
painted with the images of Love and Death and Madness; and, in his
trimmed jerkin and jewelled cap and acanthus-like curls, Grifonetto
Baglioni, who slew Astorre with his bride, and Simonetto with his page,
and whose comeliness was such that, as he lay dying in the yellow piazza
of Perugia, those who had hated him could not choose but weep, and
Atalanta, who had cursed him, blessed him.

There was a horrible fascination in them all. He saw them at night,
and they troubled his imagination in the day. The Renaissance knew of
strange manners of poisoning—poisoning by a helmet and a lighted torch,
by an embroidered glove and a jewelled fan, by a gilded pomander and
by an amber chain. Dorian Gray had been poisoned by a book.[3] There

9. Barbi (1464–71) was Pope, patronized the arts, helped beautify Rome, and collected antiquities. Borgia, below (1476–1507), soldier-politician, was the prototype for Machiavelli's *The Prince*. In the line above, the phrase "that her lover . . . he fondled" had been removed from the TS by Stoddart before *Lippincott's* publication. Its reappearance here can be explained best if we assume that Wilde had either the MS with him or, more likely, the revised TS when he was preparing the expanded edition. Wilde performed several restorations of this kind in the expanded edition.

1. An Italian Ghibelline leader (1194–1259),

remembered as a tyrant and for the prominent place assigned to him in hell by Dante. Ganymede was a favorite of Zeus. Hylas sailed with Hercules aboard the Argo. Cibo was Pope from 1484 to 1492.

2. Malatesta (1416–68) was a despotic Italian Renaissance prince. Charles VI, known as "Charles the Mad," reigned from 1380 to 1422. The Baglioni family were famous for their bloody family feuds.

3. This was, to be sure, one of Wilde's favorite myths when applied to himself, as a number of friends and biographers have attested. Speculation has not been lacking for nominations, but critics

were moments when he looked on evil simply as a mode through which he could realize his conception of the beautiful.

Chapter XII.[1]

It was on the ninth of November, the eve of his own thirty-eighth birthday,[2] as he often remembered afterwards.

He was walking home about eleven o'clock from Lord Henry's, where he had been dining, and was wrapped in heavy furs, as the night was cold and foggy. At the corner of Grosvenor Square and South Audley Street a man passed him in the mist, walking very fast, and with the collar of his grey ulster turned up. He had a bag in his hand. Dorian recognized him. It was Basil Hallward. A strange sense of fear, for which he could not account, came over him. He made no sign of recognition, and went on quickly, in the direction of his own house.

But Hallward had seen him. Dorian heard him first stopping on the pavement and then hurrying after him. In a few moments his hand was on his arm.

"Dorian! What an extraordinary piece of luck! I have been waiting for you in your library ever since nine o'clock. Finally I took pity on your tired servant, and told him to go to bed, as he let me out. I am off to Paris by the midnight train, and I particularly wanted to see you before I left. I thought it was you, or rather your fur coat, as you passed me. But I wasn't quite sure. Didn't you recognize me?"

"In this fog, my dear Basil? Why, I can't even recognize Grosvenor Square. I believe my house is somewhere about here, but I don't feel at all certain about it. I am sorry you are going away, as I have not seen you for ages. But I suppose you will be back soon?"

"No: I am going to be out of England for six months. I intend to take a studio in Paris, and shut myself up till I have finished a great picture I have in my head. However, it wasn't about myself I wanted to talk. Here we are at your door. Let me come in for a moment. I have something to say to you."

"I shall be charmed. But won't you miss your train?" said Dorian Gray, languidly, as he passed up the steps and opened the door with his latch-key.

The lamp-light struggled out through the fog, and Hallward looked at

---

have as yet been unable to establish a credible title for such influence. Wilde revealed that his favorite reading when a boy was Lady Duff Gordon's translation of *The Amber Witch* and his mother's translation of *Sidonia the Sorceress*; and then there was his maternal uncle's Gothic novel *Melmoth the Wanderer*, which he certainly knew. None seems especially poisonous, however. The inference here, intended or not, is that Wilde was poisoned by Pater's *The Renaissance*. While the claim may seem excessive, we should remember that Pater himself had withdrawn the Conclusion from the second edition for fear of its bad influence on impressionable youth. The attitudes expressed in the next sentence are, however, more characteristic of Baudelaire than of Pater.

1. Formerly chapter 10.
2. Changed from November seventh in the *Lippincott's* edition. The significance is explored by Richard Ellmann in "The Critic as Artist as Wilde," *Encounter* 29 (July 1967): 33 (see below, p. 415). The change does not alter Dorian's birth sign; he remains a Scorpio of the textbook variety.

his watch. "I have heaps of time," he answered. "The train doesn't go till twelve-fifteen, and it is only just eleven. In fact, I was on my way to the club to look for you, when I met you. You see, I sha'n't have any delay about luggage, as I have sent on my heavy things. All I have with me is in this bag, and I can easily get to Victoria in twenty minutes."

Dorian looked at him and smiled. "What a way for a fashionable painter to travel! A Gladstone bag, and an ulster![3] Come in, or the fog will get into the house. And mind you don't talk about anything serious. Nothing is serious nowadays. At least nothing should be."

Hallward shook his head, as he entered, and followed Dorian into the library. There was a bright wood fire blazing in the large open hearth. The lamps were lit, and an open Dutch silver spirit-case stood, with some siphons of soda-water and large cut-glass tumblers, on a little marqueterie[4] table.

"You see your servant made me quite at home, Dorian. He gave me everything I wanted, including your best gold-tipped cigarettes. He is a most hospitable creature. I like him much better than the Frenchman you used to have. What has become of the Frenchman, by the bye?"

Dorian shrugged his shoulders. "I believe he married Lady Radley's maid, and has established her in Paris as an English dressmaker. *Anglomanie*[5] is very fashionable over there now, I hear. It seems silly of the French, doesn't it? But—do you know?—he was not at all a bad servant. I never liked him, but I had nothing to complain about. One often imagines things that are quite absurd. He was really very devoted to me, and seemed quite sorry when he went away. Have another brandy-and-soda? Or would you like hock-and-seltzer? I always take hock-and-seltzer[6] myself. There is sure to be some in the next room."

"Thanks, I won't have anything more," said the painter, taking his cap and coat off, and throwing them on the bag that he had placed in the corner. "And now, my dear fellow, I want to speak to you seriously. Don't frown like that. You make it so much more difficult for me."

"What is it all about?" cried Dorian, in his petulant way, flinging himself down on the sofa. "I hope it is not about myself. I am tired of myself to-night. I should like to be somebody else."

"It is about yourself," answered Hallward, in his grave, deep voice, "and I must say it to you. I shall only keep you half an hour."

Dorian sighed, and lit a cigarette. "Half an hour!" he murmured.

"It is not much to ask of you, Dorian, and it is entirely for your own sake that I am speaking. I think it right that you should know that the most dreadful things are being said against you in London."

3. A Gladstone bag was a hinged suitcase opening flat into two equal parts. An ulster is a long, loose overcoat. Victoria station was a rail terminus for boat-trains to France.
4. A decorative inlay design, usually of wood and ivory.
5. The love of things English.

6. Wilde's favorite drink. "Hock" is a generic term used by the British to mean a white Rhine wine (from the German *Hochheimer Wein*). Selzer was a mineral water, naturally carbonated, from the spas of Selters, a village in Prussia. The name has since become generic for carbonated mineral water, originally with a rather salty tang.

"I don't wish to know anything about them. I love scandals about other people, but scandals about myself don't interest me. They have not got the charm of novelty."

"They must interest you, Dorian. Every gentleman is interested in his good name. You don't want people to talk of you as something vile and degraded. Of course you have your position, and your wealth, and all that kind of thing. But position and wealth are not everything. Mind you, I don't believe these rumours at all. At least, I can't believe them when I see you. Sin is a thing that writes itself across a man's face. It cannot be concealed. People talk sometimes of secret vices. There are no such things. If a wretched man has a vice, it shows itself in the lines of his mouth, the droop of his eyelids, the moulding of his hands even. Somebody—I won't mention his name, but you know him—came to me last year to have his portrait done. I had never seen him before, and had never heard anything about him at the time, though I have heard a good deal since. He offered an extravagant price. I refused him. There was something in the shape of his fingers that I hated. I know now that I was quite right in what I fancied about him. His life is dreadful. But you, Dorian, with your pure, bright, innocent face, and your marvellous untroubled youth—I can't believe anything against you. And yet I see you very seldom, and you never come down to the studio now, and when I am away from you, and I hear all these hideous things that people are whispering about you, I don't know what to say. Why is it, Dorian, that a man like the Duke of Berwick leaves the room of a club when you enter it? Why is it that so many gentlemen in London will neither go to your house nor invite you to theirs? You used to be a friend of Lord Staveley. I met him at dinner last week. Your name happened to come up in conversation, in connection with the miniatures you have lent to the exhibition at the Dudley.[7] Staveley curled his lip, and said that you might have the most artistic tastes, but that you were a man whom no pure-minded girl should be allowed to know, and whom no chaste woman should sit in the same room with. I reminded him that I was a friend of yours, and asked him what he meant. He told me. He told me right out before everybody. It was horrible! Why is your friendship so fatal to young men? There was that wretched boy in the Guards who committed suicide. You were his great friend. There was Sir Henry Ashton, who had to leave England, with a tarnished name. You and he were inseparable. What about Adrian Singleton, and his dreadful end? What about Lord Kent's only son, and his career? I met his father yesterday in St. James's Street. He seemed broken with shame and sorrow. What about the young Duke of Perth? What sort of life has he got now? What gentleman would associate with him?"

7. A gallery named in honor of the Lord Dudley bequest, which collection of art was placed on public display in The Egyptian Hall, Piccadilly. The Egyptian Hall, still standing when *Dorian Gray* was written, was an exhibition hall whose exterior Egyptian design contrasted grotesquely with adjoining Georgian town buildings.

"Stop, Basil. You are talking about things of which you know nothing," said Dorian Gray, biting his lip, and with a note of infinite contempt in his voice, "You ask me why Berwick leaves a room when I enter it. It is because I know everything about his life, not because he knows anything about mine. With such blood as he has in his veins, how could his record be clean? You ask me about Henry Ashton and young Perth. Did I teach the one his vices, and the other his debauchery? If Kent's silly son takes his wife from the streets, what is that to me? If Adrian Singleton writes his friend's name across a bill, am I his keeper? I know how people chatter in England. The middle classes air their moral prejudices over their gross dinner-tables, and whisper about what they call the profligacies of their betters in order to try and pretend that they are in smart society, and on intimate terms with the people they slander. In this country it is enough for a man to have distinction and brains for every common tongue to wag against him. And what sort of lives do these people, who pose as being moral, lead themselves? My dear fellow, you forget that we are in the native land of the hypocrite."

"Dorian," cried Hallward, "that is not the question. England is bad enough I know, and English society is all wrong. That is the reason why I want you to be fine. You have not been fine. One has the right to judge of a man by the effect he has over his friends. Yours seem to lose all sense of honour, of goodness, of purity. You have filled them with a madness for pleasure. They have gone down into the depths. You led them there. Yes: you led them there, and yet you can smile, as you are smiling now. And there is worse behind. I know you and Harry are inseparable. Surely for that reason, if for none other, you should not have made his sister's name a by-word."

"Take care, Basil. You go too far."

"I must speak, and you must listen. You shall listen. When you met Lady Gwendolen, not a breath of scandal had ever touched her. Is there a single decent woman in London now who would drive with her in the Park? Why, even her children are not allowed to live with her. Then there are other stories—stories that you have been seen creeping at dawn out of dreadful houses and slinking in disguise into the foulest dens in London. Are they true? Can they be true? When I first heard them, I laughed. I hear them now, and they make me shudder. What about your country house, and the life that is led there? Dorian, you don't know what is said about you. I won't tell you that I don't want to preach to you. I remember Harry saying once that every man who turned himself into an amateur curate for the moment always began by saying that, and then proceeded to break his word. I do want to preach to you. I want you to lead such a life as will make the world respect you. I want you to have a clean name and a fair record. I want you to get rid of the dreadful people you associate with. Don't shrug your shoulders like that. Don't be so indifferent. You have a wonderful influence. Let it be for good, not for evil. They say that you corrupt every one with whom you become intimate, and that it is quite sufficient for you to enter a house, for shame of some kind to follow after. I don't know whether it is so or not. How should I know? But it is said of you. I am told things that it seems impossible to doubt. Lord Gloucester was one of my greatest friends at Oxford. He showed me a letter that his wife had written to him when she was dying alone in her villa at Mentone.[8] Your name was implicated in the most terrible confession I ever read. I told him that it was absurd— that I knew you thoroughly, and that you were incapable of anything of the kind. Know you? I wonder do I know you? Before I could answer that, I should have to see your soul."

"To see my soul!" muttered Dorian Gray, starting up from the sofa and turning almost white from fear.

"Yes," answered Hallward, gravely, and with deep-toned sorrow in his voice—"to see your soul. But only God can do that."

A bitter laugh of mockery broke from the lips of the younger man. "You shall see it yourself, to-night!" he cried, seizing a lamp from the table. "Come: it is your own handiwork. Why shouldn't you look at it? You can tell the world all about it afterwards, if you choose. Nobody would believe you. If they did believe you, they would like me all the better for it. I know the age better than you do, though you will prate about it so tediously. Come, I tell you. You have chattered enough about corruption. Now you shall look on it face to face."

There was the madness of pride in every word he uttered. He stamped his foot upon the ground in his boyish insolent manner. He felt a terrible joy at the thought that some one else was to share his secret, and that the man who had painted the portrait that was the origin of all his shame was to be burdened for the rest of his life with the hideous memory of what he had done.

"Yes," he continued, coming closer to him, and looking steadfastly into his stern eyes, "I shall show you my soul. You shall see the thing that you fancy only God can see."

Hallward started back. "This is blasphemy, Dorian!" he cried. "You must not say things like that. They are horrible, and they don't mean anything."

"You think so?" He laughed again.

"I know so. As for what I said to you to-night I said it for your good. You know I have been always a staunch friend to you."

"Don't touch me. Finish what you have to say."

A twisted flash of pain shot across the painter's face. He paused for a moment, and a wild feeling of pity came over him. After all, what right had he to pry into the life of Dorian Gray? If he had done a tithe of what was rumoured about him, how much he must have suffered! Then he

8. A popular French resort on the Riviera.

straightened himself up, and walked over to the fireplace, and stood there, looking at the burning logs with their frost-like ashes and their throbbing cores of flame.

"I am waiting, Basil," said the young man, in a hard, clear voice.

He turned round. "What I have to say is this," he cried. "You must give me some answer to these horrible charges that are made against you. If you tell me that they are absolutely untrue from beginning to end, I shall believe you. Deny them, Dorian, deny them! Can't you see what I am going through? My God! don't tell me that you are bad, and corrupt, and shameful."

Dorian Gray smiled. There was a curl of contempt in his lips. "Come upstairs, Basil," he said, quietly. "I keep a diary of my life from day to day, and it never leaves the room in which it is written. I shall show it to you if you come with me."

"I shall come with you, Dorian, if you wish it. I see I have missed my train. That makes no matter. I can go to-morrow. But don't ask me to read anything to-night. All I want is a plain answer to my question."

"That shall be given to you upstairs. I could not give it here. You will not have to read long."

Chapter XIII. [1]

He passed out of the room, and began the ascent, Basil Hallward following close behind. They walked softly, as men do instinctively at night. The lamp cast fantastic shadows on the wall and staircase. A rising wind made some of the windows rattle.

When they reached the top landing, Dorian set the lamp down on the floor, and taking out the key turned it in the lock. "You insist on knowing, Basil?" he asked, in a low voice.

"Yes."

"I am delighted," he answered, smiling. Then he added, somewhat harshly, "You are the one man in the world who is entitled to know everything about me. You have had more to do with my life than you think:" and, taking up the lamp, he opened the door and went in. A cold current of air passed them, and the light shot up for a moment in a flame of murky orange. He shuddered. "Shut the door behind you," he whispered, as he placed the lamp on the table.

Hallward glanced round him, with a puzzled expression. The room looked as if it had not been lived in for years. A faded Flemish tapestry, a curtained picture, an old Italian *cassone*,[2] and an almost empty bookcase—that was all that it seemed to contain, besides a chair and a table. As Dorian Gray was lighting a half-burned candle that was standing on the mantelshelf, he saw that the whole place was covered with dust, and

1. Originally chapter 11.
2. A wooden chest for storage, usually decorated or covered with tooled leather.

that the carpet was in holes. A mouse ran scuffling behind the wainscoting. There was a damp odour of mildew.

"So you think that it is only God who sees the soul, Basil? Draw that curtain back, and you will see mine."

The voice that spoke was cold and cruel. "You are mad, Dorian, or playing a part," muttered Hallward, frowning.

"You won't? Then I must do it myself," said the young man; and he tore the curtain from its rod, and flung it on the ground.

An exclamation of horror broke from the painter's lips as he saw in the dim light the hideous face on the canvas grinning at him. There was something in its expression that filled him with disgust and loathing. Good heavens! it was Dorian Gray's own face that he was looking at! The horror, whatever it was, had not entirely spoiled that marvellous beauty. There was still some gold in the thinning hair and some scarlet on the sensual mouth. The sodden eyes had kept something of the loveliness of their blue, the noble curves had not yet completely passed away from chiselled nostrils and from plastic throat. Yes, it was Dorian himself. But who had done it? He seemed to recognize his own brush-work, and the frame was his own design. The idea was monstrous, yet he felt afraid. He seized the lighted candle, and held it to the picture. In the left-hand corner was his own name, traced in long letters of bright vermilion.

It was some foul parody, some infamous, ignoble satire. He had never done that. Still, it was his own picture. He knew it, and he felt as if his blood had changed in a moment from fire to sluggish ice. His own picture! What did it mean? Why had it altered? He turned, and looked at Dorian Gray with the eyes of a sick man. His mouth twitched, and his parched tongue seemed unable to articulate. He passed his hand across his forehead. It was dank with clammy sweat.

The young man was leaning against the mantel-shelf, watching him with that strange expression that one sees on the faces of those who are absorbed in a play when some great artist is acting. There was neither real sorrow in it nor real joy. There was simply the passion of the spectator, with perhaps a flicker of triumph in his eyes. He had taken the flower out of his coat, and was smelling it, or pretending to do so.

"What does this mean?" cried Hallward, at last. His own voice sounded shrill and curious in his ears.

"Years ago, when I was a boy," said Dorian Gray, crushing the flower in his hand, "you met me, flattered me, and taught me to be vain of my good looks. One day you introduced me to a friend of yours, who explained to me the wonder of youth, and you finished a portrait of me that revealed to me the wonder of beauty. In a mad moment, that, even now, I don't know whether I regret or not, I made a wish, perhaps you would call it a prayer . . ."

"I remember it! Oh, how well I remember it! No! the thing is impossible. The room is damp. Mildew had got into the canvas. The paints I used had some wretched mineral poison in them. I tell you the thing is impossible."

"Ah, what is impossible?" murmured the young man, going over to the window, and leaning his forehead against the cold, mist-stained glass.

"You told me you had destroyed it."

"I was wrong. It has destroyed me."

"I don't believe it is my picture."

"Can't you see your ideal in it?" said Dorian, bitterly.

"My ideal, as you call it . . ."

"As you called it."

"There was nothing evil in it, nothing shameful. You were to me such an ideal as I shall never meet again. This is the face of a satyr."

"It is the face of my soul."

"Christ! what a thing I must have worshipped! It has the eyes of a devil."

"Each of us has Heaven and Hell [3] in him, Basil," cried Dorian, with a wild gesture of despair.

Hallward turned again to the portrait, and gazed at it. "My God! if it is true," he exclaimed, "and this is what you have done with your life, why, you must be worse than those who talk against you fancy you to be!" He held the light up again to the canvas, and examined it. The surface seemed to be quite undisturbed, and as he had left it. It was from within, apparently, that the foulness and horror had come. Through some strange quickening of inner life the leprosies of sin ere slowly eating the thing away. The rotting of a corpse in a watery grave was not so fearful.

His hand shook, and the candle fell from its socket on the floor, and lay there sputtering. He placed his foot on it and put it out. Then he flung himself into the rickety chair that was standing by the table and buried his face in his hands.

"Good God, Dorian, what a lesson! what an awful lesson!" There was no answer, but he could hear the young man sobbing at the window. "Pray, Dorian, pray," he murmured. "What is it that one was taught to say in one's boyhood? 'Lead us not into temptation. Forgive us our sins. Wash away our iniquities.' [4] Let us say that together. The prayer of your pride has been answered. The prayer of your repentance will be answered also. I worshipped you too much. I am punished for it. You worshipped yourself too much. We are both punished."

Dorian Gray turned slowly around, and looked at him with tear-dimmed eyes. "It is too late, Basil," he faltered.

"It is never too late, Dorian. Let us kneel down and try if we cannot

---

3. Milton, *Paradise Lost* 1.255.
4. Basil combines elements of the Lord's Prayer and the *Lavabo* prayer of the Mass (washing of hands prior to the consecration).

remember a prayer. Isn't there a verse somewhere, 'Though your sins be as scarlet, yet I will make them as white as snow'?" [5]

"Those words mean nothing to me now."

"Hush! don't say that. You have done enough evil in your life. My God! don't you see that accursed thing leering at us?"

Dorian Gray glanced at the picture, and suddenly an uncontrollable feeling of hatred for Basil Hallward came over him, as though it had been suggested to him by the image on the canvas, whispered into his ear by those grinning lips. The mad passions of a hunted animal stirred within him, and he loathed the man who was seated at the table, more than in his whole life he had ever loathed anything. He glanced wildly around. Something glimmered on the top of the painted chest that faced him. His eye fell on it. He knew what it was. It was a knife that he had brought up, some days before, to cut a piece of cord, and had forgotten to take away with him. He moved slowly towards it, passing Hallward as he did so. As soon as he got behind him, he seized it, and turned round. Hallward stirred in his chair as if he was going to rise. He rushed at him, and dug the knife into the great vein that is behind the ear, crushing the man's head down on the table, and stabbing again and again.

There was a stifled groan, and the horrible sound of some one choking with blood. Three times the outstretched arms shot up convulsively, waving grotesque stiff-fingered hands in the air. He stabbed him twice more, but the man did not move. Something began to trickle on the floor. He waited for a moment, still pressing the head down. Then he threw the knife on the table, and listened.

He could hear nothing, but the drip, drip on the threadbare carpet. He opened the door and went out on the landing. The house was absolutely quiet. No one was about. For a few seconds he stood bending over the balustrade, and peering down into the black seething well of darkness. Then he took out the key and returned to the room, locking himself in as he did so.

The thing was still seated in the chair, straining over the table with bowed head, and humped back, and long fantastic arms. Had it not been for the red jagged tear in the neck, and the clotted black pool that was slowly widening on the table, one would have said that the man was simply asleep.

How quickly it had all been done! He felt strangely calm, and, walking over to the window, opened it, and stepped out on the balcony. The wind had blown the fog away, and the sky was like a monstrous peacock's tail, starred with myriads of golden eyes. He looked down, and saw the policeman going his rounds and flashing the long beam of his lantern on the doors of the silent houses. The crimson spot of a prowling hansom gleamed at the corner, and then vanished. A woman in a fluttering

5. Isaiah 1.18.

shawl was creeping slowly by the railings, staggering as she went. Now and then she stopped, and peered back. Once, she began to sing in a hoarse voice. The policeman strolled over and said something to her. She stumbled away, laughing. A bitter blast swept across the Square. The gas-lamps flickered, and became blue, and the leafless trees shook their black iron branches to and fro. He shivered, and went back, closing the window behind him.

Having reached the door, he turned the key, and opened it. He did not even glance at the murdered man. He felt that the secret of the whole thing was not to realize the situation. The friend who had painted the fatal portrait to which all his misery had been due, had gone out of his life. That was enough.

Then he remembered the lamp. It was a rather a curious one of Moorish workmanship, made of dull silver inlaid with arabesques of burnished steel, and studded with coarse turquoises. Perhaps it might be missed by his servant, and questions would be asked. He hesitated for a moment, then he turned back and took it from the table. He could not help seeing the dead thing. How still it was! How horribly white the long hands looked! It was like a dreadful wax image.

Having locked the door behind him, he crept quietly downstairs. The woodwork creaked, and seemed to cry out as if in pain. He stopped several times, and waited. No: everything was still. It was merely the sound of his own footsteps.

When he reached the library, he saw the bag and coat in the corner. They must be hidden away somewhere. He unlocked a secret press that was in the wainscoting, a press in which he kept his own curious disguises, and put them into it. He could easily burn them afterwards. Then he pulled out his watch. It was twenty minutes to two.

He sat down, and began to think. Every year—every month, almost—men were strangled in England for what he had done. There had been a madness of murder in the air. Some red star had come too close to the earth. . . . And yet what evidence was there against him? Basil Hallward had left the house at eleven. No one had seen him come in again. Most of the servants were at Selby Royal. His valet had gone to bed. . . . Paris! Yes. It was to Paris that Basil had gone, and by the midnight train, as he had intended. With his curious reserved habits, it would be months before any suspicions would be aroused. Months! Everything could be destroyed long before then.

A sudden thought struck him. He put on his fur coat and hat, and went out into the hall. There he paused, hearing the slow heavy tread of the policeman on the pavement outside, and seeing the flash of the bull's-eye[6] reflected in the window. He waited, and held his breath.

After a few moments he drew back the latch, and slipped out, shutting the door very gently behind him. Then he began ringing the bell. In

6. Generic term for a lantern with a thick, ridged lens to magnify the light. This was probably a kerosene lamp.

about five minutes his valet appeared, half dressed, and looking very drowsy.

"I am sorry to have had to wake you up, Francis," he said, stepping in; "but I had forgotten my latch-key. What time it it?"

"Ten minutes past two, sir," answered the man, looking at the clock and blinking.

"Ten minutes past two? How horribly late! You must wake me at nine to-morrow. I have some work to do."

"All right, sir."

"Did any one call this evening?"

"Mr. Hallward, sir. He stayed here till eleven, and then he went away to catch his train."

"Oh! I am sorry I didn't see him. Did he leave any message?"

"No, sir, except that he would write to you from Paris, if he did not find you at the club."

"That will do, Francis. Don't forget to call me at nine to-morrow."

"No, sir."

The man shambled down the passage in his slippers.

Dorian Gray threw his hat and coat upon the table, and passed into the library. For a quarter of an hour he walked up and down the room biting his lip, and thinking. Then he took down the Blue Book from one of the shelves, and began to turn over the leaves. "Alan Campbell, 152, Hertford Street, Mayfair."[7] Yes; that was the man he wanted.

Chapter XIV.[1]

At nine o'clock in the next morning his servant came in with a cup of chocolate on a tray, and opened the shutters. Dorian was sleeping quite peacefully, lying on his right side, with one hand underneath his cheek. He looked like a boy who had been tired out with play, or study.

The man had to touch him twice on the shoulder before he woke, and as he opened his eyes a faint smiled passed across his lips, as though he had been lost in some delightful dream. Yet he had not dreamed at all. His night had been untroubled by any images of pleasure or of pain. But youth smiles without any reason. It is one of its chiefest charms.

He turned round, and, leaning upon his elbow, began to sip his chocolate. The mellow November sun came streaming into the room. The sky was bright, and there was a genial warmth in the air. It was almost like a morning in May.

Gradually the events of the preceding night crept with silent blood-stained feet into his brain, and reconstructed themselves there with terrible distinctness. He winced at the memory of all that he had suffered, and for a moment the same curious feeling of loathing for Basil Hallward, that had made him kill him as he sat in the chair, came back to

---

7. About half a mile south of Dorian's residence in Grosvenor Square. The Blue Book consulted by Dorian was a social directory.

1. Originally chapter 12.

him, and he grew cold with passion. The dead man was still sitting there, too, and in the sunlight now. How horrible that was! Such hideous things were for the darkness, not for the day.

He felt that if he brooded on what he had gone through he would sicken or grow mad. There were sins whose fascination was more in the memory than in the doing of them, strange triumphs that gratified the pride more than the passions, and gave to the intellect a quickened sense of joy, greater than any joy they brought, or could ever bring, to the senses. But this was not one of them. It was a thing to be driven out of the mind, to be drugged with poppies, to be strangled lest it might strangle one itself.

When the half-hour struck, he passed his hand across his forehead, and then got up hastily, and dressed himself with even more than his usual care, giving a good deal of attention to the choice of his necktie and scarf-pin, and changing his rings more than once. He spent a long time also over breakfast, tasting the various dishes, talking to his valet about some new liveries that he was thinking of getting made for the servants at Selby, and going through his correspondence. At some of the letters he smiled. Three of them bored him. One he read several times over, and then tore up with a slight look of annoyance in his face. "That awful thing, a woman's memory!" as Lord Henry had once said.

After he had drunk his cup of black coffee, he wiped his lips slowly with a napkin, motioned to his servant to wait, and going over to the table sat down and wrote two letters. One he put in his pocket, the other he handed to the valet.

"Take this round to 152, Hertford Street, Francis, and if Mr. Campbell is out of town, get his address."

As soon as he was alone, he lit a cigarette, and began sketching upon a piece of paper, drawing first flowers, and bits of architecture, and then human faces. Suddenly he remarked that every face that he drew seemed to have a fantastic likeness to Basil Hallward. He frowned, and, getting up, went over to the bookcase and took out a volume at hazard. He was determined that he would not think about what had happened until it became absolutely necessary that he should do so.

When he had stretched himself on the sofa, he looked at the title-page of the book. It was Gautier's "Émaux et Camées," Charpentier's[2] Japanese-paper edition, with the Jacquemart etching. The binding was of citron-green leather, with a design of gilt trellis-work and dotted pomegranates. It had been given to him by Adrian Singleton. As he turned over the pages his eye fell on the poem about the hand of Lacenaire, the cold yellow hand *"du supplice encore mal lavée,"*[3] with its downy

2. Wilde owned a copy of the 1881 Charpentier edition of *Émaux et Camées* (Enamels and Cameos). The first edition was printed in Paris in 1852 and contained eighteen poems. The sixth edition, the last prepared by Gautier (1872), contained forty-seven poems.

3. The poem is the second of two titled "Etudes de Mains." Lacenaire was a notorious murderer executed by guillotine, whose preserved hand was the subject of Gautier's morbid meditation on the consciousness of evil. The lines Wilde quotes are from stanzas two and three:

red hairs and its *"doigts de faune."* He glanced at his own white taper fingers, shuddering slightly in spite of himself, and passed on till he came to those lovely stanzas upon Venice:—

> *"Sur une gamme chromatique,*
> *Le sein de perles ruisselant,*
> *La Vénus de l'Adriatique*
> *Sort de l'eau son corps rose et blanc.*
>
> *Les dômes, sur l'azur des ondes*
> *Suivant la phrase au pur contour,*
> *S'enflent comme des gorges rondes*
> *Que soulève un soupir d'amour.*
>
> *L'esquif aborde et me dépose,*
> *Jetant son amarre au pilier,*
> *Devant une façade rose,*
> *Sur le marbre d'un escalier."* [4]

How exquisite they were! As one read them, one seemed to be floating down the green waterways of the pink and pearl city, seated in a black gondola with silver prow and trailing curtains. The mere lines looked to him like those straight lines of turquoise-blue that follow one as one pushes out to the Lido. [5] The sudden flashes of colour reminded him of the gleam of the opal-and-iris-throated birds that flutter round the tall honey-combed Campanile, or stalk, with such stately grace, through the dim, dust-stained arcades. Leaning back with half-closed eyes, he kept saying over and over to himself:—

> *"Devant une façade rose,*
> *Sur le marbre d'un escalier."*

The whole of Venice was in those two lines. He remembered the autumn that he had passed there, and a wonderful love that had stirred him to mad, delightful follies. There was romance in every place. But Venice,

Curiosité dépravée!
J'ai touché, malgré mes dégoûts,
Du supplice encor mal lavée,
Cette chair froide au duvet roux..

Momifée et toute jaune
Comme la main d'un pharoon,
Elle allonge ses doigts de faune
Crispés par la tentation.

[Depraved curiosity! I have touched, despite my revulsion, out of pain an evil reborn in that cold flesh with the reddish down. Mummified and completely yellowed as the hand of a pharaoh, the length of its faun-colored fingers shriveled by temptation.]
Dorian's own hand in the painting drips blood, and he achieves a perverse yet detached fascination as he compares his emotion at seeing his own hand with that generated by the voice of the poet contemplating the hand of the murderer Lacen-

aire. It must have been something very like the emotion with which Wilde contemplated himself as a sinner and criminal. Wilde's interest in murder as an art form is expressed in his essay in *Intentions*, "Pen, Pencil and Poison" (1889).
4. The three stanzas on this page are from Gautier's "Variations sur le Carnival de Venise," part 2, titled "Sur les Lagunes." They translate: As though in a chromatic scale, her pearly breast streaming, the Venus of the Adriatic emerges from the waters, her body red and white. The cathedral domes above the blue waters, following the perfectly contoured line, swell as the rounded throat that heaves a sigh of love. As the gondola arrived, I cast the rope around a piling and landed in front of a rose-colored façade upon a marble staircase.
5. Lido is a resort isle near Venice. Campanile, below, is a bell tower, probably the great bell tower of Saint Mark's Church, although Venice boasts many bell towers.

like Oxford, had kept the background for romance, and, to the true
romantic, background was everything, or almost everything. Basil had
been with him part of the time, and had gone wild over Tintoret.[6] Poor
Basil! what a horrible way for a man to die!

He sighed, and took up the volume again, and tried to forget. He read
of the swallows that fly in and out of the little café at Smyrna[7] where
the Hadjis[8] sit counting their amber beads and the turbaned merchants
smoke their long tasselled pipes and talk gravely to each other; he read
of the Obelisk in the Place de la Concorde[9] that weeps tears of granite
in its lonely sunless exile, and longs to be back by the hot lotus-covered
Nile, where there are Sphinxes, and rose-red ibises, and white vultures
with gilded claws, and crocodiles, with small beryl eyes, that crawl over
the green steaming mud; he began to brood over those verses which,
drawing music from kiss-stained marble, tell of that curious statue that
Guatier compares to a contralto voice, the *"monstre charmant"*[1] that
couches in the porphyry-room of the Louvre. But after a time the book
fell from his hand. He grew nervous, and a horrible fit of terror came
over him. What if Alan Campbell should be out of England? Days would
elapse before he could come back. Perhaps he might refuse to come.
What could he do then? Every moment was of vital importance.

They had been great friends once, five years before—almost inseparable, indeed. Then the intimacy had come suddenly to an end. When
they met in society now, it was only Dorian Gray who smiled: Alan
Campbell never did.

He was an extremely clever young man, though he had no real appreciation of the visible arts, and whatever little sense of the beauty of poetry
he possessed he had gained entirely from Dorian. His dominant intellectual passion was for science. At Cambridge he had spent a great deal
of his time working in the Laboratory, and had taken a good class in the
Natural Science Tripos of his year.[2] Indeed, he was still devoted to the

6. Jacopo Robusti, called Tintoretto (1518–94), was
a master Venetian painter greatly admired by Ruskin. The associations between Basil and Ruskin here
are specific and unmistakable. Ruskin was a grad-
uate of Oxford and later taught there. For him,
Venice was the great city of Gothic architecture
and later baroque painting. *The Stones of Venice*
was Ruskin's masterpiece, blending art and social
criticism to trace the rise and fall of Venice as
recorded in its architecture.
7. Smyrna is now called Izmir in Turkey on the
Gulf of Izmir. Dorian read of swallows in Gautier's poem "Ce Que Disent les Hirondelles" (What
the swallows told) from *Émaux et Camées*. Beginning "He read . . . each other" is a loose prose
translation of stanzas 6 and 7 of that poem.
8. Moslems who have made the Mecca pilgrim-
age. The beads are prayer beads.
9. The reference is to Gautier's "Nostalgies
d'Obelisques," and from this point to "steaming
mud," Wilde gives an effective prose summary of

"L'Obelisque de Paris," first of the two parts of the
poem. In the preceeding pages since Dorian took
up Gautier's volume of poems, Wilde has been
demonstrating an Aesthetic reading of selected
poems by Gautier as they reflect and intensify
Dorian's pathology of mind and mood.
The Obelisk is a single block of red granite about
seventy-five feet tall. It was placed before the great
temple of Luxor by Ramses II in the thirteenth
century B.C. It now stands in the center of the huge
square in Paris, a gift of the viceroy of Egypt to
King Louis Philippe in 1831.
1. The "sweet monster" of indeterminate sex is
hermaphroditic. The Louvre is the most famous
art museum in the world, located in Paris.
2. The Tripos is an examination at Cambridge for
the honors B.A. degree. Of the two great English
universities, Cambridge has traditionally excelled
in the sciences, Oxford in languages and the
humanities.

study of chemistry, and had a laboratory of his own, in which he used to shut himself up all day long, greatly to the annoyance of his mother, who had set her heart on his standing for Parliament and had a vague idea that a chemist[3] was a person who made up prescriptions. He was an excellent musician, however, as well, and played both the violin and the piano better than most amateurs. In fact, it was music that had first brought him and Dorian Gray together—music and that indefinable attraction that Dorian seemed to be able to exercise whenever he wished, and indeed exercised often without being conscious of it. They had met at Lady Berkshire's the night that Rubenstein[4] played there, and after that used to be always seen together at the Opera, and wherever good music was going on. For eighteen months their intimacy lasted. Campbell was always either at Selby Royal or in Grosvenor Square. To him, as to many others, Dorian Gray was the type of everything that is wonderful and fascinating in life. Whether or not a quarrel had taken place between them no one ever knew. But suddenly people remarked that they scarcely spoke when they met, and that Campbell seemed always to go away early from any party at which Dorian Gray was present. He had changed, too—was strangely melancholy at times, appeared almost to dislike hearing music, and would never himself play, giving as his excuse, when he was called upon, that he was so absorbed in science that he had no time left in which to practise. And this was certainly true. Every day he seemed to become more interested in biology, and his name appeared once or twice in some of the scientific reviews, in connection with certain curious experiments.

This was the man Dorian Gray was waiting for. Every second he kept glancing at the clock. As the minutes went by he became horribly agitated. At last he got up, and began to pace up and down the room, looking like a beautiful caged thing. He took long stealthy strides. His hands were curiously cold.

The suspense became unbearable. Time seemed to him to be crawling with feet of lead, while he by monstrous winds was being swept towards the jagged edge of some black cleft of precipice. He knew what was waiting for him there; saw it indeed, and, shuddering, crushed with dank hands his burning lids as though he would have robbed the very brain of sight, and driven the eyeballs back into their cave. It was useless. The brain had its own food on which it battened, and the imagination, made grotesque by terror, twisted and distorted as a living thing by pain, danced like some foul puppet on a stand, and grinned through moving masks. Then, suddenly, Time stopped for him. Yes: that blind, slow-breathing thing crawled no more, and horrible thoughts, Time being dead, raced nimbly on in front, and dragged a hideous future from its grave, and showed it to him. He stared at it. Its very horror made him stone.

3. The popular English name for a pharmacist.
4. Anton Rubenstein (1830–94), composer and piano virtuoso, whose music and style of playing were heavily romantic.

At last the door opened, and his servant entered. He turned glazed eyes upon him.

"Mr. Campbell, sir," said the man.

A sigh of relief broke from his parched lips, and the colour came back to his cheeks.

"Ask him to come in at once, Francis." He felt that he was himself again. His mood of cowardice had passed away.

The man bowed, and retired. In a few moments Alan Campbell[5] walked in, looking very stern and rather pale, his pallor being intensified by his coal-black hair and dark eyebrows.

"Alan! this is kind of you. I thank you for coming."

"I had intended never to enter your house again, Gray. But you said it was a matter of life and death." His voice was hard and cold. He spoke with slow deliberation. There was a look of contempt in the steady searching gaze that he turned on Dorian. He kept his hands in the pockets of his Astrakhan coat, and seemed not to have noticed the gesture which which he had been greeted.

"Yes: it is a matter of life and death, Alan, and to more than one person. Sit down."

Campbell took a chair by the table, and Dorian sat opposite to him. The two men's eyes met. In Dorian's there was infinite pity. He knew that what he was going to do was dreadful.

After a strained moment of silence, he leaned across and said, very quietly, but watching the effect of each word upon the face of him he had sent for, "Alan, in a locked room at the top if this house, a room to which nobody but myself has access, a dead man is seated at a table. He has been dead ten hours now. Don't stir, and don't look at me like that. Who the man is, why he died, how he died, are matters that do not concern you. What you have to do is this—"

"Stop, Gray. I don't want to know anything further. Whether what you have told me is true or not true, doesn't concern me. I entirely decline to be mixed up in your life. Keep your horrible secrets to yourself. They don't interest me any more."

"Alan, they will have to interest you. This one will have to interest you. I am awfully sorry for you, Alan. But I can't help myself. You are the one man who is able to save me. I am forced to bring you into the matter. I have no option. Alan, you are scientific. You know about chemistry, and things of that kind. You have made experiments. What you have got to do is to destroy the thing that is upstairs—to destroy it so that not a vestige of it will be left. Nobody saw this person come into the house. Indeed, at the present moment he is supposed to be in Paris. He will not be missed for months. When he is missed, there must be no trace of him found here. You, Alan, you must change him, and every-

5. The model for Alan Campbell was identified by Hesketh Pearson, in *Oscar Wilde* (New York· Harper, 1946) 318–19, as Sir Peter Chalmers Mitchell, whom, over lunch at the Café Royal, Wilde once asked to describe how to get rid of a body.

thing that belongs to him, into a handful of ashes that I may scatter in the air."

"You are mad, Dorian."

"Ah! I was waiting for you to call me Dorian."

"You are mad, I tell you—mad to imagine that I would raise a finger to help you, mad to make this monstrous confession. I will have nothing to do with this matter, whatever it is. Do you think I am going to peril my reputation for you? What is it to me what devil's work you are up to?"

"It was suicide, Alan."

"I am glad of that. But who drove him to it? You, I should fancy."

"Do you still refuse to do this for me?"

"Of course I refuse. I will have absolutely nothing to do with it. I don't care what shame comes on you. You deserve it all. I should not be sorry to see you disgraced, publicly disgraced. How dare you ask me, of all men in the world, to mix myself up in this horror? I should have thought you knew more about people's characters. Your friend Lord Henry Wotton can't have taught you much about psychology, whatever else he had taught you. Nothing will induce me to stir a step to help you. You have come to the wrong man. Go to some of your friends. Don't come to me."

"Alan, it was murder. I killed him. You don't know what he had made me suffer. Whatever my life is, he had more to do with the making or the marring of it than poor Harry has had. He may not have intended it, the result was the same."

"Murder! Good God, Dorian, is that what you have come to? I shall not inform upon you. It is not my business. Besides, without my stirring in the matter, you are certain to be arrested. Nobody ever commits a crime without doing something stupid. But I will have nothing to do with it."

"You must have something to do with it. Wait, wait a moment; listen to me. Only listen, Alan. All I ask of you is to perform a certain scientific experiment. You go to hospitals and dead-houses, and the horrors that you do there don't affect you. If in some hideous dissecting-room or fetid laboratory you found this man lying on a leaden table with red gutters scooped out in it for the blood to flow through, you would simply look upon him as an admirable subject. You would not turn a hair. You would not believe that you were doing anything wrong. On the contrary, you would probably feel that you were benefiting the human race, or increasing the sum of knowledge in the world, or gratifying intellectual curiosity, or something of that kind. What I want you to do is merely what you have often done before. Indeed, to destroy a body must be far less horrible than what you are accustomed to work at. And, remember, it is the only piece of evidence against me. If it is discovered, I am lost; and it is sure to be discovered unless you help me."

"I have no desire to help you. You forget that. I am simply indifferent to the whole thing. It has nothing to do with me."

"Alan, I entreat you. Think of the position I am in. Just before you came I almost fainted with terror. You may know terror yourself some day. No! don't think of that. Look at the matter purely from the scientific point of view. You don't inquire where the dead things on which you experiment come from. Don't inquire now. I have told you too much as it is. But I beg of you to do this. We were friends once, Alan."

"Don't speak about those days, Dorian: they are dead."

"The dead linger sometimes. The man upstairs will not go away. He is sitting at the table with bowed head and outstretched arms. Alan! Alan! if you don't come to my assistance I am ruined. Why, they will hang me, Alan! Don't you understand? They will hang me for what I have done."

"There is no good in prolonging this scene. I absolutely refuse to do anything in the matter. It is insane of you to ask me."

"You refuse?"

"Yes."

"I entreat you, Alan."

"It is useless."

The same look of pity came into Dorian Gray's eyes. Then he stretched out his hand, took a piece of paper, and wrote something on it. He read it over twice, folded it carefully, and pushed it across the table. Having done this, he got up, and went over to the window.

Campbell looked at him in surprise, and then took up the paper, and opened it. As he read it, his face became ghastly pale, and he fell back in his chair. A horrible sense of sickness came over him. He felt as if his heart was beating itself to death in some empty hollow.

After two or three minutes of terrible silence, Dorian turned round, and came and stood behind him, putting his hand upon his shoulder.

"I am so sorry for you, Alan," he murmured, "but you leave me no alternative. I have a letter written already. Here it is. You see the address. If you don't help me, I must send it. If you don't help me, I will send it. You know what the result will be. But you are going to help me. It is impossible for you to refuse now. I tried to spare you. You will do me the justice to admit that. You were stern, harsh, offensive. You treated me as no man has ever dared to treat me—no living man, at any rate. I bore it all. Now it is for me to dictate terms."

Campbell buried his face in his hands, and a shudder passed through him.

"Yes, it is my turn to dictate terms, Alan. You know what they are. The thing is quite simple. Come, don't work yourself into this fever. The thing has to be done. Face it, and do it."

A groan broke from Campbell's lips, and he shivered all over. The ticking of the clock on the mantelpiece seemed to him to be dividing Time into separate atoms of agony, each of which was too terrible to be borne. He felt as if an iron ring was being slowly tightened round his forehead, as if the disgrace with which he was threatened had already come upon him. The hand upon his shoulder weighed like a hand of lead. It was intolerable. It seemed to crush him.

"Come, Alan, you must decide at once."

"I cannot do it," he said, mechanically, as though words could alter things.

"You must. You have no choice. Don't delay."

He hesitated a moment. "Is there a fire in the room upstairs?"

"Yes, there is a gas-fire with asbestos."

"I shall have to go home and get some things from the laboratory."

"No, Alan, you must not leave the house. Write out on a sheet of note-paper what you want, and my servant will take a cab and bring the things back to you."

Campbell scrawled a few lines, blotted them, and addressed the envelope to his assistant. Dorian took the note up and read it carefully. Then he rang the bell, and gave it to his valet, with orders to return as soon as possible, and to bring the things with him.

As the hall door shut, Campbell started nervously, and, having got up from the chair, went over to the chimney-piece. He was shivering with a kind of ague. For nearly twenty minutes, neither of the men spoke. A fly buzzed noisily about the room, and the ticking of the clock was like the beat of a hammer.

As the chime struck one, Campbell turned round, and, looking at Dorian Gray, saw that his eyes were filled with tears. There was something in the purity and refinement of that sad face that seemed to enrage him. "You are infamous, absolutely infamous!" he muttered.

"Hush, Alan: you have saved my life," said Dorian.

"You life? Good heavens! what a life that is! You have gone from corruption to corruption, and now you have culminated in crime. In doing what I am going to do, what you force me to do, it is not of your life that I am thinking."

"Ah, Alan," murmured Dorian, with a sigh, "I wish you had a thousandth part of the pity for me that I have for you." He turned away as he spoke, and stood looking out at the garden. Campbell made no answer.

After about ten minutes a knock came to the door, and the servant entered, carrying a large mahogany chest of chemicals, with a long coil of steel and platinum wire and two rather curiously-shaped iron clamps. "Shall I leave the things here, sir?" he asked Campbell.

"Yes," said Dorian. "And I am afraid, Francis, that I have another errand for you. What is the name of the man at Richmond who supplies Selby with orchids?"

"Harden, sir."

"Yes—Harden. You must go down to Richmond at once, see Harden personally, and tell him to send twice as many orchids as I ordered, and to have as few white ones as possible. In fact, I don't want any white ones. It is a lovely day, Francis, and Richmond is a very pretty place, otherwise I wouldn't bother you about it."

"No trouble, sir. At what time shall I be back?"

Dorian looked at Campbell. "How long will your experiment take, Alan?" he said, in a calm, indifferent voice. The presence of a third person in the room seemed to give him extraordinary courage.

Campbell frowned, and bit his lip. "It will take about five hours," he answered.

"It will be time enough, then, if you are back at half-past seven, Francis. Or stay: just leave my things out for dressing. You can have the evening to yourself. I am not dining at home, so I shall not want you."

"Thank you, sir," said the man, leaving the room.

"Now, Alan, there is not a moment to be lost. How heavy this chest is! I'll take it for you. You bring the other things." He spoke rapidly, and in an authoritative manner. Campbell felt dominated by him. They left the room together.

When they reached the top landing, Dorian took out the key and turned it in the lock. Then he stopped, and a troubled look came into his eyes. He shuddered. "I don't think I can go in, Alan," he murmured.

"It is nothing to me. I don't require you," said Campbell, coldly.

Dorian half opened the door. As he did so, he saw the face of his portrait leering in the sunlight. On the floor in front of it the torn curtain was lying. He remembered that the night before he had forgotten, for the first time in his life, to hide the fatal canvas, and was about to rush forward, when he drew back with a shudder.

What was that loathsome red dew that gleamed, wet and glistening, on one of the hands, as though the canvas had sweated blood? How horrible it was!—more horrible, it seemed to him for the moment, than the silent thing that he knew was stretched across the table, the thing whose grotesque misshapen shadow on the spotted carpet showed him that it had not stirred, but was still there, as he had left it.

He heaved a deep breath, opened the door a little wider, and with half-closed eyes and averted head walked quickly in, determined that he would not look even once upon the dead man. Then, stooping down, and taking up the gold-and-purple hanging, he flung it right over the picture.

There he stopped, feeling afraid to turn round, and his eyes fixed themselves on the intricacies of the pattern before him. He heard Campbell bringing in the heavy chest, and the irons, and the other things that he had required for his dreadful work. He began to wonder if he and Basil Hallward had ever met, and, if so, what they had thought of each other.

"Leave me now," said a stern voice behind him.

He turned and hurried out, just conscious that the dead man had been thrust back into the chair, and that Campbell was gazing into a glistening yellow face. As he was going downstairs he heard the key being turned in the lock.

It was long after seven when Campbell came back into the library. He was pale, but absolutely calm. "I have done what you asked me to do," he muttered. "And now, good-bye. Let us never see each other again."

"You have saved me from ruin, Alan. I cannot forget that," said Dorian, simply.

As soon as Campbell left, he went upstairs. There was a horrible smell of nitric acid in the room. But the thing that had been sitting at the table was gone.

Chapter XV.[1]

That evening, at eight-thirty, exquisitely dressed, and wearing a large buttonhole of Parma violets, Dorian Gray was ushered into Lady Narborough's drawing-room by bowing servants. His forehead was throbbing with maddened nerves, and he felt wildly excited, but his manner as he bent over his hostess's hand was as easy and graceful as ever. Perhaps one never seems so much at one's ease as when one has to play a part. Certainly no one looking at Dorian Gray that night could have believed that he had passed through a tragedy as horrible as any tragedy of our age. Those finely-shaped fingers could never have clutched a knife for sin, nor those smiling lips have cried out on God and goodness. He himself could not help wondering at the calm of his demeanour, and for a moment felt keenly the terrible pleasure of a double life.

It was a small party, got up rather in a hurry by Lady Narborough,[2] who was a very clever woman, with what Lord Henry used to describe as the remains of really remarkable ugliness. She had proved an excellent wife to one of our most tedious ambassadors, and having buried her husband properly in a marble mausoleum, which she had herself designed, and married off her daughters to some rich, rather elderly men, she devoted herself now to the pleasures of French fiction, French cookery, and French *esprit*[3] when she could get it.

Dorian was one of her especial favourites, and she always told him that she was extremely glad she had not met him in early life. "I know, my dear, I should have fallen madly in love with you," she used to say, "and thrown my bonnet right over the mills for your sake. It is most fortunate that you were not thought of at the time. As it was, our bonnets were so unbecoming, and the mills were so occupied in trying to raise the wind, that I never had even a flirtation with anybody. However, that

1. Wilde wrote this and the next three chapters for this edition.
2. The original of Lady Narborough's salon is said to have been the famous weekly gatherings of Wilde's mother. Whatever the case, Pater singles out these scenes of comic satire as especially effective counterpoints to the mounting disorder of Dorian's emotions. Frank Harris also praised the social comedy in *Dorian Gray*, saying that none could thereafter deny Wilde a place among the leading comic geniuses in English. It was Harris (81) who asserted that with *Dorian Gray*, Wilde had finally justified himself as an artist.
3. Wit: in this case, witty conversation.

was all Narborough's fault. He was dreadfully short-sighted, and there is no pleasure in taking a husband who never sees anything."

Her guests this evening were rather tedious. The fact was, as she explained to Dorian, behind a very shabby fan, one of her married daughters had come up quite suddenly to stay with her, and, to make matters worse, had actually brought her husband with her. "I think it is most unkind of her, my dear," she whispered. "Of course I go and stay with them every summer after I come from Homburg,[4] but then an old woman like me must have fresh air sometimes, and, besides, I really wake them up. You don't know what an existence they lead down there. It is pure unadulterated country life. They get up early, because they have so much to do, and go to bed early because they have so little to think about. There has not been a scandal in the neighbourhood since the time of Queen Elizabeth, and consequently they all fall asleep after dinner. You sha'n't sit next either of them. You shall sit by me, and amuse me."

Dorian murmured a graceful compliment, and looked round the room. Yes: it was certainly a tedious party. Two of the people he had never seen before, and the others consisted of Ernest Harrowden, one of those middle-aged mediocrities so common in London clubs who have no enemies, but are thoroughly disliked by their friends; Lady Roxton,[5] an overdressed woman of forty-seven, with a hooked nose, who was always trying to get herself compromised, but was so peculiarly plain that to her great disappointment no one would ever believe anything against her; Mrs. Erlynne, a pushing nobody, with a delightful lisp, and Venetian-red hair; Lady Alice Chapman, his hostess's daughter, a dowdy dull girl, with one of those characteristic British faces, that, once seen, are never remembered; and her husband, a red-cheeked, white-whiskered creature who, like so many of his class, was under the impression that inordinate joviality can atone for an entire lack of ideas.

He was rather sorry he had come, till Lady Narborough, looking at the great ormolu gilt clock[6] that sprawled in gaudy curves on the mauve-draped mantelshelf, exclaimed: "How horrid of Henry Wotton to be so late! I sent round to him this morning on chance, and he promised faithfully not to disappoint me."

It was some consolation that Harry was to be there, and when the door opened and he heard his slow musical voice lending charm to some insincere apology, he ceased to feel bored.

But at dinner he could not eat anything. Plate after plate went away

---

4. A Prussian resort near Frankfurt, famous for its mineral springs.
5. The lady's surname appears in two different spellings, "Ruxton" and "Roxton." The preferred spelling is the former, even though the text here reads "Roxton." Mrs. Erlynne, below, reappears as the déclassé woman with a past in Wilde's 1892

play, *Lady Windermere's Fan*. She bears a striking resemblance in more than just appearance to a middle-aged Lillie Langtry.
6. Ormolu gilt was an alloy of copper and tin or zinc resembling gold and popular during the late Victorian period for decorating furniture, jewelry, and the like.

untasted. Lady Narborough kept scolding him for what she called "an insult to poor Adolphe, who invented the *menu* specially for you," and now and then Lord Henry looked across at him, wondering at his silence and abstracted manner. From time to time the butler filled his glass with champagne. He drank eagerly, and his thirst seemed to increase.

"Dorian," said Lord Henry, at last, as the *chaudfroid*[7] was being handed round, "what is the matter with you to-night? You are quite out of sorts."

"I believe he is in love," cried Lady Narborough, "and that he is afraid to tell me for fear I should be jealous. He is quite right. I certainly should."

"Dear Lady Narborough," murmured Dorian, smiling, "I have not been in love for a whole week—not, in fact, since Madame de Ferrol left town."

"How you men can fall in love with that woman!" exclaimed the old lady. "I really cannot understand it."

"It is simply because she remembers you when you were a little girl, Lady Narborough," said Lord Henry. "She is the one link between us and your short frocks."

"She does not remember my short frocks at all, Lord Henry. But I remember her very well at Vienna thirty years ago, and how *décolletée*[8] she was then."

"She is still *décolletée*," he answered, taking an olive in his long fingers; "and when she is in a very smart gown she looks like an *édition de luxe* of a bad French novel. She is really wonderful, and full of surprises. Her capacity for family affection is extraordinary. When her third husband died, her hair turned quite gold from grief."[9]

"How can you, Harry!" cried Dorian.

"It is a most romantic explanation," laughed the hostess. "But her third husband, Lord Henry! You don't mean to say Ferrol is the fourth?"

"Certainly, Lady Narborough."

"I don't believe a word of it."

"Well, ask Mr. Gray. He is one of her most intimate friends."

"Is it true, Mr. Gray?"

"She assures me so, Lady Narborough," said Dorian. "I asked her whether, like Marguerite de Navarre,[1] she had their hearts embalmed and hung at her girdle. She told me she didn't, because none of them had had any hearts at all."

"Four husbands! Upon my word that is *trop de zèle*."[2]

"*Trop d' audace*, I tell her," said Dorian.

"Oh! she is audacious enough for anything, my dear. And what is Ferrol like? I don't know him."

---

7. A white or brown jellied sauce used as an aspic with cold meats.
8. A low-cut or plunging neckline designed to produce a tantalizing partial exposure of the female bosom.

9. See p. 65.
1. The same person as Margaret of Valois (see p. 39, n. 5).
2. "Too much ardor." And below: "too much impudence."

"The husbands of very beautiful women belong to the criminal classes," said Lord Henry, sipping his wine.

Lady Narborough hit him with her fan. "Lord Henry, I am not at all surprised that the world says that you are extremely wicked."

"But what world says that?" asked Lord Henry, elevating his eyebrows. "It can only be the next world. This world and I are on excellent terms."

"Everybody I know says you are very wicked," cried the old lady, shaking her head.

Lord Henry looked serious for some moments. "It is perfectly monstrous," he said, at last, "the way people go about nowadays saying things against one behind one's back that are absolutely and entirely true."

"Isn't he incorrigible?" cried Dorian, leaning forward in his chair.

"I hope so," said his hostess, laughing. "But really if you all worship Madame de Ferrol in this ridiculous way, I shall have to marry again so as to be in the fashion."

"You will never marry again, Lady Narborough," broke in Lord Henry. "You were far too happy. When a woman marries again it is because she detested her first husband. When a man marries again, it is because he adored his first wife. Women try their luck; men risk theirs."

"Narborough wasn't perfect," cried the old lady.

"If he had been, you would not have loved him, my dear lady," was the rejoinder. "Women love us for our defects. If we have enough of them they will forgive us everything, even our intellects. You will never ask me to dinner again, after saying this, I am afraid, Lady Narborough; but it is quite true."

"Of course it is true, Lord Henry. If we women did not love you for your defects, where would you all be? Not one of you would ever be married. You would be a set of unfortunate bachelors. Not, however, that that would alter you much. Nowadays all the married men live like bachelors, and all the bachelors like married men."

"*Fin de siécle,*"[3] murmured Lord Henry.

"*Fin du globe,*" answered his hostess.

"I wish it were *fin du globe,*" said Dorian, with a sigh. "Life is a great disappointment."

"Ah, my dear," cried Lady Narborough, putting on her gloves, "don't tell me that you have exhausted Life. When a man says that one knows that Life has exhausted him. Lord Henry is very wicked, and I sometimes wish that I had been; but you are made to be good—you look so good. I must find you a nice wife. Lord Henry, don't you think that Mr. Gray should get married?"

"I am always telling him so, Lady Narborough," said Lord Henry, with a bow.

"Well, we must look out for a suitable match for him. I shall go

3. "End of the century" referred more to a state of mind and style of life than to the 1890's. The French phrase became synonymous with that sense of exhausted energy, lost values, and discontent with the commonplace that was the sad side of the gay nineties.

through Debrett[4] carefully to-night, and draw out a list of all the eligible young ladies."

"With their ages, Lady Narborough?" asked Dorian.

"Of course, with their ages, slightly edited. But nothing must be done in a hurry. I want it to be what *The Morning Post* calls a suitable alliance, and I want you both to be happy."

"What nonsense people talk about happy marriages!" exclaimed Lord Henry. "A man can be happy with any woman, as long as he does not love her."

"Ah! what a cynic you are!" cried the old lady, pushing back her chair, and nodding to Lady Ruxton. "You must come and dine with me soon again. You are really an admirable tonic, much better than what Sir Andrew prescribes for me. You must tell me what people you would like to meet, though. I want it to be a delightful gathering."

"I like men who have a future, and women who have a past," he answered. "Or do you think that would make it a petticoat party?"

"I fear so," she said, laughing, as she stood up. "A thousand pardons, my dear Lady Ruxton," she added, "I didn't see you hadn't finished your cigarette."

"Never mind, Lady Narborough. I smoke a great deal too much. I am going to limit myself, for the future."

"Pray don't, Lady Ruxton,"[5] said Lord Henry. "Moderation is a fatal thing. Enough is as bad as a meal. More than enough is as good as a feast."

Lady Ruxton glanced at him curiously. "You must come and explain that to me some afternoon, Lord Henry. It sounds a fascinating theory," she murmured, as she swept out of the room.

"Now, mind you don't stay too long over your politics and scandal," cried Lady Narborough from the door. "If you do, we are sure to squabble upstairs."

The men laughed, and Mr. Chapman got up solemnly from the foot of the table and came up to the top. Dorian Gray changed his seat, and went and sat by Lord Henry. Mr. Chapman began to talk in a loud voice about the situation in the House of Commons. He guffawed at his adversaries. The word *doctrinaire*[6]—word full of terror to the British mind—reappeared from time to time between his explosions. An alliterative prefix served as an ornament of oratory. He hoisted the Union Jack[7] on the pinnacles of Thought. The inherited stupidity of the race—sound English common sense he jovially termed it—was shown to be the proper bulwark for Society.

---

4. *Debrett's Peerage* was the standard reference to British and Irish aristocracy.

5. Misprinted here and below as "Roxton" in the original edition.

6. Someone obstinately devoted to a theory without regard to its appropriateness or its applicability; originally, one of the French constitutionalist party after the downfall of Napoleon.

7. The national flag of England, Scotland, and Ireland, consisting of the three crosses of each nation overlaid: the red cross of St. George, and the white crosses of St. Andrew (Scotland) and St. Patrick (Ireland) on a blue field.

A smile curved Lord Henry's lips, and he turned round and looked at Dorian.

"Are you better, my dear fellow?" he asked. "You seemed rather out of sorts at dinner."

"I am quite well, Harry. I am tired. That is all."

"You were charming last night. The little Duchess is quite devoted to you. She tells me she is going down to Selby."

"She has promised to come on the twentieth."

"Is Monmouth to be there too?"

"Oh, yes, Harry."

"He bores me dreadfully, almost as much as he bores her. She is very clever, too clever for a woman. She lacks the indefinable charm of weakness. It is the feet of clay that make the gold of the image precious. Her feet are very pretty, but they are not feet of clay. White porcelain feet, if you like. They have been through the fire, and what fire does not destroy, it hardens. She has had experiences."

"How long has she been married?" asked Dorian.

"An eternity, she tells me. I believe, according to the peerage, it is ten years, but ten years with Monmouth must have been like eternity, with time thrown in. Who else is coming?"

"Oh, the Willoughbys, Lord Rugby and his wife, our hostess, Geoffrey Clouston, the usual set. I have asked Lord Grotrian."

"I like him," said Lord Henry. "A great many people don't, but I find him charming. He atones for being occasionally somewhat over-dressed, by being always absolutely over-educated.[8] He is a very modern type."

"I don't know if he will be able to come, Harry. He may have to go to Monte Carlo with his father."

"Ah! what a nuisance people's people are! Try and make him come. By the way, Dorian, you ran off very early last night. You left before eleven. What did you do afterwards? Did you go straight home?"

Dorian glanced at him hurriedly, and frowned. "No, Harry," he said at last, "I did not get home till nearly three."

"Did you go to the club?"

"Yes," he answered. Then he bit his lip. "No, I don't mean that. I didn't go to the club. I walked about. I forget what I did. . . . How inquisitive you are, Harry! You always want to know what one has been doing. I always want to forget what I have been doing. I came in at half-past two, if you wish to know the exact time. I had left my latch-key at home, and my servant had to let me in. If you want any corroborative evidence on the subject you can ask him."

Lord Henry shrugged his shoulders. "My dear fellow, as if I cared! Let us go up to the drawing-room. No, sherry, thank you, Mr. Chapman. Something has happened to you, Dorian. Tell me what it is. You are not yourself to-night."

---

8. Another aphorism that reappears in *The Importance of Being Earnest*.

"Don't mind me, Harry. I am irritable, and out of temper. I shall come round and see you to-morrow, or next day. Make my excuses to Lady Narborough. I sha'n't go upstairs. I shall go home. I must go home."

"All right, Dorian. I dare say I shall see you to-morrow at tea-time. The Duchess is coming."

"I will try to be there, Harry," he said, leaving the room. As he drove back to his own house he was conscious that the sense of terror he thought he had strangled had come back to him. Lord Henry's casual questioning had made him lose his nerves for the moment, and he wanted his nerve still. Things that were dangerous had to be destroyed. He winced. He hated the idea of even touching them.

Yet it had to be done. He realized that, and when he had locked the door of his library, he opened the secret press into which he had thrust Basil Hallward's coat and bag. A huge fire was blazing. He piled another log on it. The smell of the singeing clothes and burning leather was horrible. It took him three-quarters of an hour to consume everything. At the end he felt faint and sick, and having lit some Algerian pastilles[9] in a pierced copper brazier, he bathed his hands and forehead with a cool musk-scented vinegar.

Suddenly he started. His eyes grew strangely bright, and he gnawed nervously at his upper-lip. Between two of the windows stood a large Florentine cabinet, made out of ebony, and inlaid with ivory and blue lapis.[1] He watched it as though it were a thing that could fascinate and make afraid, as though it held something that he longed for and yet almost loathed. His breath quickened. A mad craving came over him. He lit a cigarette and then threw it away. His eyelids drooped till the long fringed lashes almost touched his cheek. But he still watched the cabinet. At last he got up from the sofa on which he had been lying, went over to it, and, having unlocked it, touched some hidden spring. A triangular drawer passed slowly out. His fingers moved instinctively towards it, dipped in, and closed on something. It was a small Chinese box of black and gold-dust lacquer, elaborately wrought, the sides patterned with curved waves, and the silken cords hung with round crystals and tasselled in plaited metal threads. He opened it. Inside was a green paste[2] waxy in lustre, the odour curiously heavy and persistent.

He hesitated for some moments, with a strangely immobile smile upon his face. Then shivering, though the atmosphere of the room was terribly hot, he drew himself up, and glanced at the clock. It was twenty minutes to twelve. He put the box back, shutting the cabinet doors as he did so, and went into his bedroom.

As midnight was striking bronze blows upon the dusky air, Dorian Gray, dressed commonly, and with a muffler wrapped round his throat, crèpt quietly out of his house. In Bond Street he found a hansom with

9. Aromatic tablets burned as incense.
1. An opaque gemstone of varying shades of blue, similar in other respects to jade.

2. Opium in a form to be smoked, usually in a porcelain pipe.

a good horse. He hailed it, and in a low voice gave the driver an address.[3]

The man shook his head. "It is too far for me," he muttered.

"Here is a sovereign for you," said Dorian. "You shall have another if you drive fast."

"All right, sir," answered the man, "you will be there in an hour," and after his fare had got in he turned his horse round, and drove rapidly towards the river.

Chapter XVI.

A cold rain began to fall, and the blurred street-lamps looked ghastly in the dripping mist. The public-houses were just closing, and dim men and women were clustering in broken groups round their doors. From some of the bars came the sound of horrible laughter. In others, drunkards brawled and screamed.

Lying back in the hansom, with his hat pulled over his forehead, Dorian Gray watched with listless eyes the sordid shame of the great city, and now and then he repeated to himself the words that Lord Henry had said to him on the first day they had met, "To cure the soul by means of the senses, and the senses by means of the soul." Yes, that was the secret. He had often tried it, and would try it again now. There were opium-dens, where one could buy oblivion, dens of horror where the memory of old sins could be destroyed by the madness of sins that were new.

The moon hung low in the sky like a yellow skull. From time to time a huge misshapen cloud stretched a long arm across and hid it. The gaslamps grew fewer, and the streets more narrow and gloomy. Once the man lost his way, and had to drive back half a mile. A steam rose from the horse as it splashed up the puddles. The side-windows of the hansom were clogged with a grey-flannel mist.

"To cure the soul by means of the senses, and the senses by means of the soul!" How the words rang in his ears! His soul, certainly, was sick to death. Was it true that the senses could cure it? Innocent blood had been split. What could atone for that? Ah! for that there was no atonement; but though forgiveness was impossible, forgetfulness was possible still, and he was determined to forget to stamp the thing out, to crush it as one would crush the adder that had stung one. Indeed, what right had Basil to have spoken to him as he had done? Who had made him a judge over others? He had said things that were dreadful, horrible, not to be endured.

On and on plodded the hansom, going slower, it seemed to him, at each step. He thrust up the trap, and called to the man to drive faster. The hideous hunger for opium began to gnaw at him. His throat burned, and his delicate hands twitched nervously together. He struck at the

---

3. The address was evidently in London's Chinatown near the docks, where opium dens prospered.

horse madly with his stick. The driver laughed, and whipped up. He laughed in answer, and the man was silent.

The way seemed interminable, and the streets like the black web of some sprawling spider. The monotony became unbearable, and, as the mist thickened, he felt afraid.

Then they passed by lonely brickfields. The fog was lighter here, and he could see the strange bottle-shaped kilns with their orange fan-like tongues of fire. A dog barked as they went by, and far away in the darkness some wandering sea-gull screamed. The horse stumbled in a rut, then swerved aside, and broke into a gallop.

After some time they left the clay road, and rattled again over rough-paven streets. Most of the windows were dark, but now and then fantastic shadows were silhouetted against some lamp-lit blind. He watched them curiously. They moved like monstrous marionettes, and made gestures like live things.[1] He hated them. A dull rage was in his heart. As they turned a corner a woman yelled something at them from an open door, and two men ran after the hansom for about a hundred yards. The driver beat at them with his whip.

It is said that passion makes one think in a circle. Certainly with hideous iteration the bitten lips of Dorian Gray shaped and reshaped those subtle words that dealt with soul and sense, till he had found in them the full expression, as it were, of his mood, and justified, by intellectual approval, passions that without such justification would still have dominated his temper. From cell to cell of his brain crept the one thought; and the wild desire to live, most terrible of all man's appetites, quickened into force each trembling nerve and fibre. Ugliness that had once been hateful to him because it made things real, became dear to him now for that very reason. Ugliness was the one reality. The coarse brawl, the loathsome den, the crude violence of disordered life, the very vileness of thief and outcast, were more vivid, in their intense actuality of impression, than all the gracious shapes of Art, the dreamy shadows of Song. They were what he needed for forgetfulness. In three days he would be free.[2]

Suddenly the man drew up with a jerk at the top of a dark lane. Over the low roofs and jagged chimney-stacks of the houses rose the black masts of ships. Wreaths of white mist clung like ghostly sails to the yards.

"Somewhere about here, sir, ain't it?" he asked huskily through the trap.

Dorian started, and peered round. "This will do," he answered, and, having got out hastily, and given the driver the extra fare he had promised him, he walked quickly in the direction of the quay. Here and there a lantern gleamed at the stern of some huge merchantman. The light

---

1. From "Most of the windows . . . things," Wilde paraphrases a scene in his poem "The Harlot's House" (1885) 22–24. This is another instance of Wilde's habit of mediating a mood, emotion, or reflection through art.
2. Dorian's mood is one often alternately celebrated and lamented in poets like Baudelaire and Rimbaud and among the English Decadents.

shook and splintered in the puddles. A red glare came from an outward-bound steamer that was coaling. The slimy pavement looked like a wet mackintosh.

He hurried on towards the left, glancing back now and then to see if he was being followed. In about seven or eight minutes he reached a small shabby house, that was wedged in between two gaunt factories. In one of the top-windows stood a lamp. He stopped, and gave a peculiar knock.

After a little time he heard steps in the passage, and the chain being unhooked. The door opened quietly, and he went in without saying a word to the squat misshapen figure that flattened itself into the shadow as he passed. At the end of the hall hung a tattered green curtain that swayed and shook in the gusty wind which had followed him in from the street. He dragged it aside, and entered a long, low room which looked as if it had once been a third-rate dancing-saloon. Shrill flaring gas-jets, dulled and distorted in the fly-blown mirrors that faced them, were ranged round the walls. Greasy reflectors of ribbed tin backed them, making quivering discs of light. The floor was covered with ochre-coloured[3] sawdust, trampled here and there into mud, and stained with dark rings of spilt liquor. Some Malays were crouching by a little charcoal stove playing with bone counters, and showing their white teeth as they chattered. In one corner with his head buried in his arms, a sailor sprawled over a table, and by the tawdrily-painted bar that ran across one complete side stood two haggard women mocking an old man who was brushing the sleeves of his coat with an expression of disgust. "He thinks he's got red ants on him," laughed one of them, as Dorian passed by. The man looked at her in terror, and began to whimper.

At the end of the room there was a little staircase, leading to a darkened chamber. As Dorian hurried up its three ricketty steps, the heavy odour of opium met him. He heaved a deep breath, and his nostrils quivered with pleasure. When he entered, a young man with smooth yellow hair, who was bending over a lamp lighting a long thin pipe, looked up at him, and nodded in a hesitating manner.

"You here, Adrian?" muttered Dorian.

"Where else should I be?" he answered, listlessly. "None of the chaps will speak to me now."

"I thought you had left England."

"Darlington is not going to do anything. My brother paid the bill at last. George doesn't speak to me either. . . . I don't care," he added, with a sigh. "As long as one has this stuff, one doesn't want friends. I think I have had too many friends."

Dorian winced, and looked around at the grotesque things that lay in such fantastic postures on the ragged mattresses. The twisted limbs, the gaping mouths, the staring lustreless eyes, fascinated him. He knew in

3. Of an orange-yellow color produced by certain oxides of iron.

what strange heavens they were suffering, and what dull hells were teaching them the secret of some new joy. They were better off than he was. He was prisoned in thought. Memory, like a horrible malady, was eating his soul away. From time to time he seemed to see the eyes of Basil Hallward looking at him. Yet he felt he could not stay. The presence of Adrian Singleton troubled him. He wanted to be where no one would know who he was. He wanted to escape from himself.

"I am going on to the other place," he said, after a pause.

"On the wharf?"

"Yes."

"That mad-cat is sure to be there. They won't have her in this place now."

Dorian shrugged his shoulders. "I am sick of women who love one. Women who hate one are much more interesting. Besides, the stuff is better."

"Much the same."

"I like it better. Come and have something to drink. I must have something."

"I don't want anything," murmured the young man.

"Never mind."

Adrian Singleton rose up wearily, and followed Dorian to the bar. A half-caste, in a ragged turban and a shabby ulster, grinned a hideous greeting as he thrust a bottle of brandy and two tumblers in front of them. The women sidled up, and began to chatter. Dorian turned his back on them, and said something in a low voice to Adrian Singleton.

A crooked smile, like a Malay crease, writhed across the face of one of the women. "We are very proud to-night," she sneered.

"For God's sake don't talk to me," cried Dorian, stamping his foot on the ground. "What do you want? Money? Here it is. Don't ever talk to me again."

Two red sparks flashed for a moment in the woman's sodden eyes, then flickered out, and left them dull and glazed. She tossed her head, and raked the coins off the counter with greedy fingers. Her companion watched her enviously.

"It's no use," sighed Adrian Singleton. "I don't care to go back. What does it matter? I am quite happy here."

"You will write to me if you want anything, won't you?" said Dorian, after a pause.

"Perhaps."

"Good-night, then."

"Good-night," answered the young man, passing up the steps, and wiping his parched mouth with a handkerchief.

Dorian walked to the door with a look of pain in his face. As he drew the curtain aside a hideous laugh broke from the painted lips of the woman who had taken his money. "There goes the devil's bargain!" she hiccoughed, in a hoarse voice.

"Curse you!" he answered, "don't call me that."

She snapped her fingers. "Prince Charming is what you like to be called, ain't it?" she yelled after him.

The drowsy sailor leapt to his feet as she spoke, and looked wildly round. The sound of the shutting of the hall door fell on his ear. He rushed out as if in pursuit.

Dorian Gray hurried along the quay through the drizzling rain. His meeting with Adrian Singleton had strangely moved him, and he wondered if the ruin of that young life was really to be laid at his door, as Basil Hallward had said to him with such infamy of insult. He bit his lip, and for a few seconds his eyes grew sad. Yet, after all, what did it matter to him? One's days were too brief to take the burden of another's errors on one's shoulders. Each man lived his own life, and paid his own price for living it. The only pity was one had to pay so often for a single fault. One had to pay over and over again, indeed. In her dealings with man Destiny never closed her accounts.

There are moments, psychologists tell us, when the passion for sin, or for what the world calls sin, so dominates a nature, that every fibre of the body, as every cell of the brain, seems to be instinct with fearful impulses. Men and women at such moments lose the freedom of their will. They move to their terrible end as automatons move.

Choice is taken from them, and conscience is either killed, or, if it lives at all, lives but to give rebellion its fascination, and disobedience its charm. For all sins, as theologians weary not of reminding us, are sins of disobedience. When that high spirit, that morning-star of evil, fell from heaven, it was as a rebel that he fell.

Callous, concentrated on evil, with stained mind, and soul hungry for rebellion, Dorian Gray hastened on, quickening his step as he went, but as he darted aside into a dim archway, that had served him often as a short cut to the ill-famed place where he was going, he felt himself suddenly seized from behind, and before he had time to defend himself he was thrust back against the wall, with a brutal hand round his throat.

He struggled madly for life, and by a terrible effort wrenched the tightening fingers away. In a second he heard the click of a revolver, and saw the gleam of a polished barrel pointing straight at his head, and the dusky form of a short thick-set man facing him.

"What do you want?" he gasped.

"Keep quiet," said the man. "If you stir, I shoot you."

"You are mad. What have I done to you?"

"You wrecked the life of Sibyl Vane," was the answer, "and Sibyl Vane was my sister. She killed herself. I know it. Her death is at your door. I swore I would kill you in return. For years I have sought you. I had no clue, no trace. The two people who could have described you were dead. I knew nothing of you but the pet name she used to call you. I heard it to-night by chance. Make your peace with God, for to-night you are going to die."

Dorian Gray grew sick with fear. "I never knew her," he stammered. "I never heard of her. You are mad."

"You had better confess your sin, for as sure as I am James Vane, you are going to die." There was a horrible moment. Dorian did not know what to say or do. "Down on your knees!" growled the man. "I give you one minute to make your peace—no more. I go on board to-night for India, and I must do my job first. One minute. That's all."

Dorian's arms fell to his side. Paralyzed with terror, he did not know what to do. Suddenly a wild hope flashed across his brain. "Stop," he cried. "How long ago is it since your sister died? Quick, tell me!"

"Eighteen years," said the man. "Why do you ask me? What do years matter?"

"Eighteen years," laughed Dorian Gray, with a touch of triumph in his voice. "Eighteen years! Set me under the lamp and look at my face!"

James Vane hesitated for a moment, not understanding what was meant. Then he seized Dorian Gray and dragged him from the archway.

Dim and wavering as was the windblown light, yet it served to show him the hideous error, as it seemed, into which he had fallen, for the face of the man he had sought to kill had all the bloom of boyhood, all the unstained purity of youth. He seemed little more than a lad of twenty summers, hardly older, if older indeed at all, than his sister had been when they had parted so many years ago. It was obvious that this was not the man who had destroyed her life.

He loosened his hold and reeled back. "My God! my God!" he cried, "and I would have murdered you!"

Dorian Gray drew a long breath. "You have been on the brink of committing a terrible crime, my man," he said, looking at him sternly. "Let this be a warning to you not to take vengeance into your own hands."

"Forgive me, sir," muttered James Vane. "I was deceived. A chance word I heard in that damned den set me on the wrong track."

"You had better go home, and put that pistol away, or you may get into trouble," said Dorian, turning on his heel, and going slowly down the street.

James Vane stood on the pavement in horror. He was trembling from head to foot. After a little while a black shadow that had been creeping along the dripping wall, moved out into the light and came close to him with stealthy footsteps. He felt a hand laid on his arm and looked round with a start. It was one of the woman who had been drinking at the bar.

"Why didn't you kill him?" she hissed out, putting her haggard face quite close to his. "I knew you were following him when you rushed out from Daly's.[4] You fool! You should have killed him. He has lots of money, and he's as bad as bad."

"He is not the man I am looking for," he answered, "and I want no man's money. I want a man's life. The man whose life I want must be

---

4. A theater on Cranbourn Street off Leicester Square, established by the American playwright Augustin Daly in 1879, long since razed.

nearly forty now. This one is little more than a boy. Thank God, I have not got his blood upon my hands."

The woman gave a bitter laugh. "Little more than a boy!" she sneered. "Why, man, it's nigh on eighteen years since Prince Charming made me what I am."

"You lie!" cried James Vane.

She raised her hand up to heaven. "Before God I am telling the truth," she cried.

"Before God?"

"Strike me dumb if it ain't so. He is the worst one that comes here. They say he has sold himself to the devil for a pretty face. It's nigh on eighteen years since I met him. He hasn't changed much since then. I have though," she added, with a sickly leer.

"You swear this?"

"I swear it," came in hoarse echo from her flat mouth. "But don't give me away to him," she whined; "I am afraid of him. Let me have some money for my night's lodging."

He broke from her with an oath, and rushed to the corner of the street, but Dorian Gray had disappeared. When he looked back, the woman had vanished also.

Chapter XVII.

A week later Dorian Gray was sitting in the conservatory at Selby Royal talking to the pretty Duchess of Monmouth, who with her husband, a jaded-looking man of sixty, was amongst his guests. It was tea-time, and the mellow light of the huge lace-covered lamp that stood on the table lit up the delicate china and hammered silver of the service at which the Duchess was presiding. Her white hands were moving daintily among the cups, and her full red lips were smiling at something that Dorian had whispered to her. Lord Henry was lying back in a silk-draped wicker chair looking at them. On a peach-coloured divan sat Lady Narborough pretending to listen to the Duke's description of the last Brazilian beetle that he had added to his collection. Three young men in elaborate smoking-suits were handing tea-cakes to some of the women. The house-party consisted of twelve people, and there were more expected to arrive on the next day.

"What are you two talking about?" said Lord Henry, strolling over to the table, and putting his cup down. "I hope Dorian has told you about my plan for rechristening everything, Gladys. It is a delightful idea."

"But I don't want to be rechristened, Harry," rejoined the Duchess, looking up at him with her wonderful eyes. "I am quite satisfied with my own name, and I am sure Mr. Gray should be satisfied with his."

"My dear Gladys, I would not alter either name for the world. They are both perfect. I was thinking chiefly of flowers. Yesterday I cut an orchid, for my buttonhole. It was a marvellous spotted thing, as effective as the seven deadly sins. In a thoughtless moment I asked one of the gardeners what it was called. He told me it was a fine specimen of *Robinsoniana*, or something dreadful of that kind. It is a sad truth, but we have lost the faculty of giving lovely names to things. Names are everything. I never quarrel with actions. My one quarrel is with words. This is the reason I hate vulgar realism in literature. The man who could call a spade a spade should be compelled to use one. It is the only thing he is fit for."

"Then what should we call you, Harry?" she asked.

"His name is Prince Paradox," said Dorian

"I recognize him in a flash," exclaimed the Duchess.

"I won't hear of it," laughed Lord Henry, sinking into a chair. "From a label there is no escape! I refuse the title."

"Royalties may not abdicate," fell as a warning from pretty lips.

"You wish me to defend my throne, then?"

"Yes."

"I give the truths of to-morrow."

"I prefer the mistakes of to-day," she answered.

"You disarm me, Gladys," he cried, catching the willfulness of her mood.

"Of your shield, Harry: not of your spear."

"I never tilt against Beauty," he said, with a wave of his hand.

"That is your error, Harry, believe me. You value beauty far too much."

"How can you say that? I admit that I think that it is better to be beautiful than to be good.[1] But on the other hand no one is more ready than I am to acknowledge that it is better to be good than to be ugly."

"Ugliness is one of the seven deadly sins, then?" cried the Duchess. "What becomes of your simile about the orchid?"

"Ugliness is one of the seven deadly virtues, Gladys. You, as a good Tory, must not underrate them. Beer, the Bible, and the seven deadly virtues have made our England what she is."

"You don't like your country, then?" she asked.

"I live in it."

"That you may censure it the better."

"Would you have me take the verdict of Europe on it?" he enquired.

"What do they say of us."

"That Tartuffe[2] has emigrated to England and opened a shop."

"Is that yours, Harry?"

"I give it to you."

"I could not use it. It is too true."

"You need not be afraid. Our countrymen never recognize a description."

"They are practical."

1. An echo of the phrase in "The Critic as Artist": "aesthetics are higher than ethics."
2. The scheming, religious hypocrite who is the leading character in Molière's comedy of the same name.

"They are more cunning than practical. When they make up their ledger, they balance stupidity by wealth, and vice by hypocrisy."

"Still, we have done great things."

"Great things have been thrust on us,[3] Gladys."

"We have carried their burden."

"Only as far as the Stock Exchange."

She shook her head. "I believe in the race," she cried.

"It represents the survival of the pushing."[4]

"It has development."

"Decay fascinates me more."

"What of Art?" she asked.

"It is a malady."

"Love?"

"An illusion."

"Religion?"

"The fashionable substitute for Belief."

"You are a sceptic."

"Never! Scepticism is the beginning of Faith."

"What are you?"

"To define is to limit."

"Give me a clue."

"Threads snap. You would lose your way in the labyrinth."

"You bewilder me. Let us talk of some one else."

"Our host is a delightful topic. Years ago he was christened Prince Charming."

"Ah! don't remind me of that," cried Dorian Gray.

"Our host is rather horrid this evening," answered the Duchess, colouring. "I believe he thinks that Monmouth married me on purely scientific principles as the best specimen he could find of a modern butterfly."

"Well, I hope he won't stick pins into you, Duchess," laughed Dorian.

"Oh! my maid does that already, Mr. Gray, when she is annoyed with me."

"And what does she get annoyed with you about, Duchess?"

"For the most trivial things, Mr. Gray, I assure you. Usually because I come in at ten minutes to nine and tell her that I must be dressed by half-past eight."

"How unreasonable of her! You should give her warning."

"I daren't, Mr. Gray. Why, she invents hats for me. You remember the one I wore at Lady Hilstone's garden-party? You don't, but it is nice of you to pretend that you do. Well, she made it out of nothing. All good hats are made out of nothing."

"Like all good reputations, Gladys," interrupted Lord Henry. "Every

3. *Twelfth Night* 2.5.144–46.
4. Parody of Herbert Spencer's maxim "survival of the fittest," often applied by the Victorians to economic and social life and referred to as the doctrine of Social Darwinism.

effect that one produces gives one an enemy. To be popular one must be a mediocrity."

"Not with women," said the Duchess, shaking her head; "and women rule the world. I assure you we can't bear mediocrities. We women, as some one says, love with our ears, just as you men love with your eyes, if you ever love at all."

"It seems to me that we never do anything else," murmured Dorian.

"Ah! then, you never really love, Mr. Gray," answered the Duchess, with mock sadness.

"My dear Gladys!" cried Lord Henry. "How can you say that? Romance lives by repetition, and repetition converts an appetite into an art. Besides, each time that one loves is the only time one has ever loved. Difference of object does not alter singleness of passion. It merely intensifies it. We can have in life but one great experience at best, and the secret of life is to reproduce that experience as often as possible."

"Even when one has been wounded by it, Harry?" asked the Duchess, after a pause.

"Especially when one has been wounded by it," answered Lord Henry.

The Duchess turned and looked at Dorian Gray with a curious expression in her eyes. "What do you say to that, Mr. Gray?" she enquired.

Dorian hesitated for a moment. Then he threw his head back and laughed. "I always agree with Harry, Duchess."

"Even when he is wrong?"

"Harry is never wrong, Duchess."

"And does his philosophy make you happy?"

"I have never searched for happiness. Who wants happiness? I have searched for pleasure."

"And found it, Mr. Gray?"

"Often. Too often."

The Duchess sighed. "I am searching for peace," she said, "and if I don't go and dress, I shall have none this evening."

"Let me get you some orchids, Duchess," cried Dorian, starting to his feet, and walking down the conservatory.

"You are flirting disgracefully with him," said Lord Henry to his cousin. "You had better take care. He is very fascinating."

"If he were not, there would be no battle."

"Greek meets Greek, then?"

"I am on the side of the Trojans. They fought for a woman."

"They were defeated."

"There are worse things than capture," she answered.

"You gallop with a loose rein."

"Pace gives life," was the *riposte*."[5]

"I shall write it in my diary to-night."

---

5. Retort. Originally, the word referred to a return thrust in fencing. The fencing here is verbal.

"What?"

"That a burnt child loves the fire."

"I am not even singed. My wings are untouched."

"You use them for everything, except flight."

"Courage has passed from men to women. It is a new experience for us."

"You have a rival."

"Who?"

He laughed. "Lady Narborough," he whispered. "She perfectly adores him."

"You fill me with apprehension. The appeal to Antiquity is fatal to us who are romanticists."

"Romanticists! You have all the methods of science."

"Men have educated us."

"But not explained you."

"Describe us as a sex," was her challenge.

"Sphynxes without secrets."

She looked at him, smiling. "How long Mr. Gray is!" she said. "Let us go and help him. I have not yet told him the colour of my frock."

"Ah! you must suit your frock to his flowers, Gladys."

"That would be a premature surrender."

"Romantic Art begins with its climax."

"I must keep an opportunity for retreat."

"In the Parthian manner?"[6]

"They found safety in the desert. I could not do that."

"Women are not always allowed a choice," he answered, but hardly had he finished the sentence before from the far end of the conservatory came a stifled groan, followed by the dull sound of a heavy fall. Everybody started up. The Duchess stood motionless in horror. And with fear in his eyes Lord Henry rushed through the flapping palms, to find Dorian Gray lying face downwards on the tiled floor in a death-like swoon.

He was carried at once into the blue drawing-room, and laid upon one of the sofas. After a short time he came to himself, and looked round with a dazed expression.

"What has happened?" he asked. "Oh! I remember. Am I safe here, Harry?" He began to tremble.

"My dear Dorian," answered Lord Henry, "you merely fainted. That was all. You must have overtired yourself. You had better not come down to dinner. I will take your place."

"No, I will come down," he said, struggling to his feet. "I would rather come down. I must not be alone."

He went to his room and dressed. There was a wild recklessness of gaiety in his manner as he sat at table, but now and then a thrill of terror ran through him when he remembered that, pressed against the window

6. Parthians were credited with having perfected retreat as a strategy of attack by luring the enemy close enough to fire their arrows as they moved away.

of the conservatory, like a white handkerchief, he had seen the face of James Vane watching him.

Chapter XVIII.[1]

The next day he did not leave the house, and, indeed, spent most of the time in his own room, sick with a wild terror of dying, and yet indifferent to life itself. The consciousness of being hunted, snared, tracked down, had begun to dominate him. If the tapestry did but tremble in the wind, he shook. The dead leaves that were blown against the leaded panes seemed to him like his own wasted resolutions and wild regrets. When he closed his eyes, he saw again the sailor's face peering through the mist-stained glass, and horror seemed once more to lay its hand upon his heart.

But perhaps it had been only his fancy that had called vengeance out of the night, and set the hideous shapes of punishment before him. Actual life was chaos, but there was something terribly logical in the imagination. It was the imagination that set remorse to dog the feet of sin. It was the imagination that made each crime bear its misshapen brood.[2] In the common world of fact the wicked were not punished, nor the good rewarded. Success was given to the strong, failure thrust upon the weak. That was all. Besides, had any stranger been prowling round the house he would have been seen by the servants or the keepers. Had any footmarks been found on the flower-beds, the gardeners would have reported it. Yes: it had been merely fancy. Sibyl Vane's brother had not come back to kill him. He had sailed away in his ship to founder in some winter sea. From him, at any rate, he was safe. Why, the man did not know who he was, could not know who he was. The mask of youth had saved him.

And yet if it had been merely an illusion, how terrible it was to think that conscience could raise such fearful phantoms, and give them visible form, and make them move before one! What sort of life would his be if, day and night, shadows of his crime were to peer at him from silent corners, to mock him from secret places, to whisper in his ear as he sat at the feast, to wake him with icy fingers as he lay asleep! As the thought crept through his brain, he grew pale with terror, and the air seemed to him to have become suddenly colder. Oh! in what a wild hour of madness he had killed his friend! How ghastly the mere memory of the scene! He saw it all again. Each hideous detail came back to him with added horror. Out of the black cave of Time, terrible and swathed in scarlet, rose the image of his sin. When Lord Henry came in at six o'clock, he found him crying as one whose heart will break.

It was not till the third day that he ventured to go out. There was

---

1. Last of the new chapters added to this edition by Wilde.
2. A familiar emblematic conceit that allegorists have used since the Middle Ages, especially Edmund Spenser in *The Faerie Queen* 1.

something in the clear, pine-scented air of that winter morning that seemed to bring him back his joyousness and his ardour for life. But it was not merely the physical conditions of environment that had caused the change. His own nature had revolted against the excess of anguish that had sought to maim and mar the perfection of its calm. With subtle and finely-wrought temperaments it is always so. Their strong passions must either bruise or bend. They either slay the man, or themselves die. Shallow sorrows and shallow loves live on. The loves and sorrows that are great are destroyed by their own plenitdue. Besides, he had convinced himself that he had been the victim of a terror-stricken imagination, and looked back now on his fears with something of pity and not a little of contempt.

After breakfast he walked with the Duchess for an hour in the garden, and then drove across the park to join the shooting-party. The crisp frost lay like salt upon the grass. The sky was an inverted cup of blue metal. A thin film of ice bordered the flat reed-grown lake.

At the corner of the pine-wood he caught sight of Sir Geoffrey Clouston, the Duchess's brother, jerking two spent cartridges out of his gun. He jumped from the cart, and having told the groom to take the mare home, made his way towards his guest through the withered bracken and rough undergrowth.

"Have you had good sport, Geoffrey?" he asked.

"Not very good, Dorian. I think most of the birds have gone to the open. I dare say it will be better after lunch, when we get to new ground."

Dorian strolled along by his side. The keen aromatic air, the brown and red lights that glimmered in the wood, the hoarse cries of the beaters ringing out from time to time, and the sharp snaps of the guns that followed, fascinated him, and filled him with a sense of delightful freedom. He was dominated by the carelessness of happiness, by the high indifference of joy.

Suddenly from a lumpy tussock of old grass, some twenty yards in front of them, with black-tipped ears erect, and long hinder limbs throwing it forward, started a hare. It bolted for a thicket of alders. Sir Geoffrey put his gun to his shoulder, but there was something in the animal's grace of movement that strangely charmed Dorian Gray, and he cried out at once, "Don't shoot it, Geoffrey. Let it live."

"What nonsense, Dorian!" laughed his companion, and as the hare bounded into the thicket he fired. There were two cries heard, the cry of a hare in pain, which is dreadful, the cry of a man in agony, which is worse.

"Good heavens! I have hit a beater!" exclaimed Sir Geoffrey. "What an ass the man was to get in front of the guns! Stop shooting there!" he called out at the top of his voice. "A man is hurt."

The head-keeper came running up with a stick in his hand.

"Where, sir? Where is he?" he shouted. At the same time the firing ceased along the line.

"Here," answered Sir Geoffrey, angrily, hurrying towards the thicket. "Why on earth don't you keep your men back? Spoiled my shooting for the day."

Dorian watched them as they plunged into the alder-clump, brushing the lithe, swinging branches aside. In a few moments they emerged, dragging a body after them into the sunlight. He turned away in horror. It seemed to him that misfortune followed wherever he went. He heard Sir Geoffrey ask if the man was really dead, and the affirmative answer of the keeper. The wood seemed to him to have become suddenly alive with faces. There was the trampling of myriad feet, and the low buzz of voices. A great copper-breasted pheasant came beating through the boughs overhead.

After a few moments, that were to him, in his perturbed state, like endless hours of pain, he felt a hand laid on his shoulder. He started, and looked round.

"Dorian," said Lord Henry, "I had better tell them that the shooting is stopped for to-day. It would not look well to go on."

"I wish it were stopped for ever, Harry," he answered bitterly. "The whole thing is hideous and cruel. Is the man . . . ?"

He could not finish the sentence.

"I am afraid so," rejoined Lord Henry. "He got the whole charge of shot in his chest. He must have died almost instantaneously. Come; let us go home."

They walked side by side in the direction of the avenue for nearly fifty yards without speaking. Then Dorian looked at Lord Henry, and said, with a heavy sigh, "It is a bad omen, Harry, a very bad omen."

"What is?" asked Lord Henry. "Oh! this accident, I suppose. My dear fellow, it can't be helped. It was the man's own fault. Why did he get in front of the guns? Besides, it is nothing to us. It is rather awkward for Geoffrey, of course. It does not do to pepper beaters. it makes people think that one is a wild shot. And Geoffrey is not; he shoots very straight. But there is no use talking about the matter."

Dorian shook his head. "It is a bad omen, Harry. I feel as if something horrible were going to happen to some of us. To myself, perhaps," he added, passing his hand over his eyes, with a gesture of pain.

The elder man laughed. "The only horrible thing in the world is *ennui*, Dorian. That is the one sin for which there is no forgiveness. But we are not likely to suffer from it, unless these fellows keep chattering about this thing at dinner. I must tell them that the subject is to be tabooed. As for omens, there is no such thing as an omen. Destiny does not send us heralds. She is too wise or too cruel for that. Besides, what on earth could happen to you, Dorian? You have everything in the world that a man can want. There is no one who would not be delighted to change places with you."

"There is no one with whom I would not change places, Harry. Don't laugh like that. I am telling you the truth. The wretched peasant who has just died is better off than I am. I have no terror of Death. It is the coming of Death that terrifies me. Its monstrous wings seem to wheel in the leaden air around me. Good heavens! don't you see a man moving behind the trees there, watching me, waiting for me?"

Lord Henry looked in the direction in which the trembling gloved hand was pointing. "Yes," he said, smiling, "I see the gardener waiting for you. I suppose he wants to ask you what flowers you wish to have on the table to-night. How absurdly nervous you are, my dear fellow! You must come and see my doctor, when we get back to town."

Dorian heaved a sigh of relief as he saw the gardener approaching The man touched his hat, glanced for a moment at Lord Henry in a hesitating manner, and then produced a letter, which he handed to his master. "Her Grace told me to wait for an answer," he murmured.

Dorian put the letter into his pocket. "Tell her Grace that I am coming in," he said, coldly. The man turned round, and went rapidly in the direction of the house.

"How fond women are of doing dangerous things!" laughed Lord Henry. "It is one of the qualities in them that I admire most. A woman will flirt with anybody in the world as long as other people are looking on."

"How fond you are of saying dangerous things, Harry! In the present instance you are quite astray. I like the Dutchess very much, but I don't love her."

"And the Duchess loves you very much, but she likes you less, so you are excellently matched."

"You are talking scandal, Harry, and there is never basis for scandal."

"The basis of every scandal is an immoral certainty," said Lord Henry, lighting a cigarette.

"You would sacrifice anybody, Harry, for the sake of an epigram."

"The world goes to the altar of its own accord," was the answer.

"I wish I could love," cried Dorian Gray, with a deep note of pathos in his voice. "But I seem to have lost the passion, and forgotten the desire. I am too much concentrated on myself. My own personality has become a burden to me. I want to escape, to go away, to forget. It was silly of me to come down here at all. I think I shall send a wire to Harvey to have the yacht got ready. On a yacht one is safe."

"Safe from what, Dorian? You are in some trouble. Why not tell me what it is? You know I would help you."

"I can't tell you, Harry," he answered, sadly. "And I dare say it is only a fancy of mine. This unfortunate accident has upset me. I have a horrible presentiment that something of the kind may happen to me."

"What nonsense!"

"I hope it is, but I can't help feeling it. Ah! here is the Duchess, looking like Artemis[3] in a tailor-made gown. You see we have come back, Duchess."

3. In Roman mythology, goddess of fertility, twin of Apollo, Artemis frequently appeared dressed in animal hides.

"I have heard all about it, Mr. Gray," she answered. "Poor Geoffrey is terribly upset. And it seems that you asked him not to shoot the hare. How curious!"

"Yes, it was very curious. I don't know what made me say it. Some whim, I suppose. It looked the loveliest of little live things. But I am sorry they told you about the man. It is a hideous subject."

"It is an annoying subject," broke in Lord Henry. "It has no psychological value at all. Now if Geoffrey had done the thing on purpose, how interesting he would be! I should like to know some one who had committed a real murder."

"How horrid of you, Harry!" cried the Duchess. "Isn't it, Mr. Gray? Harry, Mr. Gray is ill again. He is going to faint."

Dorian drew himself up with an effort, and smiled. "It is nothing, Duchess," he murmured; "my nerves are dreadfully out of order. That is all. I am afraid I walked too far this morning. I didn't hear what Harry said. Was it very bad? You must tell me some other time. I think I must go and lie down. You will excuse me, won't you?"

They had reached the great flight of steps that led from the conservatory on to the terrace. As the glass door closed behind Dorian, Lord Henry turned and looked at the Duchess with his slumberous eyes. "Are you very much in love with him?" he asked.

She did not answer for some time, but stood gazing at the landscape. "I wish I knew," she said at last.

He shook his head. "Knowledge would be fatal. It is the uncertainty that charms one. A mist makes things wonderful."

"One may lose one's way."

"All ways end at the same point, my dear Gladys."

"What is that?"

"Disillusion."

"It was my *début* in life," she sighed.

"It came to you crowned."

"I am tired of strawberry leaves."[4]

"They become you."

"Only in public."

"You would miss them," said Lord Henry.

"I will not part with a petal."

"Monmouth has ears."

"Old age is dull of hearing."

"Has he never been jealous?"

"I wish he had been."

He glanced about as if in search of something. "What are you looking for?" she enquired.

"The button from your foil,"[5] he answered. "You have dropped it."

---

4. Since strawberry-leaf images are worked into the design of the coronet, the reference here is to Gladys's title as duchess.

5. The tip on a fencing foil was used to prevent injury during a fencing match. Dueling without the button would be a blood match.

She laughed. "I have still the mask."

"It makes your eyes lovelier," was his reply.

She laughed again. Her teeth showed like white seeds in a scarlet fruit.

Upstairs, in his own room, Dorian Gray was lying on a sofa, with terror in every tingling fibre of his body. Life had suddenly become too hideous a burden for him to bear. The dreadful death of the unlucky beater, shot in the thicket like a wild animal, had seemed to him to prefigure death for himself also. He had nearly swooned at what Lord Henry had said in a chance mood of cynical jesting.

At five o'clock he rang his bell for his servant and gave him orders to pack his things for the night-express to town, and to have the brougham at the door by eight-thirty. He was determined not to sleep another night at Selby Royal. It was an ill-omened place. Death walked there in the sunlight. The grass of the forest had been spotted with blood.

Then he wrote a note to Lord Henry, telling him that he was going up to town to consult his doctor, and asking him to entertain his guests in his absence. As he was putting it into the envelope, a knock came to the door, and his valet informed him that the head-keeper wished to see him. He frowned, and bit his lip. "Send him in," he muttered, after some moments' hesitation.

As soon as the man entered Dorian pulled his cheque-book out of a drawer, and spread it out before him.

"I suppose you have come about the unfortunate accident of this morning, Thornton?" he said, taking up a pen.

"Yes, sir," answered the gamekeeper.

"Was the poor fellow married? Had he any people dependent on him?" asked Dorian, looking bored. "If so, I should not like them to be left in want, and will send them any sum of money you may think necessary."

"We don't know who he is, sir. That is what I took the liberty of coming to you about."

"Don't know who he is?" said Dorian, listlessly. "What do you mean? Wasn't he one of your men?"

"No, sir. Never saw him before. Seems like a sailor, sir."

The pen dropped from Dorian Gray's hand, and he felt as if his heart had suddenly stopped beating. "A sailor?" he cried out. "Did you say a sailor?"

"Yes, sir. He looks as if he had been a sort of sailor; tattooed on both arms, and that kind of thing."

"Was there anything found on him?" said Dorian, leaning forward and looking at the man with startled eyes. "Anything that would tell his name?"

"Some money, sir—not much, and a six-shooter. There was no name of any kind. A decent-looking man, sir, but rough-like. A sort of sailor we think."

Dorian started to his feet. A terrible hope fluttered past him. He clutched at it madly. "Where is the body?" he exclaimed. "Quick! I must see it at once."

"It is in an empty stable at the Home Farm, sir. The folk don't like to have that sort of thing in their houses. They say a corpse brings bad luck."

"The Home Farm! Go there at once and meet me. Tell one of the grooms to bring my horse round. No. Never mind. I'll go to the stables myself. It will save time."

In less than a quarter of an hour Dorian Gray was galloping down the long avenue as hard as he could go. The trees seemed to sweep past him in spectral procession, and wild shadows to fling themselves across his path. Once the mare swerved at a white gate-post and nearly threw him. He lashed her across the neck with his crop. She cleft the dusky air like an arrow. The stones flew from her hoofs.

At least he reached the Home Farm. Two men were loitering in the yard. He leapt from the saddle and threw the reins to one of them. In the farthest stable a light was glimmering. Something seemed to tell him that the body was there, and he hurried to the door, and put his hand upon the latch.

There he paused for a moment, feeling that he was on the brink of a discovery that would either make or mar his life. Then he thrust the door open, and entered.

On a heap of sacking in the far corner was lying the dead body of a man dressed in a coarse shirt and a pair of blue trousers. A spotted handkerchief had been placed over the face. A coarse candle, stuck in a bottle, sputtered beside it.

Dorian Gray shuddered. He felt that his could not be the hand to take the handkerchief away, and called out to one of the farm-servants to come to him.

"Take that thing off the face. I wish to see it," he said, clutching at the doorpost for support.

When the farm-servant had done so, he stepped forward. A cry of joy broke from his lips. The man who had been shot in the thicket was James Vane.

He stood there for some minutes looking at the dead body. As he rode home, his eyes were full of tears, for he knew he was safe.

Chapter XIX. [1]

"There is no use your telling me that you are going to be good," cried Lord Henry, dipping his white fingers into a red copper bowl filled with rose-water. "You are quite perfect. Pray, don't change."

Dorian Gray shook his head. "No, Harry, I have done too many

---

1. Wilde divided the last chapter of the *Lippincott's* edition (13), made some additions and other changes, and turned it into the two last chapters of this edition.

dreadful things in my life. I am not going to do any more. I began my good actions yesterday."

"Where were you yesterday?"

"In the country, Harry. I was staying at a little inn by myself."

"My dear boy," said Lord Henry, smiling, "anybody can be good in the country. There are no temptations there. That is the reason why people who live out of town are so absolutely uncivilized. Civilization is not by any means an easy thing to attain to. There are only two ways by which man can reach it. One is by being cultured, the other by being corrupt. Country people have no opportunity of being either, so they stagnate."

"Culture and corruption," echoed Dorian. "I have known something of both. It seems terrible to me now that they should ever be found together. For I have a new ideal, Harry. I am going to alter. I think I have altered."

"You have not yet told me what your good action was. Or did you say you had done more than one?" asked his companion, as he split into his plate a little crimson pyramid of seeded strawberries, and through a perforated shell-shaped spoon snowed white sugar upon them.

"I can tell you, Harry. It is not a story I could tell to any one else. I spared somebody. It sounds vain, but you understand what I mean. She was quite beautiful, and wonderfully like Sibyl Vane. I think it was that which first attracted me to her. You remember Sibyl, don't you? How long ago that seems! Well, Hetty was not one of our own class of course. She was simply a girl in a village. But I really loved her. I am quite sure that I loved her. All during this wonderful May that we have been having, I used to run down and see her two or three times a week. Yesterday she met me in a little orchard. The apple-blossoms kept tumbling down on her hair, and she was laughing. We were to have gone away together this morning at dawn. Suddenly I determined to leave her as flower-like as I had found her."

"I should think the novelty of the emotion must have given you a thrill of real pleasure, Dorian," interrupted Lord Henry. "But I can finish your idyll for you. You gave her good advice, and broke her heart. That was the beginning of your reformation."

"Harry, you are horrible! You mustn't say these dreadful things. Hetty's heart is not broken. Of course she cried, and all that. But there is no disgrace upon her. She can live, like Perdita,[2] in her garden of mint and marigold."

"And weep over a faithless Florizel,"[3] said Lord Henry, laughing, as he leant back in his chair. "My dear Dorian, you have the most curiously boyish moods. Do you think this girl will ever be really contented

2. Daughter of Leontes and Hermione in Shakespeare's A *Winter's Tale*, Perdita was abandoned by her parents.
3. In A *Winter's Tale*, the son of King Polixenes who falls in love with Perdita, a supposed shepherdess. Florizel, however, remains faithful, and after several misadventures, the impediments are removed and the lovers marry.

now with any one of her own rank? I suppose she will be married some day to a rough carter or a grinning ploughman. Well, the fact of having met you, and loved you, will teach her to despise her husband, and she will be wretched. From a moral point of view, I cannot say that I think much of your great renunciation. Even as a beginning, it is poor. Besides, how do you know that Hetty isn't floating at the present moment in some star-lit mill-pond, with lovely water-lilies round her, like Ophelia?"

"I can't bear this, Harry! You mock at everything, and then suggest the most serious tragedies. I am sorry I told you now. I don't care what you say to me. I know I was right in acting as I did. Poor Hetty! As I rode past the farm this morning, I saw her white face at the window, like a spray of jasmine. Don't let us talk about it any more, and don't try to persuade me that the first good action I have done for years, the first little bit of self-sacrifice I have ever known, is really a sort of sin. I want to be better. I am going to be better. Tell me something about yourself. What is going on in town? I have not been to the club for days."

"The people are still discussing poor Basil's disappearance."

"I should have thought they had got tired of that by this time," said Dorian, pouring himself out some wine, and frowning slightly.

"My dear boy, they have only been talking about it for six weeks, and the British public are really not equal to the mental strain of having more than one topic every three months. They have been very fortunate lately, however. They have had my own divorce-case, and Alan Campbell's suicide. Now they have got the mysterious disappearance of an artist. Scotland Yard still insists that the man in the grey ulster who left for Paris by the midnight train on the ninth of November was poor Basil, and the French police declare that Basil never arrived in Paris at all. I suppose in about a fortnight we shall be told that he has been seen in San Francisco. It is an odd thing, but every one who disappears is said to be seen at San Francisco. It must be a delightful city, and possess all the attractions of the next world."[4]

"What do you think has happened to Basil?" asked Dorian, holding up his Burgundy against the light, and wondering how it was that he could discuss the matter so calmly.

"I have not the slightest idea. If Basil chooses to hide himself, it is no business of mine. If he is dead, I don't want to think about him. Death is the only thing that ever terrifies me. I hate it."

"Why?" said the younger man, wearily.

"Because," said Lord Henry, passing beneath his nostrils the gilt trellis of an open vinaigrette[5] box, "one can survive everything nowadays except that. Death and vulgarity are the only two facts in the nineteenth century that one cannot explain away. Let us have our coffee in the music-room, Dorian. You must play Chopin to me. The man with whom my

4. Wilde visited San Francisco in 1883 during his American lecture tour. The reference to the attractions of the other world is likely an ironic ref-erence to Hades or the underworld.
5. Aromatic salts.

wife ran away played Chopin[6] exquisitely. Poor Victoria! I was very fond of her. The house is rather lonely without her. Of course married life is merely a habit, a bad habit. But then one regrets the loss even of one's worst habits. Perhaps one regrets them the most. They are such an essential part of one's personality."

Dorian said nothing, but rose from the table, and, passing into the next room, sat down to the piano and let his fingers stray across the white and black ivory of the keys. After the coffee had been brought in, he stopped, and looking over at Lord Henry, said, "Harry, did it ever occur to you that Basil was murdered?"

"Lord Henry yawned. "Basil was very popular, and always wore a Waterbury watch.[7] Why should he have been murdered? He was not clever enough to have enemies. Of course he had a wonderful genius for painting. But a man can paint like Velasquez[8] and yet be as dull as possible. Basil was really rather dull. He only interested me once, and that was when he told me, years ago, that he had a wild adoration for you, and that you were the dominant motive of his art."

"I was very fond of Basil," said Dorian, with a note of sadness in his voice. "But don't people say that he was murdered?"

"Oh, some of the papers do. It does not seem to me to be at all probable. I know there are dreadful places in Paris, but Basil was not the sort of man to have gone to them. He had no curiosity. It was his chief defect."

"What would you say, Harry, if I told you that I had murdered Basil?" said the younger man. He watched him intently after he had spoken.

"I would say, my dear fellow, that you were posing for a character that doesn't suit you. All crime is vulgar, just as all vulgarity is crime. It is not in you, Dorian, to commit a murder. I am sorry if I hurt your vanity by saying so, but I assure you it is true. Crime belongs exclusively to the lower orders. I don't blame them in the smallest degree. I should fancy that crime was to them what art is to us, simply a method of procuring extraordinary sensations."

"A method of procuring sensations? Do you think, then, that a man who has once committed a murder could possibly do the same crime again? Don't tell me that."

"Oh! anything becomes a pleasure if one does it too often," cried Lord Henry, laughing. "That is one of the most important secrets of life. I should fancy, however, that murder is always a mistake. One should never do anything that one cannot talk about after dinner. But let us pass from poor Basil. I wish I could believe that he had come to such a really romantic end as you suggest; but I can't. I dare say he fell into the Seine off an omnibus, and that the conductor hushed up the scandal.

---

6. Frederic Chopin (1810–49) was one of Wilde's favorite piano composers, referred to frequently in his writing from the early poetry to *De Profundis*.
7. An inexpensive pocket watch, hence of little interest to a thief.
8. Diego Rodríguez de Silva y Velásquez (1599–1660), the great Spanish painter much admired by Wilde.

Yes: I should fancy that was his end. I see him lying now on his back under those dull-green waters with the heavy barges floating over him, and long weeds catching in his hair. Do you know, I don't think he would have done much more good work. During the last ten years his painting had gone off very much."

Dorian heaved a sigh, and Lord Henry strolled across the room and began to stroke the head of a curious Java parrot, a large grey-plumaged bird, with pink crest and tail, that was balancing itself up a bamboo perch. As his pointed fingers touched it, it dropped the white scurf of crinkled lids over black glass-like eyes, and began to sway backwards and forwards.

"Yes," he continued, turning round, and taking his handkerchief out of his pocket; "his painting had quite gone off. It seemed to me to have lost something. It had lost an ideal. When you and he ceased to be great friends, he ceased to be a great artist. What was it separated you? I suppose he bored you. If so, he never forgave you. It's a habit bores have. By the way, what has become of that wonderful portrait he did of you? I don't think I have ever seen it since he finished it. Oh! I remember your telling me years ago that you had sent it down to Selby, and that it had got mislaid or stolen on the way. You never got it back? What a pity! It was really a masterpiece. I remember I wanted to buy it. I wish I had now. It belonged to Basil's best period. Since then, his work was that curious mixture of bad painting and good intentions that always entitles a man to be called a representative British artist. Did you advertise for it? You should."

"I forget," said Dorian. "I suppose I did. But I never really liked it. I am sorry I sat for it. The memory of the thing is hateful to me. Why do you talk of it? It used to remind me of those curious lines in some play— 'Hamlet,' I think—how do they run?—

> " 'Like the painting of a sorrow,
> A face without a heart.' [9]

Yes: that is what it was like."

Lord Henry laughed. "If a man treats life artistically, his brain is his heart," he answered, sinking into an arm-chair.

Dorian Gray shook his head, and struck some soft chords on the piano. " 'Like the painting of a sorrow,' " he repeated, " 'a face without a heart.' "

The elder man lay back and looked at him with half-closed eyes. "By the way, Dorian," he said, after a pause, " 'what does it profit a man if he gain the whole world and lose—how does the quotation run?—his own soul'?" [1]

The music jarred and Dorian Gray started, and stared at his friend. "Why do you ask me that, Harry?"

9. *Hamlet* 4.7.108–9. The lines spoken by King Claudius are part of a question: "Laertes, was your father dear to you? / Or are you like the painting of a sorrow, / A face without a heart?"

1. Mark 8.36.

"My dear fellow," said Lord Henry, elevating his eyebrows in surprise, "I asked you because I thought you might be able to give me an answer. That is all. I was going through the Park last Sunday, and close by the Marble Arch there stood a little crowd of shabby-looking people listening to some vulgar street-preacher. As I passed by, I heard the man yelling out that question to his audience. It struck me as being rather dramatic. London is very rich in curious effects of that kind. A wet Sunday, an uncouth Christian in a mackintosh, a ring of sickly white faces under a broken roof of dripping umbrellas, and a wonderful phrase flung into the air by shrill, hysterical lips—it was really very good in its way, quite a suggestion. I thought of telling the prophet that Art had a soul, but that man had not. I am afraid, however, he would not have understood me."

"Don't, Harry. The soul is a terrible reality. It can be bought, and sold, and bartered away. It can be poisoned, or made perfect. There is a soul in each one of us. I know it."

"Do you feel quite sure of that, Dorian?"

"Quite sure."

"Ah! then it must be an illusion. The things one feels absolutely certain about are never true. That is the fatality of Faith, and the lesson of Romance. How grave you are! Don't be so serious. What have you or I to do with the superstitions of our age? No: we have given up our belief in the soul. Play me something. Play me a nocturne, Dorian, and, as you play, tell me, in a low voice, how you have kept your youth. You must have some secret. I am only ten years older than you are, and I am wrinkled, and worn, and yellow. You are really wonderful, Dorian. You have never looked more charming than you do to-night. You remind me of the day I saw you first. You were rather cheeky, very shy, and absolutely extraordinary. You have changed, of course, but not in appearance. I wish you would tell me your secret. To get back my youth I would do anything in the world, except take exercise, get up early, or be respectable. Youth! There is nothing like it. It's absurd to talk of the ignorance of youth. The only people to whose opinions I listen now with any respect are people much younger than myself. They seem in front of me. Life has revealed to them her latest wonder. As for the aged, I always contradict the aged. I do it on principle. If you ask them their opinion on something that happened yesterday, they solemnly give you the opinions current in 1820, when people wore high stocks,[2] believed in everything, and knew absolutely nothing. How lovely that thing you are playing is! I wonder did Chopin write it at Majorca,[3] with the sea weeping round the villa, and the salt spray dashing against the panes? It is marvellously romantic. What a blessing it is that there is one art left to us that is not imitative! Don't stop. I want music to-night. It seems to

2. Neckcloths, worn in the reign of George IV (1820–30).
3. Chopin lived there with George Sand (Aman-

dine Dupin) during their romance and wrote some of his finest and most tempestuous music during that time.

me that you are the young Apollo, and that I am Marsyas[4] listening to you. I have sorrows, Dorian, of my own, that even you know nothing of. The tragedy of old age is not that one is old, but that one is young. I am amazed sometimes at my own sincerity. Ah, Dorian, how happy you are! What an exquisite life you have led! You have drunk deeply of everything. You have crushed the grapes against your palate. Nothing has been hidden from you. And it has all been to you no more than the sound of music.[5] It has not marred you. You are still the same."

"I am not the same, Harry."

"Yes: you are the same. I wonder what the rest of your life will be. Don't spoil it by renunciations. At present you are a perfect type. Don't make yourself incomplete. You are quite flawless now. You need not shake your head: you know you are. Besides, Dorian, don't deceive yourself. Life is not governed by will or intention. Life is a question of nerves, and fibres, and slowly built-up cells in which thought hides itself and passion has its dreams.[6] You may fancy yourself safe, and think yourself strong. But a chance tone of colour in a room or a morning sky, a particular perfume that you had once loved and that brings subtle memories with it, a line from a forgotten poem that you had come across again, a cadence from a piece of music that you had ceased to play—I tell you, Dorian, that it is on things like these that our lives depend. Browning writes about that somewhere;[7] but our own senses will imagine them for us. There are moments when the odour of *lilas blanc* passes suddenly across me, and I have to live the strangest month of my life over again. I wish I could change places with you, Dorian. The world has cried out against us both, but it has always worshipped you. It always will worship you. You are the type of what the age is searching for, and what it is afraid it has found. I am so glad that you have never done anything, never carved a statue, or painted a picture, or produced anything outside of yourself! Life has been your art. You have set yourself to music. Your days are your sonnets."

Dorian rose up from the piano, and passed his hand through his hair. "Yes, life has been exquisite," he murmured, "but I am not going to have the same life, Harry. And you must not say these extravagant things to me. You don't know everything about me. I think that if you did, even you would turn from me. You laugh. Don't laugh."

"Why have you stopped playing, Dorian? Go back and give me the

---

4. Marsyas was a minor diety who challenged Apollo to a musical contest of skill. His punishment for presumption was to be flayed alive by the god. Marsyas was adopted by the Decadents as a sort of aesthetic Prometheus, symbolizing their own rebellious artistic practice.

5. An echo of Pater, who compares the world's thought and experiences to "the sound of lyres and flutes" that lives only in the expression of Mona Lisa's face and hands (see p. 307). In this as in so many other instances, Lord Henry reveals how lit-

tle he understands his protégé.

6. Perhaps to emphasize the autobiographical parallels in this scene, Lord Henry's speech on art and life here and elsewhere is a pastiche of Pater's writing. Here especially, it echoes "Leonardo Da Vinci" from *The Renaissance* (see p. 304).

7. A recurrent theme in Browning's poetry, appearing in "A Toccata of Galuppi's" and more obliquely in "Bishop Blougram's Apology," lines 183–86.

8. See p. 28.

nocturne over again. Look at that great honey-coloured moon that hangs in the dusky air. She is waiting for you to charm her, and if you play she will come closer to the earth. You won't? Let us go to the club, then. It has been a charming evening, and we must end it charmingly. There is some one at White's[8] who wants immensely to know you— young Lord Poole, Bournemouth's eldest son. He has already copied your neckties, and has begged me to introduce him to you. He is quite delightful, and rather reminds me of you."

"I hope not," said Dorian, with a sad look in his eyes. "But I am tired to-night, Harry. I sha'n't go to the club. It is nearly eleven, and I want to go to bed early."

"Do stay. You have never played so well as to-night. There was something in your touch that was wonderful. It had more expression than I had ever heard from it before."

"It is because I am going to be good," he answered, smiling. "I am a little changed already."

"You cannot change to me, Dorian," said Lord Henry. "You and I will always be friends."

"Yet you poisoned me with a book once. I should not forgive that. Harry, promise me that you will never lend that book to any one. It does harm."

"My dear boy, you are really beginning to moralize. You will soon be going about like the converted, and the revivalist, warning people against all the sins of which you have grown tired. You are much too delightful to do that. Besides, it is no use. You and I are what we are, and will be what we will be. As for being poisoned by a book, there is no such thing as that. Art has no influence upon action. It annihilates the desire to act. It is superbly sterile. The books that the world calls immoral are books that show the world its own shame. That is all.[9] But we won't discuss literature. Come round to-morrow. I am going to ride at eleven. We might go together, and I will take you to lunch afterwards with Lady Branksome. She is a charming woman, and wants to consult you about some tapestries she is thinking of buying. Mind you come. Or shall we lunch with our little Duchess? She says she never sees you now. Perhaps you are tired of Gladys? I thought you would be. Her clever tongue gets on one's nerves. Well, in any case, be here at eleven."

"Must I really come, Harry?"

"Certainly. The Park is quite lovely now. I don't think there have been such lilacs since the year I met you."

"Very well. I shall be here at eleven," said Dorian. "Good-night, Harry." As he reached the door he hesitated for a moment, as if he had something more to say. Then he sighed and went out.

---

8. See p. 28.
9. Wilde took a similar line at his first trial in

defending *Dorian Gray* against charges of its alleged pernicious influence.

Chapter XX.

It was a lovely night, so warm that he threw his coat over his arm, and did not even put his silk scarf round his throat. As he strolled home, smoking his cigarette, two young men in evening dress passed him. He heard one of them whisper to the other, "That is Dorian Gray." He remembered how pleased he used to be when he was pointed out, or stared at, or talked about. He was tired of hearing his own name now. Half the charm of the little village where he had been so often lately was that no one knew who he was. He had often told the girl whom he had lured to love him that he was poor, and she believed him. He had told her once that he was wicked, and she had laughed at him, and answered that wicked people were always very old and very ugly. What a laugh she had!—just like a thrush singing. And how pretty she had been in her cotton dresses and her large hats! She knew nothing, but she had everything that he had lost.

When he reached home, he found his servant waiting up for him. He sent him to bed, and threw himself down on the sofa in the library, and began to think over some of the things that Lord Henry had said to him.

Was it really true that one could never change? He felt a wild longing for the unstained purity of his boyhood—his rose-white boyhood, as Lord Henry had once called it. He knew that he had tarnished himself, filled his mind with corruption and given horror to his fancy; that he had been an evil influence to others, and had experienced a terrible joy in being so; and that of the lives that had crossed his own it had been the fairest and the most full of promise that he had brought to shame. But was it all irretrievable? Was there no hope for him?

Ah! in what a monstrous moment of pride and passion he had prayed that the portrait should bear the burden of his days, and he keep the unsullied splendour of eternal youth! All his failure had been due to that. Better for him that each sin of his life had brought its sure, swift penalty along with it. There was purification in punishment. Not "Forgive us our sins" but "Smite us for our iniquities" should be the prayer of man to a most just God.

The curiously-carved mirror that Lord Henry had given to him, so many years ago now, was standing on the table, and the white-limbed Cupids laughed round as of old. He took it up, as he had done on that night of horror, when he had first noted the change in the fatal picture, and with wild tear-dimmed eyes looked into its polished shield. Once, some one who had terribly loved him, had written to him a mad letter, ending with these idolatrous words: "The world is changed because you are made of ivory and gold. The curves of your lips rewrite history." The phrases came back to his memory, and he repeated them over and over to himself. Then he loathed his own beauty, and flinging the mirror on the floor crushed it into silver splinters beneath his heel. It was his beauty that had ruined him, his beauty and the youth that he had prayed for. But for those two things, his life might have been free from stain. His beauty had been to him but a mask, his youth but a mockery. What was youth at best? A green, an unripe time, a time of shallow moods, and sickly thoughts. Why had he worn its livery? Youth had spoiled him.

It was better not to think of the past. Nothing could alter that. It was of himself, and of his own future, that he had to think. James Vane was hidden in a nameless grave in Selby churchyard. Alan Campbell had shot himself one night in his laboratory, but had not revealed the secret that he had been forced to know. The excitement, such as it was, over Basil Hallward's disappearance would soon pass away. It was already waning. He was perfectly safe there. Nor, indeed, was it the death of Basil Hallward that weighed most upon his mind. It was the living death of his own soul that troubled him. Basil had painted the portrait that had marred his life. He could not forgive him that. It was the portrait that had done everything. Basil had said things to him that were unbearable, and that he had yet borne with patience. The murder had been simply the madness of a moment. As for Alan Campbell, his suicide had been his own act. He had chosen to do it. It was nothing to him.

A new life! That was what he wanted. That was what he was waiting for. Surely he had begun it already. He had spared one innocent thing, at any rate. He would never again tempt innocence. He would be good.

As he thought of Hetty Merton, he began to wonder if the portrait in the locked room had changed. Surely it was not still so horrible as it had been? Perhaps if his life became pure, he would be able to expel every sign of evil passion from the face. Perhaps the signs of evil had already gone away. He would go and look.

He took the lamp from the table and crept upstairs. As he unbarred the door, a smile of joy flitted across his strangely young-looking face and lingered for a moment about his lips. Yes, he would be good, and the hideous thing that he had hidden away would no longer be a terror to him. He felt as if the load had been lifted from him already.

He went in quietly, locking the door behind him, as was his custom, and dragged the purple hanging from the portrait. A cry of pain and indignation broke from him. He could see no change, save that in the eyes there was a look of cunning, and in the mouth the curved wrinkle of the hypocrite. The thing was still loathsome—more loathsome, if possible, than before—and the scarlet dew that spotted the hand seemed brighter, and more like blood newly spilt. Then he trembled. Had it been merely vanity that had made him do his one good deed? Or the desire for a new sensation, as Lord Henry had hinted, with his mocking laugh? Or that passion to act a part that sometimes makes us do things finer than we are ourselves? Or, perhaps, all these? And why was the red stain larger than it had been? It seemed to have crept like a horrible disease over the wrinkled fingers. There was blood on the painted feet, as though the thing had dripped—blood even on the hand that had not held the knife. Confess? Did it mean that he was to confess? To give himself up, and be put to death? He laughed. He felt that the idea was monstrous. Besides, even if he did confess, who would believe him? There was no trace of the murdered man anywhere. Everything belonging to him had been destroyed. He himself had burned what had been below-stairs. The world would simply say that he was mad. They would shut him up if he persisted in his story. . . . Yet it was his duty to confess, to suffer public shame, and to make public atonement. There was a God who called upon men to tell their sins to earth as well as to heaven. Nothing that he could do would cleanse him till he had told his own sin. His sin? He shrugged his shoulders. The death of Basil Hallward seemed very little to him. He was thinking of Hetty Merton. For it was an unjust mirror, this mirror of his soul that he was looking at. Vanity? Curiosity? Hypocrisy? Had there been nothing more in his renunciation than that? There had been something more. At least he thought so. But who could tell? . . . No. There had been nothing more. Through vanity he had spared her. In hypocrisy he had worn the mask of goodness. For curiosity's sake he had tried the denial of self. He recognized that now.[1]

But this murder—was it to dog him all his life? Was he always to be burdened by his past? Was he really to confess? Never. There was only one bit of evidence left against him. The picture itself—that was evidence. He would destroy it. Why had he kept it so long? Once it had given him pleasure to watch it changing and growing old. Of late he had felt no such pleasure. It had kept him awake at night. When he had been away, he had been filled with terror lest other eyes should look upon it. It had brought melancholy across his passions. Its mere memory had marred many moments of joy. It had been like conscience to him. Yes, it had been conscience. He would destroy it.

He looked round, and saw the knife that had stabbed Basil Hallward. He had cleaned it many times, till there was no stain left upon it. It was bright, and glistened. As it had killed the painter, so it would kill the painter's work, and all that that meant. It would kill the past, and when that was dead he would be free. It would kill this monstrous soul-life, and without its hideous warnings, he would be at peace.[2] He seized the thing, and stabbed the picture with it.

There was a cry heard, and a crash. The cry was so horrible in its agony that the frightened servants woke, and crept out of their rooms. Two gentlemen, who were passing in the Square below, stopped, and looked up at the great house. They walked on till they met a policeman, and brought him back. The man rang the bell several times, but there was no answer. Except for a light in one of the top windows, the house was all dark. After a time, he went away, and stood in an adjoining portico and watched.

1. Wilde added the lines beginning "No. There had been nothing more . . ." to the end of the paragraph in this edition.

2. Wilde added this sentence to this edition.

"Whose house is that, constable?" asked the elder of the two gentlemen.

"Mr. Dorian Gray's, sir," answered the policeman.

They looked at each other, as they walked away, and sneered. One of
them was Sir Henry Ashtons' uncle.

Inside, in the servants' part of the house, the half-clad domestics were
talking in low whispers to each other. Old Mrs. Leaf was crying, and
wringing her hands. Francis was as pale as death.

After about a quarter of an hour, he got the coachman and one of the
footmen and crept upstairs. They knocked, but there was no reply. They
called out. Everything was still. Finally, after vainly trying to force the
door, they got on the roof, and dropped down on to the balcony. The
windows yielded easily: their bolts were old.

When they entered, they found hanging upon the wall a splendid
portrait of their master as they had last seen him, in all the wonder of
his exquisite youth and beauty. Lying on the floor was a dead man, in
evening dress, with a knife in his heart. He was withered, wrinkled, and
loathsome of visage. It was not till they had examined the rings that they
recognized who it was.

LIPPINCOTT'S
MONTHLY MAGAZINE.

JULY, 1890.   Containing

THE PICTURE OF DORIAN GRAY:
A COMPLETE NOVEL
BY OSCAR WILDE.

LONDON:

WARD, LOCK, AND CO., Salisbury Square, E.C.
J. B. LIPPINCOTT COMPANY, PHILADELPHIA.

The Picture of Dorian Gray (1890)

Chapter I.

The studio was filled with the rich odor of roses, and when the light summer wind stirred amidst the trees of the garden there came through the open door the heavy scent of the lilac, or the more delicate perfume of the pink-flowering thorn.

From the corner of the divan of Persian saddle-bags on which he was lying, smoking, as usual,[1] innumerable cigarettes, Lord Henry Wotton could just catch the gleam of the honey-sweet and honey-colored blossoms of the laburnum, whose tremulous branches seemed hardly able to bear the burden of a beauty so flame-like as theirs; and now and then the fantastic shadows of birds in flight flitted across the long tussore-silk curtains that were stretched in front of the huge window, producing a kind of momentary Japanese effect, and making him think of those pallid jade-faced painters who, in an art that is necessarily immobile,[2] seek to convey the sense of swiftness and motion. The sullen murmur of the bees shouldering their way through the long unmown grass, or circling with monotonous insistence round the black-crocketed spires of the early June hollyhocks,[3] seemed to make the stillness more oppressive, and the dim roar of London was like the bourdon note of a distant organ.

In the centre of the room, clamped to an upright easel, stood the full-length portrait of a young man of extraordinary personal beauty, and in front of it, some little distance away, was sitting the artist himself, Basil Hallward, whose sudden disappearance some years ago caused, at the time, such public excitement, and gave rise to so many strange conjectures.

As he looked at the gracious and comely form he had so skilfully mirrored in his art, a smile of pleasure passed across his face, and seemed about to linger there. But he suddenly started up, and, closing his eyes, placed his fingers upon the lids, as though he sought to imprison within his brain some curious dream from which he feared he might awake.

"It is your best work, Basil, the best thing you have ever done," said

---

1. Changed to "as was his custom" in 1891.
2. Several refinements are made in this description in 1891.

3. "black-crocketed . . . hollyhocks" changed to "dusty gilt horns of the straggling woodbine" in 1891.

Lord Henry, languidly. "You must certainly send it next year to the Grosvenor. The Academy is too large and too vulgar. The Grosvenor is the only place."[4]

"I don't think I will[5] send it anywhere," he answered, tossing his head back in that odd way that used to make his friends laugh at him at Oxford. "No: I won't send it anywhere."[6]

Lord Henry elevated his eyebrows, and looked at him in amazement through the thin blue wreaths of smoke that curled up in such fanciful whorls from his heavy opium-tainted cigarette. "Not send it anywhere? My dear fellow, why? Have you any reason? What odd chaps you painters are! You do anything in the world to gain a reputation. As soon as you have one, you seem to want to throw it away. It is silly of you, for there is only one thing in the world worse than being talked about, and that is not being talked about. A portrait like this would set you far above all the young men in England, and make the old men quite jealous, if old men are ever capable of any emotion."

"I know you will laugh at me," he replied, "but I really can't exhibit it. I have put too much of myself into it."

Lord Henry stretched his long legs out on the divan and shook with laughter.[7]

"Yes, I knew you would laugh; but it is quite true, all the same."

"Too much of yourself in it! Upon my word, Basil, I didn't know you were so vain; and I really can't see any resemblance between you, with your rugged strong face and your coal-black hair, and this young Adonis, who looks as if he was made of ivory and rose-leaves. Why, my dear Basil, he is a Narcissus and you—well, of course you have an intellectual expression, and all that. But beauty, real beauty, ends where an intellectual expression begins. Intellect is in itself an exaggeration,[8] and destroys the harmony of any face. The moment one sits down to think, one becomes all nose, or all forehead, or something horrid. Look at the successful men in any of the learned professions. How perfectly hideous they are! Except, of course, in the Church. But then in the Church they don't think. A bishop keeps on saying at the age of eighty what he was told to say when he was a boy of eighteen, and consequently[9] he always looks absolutely delightful. Your mysterious young friend, whose name you have never told me, but whose picture really fascinates me, never thinks. I feel quite sure of that. He is a brainless, beautiful thing, who should be always here in winter when we have no flowers to look at, and always here in summer when we want something to chill our intelligence. Don't flatter yourself, Basil: you are not in the least like him."

"You don't understand me, Harry. Of course I am not like him. I know

---

4. This last sentence omitted in 1891.
5. Wilde wrote Coulson Kernahan, editor of the revised edition for Ward, Lock and Company, asking that he "look after my 'wills' and 'shalls' in proof," explaining that his "usage was Celtic not English" (*Letters* 289).
6. TS has "and yet, you are quite right about it. It is my best work."
7. This sentence slightly altered in 1891.
8. Changed to "a mode of exaggeration" in 1891.
9. Changed to "as a natural consequence" in 1891.

that perfectly well. Indeed, I should be sorry to look like him. You shrug your shoulders? I am telling you the truth. There is a fatality about all physical and intellectual distinction, the sort of fatality that seems to dog through history the faltering steps of kings.[1] It is better not to be different from one's fellows. The ugly and the stupid have the best of it in this world. They can sit quietly and gape at the play. If they know nothing of victory, they are at least spared the knowledge of defeat. They live as we all should live, undisturbed, indifferent, and without disquiet. They neither bring ruin upon others nor ever receive it from alien hands. Your rank and wealth, Harry; my brains, such as they are,—my fame,[2] whatever it may be worth; Dorian Gray's good looks,—we will all suffer for what the gods have given us, suffer terribly."

"Dorian Gray? is that his name?" said Lord Henry, walking across the studio towards Basil Hallward.

"Yes; that is his name. I didn't intend to tell it to you."

"But why not?"

"Oh, I can't explain. When I like people immensely I never tell their names to any one. It seems like surrendering a part of them. You know how I love secrecy. It is the only thing that can make modern life wonderful or mysterious to us.[3] The commonest thing is delightful if one only hides it. When I leave town I never tell my people where I am going. If I did, I would lose all my pleasure. It is a silly habit, I dare say, but somehow it seems to bring a great deal of romance into one's life. I suppose you think me awfully foolish about it?"

"Not at all," answered Lord Henry, laying his hand upon his shoulder;[4] "not at all, my dear Basil. You seem to forget that I am married, and the one charm of marriage is that it makes a life of deception necessary for both parties. I never know where my wife is, and my wife never knows what I am doing. When we meet,—we do meet occasionally, when we dine out together, or go down to the duke's,—we tell each other the most absurd stories with the most serious faces. My wife is very good at it,—much better, in fact, than I am. She never gets confused over her dates, and I always do. But when she does find me out, she makes no row at all. I sometimes wish she would; but she merely laughs at me."

"I hate the way you talk about your married life, Harry," said Basil Hallward, shaking his hand off,[5] and strolling towards the door that led into the garden. "I believe that you are really a very good husband, but that you are thoroughly ashamed of your own virtues. You are an extraordinary fellow. You never say a moral thing, and you never do a wrong thing. Your cynicism is simply a pose."

"Being natural is simply a pose, and the most irritating pose I know,"

1. MS has "to dog the steps of kings."
2. Changed to "art" in 1891.
3. Wilde made four stylistic changes in the first four lines of this paragraph in 1891.
4. "laying . . . shoulder" deleted in 1891. This is the first of many such deletions or rewrites eliminating descriptions of physical contact suggestive of homoerotic behavior.
5. "shaking . . . off" deleted in 1891.

cried Lord Henry, laughing; and the two young men went out into the garden together, and for a time they did not speak.[6]

After a long pause Lord Henry pulled out his watch. "I am afraid I must be going, Basil," he murmured, "and before I go I insist on your answering a question I put to you some time ago."

"What is that?" asked Basil Hallward, keeping his eyes fixed on the ground.

"You know quite well."

"I do not, Harry."

"Well, I will tell you what it is."

"Please don't."[7]

"I must. I want you to explain to me why you won't exhibit Dorian Gray's picture. I want the real reason."

"I told you the real reason."

"No, you did not. You said it was because there was too much of yourself in it. Now, that is childish."

"Harry," said Basil Hallward, looking him straight in the face,[8] "every portrait that is painted with feeling[9] is a portrait of the artist, not of the sitter. The sitter is merely the accident, the occasion. It is not he who is revealed by the painter; it is rather the painter who, on the colored canvas, reveals himself. The reason I will not exhibit this picture is that I am afraid that I have shown with it the secret of my own soul."

Lord Harry laughed. "And what is that?" he asked.

"I will tell you," said Hallward; and an expression of perplexity came over his face.

"I am all expectation, Basil," murmured his companion, looking at him.

"Oh, there is really very little to tell, Harry," answered the young painter; "and I am afraid you will hardly understand it. Perhaps you will hardly believe it."

Lord Henry smiled, and, leaning down, plucked a pink-petalled daisy from the grass, and examined it. "I am quite sure I shall understand it," he replied, gazing intently at the little golden white-feathered disk,[1] "and I can believe anything, provided that it is incredible."

The wind shook some blossoms from the trees, and the heavy lilac-blooms, with their clustering stars, moved to and fro in the languid air. A grasshopper began to chirrup in the grass, and a long thin dragon-fly floated by on its brown gauze wings.[2] Lord Henry felt as if he could hear Basil Hallward's heart beating, and he wondered what was coming.

"Well, this is incredible," repeated Hallward, rather bitterly,—

---

6. Wilde changed the last phrase in 1891.
7. This sentence and Henry's "I must" deleted in 1891.
8. Wilde canceled the phrase "taking hold of his hand" in MS.
9. Wilde changed the original "passion" to "feel-ing" in MS.

1. Wilde deleted "that had charmed all the poets from Chaucer to Tennyson" in MS and modified the style of the epigram following in 1891. The epigram appeared written in TS.
2. Several stylistic changes made here in 1891.

"incredible to me at times. I don't know what it means.[3] The story is simply this. Two months ago I went to a crush at Lady Brandon's. You know we poor painters have to show ourselves in society from time to time, just to remind the public that we are not savages. With an evening coat and a white tie, as you told me once, anybody, even a stock-broker, can gain a reputation for being civilized. Well, after I had been in the room about ten minutes, talking to huge overdressed dowagers and tedious Academicians, I suddenly became conscious that some one was looking at me. I turned half-way round, and saw Dorian Gray for the first time. When our eyes met, I felt that I was growing pale. A curious instinct of terror came over me. I knew that I had come face to face with some one whose mere personality was so fascinating that, if I allowed it to do so, it would absorb my whole nature, my whole soul, my very art itself. I did not want any external influence in my life. You know yourself, Harry, how independent I am by nature. My father destined me for the army. I insisted on going to Oxford. Then he made me enter my name at the Middle Temple. Before I had eaten half a dozen dinners I gave up the Bar, and announced my intention of becoming a painter.[4] I have always been my own master; had at least always been so, till I met Dorian Gray. Then——But I don't know how to explain it to you. Something seemed to tell me that I was on the verge of a terrible crisis in my life. I had a strange feeling that Fate had in store for me exquisite joys and exquisite sorrows. I knew that if I spoke to Dorian I would become absolutely devoted to him, and that I ought not to speak to him.[5] I grew afraid, and turned to quit the room. It was not conscience that made me do so: it was cowardice. I take no credit to myself for trying to escape."

"Conscience and cowardice are really the same things, Basil. Conscience is the trade-name of the firm. That is all."

"I don't believe that, Harry. However, whatever was my motive,—and it may have been pride, for I used to be very proud,—I certainly struggled to the door. There, of course, I stumbled against Lady Brandon. 'You are not going to run away so soon, Mr. Hallward?' she screamed out. You know her shrill horrid voice?"

"Yes; she is a peacock in everything but beauty," said Lord Henry, pulling the daisy to bits with his long, nervous fingers.

"I could not get rid of her. She brought me up to Royalties, and people with Stars and Garters, and elderly ladies with gigantic tiaras and hooked noses. She spoke of me as her dearest friend. I had only met her once before, but she took it into her head to lionize me. I believe some picture of mine had made a great success at the time, at least had been chattered about in the penny newspapers, which is the nineteenth-cen-

3. Opening lines of this paragraph deleted in 1891.
4. "My father (p. 11) . . . painter" deleted in 1891. The Middle Temple is one of four legal societies of London through which one prepared for the practice of law before the English bar.
5. "I knew . . . to him," changed in MS from "I would never leave him till either he or I were dead" and omitted from the 1891 text.

tury standard of immortality. Suddenly I found myself face to face with the young man whose personality[6] had so strangely stirred me. We were quite close, almost touching. Our eyes met again. It was mad of me, but I asked Lady Brandon to introduce me to him. Perhaps it was not so mad, after all. It was simply inevitable. We would have spoken to each other without any introduction. I am sure of that. Dorian told me so afterwards. He, too, felt that we were destined to know each other."

"And how did Lady Brandon describe this wonderful young man? I know she goes in for giving a rapid *précis* of all her guests. I remember her bringing me up to a most truculent and red-faced old gentleman covered all over with orders and ribbons, and hissing into my ear, in a tragic whisper which must have been perfectly audible to everybody in the room, something like 'Sir Humpty Dumpty—you know—Afghan frontier—Russian intrigues: very successful man—wife killed by an elephant—quite inconsolable—wants to marry a beautiful American widow—everybody does nowadays—hates Mr. Gladstone—but very much interested in beetles: ask him what he thinks of Schouvaloff.'[7] I simply fled. I like to find out people for myself. But poor Lady Brandon treats her guests exactly as an auctioneer treats his goods. She either explains them entirely away, or tells one everything about them except what one wants to know. But what did she say about Mr. Dorian Gray?"

"Oh, she murmured, 'Charming boy—poor dear mother and I quite inseparable—engaged to be married to the same man—I mean married on the same day—how very silly of me! Quite forget what he does—afraid he—doesn't do anything—oh, yes, plays the piano—or is it the violin, dear Mr. Gray?' We could neither of us help laughing, and we became friends at once."

"Laughter is not a bad beginning for a friendship, and it is the best ending for one," said Lord Henry, plucking another daisy.

Hallward buried his face in his hands.[8] "You don't understand what friendship is, Harry," he murmured,—"or what enmity is, for that matter. You like every one; that is to say, you are indifferent to every one."

"How horribly unjust of you!" cried Lord Henry, tilting his hat back, and looking up at the little clouds that were drifting across the hollowed turquoise of the summer sky, like ravelled skeins of glossy white silk. "Yes; horribly unjust of you. I make a great difference between people. I choose my friends for their good looks, my acquaintances for their characters, and my enemies for their brains.[9] A man can't be too careful

6. Changed in MS from "beauty had so stirred me."
7. "Something like . . . Schouvaloff" removed from 1891 text. Lady Brandon's rapid precis is cited by Sherard, Harris, and others as a parody of the speech of Lady Wilde, Oscar's mother. She was noted for her salons when the family lived in Dublin and later, more modestly, in London. William Gladstone (1809–98), English statesman and four-

time prime minister, was known as a social and political reformer. Count Peter Schouvaloff (1827–89), Russian envoy to London from 1873 to 1879, helped preserve amicable relations with England during the Russo-Turkish War (1877–78).
8. Wilde made several stylistic changes in the preceding eight lines in the 1891 text.
9. Another epigram Wilde touched up a little in 1891.

in the choice of his enemies. I have not got one who is a fool. They are all men of some intellectual power, and consequently they all appreciate me. Is that very vain of me? I think it is rather vain."

"I should think it was, Harry. But according to your category I must be merely an acquaintance."

"My dear old Basil, you are much more than an acquaintance."

"And much less than a friend. A sort of brother, I suppose?"

"Oh, brothers! I don't care for brothers. My elder brother won't die, and my younger brothers seem never to do anything else."

"Harry!"

"My dear fellow, I am not quite serious. But I can't help detesting my relations. I suppose it comes from the fact that we can't stand other people having the same faults as ourselves. I quite sympathize with the rage of the English democracy against what they call the vices of the upper classes. They feel that drunkenness, stupidity, and immorality should be their own special property, and that if any one of us makes an ass of himself he is poaching on their preserves. When poor Southwark got into the Divorce Court, their indignation was quite magnificent. And yet I don't that ten per cent. of the lower orders live correctly."[1]

"I don't agree with a single word that you have said, and, what is more, Harry, I don't believe you do either."

Lord Henry stroked his pointed brown beard, and tapped the toe of his patent-leather boot with a tasselled malacca cane. "How English you are, Basil! If one puts forward an idea to a real Englishman,—always a rash thing to do,—he never dreams of considering whether the idea is right or wrong.[2] The only thing he considers of any importance is whether one believes it one's self. Now, the value of an idea has nothing whatsoever to do with the sincerity of the man who expresses it. Indeed, the probabilities are that the more insincere the man is, the more purely intellectual will the idea be, as in that case it will not be colored by either his wants, his desires, or his prejudices. However, I don't propose to discuss politics, sociology, or metaphysics with you. I like persons better than principles. Tell me more about Dorian Gray. How often do you see him?"

"Every day. I couldn't be happy if I didn't see him every day. Of course sometimes it is only for a few minutes. But a few minutes with somebody one worships mean a great deal."

"But you don't really worship him?"

"I do."

"How extraordinary! I thought you would never care for anything but

1. J. M. Stoddart, *Lippincott's* editor, changed TS reading "live with their wives," removing an expression inadmissible to the American public. Wilde let these and similar changes stand even though they are clearly inferior to his original.
2. Wilde altered details here and in the preceding two paragraphs in 1891. Lord Henry originally owned a "straw colored moustache" and a "Henry Deux" beard, but lost them both in MS. Both were features of the appearance of Lord Ronald Sutherland-Gower, a candidate for the original of Lord Henry.

your painting,—your art, I should say. Art sounds better, doesn't it?"[3]

"He is all my art to me now. I sometimes think, Harry, that there are only two eras of any importance in the history of the world. The first is the appearance of a new medium for art, and the second is the appearance of a new personality for art also. What the invention of oil-painting was to the Venetians, the face of Antinoüs was to late Greek sculpture, and the face of Dorian Gray will some day be to me. It is not merely that I paint from him, draw from him, model from him. Of course I have done all that. He has stood as Paris in dainty armor, and as Adonis with huntsman's cloak and polished boar-spear. Crowned with heavy lotus-blossoms, he has sat on the prow of Adrian's barge, looking into the green, turbid Nile. He has leaned over the still pool of some Greek woodland, and seen in the water's silent silver the wonder of his own beauty.[4] But he is much more to me than that. I won't tell you that I am dissatisfied with what I have done of him, or that his beauty is such that art cannot express it. There is nothing that art cannot express, and I know that the work I have done since I met Dorian Gray is good work, is the best work of my life. But in some curious way—I wonder will you understand me?—his personality has suggested to me an entirely new manner in art, an entirely new mode of style. I see things differently, I think of them differently. I can now re-create life in a way that was hidden from me before. 'A dream of form in days of thought,'—who is it who says that? I forget; but it is what Dorian Gray has been to me. The merely visible presence of this lad,[5]—for he seems to me little more than a lad, though he is really over twenty,—his merely visible presence,—ah! I wonder can you realize all that that means? Unconsciously he defines for me the lines of a fresh school, a school that is to have in itself all the passion of the romantic spirit, all the perfection of the spirit that is Greek. The harmony of soul and body,—how much that is! We in our madness have separated the two, and have invented a realism that is bestial, an ideality that is void. Harry! Harry! if you only knew what Dorian Gray is to me! You remember that landscape of mine, for which Agnew offered me such a huge price, but which I would not part with? It is one of the best things I have ever done. And why is it so? Because, while I was painting it, Dorian Gray sat beside me."[6]

"Basil, this is quite wonderful! I must see Dorian Gray."[7]

---

3. Wilde revised the dialogue above in 1891, leaving out "worship" and muting the homoerotic overtones.

4. "He stood . . . beauty" was moved by Wilde to another context in 1891 (see p. 89).

5. "Lad" substituted for "boy" here and in several other places in MS. Wilde removed "Though twenty summers have shown him roses less scarlet than his lips" in MS.

6. Wilde made several changes in this paragraph in 1891. In MS, Wilde deleted "and as he leaned across to look at it, his lips just touched my hand. The world becomes young to me when I hold his

hand. . . ." In 1891, Wilde added another sentence here emphasizing Dorian's influence on Basil's art.

7. Henry's response in MS is too heavily blotted to read fully, but he protests Basil's being in Dorian's power: "to make yourself the slave of your slave. It is worse than wicked, it is silly. I hate Dorian Gray!" In one stroke, Wilde rid himself of some silly dialogue and removed a clue, perhaps, to the nature of the relationship between Dorian and Basil as a form of homoerotic bondage so fashionable among the English that the French referred to it as *le vice anglais*.

Hallward got up from the seat, and walked up and down the garden.[8] After some time he came back. "You don't understand, Harry," he said. "Dorian Gray is merely to me a motive in art. He is never more present in my work than when no image of him is there. He is simply a suggestion, as I have said, of a new manner. I see him in the curves of certain lines, in the loveliness and the subtleties of certain colors. That is all."

"Then why won't you exhibit his portrait?"

"Because I have put into it all the extraordinary romance of which, of course, I have never dared to speak to him. He knows nothing about it. He will never know anything about it. But the world might guess it; and I will not bare my soul to their shallow, prying eyes. My heart shall never be put under their microscope. There is too much of myself in the thing, Harry,—too much of myself!"[9]

"Poets are not so scrupulous as you are. They know how useful passion is for publication. Nowadays a broken heart will run to many editions."

"I hate them for it. An artist should create beautiful things, but should put nothing of his own life into them. We live in an age when men treat art as if it were meant to be a form of autobiography. We have lost the abstract sense of beauty. If I live, I will show the world what it is; and for that reason the world shall never see my portrait of Dorian Gray."

"I think you are wrong, Basil, but I won't argue with you. It is only the intellectually lost who ever argue. Tell me, is Dorian Gray very fond of you?"

Hallward considered for a few moments. "He likes me," he answered, after a pause; "I know he likes me. Of course I flatter him dreadfully. I find a strange pleasure in saying things to him that I know I shall be sorry for having said. I give myself away.[1] As a rule, he is charming to me, and we walk home together from the club arm in arm, or sit in the studio and talk of a thousand things. Now and then, however, he is horribly thoughtless, and seems to take a real delight in giving me pain. Then I feel, Harry, that I have given away my whole soul to some one[2] who treats it as if it were a flower to put in his coat, a bit of decoration to charm his vanity, an ornament for a summer's day."

"Days in summer, Basil, are apt to linger. Perhaps you will tire sooner than he will. It is a sad thing to think of, but there is no doubt that Genius lasts longer than Beauty. That accounts for the fact that we all

8. Wilde canceled the following at this point in MS: "A curious smile crossed his face. He seemed like a man in a dream."

9. Wilde altered this and the preceding paragraphs in every revision. He removed from MS (after "the world might guess it") "where there is merely love, they would see something evil. Where there is spiritual passion, they would suggest something vile."

1. Wilde dropped this sentence from the 1891 text together with the phrase "walk home together from the club arm in arm" from the next sentence.

2. The following lines were canceled at this point in MS: "who seems to take a real delight in giving me pain. I seem quite adjusted to it. I can imagine myself doing it. But not to him, not to him. Once or twice we have been away together. Then I have had him all to myself. I am horribly jealous of him, of course. I never let him talk to me of the people he knows. I like to isolate him from the rest of life and to think that he absolutely belongs to me. He does not, I know. But it gives me pleasure to think he does."

take such pains to over-educate ourselves. In the wild struggle for existence, we want to have something that endures, and so we fill our minds
with rubbish and facts, in the silly hope of keeping our place. The thoroughly well informed man,—that is the modern ideal. And the mind of
the thoroughly well informed man is a dreadful thing. It is like a bric-à-
brac shop, all monsters and dust, and everything priced above its proper
value. I think you will tire first, all the same. Some day you will look at
Gray, and he will seem to you to be a little out of drawing, or you won't
like his tone of color, or something. You will bitterly reproach him in
your own heart, and seriously think that he has behaved very badly to
you. The next time he calls, you will be perfectly cold and indifferent.
It will be a great pity, for it will alter you. The worst of having a romance
is that it leaves one so unromantic."[3]

"Harry, don't talk like that.[4] As long as I live, the personality of Dorian
Gray will dominate me. You can't feel what I feel. You change too
often."

"Ah, my dear Basil, that is exactly why I can feel it. Those who are
faithful know only the pleasures of love: it is the faithless who know
love's tragedies." And Lord Henry struck a light on a dainty silver case,
and began to smoke a cigarette with a self-conscious and self-satisfied
air, as if he had summed up life in a phrase. There was a rustle of
chirruping sparrows in the ivy, and the blue cloud-shadows chased
themselves across the grass like swallows. How pleasant it was in the
garden! And how delightful other people's emotions were!—much more
delightful than their ideas, it seemed to him. One's own soul, and the
passions of one's friends,—those were the fascinating things in life. He
thought with pleasure of the tedious luncheon that he had missed by
staying so long with Basil Hallward. Had he gone to his aunt's, he would
have been sure to meet Lord Goodbody there, and the whole conversation would have been about the housing of the poor, and the necessity
for model lodging-houses.[5] It was charming to have escaped all that! As
he thought of his aunt, an idea seemed to strike him. He turned to
Hallward, and said, "My dear fellow, I have just remembered."

"Remembered what, Harry?"

"Where I heard the name of Dorian Gray."

"Where was it?" asked Hallward, with a slight frown.

"Don't look so angry, Basil. It was at my aunt's, Lady Agatha's. She
told me she had discovered a wonderful young man, who was going to
help her in the East End, and that his name was Dorian Gray. I am

3. In 1891, Wilde added the mitigating phrase "of
any kind" after "having a romance."
4. The following lines were canceled in MS: "I
am not afraid of things, but I am afraid of words. I
cannot understand how it is that no prophecy has
ever been fulfilled. None has I know. And yet it
seems to me that to say a thing is to bring it to pass.
Whatever has found expression becomes true, and
what has not found expression can never happen.

As for genius lasting longer than beauty, it is only
the transitory that stirs me. What is permanent is
monstrous and produces no effect. Our senses
become dulled by what is always with us." These
lines have a strong flavor of Pater about them.
5. Wilde made several alterations here in 1891,
including the addition of the aphorism beginning
"each class . . ." (see p. 16).

bound to state that she never told me he was good-looking. Women have no appreciation of good looks. At least, good women have not. She said that he was very earnest, and had a beautiful nature. I at once pictured to myself a creature with spectacles and lank hair, horridly freckled, and tramping about on huge feet. I wish I had known it was your friend."

"I am very glad you didn't, Harry."

"Why?"

"I don't want you to meet him."

"Mr. Dorian Gray is in the studio, sir," said the butler, coming into the garden.

"You must introduce me now," cried Lord Henry, laughing.

Basil Hallward turned to the servant, who stood blinking in the sunlight. "Ask Mr. Gray to wait, Parker: I will be in in a few moments." The man bowed, and went up the walk.

Then he looked at Lord Henry. "Dorian Gray is my dearest friend," he said. "He has a simple and a beautiful nature. Your aunt was quite right in what she said of him. Don't spoil him for me. Don't try to influence him. Your influence would be bad. The world is wide, and has many marvellous people in it. Don't take away from me the one person that makes life absolutely lovely to me, and that gives to my art whatever wonder or charm it possesses.[6] Mind, Harry, I trust you." He spoke very slowly, and the words seemed wrung out of him almost against his will.

"What nonsense you talk!" said Lord Henry, smiling, and, taking Hallward by the arm, he almost led him into the house.[7]

Chapter II.

As they entered they saw Dorian Gray. He was seated at the piano, with his back to them, turning over the pages of a volume of Schumann's "Forest Scenes." "You must lend me these, Basil," he cried. "I want to learn them. They are perfectly charming."

"That entirely depends on how you sit to-day, Dorian."

"Oh, I am tired of sitting, and I don't want a life-sized portrait of myself," answered the lad, swinging round on the music-stool, in a wilful, petulant manner. When he caught sight of Lord Henry, a faint blush colored his cheeks for a moment, and he started up. "I beg your pardon, Basil, but I didn't know you had any one with you."

"This is Lord Henry Wotton, Dorian, an old Oxford friend of mine. I have just been telling him what a capital sitter you were, and now you have spoiled everything."

"You have not spoiled my pleasure in meeting you, Mr. Gray," said Lord Henry, stepping forward and shaking him by the hand. "My aunt

6. "that makes . . . me" and "or wonder" in the next line were dropped in 1891; following "possess," Wilde added "my life as an artist depends on him."

7. The original conclusion of the chapter, canceled in MS, read: " 'I don't suppose I shall care for him, and I am quite sure he won't care for me,' replied Lord Henry, smiling. . . ."

has often spoken to me about you. You are one of her favorites, and, I am afraid, one of her victims also."

"I am in Lady Agatha's black books at present," answered Dorian, with a funny look of penitence. "I promised to go to her club in White-chapel with her last Tuesday, and I really forgot all about it. We were to have played a duet together,—three duets, I believe. I don't know what she will say to me. I am far too frightened to call."

"Oh, I will make your peace with my aunt. She is quite devoted to you. And I don't think it really matters about your not being there. The audience probably thought it was a duet. When Aunt Agatha sits down to the piano she makes quite enough noise for two people."

"That is very horrid to her, and not very nice to me," answered Dorian, laughing.

Lord Henry looked at him. Yes, he was certainly wonderfully hand-some, with his finely-curved scarlet lips, his frank blue eyes, his crisp gold hair. There was something in his face that made one trust him at once. All the candor of youth was there, as well as all youth's passionate purity. One felt that he had kept himself unspotted from the world. No wonder Basil Hallward worshipped him. He was made to be wor-shipped.[1]

"You are too charming to go in for philanthropy, Mr. Gray,—far too charming." And Lord Henry flung himself down on the divan, and opened his cigarette-case.

Hallward had been busy mixing his colors and getting his brushes ready. He was looking worried, and when he heard Lord Henry's last remark he glanced at him, hesitated for a moment, and then said, "Harry, I want to finish this picture to-day. Would you think it awfully rude of me if I asked you to go away?"

Lord Henry smiled, and looked at Dorian Gray. "Am I to go, Mr. Gray?" he asked.

"Oh, please don't, Lord Henry. I see that Basil is in one of his sulky moods; and I can't bear him when he sulks. Besides, I want you to tell me why I should not go in for philanthropy."

"I don't know that I shall tell you that, Mr. Gray.[2] But I certainly will not run away, now that you have asked me to stop. You don't really mind, Basil, do you? You have often told me that you liked your sitters to have some one to chat to."

Hallward bit his lip. "If Dorian wishes it, of course you must stay. Dorian's whims are laws to everybody, except himself."

Lord Henry took up his hat and gloves. "You are very pressing, Basil, but I am afraid I must go. I have promised to meet a man at the Orle-ans.—Good-by, Mr. Gray. Come and see me some afternoon in Cur-zon Street. I am nearly always at home at five o'clock. Write to me when you are coming. I should be sorry to miss you."

---

1. This last sentence was removed in 1891.   2. Wilde added an epigram here in 1891.

"Basil," cried Dorian Gray, "if Lord Henry goes I shall go too. You never open your lips while you are painting, and it is horribly dull standing on a platform and trying to look pleasant. Ask him to stay. I insist upon it."

"Stay, Harry, to oblige Dorian, and to oblige me," said Hallward, gazing intently at his picture. "It is quite true, I never talk when I am working, and never listen either, and it must be dreadfully tedious for my unfortunate sitters. I beg you to stay."

"But what about my man at the Orleans?"

Hallward laughed. "I don't think there will be any difficulty about that. Sit down again, Harry.—And now, Dorian, get up on the platform, and don't move about too much, or pay any attention to what Lord Henry says. He has a very bad influence over all his friends, with the exception of myself."

Dorian stepped up on the dais, with the air of a young Greek martyr, and made a little *moue* of discontent to Lord Henry, to whom he had rather taken a fancy. He was so unlike Hallward. They made a delightful contrast. And he had such a beautiful voice.[3] After a few moments he said to him, "Have you really a very bad influence, Lord Henry? As bad as Basil says?"

"There is no such thing as a good influence, Mr. Gray. All influence is immoral,—immoral from the scientific point of view."

"Why?"

"Because to influence a person is to give him one's own soul. He does not think his natural thoughts, or burn with his natural passions. His virtues are not real to him. His sins, if there are such things as sins, are borrowed. He becomes an echo of some one else's music, an actor of a part that has not been written for him. The aim of life is self-development. To realize one's nature perfectly,—that is what each of us is here for. People are afraid of themselves, nowadays. They have forgotten the highest of all duties, the duty that one owes to one's self. Of course they are charitable. They feed the hungry, and clothe the beggar. But their own souls starve, and are naked. Courage has gone out of our race. Perhaps we never really had it. The terror of society, which is the basis of morals, the terror of God, which is the secret of religion,—these are the two things that govern us. And yet——"

"Just turn your head a little more to the right, Dorian, like a good boy," said Hallward, deep in his work, and conscious only that a look had come into the lad's face that he had never seen there before.

"And yet," continued Lord Henry, in his low, musical voice, and with that graceful wave of the hand that was always so characteristic of him, and that he had even in his Eton days, "I believe that if one man were to live his life out fully and completely, were to give form to every feeling, expression to every thought, reality to every dream,—I believe

3. Wilde added "to whom . . . voice" in TS.

that the world would gain such a fresh impulse of joy that we would
forget all the maladies of mediævalism, and return to the Hellenic ideal,—
to something finer, richer, than the Hellenic ideal, it may be. But the
bravest man among us is afraid of himself. The mutilation of the savage
has its tragic survival in the self-denial that mars our lives. We are punished for our refusals. Every impulse that we strive to strangle broods in
the mind, and poisons us. The body sins once, and has done with its
sin, for action is a mode of purification. Nothing remains then but the
recollection of a pleasure, or the luxury of a regret. The only way to get
rid of a temptation is to yield to it. Resist it, and your soul grows sick
with longing for the things it has forbidden to itself, with desire for what
its monstrous laws have made monstrous and unlawful. It has been said
that the great events of the world take place in the brain. It is in the
brain, and the brain only, that the great sins of the world take place also.
You, Mr. Gray, you yourself, with your rose-red youth and your rose-
white boyhood, you have had passions that have made you afraid, thoughts
that have filled you with terror, day-dreams and sleeping dreams whose
mere memory might stain your cheek with shame——"

"Stop!" murmured Dorian Gray, "stop! you bewilder me. I don't know
what to say. There is some answer to you, but I cannot find it. Don't
speak, Let me think, or, rather, let me try not to think."[4]

For nearly ten minutes he stood there motionless, with parted lips,
and eyes strangely bright. He was dimly conscious that entirely fresh
impulses[5] were at work within him, and they seemed to him to have
come really from himself. The few words that Basil's friend had said to
him—words spoken by chance, no doubt, and with wilful paradox in
them—had yet touched some secret chord, that had never been touched
before, but that he felt was now vibrating and throbbing to curious pulses.

Music had stirred him like that. Music had troubled him many times.
But music was not articulate. It was not a new world, but rather a new
chaos, that it created in us. Words! Mere words! How terrible they were!
How clear, and vivid, and cruel! One could not escape from them. And
yet what a subtle magic there was in them! They seemed to be able to
give a plastic form to formless things, and to have a music of their own
as sweet as that of viol or of lute. Mere words! Was there anything so
real as words?

Yes; there had been things in his boyhood that he had not understood.
He understood them now. Life suddenly became fiery-colored to him.
It seemed to him that he had been walking in fire. Why had he not
known it?

Lord Henry watched him, with his sad smile. He knew the precise
psychological moment when to say nothing. He felt intensely interested.
He was amazed at the sudden impression that his words had produced,

4. Wilde added this and the following five paragraphs to TS on an inserted page and in a long
marginal note ending with ". . . of the silence."

5. Wilde changed this word to "influences" in
1891.

and, remembering a book that he had read when he was sixteen, which had revealed to him much that he had not known before, he wondered whether Dorian Gray was passing through the same experience. He had merely shot an arrow into the air. Had it hit the mark? How fascinating the lad was!

Hallward painted away with that marvellous bold touch of his, that had the true refinement and perfect delicacy that come only from strength. He was unconscious of the silence.

"Basil, I am tired of standing," cried Dorian Gray, suddenly. "I must go out and sit in the garden. The air is stifling here."

"My dear fellow, I am so sorry. When I am painting, I can't think of anything else. But you never sat better. You were perfectly still. And I have caught the effect I wanted,—the half-parted lips, and the bright look in the eyes. I don't know what Harry has been saying to you, but he has certainly made you have the most wonderful expression. I suppose he has been paying you compliments. You mustn't believe a word that he says."

"He has certainly not been paying me compliments. Perhaps that is the reason I don't think I believe anything he has told me."

"You know you believe it all," said Lord Henry, looking at him with his dreamy, heavy-lidded eyes. "I will go out to the garden with you. It is horridly hot in the studio.—Basil, let us have something iced to drink, something with strawberries in it."

"Certainly, Harry. Just touch the bell, and when Parker comes I will tell him what you want. I have got to work up this background, so I will join you later on. Don't keep Dorian too long. I have never been in better form for painting than I am to-day. This is going to be my masterpiece. It is my masterpiece as it stands."

Lord Henry went out to the garden, and found Dorian Gray burying his face in the great cool lilac-blossoms, feverishly drinking in their perfume as if it had been wine. He came close to him, and put his hand upon his shoulder. "You are quite right to do that," he murmured. "Nothing can cure the soul but the senses, just as nothing can cure the senses but the soul."

The lad started and drew back. He was bareheaded, and the leaves had tossed his rebellious curls and tangled all their gilded threads. There was a look of fear in his eyes, such as people have when they are suddenly awakened. His finely-chiselled nostrils quivered, and some hidden nerve shook the scarlet of his lips and left them trembling.

"Yes," continued Lord Henry, "that is one of the great secrets of life,—to cure the soul by means of the senses, and the senses by means of the soul. You are a wonderful creature. You know more than you think you know, just as you know less than you want to know."

Dorian Gray frowned and turned his head away. he could not help liking the tall, graceful young man who was standing by him. His romantic olive-colored face and worn expression interested him. There was something in his low, languid voice that was absolutely fascinating. His cool, white, flower-like hands, even, had a curious charm. They moved, as he spoke, like music, and seemed to have a language of their own. But he felt afraid of him, and ashamed of being afraid. Why had it been left for a stranger to reveal him to himself? He had known Basil Hallward for months, but the friendship between then had never altered him. Suddenly there had come some one across his life who seemed to have disclosed to him life's mystery. And, yet, what was there to be afraid of? He was not a school-boy, or a girl. It was absurd to be frightened.

"Let us go and sit in the shade," said Lord Henry. "Parker has brought out the drinks, and if you stay any longer in this glare you will be quite spoiled, and Basil will never paint you again. You really must not let yourself become sunburnt. It would be very unbecoming to you."

"What does it matter?" cried Dorian, laughing, as he sat down on the seat at the end of the garden.

"It should matter everything to you, Mr. Gray."

"Why?"

"Because you have now the most marvellous youth, and youth is the one thing worth having."

"I don't feel that, Lord Henry."

"No, you don't feel it now. Some day, when you are old and wrinkled and ugly, when thought has seared your forehead with its lines, and passion branded your lips with its hideous fires, you will feel it, you will feel it terribly.[6] Now, wherever you go, you charm the world. Will it always be so?

"You have a wonderfully beautiful face, Mr. Gray. Don't frown. You have. And Beauty is a form of Genius,—is higher, indeed, than Genius, as it needs no explanation. It is one of the great facts of the world, like sunlight, or spring-time, or the reflection in dark waters of that silver shell we call the moon.[7] It cannot be questioned. It has its divine right of sovereignty. It makes princes of those who have it. You smile? Ah! when you have lost it you won't smile.

"People say sometimes that Beauty is only superficial. That may be so. But at least it is not so superficial as Thought. To me, Beauty is the wonder of wonders. It is only shallow people who do not judge by appearances. The true mystery of the world is the visible, not the invisible.

"Yes, Mr. Gray, the gods have been good to you. But what the gods give they quickly take away. You have only a few years in which really to live. When your youth goes, your beauty will go with it, and then you will suddenly discover that there are no triumphs left for you, or have to content yourself with those mean triumphs that the memory of

6. Wilde canceled these lines here in TS: "If you set yourself to know life, you will look evil; if you are afraid of life you will look common."

7. The lines "Beauty is a form of genius . . . the moon" were originally spoken by Basil in the previous chapter. Wilde relocated them here in MS and transferred them to Henry.

your past will make more bitter than defeats. Every month as it wanes brings you nearer to something dreadful. Time is jealous of you, and wars against your lilies and your roses. You will become sallow, and hollow-cheeked, and dull-eyed. You will suffer horribly.

"Realize your youth while you have it. Don't squander the gold of your days, listening to the tedious, trying to improve the hopeless failure, or giving away your life to the ignorant, the common, and the vulgar, which are the aims, the false ideals, of our age. Live! Live the wonderful life that is in you! Let nothing be lost upon you. Be always searching for new sensations. Be afraid of nothing.

"A new hedonism,—that is what our century wants. You might be its visible symbol. With your personality there is nothing you could not do. The world belongs to you for a season.

"The moment I met you I saw that you were quite unconscious of what you really are, what you really might be. There was so much about you that charmed me that I felt I must tell you something about yourself. I thought how tragic it would be if you were wasted. For there is such a little time that your youth will last,—such a little time.

"The common hill-flowers wither, but they blossom again. The laburnum will be as golden next June as it is now. In a month there will be purple stars on the clematis, and year after year the green night of its leaves will have its purple stars. But we never get back our youth. The pulse of joy that beats in us at twenty, becomes sluggish. Our limbs fail, our senses rot. We degenerate into hideous puppets, haunted by the memory of the passions of which we were too much afraid, and the exquisite temptations that we did not dare to yield to. Youth! Youth! There is absolutely nothing in the world but youth!"

Dorian Gray listened, open-eyed and wondering. The spray of lilac fell from his hand upon the gravel. A furry bee came and buzzed round it for a moment. Then it began to scramble all over the fretted purple of the tiny blossoms. He watched it with that strange interest in trivial things that we try to develop when things of high import make us afraid, or when we are stirred by some new emotion, for which we cannot find expression, or when some thought that terrifies us lays sudden siege to the brain and calls on us to yield.[8] After a time it flew away. He saw it creeping into the stained trumpet of a Tyrian convolvulus. The flower seemed to quiver, and then swayed gently to and fro.

Suddenly Hallward appeared at the door of the studio, and made frantic signs for them to come in. They turned to each other, and smiled.

"'I am waiting,'" cried Hallward. "Do come in. The light is quite perfect, and you can bring your drinks."

They rose up, and sauntered down the walk together. Two green-and-white butterflies fluttered past them, and in the pear-tree at the end of the garden a thrush began to sing.

8. Wilde added "or when we are stirred . . . to yield" in the margin of TS.

"You are glad you have met me, Mr. Gray," said Lord Henry, looking at him.

"Yes, I am glad now. I wonder shall I always be glad?"

"Always! That is a dreadful word. It makes me shudder when I hear it. Women are so fond of using it. They spoil every romance by trying to make it last forever.[9] It is a meaningless word, too. The only difference between a caprice and a life-long passion is that the caprice lasts a little longer."

As they entered the studio, Dorian Gray put his hand upon Lord Henry's arm. "In that case, let our friendship be a caprice," he murmured, flushing at his own boldness, then stepped upon the platform and resumed his pose.

Lord Henry flung himself into a large wicker arm-chair, and watched him. The sweep and dash of the brush on thee canvas made the only sound that broke the stillness, except when Hallward stepped back now and then to look at his work from a distance. In the slanting beams that streamed through the open door-way the dust danced and was golden. The heavy scent of the roses seemed to brood over everything.

After about a quarter of an hour, Hallward stopped painting, looked for a long time at Dorian Gray, and then for a long time at the picture, biting the end of one of his huge brushes, and smiling. "It is quite finished," he cried, at last, and stooping down he wrote his name in thin vermilion letters on the left-hand corner of the canvas.

Lord Henry came over and examined the picture. It was certainly a wonderful work of art, and a wonderful likeness as well.[1]

"My dear fellow, I congratulate you most warmly," he said.—"Mr. Gray, come and look at yourself."

The lad started, as if awakened from some dream. "Is it really finished?" he murmured, stepping down from the platform.

"Quite finished," said Hallward. "And you have sat splendidly to-day. I am awfully obliged to you."

"That is entirely due to me," broke in Lord Henry. "Isn't it, Mr. Gray?"

Dorian made no answer, but passed listlessly in front of his picture and turned towards it. When he saw it he drew back, and his cheeks flushed for a moment with pleasure. A look of joy came into his eyes, as if he had recognized himself for the first time. He stood there motionless, and in wonder, dimly conscious that Hallward was speaking to him, but not catching the meaning of his words. The sense of his own beauty came on him like a revelation. He had never felt it before. Basil Hall-

9. Wilde canceled the following at this point in MS: "Like priests, they terrify one at the prospect of certain eternity, attempt to terrify one, I should say."
1. Wilde canceled here the following passage in MS: "Most modern portrait painting comes under the head of elegant fiction or if it aims at realism, gives one something between a caricature and a photograph. But this was different. It had all the mystery of life, and all the mystery of beauty. Within the world, as men know it, there is a finer world that only artists know of—artists or those to whom the temperament of the artist has been given. Creation within creation—that is what Basil Hallward named it, that is what he had attained to."

ward's compliments had seemed to him to be merely the charming exaggerations of friendship. He had listened to them, laughed at them, forgotten them. They had not influenced his nature. Then had come Lord Henry, with his strange panegyric on youth, his terrible warning of its brevity. That had stirred him at the time, and now, as he stood gazing at the shadow of his own loveliness, the full reality of the description flashed across him. Yes, there would be a day when his face would be wrinkled and wizen, his eyes dim and colorless, the grace of his figure broken and deformed. The scarlet would pass away from his lips, and the gold steal from his hair. The life that was to make his soul would mar his body. He would become ignoble,[2] hideous, and uncouth.

As he thought of it, a sharp pang of pain struck like a knife across him, and made each delicate fibre of his nature quiver. His eyes deepened into amethyst, and a mist of tears came across them. He felt as if a hand of ice had been laid upon his heart.

"Don't you like it?" cried Hallward at last, stung a little by the lad's silence, and not understanding what it meant.

"Of course he likes it," said Lord Henry. "Who wouldn't like it? It is one of the greatest things in modern art. I will give you anything you like to ask for it. I must have it."

"It is not my property, Harry."

"Whose property is it?"

"Dorian's, of course."

"He is a very lucky fellow."

"How sad it is!" murmured Dorian Gray, with his eyes still fixed upon his own portrait. "How sad it is! I shall grow old, and horrid, and dreadful. But this picture will remain always young. It will never be older than this particular day of June. . . . If it was only the other way! If it was I who were to be always young, and the picture that were to grow old! For this—for this—I would give everything! Yes, there is nothing in the whole world I would not give!"[3]

"You would hardly care for that arrangement, Basil," cried Lord Henry, laughing. "It would be rather hard lines on you."

"I should object very strongly, Harry."

Dorian Gray turned and looked at him. "I believe you would, Basil. You like your art better than your friends. I am no more to you than a green bronze figure. Hardly as much, I dare say."

Hallward stared in amazement. It was so unlike Dorian to speak like that. What had happened? He seemed almost angry. His face was flushed and his cheeks burning.

"Yes," he continued, "I am less to you than your ivory Hermes[4] or

---

2. Wilde changed this to "dreadful" in 1891.
3. Wilde altered this passage each time he revised his text. In MS, he canceled after "dreadful" the following: "Life will send its lines across my face. Passion will crease it and thought twist it from its form." In TS, Wilde added "Yes, there is nothing

. . . give!" He added to it again in 1891: "I would give my soul for that."
4. Originally "Sylvanus" in MS, but changed there. Sylvanus was a Latin divinity, a variation of Pan, god of woods, fields, and grottoes, who looked young despite his antiquity.

your silver Faun. You will like them always. How long will you like me? Till I have my first wrinkle, I suppose. I know, now, that when one loses one's good looks, whatever they may be, one loses everything. Your picture has taught me that. Lord Henry is perfectly right. Youth is the only thing worth having. When I find that I am growing old, I will kill myself."[5]

Hallward turned pale, and caught his hand. "Dorian! Dorian!" he cried, "don't talk like that. I have never had such a friend as you, and I shall never have such another. You are not jealous of material things, are you?"

"I am jealous of everything whose beauty does not die. I am jealous of the portrait you have painted of me. Why should it keep what I must lose? Every moment that passes takes something from me, and gives something to it. Oh, if it was only the other way! If the picture could change, and I could be always what I am now! Why did you paint it? It will mock me some day,—mock me horribly!"[6] The hot tears welled into his eyes; he tore his hand away, and, flinging himself on the divan, he buried his face in the cushions, as if he was praying.

"This is your doing, Harry," said Hallward, bitterly.

"My doing?"

"Yes, yours, and you know it."[7]

Lord Henry shrugged his shoulders. "It is the real Dorian Gray,—that is all," he answered.

"It is not."

"If it is not, what have I to do with it?"[8]

"You should have gone away when I asked you."

"I stayed when you asked me."

"Harry, I can't quarrel with my two best friends at once, but between you both you have made me hate the finest piece of work I have ever done, and I will destroy it. What is it but canvas and color? I will not let it come across our three lives and mar them."

Dorian Gray lifted his golden head from the pillow, and looked at him with pallid face and tear-stained eyes, as he walked over to the deal painting-table that was set beneath the large curtained window. What was he doing there? His fingers were straying about among the litter of tin tubes and dry brushes, seeking for something. Yes, it was the long palette-knife, with its thin blade of lithe steel. He had found it at last. He was going to rip up the canvas.

With a stifled sob he leaped from the couch, and, rushing over to Hallward, tore the knife out of his hand, and flung it to the end of the studio. "Don't Basil, don't!" he cried. "It would be murder!"

"I am glad you appreciate my work at last, Dorian," said Hallward,

5. Wilde added this sentence in TS.
6. "Oh, if it was only . . . horribly!" was added by Wilde in TS.
7. Wilde dropped Henry's question and Basil's

answer in 1891.
8. Wilde wrote this into TS after removing "*comme vous voulez, mon cher.*"

coldly, when he had recovered from his surprise. "I never thought you would."

"Appreciate it? I am in love with it, Basil. It is part of myself, I feel that."

"Well, as soon as you are dry, you shall be varnished, and framed, and sent home. Then you can do what you like with yourself." And he walked across the room and rang the bell for tea. "You will have tea, of course, Dorian? And so will you, Harry? Tea is the only simple pleasure left to us."

"I don't like simple pleasures," said Lord Henry. "And I don't like scenes, except on the stage. What absurd fellows you are, both of you! I wonder who it was defined man as a rational animal. It was the most premature definition ever given. Man is many things, but he is not rational. I am glad he is not, after all: though I wish you chaps would not squabble over the picture. You had much better let me have it, Basil. This silly boy doesn't really want it, and I do."

"If you let any one have it but me, Basil, I will never forgive you!" cried Dorian Gray. "And I don't allow people to call me a silly boy."

"You know the picture is yours, Dorian. I gave it to you before it existed."

"And you know you have been a little silly, Mr. Gray, and that you don't really mind being called a boy."

"I should have minded very much this morning, Lord Henry."

"Ah! this morning! You have lived since then."[9]

There came a knock to the door, and the butler entered with the tea-tray and set it down upon a small Japanese table. There was a rattle of cups and saucers and the hissing of a fluted Georgian urn. Two globe-shaped china dishes were brought in by a page. Dorian Gray went over and poured the tea out. The two men sauntered languidly to the table, and examined what was under the covers.

"Let us go to the theatre to-night," said Lord Henry. "There is sure to be something on, somewhere. I have promised to dine at White's, but it is only with an old friend, so I can send him a wire and say that I am ill, or that I am prevented from coming in consequence of a subsequent engagement. I think that would be a rather nice excuse: it would have the surprise of candor."

"It is such a bore putting on one's dress-clothes," muttered Hallward. "And, when one has them on, they are so horrid."

"Yes," answered Lord Henry, dreamily, "the costume of our day is detestable. It is so sombre, so depressing. Sin is the only color-element left in modern life."

"You really must not say things like that before Dorian, Harry."

"Before which Dorian? The one who is pouring out tea for us, or the one in the picture?"

9. Wilde wrote the preceding three sentences into TS.

"Before either."

"I should like to come to the theatre with you, Lord Henry," said th lad.

"Then you shall come; and you will come too, Basil, won't you?"

"I can't really. I would sooner not. I have a lot of work to do."

"Well, then, you and I will go alone, Mr. Gray."

"I should like that awfully."

Basil Hallward bit his lip and walked over, cup in hand, to the picture. "I will stay with the real Dorian," he said, sadly.

"Is it the real Dorian?" cried the original of the portrait, running across to him. "Am I really like that?"

"Yes; you are just like that."

"How wonderful, Basil!"[1]

"At least you are like it in appearance. But it will never alter," said Hallward. "That is something."

"What a fuss people make about fidelity!" murmured Lord Henry. "And, after all, it is purely a question for physiology. It has nothing to do with our own will. It is either an unfortunate accident, or an unpleasant result of temperament.[2] Young men want to be faithful, and are not; old men want to be faithless, and cannot: that is all one can say."

"Don't go to the theatre to-night, Dorian," said Hallward. "Stop and dine with me."

"I can't, really."

"Why?"

"Because I have promised Lord Henry to go with him."

"He won't like you better for keeping your promises. He always breaks his own. I beg you not to go."

Dorian Gray laughed and shook his head.

"I entreat you."

The lad hesitated, and looked over at Lord Henry, who was watching them from the tea-table with an amused smile.

"I must go, Basil," he answered.

"Very well," said Hallward; and he walked over and laid his cup down on the tray. "It is rather late, and, as you have to dress, you had better lose no time. Good-by, Harry; good-by, Dorian. Come and see me soon. Come to-morrow."

"Certainly."

"You won't forget?"

"No, of course not."

"And . . . Harry!"

"Yes, Basil?"

"Remember what I asked you, when in the garden this morning."

"I have forgotten it."

"I trust you."

1. Wilde added this and the preceding two sentences to TS.

2. Wilde dropped this sentence in 1891 and made some alterations to the sentence preceding it.

"I wish I could trust myself," said Lord Henry, laughing.—"Come, Mr. Gray, my hansom is outside, and I can drop you at your own place.— Good-by, Basil. It has been a most interesting afternoon."

As the door closed behind them, Hallward flung himself down on a sofa, and a look of pain came into his face.

Chapter III.[1]

One afternoon, a month later, Dorian Gray was reclining in a luxurious arm-chair, in the little library of Lord Henry's house in Curzon Street. It was, in its way, a very charming room, with its high panelled wainscoting of olive-stained oak, its cream-colored frieze and ceiling of raised plaster-work, and its brick-dust felt carpet strewn with long-fringed silk Persian rugs. On a tiny satinwood table stood a statuette by Clodion, and beside it lay a copy of "Les Cent Nouvelles," bound for Margaret of Valois by Clovis Eve, and powdered with the gilt daisies that the queen had selected for her device. Some large blue china jars, filled with parrot-tulips, were ranged on the mantel-shelf, and through the small leaded panes of the window streamed the apricot-colored light of a summer's day in London.

Lord Henry had not come in yet. He was always late on principle, his principle being that punctuality is the thief of time. So the lad was looking rather sulky, as with listless fingers he turned over the pages of an elaborately-illustrated edition of "Manon Lescaut" that he had found in one of the bookcases. The formal monotonous ticking of the Louis Quatorze clock annoyed him. Once or twice he thought of going away.

At last he heard a light step outside, and the door opened. "How late you are, Harry!" he murmured.

"I am afraid it is not Harry, Mr. Gray," said a woman's voice.

He glanced quickly round, and rose to his feet. "I beg your pardon. I thought——"

"You thought it was my husband. It is only his wife. You must let me introduce myself. I know you quite well by your photographs. I think my husband has got twenty-seven of them."

"Not twenty-seven, Lady Henry?"

"Well, twenty-six, then.[2] And I saw you with him the other night at the Opera." She laughed nervously, as she spoke, and watched him with her vague forget-me-not eyes. She was a curious woman, whose dresses always looked as if they had been designed in a rage and put on in a tempest. She was always in love with somebody, and, as her passion was never returned, she had kept all her illusions. She tried to look picturesque, but only succeeded in being untidy. Her name was Victoria, and she had a perfect mania for going to church.

"That was at 'Lohengrin,' Lady Henry, I think?"

1. First of the new chapters added in 1891 was inserted before the original chapter 3 here.

2. Wilde changed the number of photographs for humorous effect in 1891.

"Yes; it was at dear 'Lohengrin.' I like Wagner's music better than any other music. It is so loud that one can talk the whole time, without people hearing what one says. That is a great advantage: don't you think so, Mr. Gray?"

The same nervous staccato laugh broke from her thin lips, and her fingers began to play with a long paper-knife.

Dorian smiled, and shook his head: "I am afraid I don't think so, Lady Henry. I never talk during music,—at least during good music. If one hears bad music, it is one's duty to drown it by conversation."

"Ah! that is one of Harry's views, isn't it, Mr. Gray? But you must not think I don't like good music. I adore it, but I am afraid of it. It makes me too romantic. I have simply worshipped pianists,—two at a time, sometimes. I don't know what it is about them. Perhaps it is that they are foreigners. They all are, aren't they? Even those that are born in England become foreigners after a time, don't they? It is so clever of them, and such a compliment to art. Makes it quite cosmopolitan, doesn't it? You have never been to any of my parties, have you, Mr. Gray? You must come. I can't afford orchids, but I spare no expense in foreigners. They make one's rooms look so picturesque. But here is Harry!—Harry, I came in to look for you, to ask you something,—I forget what it was,— and I found Mr. Gray here. We have had such a pleasant chat about music. We have quite the same views. No; I think our views are quite different. But he has been most pleasant. I am so glad I've seen him."

"I am charmed, my love, quite charmed," said Lord Henry, elevating his dark crescent-shaped eyebrows and looking at them both with an amused smile.—"So sorry I am late, Dorian. I went to look after a piece of old brocade in Wardour Street, and had to bargain for hours for it. Nowadays people know the price of everything, and the value of nothing."[3]

"I am afraid I must be going," exclaimed Lady Henry, after an awkward silence, with her silly sudden laugh. "I have promised to drive with the duchess.—Good-by, Mr. Gray.—Good-by, Harry. You are dining out, I suppose? So am I. Perhaps I shall see you at Lady Thornbury's."

"I dare say, my dear," said Lord Henry, shutting the door behind her, as she flitted out of the room, looking like a bird-of-paradise that had been out in the rain, and leaving a faint odor of patchouli[4] behind her. Then he shook hand with Dorian Gray, lit a cigarette, and flung himself down on the sofa.

"Never marry a woman with straw-colored hair, Dorian," he said, after a few puffs.

"Why, Harry?"

"Because they are so sentimental."

---

3. This well-known epigram was added in TS. It reappeared again in *Lady Windermere's Fan* and for an encore in *The Importance of Being Earnest*. Wilde did not believe in running dead horses, only live ones.

4. Wilde changed the perfume to frangipanni in 1891. Patchouli was a scent identified with London prostitutes.

"But I like sentimental people."

"Never marry at all, Dorian. Men marry because they are tired; women, because they are curious: both are disappointed."

"I don't think I am likely to marry, Harry. I am too much in love. That is one of your aphorisms. I am putting it into practice, as I do everything you say."[5]

"Whom are you in love with?" said Lord Henry, looking at him with a curious smile.

"With an actress," said Dorian Gray, blushing.

Lord Henry shrugged his shoulders. "That is a rather common-place *début*," he murmured.

"You would not say so if you saw her, Harry."

"Who is she?"

"Her name is Sibyl[6] Vane."

"Never heard of her."

"No one has. People will some day, however, She is a genius."

"My dear boy, no woman is a genius: women are a decorative sex. They never have anything to say, but they say it charmingly. They represent the triumph of matter over mind, just as we men represent the triumph of mind over morals. There are only two kinds of women, the plain and the colored. The plain women are very useful. If you want to gain a reputation for respectability, you have merely to take them down to supper. The other women are very charming. They commit one mistake, however. They paint in order to try to look young. Our grandmothers painted in order to try to talk brilliantly. *Rouge* and *esprit* used to go together. That has all gone out now. As long as a woman can look ten years younger than her own daughter, she is perfectly satisfied. As for conversation, there are only five women in London worth talking to, and two of these can't be admitted into decent society. However, tell me about your genius. How long have you known her?"

"About three weeks. Not so much. About two weeks and two days."

"How did you come across her?"

"I will tell you, Harry; but you mustn't be unsympathetic about it. After all, it never would have happened if I had not met you. You filled me with a wild desire to know everything about life. For days after I met you, something seemed to throb in my veins. As I lounged in the Park, or strolled down Piccadilly, I used to look at every one who passed me, and wonder with a mad curiosity what sort of lives they led. Some of them fascinated me. Others filled me with terror. There was an exquisite poison in the air. I had a passion for sensations.

"One evening about seven o'clock I determined to go out in search of some adventure. I felt that this gray, monstrous London of ours, with its myriads of people, its splendid sinners, and its sordid sins, as you once said, must have something in store for me. I fancied a thousand things.

---

5. This sentence was added in TS.
6. Stoddart changed the spelling from Wilde's

"Sybil" here and throughout the text of this edition, and it remained "Sibyl" in the 1891 text.

The mere danger gave me a sense of delight. I remembered what you had said to me on that wonderful night when we first dined together, about the search for beauty being the poisonous secret of life. I don't know what I expected, but I went out, and wandered eastward, soon losing my way in a labyrinth of grimy streets and black, grassless squares. About half-past eight I passed by a little third-rate theatre, with great flaring gas-jets and gaudy play-bills. A hideous Jew,[7] in the most amazing waistcoat I ever beheld in my life, was standing at the entrance, smoking a vile cigar. He had greasy ringlets, and an enormous diamond blazed in the centre of a soiled shirt. ' 'Ave a box, my lord?' he said, when he saw me, and he took off his hat with an act of gorgeous servility. There was something about him, Harry, that amused me. He was such a monster. You will laugh at me, I know, but I really went in and paid a whole guinea for the stage-box. To the present day I can't make out why I did so; and yet if I hadn't!—my dear Harry, if I hadn't, I would have missed the greatest romance of my life. I see you are laughing. It is horrid of you!"

"I am not laughing, Dorian; at least I am not laughing at you. But you should not say the greatest romance of your life. You should say the first romance of your life. You will always be loved, and you will always be in love with love.[8] There are exquisite things in store for you. This is merely the beginning."

"Do you think my nature so shallow?" cried Dorian Gray, angrily.

"No; I think your nature so deep."

"How do you mean?"

"My dear boy, people who only love once in their lives are really shallow people. What they call their loyalty, and their fidelity, I call either the lethargy of custom or the lack of imagination. Faithlessness is to the emotional life what consistency is to the intellectual life,—simply a confession of failure.[9] But I don't want to interrupt you. Go on with your story."

"Well, I found myself seated in a horrid little private box, with a vulgar drop-scene staring me in the face. I looked out behind the curtain, and surveyed the house. It was a tawdry affair, all Cupids and cornucopias, like a third-rate wedding-cake. The gallery and pit were fairly full, but the two rows of dingy stalls were quite empty, and there was hardly a person in what I suppose they called the dress-circle. Women went about with oranges and ginger-beer, and there was a terrible consumption of nuts going on."

"It must have been just like the palmy days of the British Drama."

"Just like, I should fancy, and very horrid. I began to wonder what on

---

7. An example of modern censorship of *Dorian Gray* may be found in some recent paperback editions (Dell and Signet) in which "Jew" is silently changed to "man" here and to other equally neutral nouns throughout.

8. Wilde added three more sentences here in 1891.

9. Wilde added this epigram in TS and followed it up with four additional sentences in 1891.

earth I should do, when I caught sight of the play-bill. What do you think the play was, Harry?"

"I should think 'The Idiot Boy, or Dumb but Innocent.' Our fathers used to like that sort of piece, I believe. The longer I live, Dorian, the more keenly I feel that whatever was good enough for our fathers is not good enough for us. In art, as in politics, *les grandpères ont toujours tort.*"

"This play was good enough for us, Harry. It was 'Romeo and Juliet.' I must admit I was rather annoyed at the idea of seeing Shakespeare done in such a wretched hole of a place. Still, I felt interested, in a sort of way. At any rate, I determined to wait for the first act. There was a dreadful orchestra, presided over by a young Jew who sat at a cracked piano, that nearly drove me away, but at last the drop-scene was drawn up, and the play began. Romeo was a stout elderly gentleman, with corked eyebrows, a husky tragedy voice, and a figure like a beer-barrel. Mercutio was almost as bad. He was played by the low-comedian, who had introduced gags of his own and was on most familiar terms with the pit. They were as grotesque as the scenery, and that looked as if it had come out of a pantomime of fifty years ago. But Juliet! Harry, imagine a girl, hardly seventeen years of age, with a little flower-like face, a small Greek head with plaited coils of dark-brown hair, eyes that were violet wells of passion, lips that were like the petals of a rose. She was the loveliest thing I had ever seen in my life. You said to me once that pathos left you unmoved, but that beauty, mere beauty, could fill your eyes with tears. I tell you, Harry, I could hardly see this girl for the mist of tears that came across me. And her voice,—I never heard such a voice. It was very low at first, with deep mellow notes, that seemed to fall singly upon one's ear. Then it became a little louder, and sounded like a flute or a distant hautbois. In the garden-scene it had all the tremulous ecstasy that one hears just before dawn when nightingales are singing. There were moments, later on, when it had the wild passion of violins. You know how a voice can stir one. Your voice and the voice of Sibyl Vane are two things that I shall never forget. When I close my eyes, I hear them, and each of them says something different. I don't know which to follow. Why should I not love her? Harry, I do love her. She is everything to me in life. Night after night I go to see her play. One evening she is Rosalind, and the next evening she is Imogen. I have seen her die in the gloom of an Italian tomb, sucking the poison from her lover's lips. I have watched her wandering through the forest of Arden, disguised as a pretty boy in hose and doublet and dainty cap. She has been mad, and has come into the presence of a guilty king, and given him rue to wear, and bitter herbs to taste of. She has been innocent, and the black hands of jealousy have crushed her reed-like throat. I have seen her in every age and in every costume. Ordinary women never appeal to one's imagination. They are limited to their century. No glamour ever transfigures them. One knows their minds as easily as one knows their bonnets. One can always find them. There is no mystery in one of them. They ride in the Park in the morning, and chatter at tea-parties in the afternoon. They have their stereotyped smile, and their fashionable manner. They are quite obvious. But an actress! How different an actress is! Why didn't you tell me that the only thing worth loving is an actress?"

"Because I have loved so many of them, Dorian."

"Oh, yes, horrid people with dyed hair and painted faces."

"Don't run down dyed hair and painted faces. There is an extraordinary charm in them, sometimes."

"I wish now I had not told you about Sibyl Vane."

"You could not have helped telling me, Dorian. All through your life you will tell me everything you do."

"Yes, Harry, I believe that is true. I cannot help telling you things. You have a curious influence over me. If I ever did a crime, I would come and confide it to you. You would understand me."

"People like you—the wilful sunbeams of life—don't commit crimes, Dorian. But I am much obliged for the compliment, all the same. And now tell me,—reach me the matches, like a good boy: thanks,—tell me, what are your relations with Sibyl Vane?"[1]

Dorian Gray leaped to his feet, with flushed cheeks and burning eyes.[2] "Harry, Sibyl Vane is sacred!"

"It is only the sacred things that are worth touching, Dorian," said Lord Henry, with a strange touch of pathos in his voice. "But why should you be annoyed? I suppose she will be yours[3] some day. When one is in love, one always begins by deceiving one's self, and one always ends by deceiving others. That is what the world calls romance. You know her, at any rate, I suppose?"

"Of course I know her. On the first night I was at the theatre, the horrid old Jew came round to the box after the performance was over, and offered to bring me behind the scenes and introduce me to her. I was furious with him, and told him that Juliet had been dead for hundreds of years, and that her body was lying in a marble tomb in Verona. I think, from his blank look of amazement, that he thought I had taken too much champagne, or something."

"I am not surprised."

"I was not surprised either. Then he asked me if I wrote for any of the newspapers. I told him I never even read them. He seemed terribly disappointed at that, and confided to me that all the dramatic critics were in a conspiracy against him, and that they were all to be bought."

1. This is another of the series of bowdlerizations by Stoddart. This line was written by Wilde: "is Sybil Vane your mistress?" Stoddart simply rewrote it in its present form, and although Wilde made an addition in 1891, he did not restore the original reading.

2. Stoddart changed TS: "How dare you suggest such a thing, Harry? It is horrible."

3. Stoddart changed this from TS: "your mistress." Wilde altered the Stoddart emendation in 1891, making it a little stronger.

"I believe he was quite right there. But, on the other hand, most of them are not at all expensive."[4]

"Well, he seemed to think they were beyond his means. By this time the lights were being put out in the theatre, and I had to go. He wanted me to try some cigars which he strongly recommended. I declined. The next night, of course, I arrived at the theatre again. When he saw me he made me a low bow, and assured me that I was a patron of art. He was a most offensive brute, though he had an extraordinary passion for Shakespeare. He told me once, with an air of pride, that his three bankruptcies were entirely due to the poet, whom he insisted on calling 'The Bard.'[5] He seemed to think it a distinction."

"It was a distinction, my dear Dorian,—a great distinction. But when did you first speak to Miss Sibyl Vane?"

"The third night. She had been playing Rosalind. I could not help going round. I had thrown her some flowers, and she had looked at me; at least I fancied that she had. The old Jew was persistent. He seemed determined to bring me behind, so I consented. It was curious my not wanting to know her, wasn't it?"

"No; I don't think so."

"My dear Harry, why?"

"I will tell you some other time. Now I want to know about the girl."

"Sibyl? Oh, she was so shy, and so gentle. There is something of a child about her. Her eyes opened wide in exquisite wonder when I told her what I thought of her performance, and she seemed quite unconscious of her power. I think we were both rather nervous. The old Jew stood grinning at the door-way of the dusty greenroom, making elaborate speeches about us both, while we stood looking at each other like children. He would insist on calling me 'My Lord,' so I had to assure Sibyl that I was not anything of the kind. She said quite simply to me, 'You look more like a prince.' "

"Upon my word, Dorian, Miss Sibyl knows how to pay compliments."

"You don't understand her, Harry. She regarded me merely as a person in a play. She knows nothing of life. She lives with her mother, a faded tired woman who played Lady Capulet in a sort of magenta dressing-wrapper on the first night, and who looks as if she had seen better days."

"I know that look. It always depresses me."

"The Jew wanted to tell me her history, but I said it did not interest me."

"You were quite right. There is always something infinitely mean about other people's tragedies."

"Sibyl is the only thing I care about. What is it to me where she came from? From her little head to her little feet, she is absolutely and entirely

4. Wilde altered this passage slightly in 1891.
5. Wilde substituted this phrase in TS for "Shake-

speare." In 1891, the number of bankruptcies was increased to five.

divine. I go to see her act every night of my life, and every night she is more marvellous."

"That is the reason, I suppose, that you will never dine with me now. I thought you must have some curious romance on hand. You have; but it is not quite what I expected."

"My dear Harry, we either lunch or sup together every day, and I have been to the Opera with you several times."

"You always come dreadfully late."

"Well, I can't help going to see Sibyl play, even if it is only for an act. I get hungry for her presence; and when I think of the wonderful soul that is hidden away in that little ivory body, I am filled with awe."

"You can dine with me to-night, Dorian, can't you?"

He shook his head. "To night she is Imogen," he answered, "and to-morrow night she will be Juliet."

"When is she Sibyl Vane?"

"Never."

"I congratulate you."

"How horrid you are! She is all the great heroines of the world in one. She is more than an individual. You laugh, but I tell you she has genius. I love her, and I must make her love me. You, who know all the secrets of life, tell me how to charm Sibyl Vane to love me! I want to make Romeo jealous. I want the dead lovers of the world to hear our laughter, and grow sad. I want a breath of our passion to stir their dust into consciousness, to wake their ashes into pain. My God, Harry, how I worship her!" He was walking up and down the room as he spoke. Hectic spots of red burned on his cheeks. He was terribly excited.

Lord Henry watched him with a subtle sense of pleasure. How different he was now from the shy, frightened boy he had met in Basil Hallward's studio! His nature had developed like a flower, had borne blossoms of scarlet flame. Out of its secret hiding-place had crept his Soul, and Desire had come to meet it on the way.

"And what do you propose to do?" said Lord Henry, at last.

"I want you and Basil to come with me some night and see her act. I have not the slightest fear of the result. You won't be able to refuse to recognize her genius. Then we must get her out of the Jew's hands. She is bound to him for three years—at least for two years and eight months—from the present time. I will have to pay him something, of course. When all that is settled, I will take a West-End theatre and bring her out properly. She will make the world as mad as she has made me."

"Impossible, my dear boy!"

"Yes, she will. She has not merely art, consummate art-instinct, in her, but she has personality also; and you have often told me that it is personalities, not principles, that move the age."

"Well, what night shall we go?"

"Let me see. To-day is Tuesday. Let us fix to-morrow. She plays Juliet to-morrow."

"All right. The Bristol at eight o'clock; and I will get Basil."

"Not eight, Harry, please. Half-past six. We must be there before the curtain rises. You must see her in the first act, where she meets Romeo."

"Half-past six! What an hour! It will be like having a meat-tea. However, just as you wish. Shall you see Basil between this and then? Or shall I write to him?"

"Dear Basil! I have not laid eyes on him for a week. It is rather horrid of me, as he has sent me my portrait in the most wonderful frame, designed by himself, and, though I am a little jealous of it for being a whole month younger than I am, I must admit that I delight in it. Perhaps you had better write to him. I don't want to see him alone. He says things that annoy me."

Lord Henry smiled. "He gives you good advice, I suppose. People are very fond of giving away what they need most themselves."

"You don't mean to say that Basil has got any passion or any romance in him?"

"I don't know whether he has any passion, but he certainly has romance," said Lord Henry, with an amused look in his eyes. "Has he never let you know that?"

"Never. I must ask him about it. I am rather surprised to hear it.[6] He is the best of fellows, but he seems to me to be just a bit of a Philistine. Since I have known you, Harry, I have discovered that."

"Basil, my dear boy, puts everything that is charming in him into his work. The consequence is that he has nothing left for life but his prejudices, his principles, and his common sense. The only artists I have ever known who are personally delightful are bad artists. Good artists give everything to their art, and consequently are perfectly uninteresting in themselves.[7] A great poet, a really great poet, is the most unpoetical of all creatures. But inferior poets are absolutely fascinating. The worse their rhymes are, the more picturesque they look. The mere fact of having published a book of second-rate sonnets makes a man quite irresistible. He lives the poetry that he cannot write. The others write the poetry that they dare not realize."

"I wonder is that really so, Harry?" said Dorian Gray, putting some perfume on his handkerchief out of a large gold-topped bottle that stood on the table. "It must be, if you say so. And now I must be off. Imogen is waiting for me. Don't forget about to-morrow. Good-by."

As he left the room, Lord Henry's heavy eyelids drooped, and he began to think. Certainly few people had ever interested him so much as Dorian Gray, and yet the lad's mad adoration of some one else caused him not the slightest pang of annoyance or jealousy. He was pleased by it. It made him a more interesting study. He had been always enthralled

---

6. Wilde altered the preceding lines after "You don't mean to say . . ." in TS and again in 1891. Originally, Dorian asked whether "Basil has got a passion for somebody?" Lord Henry answered, "Yes, he has. Has he never told you?" This dialogue was canceled, and Wilde wrote the changes in the margin.

7. Wilde rewrote this sentence in 1891.

by the methods of science, but the ordinary subject-matter of science had seemed to him trivial and of no import. And so he had begun by vivisecting himself, as he had ended by vivisecting others. Human life,— that appeared to him the one thing worth investigating. There was nothing else of any value, compared to it. It was true that as one watched life in its curious crucible of pain and pleasure, one could not wear over one's face a mask of glass, or keep the sulphurous fumes from troubling the brain and making the imagination turbid with monstrous fancies and misshapen dreams. There were poisons so subtle that to know their properties one had to sicken of them. There were maladies so strange that one had to pass through them if one sought to understand their nature. And, yet, what a great reward one received! How wonderful the whole world became to one! To note the curious hard logic of passion, and the emotional colored life of the intellect,—to observe where they met, and where they separated, at what point they became one, and at what point they were at discord,—there was a delight in that! What matter what the cost was? One could never pay too high a price for any sensation.

He was conscious—and the thought brought a gleam of pleasure into his brown agate eyes—that it was through certain words of his, musical words said with musical utterance, that Dorian Gray's soul had turned to this white girl and bowed in worship before her. To a large extent, the lad was his own creation. He had made him premature. That was something. Ordinary people waited till life disclosed to them its secrets, but to the few, to the elect, the mysteries of life were revealed before the veil was drawn away. Sometimes this was the effect of art, and chiefly of the art of literature, which dealt immediately with the passions and the intellect. But now and then a complex personality took the place and assumed the office of art, was indeed, in its way, a real work of art, Life having its elaborate masterpieces, just as poetry has, or sculpture, or painting.

Yes, the lad was premature. He was gathering his harvest while it was yet spring. The pulse and passion of youth were in him, but he was becoming self-conscious. It was delightful to watch him. With his beautiful face, and his beautiful soul, he was a thing to wonder at. It was no matter how it all ended, or was destined to end. He was like one of those gracious figures in a pageant or a play, whose joys seem to be remote from one, but whose sorrows stir one's sense of beauty, and whose wounds are like red roses.

Soul and body, body and soul—how mysterious they were![8] There was animalism in the soul, and the body had its moments of spirituality. The senses could refine, and the intellect could degrade. Who could say where the fleshly impulse ceased, or the psychical impulse began? How shallow were the arbitrary definitions of ordinary psychologists! And yet how difficult to decide between the claims of the various schools! Was

8. This sentence was a marginal addition in MS.

the soul a shadow seated in the house of sin? Or was the body really in the soul, as Giordano Bruno thought? The separation of spirit from matter was a mystery, and the union of spirit with matter was a mystery also.

He began to wonder whether we should ever make psychology so absolute a science that each little spring of life would be revealed to us. As it was, we always misunderstood ourselves, and rarely understood others. Experience was of no ethical value. It was merely the name we gave to our mistakes. Men had, as a rule, regarded it as a mode of warning, had claimed for it a certain moral efficacy in the formation of character, had praised it as something that taught us what to follow and showed us what to avoid. But there was no motive power in experience. It was as little of an active cause as conscience itself. All that it really demonstrated was that our future would be the same as our past, and that the sin we had done once, and with loathing, we would do many times, and with joy.

It was clear to him that the experimental method was the only method by which one could arrive at any scientific analysis of the passions; and certainly Dorian Gray was a subject made to his hand, and seemed to promise rich and fruitful results. His sudden mad love for Sibyl Vane was a psychological phenomenon of no small interest. There was no doubt that curiosity had much to do with it, curiosity and the desire for new experiences; yet it was not a simple but rather a very complex passion. What there was in it of the purely sensuous instinct of boyhood had been transformed by the workings of the imagination, changed into something that seemed to the boy himself to be remote from sense, and was for that very reason all the more dangerous. It was the passions about whose origin we deceived ourselves that tyrannized most strongly over us. Our weakest motives were those of whose nature we were conscious. It often happened that when we thought we were experimenting on others we were really experimenting on ourselves.

While Lord Henry sat dreaming on these things, a knock came to the door, and his valet entered, and reminded him it was time to dress for dinner. He got up and looked out into the street. The sunset had smitten into scarlet gold the upper windows of the houses opposite. The panes glowed like plates of heated metal. The sky above was like a faded rose. He thought of Dorian Gray's young fiery-colored life, and wondered how it was all going to end.

When he arrived home, about half-past twelve o'clock, he saw a telegram lying on the hall-table. He opened it and found it was from Dorian. It was to tell him that he was engaged to be married to Sibyl Vane.

Chapter IV.[1]

"I suppose you have heard the news, Basil?" said Lord Henry on the following evening, as Hallward was shown into a little private room at

1. Wilde added another chapter (6) here in 1891.

the Bristol where dinner had been laid for three.

"No, Harry," answered Hallward, giving his hat and coat to the bowing waiter. "What is it? Nothing about politics, I hope? They don't interest me. There is hardly a single person in the House of Commons worth painting; though many of them would be the better for a little white-washing."

"Dorian Gray is engaged to be married," said Lord Henry, watching him as he spoke.

Hallward turned perfectly pale, and a curious look flashed for a moment into his eyes, and then passed away, leaving them dull.[2] "Dorian engaged to be married!" he cried. "Impossible!"

"It is perfectly true."

"To whom?"

"To some little actress or other."

"I can't believe it. Dorian is far too sensible."

"Dorian is far too wise not to do foolish things now and then, my dear Basil."

"Marriage is hardly a thing that one can do now and then, Harry," said Hallward, smiling.

"Except in America.[3] But I didn't say he was married. I said he was engaged to be married. There is a great difference. I have a distinct remembrance of being married, but I have no recollection at all of being engaged.[4] I am inclined to think that I never was engaged."

"But think of Dorian's birth, and position, and wealth. It would be absurd for him to marry so much beneath him."

"If you want him to marry this girl, tell him that, Basil. He is sure to do it then.[5] Whenever a man does a thoroughly stupid thing, it is always from the noblest motives."

"I hope the girl is good, Harry. I don't want to see Dorian tied to some vile creature, who might degrade his nature and ruin his intellect."

"Oh, she is more than good—she is beautiful," murmured Lord Henry, sipping a glass of vermouth and orange-bitters. "Dorian says she is beautiful; and he is not often wrong about things of that kind. Your portrait of him has quickened his appreciation of the personal appearance of other people. It has had that excellent effect, among others. We are to see her to-night, if that boy doesn't forget his appointment."[6]

"But do you approve of it, Harry?" asked Hallward, walking up and down the room, and biting his lip. "You can't approve of it, really. It is some silly infatuation."

"I never approve, or disapprove, of anything now. It is an absurd attitude to take towards life. We are not sent into the world to air our moral prejudices. I never take any notice of what common people say,

2. Wilde changed these lines in 1891, muting Basil's reaction.
3. Wilde added this in TS.
4. "I have a distinct . . . being engaged" was added in TS.

5. "But think of Dorian's birth . . . do it then" was added in MS margin, and the following sentence was added in TS.
6. Wilde added several lines here in 1891.

and I never interfere with what charming people do. If a personality fascinates me, whatever the personality chooses to do is absolutely delightful to me. Dorian Gray falls in love with a beautiful girl who acts Shakespeare, and proposes to marry her. Why not? If he wedded Messalina he would be none the less interesting. You know I am not a champion of marriage. The real drawback to marriage is that it makes one unselfish. And unselfish people are colorless. They lack individuality. Still, there are certain temperaments that marriage makes more complex. They retain their egotism, and add to it many other egos. They are forced to have more than one life. They become more highly organized. Besides, every experience is of value, and, whatever one may say against marriage, it is certainly an experience. I hope that Dorian Gray will make this girl his wife, passionately adore her for six months, and then suddenly become fascinated by some one else. He would be a wonderful study."[7]

"You don't mean all that, Harry; you know you don't. If Dorian Gray's life were spoiled, no one would be sorrier than yourself. You are much better than you pretend to be."

Lord Henry laughed. "The reason we all like to think so well of others is that we are all afraid for ourselves. The basis of optimism is sheer terror. We think that we are generous because we credit our neighbor with those virtues that are likely to benefit ourselves. We praise the banker that we may overdraw our account, and find good qualities in the highwayman in the hope that he may spare our pockets.[8] I mean everything that I have said. I have the greatest contempt for optimism.[9] And as for a spoiled life, no life is spoiled but one whose growth is arrested. If you want to mar a nature, you have merely to reform it. But here is Dorian himself. He will tell you more than I can."

"My dear Harry, my dear Basil, you must both congratulate me!" said the boy, throwing off his evening cape with its satin-lined wings, and shaking each of his friends by the hand in turn. "I have never been so happy. Of course it is sudden: all really delightful things are. And yet it seems to me to be the one thing I have been looking for all my life." He was flushed with excitement and pleasure, and looked extraordinarily handsome.

"I hope you will always be very happy, Dorian," said Hallward, "but I don't quite forgive you for not having let me know of your engagement. You let Harry know."

"And I don't forgive you for being late for dinner," broke in Lord Henry, putting his hand on the lad's shoulder, and smiling as he spoke. "Come, let us sit down and try what the new *chef* here is like, and then you will tell us how it all came about."

---

7. Wilde made several minor changes in this paragraph in 1891.
8. "and find good qualities . . . pockets" added in TS.
9. This sentence and the four immediately following were added in TS.

"There is really not much to tell," cried Dorian, as they took their seats at the small round table. "What happened was simply this. After I left you yesterday evening, Harry, I had some dinner at that curious little Italian restaurant in Rupert Street,[1] you introduced me to, and went down afterwards to the theatre. Sibyl was playing Rosalind. Of course the scenery was dreadful, and the Orlando absurd. But Sibyl! You should have seen her! When she came on in her boy's dress she was perfectly wonderful. She wore a moss-colored velvet jerkin with cinnamon sleeves, slim brown cross-gartered hose, a dainty little green cap with a hawk's feather caught in a jewel, and a hooded cloak lined with dull red. She had never seemed to me more exquisite. She had all the delicate grace of that Tanagra figurine that you have in your studio, Basil. Her hair clustered round her face like dark leaves round a pale rose. As for her acting—well, you will see her to-night. She is simply a born artist. I sat in the dingy box absolutely enthralled. I forgot that I was in London and in the nineteenth century. I was away with my love in a forest that no man had ever seen. After the performance was over I went behind, and spoke to her. As we were sitting together, suddenly there came a look into her eyes that I had never seen there before. My lips moved towards hers. We kissed each other. I can't describe to you what I felt at that moment. It seemed to me that all my life had been narrowed to one perfect point of rose-colored joy. She trembled all over, and shook like a white narcissus. Then she flung herself on her knees and kissed my hands. I feel that I should not tell you all this, but I can't help it. Of course our engagement is a dead secret. She has not even told her own mother. I don't know what my guardians will say. Lord Radley is sure to be furious. I don't care. I shall be of age in less than a year, and then I can do what I like. I have been right, Basil, haven't I, to take my love out of poetry, and to find my wife in Shakespeare's plays? Lips that Shakespeare taught to speak have whispered their secret in my ear. I have had the arms of Rosalind around me, and kissed Juliet on the mouth."

"Yes, Dorian, I suppose you were right," said Hallward, slowly.

"Have you seen her to-day?" asked Lord Henry.

"Dorian Gray shook his head. "I left her in the forest of Arden, I shall find her in an orchard in Verona."

Lord Henry sipped his champagne in a meditative manner. "At what particular point did you mention the word marriage, Dorian? and what did she say in answer? Perhaps you forgot all about it."

"My dear Harry, I did not treat it as a business transaction, and I did not make any formal proposal. I told her that I loved her, and she said she was not worthy to be my wife. Not worthy! Why, the whole world is nothing to me compared to her."

"Women are wonderfully practical," murmured Lord Henry,—"much

1. Wilde added this detail in TS.

more practical than we are. In situations of that kind we often forget to say anything about marriage, and they always remind us."

Hallward laid his hand upon his arm. "Don't, Harry. You have annoyed Dorian. He is not like other men. He would never bring misery upon any one. His nature is too fine for that."

Lord Henry looked across the table. "Dorian is never annoyed with me," he answered. "I asked the question for the best reason possible, for the only reason, indeed, that excuses one for asking any question,— simple curiosity. I have a theory that it is always the women who propose to us, and not we who propose to the women, except, of course, in middle-class life. But then the middle classes are not modern."

Dorian Gray laughed, and tossed his head. "You are quite incorrigible, Harry; but I don't mind. It is impossible to be angry with you. When you see Sibyl Vane you will feel that the man who could wrong her would be a beast without a heart. I cannot understand how any one can wish to shame what he loves. I love Sibyl Vane. I wish to place her on a pedestal of gold, and to see the world worship the woman who is mine. What is marriage? An irrevocable vow. And it is an irrevocable vow that I want to take.[2] Her trust makes me faithful, her belief makes me good. When I am with her, I regret all that you have taught me. I become different from what you have known me to be. I am changed, and the mere touch of Sibyl Vane's hand makes me forget you and all your wrong, fascinating, poisonous, delightful[3] theories."

"You will always like me, Dorian," said Lord Henry. "Will you have some coffee, you fellows?—Waiter, bring coffee, and *fine-champagne*, and some cigarettes. No: don't mind the cigarettes; I have some.—Basil, I can't allow you to smoke cigars. You must have a cigarette. A cigarette is the perfect type of a perfect pleasure. It is exquisite, and it leaves one unsatisfied. What more can you want?—Yes, Dorian, you will always be fond of me. I represent to you all the sins you have never had the courage to commit."

"What nonsense you talk, Harry!" cried Dorian Gray, lighting his cigarette from a fire-breathing silver dragon that the waiter had placed on the table. "Let us go down to the theatre. When you see Sibyl you will have a new ideal of life. She will represent something to you that you have never known."

"I have known everything," said Lord Henry, with a sad[4] look in his eyes, "but I am always ready for a new emotion. I am afraid that there is no such thing, for me at any rate. Still, your wonderful girl may thrill me. Dorian, you will come with me.—I am so sorry, Basil, but there is only room for two in the brougham. You must follow us in a hansom."

They got up and put on their coats, sipping their coffee standing.

2. Wilde crossed out the following in MS: "Why she would loathe me if she thought I merely meant to use her till I grew weary of her and then throw her away."

3. "Delightful" added in TS. Wilde inserted almost two additional pages at this point in 1891.

4. Changed to "tired" in 1891.

Hallward was silent and preoccupied. There was a gloom over him. He could not bear this marriage, and yet it seemed to him to be better than many other things that might have happened. After a few moments, they all passed down-stairs. He drove off by himself, as had been arranged, and watched the flashing lights of the little brougham in front of him. A strange sense of loss came over him. He felt that Dorian Gray would never again be to him all that he had been in the past. His eyes darkened,[5] and the crowded flaring streets became blurred to him. When the cab drew up at the doors of the theatre, it seemed to him that he had grown years older.

Chapter V.

For some reason or other, the house was crowded that night, and the fat Jew manager who met them at the door was beaming from ear to ear with an oily, tremulous smile. He escorted them to their box with a sort of pompous humility, waving his fat jewelled hands, and talking at the top of his voice. Dorian Gray loathed him more than ever. He felt as if he had come to look for Miranda and had been met by Caliban. Lord Henry, upon the other hand, rather liked him. At least he declared he did, and insisted on shaking him by the hand, and assured him that he was proud to meet a man who had discovered a real genius and gone bankrupt over Shakespeare. Hallward amused himself with watching the faces in the pit. The heat was terribly oppressive, and the huge sunlight flamed like a monstrous dahlia with petals of fire. The youths in the gallery had taken off their coats and waistcoats and hung them over the side. They talked to each other across the theatre, and shared their oranges with the tawdry painted girls who sat by them. Some women were laughing in the pit; their voices were horribly shrill and discordant. The sound of the popping of corks came from the bar.

"What a place to find one's divinity in!" said Lord Henry.

"Yes!" answered Dorian Gray. "It was here I found her, and she is divine beyond all living things. When she acts you will forget everything. These common people here, with their coarse faces and brutal gestures, become quite different when she is on the stage. They sit silently and watch her. They weep and laugh as she wills them to do. She makes them as responsive as a violin. She spiritualizes them, and one feels that they are of the same flesh and blood as one's self."

"Oh, I hope not!" murmured Lord Henry, who was scanning the occupants of the gallery through his opera-glass.

"Don't pay any attention to him, Dorian," said Hallward. "I understand what you mean, and I believe in this girl. Any one you love must be marvellous, and any girl that has the effect you describe must be fine and noble. To spiritualize one's age,—that is something worth doing. If

---

5. Wilde substituted "darkened" for "filled with tears" in MS.

this girl can give a soul to those who have lived without one, if she can create the sense of beauty in people whose lives have been sordid and ugly, if she can strip them of their selfishness and lend them tears for sorrows that are not their own, she is worthy of all your adoration, worthy of the adoration of the world. This marriage is quite right. I did not think so at first, but I admit it now. God[1] made Sibyl Vane for you. Without her you would have been incomplete.

"Thanks, Basil," answered Dorian Gray, pressing his hand. "I knew that you would understand me. Harry is so cynical, he terrifies me. But here is the orchestra. It is quite dreadful, but it only lasts for about five minutes. Then the curtain rises, and you will see the girl to whom I am going to give all my life, to whom I have given everything that is good in me."

A quarter of an hour afterwards, amidst an extraordinary turmoil of applause, Sibyl Vane stepped on to the stage. Yes, she was certainly lovely to look at—one of the loveliest creatures, Lord Henry thought, that he had ever seen. There was something of the fawn in her shy grace and startled eyes. A faint blush, like the shadow of a rose in a mirror of silver, came to her cheeks as she glanced at the crowded, enthusiastic house. She stepped back a few paces, and her lips seemed to tremble. Basil Hallward leaped to his feet and began to applaud. Dorian Gray sat motionless, gazing on her, like a man in a dream. Lord Henry peered through his opera-glass, murmuring, "Charming! charming!"

The scene was the hall of Capulet's house, and Romeo in his pilgrim's dress had entered with Mercutio and his friends. The band, such as it was, struck up a few bars of music, and the dance began. Through the crowd of ungainly, shabbily-dressed actors, Sibyl Vane moved like a creature from a finer world. Her body swayed, as she danced, as a plant sways in the water. The curves of her throat were like the curves of a white lily. Her hands seemed to be made of cool ivory.

Yet she was curiously listless. She showed no sign of joy when her eyes rested on Romeo. The few lines she had to speak,—

> Good pilgrim, you do wrong your hand too much,
>   Which mannerly devotion shows in this;
> For saints have hands that pilgrims' hands do touch,
>   And palm to palm is holy palmers' kiss,—

with the brief dialogue that follows, were spoken in a thoroughly artificial manner. The voice was exquisite, but from the point of view of tone it was absolutely false. It was wrong in color. It took away all the life from the verse. It made the passion unreal.

Dorian Gray grew pale as he watched her. Neither of his friends dared to say anything to him. She seemed to them to be absolutely incompetent. They were horribly disappointed.

1. Changed to "the gods" in 1891.

Yet they felt that the true test of any Juliet is the balcony scene of the second act. They waited for that. If she failed there, there was nothing in her.

She looked charming as she came out in the moonlight. That could not be denied. But the staginess of her acting was unbearable, and grew worse as she went on. Her gestures became absurdly artificial. She over-emphasized everything that she had to say. The beautiful passage,—

> Thou knowest the mask of night is on my face,
> Else would a maiden blush bepaint my cheek
> For that which thou hast heard me speak to-night,—

was declaimed with the painful precision of a school-girl who has been taught to recite by some second-rate professor of elocution. When she leaned over the balcony and came to those wonderful lines,—

> Although I joy in thee,
> I have no joy of this contract to-night:
> It is too rash, too unadvised, too sudden;
> Too like the lightning, which doth cease to be
> Ere one can say, "It lightens." Sweet, good-night!
> This bud of love by summer's ripening breath
> May prove a beauteous flower when next we meet,—

she spoke the words as if they conveyed no meaning to her. It was not nervousness. Indeed, so far from being nervous, she seemed absolutely self-contained. It was simply bad art. She was a complete failure.

Even the common uneducated audience of the pit and gallery lost their interest in the play. They got restless, and began to talk loudly and to whistle. The Jew manager, who was standing at the back of the dress-circle, stamped and swore with rage. The only person unmoved was the girl herself.

When the second act was over there came a storm of hisses, and Lord Henry got up from his chair and put on his coat. "She is quite beautiful, Dorian," he said, "but she can't act. Let us go."

"I am going to see the play through," answered the lad, in a hard, bitter voice. "I am awfully sorry that I have made you waste an evening, Harry. I apologize to both of you."

"My dear Dorian, I should think Miss Vane was ill," interrupted Hallward. "We will come some other night."

"I wish she was ill," he rejoined. "But she seems to me to be simply callous and cold. She has entirely altered. Last night she was a great artist. To-night she is merely a commonplace, mediocre actress."

"Don't talk like that about any one you love, Dorian. Love is a more wonderful thing than art."

"They are both simply forms of imitation," murmured Lord Henry. "But do let us go. Dorian, you must not stay here any longer. It is not good for one's morals to see bad acting. Besides, I don't suppose you will want your wife to act. So what does it matter if she plays Juliet like a wooden doll? She is very lovely, and if she knows as little about life as she does about acting, she will be a delightful experience. There are only two kinds of people who are really fascinating,—people who know absolutely everything, and people who know absolutely nothing. Good heavens, my dear boy, don't look so tragic! The secret of remaining young is never to have an emotion that is unbecoming. Come to the club with Basil and myself. We will smoke cigarettes and drink to the beauty of Sibyl Vane. She is beautiful. What more can you want?"

"Please go away, Harry," cried the lad. "I really want to be alone.— Basil, you don't mind my asking you to go? Ah! can't you see that my heart is breaking?" The hot tears came to his eyes. His lips trembled, and, rushing to the back of the box, he leaned up against the wall, hiding his face in his hands.

"Let us go, Basil," said Lord Henry, with a strange tenderness in his voice; and the two young men passed out together.

A few moments afterwards the footlights flared up, and the curtain rose on the third act. Dorian Gray went back to his seat. He looked pale, and proud, and indifferent. The play dragged on, and seemed interminable. Half of the audience went out, tramping in heavy boots, and laughing. The whole thing was a *fiasco*. The last act was played to almost empty benches.

As soon as it was over, Dorian Gray rushed behind the scenes into the greenroom. The girl was standing alone there, with a look of triumph on her face. Her eyes were lit with an exquisite fire. There was a radiance about her. Her parted lips were smiling over some secret of their own.

When he entered, she looked at him, and an expression of infinite joy came over her. "How badly I acted to-night, Dorian!" she cried.

"Horribly!" he answered, gazing at her in amazement,—"horribly! It was dreadful. Are you ill? You have no idea what it was. You have no idea what I suffered."

The girl smiled. "Dorian," she answered, lingering over his name with long-drawn music in her voice, as though it were sweeter than honey to the red petals of her lips,—"Dorian, you should have understood. But you understand now, don't you?"

"Understand what?" he asked, angrily.

"Why I was so bad to-night. Why I shall always be bad. Why I shall never act well again."

He shrugged his shoulders. "You are ill, I suppose. When you are ill you shouldn't act. You make yourself ridiculous. My friends were bored. I was bored."

She seemed not to listen to him. She was transfigured with joy. An ecstasy of happiness dominated her.

"Dorian, Dorian," she cried, "before I knew you, acting was the one reality of my life. It was only in the theatre that I lived. I thought that it was all true. I was Rosalind one night, and Portia the other. The joy of Beatrice was my joy, and the sorrows of Cordelia were mine also.[2] I believed in everything. The common people who acted with me seemed to me to be godlike. The painted scenes were my world. I knew nothing but shadows, and I thought them real. You came,—oh, my beautiful love!—and you freed my soul from prison. You taught me what reality really is. To-night, for the first time in my life, I saw through the hollowness, the sham, the silliness, of the empty pageant in which I had always played. To-night, for the first time, I became conscious that the Romeo was hideous, and old, and painted, that the moonlight in the orchard was false, that the scenery was vulgar, and that the words I had to speak were unreal, were not my words, not what I wanted to say. You had brought me something higher, something of which all art is but a reflection. You have made me understand what love really is. My love! my love! I am sick of shadows. You are more to me than all art can ever be. What have I to do with the puppets of a play? When I came on to-night, I could not understand how it was that everything had gone from me. Suddenly it dawned on my soul what it all meant. The knowledge was exquisite to me. I heard them hissing, and I smiled. What should they know of love? Take me away, Dorian—take me away with you, where we can be quite alone. I hate the stage. I might mimic a passion that I do not feel, but I cannot mimic one that burns me like fire. Oh, Dorian, Dorian, you understand now what it all means? Even if I could do it, it would be profanation for me to play at being in love. You have made me see that."

He flung himself down on the sofa, and turned away his face. "You have killed my love," he muttered.

She looked at him in wonder, and laughed. He made no answer. She came across to him, and stroked his hair with her little fingers. She knelt down and pressed his hands to her lips. He drew them away, and a shudder ran through him.

Then he leaped up, and went to the door. "Yes," he cried, "you have killed my love. You used to stir my imagination. Now you don't even stir my curiosity. You simply produce no effect. I loved you because you were wonderful, because you had genius and intellect, because you realized the dreams of great poets and gave shape and substance to the shadows of art. You have thrown it all away. You are shallow and stupid. My God! how mad I was to love you! What a fool I have been! You are nothing to me now. I will never see you again. I will never think of you. I will never mention your name. You don't know what you were to me, once. Why, once. . . . Oh, I can't bear to think of it! I wish I had never laid eyes upon you! You have spoiled the romance of my life. How little you can know of love, if you say it mars your art! What are you without your art? Nothing. I would have made you famous, splendid, magnifi-

---

2. Wilde rewrote this line in TS, changing it from "If I died as Desdemona, I came back as Juliet."

cent. The world would have worshipped you, and you would have belonged to me. What are you now? A third-rate actress with a pretty face."

The girl grew white, and trembled. She clinched her hands together, and her voice seemed to catch in her throat. "You are not serious, Dorian?" she murmured. "You are acting."

"Acting! I leave that to you. You do it so well," he answered, bitterly.

She rose from her knees, and, with a piteous expression of pain in her face, came across the room to him. She put her hand upon his arm, and looked into his eyes. He thrust her back. "Don't touch me!" he cried.

A low moan broke from her, and she flung herself at his feet, and lay there like a trampled flower. "Dorian, Dorian, don't leave me!" she whispered. "I am so sorry I didn't act well. I was thinking of you all the time. But I will try,—indeed, I will try. It came so suddenly across me, my love for you. I think I should never have known it if you had not kissed me,—if we had not kissed each other. Kiss me again, my love. Don't go away from me. I couldn't bear it.[3] Can't you forgive me for to-night? I will work so hard, and try to improve. Don't be cruel to me because I love you better than anything in the world. After all, it is only once that I have not pleased you. But you are quite right, Dorian. I should have shown myself more of an artist. It was foolish of me; and yet I couldn't help it. Oh, don't leave me, don't leave me." A fit of passionate sobbing choked her. She crouched on the floor like a wounded thing, and Dorian Gray, with his beautiful eyes, looked down at her, and his chiselled lips curled in exquisite disdain. There is always something ridiculous about the passions of people whom one has ceased to love. Sibyl Vane seemed to him to be absurdly melodramatic. Her tears and sobs annoyed him.

"I am going," he said at last, in his calm, clear voice. "I don't wish to be unkind, but I can't see you again. You have disappointed me."

She wept silently, and made no answer, but crept nearer to him. Her little hands stretched blindly out, and appeared to be seeking for him.[4] He turned on his heel, and left the room. In a few moments he was out of the theatre.

Where he went to, he hardly knew. He remembered wandering through dimly-lit streets with gaunt black-shadowed archways and evil-looking houses. Women with hoarse voices and harsh laughter had called after him. Drunkards had reeled by cursing, and chattering to themselves like monstrous apes.[5] He had seen grotesque children huddled upon doorsteps, and had heard shrieks and oaths from gloomy courts.

When the dawn was just breaking, he found himself at Covent Gar-

3. Wilde added foreshadowing here in 1891.
4. This sentence added in TS.
5. Wilde wrote in TS, then crossed out the following lines: "A man with curious eyes had suddenly peered into his face and then dogged him with stealthy footsteps, passing and repassing him many times." It is likely that Sibyl's avenging brother, James, added in 1891, may have originated in these lines.

den. Huge carts filled with nodding lilies rumbled slowly down the polished empty street. The air was heavy with the perfume of the flowers, and their beauty seemed to bring him an anodyne for his pain. He followed into the market, and watched the men unloading their wagons. A white-smocked carter offered him some cherries. He thanked him, wondered why he refused to accept any money for them, and began to eat them listlessly. They had been plucked at midnight, and the coldness of the moon had entered into them. A long line of boys carrying crates of striped tulips, and of yellow and red roses, defiled in front of him, threading their way through the huge jade-green piles of vegetables. Under the portico, with its gray sun-bleached pillars, loitered a troop of draggled bareheaded girls, waiting for the auction to be over.[6] After some time he hailed a hansom and drove home. The sky was pure opal now, and the roofs of the houses glistened like silver against it.[7] As he was passing through the library towards the door of his bedroom, his eye fell upon the portrait Basil Hallward had painted of him. He started back in surprise,[8] and then went over to it and examined it. In the dim arrested light that struggled through the cream-colored silk blinds, the face seemed to him to be a little changed. The expression looked different. One would have said that there was a touch of cruelty in the mouth. It was certainly curious.

He turned round, and, walking to the window, drew the blinds up. The bright dawn flooded the room, and swept the fantastic shadows into dusky corners, where they lay shuddering. But the strange expression that he had noticed in the face of the portrait seemed to linger there, to be more intensified even. The quivering, ardent sunlight showed him the lines of cruelty round the mouth as clearly as if he had been looking into a mirror after he had done some dreadful thing.

He winced, and, taking up from the table an oval glass framed in ivory Cupids, that Lord Henry had given him, he glanced hurriedly into it. No line like that warped his red lips. What did it mean?

He rubbed his eyes, and came close to the picture, and examined it again. There were no signs of change when he looked into the actual painting, and yet there was no doubt that the whole expression had altered. It was not a mere fancy of his own. The thing was horribly apparent.

He threw himself into a chair, and began to think. Suddenly there flashed across his mind what he had said in Basil Hallward's studio the day the picture had been finished. Yes, he remembered it perfectly. He had uttered a mad wish that he himself might remain young, and the portrait grow old; that his own beauty might be untarnished, and the face on the canvas bear the burden of his passions and his sins; that the painted image might be seared with the lines of suffering and thought,

---

6. "A long line . . . to be over" added in TS.
7. This sentence also added in TS. Wilde expanded and revised the rest of the paragraph in 1891.
8. In MS, the following lines were canceled at this point: "then he smiled to himself and went on into his bedroom. 'It is merely an effect of light,' he murmured. 'I did not know that the dawn was so unbecoming.'"

and that he might keep all the delicate bloom and loveliness of his then just conscious boyhood. Surely his prayer had not been answered? Such things were impossible. It seemed monstrous even to think of them. And, yet, there was the picture before him, with the touch of cruelty in the mouth.

Cruelty! Had he been cruel? It was the girl's fault, not his. He had dreamed of her as a great artist, had given his love to her because he had thought her great. Then she had disappointed him. She had been shallow and unworthy. And, yet, a feeling of infinite regret came over him, as he thought of her lying at his feet sobbing like a little child. He remembered with what callousness he had watched her. Why had he been made like that? Why had such a soul been given to him? But he had suffered also. During the three terrible hours that the play had lasted, he had lived centuries of pain, æon upon æon of torture. His life was well worth hers. She had marred him for a moment, if he had wounded her for an age. Besides, women were better suited to bear sorrow than men. They lived on their emotions. They only thought of their emotions. When they took lovers, it was merely to have some one with whom they could have scenes. Lord Henry had told him that, and Lord Henry knew what women were. Why should he trouble about Sibyl Vane? She was nothing to him now.

But the picture? What was he to say of that?[9] It held the secret of his life, and told his story. It had taught him to love his own beauty. Would it teach him to loathe his own soul? Would he ever look at it again?

No; it was merely an illusion wrought on the troubled senses. The horrible night that he had passed had left phantoms behind it. Suddenly there had fallen upon his brain that tiny scarlet speck that makes men mad. The picture had not changed. It was folly to think so.

Yet it was watching him, with its beautiful marred face and its cruel smile. Its bright hair gleamed in the early sunlight. Its blue eyes met his own. A sense of infinite pity, not for himself, but for the painted image of himself, came over him. It had altered already, and would alter more. Its gold would wither into gray. Its red and white roses would die. For every sin that he committed, a stain would fleck and wreck its fairness. But he would not sin. The picture, changed or unchanged, would be to him the visible emblem of conscience. He would resist temptation. He would not see Lord Henry any more—would not, at any rate, listen to those subtle poisonous theories that in Basil Hallward's garden had first stirred within him the passion for impossible things. He would go back to Sibyl Vane, make her amends, marry her, try to love her again. Yes, it was his duty to do so. She must have suffered more than he had. Poor child! He had been selfish and cruel to her. The fascination that she had exercised over him would return. They would be happy together. His life with her would be beautiful and pure.

9. Wilde canceled the following in TS: "Where was he to hide it? It could not be left for common eyes to gaze at."

He got up from his chair, and drew a large screen right in front of the portrait, shuddering as he glanced at it. "How horrible!" he murmured to himself, and he walked across to the window and opened it. When he stepped out on the grass, he drew a deep breath. The fresh morning air seemed to drive away all his sombre passions. He thought only of Sibyl Vane. A faint echo of his love came back to him. He repeated her name over and over again. The birds that were singing in the dew-drenched garden seemed to be telling the flowers about her.

Chapter VI.

It was long past noon when he awoke. His valet had crept several times into the room on tiptoe to see if he was stirring, and had wondered what made his young master sleep so late. Finally his bell sounded, and Victor came in softly with a cup of tea, and a pile of letters, on a small tray of old Sèvres china, and drew back the olive-satin curtains, with their shimmering blue lining, that hung in front of the three tall windows.

"Monsieur has well slept this morning," he said, smiling.

"What o'clock is it, Victor?"[1] asked Dorian Gray, sleepily.

"One hour and a quarter, monsieur."

How late it was! He sat up, and, having sipped some tea, turned over his letters. One of them was from Lord Henry, and had been brought by hand that morning. He hesitated for a moment, and then put it aside. The others he opened listlessly. They contained the usual collection of cards, invitations to dinner, tickets for private views, programmes of charity concerts, and the like, that are showered on fashionable young men every morning during the season. There was a rather heavy bill, for a chased silver Louis-Quinze toilet-set, that he had not yet had the courage to send on to his guardians, who were extremely old-fashioned people and did not realize that we live in an age when only unnecessary things are absolutely necessary to us; and there were several very courteously worded communications from Jermyn Street money-lenders offering to advance any sum of money at a moment's notice and at the most reasonable rates of interest.

After about ten minutes he got up, and, throwing on an elaborate dressing-gown, passed into the onyx-paved bath-room. The cool water refreshed him after his long sleep. He seemed to have forgotten all that he had gone through. A dim sense of having taken part in some strange tragedy came to him once of twice, but there was the unreality of a dream about it.

As soon as he was dressed, he went into the library and sat down to a light French breakfast, that had been laid out for him on a small round

1. In MS the valet was named Jacques. The conversation was in French, as it was whenever Dorian and Jacques spoke. Wilde changed this to English in stages: first, Dorian's speech in MS, then name of the valet and his dialogue.

table close to an open window. It was an exquisite day. The warm air seemed laden with spices. A bee flew in, and buzzed round the blue-dragon bowl, filled with sulphur-yellow roses, that stood in front of him. He felt perfectly happy.

Suddenly his eye fell on the screen that he had placed in front of the portrait, and he started.

"Too cold for Monsieur?" asked his valet, putting an omelette on the table. "I shut the window?"

Dorian shook his head. "I am not cold," he murmured.

Was it all true? Had the portrait really changed? Or had it been simply his own imagination that had made him see a look of evil where there had been a look of joy? Surely a painted canvas could not alter? The thing was absurd. It would serve as a tale to tell Basil some day. It would make him smile.

And, yet, how vivid was his recollection of the whole thing! First in the dim twilight, and then in the bright dawn, he had seen the touch of cruelty in the warped lips. He almost dreaded his valet leaving the room. He knew that when he was alone he would have to examine the portrait. He was afraid of certainty. When the coffee and cigarettes had been brought and the man turned to go, he felt a mad desire to tell him to remain. As the door closed behind him he called him back. The man stood waiting for his orders. Dorian looked at him for a moment. "I am not at home to any one, Victor," he said, with a sigh. The man bowed and retired.

He rose from the table, lit a cigarette, and flung himself down on a luxuriously-cushioned couch that stood facing the screen. The screen was an old one of gilt Spanish leather, stamped and wrought with a rather florid Louis-Quatorze pattern. He scanned it curiously, wondering if it had ever before concealed the secret of a man's life.

Should he move it aside, after all? Why not let it stay there? What was the use of knowing? If the thing was true, it was terrible. If it was not true, why trouble about it? But what if, by some fate or deadlier chance, other eyes than his spied behind, and saw the horrible change? What should he do if Basil Hallward came and asked to look at his own picture? He would be sure to do that. No; the thing had to be examined, and at once. Anything would be better than this dreadful state of doubt.

He got up, and locked both doors. At least he would be alone when he looked upon the mask of his shame. Then he drew the screen aside, and saw himself face to face. It was perfectly true. The portrait had altered.

As he often remembered afterwards, and always with no small wonder, he found himself at first gazing at the portrait with a feeling of almost scientific interest.[2] That such a chance should have taken place was incredible to him. And yet it was a fact. Was there some subtle

---

2. Originally, the MS read, "He was strangely calm at this moment."

affinity between the chemical atoms, that shaped themselves into form and color on the canvas, and the soul that was within him? Could it be that what that soul thought, they realized?—that what it dreamed, they made true? Or was there some other, more terrible reason? He shuddered, and felt afraid, and, going back to the couch, lay there, gazing at the picture in sickened horror.[3]

One thing, however, he felt that it had done for him. It had made him conscious how unjust, how cruel, he had been to Sibyl Vane. It was not too late to make reparation for that. She could still be his wife. His unreal and selfish love would yield to some higher influence, would be transformed into some nobler passion, and the portrait that Basil Hallward had painted of him would be a guide to him through life, would be to him what holiness was to some, and conscience to others, and the fear of God to us all. There were opiates for remorse, drugs that could lull the moral sense to sleep. But here was a visible symbol of the degradation of sin. Here was an ever-present sign of the ruin men brought upon their souls.

Three o'clock struck, and four, and half-past four, but he did not stir. He was trying to gather up the scarlet threads of life, and to weave them into a pattern; to find his way through the sanguine labyrinth of passion through which he was wandering. He did not know what to do, or what to think.[4] Finally, he went over to the table and wrote a passionate letter to the girl he had loved, imploring her forgiveness, and accusing himself of madness. He covered page after page with wild words of sorrow, and wilder words of pain.[5] There is a luxury in self-reproach. When we blame ourselves we feel that no one else has a right to blame us. It is the confession, not the priest, that gives us absolution. When Dorian Gray had finished the letter, he felt that he had been forgiven.

Suddenly there came a knock to the door, and he heard Lord Henry's voice outside. "My dear Dorian, I must see you. Let me in at once. I can't bear your shutting yourself up like this."

He made no answer at first, but remained quite still. The knocking still continued, and grew louder. Yes, it was better to let Lord Henry in, and to[6] explain to him the new life he was going to lead, to quarrel with him if it became necessary to quarrel, to part if parting was inevitable. He jumped up, drew the screen hastily across the picture, and unlocked the door.

"I am so sorry for it all, my dear boy," said Lord Henry, coming in. "But you must not think about it too much."

"Do you mean about Sibyl Vane?" asked Dorian.

"Yes, of course," answered Lord Henry, sinking into a chair, and slowly pulling his gloves off. "It is dreadful, from one point of view, but

---

3. Wilde added the last two sentences of this paragraph in TS.
4. Wilde added to TS the first three sentences of this paragraph.

5. This sentence added in TS.
6. TS originally read "to sever their friendship at once."

it was not your fault.[7] Tell me, did you go behind and see her after the play was over?"

"Yes."

"I felt sure you had. Did you make a scene with her?"

"I was brutal, Harry,—perfectly brutal. But it is all right now. I am not sorry for anything that has happened. It has taught me to know myself better."

"Ah, Dorian, I am so glad you take it in that way! I was afraid I would find you plunged in remorse, and tearing your nice hair."

"I have got through all that," said Dorian, shaking his head, and smiling. "I am perfectly happy now. I know what conscience is, to begin with. It is not what you told me it was. It is the divinest thing in us. Don't sneer at it, Harry, any more,—at least not before me. I want to be good. I can't bear the idea of my soul being hideous."

"A very charming artistic basis for ethics, Dorian! I congratulate you on it. But how are you going to begin?"

"By marrying Sibyl Vane."

"Marrying Sibyl Vane!" cried Lord Henry, standing up, and looking at him in perplexed amazement. "But, my dear Dorian——"

"Yes, Harry, I know what you are going to say. Something dreadful about marriage. Don't say it. Don't ever say things of that kind to me again. Two days ago I asked Sibyl to marry me. I am not going to break my word to her. She is to be my wife."

"Your wife! Dorian! . . . Didn't you get my letter? I wrote to you this morning, and sent the note down, by my own man."

"Your letter? Oh, yes, I remember. I have not read it yet, Harry. I was afraid there might be something in it that I wouldn't like."

Lord Henry walked across the room, and, sitting down by Dorian Gray, took both his hands in his, and held them tightly. "Dorian," he said, "my letter—don't be frightened—was to tell you that Sibyl Vane is dead."

A cry of pain rose from the lad's lips, and he leaped to his feet, tearing his hands away from Lord Henry's grasp. "Dead! Sibyl dead! It is not true! It is a horrible lie!"

"It is quite true, Dorian," said Lord Henry, gravely. "It is in all the morning papers. I wrote down to you to ask you not to see any one till I came. There will have to be an inquest, of course, and you must not be mixed up in it. Things like that make a man fashionable in Paris. But in London people are so prejudiced. Here, one should never make one's *début* with a scandal. One should reserve that to give an interest to one's old age. I don't suppose they know your name at the theatre. If they don't, it is all right. Did any one see you going round to her room? That is an important point."

Dorian did not answer for a few moments. He was dazed with horror.

---

7. Wilde canceled in TS the following: "And besides, no one knows that you were at the theatre last night." The *Lippincott's* text misprinted "slowing pulling his gloves off."

Finally he murmured, in a stifled voice, "Harry, did you say an inquest? What did you mean by that? Did Sibyl——? Oh, Harry, I can't bear it! But be quick. Tell me everything at once."

"I have no doubt it was not an accident, Dorian, though it must be put in that way to the public. As she was leaving the theatre with her mother, about half-past twelve or so, she said she had forgotten something up-stairs. They waited some time for her, but she did not come down again. They ultimately found her lying dead on the floor of her dressing-room. She had swallowed something by mistake, some dreadful thing they use at theatres. I don't know what it was, but it had either prussic acid or white lead in it. I should fancy it was prussic acid, as she seems to have died instantaneously. It is very tragic, of course, but you must not get yourself mixed up in it. I see by the *Standard* that she was seventeen. I should have thought she was almost younger than that. She looked such a child, and seemed to know so little about acting. Dorian, you mustn't let this thing get on your nerves. You must come and dine with me, and afterwards we will look in at the Opera. It is a Patti night, and everybody will be there. You can come to my sister's box. She has got some smart women with her."

"So I have murdered Sibyl Vane," said Dorian Gray, half to himself,—"murdered her as certainly as if I had cut her little throat with a knife. And the roses are not less lovely for all that. The birds sing just as happily in my garden. And to-night I am to dine with you, and then go on to the Opera, and sup somewhere I suppose, afterwards. How extraordinarily dramatic life is! If I had read all this in a book, Harry, I think I would have wept over it. Somehow, now that it has happened actually, and to me, it seems far too wonderful for tears. Here is the first passionate love-letter I have ever written in my life. Strange, that my first passionate love-letter should have been addressed to a dead girl. Can they feel, I wonder, those white silent people we call the dead? Sibyl! Can she feel, or know, or listen? Oh, Harry, how I loved her once! It seems years ago to me now. She was everything to me. Then came that dreadful night—was it really only last night?—when she played so badly, and my heart almost broke. She explained it all to me. It was terribly pathetic. But I was not moved a bit. I thought her shallow. Then something happened that made me afraid. I can't tell you what it was, but it was awful. I said I would go back to her. I felt I had done wrong. And now she is dead. My God! my God! Harry, what shall I do? You don't know the danger I am in, and there is nothing to keep me straight. She would have done that for me. She had no right to kill herself. It was selfish of her."

"My dear Dorian, the only way a woman can ever reform a man is by boring him so completely that he loses all possible interest in life. If you had married this girl you would have been wretched. Of course you would have treated her kindly. One can always be kind to people about whom one cares nothing. But she would have soon found out that you were absolutely indifferent to her. And when a woman finds that out about her husband, she either becomes dreadfully dowdy, or wears very smart bonnets that some other woman's husband has to pay for. I say nothing about the social mistake, but I assure you that in any case the whole thing would have been an absolute failure."

"I suppose it would," muttered the lad, walking up and down the room, and looking horribly pale. "But I thought it was my duty. It is not my fault that this terrible tragedy has prevented my doing what was right. I remember your saying once that there is a fatality about good resolutions—that they are always made too late. Mine certainly were."

"Good resolutions are simply a useless attempt to interfere with scientific laws. Their origin is pure vanity. Their result is absolutely *nil*. They give us, now and then, some of those luxurious sterile emotions that have a certain charm for us. That is all that can be said for them."

"Harry," cried Dorian Gray, coming over and sitting down beside him, "why is it that I cannot feel this tragedy as much as I want to? I don't think I am heartless. Do you?"

"You have done too many foolish things in your life[8] to be entitled to give yourself that name, Dorian," answered Lord Henry, with his sweet, melancholy smile.

The lad frowned. "I don't like that explanation, Harry," he rejoined, "but I am glad you don't think I am heartless. I am nothing of the kind. I know I am not. And yet I must admit that this thing that has happened does not affect me as it should. It seems to me to be simply like a wonderful ending to a wonderful play. It has all the terrible beauty of a great tragedy, in which I took part, a tragedy, but by which I have not been wounded."

"It is an interesting question," said Lord Henry, who found an exquisite pleasure in playing on the lad's unconscious egotism,—"an extremely interesting question. I fancy that the explanation is this. It often happens that the real tragedies of life occur in such an inartistic manner that they hurt us by their crude violence, their absolute incoherence, their absurd want of meaning, their entire lack of style. They affect us just as vulgarity affects us. They give us an impression of sheer brute force, and we revolt against that. Sometimes, however, a tragedy that has artistic elements of beauty crosses our lives. If these elements of beauty are real, the whole thing simply appeals to our sense of dramatic effect. Suddenly we find that we are no longer the actors but the spectators of the play. Or rather we are both. We watch ourselves, and the mere wonder of the spectacle enthralls us. In the present case, what is it that has really happened? Some one has killed herself for love of you. I wish I had ever had such an experience. It would have made me in love with love for the rest of my life. The people who have adored me—there have not been very many, but there have been some—have always insisted on

8. Wilde made a change here in 1891.

living on, long after I had ceased to care for them, or they to care for me. They have become stout and tedious, and when I meet them they go in at once for reminiscences. That awful memory of woman! What a fearful thing it is! And what an utter intellectual stagnation it reveals! One should absorb the color of life, but one should never remember its details. Details are always vulgar.

"Of course, now and then things linger. I once wore nothing but violets all through one season, as mourning for a romance that would not die. Ultimately, however, it did die. I forget what killed it. I think it was her proposing to sacrifice the whole world for me. That is always a dreadful moment. It fills one with the terror of eternity. Well,—would you believe it?—a week ago, at Lady Hampshire's, I found myself seated at dinner next the lady in question, and she insisted on going over the whole thing again, and digging up the past, and raking up the future. I had buried my romance in a bed of poppies. She dragged it out again, and assured me that I had spoiled her life. I am bound to state that she ate an enormous dinner, so I did not feel any anxiety. But what a lack of taste she showed! The one charm of the past is that it is the past. But women never know when the curtain has fallen. They always want a sixth act, and as soon as the interest of the play is entirely over they propose to continue it. If they were allowed to have their way, every comedy would have a tragic ending, and every tragedy would culminate in a farce. They are charmingly artificial, but they have no sense of art. You are more fortunate than I am. I assure you, Dorian, that not one of the women I have known would have done for me what Sibyl Vane did for you. Ordinary women always console themselves. Some of them do it by going in for sentimental colors. Never trust a woman who wears mauve, whatever her age may be, or a woman over thirty-five who is fond of pink ribbons. It always means that they have a history. Others find a great consolation in suddenly discovering the good qualities of their husbands. They flaunt their conjugal felicity in one's face, as if it was the most fascinating sins. Religion consoles some. Its mysteries have all the charm of a flirtation, a woman once told me; and I can quite understand it. Besides, nothing makes one so vain as being told that one is a sinner. There is really no end to the consolations that women find in modern life. Indeed, I have not mentioned the most important one of all."

"What is that, Harry?" said Dorian Gray, listlessly.

"Oh, the obvious one. Taking some one else's admirer when one loses one's own. In good society that always whitewashes a woman. But really, Dorian, how different Sibyl Vane must have been from all the women one meets! There is something to me quite beautiful about her death. I am glad I am living in a century when such wonders happen. They make one believe in the reality of the things that shallow, fashionable people play with, such as romance, passion, and love."

"I was terribly cruel to her. You forget that."

"I believe that women appreciate cruelty more than anything else. They have wonderfully primitive instincts. We have emancipated them, but they remain slaves looking for their masters, all the same. They love being dominated. I am sure you were splendid. I have never seen you angry, but I can fancy how delightful you looked. And, after all, you said something to me the day before yesterday that seemed to me at the time to be merely fanciful, but that I see now was absolutely true, and it explains everything."

"What was that, Harry?"

"You said to me that Sibyl Vane represented to you all the heroines of romance—that she was Desdemona one night, and Ophelia the other; that if she died as Juliet, she came to life as Imogen."

"She will never come to life again now," murmured the lad, buying his face in his hands.

"No, she will never come to life. She has played her last part. But you must think of that lonely death in the tawdry dressing-room simply as a strange lurid fragment from some Jacobean tragedy, as a wonderful scene from Webster, or Ford, or Cyril Tourneur. The girl never really lived, and so she has never really died. To you at least she was always a dream, a phantom that flitted through Shakespeare's plays and left them lovelier for its presence, a reed through which Shakespeare's music sounded richer and more full of joy. The moment she touched actual life, she marred it, and it marred her, and so she passed away. Mourn for Ophelia, if you like. Put ashes on your head because Cordelia was strangled. Cry out against Heaven because the daughter of Brabantio died. But don't waste your tears over Sibyl Vane. She was less real than they are."

There was a silence. The evening darkened in the room. Noiselessly, and with silver feet, the shadows crept in from the garden. The colors faded wearily out of things.

After some time Dorian Gray looked up. "You have explained me to myself, Harry," he murmured, with something of a sigh of relief. "I felt all that you have said, but somehow I was afraid of it, and I could not express it to myself. How well you know me! But we will not talk again of what has happened. It has been a marvellous experience. That is all. I wonder if life has still in store for me anything as marvellous."

"Life has everything in store for you, Dorian. There is nothing that you, with your extraordinary good looks, will not be able to do."

"But suppose, Harry, I became haggard, and gray, and wrinkled? What then?"

"Ah, then," said Lord Henry, rising to go,—"then, my dear Dorian, you would have to fight for your victories. As it is, they are brought to you. No, you must keep your good looks. We live in an age that reads too much to be wise, and that thinks too much to be beautiful. We cannot spare you. And now you had better dress, and drive down to the club. We are rather late, as it is."

"I think I shall join you at the Opera, Harry. I feel too tired to eat anything. What is the number of your sister's box?"

"Twenty-seven, I believe. It is on the grand tier. You will see her name on the door. But I am sorry you won't come and dine."

"I don't feel up to it," said Dorian, wearily. "But I am awfully obliged to you for all that you have said to me. You are certainly my best friend. No one has ever understood me as you have."

"We are only at the beginning of our friendship, Dorian," answered Lord Henry, shaking him by the hand. "Good-by. I shall see you before nine-thirty, I hope. Remember, Patti is singing."

As he closed the door behind him, Dorian Gray touched the bell, and in a few minutes Victor appeared with the lamps and drew the blinds down. He waited impatiently for him to go. The man seemed to take an interminable time about everything.

As soon as he had left, he rushed to the screen, and drew it back. No; there was no further change in the picture. It had received the news of Sibyl Vane's death before he had known of it himself. It was conscious of the events of life as they occurred. The vicious cruelty that marred the fine lines of the mouth had, no doubt, appeared at the very moment that the girl had drunk the poison, whatever it was. Or was it indifferent to results? Did it merely take cognizance of what passed within the soul? he wondered, and hoped that some day he would see the change taking place before his very eyes, shuddering as he hoped it.

Poor Sibyl! what a romance it had all been! She had often mimicked death on the stage, and at last Death himself had touched her, and brought her with him. How had she played that dreadful scene? Had she cursed him, as she died? No; she had died for love of him, and love would always be a sacrament to him now. She had atoned for everything, by the sacrifice she had made of her life. He would not think any more of what she had made him go through, that horrible night at the theatre. When he thought of her, it would be as a wonderful tragic figure to show Love had been a great reality. A wonderful tragic figure? Tears came to his eyes as he remembered her child-like look and winsome fanciful ways and shy tremulous grace. He wiped them away hastily, and looked again at the picture.[9]

He felt that the time had really come for making his choice. Or had his choice already been made? Yes, life had decided that for him,—life, and his own infinite curiosity about life. Eternal youth, infinite passion, pleasures subtle and secret, wild joys and wilder sins,—he was to have all these things. The portrait was to bear the burden of his shame: that was all.

A feeling of pain came over him as he thought of the desecration that was in store for the fair face on the canvas. Once, in boyish mockery of Narcissus, he had kissed, or feigned to kiss, those painted lips that now

9. This paragraph added in TS.

smiled so cruelly at him. Morning after morning he had sat before the portrait wondering at its beauty, almost enamoured of it, as it seemed to him at times. Was it to alter now with every mood to which he yielded? Was it to become a hideous and loathsome thing, to be hidden away in a locked room, to be shut out from the sunlight that had so often touched to brighter gold the waving wonder of the hair? The pity of it! the pity of it!

For a moment he thought of praying that the horrible sympathy that existed between him and the picture might cease. It had changed in answer to a prayer; perhaps in answer to a prayer it might remain unchanged. And, yet, who, that knew anything about Life, would surrender the chance of remaining always young, however fantastic that chance might be, or with what fateful consequences it might be fraught? Besides, was it really under his control? Had it indeed been prayer that had produced the substitution? Might there not be some curious scientific reason for it all? If thought could exercise its influence upon a living organism, might not thought exercise an influence upon dead and inorganic things? Nay, without thought or conscious desire, might not things external to ourselves vibrate in unison with our moods and passions, atom calling to atom, in secret love or strange affinity? But the reason was of no importance. He would never again tempt by a prayer any terrible power. If the picture was to alter, it was to alter. That was all. Why inquire too closely into it?[1]

For there would be a real pleasure in watching it. He would be able to follow his mind into its secret places. This portrait would be to him the most magical of mirrors. As it had revealed to him him own body, so it would reveal to him his own soul. And when winter came upon it, he would still be standing where spring trembles on the verge of summer. When the blood crept from its face, and left behind a pallid mask of chalk with leaden eyes, he would keep the glamour of boyhood. Not one blossom of his loveliness would ever fade. Not one pulse of his life would ever weaken. Like the gods of the Greeks, he would be strong, and fleet, and joyous. What did it matter what happened to the colored image on the canvas? He would be safe. That was everything.

He drew the screen back into its former place in front of the picture, smiling as he did so, and passed into his bedroom, where his valet was already waiting for him. An hour later he was at the Opera, and Lord Henry was leaning over his chair.

Chapter VII.

As he was sitting at breakfast next morning, Basil Hallward was shown into the room.

"I am so glad I have found you, Dorian," he said, gravely. "I called

1. This paragraph added in TS.

last night, and they told me you were at the Opera. Of course I knew that was impossible. But I wish you had left word where you had really gone to. I passed a dreadful evening, half afraid that one tragedy might be followed by another. I think you might have telegraphed for me when you heard of it first. I read of it quite by chance in a late edition of the *Globe*, that I picked up at the club. I came here at once, and was miserable at not finding you. I can't tell you how heart-broken I am about the whole thing. I know what you must suffer. But where were you? Did you go down and see the girl's mother? For a moment I thought of following you there. They gave the address in the paper. Somewhere in the Euston Road, isn't it? But I was afraid of intruding upon a sorrow that I could not lighten. Poor woman! What a state she must be in! And her only child, too![1] What did she say about it all?"

"My dear Basil, how do I know?" murmured Dorian, sipping some pale-yellow wine from a delicate gold-beaded bubble of Venetian glass, and looking dreadfully bored. "I was at the Opera. You should have come on there. I met Lady Gwendolen, Harry's sister, for the first time. We were in her box. She is perfectly charming; and Patti sang divinely. Don't talk about horrid subjects. If one doesn't talk about a thing, it has never happened. It is simply expression, as Harry says, that gives reality to things. Tell me about yourself and what you are painting."

"You went to the Opera?" said Hallward, speaking very slowly, and with a strained touch of pain in his voice. "You went to the Opera while Sibyl Vane was lying dead in some sordid lodging? You can talk to me of other women being charming, and of Patti singing divinely, before the girl you loved has even the quiet of a grave to sleep in? Why, man, there are horrors in store for that little white body of hers!"

"Stop, Basil! I won't hear it!" cried Dorian, leaping to his feet. "You must not tell me about things. What is done is done. What is past is past."

"You call yesterday the past?"

"What has the actual lapse of time got to do with it? It is only shallow people who require years to get rid of an emotion. A man who is master of himself can end a sorrow as easily as he can invent a pleasure. I don't want to be at the mercy of my emotions. I want to use them, to enjoy them, and to dominate them."

"Dorian, this is horrible! Something has changed you completely. You look exactly the same wonderful boy who used to come down to my studio, day after day, to sit for his picture. But you were simple, natural, and affectionate then. You were the most unspoiled creature in the whole world. Now, I don't know what has come over you. You talk as if you had no heart, no pity in you. It is all Harry's influence. I see that."

The lad flushed up, and, going to the window, looked out on the

1. Wilde let this stand in 1891, but added Dorian's reply below that Sibyl had a brother (an invention of the revised edition; see p. 85).

green, flickering garden for a few moments. "I owe a great deal to Harry, Basil," he said, at last,—"more than I owe to you. You only taught me to be vain."

"Well, I am punished for that, Dorian,—or shall be some day."

"I don't know what you mean, Basil," he exclaimed, turning round. "I don't know what you want. What do you want?"

"I want the Dorian Gray I used to know."

"Basil," said the lad, going over to him, and putting his hand on his shoulder, "you have come too late. Yesterday when I heard that Sibyl Vane had killed herself——"

"Killed herself! Good heavens! is there no doubt about that?" cried Hallward, looking up at him with an expression of horror.

"My dear Basil! Surely you don't think it was a vulgar accident? Of course she killed herself.[2] It is one of the great romantic tragedies of the age. As a rule, people who act lead the most commonplace lives. They are good husbands, or faithful wives, or something tedious. You know what I mean,—middle-class virtue, and all that kind of thing. How different Sibyl was! She lived her finest tragedy. She was always a heroine. The last night she played—the night you saw her—she acted badly because she had known the reality of love. When she knew its unreality, she died, as Juliet might have died. She passed again into the sphere of art. There is something of the martyr about her. Her death has all the pathetic uselessness of martyrdom, all its wasted beauty. But, as I was saying, you must not think I have not suffered. If you had come in yesterday at a particular moment,—about half-past five, perhaps, or a quarter to six,— you would have found me in tears. Even Harry, who was here, who brought me the news, in fact, had no idea what I was going through. I suffered immensely, then it passed away. I cannot repeat an emotion. No one can, except sentimentalists. And you are awfully unjust, Basil. You come down here to console me. That is charming of you. You find me consoled, and you are furious. How like a sympathetic person! You remind me of a story Harry told me about a certain philanthropist who spent twenty years of his life in trying to get some grievance redressed, or some unjust law altered,—I forget exactly what it was. Finally he succeeded, and nothing could exceed his disappointment. He had absolutely nothing to do, almost died of *ennui*, and became a confirmed misanthrope. And besides, my dear old Basil, if you really want to console me, teach me rather to forget what has happened, or to see it from a proper artistic point of view. Was it not Gautier who used to write about *la consolation des arts?* I remember picking up a little vellum-covered book in your studio one day and chancing on that delightful phrase. Well, I am not like that young man you told me of when we were down at Marlowe together, the young man who used to say that yellow satin could console one for all the miseries of life. I love beautiful

2. Wilde added lines here in 1891.

things that one can touch and handle. Old brocades, green bronzes, lacquer-work, carved ivories, exquisite surroundings, luxury, pomp,— there is much to be got from all these. But the artistic temperament that they create, or at any rate reveal, is still more to me. To become the spectator of one's own life, as Harry says, is to escape the suffering of life. I know you are surprised at my talking to you like this. You have not realized how I have developed. I was a school-boy when you knew me. I am a man now. I have new passions, new thoughts, new ideas. I am different, but you must not like me less. I am changed, but you must always be my friend. Of course I am very fond of Harry. But I know that you are better than he is. You are not stronger,—you are too much afraid of life,—but you are better. And how happy we used to be together! Don't leave me, Basil, and don't quarrel with me. I am what I am. There is nothing more to be said."

Hallward felt strangely moved. Rugged and straightforward as he was, there was something in his nature that was purely feminine in its tenderness.[3] The lad was infinitely dear to him, and his personality had been the great turning-point in his art. He could not bear the idea of reproaching him any more. After all, his indifference was probably merely a mood that would pass away. There was so much in him that was good, so much in him that was noble.

"Well, Dorian," he said, at length, with a sad smile, "I won't speak to you again about this horrible thing, after to-day. I only trust your name won't be mentioned in connection with it. The inquest is to take place this afternoon. Have they summoned you?"

Dorian shook his head, and a look of annoyance passed over his face at the mention of the word "inquest." There was something so crude and vulgar about everything of the kind. "They don't know my name," he answered.

"But surely she did?"

"Only my Christian name, and that I am quite sure she never mentioned to any one. She told me once that they were all rather curious to learn who I was, and that she invariably told them my name was Prince Charming. It was pretty of her. You must do me a drawing of her, Basil. I should like to have something more of her than the memory of a few kisses and some broken pathetic words."

"I will try and do something, Dorian, if it would please you. But you must come and sit to me yourself again. I can't get on without you."

"I will never sit to you again, Basil. It is impossible!" he exclaimed, starting back.

Hallward stared at him, "My dear boy, what nonsense!" he cried. "Do you mean to say you don't like what I did of you? Where is it? Why have you pulled the screen in front of it? Let me look at it. It is the best thing I have ever painted. Do take that screen away, Dorian. It is simply horrid

3. This sentence deleted in 1891.

of your servant hiding my work like that. I felt the room looked different as I came in."

"My servant has nothing to do with it, Basil. You don't imagine I let him arrange my room for me? He settles my flowers for me sometimes,—that is all. No; I did it myself. The light was too strong on the portrait."

"Too strong! Impossible, my dear fellow! It is an admirable place for it. Let me see it." And Hallward walked towards the corner of the room.

A cry of terror broke from Dorian Gray's lips, and he rushed between Hallward and the screen. "Basil," he said, looking very pale, "you must not look at it. I don't wish you to."

"Not look at my own work! you are not serious. Why shouldn't I look at it?" exclaimed Hallward, laughing.

"If you try to look at it, Basil, on my word of honor I will never speak to you again as long as I live. I am quite serious. I don't offer any explanation, and you are not to ask for any. But, remember, if you touch this screen, everything is over between us."

Hallward was thunderstruck. He looked at Dorian Gray in absolute amazement. He had never seen him like this before. The lad was absolutely pallid with rage. His hands were clinched, and the pupils of his eyes were like disks of blue fire. He was trembling all over.

"Dorian!"

"Don't speak!"

"But what is the matter? Of course I won't look at it if you don't want me to," he said, rather coldly, turning on his heel, and going over towards the window. "But, really, it seems rather absurd that I shouldn't see my own work, especially as I am going to exhibit it in Paris in the autumn. I shall probably have to give it another coat of varnish before that, so I must see it some day, and why not to-day?"

"To exhibit it! You want to exhibit it?" exclaimed Dorian Gray, a strange sense of terror creeping over him. Was the world going to be shown his secret? Were people to gape at the mystery of his life? That was impossible. Something—he did not know what—had to be done at once.

"Yes: I don't suppose you will object to that. Georges Petit is going to collect all my best pictures for a special exhibition in the Rue de Sèze, which will open the first week in October. The portrait will only be away a month. I should think you could easily spare it for that time. In fact, you are sure to be out of town. And if you hide it always behind a screen, you can't care much abut it."

Dorian Gray passed his hand over his forehead. There were beads of perspiration there. He felt that he was on the brink of a horrible danger. "You told me a month ago that you would never exhibit it," he said. "Why have you changed your mind? You people who go in for being consistent have just as many moods as others. The only difference is that your moods are rather meaningless. You can't have forgotten that you assured me most solemnly that nothing in the world would induce you to send it to any exhibition. You told Harry exactly the same thing." He stopped suddenly, and a gleam of light came into his eyes. He remembered that Lord Henry had said to him once, half seriously and half in jest, "If you want to have an interesting quarter of an hour, get Basil to tell you why he won't exhibit your picture. He told me why he wouldn't, and it was a revelation to me." Yes, perhaps Basil, too, had his secret. He would ask him and try.

"Basil," he said, coming over quite close, and looking him straight in the face, "we have each of us a secret. Let me know yours, and I will tell you mine. What was your reason for refusing to exhibit my picture?"

Hallward shuddered in spite of himself. "Dorian, if I told you, you might like me less than you do, and you would certainly laugh at me. I could not bear your doing either of those two things. If you wish me never to look at your picture again, I am content. I have always you to look at. If you wish the best work I have ever done to be hidden from the world, I am satisfied. Your friendship is dearer to me than any fame or reputation."

"No, Basil, you must tell me," murmured Dorian Gray. "I think I have a right to know." His feeling of terror had passed away, and curiosity had taken its place. He was determined to find out Basil Hallward's mystery.

"Let us sit down, Dorian," said Hallward, looking pale and pained. "Let us sit down. I will sit in the shadow, and you shall sit in the sunlight. Our lives are like that. Just answer me one question. Have you noticed in the picture something that you did not like?—something that probably at first did not strike you, but that revealed itself to you suddenly?"[4]

"Basil!" cried the lad, clutching the arms of his chair with trembling hands, and gazing at him with wild, startled eyes.

"I see you did. Don't speak. Wait till you hear what I have to say. It is quite true that I have worshipped you with far more romance of feeling than a man usually[5] gives to a friend. Somehow, I had never loved a woman. I suppose I never had time. Perhaps, as Harry says, a really 'grande passion' is the privilege of those who have nothing to do, and that is the use of the idle classes in a country. Well, from the moment I met you, your personality had the most extraordinary influence over me. I quite admit that I adored you madly, extravagantly, absurdly. I was jealous of every one to whom you spoke. I wanted to have you all to myself. I was only happy when I was with you. When I was away from you, you were still present in my art. It was all wrong and foolish. It is all wrong and foolish still. Of course I never let you know anything about this. It would have been impossible. You would not have under-

4. Wilde deleted the following in MS: "Something that filled you perhaps with a sense of shame?" and made further alterations in 1891.

5. Stoddart changed Wilde's "should ever give" to this reading in TS.

stood it; I did not understand it myself. One day I determined to paint a wonderful portrait of you. It was to have been my masterpiece. It is my masterpiece. But, as I worked at it, every flake and film of color seemed to me to reveal my secret.[6] I grew afraid that the world would know of my idolatry. I felt, Dorian, that I had told too much. Then it was that I resolved never to allow the picture to be exhibited. You were a little annoyed; but then you did not realize all that it meant to me. Harry, to whom I talked about it, laughed at me. But I did not mind that. When the picture was finished, and I sat alone with it, I felt that I was right. Well, after a few days the portrait left my studio, and as soon as I had got rid of the intolerable fascination of its presence it seemed to me that I had been foolish in imagining that I had said anything in it, more than that you were extremely good-looking and that I could paint. Even now I cannot help feeling that it is a mistake to think that the passion one feels in creation is ever really shown in the work one creates. Art is more abstract than we fancy. Form and color tell us of form and color—that is all. It often seems to me that art conceals the artist far more completely than it ever reveals him. And so when I got this offer from Paris I determined to make your portrait the principal thing in my exhibition. It never occurred to me that you would refuse. I see now that you were right. The picture must not be shown. You must not be angry with me, Dorian, for what I have told you. As I said Harry, once, you are made to be worshipped."[7]

Dorian Gray drew a long breath. The color came back to his cheeks, and a smile played about his lips. The peril was over. He was safe for the time. Yet he could not help feeling infinite pity for the young man who had just made this strange confession to him. He wondered if he would ever be so dominated by the personality of a friend. Lord Harry had the charm of being very dangerous. But that was all.[8] He was too clever and too cynical to be really fond of. Would there ever be some one who would fill him with a strange idolatry? Was that one of the things that life had in store?

"It is extraordinary to me, Dorian," said Hallward, "that you should have seen this in the picture.[9] Did you really see it?"

"Of course I did."

"Well, you don't mind my looking at it now?"

Dorian shook his head. "You must not ask me that, Basil. I could not possibly let you stand in front of that picture."

"You will some day, surely?"

"Never."

6. Stoddart canceled the following in TS: "There was love in every line, and in every touch there was passion."
7. Wilde made extensive revisions to this paragraph in 1891, deleting two passages, "It is quite true . . . country" and "I quite admit . . . was with you," and adding as much as he removed, including a passage transposed from page 180 (see n. 4).

Carson made much of such passages during the first cross-examination of Wilde at the libel trial.
8. Wilde canceled "He felt no romance for him" in TS.
9. A canceled passage in MS reads: "Perhaps you did not see it. But you suspected it. You were conscious of something you did not like."

"Well, perhaps you are right. And now good-by, Dorian. You have been the one person in my life of whom I have been really fond.[1] I don't suppose I shall often see you again. You don't know what it cost me to tell you all that I have told you."

"My dear Basil," cried Dorian, "what have you told me? Simply that you felt that you liked me too much. That is not even a compliment."

"It was not intended as a compliment. It was a confession."

"A very disappointing one."

"Why, what did you expect, Dorian? You didn't see anything else in the picture, did you? There was nothing else to see?"

"No: there was nothing else to see. Why do you ask? But you mustn't talk about not meeting me again, or anything of that kind. You and I are friends, Basil, and we must always remain so."

"You have got Harry," said Hallward, sadly.

"Oh, Harry!" cried the lad, with a ripple of laughter. "Harry spends his days in saying what is incredible, and his evenings in doing what is improbable. Just the sort of life I would like to lead. But still I don't think I would go to Harry if I was in trouble. I would sooner go to you, Basil."

"But you won't sit to me again?"

"Impossible!"

"You spoil my life as an artist by refusing, Dorian. No man comes across two ideal things. Few come across one."

"I can't explain it to you, Basil, but I must never sit to you again. I will come and have tea with you. That will be just as pleasant."

"Pleasanter for you, I am afraid," murmured Hallward, regretfully. "And now good-by. I am sorry you won't let me look at the picture once again. But that can't be helped. I quite understand what you feel about it."

As he left the room, Dorian Gray smiled to himself. Poor Basil! how little he knew of the true reason! And how strange it was that, instead of having been forced to reveal his own secret, he had succeeded, almost by chance, in wresting a secret from his friend! How much that strange confession explained to him! Basil's absurd fits of jealousy, his wild devotion, his extravagant panegyrics, his curious reticences,—he understood them all now, and he felt sorry. There was something tragic in a friendship so colored by romance.[2]

He sighed, and touched the bell. The portrait must be hidden away at all costs. He could not run such a risk of discovery again. It had been mad of him to have the thing remain, even for an hour, in a room to which any of his friends had access.

---

1. MS originally had "whom I have loved."
2. Stoddart changed the original reading in TS: "something infinitely tragic in a romance that was at once so passionate and so sterile," to this more circumspect version.

Chapter VIII.

When his servant entered, he looked at him steadfastly, and wondered if he had thought of peering behind the screen. The man was quite impassive, and waited for his orders. Dorian lit a cigarette, and walked over to the glass and glanced into it. He could see the reflection of Victor's face perfectly. It was like a placid mask of servility. There was nothing to be afraid of, there. Yet he thought it best to be on his guard.

Speaking very slowly, he told him to tell the housekeeper that he wanted to see her, and then to go to the frame-maker's and ask him to send two of his men round at once. It seemed to him that as the man left the room he peered in the direction of the screen. Or was that only his fancy?[1]

After a few moments, Mrs. Leaf, a dear old lady in a black silk dress, with a photograph of the late Mr. Leaf framed in a large gold brooch at her neck, and old-fashioned thread mittens on her wrinkled hands, bustled into the room.

"Well, Master Dorian," she said, "what can I do for you?[2] I beg your pardon, sir,"—here came a courtesy,—"I shouldn't call you Master Dorian any more. But, Lord bless you, sir, I have known you since you were a baby, and many's the trick you've played on poor old Leaf. Not that you were not always a good boy, sir; but boys will be boys, Master Dorian, and jam is a temptation to the young, isn't it, sir?"

He laughed. "You must always call me Master Dorian, Leaf. I will be very angry with you if you don't. And I assure you I am quite as fond of jam now as I used to be. Only when I am asked out to tea I am never offered any. I want you to give me the key of the room at the top of the house."

"The old school-room, Master Dorian? Why, it's full of dust. I must get it arranged and put straight before you go into it. It's not fit for you to see, Master Dorian. It is not, indeed."

"I don't want it put straight, Leaf. I only want the key."

"Well, Master Dorian, you'll be covered with cobwebs if you goes into it. Why, it hasn't been opened for nearly five years—not since his lordship died."

He winced at the mention of his dead uncle's name. He had hateful memories of him. "That does not matter, Leaf," he replied. "All I want is the key."

"And here is the key, Master Dorian," said the old lady, after going over the contents of her bunch with tremulously uncertain hands. "Here is the key. I'll have it off the ring in a moment. But you don't think of living up there, Master Dorian, and you so comfortable here?"

1. Wilde added this effect in TS, which originally read, "the man bowed and retired."
2. Wilde's 1891 revision all but removed the comic side of Leaf's personality found here. Most of her dialogue and Dorian's replies were changed in both substance and tone. This is the lone instance when Wilde eclipsed a character or diluted a scene in his last revision.

"No, Leaf, I don't. I merely want to see the place, and perhaps store something in it,—that is all. Thank you, Leaf. I hope your rheumatism is better; and mind you send me up jam for breakfast."

Mrs. Leaf shook her head. "Them foreigners doesn't understand jam, Master Dorian. They calls it 'compot.' But I'll bring it to you myself some morning, if you lets me."

"That will be very kind of you, Leaf," he answered, looking at the key; and, having made him an elaborate courtesy, the old lady left the room, her face wreathed in smiles. She had a strong objection to the French valet. It was a poor thing, she felt, for any one to be born a foreigner.

As the door closed, Dorian put the key in his pocket, and looked round the room. His eye fell on a large purple satin coverlet heavily embroidered with gold, a splendid piece of late seventeenth-century Venetian work that his uncle had found in a convent near Bologna. Yes, that would serve to wrap the dreadful thing in. It had perhaps served often as a pall for the dead. Now it was to hide something that had a corruption of its own, worse than the corruption of death itself,—something that would breed horrors and yet would never die. What the worm was to the corpse, his sins would be to the painted image on the canvas. They would mar its beauty, and eat away its grace. They would defile it, and make it shameful. And yet the thing would still live on. It would be always alive.

He shuddered, and for a moment he regretted that he had not told Basil the true reason why he had wished to hide the picture away. Basil would have helped him to resist Lord Henry's influence, and the still more poisonous influences that came from his own temperament. The love that he bore him—for it was really love—and something noble and intellectual in it. It was not that mere physical admiration of beauty that is born of the senses, and that does when the senses tire. It was such love as Michael Angelo had known, and Montaigne, and Winckelmann, and Shakespeare himself. Yes, Basil could have saved him. But it was too late now. The past could always be annihilated. Regret, denial, or forgetfulness could do that. But the future was inevitable. There were passions in him that would find their terrible outlet, dreams that would make the shadow of their evil real.

He took up from the couch the great purple-and-gold texture that covered it, and, holding it in his hands, passed behind the screen. Was the face on the canvas viler than before? It seemed to him that it was unchanged; and yet his loathing of it was intensified. Gold hair, blue eyes, and rose-red lips,—they all were there. It was simply the expression that had altered. That was horrible in its cruelty. Compared to what he saw in it of censure or rebuke, how shallow Basil's reproaches about Sibyl Vane had been!—how shallow, and of what little account! His own soul was looking out at him from the canvas and calling him to judgment. A look of pain came across him, and he flung the rich pall over the picture. As he did so, a knock came to the door. He passed out as his servant entered.

"The persons are here, monsieur."[3]

He felt that the man must be got rid of at once. He must not be allowed to know where the picture was being taken to. There was something sly about him, and he had thoughtful, treacherous eyes. Sitting down at the writing-table, he scribbled a note to Lord Henry, asking him to send him round something to read, and reminding him that they were to meet at eight-fifteen that evening.

"Wait for an answer," he said, handing it to him, "and show the men in here."

In two or three minutes there was another knock, and Mr. Ashton himself, the celebrated frame-maker of South Audley Street, came in with a somewhat rough-looking young assistant. Mr. Ashton was a florid, red-whiskered little man, whose admiration for art was considerably tempered by the inveterate impecuniosity of most of the artists who dealt with him. As a rule, he never left his shop. He waited for people to come to him. But he always made an exception in favor of Dorian Gray. There was something about Dorian that charmed everybody. It was a pleasure even to see him.

"What can I do for you, Mr. Gray?" he said, rubbing his fat freckled hands. "I thought I would do myself the honor of coming round in person. I have just got a beauty of a frame, sir. Picked it up at a sale. Old Florentine. Came from Fonthill, I believe. Admirably suited for a religious picture, Mr. Gray."

"I am so sorry you have given yourself the trouble of coming round, Mr. Ashton. I will certainly drop in and look at the frame,—though I don't go in much for religious art,—but to-day I only want a picture carried to the top of the house for me. It is rather heavy, so I thought I would ask you to lend me a couple of your men."

"No trouble at all, Mr. Gray. I am delighted to be of any service to you. Which is the work of art, sir?"

"This," replied Dorian, moving the screen back. "Can you move it, covering and all, just as it is? I don't want it to get scratched going upstairs."

"There will be no difficulty, sir," said the genial frame-maker, beginning, with the aid of his assistant, to unhook the picture from the long brass chains by which it was suspended. "And, now, where shall we carry it to, Mr. Gray?"

"I will show you the way, Mr. Ashton, if you will kindly follow me. Or perhaps you had better go in front. I am afraid it is right at the top of the house. We will go up by the front staircase, as it is wider."

He held the door open for them, and they passed out into the hall

3. Victor originally spoke in French in MS. This was followed by Dorian's directions given in French to take a letter round to Lord Henry in Curzon Street and to ask for the "French book of which he had spoken to him."

and began the ascent. The elaborate character of the frame had made the picture extremely bulky, and now and then, in spite of the obsequious protests of Mr. Ashton, who had a true tradesman's dislike of seeing a gentleman doing anything useful, Dorian put his hand to it so as to help them.

"Something of a load to carry, sir," gasped the little man, when they reached the top landing. And he wiped his shiny forehead.

"A terrible load to carry,"[4] murmured Dorian, as he unlocked the door that opened into the room that was to keep for him the curious secret of his life and hide his soul from the eyes of men.

He had not entered the place for more than four years,—not, indeed, since he had used it first as a play-room when he was a child and then as a study when he grew somewhat older. It was a large, well-proportioned room, which had been specially built by the last Lord Sherard for the use of the little nephew whom, being himself childless, and perhaps for other reasons, he had always hated and desired to keep at a distance. It did not appear to Dorian to have much changed. There was the huge Italian *cassone*, with its fantastically-painted panels and its tarnished gilt mouldings, in which he had so often hidden himself as a boy. There was the satinwood bookcase filled with his dog-eared school-books. On the wall behind it was hanging the same ragged Flemish tapestry where a faded king and queen were playing chess in a garden, while a company of hawkers rode by, carrying hooded birds of their gauntleted wrists. How well he recalled it all! Every moment of his lonely childhood came back to him, as he looked round. He remembered the stainless purity of his boyish life, and it seemed horrible to him that it was here that the fatal portrait was to be hidden away. How little he had thought, in those dead days, of all that was in store for him!

But there was no other place in the house to secure from prying eyes as this. He had the key, and no one else could enter it. Beneath its purple pall, the face painted on the canvas could grow bestial, sodden, and unclean. What did it matter? No one could see it. He himself would not see it. Why should he watch the hideous corruption of his soul? He kept his youth,—that was enough. And, besides, might not his nature grow finer, after all? There was no reason that the future should be so full of shame. Some love might come across his life, and purify him, and shield him from those sins that seemed to be already stirring in spirit and in flesh,—those curious unpictured sins whose very mystery lent them their subtlety and their charm. Perhaps, some day, the cruel look would have passed away from the scarlet sensitive mouth, and he might show to the world Basil Hallward's masterpiece.

No; that was impossible. The thing upon the canvas was growing old, hour by hour, and week by week. Even if it escaped the hideousness of

4. Wilde changed this line three times. In TS there was another sort of pun in Dorian's reply: "There is a good deal of heaviness in modern art." In 1891, Wilde changed it again to the deliberately prosaic "I am afraid it is rather heavy," emphasizing a different mood entirely.

sin, the hideousness of age was in store for it. The cheeks would become hollow or flaccid. Yellow crow's-feet would creep round the fading eyes and make them horrible. The hair would lose its brightness, the mouth would gape or droop, would be foolish or gross, as the mouths of old men are. There would be the wrinkled throat, the cold blue-veined hands, the twisted body, that he remembered in the uncle who had been so stern to him in his boyhood. The picture had to be concealed. There was no help for it.

"Bring it in, Mr. Ashton, please," he said, wearily, turning round. "I am sorry I kept you so long. I was thinking of something else."

"Always glad to have a rest, Mr. Gray," answered the frame-maker, who was still gasping for breath. "Where shall we put it, sir?"

"Oh, anywhere, Here, this will do. I don't want to have it hung up. Just lean it against the wall. Thanks."

"Might one look at the work of art, sir?"

Dorian started. "It would not interest you, Mr. Ashton," he said, keeping his eye on the man. He felt ready to leap upon him and fling him to the ground if he dared to lift the gorgeous hanging that concealed the secret of his life. "I won't trouble you any more now. I am much obliged for your kindness in coming round."

"Not at all, not at all, Mr. Gray. Ever ready to do anything for you, sir." And Mr. Ashton tramped down-stairs, followed by the assistant, who glanced back at Dorian with a look of shy wonder in his rough, uncomely face. He had never seen any one so marvellous.

When the sound of their footsteps had died away, Dorian locked the door, and put the key in his pocket. He felt safe now. No one would ever look on the horrible thing. No eye but his would ever see his shame.

On reaching the library he found that it was just after five o'clock, and that the tea had been already brought up. On a little table of dark perfumed wood thickly incrusted with nacre, a present from his guardian's wife, Lady Radley, who had spent the preceding winter in Cairo, was lying a note from Lord Henry, and beside it was a book bound in yellow paper, the cover slightly torn and the edges soiled. A copy of the third edition of the *St. James's Gazette* had been placed on the tea-tray. It was evident that Victor had returned. He wondered if he had met the men in the hall as they were leaving the house and had wormed out of them what they had been doing. He would be sure to miss the picture,— had no doubt missed it already, while he had been laying the tea-things. The screen had not been replaced, and the blank space on the wall was visible. Perhaps some night he might find him creeping up-stairs and trying to force the door of the room. It was a horrible thing to have a spy in one's house. He had heard of rich men who had been blackmailed all their lives by some servant who had read a letter, or overheard a conversation, or picked up a card with an address, or found beneath a pillow a withered flower or a bit of crumpled lace.

He sighed, and, having poured himself out some tea, opened Lord

Henry's note. It was simply to say that he sent him round the evening paper, and a book that might interest him, and that he would be at the club at eight-fifteen. He opened the *St. James's* languidly, and looked through it. A red pencil-mark on the fifth page caught his eye. He read the following paragraph:

> "INQUEST ON AN ACTRESS.—An inquest was held this morning at the Bell Tavern, Hoxton Road, by Mr. Danby, the District Coroner, on the body of Sibyl Vane, a young actress recently engaged at the Royal Theatre, Holborn. A verdict of death by misadventure was returned. Considerable sympathy was expressed for the mother of the deceased, who was greatly affected during the giving of her own evidence, and that of Dr. Birrell, who had made the post-mortem examination of the deceased."

He frowned slightly, and, tearing the paper in two, went across the room and flung the pieces into a gilt basket.[5] How ugly it all was! And how horribly real ugliness made things! He felt a little annoyed with Lord Henry for having sent him the account. And it was certainly stupid of him to have marked it with red pencil. Victor might have read it. The man knew more than enough English for that.[6]

Perhaps he had read it, and had begun to suspect something. And, yet, what did it matter? What had Dorian Gray to do with Sibyl Vane's death? There was nothing to fear. Dorian Gray had not killed her.

His eye fell on the yellow book that Lord Henry had sent him. What was it, he wondered. He went towards the little pearl-colored octagonal stand, that had always looked to him like the work of some strange Egyptian bees who wrought in silver, and took the volume up.[7] He flung himself into an arm-chair, and began to turn over the leaves. After a few minutes, he became absorbed. It was the strangest book he had ever read. It seemed to him that in exquisite raiment, and to the delicate sound of flutes, the sins of the world were passing in dumb show before him. Things that he had dimly dreamed of were suddenly made real to him. Things of which he had never dreamed were gradually revealed.

It was a novel without a plot, and with only one character, being, indeed, simply a psychological study of a certain young Parisian, who spent his life trying to realize in the nineteenth century all the passions and modes of thought that belonged to every century except his own,

5. Wilde reduced this to "flung away" in 1891.
6. A vestige of Jacques, the French valet, in MS.
7. Stoddart canceled the following here: "*Le Secret de Raoul* par Catulle Sarrazin. What a curious title." All subsequent references to the title of the notorious yellow book were also removed by Stoddart. The author and title are fictitious, although Wilde knew a Gabriel Sarrazin, a French writer who reviewed for Wilde's *Woman's World* magazine. The title may have suggested to Stoddart the scandalous French novel by Rachilde (Marguerite Vallette) *Monsieur Venus* (1889), in which there is a character, M. Raoule de Vénérande. The fictitious title may have had its origin in a letter Wilde sent to Robert Ross in July 1889, following publication of "The Portrait of Mr. W. H." in *Blackwood's:* "Now that Willie Hughes has been revealed to the world, we must have another secret" (*Letters* 247). That is the kind of inside joke Wilde enjoyed playing in his fiction for the benefit of friends. Willie Hughes is the hypothetical original of the "Mr. W. H." to whom Shakespeare dedicated his sonnets.

and to sum up, as it were, in himself the various moods through which the world-spirit had ever passed, loving for their mere artificiality those renunciations that men have unwisely called virtue, as much as those natural rebellions that wise men still call sin. The style in which it was written was that curious jewelled style, vivid and obscure at once, full of *argot* and of archaisms, of technical expressions and of elaborate paraphrases, that characterizes the work of some of the finest artists of the French school of *Décadents*.[8] There were in it metaphors as monstrous as orchids, and as evil in color. The life of the senses was described in the terms of mystical philosophy. One hardly knew at times whether one was reading the spiritual ecstasies of some mediæval saint or the morbid confessions of a modern sinner. It was a poisonous book. The heavy odor of incense seemed to cling about its pages and to trouble the brain. The mere cadence of the sentences, the subtle monotony of their music, so full as it was of complex refrains and movements elaborately repeated, produced in the mind of the lad, as he passed from chapter to chapter, a form of revery, a malady of dreaming, that made him unconscious of the falling day and the creeping shadows.

Cloudless, and pierced by one solitary star, a copper-green sky gleamed through the windows. He read on by its wan light till he could read no more. Then, after his valet had reminded him several times of the lateness of the hour, he got up, and, going into the next room, placed the book on the little Florentine table that always stood at his bedside, and began to dress for dinner.

It was almost nine o'clock before he reached the club, where he found Lord Henry sitting alone, in the morning-room, looking very bored.

"I am so sorry, Harry," he cried, "but really it is entirely your fault. That book you sent me so fascinated me that I forgot what the time was."

"I thought you would like it," replied his host, rising from his chair.

"I didn't say I liked it, Harry. I said it fascinated me. There is a great difference."

"Ah, if you have discovered that, you have discovered a great deal," murmured Lord Henry, with his curious smile. "Come, let us go in to dinner. It is dreadfully late, and I am afraid the champagne will be too much iced."[9]

Chapter IX.

For years, Dorian Gray could not free himself from the memory of this book. Or perhaps it would be more accurate to say that he never sought to free himself from it. He procured from Paris no less than five large-paper copies of the first edition, and had them bound in different colors, so that they might suit his various moods and the changing fan-

8. Wilde added "full of *argot* . . . elaborate paraphrases" and "the work . . . artists of" in TS. *Décadents* was changed to *Symbolistes* in 1891.

9. Wilde shortened and simplified the last paragraph in 1891, changing its focus.

cies of a nature over which he seemed, at times, to have almost entirely lost control. The hero, the wonderful young Parisian, in whom the romantic temperament and the scientific temperament were so strangely blended, became to him a kind of prefiguring type of himself. And, indeed, the whole book seemed to him to contain the story of his own life, written before he had lived it.

In one point he was more fortunate than the book's[1] fantastic hero. He never knew—never, indeed, had any cause to know—that somewhat grotesque dread of mirrors, and polished metal surfaces, and still water, which came upon the young Parisian[2] so early in his life, and was occasioned by the sudden decay of a beauty that had once, apparently, been so remarkable. It was with an almost cruel joy—and perhaps in nearly every joy, as certainly in every pleasure, cruelty has its place—that he used to read the latter part[3] of the book, with its really tragic, if somewhat over-emphasized, account of the sorrow and despair of one who had himself lost what in others, and in the world, he had most valued.

He, at any rate, had no cause to fear that. The boyish beauty that had so fascinated Basil Hallward, and many others besides him, seemed never to leave him. Even those who had heard the most evil things against him (and from time to time strange rumors about his mode of life crept through London and became the chatter of the clubs) could not believe anything to his dishonor when they saw him. He had always the look of one who had kept himself unspotted from the world. Men who talked grossly became silent when Dorian Gray entered the room. There was something in the purity of his face that rebuked them. His mere presence seemed to recall to them the innocence that they had tarnished. They wondered how one so charming and graceful as he was could have escaped the stain of an age that was at once sordid and sensuous.

He himself, on returning home from one of those mysterious and prolonged absences that gave rise to such strange conjecture among those who were his friends, or thought that they were so, would creep up-stairs to the locked room, open the door with the key that never left him, and stand, with a mirror, in front of the portrait that Basil Hallward had painted of him, looking now at the evil and aging face on the canvas, and now at the fair young face that laughed back at him from the polished glass. The very sharpness of the contrast used to quicken his sense of pleasure. He grew more and more enamoured of his own beauty, more and more interested in the corruption of his own soul. He would examine with minute care, and often with a monstrous and terrible delight, the hideous lines that seared the wrinkling forehead or crawled around the heavy sensual mouth, wondering sometimes which were the more horrible, the signs of sin or the signs of age. He would place his white

1. Stoddart changed from "Catulle Sarrazin's."
2. Stoddart's substitute for Wilde's "Raoul."
3. Canceled in MS: "twelfth and thirteenth chapters." No parallels seem to exist in these and other allusions between the contents of the yellow book and either *A Rebours* or *Monsieur Venus* except for similarities in tone, general subject matter, and angle of treatment.

hands beside the coarse bloated hands of the picture, and smile. He mocked the misshapen body and the failing limbs.

There were moments, indeed, at night, when, lying sleepless in his own delicately-scented chamber, or in the sordid room of the little ill-famed tavern near the Docks, which, under an assumed name, and in disguise, it was his habit to frequent, he would think of the ruin he had brought upon his soul, with a pity that was all the more poignant because it was purely selfish. But moments such as these were rare. That curiosity about life that, many years before, Lord Henry had first stirred in him, as they sat together in the garden of their friend, seemed to increase with gratification. The more he knew, the more he desired to know. He had mad hungers that grew more ravenous as he fed them.

Yet he was not really reckless, at any rate in his relations to society. Once or twice every month during the winter, and on each Wednesday evening while the season lasted, he would throw open to the world his beautiful house and have the most celebrated musicians of the day to charm his guests with the wonders of their art. His little dinners, in the settling of which Lord Henry always assisted him, were noted as much for the careful selection and placing of those invited, as for the exquisite taste shown in the decoration of the table, with its subtle symphonic arrangements of exotic flowers, and embroidered cloths, and antique plate of gold and silver. Indeed, there were many, especially among the very young men, who saw, or fancied that they saw, in Dorian Gray the true realization of a type of which they had often dreamed in Eton or Oxford days, a type that was to combine something of the real culture of the scholar with all the grace and distinction and perfect manner of a citizen of the world. To them he seemed to belong to those whom Dante describes as having sought to "make themselves perfect by the worship of beauty." Like Gautier, he was one for whom "the visible world existed."

And, certainly, to him life itself was the first, the greatest, of the arts, and for it all the other arts seemed to be but a preparation. Fashion, by which what is really fantastic becomes for a moment universal, and Dandyism, which, in its own way, is an attempt to assert the absolute modernity of beauty, had, of course, their fascination for him. His mode of dressing, and the particular styles that he affected from time to time, had their marked influence on the young exquisites of the Mayfair balls and Pall Mall club windows, who copied him in everything that he did, and tried to reproduce the accidental charm of his graceful, though to him only half-serious, fopperies.

For, while he was but too ready to accept the position that was almost immediately offered to him on his coming of age, and found, indeed, a subtle pleasure in the thought that he might really become to the London of his own day what to imperial Neronian Rome the author of the "Satyricon" had once been, yet in his inmost heart he desired to be something more than a mere *arbiter elegantiarum*, to be consulted on the wearing of a jewel, or the knotting of a necktie, or the conduct of a cane. He sought to elaborate some new scheme of life that would have its reasoned philosophy and its ordered principles and find in the spiritualizing of the senses its highest realization.

The worship of the senses has often, and with much justice, been decried, men feeling a natural instinct of terror about passions and sensations that seem stronger than ourselves, and that we are conscious of sharing with the less highly organized forms of existence. But it appeared to Dorian Gray that the true nature of the senses had never been understood, and that they had remained savage and animal merely because the world had sought to starve them into submission or to kill them by pain, instead of aiming at making them elements of a new spirituality, of which a fine instinct for beauty was to be the dominant characteristic. As he looked back upon man moving through History, he was haunted by a feeling of loss. So much had been surrendered! and to such little purpose! There had been mad wilful rejections, monstrous forms of self-torture and self-denial, whose origin was fear, and whose result was a degradation infinitely more terrible than that fancied degradation from which, in their ignorance, they had sought to escape, Nature in her wonderful irony driving the anchorite out to herd with the wild animals of the desert and giving to the hermit the beasts of the field as his companions.

Yes, there was to be, as Lord Henry had prophesied, a new hedonism that was to re-create life, and to save it from that harsh, uncomely puritanism that is having, in our own day, its curious revival. It was to have its service of the intellect, certainly; yet it was never to accept any theory or system that would involve the sacrifice of any mode of passionate experience. Its aim, indeed, was to be experience itself, and not the fruits of experience, sweet or bitter as they might be. Of the asceticism that deadens the senses, as of the vulgar profligacy that dulls them, it was to know nothing. But it was to teach man to concentrate himself upon the moments of a life that is itself but a moment.

There are few of us who have not sometimes wakened before dawn, either after one of those dreamless nights that make one almost enamoured of death, or one of those nights of horror and misshapen joy, when through the chambers of the brain sweep phantoms more terrible than reality itself, and instinct with that vivid life that lurks in all grotesques, and that lends to Gothic art its enduring vitality, this art being, one might fancy, especially the art of those whose minds have been troubled with the malady of revery. Gradually white fingers creep through the curtains, and they appear to tremble. Black fantastic shadows crawl into the corners of the room, and crouch there. Outside, there is the stirring of birds among the leaves, or the sound of men going forth to their work, or the sigh and sob of the wind coming down from the hills, and wandering round the silent house, as though it feared to wake the sleepers. Veil after veil of thin dusky gauze is lifted, and by degrees the forms and colors of things are restored to them, and we watch the dawn remaking the world in its antique pattern. The wan mirrors get back their mimic life. The flameless tapers stand where we have left them, and beside them lies the half-read book that we had been studying, or the wired flower that we had worn at the ball, or the letter that we had been afraid to read, or that we had read too often. Nothing seems to us changed. Out of the unreal shadows of the night comes back the real life that we had known. We have to resume it where we had left off, and there steals over us a terrible sense of the necessity for the continuance of energy in the same wearisome round of stereotyped habits, or a wild longing, it may be, that our eyelids might open some morning upon a world that had been re-fashioned anew for our pleasure in the darkness, a world in which things would have fresh shapes and colors, and be changed, or have other secrets, a world in which the past would have little or no place, or survive, at any rate, in no conscious form of obligation or regret, the remembrance even of joy having its bitterness, and the memories of pleasure their pain.

It was the creation of such worlds as these that seemed to Dorian Gray to be the true object, or among the true objects, of life; and in his search for sensations that would be at once new and delightful, and possess that element of strangeness that is so essential to romance, he would often adopt certain modes of thought that he knew to be really alien to his nature, abandon himself to their subtle influences, and then, having, as it were, caught their color and satisfied his intellectual curiosity, leave them with that curious indifference that is not incompatible with a real ardor of temperament, and that indeed, according to certain modern psychologists, is often a condition of it.

It was rumored of him once that he was about to join the Roman Catholic communion; and certainly the Roman ritual had always a great attraction for him. The daily sacrifice, more awful really than all the sacrifices of the antique world, stirred him as much by its superb rejection of the evidence of the senses as by the primitive simplicity of its elements and the eternal pathos of the human tragedy that it sought to symbolize. He loved to kneel down on the cold marble pavement, and with the priest, in his stiff flowered cope,[4] slowly and with white hands moving aside the veil of the tabernacle, and raising aloft the jewelled lantern-shaped monstrance with that pallid wafer that at times, one would fain think, is indeed the "panis cælestis," the bread of angels, or, robed in the garments of the Passion of Christ, breaking the Host into the chalice, and smiting his breast for his sins. The fuming censers, that the grave boys, in their lace and scarlet, tossed into the air like great gilt flowers, had their subtle fascination for him. As he passed out, he used to look with wonder at the black confessionals, and long to sit in the dim shadow of one of them and listen to men and women whispering through the tarnished grating the true story of their lives.

4. Changed to "dalmatic" in 1891.

But he never fell into the error of arresting his intellectual development by any formal acceptance of creed or system, or of mistaking, for a house in which to live, an inn that is but suitable for the sojourn of a night, or for a few hours of a night in which there are no stars and the moon is in travail. Mysticism, with its marvellous power of making common things strange to us, and the subtle antinomianism that always seems to accompany it, moved him for a season; and for a season he inclined to the materialistic doctrines of the *Darwinismus* movement in Germany, and found a curious pleasure in tracing the thoughts and passions of men to some pearly cell in the brain, or some white nerve in the body,[5] delighting in the conception of the absolute dependence of the spirit on certain physical conditions, morbid or healthy, normal or diseased. Yet, as has been said of him before, no theory of life seemed to him to be of any importance compared with life itself. He felt keenly conscious of how barren all all intellectual speculation is when separated from action and experiment. He knew that the senses, no less than the soul, have their mysteries to reveal.

And so he would now study perfumes, and the secrets of their manufacture, distilling heavily-scented oils, and burning odorous gums from the East. He saw that there was no mood of the mind that had not its counterpart in the sensuous life, and set himself to discover their true relations, wondering what there was in frankincense that made one mystical, and in ambergris that stirred one's passions, and in violets that woke the memory of dead romances, and in musk that troubled the brain, and in champak that stained the imagination; and seeking often to elaborate a real psychology of perfumes, and to estimate the several influences of sweet-smelling roots, and scented pollen-laden flowers, of aromatic balms, and of dark and fragrant woods, of spikenard that sickens, of hovenia that makes men mad, and of aloes that are said to be able to expel melancholy from the soul.

At another time he devoted himself entirely to music, and in a long latticed room, with a vermilion-and-gold ceiling and walls of olive-green lacquer, he used to give curious concerts in which mad gypsies tore wild music from little zithers, or grave yellow-shawled Tunisians plucked at the strained strings of monstrous lutes, while grinning negroes beat monotonously upon copper drums, or turbaned Indians, crouching upon scarlet mats, blew through long pipes of reed or brass, and charmed, or feigned to charm, great hooded snakes and horrible horned adders. The harsh intervals and shrill discords of barbaric music stirred him at times when Schubert's grace, and Chopin's beautiful sorrows, and the mighty harmonies of Beethoven himself, fell unheeded on his ear. He collected together from all parts of the world the strangest instruments that could be found, either in the tombs of dead nations or among the few savage tribes that have survived contact with Western civilizations, and loved

5. Stoddart or another editor at *Lippincott's* knew anatomy better than Wilde and revised the TS from Wilde's "ivory cell . . . or scarlet nerve."

to touch and try them. He had the mysterious *juruparis* of the Rio Negro Indians, that women are not allowed to look at, and that even youths may not see till they have been subjected to fasting and scourging, and the earthen jars of the Peruvians that have the shrill cries of birds, and flutes of human bones such as Alfonso de Ovalle heard in Chili, and the sonorous green stones that are found near Cuzco and give forth a note of singular sweetness. He had painted gourds filled with pebbles that rattled when they were shaken; the long *clarin* of the Mexicans, into which the performer does not blow, but through which he inhales the air; the harsh *turé* of the Amazon tribes, that is sounded by the sentinels who sit all day long in trees, and that can be heard, it is said, at a distance of three leagues; the *teponaztli*, that has two vibrating tongues of wood, and is beaten with sticks that are smeared with an elastic gum obtained from the milky juice of plants; the *yotl*-bells of the Aztecs, that are hung in clusters like grapes; and a huge cylindrical drum, covered with the skins of great serpents, like the one that Bernal Diaz saw when he went with Cortes into the Mexican temple, and of whose doleful sound he has left us so vivid a description. The fantastic character of these instruments fascinated him, and he felt a curious delight in the thought that Art, like Nature, has her monsters, things of bestial shape and with hideous voices. Yet, after some time, he wearied of them, and would sit in his box at the Opera, either alone or with Lord Henry, listening in rapt pleasure to "Tannhäuser," and seeing in that great work of art a presentation of the tragedy of his own soul.

On another occasion he took up the study of jewels, and appeared at a costume ball as Anne de Joyeuse, Admiral of France, in a dress covered with five hundred and sixty pearls. He would often spend a whole day settling and resettling in their cases the various stones that he had collected, such as the olive-green chrysoberyl that turns red by lamplight, the cymophane with its wire-like line of silver, the pistachio-colored peridot, rose-pink and wine-yellow topazes, carbuncles of fiery scarlet with tremulous four-rayed stars, flame-red cinnamon-stones, orange and violet spinels, and amethysts with their alternate layers of ruby and sapphire. He loved the red gold of the sunstone, and the moonstone's pearly whiteness, and the broken rainbow of the milky opal. He procured from Amsterdam three emeralds of extraordinary size and richness of color, and had a turquoise *de la vieille roche* that was the envy of all the connoisseurs.

He discovered wonderful stories, also, about jewels.[6] In Alphonso's "Clericalis Disciplina" a serpent was mentioned with eyes of real jacinth,

6. Wilde added four paragraphs here in three long MS pages to TS beginning "He discovered wonderful stories . . ." and ending "luxury of the dead was wonderful" on the next page. The following lines of the insert never appeared in print. Since there were no instructions from Stoddart or other editorial marks, the omission may have been a typesetting error or a deliberate omission to avoid an ambiguity of reference or syntax: "It was a pearl that Julius Caesar had given to Servilia when he loved her. Their child had been Brutus. [New paragraph] The young priest of the Sun, who while yet a boy had been slain for his sins, used to walk in jewelled shoes on dust of gold and silver."

and in the romantic history of Alexander he was said to have found
snakes in the vale of Jordan "with collars of real emeralds growing on
their backs." There was a gem in the brain of the dragon, Philostratus
told us, and "by the exhibition of golden letters and a scarlet robe" the
monster could be thrown into a magical sleep, and slain. According to
the great alchemist Pierre de Boniface, the diamond rendered a man
invisible, and the agate of India made him eloquent. The cornelian
appeased anger, and the hyacinth provoked sleep, and the amethyst drove
away the fumes of wine. The garnet cast out demons, and the hydropicus deprived the moon of her color. The selenite waxed and waned with
the moon, and the meloceus, that discovers thieves, could be affected
only by the blood of kids. Leonardus Camillus had seen a white stone
taken from the brain of a newly-killed toad, that was a certain antidote
against poison. The bezoar, that was found in the heart of the Arabian
deer, was a charm that could cure the plague. In the nests of Arabian
birds was the aspilates, that, according to Democritus, kept the wearer
from any danger by fire.

The King of Ceilan rode through his city with a large ruby in his
hand, as the ceremony of his coronation. The gates of the palace of John
the Priest were "made of sardius, with the horn of the horned snake
inwrought, so that no man might bring poison within." Over the gable
were "two golden apples, in which were two carbuncles," so that the
gold might shine by day, and the carbuncles by night. In Lodge's strange
romance "A Margarite of America" it was stated that in the chamber of
Margarite were seen "all the chaste ladies of the world, inchased out of
silver, looking through fair mirrours of chrysolites, carbuncles, sapphires, and greene emeraults." Marco Polo had watched the inhabitants
of Zipangu place a rose-colored pearl in the mouth of the dead. A sea-
monster had been enamoured of the pearl that the diver brought to King
Perozes, and had slain the thief, and mourned for seven moons over his
loss. When the Huns lured the king into the great pit, he flung it away,—
Procopius tells the story,—nor was it ever found again, though the
Emperor Anastasius offered five hundred-weight of gold pieces for it.
The King of Malabar had shown a Venetian a rosary of one hundred
and four pearls, one for every god that he worshipped.[7]

When the Duke de Valentinois, son of Alexander VI., visited Louis
XII. of France, his horse was loaded with gold leaves, according to Brantôme, and his cap had double rows of rubies that threw out a great light.
Charles of England had ridden in stirrups hung with three hundred and
twenty-one diamonds. Richard II. had a coat, valued at thirty thousand
marks, which was covered with balas rubies. Hall described Henry VIII.,
on his way to the Tower previous to his coronation, as wearing "a jacket
of raised gold, the placard embroidered with diamonds and other rich

7. Wilde changed this to "three hundred and four pearls" in 1891.

stones, and a great bauderike about his neck of large balasses." The favorites of James I. wore ear-rings of emeralds set in gold filigrane. Edward II. gave to Piers Gaveston a suit of red-gold armor studded with jacinths, and a collar of gold roses set with turquoise-stones, and a skull-cap *parsemé* with pearls. Henry II. wore jewelled gloves reaching to the elbow, and had a hawk-glove set with twelve rubies and fifty-two great pearls. The ducal hat of Charles the Rash, the last Duke of Burgundy of his race, was studded with sapphires and hung with pear-shaped pearls.

How exquisite life had once been! How gorgeous in its pomp and decoration! Even to read of the luxury of the dead was wonderful.

Then he turned his attention to embroideries, and to the tapestries that performed the office of frescos in the chill rooms of the Northern nations of Europe. As he investigated the subject,—and he always had an extraordinary faculty of becoming absolutely absorbed for the moment in whatever he took up,—he was almost saddened by the reflection of the ruin that time brought on beautiful and wonderful things. He, at any rate, had escaped that. Summer followed summer, and the yellow jonquils bloomed and died many times, and nights of horror repeated the story of their shame, but he was unchanged. No winter marred his face or stained his flower-like bloom. How different it was with material things! Where had they gone to? Where was the great crocus-colored robe, on which the gods fought against the giants, that had been worked for Athena? Where the huge velarium that Nero had stretched across the Colosseum at Rome, on which were represented the starry sky, and Apollo driving a chariot drawn by white gilt-reined steeds? He longed to see the curious table-napkins wrought for Elagabalus,[8] on which were displayed all the dainties and viands that could be wanted for a feast; the mortuary cloth of King Chilperic, with its three hundred golden bees; the fantastic robes that excited the indignation of the Bishop of Pontus, and were figured with "lions, panthers, bears, dogs, forests, rocks, hunters,—all, in fact, that a painter can copy from nature;" and the coat that Charles of Orleans once wore, on the sleeves of which were embroidered the verses of a song beginning *"Madame, je suis tout joyeux,"* the musical accompaniment of the words being wrought in gold thread, and each note, a square shape in those days, formed with four pearls. He read of the room that was prepared at the palace at Rheims for the use of Queen Joan of Burgundy, and was decorated with "thirteen hundred and twenty-one parrots, made in broidery, and blazoned with the king's arms, and five hundred and sixty-one butterflies, whose wings were similarly ornamented with the arms of the queen, the whole worked in gold." Catherine de Médicis had a mourning-bed made for her of black velvet powdered with crescents and suns. Its curtains were of damask, with leafy wreaths and garlands, figured upon a gold and silver ground, and

8. Wilde changed this to "Priest of the Sun" in 1891. Elagabalus was priest of the sun god at Emesa and later Roman emperor under the name Marcus Aurelius Antoninus.

fringed along the edges with broideries of pearls, and it stood in a room hung with rows of the queen's devices in cut black velvet upon cloth of silver. Louis XIV. had gold-embroidered caryatides fifteen feet high in his apartment. The state bed of Sobieski, King of Poland, was made of Smyrna gold brocade embroidered in turquoises with verses from the Koran. Its supports were of silver gilt, beautifully chased, and profusely set with enamelled and jewelled medallions. It had been taken from the Turkish camp before Vienna, and the standard of Mohammed had stood under it.

And so, for a whole year, he sought to accumulate the most exquisite specimens that he could find of textile and embroidered work, getting the dainty Delhi muslins, finely wrought, with gold-threat palmates, and stitched over with irridescent beetles' wings; the Dacca gauzes, that from their transparency are known in the East as "woven air," and "running water," and "evening dew;" strange figured cloths from Java; elaborate yellow Chinese hangings; books bound in tawny satins or fair blue silks and wrought with *fleurs de lys*, birds, and images; veils of *lacis* worked in Hungary point; Sicilian brocades, and stiff Spanish velvets; Georgian work with its gilt coins, and Japanese *Foukousas* with their green-toned golds and their marvellously-plumaged birds.

He had a special passion, also, for ecclesiastical vestments, as indeed he had for everything connected with the service of the Church. In the long cedar chests that lined the west gallery of his house he had stored away many rare and beautiful specimens of what is really the raiment of the Bride of Christ, who must wear purple and jewels and fine linen that she may hide the pallid macerated body that is worn by the suffering that she seeks for, and wounded by self-inflicted pain. He had a gorgeous cope of crimson silk and gold-thread damask, figured with a repeating pattern of golden pomegranates set in six-petalled formal blossoms, beyond which on either side was the pine-apple device wrought in seed-pearls. The orphreys were divided into panels representing scenes from the life of the Virgin, and the coronation of the Virgin was figured in colored silks upon the hood. This was Italian work of the fifteenth century. Another cope was of green velvet, embroidered with heart-shaped groups of acanthus-leaves, from which spread long-stemmed white blossoms, the details of which were picked out with silver thread and colored crystals. The morse bore a seraph's head in gold-thread raised work. The orphreys were woven in a diaper of red and gold silk, and were starred with medallions of many saints and martyrs, among whom was St. Sebastian. He had chasubles, also, of amber-colored silk, and blue silk and gold brocade, and yellow silk damask and cloth of gold, figured with representations of the Passion and Crucifixion of Christ, and embroidered with lions and peacocks and other emblems; dalmatics of white satin and pink silk damask, decorated with tulips and dolphins and *fleurs de lys*; altar frontals of crimson velvet and blue linen; and many corporals, chalice-veils, and sudaria. In the mystic offices to which these things were put there was something that quickened his imagination.[9]

For these things, and everything that he collected in his lovely house, were to be to him means of forgetfulness, modes by which he could escape, for a season, from the fear that seemed to him at times to be almost too great to be borne. Upon the walls of the lonely locked room where he had spent so much of his boyhood, he had hung with his own hands the terrible portrait whose changing features showed him the real degradation of his life, and had draped the purple-and-gold pall in front of it as a curtain. For weeks he would not go there, would forget the hideous painted thing, and get back his light heart, his wonderful joyousness, his passionate pleasure in mere existence. Then, suddenly, some night he would creep out of the house, go down to dreadful places near Blue Gate Fields,[1] and stay there, day after day, until he was driven away.[2] On his return he would sit in front of the picture, sometimes loathing it and himself, but filled, at other times, with that pride of rebellion that is half the fascination of sin, and smiling, with secret pleasure, at the misshapen shadow that had to bear the burden that should have been his own.

After a few years he could not endure to be long out of England, and gave up the villa that he had shared at Trouville with Lord Henry, as well as the little white walled-in house at Algiers where he had more than once spent his winter. He hated to be separated from the picture that was such a part of his life, and he was also afraid that during his absence some one might gain access to the room, in spite of the elaborate bolts and bars that he had caused to be placed upon the door.

He was quite conscious that this would tell them nothing. It was true that the portrait still preserved, under all the foulness and ugliness of the face, its marked likeness to himself; but what could they learn from that? He would laugh at any one who tried to taunt him. He had not painted it. What was it to him how vile and full of shame it looked? Even if he told them, would they believe it?

Yet he was afraid. Sometimes when he was down at his great house in Nottinghamshire, entertaining the fashionable young men of his own rank who were his chief companions, and astounding the county by the wanton luxury and gorgeous splendor of his mode of life, he would suddenly leave his guests and rush back to town to see that the door had not been tampered with and that the picture was still there. What if it should be stolen? The mere thought made him cold with horror. Surely the world would know his secret then. Perhaps the world already suspected it.

For, while he fascinated many, there were not a few who distrusted him. He was blackballed at a West End club of which his birth and social position fully entitled him to become a member, and on one

9. Wilde added this paragraph on two handwritten pages inserted into TS.
1. Wilde originally wrote "the Docks."

2. The last phrase is Stoddart's. The original read, "till they almost drove him out in horror and had to be appeased with monstrous bribes."

occasion, when he was brought by a friend into the smoking-room of the Carlton,[3] the Duke of Berwick and another gentleman got up in a marked manner and went out. Curious stories became current about him after he had passed his twenty-fifth year. It was said that he had been seen brawling with foreign sailors in a low den in the distant parts of Whitechapel, and that he consorted with thieves and coiners and knew the mysteries of their trade. His extraordinary absences became notorious, and, when he used to reappear again in society, men[4] would whisper to each other in corners, or pass him with a sneer, or look at him with cold searching eyes, as if they were determined to discover his secret.

Of such insolences and attempted slights he, of course, took no notice, and in the opinion of most people his frank debonair manner, his charming boyish smile, and the infinite grace of that wonderful youth that seemed never to leave him, were in themselves a sufficient answer to the calumnies (for so they called them) that were circulated about him. It was remarked, however, that those who had been most intimate with him appeared, after a time, to shun him. Of all his friends, or so-called friends, Lord Henry Wotton was the only one who remained loyal to him.[5] Women who had wildly adored him, and for his sake had braved all social censure and set convention at defiance, were seen to grow pallid with shame or horror if Dorian Gray entered the room.[6]

Yet these whispered scandals only lent him, in the eyes of many, his strange and dangerous charm. His great wealth was a certain element of security. Society, civilized society at least, is never very ready to believe anything to the detriment of those who are both rich and charming. It feels instinctively that manners are of more importance than morals, and the highest respectability is of less value in its opinion that the possession of a good *chef*. And, after all, it is a very poor consolation to be told that the man who has given one a bad dinner, or poor wine, is irreproachable in his private life. Even the cardinal virtues cannot atone for cold *entrées*, as Lord Henry remarked once, in a discussion on the subject; and there is possibly a good deal to be said for his view. For the canons of good society are, or should be, the same as the canons of art. Form is absolutely essential to it. It should have the dignity of a ceremony, as well as its unreality, and should combine the insincere character of a romantic play with the wit and beauty that make such plays charming. Is insincerity such a terrible thing? I think not. It is merely a method by which we can multiply our personalities.

3. Changed in 1891. The Carlton was a famous conservative political club located in Pall Mall.
4. Stoddart canceled the following here: "who were jealous of the strange love he inspired in women."
5. Stoddart also canceled the following marginal insert that ended the sentence: "and in the eyes of some it was a question whether that was an honor or a disgrace."
6. The conclusion of this paragraph, crossed out

by Stoddart in TS, was as follows: "It was said that even the sinful creatures who prowl the streets at night had cursed him as he passed by, seeing in him a corruption greater than their own and knowing but too well the horror of his real life." An additional passage in the same spirit, which Wilde blotted out in MS, described Dorian's appeal in terms of his "strange and dangerous charm."

Such, at any rate, was Dorian Gray's opinion. He used to wonder at the shallow psychology of those who conceive the Ego in man as a thing simple, permanent, reliable, and of one essence. To him, man was a being with myriad lives and myriad sensations, a complex-multi-form creature that bore within itself strange legacies of thought and passion, and whose very flesh was tainted with the monstrous maladies of the dead. He loved to stroll through the gaunt cold picture-gallery of his country-house and look at the various portraits of those whose blood flowed in his veins. Here was Philip Herbert, described by Francis Osborne, in his "Memories on the Reigns of Queen Elizabeth and King James," as one who was "caressed by the court for his handsome face, which kept him not long company." Was it young Herbert's life that he sometimes led? Had some strange poisonous germ crept from body to body till it had reached his own? Was it some dim sense of that ruined grace that had made him so suddenly, and almost without cause, give utterance, in Basil Hallward's studio, to that mad prayer that had so changed his life? Here, in gold-embroidered red doublet, jewelled sur-coat, and gilt-edged ruff and wrist-bands, stood Sir Anthony Sherard, with his silver-and-black armor piled at his feet. What had this man's legacy been? Had the lover of Giovanna of Naples bequeathed him some inheritance of sin and shame? Were his own actions merely the dreams that the dead man had not dared to realize? Here, from the fading can-vas, smiled Lady Elizabeth Devereux, in her gauze hood, pearl stom-acher, and pink slashed sleeves. A flower was in her right hand, and her left clasped an enamelled collar of white and damask roses. On a table by her side lay a mandolin and an apple. There were large green rosettes upon her little pointed shoes. He knew her life, and the strange stories that were told about her lovers.[7] Had he something of her temperament in him? Those oval heavy-lidded eyes seemed to look curiously at him. What of George Willoughby, with his powdered hair and fantastic patches? How evil he looked! The face was saturnine and swarthy, and the sen-sual lips seemed to be twisted with disdain. Delicate lace ruffles fell over the lean yellow hands that were so overladen with rings. He had been a macaroni of the eighteenth century, and the friend, in his youth, of Lord Ferrars. What of the second Lord Sherard, the companion of the Prince Regent in his wildest days, and one of the witnesses at the secret marriage with Mrs. Fitzherbert? How proud and handsome he was, with his chestnut curls and insolent pose! What passions had he bequeathed? The world had looked upon him as infamous. He had led the orgies at Carlton House. The star of the Garter glittered upon his breast. Beside him hung the portrait of his wife, a pallid, thin-lipped woman in black. Her blood, also, stirred within him. How curious it all seemed!

Yet one had ancestors in literature, as well as in one's own race, nearer perhaps in type and temperament, many of them, and certainly with an

7. Wilde added and Stoddart canceled the following, thus reinstating the original reading: "the deaths of those whom she had granted her favors."

influence of which one was more absolutely conscious. There were times when it seemed to Dorian Gray that the whole of history was merely the record of his own life, not as he had lived it in act and circumstance, but as his imagination had created it for him, as it had been in his brain and in his passions. He felt that he had known them all, those strange terrible figures that had passed across the stage of the world and made sin so marvellous and evil so full of wonder. It seemed to him that in some mysterious way their lives had been his own.

The hero[8] of the dangerous novel that had so influenced his life had himself had this curious fancy. In a chapter[9] of the book he tells how, crowned with a laurel, lest lightning might strike him, he had sat, as Tiberius, in a garden at Capri, reading the shameful books of Elephantis, while dwarfs and peacocks strutted round him and the flute-player mocked the swinger of the censer; and, as Caligula,[1] had caroused with the green-shirted jockeys in their stables, and supped in an ivory manger with a jewel-frontleted horse; and, as Domitian, had wandered through a corridor lined with marble mirrors, looking round with haggard eyes for the reflection of the dagger that was to end his days, and sick with that ennui, that *tædium vitæ*, that comes on those to whom life denies nothing; and had peered through a clear emerald at the red shambles of the Circus, and then, in a litter of pearl and purple drawn by silver-shod mules, been carried through the Street of Pomegranates to a House of Gold, and heard men cry on Nero Cæsar as he passed by; and, as Elagabalus, had painted his face with colors, and plied the distaff among the women, and brought the Moon from Carthage, and given her in mystic marriage to the Sun.

Over and over again Dorian used to read this fantastic chapter,[2] and the chapter immediately following, in which the hero describes the curious tapestries that he had had woven for him from Gustave Moreau's[3] designs, and on which were pictured the awful and beautiful forms of those whom Vice and Blood and Weariness had made monstrous or mad.[4] Filippo, Duke of Milan, who slew his wife, and painted her lips with a scarlet poison; Pietro Barbi, the Venetian, known as Paul the Second, who sought in his vanity to assume the title of Formosus, and whose tiara, valued at two hundred thousand florins, was bought at the price of a terrible sin; Gian Maria Visconti, who used hounds to chase living men, and whose murdered body was covered with roses by a harlot

8. Originally "Raoul" in TS. In 1891 Wilde changed "dangerous" to "wonderful."

9. "Fourth" is canceled in TS and changed by Wilde to "seventh" in 1891.

1. Stoddart deleted "had drank the live philter of Caesonia, and wore the habit of Venus by night, and by day a false gilded beard."

2. Changed by Wilde from "passage" in TS. In the next line, Stoddart substituted "the hero" for "Raoul."

3. Gustave Moreau (1826–98) was a famous painter

of Decadent themes and subjects whose style became synonymous with the movement. Wilde added his name in TS and removed it in 1891.

4. Stoddart changed the original "Lust" to "Vice" in the line above, deleted "here was Manfred, King of Apulia who dressed always in green, and consorted only with cortezans and buffoons," and in the line below, after "scarlet poison," canceled "that her guilty lover might suck swift death from the dead thing he had fondled."

who had loved him; the Borgia on his white horse, with Fratricide[5] riding beside him, and his mantle stained with the blood of Perotto; Pietro Riario, the young Cardinal Archbishop of Florence, child and minion of Sixtus IV., whose beauty was equalled only by his debauchery, and who received Leonora of Aragon in a pavilion of white and crimson silk, filled with nymphs and centaurs, and gilded a boy that he might serve her at the feast as Ganymede or Hylas; Ezzelin, whose melancholy could be cured only by the spectacle of death, and who had a passion for red blood, as other men have for red wine,—the son of the Fiend, as was reported, and one who had cheated his father at dice when gambling with him for his own soul; Giambattista Cibo, who in mockery took the name of Innocent, and into whose torpid veins the blood of three lads was infused by a Jewish doctor; Sigismondo Malatesta, the lover of Isotta, and the lord of Rimini, whose effigy was burned at Rome as the enemy of God and man, who strangled Polyssena with a napkin, and gave poison to Ginerva d'Este in a cup of emerald, and in honor of a shameful passion built a pagan church for Christian worship; Charles VI., who had so wildly adored his brother's wife that a leper had warned him of the insanity that was coming on him, and who could only be soothed by Saracen cards painted with the images of Love and Death and Madness; and, in his trimmed jerkin and jewelled cap and acanthus-like curls, Grifonetto Baglioni, who slew Astorre with his bride, and Simonetto with his page, and whose comeliness was such that, as he lay dying in the yellow piazza of Perugia, those who had hated him could not choose but weep, and Atalanta, who had cursed him, blessed him.

There was a horrible fascination in them all. He saw them at night, and they troubled his imagination in the day. The Renaissance knew of strange manners of poisoning,—poisoning by a helmet and a lighted torch, by an embroidered glove and a jewelled fan, by a gilded pomander and by an amber chain. Dorian Gray had been poisoned by a book.[6] There were moments when he looked on evil simply as a mode through which he could realize his conception of the beautiful.

Chapter X.

It was on the 7th[1] of November, the eve of his own thirty-second birthday, as he often remembered afterwards.

He was walking home about eleven o'clock from Lord Henry's, where he had been dining, and was wrapped in heavy furs, as the night was cold and foggy. At the corner of Grosvenor Square and South Audley Street a man passed him in the mist, walking very fast, and with the collar of his gray ulster turned up. He had a bag in his hand. He recog-

5. Stoddart removed "Incest and" here in TS. Wilde restored "harlot" to the line above after Stoddart had changed it to "one."
6. The original ending of the chapter read: "Lord Henry had given him one, and Basil Hallward had

painted the other." Wilde then moved the lines beginning "The Renaissance . . ." to their present location on the page.
1. Changed to "9th" in 1891 and the birthday from the "thirty-second" to "thirty-eighth."

nized him. It was Basil Hallward. A strange sense of fear, for which he could not account, came over him. He made no sign of recognition, and went on slowly, in the direction of his own house.

But Hallward had seen him. Dorian heard him first stopping, and then hurrying after him. In a few moments his hand was on his arm.

"Dorian! What an extraordinary piece of luck! I have been waiting for you ever since nine o'clock in your library. Finally I took pity on your tired servant, and told him to go to bed, as he let me out. I am off to Paris by the midnight train, and I wanted particularly to see you before I left. I thought it was you, or rather your fur coat, as you passed me. But I wasn't quite sure. Didn't you recognize me?"

"In this fog, my dear Basil? Why, I can't even recognize Grosvenor Square. I believe my house is somewhere about here, but I don't feel at all certain about it. I am sorry you are going away, as I have not seen you for ages. But I suppose you will be back soon?"

"No: I am going to be out of England for six months. I intend to take a studio in Paris, and shut myself up till I have finished a great picture I have in my head. However, it wasn't about myself I wanted to talk. Here we are at your door. Let me come in for a moment. I have something to say to you."

"I shall be charmed. But won't you miss your train?" said Dorian Gray, languidly, as he passed up the steps and opened the door with his latch-key.

The lamp-light struggled out through the fog, and Hallward looked at his watch. "I have heaps of time," he answered. "The train doesn't go till twelve-fifteen, and it is only just eleven. In fact, I was on my way to the club to look for you, when I met you. You see, I shan't have any delay about luggage, as I have sent on my heavy things. All I have with me is in this bag, and I can easily get to Victoria in twenty minutes."

Dorian looked at him and smiled. "What a way for a fashionable painter to travel! A Gladstone bad, and an ulster! Come in, or the fog will get into the house. And mind you don't talk about anything serious. Nothing is serious nowadays. At least nothing should be."

Hallward shook his head, as he entered, and followed Dorian into the library. There was a bright wood fire blazing in the large open hearth. The lamps were lit, and an open Dutch silver spirit-case stood, with some siphons of soda-water and large cut-glass tumblers, on a little table.

"You see your servant made me quite at home, Dorian. He gave me everything I wanted, including your best cigarettes. He is a most hospitable creature. I like him much better than the Frenchman you used to have. What has become of the Frenchman, by the bye?"

Dorian shrugged his shoulders. "I believe he married Lady Ashton's maid, and has established her in Paris as an English dressmaker. *Anglomanie* is very fashionable over there now, I hear. It seems silly of the French, doesn't it? But—do you know?—he was not at all a bad servant. I never liked him, but I had nothing to complain about. One often imagines things that are quite absurd. He was really very devoted to me, and seemed quite sorry when he went away. Have another brandy-and-soda? Or would you like hock-and-seltzer? I always take hock-and-seltzer myself. There is sure to be some in the next room."

"Thanks, I won't have anything more," said Hallward, taking his cap and coat off, and throwing them on the bag that he had placed in the corner. "And now, my dear fellow, I want to speak to you seriously. Don't frown like that. You make it so much more difficult for me."

"What is it all about?" cried Dorian, in his petulant way, flinging himself down on the sofa. "I hope it is not about myself. I am tired of myself to-night. I should like to be somebody else."

"It is about yourself," answered Hallward, in his grave, deep voice, "and I must say it to you. I shall only keep you half an hour."

Dorian sighed, and lit a cigarette. "Half an hour!" he murmured.

"It is not much to ask of you, Dorian, and it is entirely for your own sake that I am speaking. I think it right that you should know that the most dreadful things are being said about you in London,—things that I could hardly repeat to you."[2]

"I don't wish to know anything about them. I love scandals about other people, but scandals about myself don't interest me. They have not got the charm of novelty."

"They must interest you, Dorian. Every gentleman is interested in his good name. You don't want people to talk of you as something vile and degraded. Of course you have your position, and your wealth, and all that kind of thing. But position and wealth are not everything. Mind you, I don't believe these rumors at all. At least, I can't believe them when I see you. Sin is a thing that writes itself across a man's face. It cannot be concealed. People talk of secret vices. There are no such things as secret vices. If a wretched man has a vice, it shows itself in the lines of his mouth, the droop of his eyelids, the moulding of his hands, even. Somebody—I won't mention his name, but you know him—came to me last year to have his portrait done. I had never seen him before, and had never heard anything about him at the time, though I have heard a good deal since. He offered an extravagant price. I refused him. There was something in the shape of his fingers that I hated. I know now that I was quite right in what I fancied about him. His life is dreadful. But you, Dorian, with your pure, bright, innocent face, and your marvellous untroubled youth,—I can't believe anything against you. And yet I see you very seldom, and you never come down to the studio now, and when I am away from you, and I hear all these hideous things that people are whispering about you, I don't know what to say. Why is it, Dorian, that a man like the Duke of Berwick leaves the room of a club when you enter it? Why is it that so many gentlemen in London will neither go to your house nor invite you to theirs? You used to be a friend

2. This line was dropped in 1891.

of Lord Cawdor. I met him at dinner last week. Your name happened
to come up in conversation, in connection with the miniatures you have
lent to the exhibition at the Dudley. Cawdor curled his lip, and said that
you might have the most artistic tastes, but that you were a man whom
no pure-minded girl should be allowed to know, and whom no chaste
woman should sit in the same room with. I reminded him that I was a
friend of yours, and asked him what he meant. He told me. He told me
right out before everybody. It was horrible! Why is your friendship so
fateful to young men?[3] There was that wretched boy in the Guards who
committed suicide. You were his great friend. There was Sir Henry Ashton, who had to leave England, with a tarnished name. You and he
were inseparable. What about Adrian Singleton, and his dreadful end?
What about Lord Kent's only son, and his career? I met his father yesterday in St. James Street. He seemed broken with shame and sorrow.
What about the young Duke of Perth? What sort of life has he got now?
What gentleman would associate with him?[4] Dorian, Dorian, your reputation is infamous. I know you and Harry are great friends. I say nothing about that now, but surely you need not have made his sister's name
a by-word. When you met Lady Gwendolen, not a breath of scandal
had ever touched her. Is there a single decent woman in London now
who would drive with her in the Park? Why, even her children are not
allowed to live with her. Then there are other stories,—stories that you
have been seen creeping at dawn out of dreadful houses and slinking in
disguise into the foulest dens in London. Are they true? Can they be
true? When I first heard them, I laughed. I hear them now, and they
make me shudder. What about your country-house, and the life that is
led there? Dorian, you don't know what is said about you.[5] I won't tell
you that I don't want to preach to you. I remember Harry saying once
that every man who turned himself into an amateur curate for the moment
always said that, and then broke his word. I do want to preach to you. I
want you to lead such a life as will make the world respect you. I want
you to have a clean name and a fair record. I want you to get rid of the
dreadful people you associate with. Don't shrug your shoulders like that.
Don't be so indifferent. You have a wonderful influence. Let it be for
good, not evil. They say that you corrupt every one whom you become
intimate with, and that it is quite sufficient for you to enter a house, for
shame of some kind to follow after you. I don't know whether it is so or
not. How should I know? But it is said of you. I am told things that it
seems impossible to doubt. Lord Gloucester was one of my greatest friends
at Oxford. He showed me a letter that his wife had written to him when
she was dying alone in her villa at Mentone. Your name was implicated

3. Stoddart substituted the rest of the sentence after
"why is" for the original reading: "why is it that
every young man that you take up seems to come
to grief, to go to the bad at once?"
4. Wilde added a new paragraph here in 1891.

5. Stoddart canceled the following in TS: "It is
quite sufficient to say of a young man that he goes
to stay at Selby Royal, for people to sneer and titter."

in [6] the most terrible confession I ever read. I told him that it was absurd,—
that I knew you thoroughly, and that you were incapable of anything of
the kind. Know you? I wonder do I know you? Before I could answer
that, I should have to see your soul."

"To see my soul!" muttered Dorian Gray, starting up from the sofa
and turning almost white from fear.

"Yes," answered Hallward, gravely, and with infinite sorrow in his
voice,—"to see your soul. But only God can do that."

A bitter laugh of mockery broke from the lips of the younger man.
"You shall see it yourself, to-night!" he cried, seizing a lamp from the
table. "Come: it is your own handiwork. Why shouldn't you look at it?
You can tell the world all about it afterwards, if you choose. Nobody
would believe you. If they did believe you, they'd like me all the better
for it. I know the age better than you do, though you will prate about it
so tediously. Come, I tell you. You have chattered enough about corruption. Now you shall look on it face to face." [7]

There was the madness of pride in every word he uttered. He stamped
his foot upon the ground in his boyish insolent manner. He felt a terrible
joy at the thought that some one else was to share his secret, and that
the man who had painted the portrait that was the origin of all his shame
was to be burdened for the rest of his life with the hideous memory of
what he had done.

"Yes," he continued, coming closer to him, and looking steadfastly
into his stern eyes, "I will show you my soul. You shall see the thing
that you fancy only God can see."

Hallward started back. "This is blasphemy, Dorian!" he cried. "You
must not say things like that. They are horrible, and they don't mean
anything."

"You think so?" He laughed again.

"I know so. As for what I said to you to-night, I said it for your good.
You know I have been always devoted [8] to you."

"Don't touch me. Finish what you have to say."

A twisted flash of pain shot across Hallward's face. He paused for a
moment, and a wild feeling of pity came over him. After all, what right
had he to pry into the life of Dorian Gray? If he had done a tithe of what
was rumored about him, how much he must have suffered! Then he
straightened himself up, and walked over to the fireplace, and stood
there, looking at the burning logs with their frost-like ashes and their
throbbing cores of flame.

"I am waiting, Basil," said the young man, in a hard, clear voice.

He turned round. "What I have to say is this," he cried. "You must
give me some answer to these horrible charges that are made against

6. Stoddart changed this from "It was" and then
canceled the next sentence, which read: "He said
that he suspected you."
7. Wilde canceled these lines in MS: "Now, I will

show you my soul. You shall see the thing you
fancy only God can see."
8. Changed to "a staunch friend" in 1891.

you. If you tell me that they are absolutely untrue from beginning to end, I will believe you. Deny them, Dorian, deny them! Can't you see what I am going through? My God! don't tell me that you are infamous!"[9]

Dorian Gray smiled. There was a curl of contempt in his lips. "Come up-stairs, Basil," he said, quietly. "I keep a diary of my life from day to day, and it never leaves the room in which it is written. I will show it to you if you come with me."

"I will come with you, Dorian, if you wish it. I see I have missed my train. That makes no matter. I can go to-morrow. But don't ask me to read anything to-night. All I want is a plain answer to my question."

"That will be given to you up-stairs. I could not give it here. You won't have to read long. Don't keep me waiting."

Chapter XI.

He passed out of the room, and began the ascent, Basil Hallward following close behind. They walked softly, as men instinctively do at night. The lamp cast fantastic shadows on the wall and staircase. A rising wind made some of the windows rattle.

When they reached the top landing, Dorian set the lamp down on the floor, and taking out the key turned it in the lock. "You insist on knowing, Basil?" he asked, in a low voice.

"Yes."

"I am delighted," he murmured, smiling. Then he added, somewhat bitterly, "You are the one man in the world who is entitled to know everything about me. You have had more to do with my life than you think." And, taking up the lamp, he opened the door and went in. A cold current of air passed them, and the light shot up for a moment in a flame of murky orange. He shuddered. "Shut the door behind you," he said, as he placed the lamp on the table.

Hallward glanced round him, with a puzzled expression. The room looked as if it had not been lived in for years. A faded Flemish tapestry, a curtained picture, an old Italian *cassone*, and an almost empty book-case,—that was all that it seemed to contain, besides a chair and a table. As Dorian Gray was lighting a half-burned candle that was standing on the mantel-shelf, he saw that the whole place was covered with dust, and that the carpet was in holes. A mouse ran scuffling behind the wainscoting. There was a damp odor of mildew.

"So you think that it is only God who sees the soul, Basil? Draw that curtain back, and you will see mine."

The voice that spoke was cold and cruel. "You are mad, Dorian, or playing a part," muttered Hallward, frowning.

"You won't? Then I must do it myself," said the young man; and he tore the curtain from its rod, and flung it on the ground.

9. Wilde made a change here in 1891.

An exclamation of horror broke from Hallward's lips as he saw in the dim light the hideous thing on the canvas leering at him.[1] There was something in its expression that filled him with disgust and loathing. Good heavens! it was Dorian Gray's own face that he was looking at! The horror, whatever it was, had not yet entirely marred that marvellous beauty. There was still some gold in the thinning hair and some scarlet on the sensual lips. The sodden eyes had kept something of the loveliness of their blue, the noble curves had not yet passed entirely away from chiselled nostrils and from plastic throat. Yes, it was Dorian himself. But who had done it? He seemed to recognize his own brush-work, and the frame was his own design. The idea was monstrous, yet he felt afraid. He seized the lighted candle, and held it to the picture. In the left-hand corner was his own name, traced in long letters of bright vermilion.

It was some foul parody, some infamous, ignoble satire. He had never done that. Still, it was his own picture. He knew it, and he felt as if his blood had changed from fire to sluggish ice in a moment. His own picture! What did it mean? Why had it altered? He turned, and looked at Dorian Gray with the eyes of a sick man. His mouth twitched, and his parched tongue seemed unable to articulate. He passed his hand across his forehead. It was dank with clammy sweat.

The young man was leaning against the mantel-shelf, watching him with that strange expression that is on the faces of those who are absorbed in a play when a great artist is acting. There was neither real sorrow in it nor real joy. There was simply the passion of the spectator, with perhaps a flicker of triumph in the eyes. He had taken the flower out of his coat, and was smelling it, or pretending to do so.

"What does this mean?" cried Hallward, at last. His own voice sounded shrill and curious in his ears.

"Years ago, when I was a boy," said Dorian Gray, "you met me, devoted yourself to me, flattered me, and taught me to be vain of my good looks. One day you introduced me to a friend of yours, who explained to me the wonder of youth, and you finished a portrait of me that revealed to me the wonder of beauty. In a mad moment, that I don't know, even now, whether I regret or not, I made a wish. Perhaps you would call it a prayer. . . ."

"I remember it! Oh, how well I remember it! No! the thing is impossible. The room is damp. The mildew has got into the canvas. The paints I used had some wretched mineral poison in them. I tell you the thing is impossible."[2]

"Ah, what is impossible?" murmured the young man, going over to the window, and leaning his forehead against the cold, mist-stained glass.

---

1. To compare this and the following paragraphs with the revised, 1891 text (see p. 121) is to appreciate how many little improvements Wilde made in revising the first printed version. The evidence of the texts therefore contradicts the myth that Wilde tossed off his work carelessly and hastily.

2. Wilde added in TS margin, "The room is damp . . . impossible."

"You told me you had destroyed it."

"I was wrong. It has destroyed me."

"I don't believe it is my picture."

"Can't you see your romance in it?" said Dorian, bitterly.[3]

"My romance, as you call it . . ."

"As you called it."

"There was nothing evil in it, nothing shameful. This is the face of a satyr."

"It is the face of my soul."

"God![4] what a thing I must have worshipped! This has the eyes of a devil."

"Each of us has Heaven and Hell in him, Basil," cried Dorian, with a wild gesture of despair.

Hallward turned again to the portrait, and gazed at it. "My God! if it is true," he exclaimed, "and this is what you have done with your life, why, you must be worse even than those who talk against you fancy you to be!" He held the light up again to the canvas, and examined it. The surface seemed to be quite undisturbed, and as he had left it. It was from within, apparently, that the foulness and horror had come. Through some strange quickening of inner life the leprosies of sin were slowly eating the thing away. The rotting of a corpse in a watery grave was not so fearful.

His hand shook, and the candle fell from its socket on the floor, and lay there sputtering. He placed his foot on it and put it out. Then he flung himself into the rickety chair that was standing by the table and buried his face in his hands.

"Good God, Dorian, what a lesson! what an awful lesson!" There was no answer, but he could hear the young man sobbing at the window.

"Pray, Dorian, pray," he murmured. "What is it that one was taught to say in one's boyhood? 'Lead us not into temptation. Forgive us our sins. Wash away our iniquities.' Let us say that together. The prayer of your pride has been answered. The prayer of your repentance will be answered also. I worshipped you too much. I am punished for it. You worshipped yourself too much. We are both punished."

Dorian Gray turned slowly around, and looked at him with tear-dimmed eyes. "It is too late, Basil," he murmured.

"It is never too late, Dorian. Let us kneel down and try if we can remember a prayer. Isn't there a verse somewhere, 'Though your sins be as scarlet, you I will make them white as snow'?"

"Those words mean nothing to me now."

"Hush! don't say that. You have done enough evil in your life. My God! don't you see that accursed thing leering at us?"

Dorian Gray glanced at the picture, and suddenly an uncontrollable

3. Wilde changed "romance" to "ideal" in 1891 and added another line further down (see p. 122). 4. Stoddart changed the original "Christ!" here, but Wilde put it back into the 1891 text.

feeling of hatred for Basil Hallward came over him.[5] The mad passions of a hunted animal stirred within him, and he loathed the man who was seated at the table, more than he had ever loathed anything in his whole life. He glanced wildly around. Something glimmered on the top of the painted chest that faced him. His eye fell on it. He knew what it was. It was a knife that he had brought up, some days before, to cut a piece of cord, and had forgotten to take away with him. He moved slowly towards it, passing Hallward as he did so. As soon as he got behind him, he seized it, and turned round. Hallward moved in his chair as if he was going to rise. He rushed at him, and dug the knife into the great vein that is behind the ear, crushing the man's head down on the table, and stabbing again and again.

There was a stifled groan, and the horrible sound of some one choking with blood. The outstretched arms shot up convulsively three times, waving grotesque stiff-fingered hands in the air. He stabbed him once more, but the man did not move. Something began to trickle on the floor. He waited for a moment, still pressing the head down. Then he threw the knife on the table, and listened.

He could hear nothing, but the drip, drip on the threadbare carpet. He opened the door, and went out on the landing. The house was quite quiet. No one was stirring.

He took out the key, and returned to the room, locking himself in as he did so.

The thing was still seated in the chair, straining over the table with bowed head, and humped back, and long fantastic arms. Had it not been for the red jagged tear in the neck, and the clotted black pool that slowly widened on the table, one would have said that the man was simply asleep.

How quickly it had all been done! He felt strangely calm, and, walking over to the window, opened it, and stepped out on the balcony. The wind had blown the fog away, and the sky was like a monstrous peacock's tail, starred with myriads of golden eyes. He looked down, and saw the policeman going his rounds and flashing a bull's-eye lantern on the doors of the silent houses. The crimson spot of a prowling hansom gleamed at the corner, and then vanished. A woman in a ragged shawl was creeping round by the railings, staggering as she went. Now and then she stopped, and peered back. Once, she began to sing in a hoarse voice. The policeman strolled over and said something to her. She stumbled away, laughing. A bitter blast swept across the Square. The gas-lamps flickered, and became blue, and the leafless trees shook their black iron branches as if in pain.[6] He shivered, and went back, closing the window behind him.

He passed to the door, turned the key, and opened it. He did not even

---

5. Wilde added as "though . . . grinning lips" in 1891.
6. Wilde changed this from "in the uncertain gloom" in TS and made another alteration in the effect in 1891.

glance at the murdered man. he felt that the secret of the whole thing was not to realize the situation. The friend who had painted the fatal portrait, the portrait to which all his misery had been due, had gone out of his life. That was enough.

Then he remembered the lamp. It was a rather curious one of Moorish workmanship, made of dull silver inlaid with arabesques of burnished steel. Perhaps it might be missed by his servant, and questions would be asked. He turned back, and took it from the table. How still the man was! How horribly white the long hands looked! He was like a dreadful wax image.

He locked the door behind him, and crept quietly down-stairs. The wood-work creaked, and seemed to cry out as if in pain. He stopped several times, and waited. No: everything was still. It was merely the sound of his own footsteps.

When he reached the library, he saw the bag and coat in the corner. They must be hidden away somewhere. He unlocked a secret press that was in the wainscoting, and put them into it. He could easily burn them afterwards. Then he pulled out his watch. It was twenty minutes to two.

He sat down, and began to think. Every year—every month, almost—men were strangled in England for what he had done. There had been a madness of murder in the air. Some red star had come too close to the earth.

Evidence? What evidence was there against him? Basil Hallward had left the house at eleven. No one had seen him come in again. Most of the servants were at Selby Royal. His valet had gone to bed.

Paris! Yes. It was to Paris that Basil had gone, by the midnight train, as he had intended. With his curious reserved habits, it would be months before any suspicions would be aroused. Months? Everything could be destroyed long before then.

A sudden thought struck him. He put on his fur coat and hat, and went out into the hall. There he paused, hearing the slow heavy tread of the policeman outside on the pavement, and seeing the flash of the lantern reflected in the window. He waited, holding his breath.

After a few moments he opened the front door, and slipped out, shutting it very gently behind him. Then he began ringing the bell. In about ten minutes his valet appeared, half dressed, and looking very drowsy.

"I am sorry to have had to wake you up, Francis," he said, stepping in' "but I had forgotten my latch-key. What time is it?"

"Five minutes past two, sir," answered the man, looking at the clock and yawning.

"Five minutes past two? How horribly late! You must wake me at nine to-morrow. I have some work to do."

"All right, sir."

"Did any one call this evening?"

"Mr. Hallward, sir. He stayed here till eleven, and then he went away to catch his train."

"Oh! I am sorry I didn't see him. Did he leave any message?"

"No, sir, except that he would write to you."[7]

"That will do, Francis. Don't forget to call me at nine tomorrow."

"No, sir."

The man shambled down the passage in his slippers.

Dorian Gray threw his hat and coat upon the yellow marble table, and passed into the library. He walked up and down the room for a quarter of an hour, biting his lip, and thinking.[8] Then he took the Blue Book down from one of the shelves, and began to turn over the leaves. "Alan Campbell, 152, Hertford Street, Mayfair." Yes; that was the man he wanted.

Chapter XII.

At nine o'clock the next morning his servant came in with a cup of chocolate on a tray, and opened the shutters. Dorian was sleeping quite peacefully, lying on his right side, with one hand underneath his cheek. He looked like a boy who had been tired out with play, or study.

The man had to touch him twice on the shoulder before he woke, and as he opened his eyes a faint smile passed across his lips, as though he had been having some delightful dream. yet he had not dreamed at all. His night had been untroubled by any images of pleasure or of pain. But youth smiles without any reason. It is one of its chiefest charms.[1]

He turned round, and, leaning on his elbow, began to drink his chocolate. The mellow November sun was streaming into the room. The sky was bright blue, and there was a genial warmth in the air. It was almost like a morning in May.

Gradually the events of the preceding night crept with silent blood-stained feet into his brain, and reconstructed themselves there with terrible distinctness. He winced at the memory of all that he had suffered, and for a moment the same curious feeling of loathing for Basil Hallward, that had made him kill him as he sat in the chair, came back to him, and he grew cold with passion. The dead man was still sitting there, too, and in the sunlight now. How horrible that was! Such hideous things were for the darkness, not for the day.

He felt that if he brooded on what he had gone through he would sicken or grow mad. There were sins whose fascination was more in the memory than in the doing of them, strange triumphs that gratified the pride more than the passions, and gave to the intellect a quickened sense of joy, greater than any joy they brought, or could ever bring, to the senses. But this was not one of them. It was a thing to be driven out of the mind, to be drugged with poppies, to be strangled lest it might strangle one itself.

7. Wilde added "except . . . you" in TS.   1. Wilde added the last two sentences in TS.
8. Wilde added this sentence in TS.

He passed his hand across his forehead, and then got up hastily,[2] and dressed himself with even more than his usual attention, giving a good deal of care to the selection of his necktie and scarf-pin, and changing his rings more than once.

He spent a long time over breakfast, tasting the various dishes, talking to his valet about some new liveries that he was thinking of getting made for the servants at Selby, and going through his correspondence. Over some of the letters he smiled. Three of them bored him. One he read several times over, and then tore up with a slight look of annoyance in his face. "That awful thing, a woman's memory!" as Lord Henry had once said.

When he had drunk his coffee, he sat down at the table, and wrote two letters. One he put in his pocket, the other he handed to the valet.

"Take this round to 152, Hertford Street, Francis, and if Mr. Campbell is out of town, get his address."

As soon as he was alone, he lit a cigarette, and began sketching upon a piece of paper, drawing flowers, and bits of architecture, first, and then faces. Suddenly he remarked that every face that he drew seemed to have an extraordinary likeness to Basil Hallward. he frowned, and, getting up, went over to the bookcase and took out a volume at hazard. He was determined that he would not think about what had happened, till it became absolutely necessary to do so.

When he had stretched himself on the sofa, he looked at the title-page of the book. It was Gautier's "Émaux et Camées,"[3] Charpentier's Japanese-paper edition, with the Jacquemart etching. The binding was of citron-green leather with a design of gilt trellis-work and dotted pomegranates. It had been given to him by Adrian Singleton.[4] As he turned over the pages his eye fell on the poem about the hand of Lacenaire, the cold yellow hand *"du supplice encore mal lavée,"* with its downy red hairs and its *"doigts de faune."* He glanced at his own white taper fingers, and passed on, till he came to those lovely verses upon Venice:

> Sur une gamme chromatique,
>   Le sein de perles ruisselant,
> La Vénus de l'Adriatique
>   Sort de l'eau son corps rose et blanc.
>
> Les dômes, sur l'azur des ondes
>   Suivant la phrase au pur contour,
> S'enflent comme des gorges rondes
>   Que soulève un soupir d'amour.
>
> L'esquif aborde et me dépose,
>   Jetant son amarre au pilier,

2. Here Wilde canceled the following in TS: "and having thrown on his heavy white dressing gown, passed into the bathroom. When he came out again, he felt calmer."

3. Wilde's original choice in MS was a volume of "sonnets by Verlaine."

4. Wilde added "the binding . . . Singleton" in MS.

> Devant une façade rose,
> Sur le marbre d'un escalier.

How exquisite they were! As one read them, one seemed to be floating down the green water-ways of the pink and pearl city, lying in a black gondola with silver prow and trailing curtains. The mere lines looked to him like those straight lines of turquoise-blue that follow one as one pushes out to the Lido. The sudden flashes of color reminded him of the gleam of the opal-and-iris-throated birds that flutter round the tall honey-combed Campanile, or stalk, with such stately grace, through the dim arcades. Leaning back with half-closed eyes, he kept saying over and over to himself,—

> Devant une façade rose,
> Sur le marbre d'un escalier.

The whole of Venice was in those two lines. He remembered the autumn that he had passed there, and a wonderful love that had stirred him to delightful fantastic follies. There was romance in every place. But Venice, like Oxford, had kept the background for romance, and background was everything, or almost everything. Basil had been with him part of the time, and had gone wild over Tintoret. Poor Basil! what a horrible way for a man to die!

He sighed, and took up the book again, and tried to forget. He read of the swallows that fly in and out of the little café at Smyrna where the Hadjis sit counting their amber beads and the turbaned merchants smoke their long tasselled pipes and talk gravely to each other; of the Obelisk in the Place de la Concorde that weeps tears of granite in its lonely sunless exile, and longs to be back by the hot lotus-covered Nile, where there are Sphinxes, and rose-red ibises, and white vultures with gilded claws, and crocodiles, with small beryl eyes, that crawl over the green steaming mud; and of that curious statue that Gautier compares to a contralto voice, the *"monstre charmant"* that couches in the porphyry-room of the Louvre. But after a time the book fell from his hand. He grew nervous, and a horrible fit of terror came over him. What if Alan Campbell should be out of England? Days would elapse before he could come back. Perhaps he might refuse to come. What could he do then? Every moment was of vital importance.

They had been great friends once, five years before,—almost inseparable, indeed. Then the intimacy had come suddenly to an end. When they met in society now, it was only Dorian Gray who smiled: Alan Campbell never did.

He was an extremely clever young man, though he had no real appreciation of the visible arts, and whatever little sense of the beauty of poetry he possessed he had gained entirely from Dorian. His dominant intellectual passion was for science. At Cambridge he had spent a great deal of his time working in the Laboratory, and had taken a good class in the

Natural Science tripos of his year. Indeed, he was still devoted to the study of chemistry, and had a laboratory of his own, in which he used to shut himself up all day long, greatly to the annoyance of his mother, who had set her heart on his standing for Parliament and had a vague idea that a chemist was a person who made up prescriptions. He was an excellent musician, however, as well, and played both the violin and the piano better than most amateurs. In fact, it was music that had first brought him and Dorian Gray together,—music and that indefinable attraction that Dorian seemed to be able to exercise whenever he wished, and indeed exercised often without being conscious of it. They had met at Lady Berkshire's the night that Rubinstein played there, and after that used to be always seen together at the Opera, and wherever good music was going on. For eighteen months their intimacy lasted. Campbell was always either at Selby Royal or in Grosvenor Square. To him, as to many others, Dorian Gray was the type of everything that is wonderful and fascinating in life. Whether or not a quarrel had taken place between them no one ever knew. But suddenly people remarked that they scarcely spoke when they met, and that Campbell seemed always to go away early from any party at which Dorian Gray was present. He had changed, too,—was strangely melancholy at times, appeared almost to dislike hearing music of any passionate character, and would never himself play, giving as his excuse, when he was called upon, that he was so absorbed in science that he had no time left in which to practise. And this was certainly true. Every day he seemed to become more interested in biology, and his name appeared once or twice in some of the scientific reviews, in connection with certain curious experiments.

This was the man that Dorian Gray was waiting for, pacing up and down the room, glancing every moment at the clock, and becoming horribly agitated as the minutes went by. At last the door opened, and his servant entered.[5]

"Mr. Alan Campbell, sir."

A sigh of relief broke from his parched lips, and the color came back to his cheeks.

"Ask him to come in at once, Francis."

The man bowed, and retired. In a few moments, Alan Campbell walked in, looking very stern and rather pale, his pallor being intensified by his coal-black hair and dark eyebrows.

"Alan! this is kind of you. I thank you for coming."

"I had intended never to enter your house again, Gray. But you said it was a matter of life and death." His voice was hard and cold. He spoke with slow deliberation. There was a look of contempt in the steady searching gaze that he turned on Dorian. He kept his hands in the pockets of his Astrakhan coat, and appeared not to have noticed the gesture with which he had been greeted.

5. Wilde made alterations and additions here in 1891.

"It is a matter of life and death, Alan, and to more than one person. Sit down."

Campbell took a chair by the table, and Dorian sat opposite to him. The two men's eyes met. In Dorian's there was infinite pity. He knew that what he was going to do was dreadful.

After a strained moment of silence, he leaned across and said, very quietly, but watching the effect of each word upon the face of the man he had sent for,[6] "Alan, in a locked room at the top of this house, a room to which nobody but myself has access, a dead man is seated at a table. He has been dead ten hours now. Don't stir, and don't look at me like that. Who the man is, why he died, how he died, are matters that do not concern you. What you have to do is this——"

"Stop, Gray. I don't want to know anything further. Whether what you have told me is true or not true, doesn't concern me. I entirely decline to be mixed up in your life. Keep your horrible secrets to yourself. They don't interest me any more."

"Alan, they will have to interest you. This one will have to interest you. I am awfully sorry for you, Alan. But I can't help myself. You are the one man who is able to save me. I am forced to bring you into the matter. I have no option. Alan, you are a scientist. You know about chemistry, and things of that kind. You have made experiments. What you have got to do is to destroy the thing that is up-stairs,—to destroy it so that not a vestige will be left of it. Nobody saw this person come into the house. Indeed, at the present moment he is supposed to be in Paris. He will not be missed for months. When he is missed, there must be no trace of him found here. You, Alan, you must change him, and everything that belongs to him, into a handful of ashes that I may scatter in the air."

"You are mad, Dorian."

"Ah! I was waiting for you to call me Dorian."

"You are mad, I tell you,—mad to imagine that I would raise a finger to help you, mad to make this monstrous confession. I will have nothing to do with this matter, whatever it is. Do you think I am going to peril my reputation for you? What is it to me what devil's work you are up to?"

"It was a suicide, Alan."

"I am glad of that. But who drove him to it? You, I should fancy."

"Do you still refuse to do this, for me?"

"Of course I refuse. I will have absolutely nothing to do with it. I don't care what shame comes on you. You deserve it all. I should not be sorry to see you disgraced, publicly disgraced. How dare you ask me, of all men in the world, to mix myself up in this horror? I should have thought you knew more about people's characters. Your friend Lord Henry Wotton can't have taught you much about psychology, whatever

6. Wilde added "very quietly . . . sent for" in TS.

else he has taught you. Nothing will induce me to stir a step to help you. You have come to the wrong man. Go to some of your friends. Don't come to me."

"Alan, it was murder. I killed him. You don't know what he had made me suffer. Whatever my life is, he had more to do with the making or the marring of it than poor Harry has had. he may not have intended it, the result was the same."

"Murder! Good God, Dorian, is that what you have come to? I shall not inform upon you. It is not my business. Besides, you are certain to be arrested, without my stirring in the matter. Nobody ever commits a murder without doing something stupid. But I will have nothing to do with it."

"All I ask of you is to perform a certain scientific experiment. You go to hospitals and dead-houses, and the horrors that you do there don't affect you. If in some hideous dissecting-room or fetid laboratory you found this man lying on a leaden table with red gutters scooped out in it, you would simply look upon him as an admirable subject. You would not turn a hair. You would not believe that you were doing anything wrong. On the contrary, you would probably feel that you were benefiting the human race, or increasing the sum of knowledge in the world, or gratifying intellectual curiosity, or something of that kind. What I want you to do is simply what you have often done before. Indeed, to destroy a body must be less horrible than what you are accustomed to work at. And, remember, it is the only piece of evidence against me. If it is discovered, I am lost; and it is sure to be discovered unless you help me."

"I have no desire to help you. You forget that.[7] I am simply indifferent to the whole thing. It has nothing to do with me."

"Alan, I entreat you. Think of the position I am in. Just before you came I almost fainted with terror. No! don't think of that. Look at the matter purely from the scientific point of view. You don't inquire where the dead things on which you experiment come from. Don't inquire now. I have told you too much as it is. But I beg of you to do this. We were friends once, Alan."

"Don't speak about those days, Dorian: they are dead."

"The dead linger sometimes. The man up-stairs will not go away. He is sitting at the table with bowed head and outstretched arms. Alan! Alan! if you don't come to my assistance I am ruined. Why, they will hang me, Alan! Don't you understand? They will hang me for what I have done."[8]

"There is no good in prolonging this scene. I refuse absolutely to do anything in the matter. It is insane of you to ask me."

"You refuse absolutely?"

7. Wilde canceled "Had this happened three years ago, I might have consented to be your accomplice" in MS.

8. Wilde added "Why, they . . . have done" in TS.

"Yes."

The same look of pity came into Dorian's eyes, then he stretched out his hand, took a piece of paper, and wrote something on it. He read it over twice, folded it carefully, and pushed it across the table. Having done this, he got up, and went over to the window.

Campbell looked at him in surprise, and then took up the paper, and opened it. As he read it, his face became ghastly pale, and he fell back in his chair. A horrible sense of sickness came over him. He felt as if his heart was beating itself to death in some empty hollow.[9]

After two or three minutes of terrible silence, Dorian turned round, and came and stood behind him, putting his hand upon his shoulder.

"I am so sorry, Alan," he murmured, "but you leave me no alternative. I have a letter written already. Here it is. You see the address. If you don't help me, I must send it. You know what the result will be. But you are going to help me. It is impossible for you to refuse now. I tried to spare you. You will do me the justice to admit that. You were stern, harsh, offensive. You treated me as no man has ever dared to treat me,—no living man, at any rate. I bore it all. Now it is for me to dictate terms."

Campbell buried his face in his hands, and a shudder passed through him.

"Yes, it is my turn to dictate terms, Alan. You know what they are. The thing is quite simple. Come, don't work yourself into this fever. The thing has to be done. Face it, and do it."

A groan broke from Campbell's lips, and he shivered all over. The ticking of the clock on the mantel-piece seemed to him to be dividing time into separate atoms of agony, each of which was too terrible to be borne. He felt as if an iron ring was being slowly tightened round his forehead, and as if the disgrace with which he was threatened had already come upon him. The hand upon his shoulder weighed like a hand of lead. It was intolerable. It seemed to crush him.

"Come, Alan, you must decide at once."

He hesitated a moment. "Is there a fire in the room up-stairs?" he murmured.

"Yes, there is a gas-fire with asbestos."

"I will have to go home and get some things from the laboratory."

"No, Alan, you will not leave the house. Write on a sheet of note-paper what you want, and my servant will take a cab and bring the things back to you."

Campbell wrote a few lines, blotted them, and addressed an envelope to his assistant. Dorian took the note up and read it carefully. Then he rang the bell, and gave it to his valet, with orders to return as soon as possible, and to bring the things with him.

When the hall door shut, Campbell started, and, having got up from

---

9. Wilde canceled "He tried to speak, but his tongue seemed to be paralyzed" in TS.

the chair, went over to the chimney-piece.[1] He was shivering with a sort of ague. For nearly twenty minutes, neither of the men spoke. A fly buzzed noisily about the room, and the ticking of the clock was like the beat of a hammer.

As the chime struck one, Campbell turned around, and, looking at Dorian Gray, saw that his eyes were filled with tears. There was something in the purity and the refinement of that sad face that seemed to enrage him. "You are infamous, absolutely infamous!" he muttered.

"Hush, Alan: you have saved my life," said Dorian.

"*Your* life? Good heavens! what a life that is! You have gone from corruption to corruption, and now you have culminated in crime. In doing what I am going to do, what you force me to do, it is not of *your* life that I am thinking."

"Ah, Alan," murmured Dorian, with a sigh, "I wish you had a thousandth part of the pity for me that I have for you." He turned away, as he spoke, and stood looking out at the garden. Campbell made no answer.

After about ten minutes a knock came to the door, and the servant entered, carrying a mahogany chest of chemicals, with a small electric battery set on top of it. He placed it on the table, and went out again, returning with a long coil of steel and platinum wire and two rather curiously-shaped iron clamps.

"Shall I leave the things here, sir?" he asked Campbell.

"Yes," said Dorian. "And I am afraid, Francis, that I have another errand for you. What is the name of the man at Richmond who supplies Selby with orchids?"

"Harden, sir?"

"Yes,—Harden. You must go down to Richmond at once, see Harden personally, and tell him to send twice as many orchids as I ordered, and to have as few white ones as possible. In fact, I don't want any white ones. It is a lovely day, Francis, and Richmond is a very pretty place, otherwise I wouldn't bother you about it."

"No trouble, sir. At what time shall I be back?"

Dorian looked at Campbell. "How long will your experiment take, Alan?" he said, in a calm, indifferent voice. The presence of a third person in the room seemed to give him extraordinary courage.

Campbell frowned, and bit his lip. "It will take about five hours," he answered.

"It will be time enough, then, if you are back at half-past seven, Francis. Or stay: just leave my things out for dressing. You can have the evening to yourself. I am not dining at home, so I shall not want you."

"Thank you, sir," said the man, leaving the room.

"Now, Alan, there is not a moment to be lost. How heavy this chest is! I'll take it for you. You bring the other things." He spoke rapidly, and

---

1. Wilde canceled "The pain in his forehead was less than it had been but" in TS.

in an authoritative manner. Campbell felt dominated by him. They left the room together.

When they reached the top landing, Dorian took out the key and turned it in the lock. Then he stopped, and a troubled look came into his eyes. He shuddered. "I don't think I can go in, Alan," he murmured.

"It is nothing to me. I don't require you," said Campbell, coldly.

Dorian half opened the door. As he did so, he saw the face of the portrait grinning in the sunlight. On the floor in front of it the torn curtain was lying. He remembered that the night before, for the first time in his life, he had forgotten to hide it, when he crept out of the room.[2]

But what was that loathsome red dew that gleamed, wet and glistening, on one of the hands, as though the canvas had sweated blood? How horrible it was!—more horrible, it seemed to him for the moment, than the silent thing that he knew was stretched across the table, the thing whose grotesque misshapen shadow on the spotted carpet showed him that it had not stirred, but was still there, as he had left it.

He opened the door a little wider, and walked quickly in, with half-closed eyes and averted head, determined that he would not look even once upon the dead man. Then, stooping down, and taking up the gold-and-purple hanging, he flung it over the picture.

He stopped, feeling afraid to turn round, and his eyes fixed themselves on the intricacies of the pattern before him. He heard Campbell bringing in the heavy chest, and the irons, and the other things that he had required for his dreadful work. He began to wonder if he and Basil Hallward had ever met, and, if so, what they had thought of each other.

"Leave me now," said Campbell.

He turned and hurried out, just conscious that the dead man had been thrust back into the chair and was sitting up in it, with Campbell gazing into the glistening yellow face. As he was going downstairs he heard the key being turned in the lock.

It was long after seven o'clock when Campbell came back into the library. He was pale, but absolutely calm. "I have done what you asked me to do," he muttered. "And now, good-by. Let us never see each other again."

"You have saved me from ruin, Alan. I cannot forget that," said Dorian, simply.

As soon as Campbell had left, he went up-stairs. There was a horrible smell of chemicals in the room. But the thing that had been sitting at the table was gone.

---

2. Wilde made some changes here in 1891.

Chapter XIII. [1]

"There is no good telling me you are going to be good, Dorian," cried Lord Henry, dipping his white fingers into a red copper bowl filled with rose-water. "You are quite perfect. Pray don't change."

Dorian shook his head. "No, Harry, I have done too many dreadful things in my life. I am not going to do any more. I began my good actions yesterday."

"Where were you yesterday?"

"In the country, Harry. I was staying at a little inn by myself."

"My dear boy," said Lord Henry smiling, "anybody can be good in the country. There are no temptations there. That is the reason why people who live out of town are so uncivilized. There are only two ways, as you know, of becoming civilized. One is by being cultured, the other is by being corrupt. Country-people have no opportunity of being either, so they stagnate."

"Culture and corruption," murmured Dorian. "I have known something of both. It seems to me curious now that they should ever be found together. For I have a new ideal, Harry. I am going to alter. I think I have altered."

"You have not told me yet what your good action was. Or did you say you had done more than one?"

"I can tell you, Harry. It is not a story I could tell to any one else. I spared somebody. It sounds vain, but you understand what I mean. She was quite beautiful, and wonderfully like Sibyl Vane. I think it was that which first attracted me to her. you remember Sibyl, don't you? How long ago that seems! Well, Hetty [2] was not one of our own class, of course. She was simply a girl in a village. But I really loved her. I am quite sure that I loved her. All during this wonderful May that we have been having, I used to run down and see her two or three times a week. [3] Yesterday she met me in a little orchard. The apple-blossoms kept tumbling down on her hair, and she was laughing. We were to have gone away together this morning at dawn. Suddenly I [4] determined to leave her as flower-like as I had found her."

"I should think the novelty of the emotion must have given you a thrill of real pleasure, Dorian," interrupted Lord Henry. "But I can finish your idyl for you. You gave her good advice, and broke her heart. That was the beginning of your reformation."

"Harry, you are horrible! You mustn't say these dreadful things. Hetty's heart is not broken. Of course she cried, and all that. But [5] there is

---

1. Wilde added chapters 15–18 here in 1891. *Lippincott's* chapter 13 was then divided into 19 and 20 (1891).
2. Wilde reconstructed the first part of this paragraph in TS, adding "to her. . . . Well, Hetty" in TS.
3. Stoddart canceled "Finally, she promised to come with me to town. I had taken a house for

her, and arranged everything." Wilde canceled Stoddart's emendation: "She would have come away with me."
4. Stoddart canceled "said to myself, 'I won't ruin this girl. I won't bring her to shame. And I . . .' " in TS.
5. Stoddart canceled "her life is not spoiled" here in TS.

no disgrace upon her. She can live, like Perdita, in her garden."

"And weep over a faithless Florizel," said Lord Henry, laughing. "My dear Dorian, you have the most curious boyish moods. Do you think this girl will ever be really contented now with any one of her own rank? I suppose she will be married some day to a rough carter or a grinning ploughman. Well, having met you, and loved you, will teach her to despise her husband, and she will be wretched.[6] From a moral point of view I really don't think much of your great renunciation. Even as a beginning, it is poor. Besides, how do you know that Hetty isn't floating at the present moment in some mill-pond, with water-lilies round her, like Ophelia?"

"I can't bear this, Harry! You mock at everything, and then suggest the most serious tragedies. I am sorry I told you now. I don't care what you say to me, I know I was right in acting as I did. Poor Hetty! As I rode past the farm this morning, I saw her white face at the window, like a spray of jasmine. Don't let me talk about it any more, and don't try to persuade me that the first good action I have done for years, the first little bit of self-sacrifice I have ever known, is really a sort of sin. I want to be better. I am going to be better. Tell me something about yourself. What is going on in town? I have not been to the club for days."

"The people are still discussing poor Basil's disappearance."

"I should have thought they had got tired of that by this time," said Dorian, pouring himself out some wine, and frowning slightly.

"My dear boy, they have only been talking about it for six weeks, and the public are really not equal to the mental strain of having more than one topic every three months. They have been very fortunate lately, however. They have had my own divorce-case, and Alan Campbell's suicide. Now they have got the mysterious disappearance of an artist. Scotland Yard still insists that the man in the gray ulster who left Victoria by the midnight train on the 7th of November was poor Basil, and the French police declare that Basil never arrived in Paris at all. I suppose in about a fortnight we will be told that he has been seen in San Francisco. It is an odd thing, but every one who disappears is said to be seen at San Francisco. It must be a delightful city, and possess all the attractions of the next world."

"What do you think has happened to Basil?" asked Dorian, holding up his Burgundy against the light, and wondering how it was that he could discuss the matter so calmly.

"I have not the slightest idea. If Basil chooses to hide himself, it is no business of mine. If he is dead, I don't want to think about him. Death is the only thing that ever terrifies me. I hate it. One can survive every-

6. Stoddart again canceled a passage, this one a marginal addition by Wilde: "Upon the other hand, had she become your mistress, she would have lived in the society of charming and cultivated men. You would have educated her, taught her how to dress, how to talk, how to move. You would have made her perfect, and she would have been extremely happy. After a time, no doubt, you would have grown tired of her. She would have made a scene. You would have made a settlement. Then a new career would have begun for her."

thing nowadays except that. Death and vulgarity are the only two facts in the nineteenth century that one cannot explain away. Let us have our coffee in the music-room, Dorian. You must play Chopin to me. The man with whom my wife ran away played Chopin exquisitely. Poor Victoria![7] I was very fond of her. The house is rather lonely without her."

Dorian said nothing, but rose from the table, and, passing into the next room, sat down to the piano and let his fingers stray across the keys. After the coffee had been brought in, he stopped, and, looking over at Lord Henry, said, "Harry, did it ever occur to you that Basil was murdered?"

Lord Henry yawned. "Basil had no enemies, and always wore a Waterbury watch. Why should he be murdered?[8] He was not clever enough to have enemies. Of course he had a wonderful genius for painting. But a man can paint like Velasquez and yet be as dull as possible. Basil was really rather dull. He only interested me once, and that was when he told me, years ago, that he had a wild adoration for you."

"I was very fond of Basil," said Dorian, with a sad look in his eyes. "But don't people say that he was murdered?"

"Oh, some of the papers do. It does not seem to be probable. I know there are dreadful places in Paris, but Basil was not the sort of man to have gone to them. He had no curiosity. It was his chief defect.[9] Play me a nocturne, Dorian, and, as you play, tell me, in a low voice, how you have kept your youth. You must have some secret. I am only ten years older than you are, and I am wrinkled, and bald, and yellow. You are really wonderful, Dorian. You have never looked more charming than you do to-night. You remind me of the day I saw you first. You were rather cheeky, very shy, and absolutely extraordinary. You have changed, of course, but not in appearance. I wish you would tell me your secret. To get back my youth I would do anything in the world, except take exercise, get up early, or be respectable. Youth! There is nothing like it. It's absurd to talk of the ignorance of youth. The only people whose opinions I listen to now with any respect are people much younger than myself. They seem in front of me. Life has revealed to them her last wonder. As for the aged, I always contradict the aged. I do it on principle. If you ask them their opinion on something that happened yesterday, they solemnly give you the opinions current in 1820, when people wore high stocks and knew absolutely nothing. How lovely that thing you are playing is! I wonder did Chopin write it at Majorca, with the sea weeping round the villa, and the salt spray dashing against

7. Stoddart canceled the following: "She was desperately in love with you at one time, Dorian. It used to amuse me to watch her paying you compliments. You were so charmingly indifferent. Do you know I really miss her? She never bored me. She was so delightfully improbable in everything that she did." Wilde added several lines here in 1891.

8. Wilde added "and always . . . murdered?" in TS.

9. Wilde added about four new pages here in 1891, beginning "what would you say, Harry" and ending with "given up our belief in the soul" (see pp. 162–64).

the panes? It is marvelously romantic. What a blessing it is that there is one art left to us that is not imitative! Don't stop. I want music to-night. It seems to me that you are the young Apollo, and that I am Marsyas listening to you. I have sorrows, Dorian, of my own, that even you know nothing of.[1] The tragedy of old age is not that one is old, but that one is young.[2] I am amazed sometimes at my own sincerity. Ah, Dorian, how happy you are! What an exquisite life you have had![3] You have drunk deeply of everything. You have crushed the grapes against your palate. Nothing has been hidden from you. But it has all been to you no more than the sound of music. It has not marred you. You are still the same.

"I wonder what the rest of your life will be. Don't spoil it by renunciations. At present you are a perfect type. Don't make yourself incomplete. You are quite flawless now. You need not shake your head: you know you are. Besides, Dorian, don't deceive yourself. Life is not governed by will or intention. Life is a question of nerves, and fibres, and slowly-built-up cells in which thought hides itself and passion has its dreams. You may fancy yourself safe, and think yourself strong. But a chance tone of color in a room or a morning sky, a particular perfume that you had once loved and that brings strange memories with it, a line from a forgotten poem that you had come across again, a cadence from a piece of music that you had ceased to play,—I tell you, Dorian, that it is on things like these that our lives depend. Browning writes about that somewhere; but our own senses will imagine them for us. There are moments when the odor of heliotrope passes suddenly across me, and I have to live the strangest year of my life over again.[4]

"I wish I could change places with you, Dorian. The world has cried out against us both, but it has always worshipped you. It always will worship you. You are the type of what the age is searching for, and what it is afraid it has found. I am so glad that you have never done anything, never carved a statue, or painted a picture, or produced anything outside of yourself! Life has been your art. You have set yourself to music. Your days have been your sonnets."

Dorian rose up from the piano, and passed his hand through his hair. "Yes, life has been exquisite," he murmured, "but I am not going to have the same life, Harry. And you must not say these extravagant things to me. You don't know everything about me. I think that if you did, even you would turn from me. You laugh. Don't laugh."

"Why have you stopped playing, Dorian? Go back and play the nocturne over again. Look at that great honey-colored moon that hangs in the dusky air. She is waiting for you to charm her, and if you play she will come closer to the earth. You won't? Let us go to the club, then. It has been a charming evening, and we must end it charmingly. There is

---

1. Wilde canceled in MS "moments of anguish and regret" here.
2. Wilde added this epigram in TS.
3. Wilde canceled the following in TS: "I have

always been too much of a critic. I have been afraid of things wounding me, and have looked on."
4. Wilde made alterations here in 1891 (see p. 165).

some one at the club who wants immensely to know you,—young Lord
Poole, Bournemouth's eldest son. He has already copied your neckties,
and has begged me to introduce him to you. He is quite delightful, and
rather reminds me of you."

"I hope not," said Dorian, with a touch of pathos in his voice. "But I
am tired to-night, Harry. I won't go to the club. It is nearly eleven, and
I want to go to bed early."

"Do stay. You have never played so well as to-night. There was something in your touch that was wonderful. It had more expression than I
had ever heard from it before."

"It is because I am going to be good," he answered, smiling. "I am a
little changed already."

"Don't change, Dorian; at any rate, don't change to me. We must
always be friends."

"Yet you poisoned me with a book once. I should not forgive that.
Harry, promised me that you will never lend that book to any one. It
does harm."

"My dear boy, you are really beginning to moralize. You will soon be
going about warning people against all the sins of which you have grown
tired. You are much too delightful to do that. Besides, it is no use. You
and I are what we are, and will be what we will be.[5] Come round to-
morrow. I am going to ride at eleven, and we might go together. The
Park is quite lovely now. I don't think there have been such lilacs since
the year I met you."

"Very well. I will be here at eleven," said Dorian. "Good-night, Harry."
As he reached the door he hesitated for a moment, as if he had something more to say. Then he sighed and went out.[6]

It was a lovely night, so warm that he threw his coat over his arm,
and did not even put his silk scarf round his throat. As he strolled home,
smoking his cigarette, two young men in evening dress passed him. He
heard one of them whisper to the other, "That is Dorian Gray." He
remembered how pleased he used to be when he was pointed out, or
stared at, or talked about. He was tired of hearing his own name now.
Half the charm of the little village where he had been so often lately was
that no one knew who he was. He had told the girl whom he had made
love him that he was poor, and she had believed him. He had told her
once that he was wicked, and she had laughed at him, and told him that
wicked people were always very old and very ugly. What a laugh she
had!—just like a thrush singing. And how pretty she had been in her
cotton dresses and her large hats! She knew nothing, but she had everything that he had lost.

When he reached home, he found his servant waiting up for him. He
sent him to bed, and threw himself down on the sofa in the library, and
began to think over some of the things that Lord Henry had said to him.

5. A dozen lines or so were added here in 1891, nearly half of which argue against art influencing human action.
6. Chapter 19 (1891) ends here.

Was it really true that one could never change? He felt a wild longing for the unstained purity of his boyhood,—his rose-white boyhood, as Lord Henry had once called it. He knew that he had tarnished himself, filled his mind with corruption, and given horror to his fancy; that he had been an evil influence to others, and had experienced a terrible joy in being so; and that of the lives that had crossed his own it had been the fairest and the most full of promise that he had brought to shame. But was it all irretrievable? Was there no hope for him? [7]

It was better not to think of the past. Nothing could alter that. It was of himself, and of his own future, that he had to think. [8] Alan Campbell had shot himself one night in his laboratory, but had not revealed the secret that he had been forced to know. The excitement, such as it was, over Basil Hallward's disappearance would soon pass away. It was already waning. He was perfectly safe there. Nor, indeed, was it the death of Basil Hallward that weighed most upon his mind. It was the living death of his own soul that troubled him. Basil had painted the portrait that had marred his life. He could not forgive him that. It was the portrait that had done everything. Basil had said things to him that were unbearable, and that he had yet borne with patience. The murder had been simply the madness of a moment. As for Alan Campbell, his suicide had been his own act. He had chosen to do it. It was nothing to him.

A new life! That was what he wanted. That was what he was waiting for. Surely he had begun it already. He had spared one innocent thing, at any rate. He would never again tempt innocence. He would be good.

As he thought of Hetty Merton, he began to wonder if the portrait in the locked room had changed. Surely it was not still so horrible as it had been? Perhaps if his life became pure, he would be able to expel every sign of evil passion from the face. Perhaps the signs of evil had already gone away. He would go and look.

He took the lamp from the table and crept up-stairs. As he unlocked the door, a smile of joy flitted across his young face and lingered for a moment about his lips. Yes, he would be good, and the hideous thing that he had hidden away would no longer be a terror to him. He felt as if the load had been lifted from him already.

He went in quietly, locking the door behind him, as was his custom, and dragged the purple hanging from the portrait. A cry of pain and indignation broke from him. He could see no change, unless that in the eyes there was a look of cunning, and in the mouth the curved wrinkle of the hypocrite. The thing was still loathsome,—more loathsome, if possible, than before,—and the scarlet dew that spotted the hand seemed brighter, and more like blood newly spilt.

Had it been merely vanity that had made him do his one good deed? Or the desire of a new sensation, as Lord Henry had hinted, with his mocking laugh? Or that passion to act a part that sometimes makes us

---

7. Wilde added two paragraphs here in 1891.
8. Wilde added a reference to Sibyl's brother here in 1891.

do things finer than we are ourselves? Or, perhaps, all these?

Why was the red stain larger than it had been? It seemed to have crept like a horrible disease over the wrinkled fingers. There was blood on the painted feet, as though the thing had dripped,—blood even on the hand that had not held the knife.

Confess? Did it mean that he was to confess? To give himself up, and be put to death? He laughed. He felt that the idea was monstrous. Besides, who would believe him, even if he did confess? There was no trace of the murdered man anywhere. Everything belonging to him had been destroyed. He himself had burned what had been below-stairs. The world would simply say he was mad. They would shut him up if he persisted in his story.

Yet it was his duty to confess, to suffer public shame, and to make public atonement. There was a God who called upon men to tell their sins to earth as well as to heaven. Nothing that he could do would cleanse him till he had told his own sin. His sin? He shrugged his shoulders. The death of Basil Hallward seemed very little to him. He was thinking of Hetty Merton.

It was an unjust mirror, this mirror of his soul that he was looking at. Vanity? Curiosity? Hypocrisy? Had there been nothing more in his renunciation than that? There had been something more. At least he thought so. But who could tell? [9]

And this murder,—was it to dog him all his life? Was he never to get rid of the past? Was he really to confess? No. There was only one bit of evidence left against him. The picture itself,—that was evidence.

He would destroy it. Why had he kept it so long? It had given him pleasure once to watch it changing and growing old. Of late he had felt no such pleasure. It had kept him awake at night. When he had been away, he had been filled with terror lest other eyes should look upon it. It had brought melancholy across his passions. Its mere memory had marred many moments of joy. It had been like conscience to him. Yes, it had been conscience. He would destroy it.

He looked round, and saw the knife that had stabbed Basil Hallward. He had cleaned it many times, till there was no stain left upon it. It was bright, and glistened. [1] As it had killed the painter, so it would kill the painter's work, and all that that meant. It would kill the past, and when that was dead he would be free. [2] He seized it, and stabbed the canvas with it, ripping the thing right up from top to bottom. [3]

There was a cry heard, and a crash. The cry was so horrible in its agony that the frightened servants woke, and crept out of their rooms. Two gentlemen, who were passing in the Square below, stopped, and looked up at the great house. They walked on till they met a policeman,

9. Wilde added five lines here in 1891.
1. Wilde canceled in MS "He took it up and darted it into the canvas."
2. Wilde added this sentence in TS and another in 1891.
3. Wilde deleted "ripping . . . bottom," after changing "canvas" to "picture."

and brought him back. The man rang the bell several times, but there was no answer. The house was all dark, except for a light in one of the top windows. After a time, he went away, and stood in the portico of the next house and watched.

"Whose house is that, constable?" asked the elder of the two gentlemen.

"Mr. Dorian Gray's, sir," answered the policeman.

They looked at each other, as they walked away, and sneered. One of them was Sir Henry Ashton's uncle.

Inside, in the servants' part of the house, the half-clad domestics were talking in low whispers to each other. Old Mrs. Leaf was crying, and wringing her hands.[4] Francis was as pale as death.

After about a quarter of an hour, he got the coachman and one of the footmen and crept up-stairs. They knocked, but there was no reply. They called out. Everything was still. Finally, after vainly trying to force the door, they got on the roof, and dropped down on to the balcony. The windows yielded easily: the bolts were old.

When they entered, they found hanging upon the wall a splendid portrait of their master as they had last seen him, in all the wonder of his exquisite youth and beauty. Lying on the floor was a dead man in evening dress, with a knife in his heart. He was withered, wrinkled and loathsome of visage. It was not till they had examined the ring that they recognized who it was.[5]

4. Wilde changed TS from "One of the maids was crying."

5. Wilde altered the original ending in TS, which read: "When they entered, they found on the wall the portrait of a young man of extraordinary personal beauty, their master as they had last seen him. Lying on the floor was a dead body, withered, wrinkled, and loathsome of visage with a knife in its heart."

BACKGROUNDS

The Picture of Dorian Gray is in many ways a pivotal work in Oscar Wilde's life and career, summing up the major influences of his literary apprenticeship, exploring in tone and manner the themes of his social criticism, and anticipating the style and pacing of the celebrated comedies to come.

In *Dorian Gray* (as well as in *Intentions,* Wilde's collection of four essays, published in 1890), Wilde outgrew the dominant influences of his post-Oxford career of the 1870's and 1880's by absorbing them into his personality and expressing them in a style and manner distinctively his own. He had always been a great borrower and collector of literary culture, but in his prose he transformed everything he touched into new effects and moods. Gautier, Swinburne, and Pater are the eminences standing offstage behind the painting. However, other presences may also be felt: chiefly, Ruskin, a faded but still patronizing saint of art; James Abbott McNeill Whistler, the butterfly; and still more remotely, Matthew Arnold. Other shadows are cast in Dorian's nursery by the more specific influences of Huysmans's *A Rebours* and Maturin's *Melmoth the Wanderer,* together with glimmerings of reference works, treatises, and catalogs into which Wilde dipped his pen for aesthetic ornamentation.

For Wilde the art of decoration was the blending of original invention and existing art into a design that would yield new effects quite different from the elements taken separately. In exercising his instinct for collecting and reproducing effects borrowed from other writers, Wilde was more the artist than many of his contemporary and later critics gave him credit. He was not above pilferage, as the notorious cataloging of aesthetic bric-a-brac attests in chapter 11 (1891); but at its best, his borrowing could produce variations either subtle or spectacular, depending on the intended effect. His use of Pater and Gautier in *Dorian Gray* exemplifies how Wilde made of purloined, paraphrased, or directly quoted passages a mode of creativity that few writers have practiced as successfully. Wilde was an accomplished scholar, though less pedantic about it than writers of the next generation, such as Pound and Eliot. His range of interests expressed in *Dorian Gray* alone extended from classic Greek and Latin masters to contemporary English, French, and German writers; and few English writers were more influenced by the King James Bible.

If placed in historic perspective, Wilde's anthologizing instincts anticipate the practice of modern writers who sought either to create or to preserve an eclectic cultural tradition. Wilde's practice surely derives from Gautier's fiction in French, and in English from Ruskin, Arnold, Swinburne, and Pater. The effect in Wilde is different from that of, say, a T. S. Eliot or an Ezra Pound, belonging more to the decorative taste of Decadence than to the existential cultural interests of the twentieth century. However, unless he is featuring them, Wilde's inlaid borrowings are less intrusive than they are in modern eclectics. When he wished to be obvious, Wilde most often quoted from the Bible, Shakespeare, Gautier, Pater, Keats, and Swinburne; but the full tally of the writers Wilde works into *The Picture of Dorian Gray* would be a very long one.

Perhaps today's reader will be less distracted by Wilde's eclecticism than were his contemporaries, whose devotion to philistine ideas of originality is legendary. In using what Pater termed "accessory detail taken from culture" for his decorative effects, Wilde was both more restrained than Gautier and less obsessive than Huysmans. It was for Wilde, then, as for many other Aesthetes and Decadents, an article of faith that the presence, even the profusion, of cultural and literary touchstones served to stimulate or call out the artistic instincts of the reader. This view is not far in theory, at least, from either Ruskin's or Pater's views on the powers of art, but whereas they saw this power as fundamentally moral, Wilde preferred to maintain (in his critical and reflective mode) that the moral and the aesthetic motives of art were, in theory anyway, absolutely in separate spheres. The reader will be quick to point out that in *Dorian Gray*, Wilde seems to be in flagrant violation of his own doctrine. Perhaps the reader will want to agree with Pater that the success of *Dorian Gray* as a work of art lies in the tension that the author maintains between attitudes and forces at once complementary and opposing.

The following collection of backgrounds to *Dorian Gray* attempts to illustrate some specific influences, running in both directions, in the work of other writers, and in Wilde's own work.

Although the expunged details of the "yellow book" in the manuscript and typescript reveal that *A Rebours* (Against nature) was less definitively influential on the writing of *Dorian Gray* than critics had once supposed, there is no denying that its influence was both important and direct. That is why a representative chapter is included here in translation. As Wilde admitted in a letter of April 15, 1892: "The book in *Dorian Gray* is one of the many books I have never written, but it is partly suggested by Huysmans's *A Rebours*, which you will get at any French booksellers" (313). The chief parallels between *A Rebours* and *Dorian Gray* may be summarized briefly: Each develops an interest in curious and even arcane history; each emphasizes the aesthetic and even sensuous dimensions of church ritual and pageantry; each reflects a love of Renaissance demonology and the baroque temper in art and in mores; each shows devotion to the exotic, to sensation, and to decadent taste; each offers the reader extensive if not tedious inventories of jewels, perfumes, and other luxuries of art; and each hints at a spectrum of forbidden practices, especially homoeroticism. But for all these similarities, we should recall that unlike Des Esseintes, the hero of *A Rebours*, Dorian does not cultivate mere vicarious pleasures, even though he certainly does indulge in sensations artificially produced. The approaches to life of the two self-destructive protagonists are quite distinct. Each fails for different reasons in his quest to create a life that is an extension of art, and the fatal miscalculation in both cases was the willful confusion of art with life.

The selections from Walter Pater's *The Renaissance* reveal two kinds of influence. The direct borrowings, paraphrasings, and echoes of *The Renaissance* are many, but perhaps no single chapter served as a more obvious source for some of the most telling effects than "Leonardo Da Vinci," as the notes testify. Almost the entire chapter is reprinted here to give the reader the sense of the whole out of which Wilde selected some of the most famous and also most appropriate passages to express his own intentions.

The famous Conclusion of *The Renaissance* was for Wilde what Ruskin's chapter "On the Nature of Gothic" was for William Morris. It contained the outline of a philosophy of art that was quickly taken by Pater's disciples as a philosophy of life. While it may be argued that Morris understood and followed Ruskin more faithfully than Wilde interpreted Pater, the Conclusion was a document that interpreted past culture from a perspective whose assumptions and very language were conspicuously modern. It seemed in a few pages to synthesize classic tenets of hedonism, Renaissance cultural enlightenment, modern science, and liberalism. It was in its way a foreshadowing of modern existentialism, only with art at the center of life rather than ethical idealism. Pater was well enough aware of the possible seductiveness of the philosophy espoused in the Conclusion and so removed what was perhaps the book's most famous chapter from the second edition. It was reinstated by Pater in the third and subsequent editions. Wilde's application of Pater's speculations in the practical sphere is evident enough in the two fictional lives he was creating at the time: Dorian's and his own.

Those selections from Wilde's own essays offer the reader an opportunity to assess the extent to which the ideas and themes of *Dorian Gray* occupied the mind and imagination of Wilde during the years from 1889 to 1891. The portions of Wilde's essays reprinted here emphasize the cross-fertilization taking place during this period among his poems, short stories, essays, novel, and even plays. A comparison between essays and novel will reveal the ways Wilde expressed and developed his ideas in these different genres.

A brief comment should be offered here on the tradition of source study. From its first appearance in the spring of 1890, *Dorian Gray* has suggested to readers parallels to other works, ancient and contemporary, in half a dozen languages, Classical and modern. The complexity and richness of this tradition is suggested by the variety of studies, some of which are listed in the bibliography at the end of this volume. If a single judgment is to be risked on the contribution of such studies to an understanding of *Dorian Gray*, it is that surely we are dealing with something other than and probably something more than identifying possible points of origin for elements of *Dorian Gray*. It is contrary to reason to supposed that Wilde read all alleged sources or could have used them all. The tradition of source hunting has established, unintentionally to be sure, that *Dorian Gray* is one example, and an important one, of a tradition in literature that persists from Greco-Roman times to the present and includes many of the world's great mythic works of imagination. Perhaps it is from this tradition that an accounting may some day be given of the enduring power of Wilde's gothic morality tale to appeal so persistently to the modern imagination. Few literary productions of the nineteenth century have retained the power that can move contemporary readers, theater- or moviegoers, and scholars at the same time.

JORIS KARL HUYSMANS

From *Against Nature*†

*   *   *

Sinking into an armchair, he gave himself up to his thoughts.

For years now he had been an expert in the science of perfumes; he maintained that the sense of smell could procure pleasures equal to those obtained through sight or hearing, each of the senses being capable, by virtue of a natural aptitude supplemented by an erudite education, of perceiving new impressions, magnifying these tenfold, and co-ordinating them to compose the whole that constitutes a work of art. After all, he argued, it was no more abnormal to have an art that consisted of picking out odorous fluids than it was to have other arts based on a selection of sound waves or the impact of variously coloured rays on the retina of the eye; only, just as no one, without a special intuitive faculty developed by study, could distinguish a painting by a great master from a paltry daub, or a Beethoven theme from a tune by Clapisson, so no one, without a preliminary initiation, could help confusing at first a *bouquet* created by a true artist with a potpourri concocted by a manufacturer for sale in grocers' shops and cheap bazaars.

One aspect of this art of perfumery had fascinated him more than any other, and that was the degree of accuracy it was possible to reach in imitating the real thing.

Hardly ever, in fact, are perfumes produced from the flowers whose names they bear; and any artist foolish enough to take his raw materials from Nature alone would get only a hybrid result, lacking both conviction and distinction, for the very good reason that the essence obtained by distillation from the flower itself cannot possibly offer more than a very distant, very vulgar analogy with the real aroma of the living flower, rooted in the ground and spreading its effluvia through the open air.

Consequently, with the solitary exception of the inimitable jasmine, which admits of no counterfeit, no likeness, no approximation even, all the flowers in existence are represented to perfection by combinations of alcoholates and essences, extracting from the model its distinctive personality and adding that little something, that extra tang, that heady savour, that rare touch which makes a work of art.

In short, the artist in perfumery completes the original natural odour, which, so to speak, he cuts and mounts as a jeweller improves and brings out the water of a precious stone.

Little by little the arcana of this art, the most neglected of them all, had been revealed to Des Esseintes, who could now decipher its com-

†From Joris Karl Huysmans, *Against Nature* (A rebours), trans. Robert Baldick (Baltimore: Penguin, 1959) 118–29. This is the tenth chapter.

plex language that was as subtle as any human tongue, yet wonderfully concise under its apparent vagueness and ambiguity.

To do this he had first had to master the grammar, to understand the syntax of smells, to get a firm grasp on the rules that govern them, and, once he was familiar with this dialect, to compare the works of the great masters, the Atkinsons and Lubins, the Chardins and Violets, the Legrands and Piesses, to analyse the construction of their sentences, to weigh the proportion of their words, to measure the arrangement of their periods.

The next stage in his study of this idiom of essences had been to let experience come to the aid of theories that were too often incomplete and commonplace.

Classical perfumery was indeed little diversified, practically colourless, invariably cast in a mould fashioned by chemists of olden times; it was still drivelling away, still clinging to its old alembics, when the Romantic epoch dawned and, no less than the other arts, modified it, rejuvenated it, made it more malleable and more supple.

Its history followed that of the French language step by step. The Louis XIII style in perfumery, composed of the elements dear to that period—orris-powder, musk, civet, and myrtle-water, already known by the name of angel-water—was scarcely adequate to express the cavalierish graces, the rather crude colours of the time which certain sonnets by Saint-Amand have preserved for us. Later on, with the aid of myrrh and frankincense, the potent and austere scents of religion, it became almost possible to render the stately pomp of the age of Louis XIV, the pleonastic artifices of classical oratory, the ample, sustained, wordy style of Bossuet and the other masters of the pulpit. Later still, the blasé, sophisticated graces of French society under Louis XV found their interpreters more easily in frangipane and *maréchale*, which offered in a way the very synthesis of the period. And then, after the indifference and incuriosity of the First Empire, which used eau-de-Cologne and rosemary to excess, perfumery followed Victor Hugo and Gautier and went for inspiration to the lands of the sun; it composed its own Oriental verses, its own highly spiced salaams, discovered new intonations and audacious antitheses, sorted out and revived forgotten nuances which it complicated, subtilized and paired off, and in short resolutely repudiated the voluntary decrepitude to which it had been reduced by its Malesherbes, its Boileaus, its Andrieux, its Baour-Lormians, the vulgar distillers of its poems.

But the language of scents had not remained stationary since the 1830 epoch. It had continued to develop, had followed the march of the century, had advanced side-by-side with the other arts. Like them, it had adapted itself to the whims of artists and connoisseurs, joining in the cult of things Chinese and Japanese, inventing scented albums, imitating the flower-posies of Takeoka, mingling lavender and clove to produce the perfume of the Rondeletia, marrying patchouli and camphor to obtain the singular aroma of China ink, combining citron, clove, and neroli to arrive at the odour of the Japanese Hovenia.

Des Esseintes studied and analysed the spirit of these compounds and worked on an interpretation of these texts; for his own personal pleasure and satisfaction he took to playing the psychologist, to dismantling the mechanism of a work and reassembling it, to unscrewing the separate pieces forming the structure of a composite odour, and as a result of these operations his sense of smell had acquired an almost infallible flair.

Just as a wine-merchant can recognize a vintage from the taste of a single drop; just as a hop-dealer, the moment he sniffs at a sack, can fix the precise value of the contents; just as a Chinese trader can tell at once the place of origin of the teas he has to examine, can say on what estate in the Bohea hills or in what Buddhist monastery each sample was grown and when the leaves were picked, can state precisely the degree of tor-refaction involved and the effect produced on the tea by contact with plum blossom, with the Aglaia, with the Olea fragrans, indeed with any of the perfumes used to modify its flavour, to give it an unexpected piquancy, to improve its somewhat dry smell with a whiff of fresh and foreign flowers; so Des Esseintes, after one brief sniff at scent, could promptly detail the amounts of its constituents, explain the psychology of its composition, perhaps even give the name of the artist who created it and marked it with the personal stamp of his style.

It goes without saying that he possessed a collection of all the products used by perfumers; he even had some of the genuine Balsam of Mecca, a balm so rare that it can be obtained only in certain regions of Arabia Petraea and remains a monopoly of the Grand Turk.

Sitting now at his dressing-room table, he was toying with the idea of creating a new *bouquet* when he was afflicted with that sudden hesitation so familiar to writers who, after months of idleness, make ready to embark on a new work.

Like Balzac, who was haunted by an absolute compulsion to blacken reams of paper in order to get his hand in, Des Esseintes felt that he ought to get back into practice with a few elementary exercises. He thought of making some heliotrope and picked up two bottles of almond and vanilla; then he changed his mind and decided to try sweet pea instead.

The relevant formula and working method escaped his memory, so that he had to proceed by trial and error. He knew, of course, that in the fragrance of this particular flower, orange-blossom was the dominant element; and after trying various combinations he finally hit on the right tone by mixing the orange-blossom with tuberose and rose, binding the three together with a drop of vanilla.

All his uncertainty vanished; a little fever of excitement took hold of him and he felt ready to set to work again. First he made some tea with a compound of cassia and iris; then, completely sure of himself, he resolved to go ahead, to strike a reverberating chord whose majestic thunder would drown the whisper of that artful frangipane which was still steal-ing stealthily into the room.

He handled, one after the other, amber, Tonquin musk, with its over-powering smell, and patchouli, the most pungent of all vegetable per-fumes, whose flower, in its natural state, gives off an odour of mildew and mould. Do what he would, however, visions of the eighteenth cen-tury haunted him: gowns with panniers and flounces danced before his eyes; Boucher Venuses, all flesh and no bone, stuffed with pink cotton-wool, looked down at him from every wall; memories of the novel *Thém-idore*, and especially of the exquisite Rosette with her skirts hoisted up in blushing despair, pursued him. He sprang to his feet in a fury, and to rid himself of these obsessions he filled his lungs with that unadulterated essence of spikenard which is so dear to Orientals and so abhorrent to Europeans on account of its excessive valerian content. He was stunned by the violence of the shock this gave him. The filigree of the delicate scent which had been troubling him vanished as if it had been pounded with a hammer; and he took advantage of this respite to escape from past epochs and antiquated odours in order to engage, as he had been used to do in other days, in less restricted and more up-to-date operations.

At one time he had enjoyed soothing his spirit with scented harmon-ies. He would use effects similar to those employed by the poets, follow-ing as closely as possible the admirable arrangements of certain poems by Baudelaire such as *L'Irréparable* and *Le Balcon*, in which the last of the five lines in each verse echoes the first, returning like a refrain to drown the soul in infinite depths of melancholy and languor. He used to roam haphazardly through the dreams conjured up for him by these aromatic stanzas, until he was suddenly brought back to his starting point, to the motif of his meditation, by the recurrence of the initial theme, reappearing at fixed intervals in the fragrant orchestration of the poem.

At present his ambition was to wander at will across a landscape full of changes and surprises, and he began with a simple phrase that was ample and sonorous, suddenly opening up an immense vista of country-side.

With his vaporizers he injected into the room an essence composed of ambrosia, Mitcham lavender, sweet pea, and other flowers—an extract which, when it is distilled by a true artist, well merits the name it has been given of 'extract of meadow blossoms'. Then into this meadow he introduced a carefully measured amalgam of tuberose, orange, and almond blossom; and immediately artificial lilacs came into being, while linden-trees swayed in the wind, shedding on the ground about them their pale emanations, counterfeited by the London extract of tilia.

Once he had roughed out this background in its main outlines, so that it stretched away into the distance behind his closed eyelids, he sprayed the room with a light rain of essences that were half-human, half-feline, smacking of the petticoat, indicating the presence of woman in her paint and powder—stephanotis, ayapana, opopanax, chypre, champaka, and schoenanthus—on which he superimposed a dash of syringa, to give the factitious, cosmetic, indoor life they evoked the natural appearance of laughing, sweating, rollicking pleasures out in the sun.

Next he let these fragrant odours, escape through a ventilator, keeping only the country scent, which he renewed, increasing the dose so as to force it to return like a ritornel at the end of each stanza.

The women he had conjured up had gradually disappeared, and the countryside was once more uninhabited. Then, as if by magic, the horizon was filled with factories, whose fearsome chimneys belched fire and flame like so many bowls of punch.

A breath of industry, a whiff of chemical products now floated on the breeze he raised by fanning the air, though Nature still poured her sweet effluvia into this foul-smelling atmosphere.

Des Esseintes was rubbing a pellet of styrax between his fingers, warming it so that it filled the room with a most peculiar smell, an odour at once repugnant and delightful, blending the delicious scent of the jonquil with the filthy stench of gutta-percha and coal tar. He disinfected his hands, shut away his resin in a hermetically-sealed box, and the factories disappeared in their turn.

Now, in the midst of the revivified effluvia of linden-trees and meadow flowers, he sprinkled a few drops of the perfume 'New-mown Hay', and on the magic spot momentarily stripped of its lilacs there rose piles of hay, bringing a new season with them, spreading summer about them in these delicate emanations.

Finally, when he had sufficiently savoured this spectacle, he frantically scattered exotic perfumes around him, emptied his vaporizers, quickened all his concentrated essences and gave free rein to all his balms, with the result that the suffocating room was suddenly filled with an insanely sublimated vegetation, emitting powerful exhalations, impregnating an artificial breeze with raging alcoholates—an unnatural yet charming vegetation, paradoxically uniting tropical spices such as the pungent odours of Chinese sandalwood and Jamaican hediosmia with French scents such as jasmine, hawthorn, and vervain; defying climate and season to put forth trees of different smells and flowers of the most divergent colours and fragrances; creating out of the union or collision of all these tones one common perfume, unnamed, unexpected, unusual, in which there reappeared, like a persistent refrain, the decorative phrase he had started with, the smell of the great meadow and the swaying lilacs and linden-trees.

All of a sudden he felt a sharp stab of pain, as if a drill were boring into his temples. He opened his eyes, to find himself back in the middle of his dressing-room, sitting at his table; he got up and, still in a daze, stumbled across to the window, which he pushed ajar. A gust of air blew in and freshened up the stifling atmosphere that enveloped him. He walked up and down to steady his legs, and as he went to and fro he looked up at the ceiling, on which crabs and salt-encrusted seaweed stood out in relief against a grained background as yellow as the sand on a beach. A similar design adorned the plinths bordering the wall panels, which in their turn were covered with Japanese crape, a water green in colour and slightly crumpled to imitate the surface of a river rippling in the wind, while down the gentle current floated a rose petal round which there twisted and turned a swarm of little fishes sketched in with a couple of strokes of the pen.

But his eyes were still heavy, and so he stopped pacing the short distance between font and bath and leaned his elbows on the window-sill. Soon his head cleared, and after carefully putting the stoppers back in all his scent-bottles, he took the opportunity to tidy up his cosmetic preparations. He had not touched these things since his arrival at Fontenay, and he was almost surprised to see once again this collection to which so many women had had recourse. Phials and jars were piled on top of each other in utter confusion. Here was a box of green porcelain containing schnouda, that marvellous white cream which, once it is spread on the cheeks, changes under the influence of the air to a delicate pink, then to a flesh colour so natural that it produces an entirely convincing illusion of a flushed complexion; there, lacquered jars inlaid with mother-of-pearl held Japanese gold and Athens green the colour of a blister-fly's wing, golds and greens that turn dark crimson as soon as they are moistened. And beside pots of filbert paste, of harem serkis, of Kashmir-lily emulsions, of strawberry and elder-berry lotions for the skin, next to little bottles full of China-ink and rose-water solutions for the eyes, lay an assortment of instruments fashioned out of ivory and mother-of-pearl, silver and steel, mixed up with lucern brushes for the gums—pincers, scissors, strigils, stumps, hair-pads, powder-puffs, back-scratchers, beauty-spots, and files.

He poked around among all this apparatus, bought long ago to please a mistress of his who used to go into raptures over certain aromatics and certain balms—an unbalanced, neurotic woman who loved to have her nipples macerated in scent, but who only really experienced complete and utter ecstasy when her scalp was scraped with a comb or when a lover's caresses were mingled with the smell of soot, of wet plaster from houses being built in rainy weather, or of dust thrown up by heavy raindrops in a summer thunderstorm.

As he mused over these recollections, one memory in particular haunted him, stirring up a forgotten world of old thoughts and ancient perfumes—the memory of an afternoon he had spent with this woman at Pantin, partly for want of anything better to do and partly out of curiosity, at the house of one of her sisters. While the two women were chattering away and showing each other their frocks, he had gone to the

window and, through the dusty panes, had seen the muddy street stretching
into the distance and heard it echo with the incessant beat of galoshes
tramping through the puddles.

This scene, though it belonged to a remote past, suddenly presented
itself to him in astonishing detail. Pantin was there before him, bustling
and alive in the dead green water of the moon-rimmed mirror into which
his unthinking gaze was directed. An hallucination carried him away far
from Fontenay; the looking-glass conjured up for him not only the Pantin street but also the thoughts that street had once evoked; and lost in a
dream, he said over to himself the ingenious, melancholy, yet consoling
anthem he had composed that day on getting back to Paris:

'Yes, the season of the great rains is upon us; hearken to the song of
the gutter-pipes retching under the pavements; behold the horse-dung
floating in the bowls of coffee hollowed out of the macadam; everywhere
the foot-baths of the poor are overflowing.

'Under the lowering sky, in the humid atmosphere, the houses ooze
black sweat and their ventilators breathe foul odours; the horror of life
becomes more apparent and the grip of spleen more oppressive; the seeds
of iniquity that lie in every man's heart begin to germinate; a craving for
filthy pleasures takes hold of the puritanical, and the minds of respected
citizens are visited by criminal desires.

'And yet, here I am, warming myself in front of a blazing fire, while
a basket of full-blown flowers on the table fills the room with the scent
of benzoin, geranium, and vetiver. In mid-November it is still spring-
time at Pantin in the Rue de Paris, and I can enjoy a quiet laugh at the
expense of those timorous families who, in order to avoid the approach
of winter, scuttle away at full speed to Antibes or to Cannes.

'Inclement Nature has nothing to do with this extraordinary phenomenon; let it be said at once that it is to industry, and industry alone, that
Pantin owes this factitious spring.

'The truth is that these flowers are made of taffeta and mounted on
binding wire, while this vernal fragrance has come filtering in through
cracks in the window-frame from the neighbouring factories where the
Pinaud and St. James perfumes are made.

'For the artisan worn out by the hard labour of the workshops, for the
little clerk blessed with too many offspring, the illusion of enjoying a
little fresh air is a practical possibility—thanks to these manufacturers.

'Indeed, out of this fabulous counterfeit of the countryside a sensible
form of medical treatment could be developed. At present, gay dogs
suffering from consumption who are carted away to the south generally
die down there, finished off by the change in their habits, by their nostalgic longing for the Parisian pleasures that have laid them low. Here,
in an artificial climate maintained by open stoves, their lecherous memories would come back to them in a mild and harmless form, as they
breathed in the languid feminine emanations given off by the scent factories. By means of this innocent deception, the physician could supply

his patient platonically with the atmosphere of the boudoirs and brothels of Paris, in place of the deadly boredom of provincial life. More often than not, all that would be needed to complete the cure would be for the sick man to show a little imagination.

'Seeing that nowadays there is nothing wholesome left in this world of ours; seeing that the wine we drink and the freedom we enjoy are equally adulterate and derisory; and finally, seeing that it takes a considerable degree of goodwill to believe that the governing classes are worthy of respect and that the lower classes are worthy of help or pity, it seems to me,' concluded Des Esseintes, 'no more absurd or insane to ask of my fellow men a sum total of illusion barely equivalent to that which they expend every day on idiotic objects, to persuade themselves that the town of Pantin is an artificial Nice, a factitious Menton.'

'All that,' he muttered, interrupted in his reflections by a sudden feeling of faintness, 'doesn't alter the fact that I shall have to beware of these delicious, atrocious experiments, which are just wearing me out.'

He heaved a sigh.

'Ah, well, that means more pleasures to cut down on, more precautions to take!'—and he shut himself up in his study, hoping that there he would find it easier to escape from the obsessive influence of all these perfumes.

He threw the window wide open, delighted to take a bath of fresh air; but suddenly it struck him that the breeze was bringing with it a whiff of bergamot oil, mingled with a smell of jasmine, cassia, and rose-water. He gave a gasp of horror, and began to wonder whether he might not be in the grip of one of those evil spirits they used to exorcize in the Middle Ages. Meanwhile the odour, though just as persistent, underwent a change. A vague scent of tincture of Tolu, Peruvian balsam, and saffron, blended with a few drops of musk and amber, now floated up from the sleeping village at the foot of the hill; then all at once the metamorphosis took place, these scattered whiffs of perfume came together, and the familiar scent of frangipane, the elements of which his sense of smell had detected and recognized, spread from the valley of Fontenay all the way to the Fort, assailing his jaded nostrils, shaking anew his shattered nerves, and throwing him into such a state of prostration that he fell fainting, almost dying, across the window-sill.

WALTER PATER

From "Leonardo Da Vinci" †

*   *   *

* * * But it is still by a certain mystery in his work, and something enigmatical beyond the usual measure of great men, that he fascinates, or perhaps half repels. His life is one of sudden revolts, with intervals in which he works not at all, or apart from the main scope of his work. By a strange fortune the works on which his more popular fame rested disappeared early from the world, as the *Battle of the Standard*; or are mixed obscurely with the work of meaner hands, as the *Last Supper*. His type of beauty is so exotic that it fascinates a larger number than it delights, and seems more than that of any other artist to reflect ideas and views and some scheme of the world within; so that he seemed to his contemporaries to be the possessor of some unsanctified and secret wisdom; as, to Michelet and others, to have anticipated modern ideas. He trifles with his genius, and crowds all his chief work into a few tormented years of later life; yet he is so possessed by his genius that he passes unmoved through the most tragic events, overwhelming his country and friends, like one who comes across them by change on some secret errand.

His *legend*, as the French say, with the anecdotes which everyone knows, is one of the most brilliant in Vasari. Later writers merely copied it, until, in 1804, Carlo Amoretti applied to it a criticism which left hardly a date fixed, and not one of those anecdotes untouched. The various questions thus raised have since that time become, one after another, subjects of special study, and mere antiquarianism has in this direction little more to do. For others remain the editing of the thirteen books of his manuscripts, and the separation by technical criticism of what in his reputed works is really his, from what is only half his, or the work of his pupils. But a lover of strange souls may still analyze for himself the impression made on him by those works, and try to reach through it a definition of the chief elements of Leonardo's genius. The *legend*, corrected and enlarged by its critics, may now and then intervene to support the results of this analysis.

His life has three divisions—thirty years at Florence, nearly twenty years at Milan, then nineteen years of wandering, till he sinks to rest under the protection of Francis the First at the Château de Cloux. The dishonor of illegitimacy hangs over his birth. Piero Antonio, his father, was of a noble Florentine house, of Vinci in the Val d'Arno, and Leonardo, brought up delicately among the true children of that house, was

† Of the ten chapters in the 1888 edition of Pater's *The Renaissance: Studies in Art and Poetry*, this is the sixth, a chapter famous for its description of Leonardo's "Mona Lisa." It is followed here by the Conclusion.

the love child of his youth, with the keen, puissant nature such children often have. We see him in his youth fascinating all men by his beauty, improvising music and songs, buying the caged birds and setting them free, as he walked the streets of Florence, fond of odd bright dresses and spirited horses.

From his earliest years he designed many objects, and constructed models in relief, of which Vasari mentions some of women smiling. His father, pondering over this promise in the child, took him to the workshop of Andrea del Verrocchio, then the most famous artist in Florence. Beautiful objects lay about there—reliquaries, pyxes, silver images for the pope's chapel at Rome, strange fancywork of the Middle Ages, keeping odd company with fragments of antiquity, then but lately discovered. Another student Leonardo may have seen there—a boy into whose soul the level light and aerial illusions of Italian sunsets had passed, in after days famous as Perugino, Verrocchio was an artist of the earlier Florentine type, carver, painter, and worker in metals, in one; designer, not of pictures only, but of all things for sacred or household use, drinking vessels, ambries, instruments of music, making them all fair to look upon, filling the common ways of life with the reflection of some faroff brightness; and years of patience had refined his hand till his work was now sought after from distant places.

It happened that Verrocchio was employed by the brethren of Vallombrosa to paint the Baptism of Christ, and Leonardo was allowed to finish the angel in the left-hand corner. It was one of those moments in which the progress of a great thing—here, that of the art of Italy—presses hard and sharp on the happiness of an individual, through whose discouragement and decrease, humanity, in more fortunate persons, comes a step nearer to its final success.

For beneath the cheerful exterior of the mere well-paid craftsman, chasing brooches for the copes of Santa Maria Novella, or twisting metal screens for the tombs of the Medici, lay the ambitious desire of expanding the destiny of Italian art by a larger knowledge and insight into things, a purpose in art not unlike Leonardo's still unconscious purpose; and often, in the modeling of drapery, or of a lifted arm, or of hair cast back from the face there came to him something of the freer manner and richer humanity of a later age. But in this *Baptism* the pupil had surpassed the master; and Verrocchio turned away as one stunned, and as if his sweet earlier work must thereafter be distasteful to him, from the bright animated angel of Leonardo's hand.

The angel may still be seen in Florence, a space of sunlight in the cold, labored old picture; but the legend is true only in sentiment, for painting had always been the art by which Verrocchio set least store. And as in a sense he anticipates Leonardo, so to the last Leonardo recalls the studio of Verrocchio, in the love of beautiful toys, such as the vessel of water for a mirror, and lovely needlework about the implicated hands in the *Modesty and Vanity*, and of reliefs, like those cameos which in the *Virgin of the Balances* hang all round the girdle of Saint Michael, and of bright variegated stones, such as the agates in the *Saint Anne*, and in a hieratic preciseness and grace, as of a sanctuary swept and garnished. Amid all the cunning and intricacy of his Lombard manner this never left him. Much of it there must have been in that lost picture of *Paradise*, which he prepared as a cartoon for tapestry, to be woven in the looms of Flanders. It was the perfection of the older Florentine style of miniature painting, with patient putting of each leaf upon the trees and each flower in the grass, where the first man and woman were standing.

And because it was the perfection of that style, it awoke in Leonardo some seed of discontent which lay in the secret places of his nature. For the way to perfection is through a series of disgusts; and this picture—all that he had done so far in his life at Florence—was after all in the old slight manner. His art, if it was to be something in the world, must be weighted with more of the meaning of nature and purpose of humanity. Nature was "the true mistress of higher intelligences." So he plunged into the study of nature. And in doing this he followed the manner of the older students; he brooded over the hidden virtues of plants and crystals, the lines traced by the stars as they moved in the sky, over the correspondences which exist between the different orders of living things, through which, to eyes opened, they interpret each other; and for years he seemed to those about him as one listening to a voice, silent for other men.

He learned here the art of going deep, of tracking the sources of expression to their subtlest retreats, the power of an intimate presence in the things he handled. He did not at once or entirely desert his art; only he was no longer the cheerful, objective painter, through whose soul, as through clear glass, the bright figures of Florentine life, only made a little mellower and more pensive by the transit, passed onto the white wall. He wasted many days in curious tricks of design, seeming to lose himself in the spinning of intricate devices of lines and colors. He was smitten with a love of the impossible—the perforation of mountains, changing the course of rivers, raising great buildings, such as the church of San Giovanni, in the air; all those feats for the performance of which natural magic professes to have the key. Later writers, indeed, see in these efforts an anticipation of modern mechanics; in him they were rather dreams, thrown off by the overwrought and laboring brain. Two ideas were especially fixed in him, as reflexes of things that had touched his brain in childhood beyond the measure of other impressions—the smiling of women and the motion of great waters.

And in such studies some interfusion of the extremes of beauty and terror shaped itself, as an image that might be seen and touched, in the mind of this gracious youth, so fixed that for the rest of his life it never left him; and as catching glimpses of it in the strange eyes or hair of chance people, he would follow such about the streets of Florence till the sun went down, of whom many sketches of his remain. Some of these are full of a curious beauty, that remote beauty apprehended only by those who have sought it carefully; who, starting with acknowledged types of beauty, have refined as far upon these, as these refine upon the world of common forms. But mingled inextricably with this there is an element of mockery also; so that, whether in sorrow of scorn, he caricatures Dante even. Legions of grotesques sweep under his hand; for has not nature too her grotesques—the rent rock, the distorting light of evening on lonely roads, the unveiled structure of man in the embryo, or the skeleton?

All these swarming fancies unite in the *Medusa* of the Uffizi. Vasari's story of an earlier Medusa, painted on a wooden shield, is perhaps an invention; and yet, properly told, has more of the air of truth about it than anything else in the whole legend. For its real subject is not the serious work of a man, but the experiment of a child. The lizards and glowworms and other strange small creatures which haunt an Italian vineyard bring before one the whole picture of a child's life in a Tuscan dwelling, half castle, half farm; and are as a true to nature as the pretended astonishment of the father for whom the boy has prepared a surprise. It was not in play that he painted that other Medusa, the one great picture which he left behind him in Florence. The subject has been treated in various ways; Leonardo alone cuts to its center; he alone realizes it as the head of a corpse, exercising its power through all the circumstances of death. What may be called the fascination of corruption penetrates in every touch its exquisitely finished beauty. About the dainty lines of the cheek the bat flits unheeded. The delicate snakes seem literally strangling each other in terrified struggle to escape from the Medusa brain. The hue which violent death always brings with it is in the features: features singularly massive and grand, as we catch them inverted, in a dexterous foreshortening, sloping upward, almost sliding down upon us, crown foremost, like a great calm stone against which the wave of serpents breaks. But it is a subject that may well be left to the beautiful verses of Shelley.

The science of that age was all divination, clairvoyance, unsubjected to our exact modern formulas, seeking in an instant of vision to concentrate a thousand experiences. Later writers, thinking only of the well-ordered treatise on painting which a Frenchman, Raffaelle du Fresne, a hundred years afterwards, compiled from Leonardo's bewildered manuscripts, written strangely, as his manner was, from right to left, have imagined a rigid order in his inquiries. But this rigid order was little in accordance with the restlessness of his character; and if we think of him as the mere reasoner who subjects design to anatomy, and composition to mathematical rules, we shall hardly have of him that impression which those about him received from him. Poring over his crucibles, making experiments with color, trying by a strange variation of the alchemist's dream to discover the secret, not of an elixir to make man's natural life immortal, but rather of giving immortality to the subtlest and most delicate effects of painting, he seemed to them rather the sorcerer or the magician, possessed of curious secrets and a hidden knowledge, living in a world of which he alone possessed the key. What his philosophy seems to have been most like is that of Paracelsus or Cardan; and much the spirit of the older alchemy still hangs about it, with its confidence in short cuts and odd byways to knowledge. To him philosophy was to be something giving strange swiftness and double sight, divining the sources of springs beneath the earth or of expression beneath the human countenance, clairvoyant of occult gifts in common or uncommon things, in the reed at the brookside, or the star which draws near to us but once in a century. How, in this way, the clear purpose was overclouded, the fine chaser's hand perplexed, we but dimly see; the mystery which at no point quite lifts from Leonardo's life is deepest here. But it is certain that at one period of his life he had almost ceased to be an artist.

The year 1483—the year of the birth of Raphael and the thirty-first of Leonardo's life—is fixed as the date of his visit to Milan by the letter in which he recommends himself to Lodovico Sforza, and offers to tell him, for a price, strange secrets in the air of war. It was that Sforza who murdered his young nephew by slow poison, yet was so susceptible of religious impressions that he blended mere earthly passions with a sort of religious sentimentalism, and who took for his device the mulberry tree—symbol, in its long delay and sudden yielding of flowers and fruit together, of a wisdom which economizes all forces for an opportunity of sudden and sure effect. The fame of Leonardo had gone before him, and he was to model a colossal statue of Francesco, the first duke of Milan. As for Leonardo himself, he came not as an artist at all, or careful of the fame of one; but as a player on the harp, a strange harp of silver of his own construction, shaped in some curious likeness to a horse's skull. The capricious spirit of Lodovico was susceptible also of the charm of music, and Leonardo's nature had a kind of spell in it. Fascination is always the word descriptive of him. No portrait of his youth remains; but all tends to make us believe that up to this time some charms of voice and aspect, strong enough to balance the disadvantage of his birth, had played about him. His physical strength was great; it was said that he could bend a horseshoe like a coil of lead.

The Duomo, the work of artists from beyond the Alps, so fantastic to the eye of a Florentine, used to the mellow, unbroken surfaces of Giotto and Arnolfo, was then in all its freshness; and below, in the streets of Milan, moved a people as fantastic, changeful, and dreamlike. To Leonardo least of all men could there be anything poisonous in the exotic flowers of sentiment which grew there. It was a life of brilliant sins and exquisite amusements—Leonardo became a celebrated designer of pageants—and it suited the quality of his genius, composed in almost equal parts of curiosity and the desire of beauty, to take things as they came.

Curiosity and the desire of beauty—these are the two elementary forces in Leonardo's genius; curiosity often in conflict with the desire of beauty, but generating, in union with it, a type of subtle and curious grace.

The movement of the fifteenth century was twofold; partly the Renaissance, partly also the coming of what is called the "modern spirit," with its realism, its appeal to experience, it comprehended a return to antiquity, and a return to nature. Raphael represents the return to antiquity, and Leonardo the return to nature. In this return to nature, he was seeking to satisfy a boundless curiosity by her perpetual surprises, a microscopic sense of finish by her finesse, or delicacy of operation, that *subtilitas naturae* which Bacon notices. So we find him often in intimate relations with men of science, with Fra Luca Paccioli the mathematician, and the anatomist Marc Antonio della Torre. His observations and experiments fill thirteen volumes of manuscript; and those who can judge describe him as anticipating long before, by rapid intuition, the later ideas of science. He explained the obscure light of the unilluminated part of the moon, knew that the sea had once covered the mountains which contain shells, and the gathering of the equatorial waters above the polar.

He who thus penetrated into the most secret parts of nature preferred always the more to the less remote, what, seeming exceptional, was an instance of law more refined, the construction about things of a peculiar atmosphere and mixed lights. He paints flowers with such curious felicity that different writers have attributed to him a fondness for particular flowers, as Clement the cyclamen, and Rio the jasmine; while, at Venice, there is a stray leaf from his portfolio dotted all over with studies of violets and the wild rose. In him first, appears the taste for what is bizarre or *recherché* in landscape; hollow places full of the green shadow of bituminous rocks, ridged reefs of trap-rock which cut the water into quaint sheets of light—their exact antitype is in our own western seas; all the solemn effects of moving water; you may follow it springing from its distant source among the rocks on the heath of the *Madonna of the Balances*, passing as a little fall into the treacherous calm of the *Madonna of the Lake*, next, as a goodly river, below the cliffs of the *Madonna of the Rocks*, washing the white walls of its distant villages, stealing out in a network of divided streams in *La Gioconda* to the seashore of the *Saint Anne*—that delicate place, where the wind passes like the hand of some fine etcher over the surface, and the untorn shells are lying thick upon the sand, and the tops of the rocks, to which the waves never rise, are green with grass, grown as fine as hair. It is the landscape, not of dreams or of fancy, but of places far withdrawn, and hours selected from a thousand with a miracle of finesse. Through Leonardo's strange veil of sight things reach him so; in no ordinary night or day, but as in faint light of eclipse, or in some brief interval of falling rain at daybreak, or through deep water.

And not into nature only; but he plunged also into human personality, and became above all a painter of portraits; faces of a modeling more skillful than has been seen before or since, embodied with a reality which almost amounts to illusion, on dark air. To take a character as it was, and delicately sound its stops, suited one so curious in observation, curious in invention. So he painted the portraits of Lodovico's mistresses, Lucretia Crivelli and Cecilia Galerani the poetess, of Lodovico himself, and the Duchess Beatrice. The portrait of Cecilia Galerani is lost, but that of Lucretia Crivelli has been identified with *La Belle Feronière* of the Louvre, and Lodovico's pale, anxious face still remains in the Ambrosian Library. Opposite is the portrait of Beatrice d'Este, in whom Leonardo seems to have caught some presentiment of early death, painting her precise and grave, full of the refinement of the dead, in sad earth-colored raiment, set with pale stones.

Sometimes this curiosity came in conflict with the desire of beauty; it tended to make him go too far below that outside of things in which art begins and ends. This struggle between the reason and its ideas, and the senses, the desire of beauty, is the key to Leonardo's life at Milan—his restlessness, his endless retouchings, his odd experiments with color. How much must he leave unfinished, how much recommence! His problem was the transmutation of ideas into images. What he had attained so far had been the mastery of that earlier Florentine style, with its naive and limited sensuousness. Now he was to entertain in this narrow medium those divinations of a humanity too wide for it, that larger vision of the opening world, which is only not too much for the great, irregular art of Shakespeare; and everywhere the effort is visible in the work of his hands. This agitation, this perpetual delay, give him an air of weariness and ennui. To others he seems to be aiming at an impossible effect, to do something that art, that painting, can never do. Often the expression of physical beauty at this or that point seems strained and marred in the effort, as in those heavy German foreheads—too heavy and German for perfect beauty.

For there was a touch of Germany in that genius which, as Goethe said, had *müde sich gedacht* ("thought itself weary"). What an anticipation of modern Germany, for instance, in that debate on the question whether sculpture or painting is the nobler art.[1] But there is this difference between him and the German, that, with all that curious science, the German would have thought nothing more was needed; and the name of Goethe himself reminds one how great for the artist may be the danger of overmuch science; how Goethe, who, in the *Elective Affinities* and the first part of *Faust*, does transmute ideas into images, who wrought many such transmutations, did not invariably find the spell-word, and in the second part of *Faust* presents us with a mass of science which has almost no artistic characters at all. But Leonardo will never work till the

1. How princely, how characteristic of Leonardo, the answer: *Quanto più, un' arte porta seco fatica di corpo, tanto più è vilel* [To the degree an art bears the strain of the body, the lower it is—*Editor*].

happy moment comes—that moment of *bien-être*, which to imaginative men is a moment of invention. On this moment he waits; other moments are but a preparation, or aftertaste of it. Few men distinguish between them as jealously as he did. Hence, so many flaws even in the choicest work. But for Leonardo the distinction is absolute, and in the moment of *bien-être*, the alchemy complete; the idea is stricken into color and imagery; a cloudy mysticism is refined to a subdued and graceful mystery, and painting pleases the eye while it satisfies the soul.

This curious beauty is seen above all in his drawings, and in these chiefly in the abstract grace of the bounding lines. Let us take some of these drawings, and pause over them awhile; and, first, one of those at Florence—the heads of a woman and a little child, set side by side, but each in its own separate frame. First of all, there is much pathos in the reappearance in the fuller curves of the face of the child, of the sharper, more chastened lines of the worn and older face, which leaves no doubt that the heads are those of a little child and its mother. A feeling for maternity is indeed always characteristic of Leonardo; and this feeling is further indicated here by the half-humorous pathos of the diminutive, rounded shoulders of the child. You may note a like pathetic power in drawings of a young man, seated in a stooping posture, his face in his hands, as in sorrow; of a slave sitting in an uneasy inclined posture, in some brief interval of rest; of a small Madonna and Child, peeping sideways in half-reassured terror, as a mighty griffin with batlike wings, one of Leonardo's finest *inventions*, descends suddenly from the air to snatch up a lion wandering near them. But note in these, as that which especially belongs to art, the contour of the young man's hair, the poise of the slave's arm above his head, and the curves of the head of the child, following the little skull within, thin and fine as some seashell worn by the wind.

Take again another head, still more full of sentiment, but of a different kind, a little drawing in red chalk which everyone remembers who has examined at all carefully the drawings by old masters at the Louvre. It is a face of doubtful sex, set in the shadow of its own hair, the cheek-line in high light against it, with something voluptuous and full in the eyelids and the lips. Another drawing might pass for the same face in childhood, with parched and feverish lips, but with much sweetness in the loose, short-waisted childish dress, with necklace and *bulla*, and in the daintily bound hair. We might take the threat of suggestion which these two drawings offer, when thus set side by side, following it through the drawings at Florence, Venice, and Milan, construct a sort of series, illustrating better than anything else Leonardo's type of womanly beauty. Daughters of Herodias, with their fantastic headdresses knotted and folded so strangely, to leave the dainty oval of the face disengaged, they are not of the Christian family, or of Raphael's. They are the clairvoyants, through whom, as through delicate instruments, one becomes aware of the subtler forces of nature, and the modes of their action, all that is magnetic

in it, all those finer conditions wherein material things rise to that subtlety of operation which constitutes them spiritual, where only the finer
nerve and the keener touch can follow; it is as if in certain revealing
instances we actually saw them at their work on human flesh. Nervous,
electric, faint always with some inexplicable faintness, they seem to be
subject to exceptional conditions, to feel powers at work in the common
air unfelt by others, to become, as it were, receptables of them, and pass
them on to us in a chain of secret influences.

But among the more youthful heads there is one at Florence, which
Love chooses for its own—the head of a young man, which may well be
the likeness of Andrea Salaino, beloved of Leonardo for his curled and
waving hair—*belli capelli ricci e inanellati*—and afterward his favorite
pupil and servant. Of all the interests in living men and women which
may have filled his life at Milan, this attachment alone is recorded; and
in return, Salaino identified himself so entirely with Leonardo, that the
picture of *Saint Anne*, in the Louvre, has been attributed to him. It
illustrates Leonardo's usual choice of pupils, men of some natural charm
of person or intercourse like Salaino, or men of birth, and princely habits of life like Francesco Melzi—men with just enough genius to be
capable of initiation into his secret, for the sake of which they were ready
to efface their own individuality. Among them, retiring often to the villa
of the Melzi at Canonica al Vaprio, he worked at his fugitive manuscripts and sketches, working for the present hour, and for a few only,
perhaps chiefly for himself. Other artists have been as careless of present
or future applause, in self-forgetfulness, or because they set moral or
political ends above the ends of the art; but in him this solitary culture
of beauty seems to have hung upon a kind of self-love, and a carelessness
in the work of art of all but art itself. Out of the secret places of a unique
temperament he brought strange blossoms and fruits hitherto unknown;
and for him, the novel impression conveyed, the exquisite effect woven,
counted as an end in itself—a perfect end.

And these pupils of his acquired his manner so thoroughly, that though
the number of Leonardo's authentic works is very small indeed, there is
a multitude of other men's pictures, through which we undoubtedly see
him, and come very near to his genius. Sometimes, as in the little picture of the *Madonna of the Balances*, in which, from the bosom of his
mother, Christ is weighing the pebbles of the brook against the sins of
men, we have a hand, rough enough by contrast, working upon some
fine hint or sketch of his. Sometimes, as in the subjects of the *Daughter
of Herodias* and the *Head of John the Baptist*, the lost originals have
been re-echoed and varied upon again and again by Luini and others.
At other times the original remains, but has been a mere theme or motive,
a type of which the accessories might be modified or changed; and these
variations have but brought out the more the purpose, or expression of
the original. It is so with the so-called *Saint John the Baptist* of the
Louvre—one of the few naked figures Leonardo painted—whose deli-

cate brown flesh and woman's hair no one would go out into the wilderness to seek, and whose treacherous smile would have us understand something far beyond the outward gesture, or circumstance. But the long, reedlike cross in the hand, which suggests Saint John the Baptist, becomes faint in a copy of the Ambrosian Library, and disappears altogether in another, in the Palazzo Rosso at Genoa. Returning from the last to the original, we are no longer surprised by Saint John's strange likeness to the *Bacchus* which hangs near it, which set Théophile Gautier thinking of Heine's notion of decayed gods, who, to maintain themselves, after the fall of paganism, took employment in the new religion. We recognize one of those symbolical inventions in which the ostensible subject is used, not as matter for definite pictorial realization, but as the starting point of a train of sentiment, as subtle and vague as a piece of music. No one ever ruled over his subject more entirely than Leonardo, or bent it more dexterously to purely artistic ends. And so it comes to pass that though he handles sacred subjects continually, he is the most profane of painters; the given person or subject, Saint John in the Desert, or the Virgin on the knees of Saint Anne, is often merely the pretext for a kind of work which carries one quite out of the range of its conventional associations.

About the *Last Supper*, its decay and restorations, a whole literature has risen up, Goethe's pensive sketch of its sad fortunes being far the best. The death in childbirth of the Duchess Beatrice was followed in Lodovico by one of those paroxysms of religious feeling which in him were constitutional. The low, gloomy Dominican church of Saint Mary of the Graces had been the favorite shrine of Beatrice. She had spent her last days there, full of sinister presentiments; at last it had been almost necessary to remove her from it by force; and now it was here that mass was said a hundred times a day for her repose. On the damp wall of the refectory, oozing with mineral salts, Leonardo painted the *Last Supper*. A hundred anecdotes were told about it, his retouchings and delays. They show him refusing to work except at the moment of invention, scornful of whoever thought that art was a work of mere industry and rule, often coming the whole length of Milan to give a single touch. He painted it, not in fresco, where all must be impromptu, but in oils, the new method which he had been one of the first to welcome, because it allowed of so many afterthoughts, so refined a working out of perfection. It turned out that on a plastered wall no process could have been less durable. Within fifty years it had fallen into decay. And now we have to turn back to Leonardo's own studies, above all, to one drawing of the central head at the Brera, which in a union of tenderness and severity in the face lines, reminds one of the monumental work of Mino da Fiesole, to trace it as it was.

It was another effort to set a given subject out of the range of its conventional associations. Strange, after all the misrepresentations of the Middle Ages, was the effort to see it, not as the pale host of the altar,

but as one taking leave of his friends. Five years afterwards, the young
Raphael, at Florence, painted it with sweet and solemn effect in the
refectory of Saint Onofrio; but still with all the mystical unreality of the
school of Perugino. Vasari pretends that the central head was never finished; but finished or unfinished, or owing part of its effect to a mellow-
ing decay, this central head does but consummate the sentiment of the
whole company; ghosts through which you see the wall, faint as the
shadows of the leaves upon the wall on autumn afternoons—this figure
is but the faintest, most spectral of them all. It is the image of what the
history it symbolizes has been more and more ever since, paler and paler
as it recedes from us. Criticism came with its appeal from mystical
unrealities to originals, and restored no lifelike reality but these transparent shadows, spririts which have not flesh and bones.

The *Last Supper* was finished in 1497; in 1498 the French entered
Milan, and whether or not the Gascon bowman used it as a mark for
their arrows, the model of Francesco Sforza certainly did not survive.
What, in that age, such work was capable of being, of what nobility,
amid what racy truthfulness to fact, we may judge from the bronze statue
of Bartolomeo Colleoni on horseback, modeled by Leonardo's master,
Verrocchio—he died of grief, it was said, because, the mold accidentally
failing, he was unable himself to complete it—still standing in the piazza
of Saint John and Saint Paul at Venice. Some traces of the thing may
remain in certain of Leonardo's drawings, and also, perhaps, by a singular circumstance, in a faroff town of France. For Lodovico became a
prisoner, and ended his days at Loches in Touraine; allowed, it is said,
at last to breathe fresher air for awhile in one of the rooms of a high
tower there, after many years of captivity in the dungeons below, where
all seems sick with barbarous feudal memories, and where his prison is
still shown, its walls covered with strange painted arabesques, ascribed
by tradition to his hand, amused a little thus through the tedious years—
vast helmets and faces and pieces of armor, among which in great letters
the motto *Infelix Sum*, is woven in and out, and in which perhaps it is
not too fanciful to see the fruit of a wistful afterdreaming over all those
experiments with Leonardo on the armed figure of the great duke, which
had occupied the two so often, during the days of his fortune at Milan.

The remaining years of Leonardo's life are more or less years of wandering. From his brilliant life at court he had saved nothing, and he
returned to Florence a poor man. Perhaps necessity kept his spirit excited:
the next four years are one prolonged rapture or ecstasy of invention. He
painted the pictures of the Louvre, his most authentic works, which
came there straight from the cabinet of Francis the First, at Fontaine-
bleau. One picture of his, the *Saint Anne*— not the *Saint Anne* of the
Louvre, but a mere cartoon, now in London—revived for a moment a
sort of appreciation more common in an earlier time, when good pictures had still seemed miraculous; and for two days a crowd of people of
all qualities passed in naive excitement through the chamber where it

hung, and gave Leonardo a taste of Cimabue's triumph. But his work was less with the saints than with the living women of Florence; for he lived still in the polished society that he loved, and in the houses of Florence, left perhaps a little subject to light thoughts by the death of Savonarola, (the latest gossip is of an undraped Mona Lisa, found in some out-of-the-way corner of the late Orléans collection) he saw Ginevra di Benci, and Lisa, the young third wife of Francesco del Giocondo. As we have seen him using incidents of the sacred legend, not for their own sake, or as mere subjects for pictorial realization, but as a symbolical language for fancies all his own, so now he found a vent for his thoughts in taking one of these languid women, and raising her, as Leda or Pomona, Modesty or Vanity, to the seventh heaven of symbolical expression.

La Gioconda is, in the truest sense, Leonardo's masterpiece, the revealing instance of his mode of thought and work. In suggestiveness, only the *Melancholia* of Dürer is comparable to it; and no crude symbolism disturbs the effect of its subdued and graceful mystery. We all know the face and hands of the figure, set in its marble chair, in that cirque of fantastic rocks, as in some faint light under sea. Perhaps of all ancient pictures time has chilled it least.[2] As often happens with works in which invention seems to reach its limit, there is an element in it given to, not invented by, the master. In that inestimable folio of drawings, once in the possession of Vasari, were certain designs by Verrocchio, faces of such impressive beauty that Leonardo in his boyhood copied them many times. It is hard not to connect with these designs of the elder, by-passed master, as with its germinal principle, the unfathomable smile, always with a touch of something sinister in it, which plays over all Leonardo's work. Besides, the picture is a portrait. From childhood we see this image defining itself on the fabric of his dreams; and but for express historical testimony, we might fancy that this was but his ideal lady, embodied and beheld at last. What was the relationship of a living Florentine to this creature of his thought? By means of what strange affinities had the person and the dream grown up thus apart, and yet so closely together? Present from the first, incorporeal in Leonardo's thought, dimly traced in the designs of Verrocchio, she is found present at last in Il Giocondo's house. That there is much of mere portraiture in the picture is attested by the legend that by artificial means, the presence of mimes and flute players, that subtle expression was protracted on the face. Again, was it in four years, and by renewed labor never really completed, or in four months, and as by stroke of magic, that the image was projected?

The presence that thus rose so strangely beside the waters, is expressive of what in the ways of a thousand years man had come to desire. Hers is the head upon which all "the ends of the world are come," and

2. Yet for Vasari there was some further magic of crimson in the lips and cheeks, lost for us.

the eyelids are a little weary. It is a beauty wrought out from within upon the flesh, the deposit, little cell by cell, of strange thoughts and fantastic reveries and exquisite passions. Set it for a moment beside one of those white Greek goddesses or beautiful women of antiquity, and how would they be troubled by this beauty, into which the soul with all its maladies has passed? All the thoughts and experience of the world have etched and molded there, in that which they have the power to refine and make expressive the outward form, the animalism of Greece, the lust of Rome, the reverie of the Middle Ages with its spiritual ambition and imaginative loves, the return of the pagan world, the sins of the Borgias. She is older than the rocks among which she sits; like the vampire, she has been dead many times, and learned the secrets of the grave; and has been a diver in deep seas, and keeps their fallen day about her; and trafficked for strange webs with Eastern merchants; and, as Leda, was the mother of Helen of Troy, and, as Saint Anne, the mother of Mary; and all this has been to her but as the sound of lyres and flutes, and lives only in the delicacy with which it has molded the changing lineaments, and tinged the eyelids and the hands. The fancy of a perpetual life, sweeping together ten thousand experiences, is an old one; and modern thought has conceived the idea of humanity as wrought upon by, and summing up in itself, all modes of thought and life. Certainly Lady Lisa might stand as the embodiment of the old fancy, the symbol of the modern idea.

During these years at Florence, Leonardo's history is the history of his art; he himself is lost in the bright cloud of it. The outward history begins again in 1502, with a wild journey through central Italy, which he makes as the chief engineer of Cesare Borgia. The biographer, putting together the stray jottings of his manuscripts, may follow him through every day of it, up the strange tower of Siena, which looks toward Rome, elastic like a bent bow, down to the seashore at Piombino, each place appearing as fitfully as in a fever dream.

One other great work was left for him to do, a work all trace of which soon vanished, *The Battle of the Standard*, in which he had Michelangelo for his rival. The citizens of Florence, desiring to decorate the walls of the great council chamber, had offered the work for competition, and any subject might be chosen from the Florentine wars of the fifteenth century. Michelangelo chose for his cartoon an incident of the war with Pisa, in which the Florentine soldiers, bathing in the Arno, are surprised by the sound of trumpets, and run to arms. His design has reached us only in an old engraving, which perhaps helps us less than what we remember of the background of his *Holy Family* in the Uffizi to imagine in what superhuman form, such as might have beguiled the heart of an earlier world, those figures may have risen from the water. Leonardo chose an incident from the battle of Anghiari, in which two parties of soldiers fight for a standard. Like Michelangelo's, his cartoon is lost, and has come to us only in sketches, and in a fragment of Rubens. Through the accounts given we may discern some lust of terrible things in it, so that even the horses tore each other with their teeth; and yet one fragment of it, in a drawing of his at Florence, is far different—a waving field of lovely armor, the chased edgings running like lines of sunlight from side to side. Michelangelo was twenty-seven years old; Leonardo more than fifty; and Raphael, then nineteen years old, visiting Florence for the first time, came and watched them as they worked.

We catch a glimpse of him again, at Rome in 1514, surrounded by his mirrors and vials and furnaces, making strange toys that seemed alive of wax and quicksilver. The hesitation which had haunted him all through life, and made him like one under a spell, was upon him now with double force. No one had ever carried political indifferentism farther; it had always been his philosophy to "fly before the storm"; he is for the Sforzas, or against them, as the tide of their fortune turns. Yet now in the political society of Rome, he came to be suspected of concealed French sympathies. It paralyzed him to find himself among enemies; and he turned wholly to France, which had long courted him.

France was about to become an Italy more Italian than Italy itself. Francis the First, like Lewis the Twelfth before him, was attracted by the finesse of Leonardo's work; *La Gioconda* was already in his cabinet, and he offered Leonardo the little Château de Cloux, with its vineyards and meadows, in the pleasant valley of the Masse, just outside the walls of the town of Amboise, where, especially in the hunting season, the court then frequently resided. A *Monsieur Lyonard, peinteur du Roy pour Amboyse*—so the letter of Francis the First is headed. It opens a prospect, one of the most attractive in the history of art, where, under a strange mixture of lights, Italian art dies away as a French exotic.

Two questions remain, after much busy antiquarianism, concerning Leonardo's death—the question of the form of his religion, and the question whether Francis the First was present at the time. They are of about equally little importance in the estimate of Leonardo's genius. The directions in his will about the thirty masses and the great candles for the church of Saint Florentin are things of course, their real purpose being immediate and practical; and on no theory of religion could these hurried offices be of much consequence. We forget them in speculating how one who had been always so desirous of beauty, but desired it always in such definite and precise forms, as hands or flowers or hair, looked forward now into the vague land, and experienced the last curiosity.

Conclusion [to *The Renaissance*] †

Aἐγει πουʹΗράκλειτος ὅτι πάντα χωρεῖ καί οὐδὲν μένει[1]

To regard all things and principles of things as inconstant modes or fashions has more and more become the tendency of modern thought. Let us begin with that which is without—our physical life. Fix upon it in one of its more exquisite intervals, the moment, for instance, of delicious recoil from the flood of water in summer heat. What is the whole physical life in that moment but a combination of natural elements to which science gives their names? But those elements, phosphorus and lime and delicate fibres, are present not in the human body alone: we detect them in places most remote from it. Our physical life is a perpetual motion of them—the passage of the blood, the waste and repairing of the lenses of the eye, the modification of the tissues of the brain under every ray of light and sound—processes which science reduces to simpler and more elementary forces. Like the elements of which we are composed, the action of these forces extends beyond us: it rusts iron and ripens corn. Far out on every side of us those elements are broadcast, driven in many currents; and birth and gesture and death and the springing of violets from the grave are but a few out of ten thousand resultant combinations. That clear, perpetual outline of face and limb is but an image of ours, under which we group them—a design in a web, the actual threads of which pass out beyond it. This at least of flamelike our life has, that it is but the concurrence, renewed from moment to moment, of forces parting sooner or later on their ways.

Or if we begin with the inward world of thought and feeling, the whirlpool is still more rapid, the flame more eager and devouring. There it is no longer the gradual darkening of the eye, the gradual fading of colour from the wall—movements of the shore-side, where the water flows down indeed, though in apparent rest—but the race of the midstream, a drift of momentary acts of sight and passion and thought. At first sight experience seems to bury us under a flood of external objects, pressing upon us with a sharp and importunate, reality, calling us out of ourselves in a thousand forms of action. But when reflexion begins to play upon those objects they are dissipated under its influence; the cohesive force seems suspended like some trick of magic; each object is loosed into a group of impressions—colour, odour, texture—in the mind of the observer. And if we continue to dwell in thought on this world, not of objects in the solidity with which language invests them, but of impressions, unstable, flickering, inconsistent, which burn and are extinguished with our consciousness of them, it contracts still further:

---

† This brief "Conclusion" was omitted in the second edition of this book, as I conceived it might possibly mislead some of those young men into whose hands it might fall. On the whole, I have thought it best to reprint it here, with some slight changes which bring it closer to my original meaning. I have dealt more fully in *Marius the Epicurean* with the thoughts suggested by it [*Pater's note*].

1. "Heraclitus says, 'All things give way; nothing remains.' "

the whole scope of observation is dwarfed into the narrow chamber of the individual mind. Experience, already reduced to a group of impressions, is ringed round for each one of us by that thick wall of personality through which no real voice has ever pierced on its way to us, or from us to that which we can only conjecture to be without. Every one of those impressions is the impression of the individual in his isolation, each mind keeping as a solitary prisoner its own dream of a world. Analysis goes a step farther still, and assures us that those impressions of the individual mind to which, for each one of us, experience dwindles down, are in perpetual flight; that each of them is limited by time, and that as time is infinitely divisible, each of them is infinitely divisible also; all that is actual in it being a single moment, gone while we try to apprehend it, of which it may ever be more truly said that it has ceased to be than that it is. To such a tremulous wisp constantly re-forming itself on the stream, to a single sharp impression, with a sense in it, a relic more or less fleeting, of such moments gone by, what is real in our life fines itself down. It is with this movement, with the passage and dissolution of impressions, images, sensations, that analysis leaves off—that continual vanishing away, that strange, perpetual weaving and unweaving of ourselves.

Philosophiren, says Novalis, *ist dephlegmatisiren vivificiren.*[2] The service of philosophy, of speculative culture, towards the human spirit, is to rouse, to startle it to a life of constant and eager observation. Every moment some form grows perfect in hand or face; some tone on the hills or the sea is choicer than the rest; some mood of passion or insight or intellectual excitement is irresistibly real and attractive to us,—for that moment only. Not the fruit of experience, but experience itself, is the end. A counted number of pulses only is given to us of a variegated, dramatic life. How may we see in them all that is to be seen in them by the finest senses? How shall we pass most swiftly from point to point, and be present always at the focus where the greater number of vital forces unite in their purest energy?

To burn always with this hard, gemlike flame, to maintain this ecstasy, is success in life. In a sense it might even be said that our failure is to form habits: for, after all, habit is relative to a stereotyped world, and meantime it is only the roughness of the eye that makes any two persons, things, situations, seem alike. While all melts under our feet, we may well grasp at any exquisite passion, or any contribution to knowledge that seems by a lifted horizon to set the spirit free for a moment, or any stirring of the senses, strange dyes, strange colours, and curious odours, or work of the artist's hands, or the face of one's friend. Not to discriminate every moment some passionate attitude in those about us, and in the very brilliancy of their gifts some tragic dividing of forces on their ways, is, on this short day of frost and sun, to sleep before evening. With

---

2. "To philosophize is to cast off inertia, to vitalize."

this sense of the splendour of our experience and of its awful brevity, gathering all we are into one desperate effort to see and touch, we shall hardly have time to make theories about the things we see and touch. What we have to do is to be for ever curiously testing new opinions and courting new impressions, never acquiescing in a facile orthodoxy of Comte, or of Hegel, or of our own. Philosophical theories or ideas, as points of view, instruments of criticism, may help us to gather up what might otherwise pass unregarded by us. "Philosophy is the microscope of thought." The theory or idea or system which requires of us the sacrifice of any part of this experience, in consideration of some interest into which we cannot enter, or some abstract theory we have not identified with ourselves, or of what is only conventional, has no real claim upon us.

One of the most beautiful passages of Rousseau is that in the sixth book of the *Confessions*, where he describes the awakening in him of the literary sense. An undefinable taint of death had clung always about him, and now in early manhood he believed himself smitten by mortal disease. He asked himself how he might make as much as possible of the interval that remained; and he was not biassed by anything in his previous life when he decided that it must be by intellectual excitement, which he found just then in the clear, fresh writings of Voltaire. Well! we are all *condamnés*, as Victor Hugo says: we are all under sentence of death but with a sort of indefinite reprieve—*les hommes sont tous condamnés à mort avec des sursis indéfinis:* [3] we have an interval, and then our place knows us no more. Some spend this interval in listlessness, some in high passions, the wisest, at least among "the children of this world," [4] in art and song. For our one chance lies in expanding that interval, in getting as many pulsations as possible into the given time. Great passions may give us this quickened sense of life, ecstasy and sorrow of love, the various forms of enthusiastic activity, disinterested or otherwise, which come naturally to many of us. Only be sure it is passion—that it does yield you this fruit of a quickened, multiplied consciousness. Of such wisdom, the poetic passion, the desire of beauty, the love of art for its own sake, has most. For art comes to you proposing frankly to give nothing but the highest quality to your moments as they pass, and simply for those moments' sake.

3. "Men are all condemned to death with indefinite reprieves."   4. Luke 16.8.

OSCAR WILDE

From "The Critic as Artist" †

Part Two

❊   ❊   ❊

GILBERT: Yes; the critic will be an interpreter, if he chooses. He can pass from his synthetic impression of the work of art as a whole, to an analysis or exposition of the work itself, and in this lower sphere, as I hold it to be, there are many delightful things to be said and done. Yet his object will not always be to explain the work of art. He may seek rather to deepen its mystery, to raise round it, and round its maker, that mist of wonder which is dear to both gods and worshippers alike. Ordinary people are "terribly at ease in Zion." They propose to walk arm in arm with the poets, and have a glib ignorant way of saying, "Why should we read what is written about Shakespeare and Milton? We can read the plays and the poems. That is enough." But an appreciation of Milton is, as the late Rector of Lincoln remarked once, the reward of consummate scholarship. And he who desires to understand Shakespeare truly must understand the relations in which Shakespeare stood to the Renaissance and the Reformation, to the age of Elizabeth and the age of James; he must be familiar with the history of the struggle for supremacy between the old classical forms and the new spirit of romance, between the school of Sidney, and Daniel, and Johnson, and the school of Marlowe and Marlowe's greater son; he must know the materials that were at Shakespeare's disposal, and the method in which he used them, and the conditions of theatric presentation in the sixteenth and seventeenth century, their limitations and their opportunities for freedom, and the literary criticism of Shakespeare's day, its aims and modes and canons; he must study the English language in its progress, and blank or rhymed verse in its various developments; he must study the Greek drama, and the connection between the art of the creator of the Agamemnon and the art of the creator of Macbeth; in a word, he must be able to bind Elizabethan London to the Athens of Pericles, and to learn Shakespeare's true position in the history of European drama and the drama of the world. The critic will certainly be an interpreter, but he will not treat Art as a riddling Sphinx, whose shallow secret may be guessed and revealed by one whose feet are wounded and who knows not his name. Rather, he will look upon Art as a goddess whose mystery it is his province to intensify, and whose majesty his privilege to make more marvellous in the eyes of men.

And here, Ernest, this strange thing happens. The critic will indeed

† From *The Complete Works of Oscar Wilde*, rev. ed., ed. Vyvyan Holland (London: Collins, 1966) 1032–41.

be an interpreter, but he will not be an interpreter in the sense of one who simply repeats in another form a message that has been put into his lips to say. For, just as it is only by contact with the art of foreign nations that the art of a country gains that individual and separate life that we call nationality, so, by curious inversion, it is only by intensifying his own personality that the critic can interpret the personality and work of others, and the more strongly this personality enters into the interpretation, the more real the interpretation becomes, the more satisfying, the more convincing, and the more true.

ERNEST: I would have said that personality would have been a disturbing element.

GILBERT: No; it is an element of revelation. If you wish to understand others you must intensify your own individualism.

ERNEST: What, then, is the result?

GILBERT: I will tell you, and perhaps I can tell you best by definite example. It seems to me that, while the literary critic stands of course first, as having the wider range, and larger vision, and nobler material, each of the arts has a critic, as it were, assigned to it. The actor is a critic of the drama. He shows the poet's work under new conditions, and by a method special to himself. He takes the written word, and action, gesture and voice become the media of revelation. The singer or the player on lute and viol is the critic of music. The etcher of a picture robs the painting of its fair colours, but shows us by the use of a new material its true colour-quality, its tones and values, and the relations of its masses, and so is, in his way, a critic of it, for the critic is he who exhibits to us a work of art in a form different from that of the work itself, and the employment of a new material is a critical as well as a creative element. Sculpture, too, has its critic, who may be either the carver of a gem, as he was in Greek days, or some painter like Mantegna, who sought to reproduce on canvas the beauty of plastic line and the symphonic dignity of processional bas-relief. And in the case of all these creative critics of art it is evident that personality is an absolute essential for any real interpretation. When Rubinstein plays to us the *Sonata Appassionata* of Beethoven he gives us not merely Beethoven, but also himself, and so gives us Beethoven absolutely—Beethoven reinterpreted through a rich artistic nature, and made vivid and wonderful to us by a new and intense personality. When a greater actor plays Shakespeare we have the same experience. His own individuality becomes a vital part of the interpretation. People sometimes say that actors give us their own Hamlets, and not Shakespeare's; and this fallacy—for it is a fallacy—is, I regret to say, repeated by that charming and graceful writer who has lately deserted the turmoil of literature for the peace of the House of Commons; I mean the author of *Obiter Dicta*. In point of fact, there is no such thing as Shakespeare's Hamlet. If Hamlet has something of the definiteness of a work of art, he has also all the obscurity that belongs to life. There are as many Hamlets as there are melancholies.

ERNEST: As many Hamlets as there are melancholies?

GILBERT: Yes; and as art springs from personality, so it is only to personality that it can be revealed, and from the meeting of the two comes right interpretative criticism.

ERNEST: The critic, then, considered as the interpreter, will give no less than he receives, and lend as much as he borrows?

GILBERT: He will be always showing us the work of art in some new relation to our age. He will always be reminding us that great works of art are living things—are, in fact, the only things that live. So much, indeed, will he feel this, that I am certain that, as civilisation progresses and we become more highly organised, the elect spirits of each age, the critical and cultured spirits, will grow less and less interested in actual life, and *will seek to gain their impressions almost entirely from what Art has touched*. For life is terribly deficient in form. Its catastrophes happen in the wrong way and to the wrong people. There is a grotesque horror about its comedies, and its tragedies seem to culminate in farce. One is always wounded when one approaches it. Things last either too long or not long enough.

ERNEST: Poor life! Poor human life! Are you not even touched by the tears that the Roman poet tells us are part of its essence.

GILBERT: Too quickly touched by them, I fear. For when one looks back upon the life that was so vivid in its emotional intensity, and filled with such fervent moments of ecstasy or of joy, it all seems to be a dream and an illusion. What are the unreal things, but the passions that once burned one like fire? What are the incredible things, but the things that one has faithfully believed? What are the improbable things? The things that one has done oneself. No, Ernest; life cheats us with shadows, like a puppet-master. We ask it for pleasure. It gives it to us, with bitterness and disappointment in its train. We come across some noble grief that we think will lend the purple dignity of tragedy to our days, but it passes away from us, and things less noble take its place, and on some grey windy dawn, or odorous eve of silence and of silver, we find ourselves looking with callous wonder, or dull heart of stone, at the trees of gold-flecked hair that we had once so wildly worshipped and so madly kissed.

ERNEST: Life then is a failure?

GILBERT: From the artistic point of view, certainly And the chief things that makes life a failure from this artistic point of view is the thing that lends to life its sordid security, the fact that one can never repeat exactly the same emotion. How different it is in the world of Art! * * *

It is a strange thing, this transference of emotion. We sicken with the same maladies as the poets, and the singer lends us his pain. Dead lips have their message for us, and hearts that have fallen to dust can communicate their joy. We run to kiss the bleeding mouth of Fantine, and we follow Manon Lescaut over the whole world. Ours is the love-madness of the Tyrian, and the terror of Orestes is ours also. There is no passion that we cannot feel, no pleasure that we may not gratify, and we can choose the time of our initiation and the time of our freedom also. Life! Life! Don't let us go to life for our fulfillment or our experience. It is a thing narrowed by circumstances, incoherent in its utterance, and without that fine correspondence of form and spirit which is the only thing that can satisfy the artistic and critical temperament. It makes us pay too high a price for its wares, and we purchase the meanest of its secret at a cost that is monstrous and infinite.

ERNEST: Must we go, then, to Art for everything?

GILBERT: For everything. Because Art does not hurt us. The tears that we shed at a play are a type of the exquisite sterile emotions that it is the function of Art to awaken. We weep, but we are not wounded. We grieve, but our grief is not bitter. In the actual life of man, sorrow, as Spinoza says somewhere, is a passage to a lesser perfection. But the sorrow with which Art fills us both purifies and initiates, if I may quote once more from the great art critic of the Greeks. It is through Art, and through Art only, that we can realise our perfection; through Art, and through Art only, that we can shield ourselves from the sordid perils of actual existence. This results not merely from the fact that nothing that one can imagine is worth doing, and that one can imagine everything, but from the subtle law that emotional forces, like the forces of the physical sphere, are limited in extent and energy. One can feel so much, and no more. And how can it matter with what pleasure life tries to tempt one, or with what pain it seeks to maim and mar one's soul, if in the spectacle of the lives of those who have never existed one has found the true secret of joy, and wept away one's tears over their deaths who, like Cordelia and the daughter of Brabantio, can never die?

ERNEST: Stop a moment. It seems to me that in everything that you have said there is something radically immoral.

GILBERT: All art is immoral.

ERNEST: All art?

GILBERT: Yes. For emotion for the sake of emotion is the aim of art, and emotion for the sake of action is the aim of life, and of that practical organisation of life that we call society. Society, which is the beginning and basis of morals, exists simply for the concentration of human energy, and in order to ensure its own continuance and healthy stability it demands, and no doubt rightly demands, of each of its citizens that he should contribute some form of productive labour to the common weal, and toil and travail that the day's work may be done. Society often forgives the criminal; it never forgives the dreamer. The beautiful sterile emotions that art excites in us are hateful in its eyes, and so completely are people dominated by the tyranny of this dreadful social ideal that they are always coming shamelessly up to one at Private Views and other places that are open to the general public, and saying in a loud stentorian voice, "What are you doing?" whereas "What are you thinking?" is the only question that any single civilised being should ever be allowed to whisper to another. They mean well, no doubt, these honest beaming folk. Perhaps that is the reason why they are so excessively tedious. But some one should teach them what while, in the opinion of society, Contemplation is the gravest sin of which any citizen can be guilty, in the opinion of the highest culture it is the proper occupation of man.

ERNEST: Contemplation?

GILBERT: Contemplation. I said to you some time ago that it was far more difficult to talk about a thing than to do it. Let me say to you now that to do nothing at all is the most difficult thing in the world, the most difficult and the most intellectual. To Plato, with his passion for wisdom, this was the noblest form of energy. To Aristotle, with his passion for knowledge, this was the noblest form of energy also. It was to this that the passion for holiness led the saint and the mystic of mediæval days.

ERNEST: We exist, then, to do nothing?

GILBERT: It is to do nothing that the elect exist. Action is limited and relative. Unlimited and absolute is the vision of him who sits at ease and watches, who walks in loneliness and dreams. But we who are born at the close of this wonderful age are at once too cultured and too critical, too intellectually subtle and too curious of exquisite pleasures, to accept any speculations about life in exchange for life itself. To us the *città divina*[1] is colourless, and the *fruitio Dei*[2] without meaning. Metaphysics do not satisfy our temperaments, and religious ecstasy is out of date. The world through which the Academic philosopher becomes "the spectator of all time and of all existence" is not really an ideal world, but simply a world of abstract ideas. When we enter it, we starve amidst the chill mathematics of thought. The courts of the city of God are not open to us now. Its gates are guarded by Ignorance, and to pass them we have to surrender all that in our nature is most divine. It is enough that our fathers believed. They have exhausted the faith-faculty of the species. Their legacy to us is the scepticism of which they were afraid. Had they put it into words, it might not live within us as thought. No, Ernest, no. We cannot go back to the saint. There is far more to be learned from the sinner. We cannot go back to the philosopher, and the mystic leads us astray. Who, as Mr. Pater suggests somewhere, would exchange the curve of a single rose-leaf for that formless intangible Being which Plato rates so high? What to us is the Illumination of Philo, the Abyss of Eckhart, the vision of Böhme, the monstrous Heaven itself that was revealed to Swedenborg's blinded eyes? Such things are less than the yellow trumpet of one daffodil of the field, far less than the meanest of the visible arts; for just as Nature is matter struggling into mind, so Art is mind expressing itself under the conditions of matter, and thus, even in the lowliest of her manifestations, she speaks to both sense and soul alike. To the æsthetic temperament the vague is always repellent. The Greeks were a nation of artists, because they were spared the sense of

---

1. Heavenly city.   2. Enjoyment of God.

the infinite. Like Aristotle, like Goethe after he had read Kant, we desire the concrete, and nothing but the concrete can satisfy us.

ERNEST: What then do you propose?

GILBERT: It seems to me that with the development of the critical spirit we shall be able to realise, not merely our own lives, but the collective life of the race, and so to make ourselves absolutely modern, in the true meaning of the word modernity. For he to whom the present is the only thing that is present, knows nothing of the age in which he lives. To realise the nineteenth century, one must realise every century that has preceded it and that has contributed to its making. To know anything about oneself one must know all about others. There must be no mood with which one cannot sympathise, no dead mode of life that one cannot make alive. Is this impossible? I think not. By revealing to us the absolute mechanism of all action, and so freeing us from the self-imposed and trammelling burden of moral responsibility, the scientific principle of Heredity has become, as it were, the warrant for the contemplative life. It has shown us that we are never less free than when we try to act. It has hemmed us round with the nets of the hunter, and written upon the wall the prophecy of our doom. We may not watch it, for it is within us. We may not see it, save in a mirror that mirrors the soul. It is Nemesis without her mask. It is the last of the Fates, and the most terrible. It is the only one of the Gods whose real name we know.

And yet, while in the sphere of practical and external life it has robbed energy of its freedom and activity of its choice, in the subjective sphere, where the soul is at work, it comes to us, this terrible shadow, with many gifts in its hands, gifts of strange temperaments and subtle susceptibilities, gifts of wild ardours and chill moods of indifference, complex multiform gifts of thoughts that are at variance with each other, and passions that war against themselves. And so it is not our own life that we live, but the lives of the dead, and the soul that dwells within us is no single spiritual entity, making us personal and individual, created for our service, and entering into us for our joy. It is something that has dwelt in fearful places, and in ancient sepulchres has made its abode. It is sick with many maladies, and has memories of curious sins. It is wiser than we are, and its wisdom is bitter. It fills us with impossible desires, and makes us follow what we know we cannot gain. One thing, however, Ernest, it can do for us. It can lead us away from surroundings whose beauty is dimmed to us by the mist of familiarity, or whose ignoble ugliness and sordid claims are marring the perfection of our development. It can help us to leave the age in which we were born, and to pass into other ages, and find ourselves not exiled from their air. It can teach us how to escape from our experience, and to realise the experiences of those who are greater than we are. The pain of Leopardi crying out against life becomes our pain. Theocritus blows on his pipe, and we laugh with the lips of nymph and shepherd. In the wolfskin of Pierre Vidal we flee before the hounds, and in the armour of Lancelot we ride from the bower of the Queen. We have whispered the secret of our love beneath the cowl of Abelard, and in the stained raiment of Villon have put our shame into song. We can see the dawn through Shelley's eyes, and when we wander with Endymion the Moon grows amorous of our youth. Ours is the anguish of Atys, and ours the weak rage and noble sorrows of the Dane. Do you think that it is the imagination that enables us to live these countless lives? Yes; it is the imagination; and the imagination is the result of heredity. It is simply concentrated race-experience.

ERNEST: But where in this is the function of the critical spirit?

GILBERT: The culture that this transmission of racial experiences makes possible can be made perfect by the critical spirit alone, and indeed may be said to be one with it. For who is the true critic but he who bears within himself the dreams, and ideas, and feelings of myriad generations, and to whom no form of thought is alien, no emotional impulse obscure? And who the true man of culture, if not he who by fine scholarship and fastidious rejection has made instinct self-conscious and intelligent, and can separate the work that has distinction from the work that has it not, and so by contact and comparison makes himself master of the secrets of style and school, and understands their meanings, and listens to their voices, and develop that spirit of disinterested curiosity which is the real root, as it is the real flower, of the intellectual life, and thus attains to intellectual clarity, and, having learned "the best that is known and thought in the world," lives—it is not fanciful to say so— with those who are the Immortals.

* * *

From "The Decay of Lying" †

* * *

VIVIAN: * * * Personal experience is a most vicious and limited circle. All that I desire to point out is the general principle that Life imitates Art far more than Art imitates Life, and I feel sure that if you think seriously about it you will find that it is true. Life holds the mirror up to Art, and either reproduces some strange type imagined by painter or sculptor, or realises in fact what has been dreamed in fiction. Scientifically speaking, the basis of life—the energy of life, as Aristotle would call it—is simply the desire for expression, and Art is always presenting various forms through which the expression can be attained. Life seizes on them and uses them, even if they be to her own hurt. Young men have committed suicide because Rolla did so, have died by their own hand because by his own hand Werther died. Think of what we owe to

† From *The Complete Works of Oscar Wilde*, rev. ed., ed. Vyvyan Holland (London: Collins, 1966) 985–92.

the imitation of Christ, of what we owe to the imitation of Cæsar.

CYRIL: The theory is certainly a very curious one, but to make it complete you must show that Nature, no less than Life, is an imitation of Art. Are you prepared to prove that?

VIVIAN: My dear fellow, I am prepared to prove anything.

CYRIL: Nature follows the landscape painter, then, and takes her effects from him?

VIVIAN: Certainly. Where, if not from the Impressionists, do we get those wonderful brown fogs that come creeping down our streets, blurring the gas-lamps and changing the houses into monstrous shadows? To whom, if not to them and their master, do we owe the lovely silver mists that brood over our river, and turn to faint forms of fading grace curved bridge and swaying barge? The extraordinary change that has taken place in the climate of London during the last ten years is entirely due to a particular school of Art. You smile. Consider the matter from a scientific or a metaphysical point of view, and you will find that I am right. For what is Nature? Nature is no great mother who has borne us. She is our creation. It is in our brain that she quickens to life. Things are because we see them, and what we see, and how we see it, depends on the Arts that have influenced us. To look at a thing is very different from seeing a thing. One does not see anything until one sees its beauty. Then, and then only, does it come into existence. At present, people see fogs, not because there are fogs, but because poets and painters have taught them the mysterious loveliness of such effects. There may have been fogs for centuries in London. I dare say there were. But no one saw them, and so we do not know anything about them. They did not exist till Art had invented them. Now, it must be admitted, fogs are carried to excess. They have become the mere mannerism of a clique, and the exaggerated realism of their method gives dull people bronchitis. Where the cultured catch an effect, the uncultured catch cold. And so, let us be humane, and invite Art to turn her wonderful eyes elsewhere. She has done so already, indeed. That white quivering sunlight that one sees now in France, with its strange blotches of mauve, and its restless violet shadows, is her latest fancy, and, on the whole, Nature reproduces it quite admirably. Where she used to give us Corots and Daubignys, she gives us now exquisite Monets and entrancing Pissaros. Indeed there are moments, rare, it is true, but still to be observed from time to time, when Nature becomes absolutely modern. Of course she is not always to be relied upon. The fact is that she is in this unfortunate position. Art creates an incomparable and unique effect, and, having done so, passes on to other things. Nature, upon the other hand, forgetting that imitation can be made the sincerest form of insult, keeps on repeating this effect until we all become absolutely wearied of it. Nobody of any real culture, for instance, ever talks nowadays about the beauty of a sunset. Sunsets are quite old-fashioned. They belong to the time when Turner was the last note in art. To admire them is a distinct sign of provincialism of temperament. Upon the other hand they go on. Yesterday evening Mrs. Arundel insisted on my going to the window and looking at the glorious sky, as she called it. Of course I had to look at it. She is one of those absurdly pretty Philistines to whom one can deny nothing. And what was it? It was simply a very second-rate Turner, a Turner of a bad period, with all the painter's worst faults exaggerated and over-emphasised. Of course I am quite ready to admit that Life very often commits the same error. She produces her false Renés and her sham Vautrins, just as Nature gives us, on one day a doubtful Cuyp, and on another a more than questionable Rousseau. Still, Nature irritates one more when she does things of that kind. It seems so stupid, so obvious, so unnecessary. A false Vautrin might be delightful. A doubtful Cuyp is unbearable. However, I don't want to be too hard on Nature. I wish the Channel, especially at Hastings, did not look quite so often like a Henry Moore, grey pearl with yellow lights, but then, when Art is more varied, Nature will, no doubt, be more varied also. That she imitates Art, I don't think even her worst enemy would deny now. It is the one thing that keeps her in touch with civilised man. But have I proved my theory to your satisfaction?

CYRIL: You have proved it to my dissatisfaction, which is better. But even admitting this strange imitative instinct in Life and Nature, surely you would acknowledge that Art expresses the temper of its age, the spirit of its time, the moral and social conditions that surround it, and under whose influence it is produced.

VIVIAN: Certainly not! Art never expresses anything but itself. This is the principle of my new æsthetics; and it is this, more than that vital connection between form and substance, on which Mr. Pater dwells, that makes basic the type of all the arts. Of course, nations and individuals, with that healthy natural vanity which is the secret of existence, are always under the impression that it is of them that the Muses are talking, always trying to find in the calm dignity of imaginative art some mirror of their own turbid passions, always forgetting that the singer of life is not Apollo but Marsyas. Remote from reality and with her eyes turned away from the shadows of the cave, Art reveals her own perfection, and the wondering crowd that watches the opening of the marvellous many-petalled rose fancies that it is its own history that is being told to it, its own spirit that is finding expression in a new form. But it is not so. The highest art rejects the burden of the human spirit, and gains more from a new medium or a fresh material than she does from any enthusiasm for art, or from any lofty passion, or from any great awakening of the human consciousness. She develops purely on her own lines. She is not symbolic of any age. It is the ages that are her symbols.

Even those who hold that Art is representative of time and place and people cannot help admitting that the more imitative an art is the less it represents to us the spirit of its age. The evil faces of the Roman emperors look out at us from the foul porphyry and spotted jasper in which the realistic artists of the day delighted to work and we fancy that in those cruel lips and heavy sensual jaws we can find the secret of the ruin of the Empire. But it was not so. The vices of Tiberius could not destroy that supreme civilisation, any more than the virtues of the Antonines could save it. It fell for other, for less interesting reasons. The sibyls and prophets of the Sistine may indeed serve to interpret for some that new birth of the emancipated spirit that we call the Renaissance; but what do the drunken boors and bawling peasants of Dutch art tell us about the great soul of Holland? The more abstract, the more ideal an art is the more it reveals to us the temper of its age, If we wish to understand a nation by means of its art, let us look at its architecture or its music.

CYRIL: I quite agree with you there. The spirit of an age may be best expressed in the abstract ideal arts, for the spirit itself is abstract and ideal. Upon the other hand, for the visible aspect of an age, for its look, as the phrase goes, we must of course go to the arts of imitation.

VIVIAN: I don't think so. After all, what the imitative arts really give us are merely the various styles of particular artists, or of certain schools of artists. Surely you don't imagine that the people of the Middle Ages bore any resemblance at all to the figures on mediæval stained glass, or in mediæval stone and wood carving, or on mediæval metal-work, or tapestries, or illuminated MSS. They were probably very ordinary-looking people, with nothing grotesque, or remarkable, or fantastic in their appearance. The Middle Ages, as we know them in art, are simply a definite form of style, and there is no reason at all why an artist with this style should not be produced in the nineteenth century. No great artist ever sees things as they really are. If he did he would cease to be an artist. Take an example from our own day. I know that you are fond of Japanese things. Now, do you really imagine that the Japanese people, as they are presented to us in art, have any existence? If you do, you have never understood Japanese art at all. The Japanese people are the deliberate self-conscious creation of certain individual artists. If you set a picture by Hokusai or Hokkei, or any of the great native painters, beside a real Japanese gentleman or lady, you will see that there is not the slightest resemblance between them. The actual people who live in Japan are not unlike the general run of English people; that is to say, they are extremely commonplace, and have nothing curious or extraordinary about them. In fact, the whole of Japan is a pure invention. There is no such country, there are no such people. One of our most charming painters went recently to the Land of the Chrysanthemum in the foolish hope of seeing the Japanese. All he saw, all he had the chance of painting, were a few lanterns and some fans. He was quite unable to discover the inhabitants, as his delightful exhibition at Messrs. Dowdeswell's Gallery showed only too well. He did not know that the Japanese people are, as I have said, simply a mode of style, an exquisite fancy of art. And so, if you desire to see a Japanese effect, you will not behave like a tourist and go to Tokio. On the contrary, you will stay at home and steep yourself in the work of certain Japanese artists and then, when you have absorbed the spirit of their style, and caught their imaginative manner of vision, you will go some afternoon and sit in the Park or stroll down Piccadilly, and if you cannot see an absolutely Japanese effect there, you will not see it anywhere. Or, to return again to the past, take as another instance the ancient Greeks. Do you think that Greek art ever tells us what the Greek people were like? Do you believe that the Athenian women were like the stately dignified figures of the Parthenon frieze, or like those marvellous goddesses who sat in the triangular pediments of the same building? If you judge from the art, they certainly were so. But read an authority like Aristophanes, for instance. You will find that the Athenian ladies laced tightly, wore high-heeled shoes, dyed their hair yellow, painted and rouged their faces and were exactly like any silly fashionable or fallen creature of our own day. The fact is that we look back on the ages entirely through the medium of art, and art, very fortunately, has never once told us the truth.

CYRIL: But modern portraits by English painters, what of them? Surely they are like the people they pretend to represent?

VIVIAN: Quite so. They are so like them that a hundred years from now no one will believe in them. The only portraits in which one believes are portraits where there is very little of the sitter and a very great deal of the artist. Holbein's drawings of the men and women of his time impress us with a sense of their absolute reality. But this is simply because Holbein compelled life to accept his conditions, to restrain itself within his limitations, to reproduce his type and to appear as he wished it to appear. It is style that makes us believe in a thing—nothing but style. Most of our modern portrait painters are doomed to absolute oblivion. They never paint what they see. They paint what the public sees, and the public never sees anything.

CYRIL: Well, after that I think I should like to hear the end of your article.

VIVIAN: With pleasure. Whether it will do any good I really cannot say. Ours is certainly the dullest and most prosaic century possible. Why, even Sleep has played us false, and has closed up the gates of ivory, and opened the gates of horn. The dreams of the great middle classes of this country, as recorded in Mr. Myers's two bulky volumes on the subject, and in the Transactions of the Psychical Society, are the most depressing things I have ever read. There is not even a fine nightmare among them. They are commonplace, sordid and tedious. As for the Church, I cannot conceive anything better for the culture of a country than the presence in it of a body of men whose duty it is to believe in the supernatural, to perform daily miracles, and to keep alive that mythopœic faculty which is so essential for the imagination. But in the English Church a man succeeds, not through his capacity for belief, but through his capacity for disbelief. Ours is the only Church where the sceptic stands at the altar, and where St. Thomas is regarded as the ideal apostle. Many a

worthy clergyman, who passes his life in admirable works of kindly charity, lives and dies unnoticed and unknown; but it is sufficient for some
shallow uneducated passman out of either University to get up in his
pulpit and express his doubts about Noah's ark, or Balaam's ass, or Jonah
and the whale, for half of London to flock to hear him, and to sit open-
mouthed in rapt admiration at his superb intellect. The growth of common sense in the English Church is a thing very much to be regretted.
It is really a degrading concession to a low form of realism. It is silly,
too. It springs from an entire ignorance of psychology. Man can believe
the impossible, but man can never believe the improbable. However, I
must read the end of my article:—

"What we have to do, what at any rate it is our duty to do, is revive
this old art of Lying. Much, of course, may be done in the way of
educating the public, by amateurs in the domestic circle, at literary
lunches, and at afternoon teas. But this is merely the light and graceful
side of lying, such as was probably heard at Cretan dinner-parties. There
are many other forms. Lying for the sake of gaining some immediate
personal advantage, for instance—lying with a moral purpose, as it is
usually called—though of late it has been rather looked down upon, was
extremely popular with the antique world. Athena laughs when Odys-
seus tells her 'his words of sly devising,' as Mr. William Morris phrases
it, and the glory of mendacity illumines the pale brow of the stainless
hero of Euripidean tragedy, and sets among the noble women of the past
the young bride of one of Horace's most exquisite odes. Later on, what
at first had been merely a natural instinct was elevated into a self-
conscious science. Elaborate rules were laid down for the guidance of
mankind, and an important school of literature grew up round the subject. Indeed, when one remembers the excellent philosophical treatise
of Sanchez on the whole question, one cannot help regretting that no
one has ever thought of publishing a cheap and condensed edition of
the works of that great casuist. A short primer, 'When to Lie and How,'
if brought out in an attractive and not too expensive a form, would no
doubt command a large sale, and would prove of real practical service
to many earnest and deep-thinking people. Lying for the sake of the
improvement of the young, which is the basis of home education, still
lingers amongst us, and its advantages are so admirably set forth in the
early books of Plato's *Republic* that it is unnecessary to dwell upon them
here. It is a mode of lying for which all good mothers have peculiar
capabilities, but it is capable of still further development, and has been
sadly overlooked by the School Board. Lying for the sake of a monthly
salary is, of course, well known in Fleet Street, and the profession of a
political leader-writer is not without its advantages. But it is said to be a
somewhat dull occupation, and it certainly does not lead to much beyond
a kind of ostentatious obscurity. The only form of lying that is absolutely
beyond reproach is lying for its own sake, and the highest development
of this is, as we have already pointed out, Lying in Art. Just as those who

do not love Plato more than Truth cannot pass beyond the threshold of the Academe, so those who do not love Beauty more than Truth never know the inmost shrine of Art. The solid, stolid British intellect lies in the desert sands like the Sphinx in Flaubert's marvellous tale, and fantasy, *La Chimère*, dances round it, and calls to it with her false, flute-toned voice. It may not hear her now, but surely some day, when we are all bored to death with the commonplace character of modern fiction, it will hearken to her and try to borrow her wings.

"And when that day dawns, or sunset reddens, how joyous we shall be! Facts will be regarded as discreditable, Truth will be found mourning over her fetters, and Romance, with her temper of wonder, will return to the land. The very aspect of the world will change to our startled eyes. Out of the sea will rise Behemoth and Leviathan, and sail round the high-pooped galleys, as they do on the delightful maps of those ages when books on geography were actually readable. Dragons will wander about the waste places, and the phœnix will soar from her nest of fire into the air. We shall lay our hands upon the basilisk, and see the jewel in the toad's head. Champing his gilded oats, the Hippogriff will stand in our stalls, and over our heads will float the Blue Bird singing of beautiful and impossible things, of things that are lovely and that never happen, of things that are not and that should be. But before this comes to pass we must cultivate the lost art of Lying."

CYRIL: Then we must entirely cultivate it at once. But in order to avoid making any error I want you to tell me briefly the doctrines of the new æsthetics.

VIVIAN: Briefly, then, they are these. Art never expresses anything but itself. It has an independent life, just as Thought has, and develops purely on its own lines. It is not necessarily realistic in an age of realism, nor spiritual in an age of faith. So far from being the creation of its time, it is usually in direct opposition to it, and the only history that it preserves for us is the history of its own progress. Sometimes it returns upon its footsteps, and revives some antique form, as happened in the archaistic movement of late Greek Art, and in the pre-Raphaelite movement of our own day. At other times it entirely anticipates its age, and produces in one century work that it takes another century to understand, to appreciate, and to enjoy. In no case does it reproduce its age. To pass from the art of a time to the time itself is the great mistake that all historians commit.

The second doctrine is this. All bad art comes from returning to Life and Nature, and elevating them into ideals. Life and Nature may sometimes be used as part of Art's rough material, but before they are of any real service to Art they must be translated into artistic conventions. The moment Art surrenders its imaginative medium it surrenders everything. As a method Realism is a complete failure, and the two things that every artist should avoid are modernity of form and modernity of subject-matter. To us, who live in the nineteenth century, any century is a suitable subject for art except our own. The only beautiful things are the things that do not concern us. It is, to have the pleasure of quoting myself, exactly because Hecuba is nothing to us that her sorrows are so suitable a motive for a tragedy. Besides, it is only the modern that ever becomes old-fashioned. M. Zola sits down to give us a picture of the Second Empire. Who cares for the Second Empire now? It is out of date. Life goes faster than Realism, but Romanticism is always in front of Life.

The third doctrine is that Life imitates Art far more than Art imitates Life. This results not merely from Life's imitative instinct, but from the fact that the self-conscious aim of Life is to find expression, and that Art offers it certain beautiful forms through which it may realise that energy. It is a theory that has never been put forward before, but it is extremely fruitful, and throws an entirely new light upon the history of Art.

It follows, as a corollary from this, that external Nature also imitates Art. The only effects that she can show us are effects that we have already seen through poetry, or in paintings. This is the secret of Nature's charm, as well as the explanation of Nature's weakness.

The final revelation is that Lying, the telling of beautiful untrue things, is the proper aim of Art. But of this I think I have spoken at sufficient length. And now let us go out on the terrace, where "droops the milk-white peacock like a ghost," while the evening star "washes the dusk with silver." At twilight nature becomes a wonderfully suggestive effect, and is not without loveliness, though perhaps its chief use is to illustrate quotations from the poets. Come! We have talked long enough.

REVIEWS AND
REACTIONS

The Picture of Dorian Gray occupies an important place in the social and legal history of literature. The reviews, responses, and testimony collected in this section are the very raw materials of a chapter in that history, one that seems to possess a dramatic form of its own rarely found in life outside art. It was Wilde who insisted in one of his most celebrated paradoxes from "The Decay of Lying" that "life imitates art," but then in the record of controversy that followed in the wake of *Dorian Gray*, life had more than a little assistance from the artist. Seldom has a work of art reflected its times in more ways than *Dorian Gray*. It is a benchmark of Decadence in English, a key to the psychic and creative life of its author, and a mirror of the prejudices of an era that used it against its author in a court of law as evidence of his moral corruption.

We might well wish to use *Dorian Gray* to measure important cultural and social changes over the intervening years. It is necessary to remind ourselves that the novel was considered scandalous in its day by many. Wilde, eager to press the point with one eye on sales and the other on culture, insisted that his book was "poisonous but perfect," thus inflaming his critics the more. Today's sympathies are almost entirely with the author and against his critics, at least on the matter of art and morality, chronicled briefly in the following pages.

Readers who have looked into the text of the *Lippincott's* edition of the novel above will be more aware of what the fuss was all about than those who have read only the revised edition, through which the novel has been known since its publication by Ward, Lock and Company. However, even to the alerted reader, the issues and consequences of the controversy will seem disproportionate to the apparent cause, unless some of the emotional and cultural feeling of those years can be recaptured. Even American readers of *Lippincott's* gave *Dorian Gray* a far more friendly response than the London critics. In the Sunday *New York Times* for June 29, 1890, the London correspondent filed the following report on the *Dorian Gray* eruption:

> Up to the appearance of "In Darkest Africa" [Stanley's book], Oscar Wilde's novel in *Lippincott's* had monopolized the attention of Londoners who talk about books. It must have excited vastly more interest here than in America simply because since last year's exposure of what are euphemistically styled the West End scandals, Englishmen have been abnormally sensitive to the faintest suggestion of pruriency in the direction of friendships. Very likely this bestial suspicion did not cross the mind of one American reader out of ten thousand, but here the whole town leaped at it with avidity, and one moral journal called for the intervention of the Public Prosecutor. So much has been said about this phase of the book that Wilde is writing long letters to the press, not denying the imputation that his work is a study in puppydom, but insisting that such beings are more picturesque than good people.[1]

The "West End scandals" mentioned in the report received some attention in the New York press, chiefly the *Herald*, but had little to interest American readers except for the suggestion that a member of the English royal family had been mentioned in connection with "loathsome and disgusting prac-

1. *New York Times* (Sunday) June 29, 1890: 1.

tices" (one of the dysphemisms of the times for homosexuality). In the English press, however, the scandals, also referred to as the "Cleveland Street affair," nearly grew to the proportions of a Victorian Watergate, involving cover-up charges against the prime minister, Lord Salisbury, and his government; several sensational trials of telegraph boys procured for a gay brothel at 19 Cleveland Street that catered to swells and aristocrats; the scandalous involvement of Lord Arthur Somerset, a member of the Prince of Wales's household; and the rumored involvement of Prince Albert Victor ("Eddy"), eldest son of the Prince of Wales and second in line to the English throne.[2]

The most publicized of the trials arising out of the affair was a libel suit brought by Henry James Fitzroy, earl of Euston, against Ernest Parke, editor of the *North London Press*. It was tried at the Old Bailey on January 15, 1890. The guilty verdict of "libel without justification" sent Parke to prison for a year and effectively ended press coverage of the Cleveland Street affair until Labouchère's dramatic parliamentary accusations of official cover-up. On the whole, the affair had provided the press with stories of scandals in high places and degradations in low ones for about five months, carrying into March 1890, sixty days before the *Lippincott's Dorian Gray* appeared on the newsstands.

Several months before the Cleveland Street affair broke in the press, Wilde published "The Portrait of Mr. W. H." in *Blackwell's*, which contributed as much as the notoriety of the Cleveland Street affair to prejudice press critics against Wilde's aesthetic puppets. The essay offers an elegant and deliberately transparent defense of an old theory that Shakespeare's sonnets were dedicated to and written for a young actor, Willie Hughes, whose existence has never been proven. Wilde's essay is in a way a demonstration of the thesis of "The Critic as Artist" that true criticism should be creative enough to move beyond the limits of its materials to the region of artistic invention. Wilde's essay both creates and disposes of the fiction of Willy Hughes as the "Mr. W. H." to whom Shakespeare made his dedication. The Hughes theory almost perfectly explains the problem of the dedication; it is flawed only by the total absence of any evidence that Willy Hughes ever existed. The essay demonstrates in a manner deliberately paradoxical the superiority of art (in this case criticism) to life. But it was not the perverse cleverness of Wilde's argument that put his critics on notice as much as it was Wilde's espousal of a view that implied England's greatest poet was gay and, what was worse, had plenty of company among the world's geniuses.

The critics had little to say publicly on the matter of their suspicions, perhaps because Shakespeare was beyond the reach of cavil or because of the tone and manner of Wilde's witty, fictionalized scholarship. However, given the provocation of "The Portrait of Mr. W. H." and the intervening Cleveland Street scandal, it is little wonder that *Dorian Gray* produced the nearly hysterical reaction in the press that it did, especially in the *Pall Mall Gazette*, whose editor, William Stead, found muckraking and personal exposé good for circulation. To what extent Wilde expected or even counted on this reaction it is impossible to say, but he proved more than a match for his adversaries. The exchanges in the press, especially in the *St. James's Gazette*,

2. The scandal is fully discussed in H. Montgomery Hyde, *Their Good Names* (London: Hamilton, 1970); by the same author in *The Cleveland Street Scandal* (New York: Coward, 1976); and in Colin Simpson, et al., *The Cleveland Street Affair* (Boston: Little, Brown, 1976).

brought out the best of Wilde's polemical talents, as the letters in this section attest.

The criticism leveled at *Dorian Gray* stresses several points. The foremost is, of course, the morality issue, and the objection was that Wilde had published an account of male friendship that stressed inadmissable homosexual attitudes. We may openly wonder at the apparent naïveté of the Victorians and at the emotional impact Wilde's story had on so many press critics. To some extent, at least, the naïveté was an effect of the prevailing code that the way to deal with unpleasant things was to suppress any mention of them. Wilde broke that code at a time when people in the press were especially sensitive on the issue and seems to have compelled some to recognize the existence of behavior with which many of Wilde's press critics were well acquainted through practice but to which they would and could not publicly admit. To be sure, we should give the Victorian establishment its due. Wilde knew that to raise the spectre of homosexualism, however indirectly, would cause a sensation; and he said as much.

Other related charges against the morality of the story mentioned Wilde's treatment of vice and crime, the poisonous atmosphere of sin and corruption that Wilde builds up so suggestively. His defense was that this was necessary for working out Dorian's fate. Again we see in the criticism the suggestion that an author should avoid aspects of life that the Victorian middle class simply did not wish to acknowledge or think about.

The complaint that the characters are mere puppets who strike poses and converse was a criticism that Wilde himself made of the novel, along with an admission that *Dorian Gray* contained too many melodramatic incidents.[3] While he does have more changes of scene in the revised novel, the focus of the action remains London, with a brief excursion to the country estate of Selby Royal.

Two happy and important exceptions to the otherwise predictable and dreary insistence upon critical moralizing from contemporaries are included here, partly as a contrast to the art and morality debate and partly because each marks an important critical statement about the novel. The Hawthorne essay, a review of the *Lippincott's* version published in the following number, raises important issues about the novel's properties as fantasy and romance, issues that have not received the attention they deserve from subsequent critics. The Pater essay was a review of the revised, bound novel of 1891 and gives valuable insights into Wilde's intentions and practice in making his last revision of the novel. Pater was especially qualified to do this by virtue of his position as Wilde's mentor and confidant during the writing of *Dorian Gray*, and by virtue of his own powers of criticism and analysis. Although more thorough and complete studies of the novel have been produced in the intervening fourscore and ten years, Pater's review remains the best analysis of the novel.

The effect of the "art and morality" debate, as it subsequently came to be known, on Wilde's writing and life has yet to be studied in sufficient depth. However, one or two conclusions relevant to this collection may be outlined here. Certainly the debate produced the rejoinders Wilde published sepa-

---

3. The term "puppyism," used by a reviewer for the *St. James's Gazette* and by Wilde in a response, meant "affectation or excessive art in costume or posture," according to Eric Partridge, *A Dictionary of Slang and Unconventional English*, 5th ed. (New York: Macmillan, 1961) 669.

rately as "The Preface" to *Dorian Gray*, and its influence is at work both in the revised versions of the essays collected in 1891 under the title *Intentions* and in parts of "The Soul of Man under Socialism," which appeared in the *Fortnightly Review* (February 1891), the number immediately preceding that of "The Preface." The effect on Wilde's life is more difficult to assess, but his victories in the press seem to have encouraged him to live more boldly and more dangerously than he had in the past. To the extent that there is linkage, the art and morality debate and the famous defense of *Dorian Gray* at the first trial may seem to be engagements in the long war over free speech and censorship still being vigorously debated at all levels of society.

A brief account of events surrounding the trials will be useful for the contemporary reader unfamiliar with one of the juicier late Victorian scandals. The trial at which *Dorian Gray* made up the "literary part of the case" was the first of three prosecutions involving Oscar Wilde in the spring of 1895. The first trial was an action for libel brought by Wilde against the marquess of Queensberry, who had left his card at Wilde's club with the words "For Oscar Wilde posing as a somdomite [sic]" scrawled upon it. Not only was the critical word misspelled, but also the card itself had been put in an envelope by the porter and seen by no one. No action need have been taken, except that Wilde was convinced by Alfred Douglas, Queensberry's estranged son, that this was an opportunity to send his father to prison. Douglas had made a spectacle of himself both posing as and being Wilde's "boy," and Queensberry had grown more and more publicly outraged by this behavior and had threatened to make a scandal. When Wilde brought his ill-conceived charges, Queensberry pleaded justification. Although Wilde stoutly maintained the pose of one entirely innocent of the alleged libel, he was in fact guilty of a great deal more than Queensberry asserted.

Wilde had to face Edward Carson, an able criminal barrister and a former Trinity College, Dublin, classmate. Perhaps a renewal of their youthful rivalry added even more spirit to a courtroom clash that has become one of the classic duals in trial history. Although the literary phase was by no means the strong point of Carson's case, he pursued a line of questioning that raised once again the art and morality issue. Carson was determined to prove that Wilde was a corrupt person and had exercised a morally bad influence over Alfred Douglas. However, the art and morality issue was one on which Wilde was well-schooled, and he clearly got the better of the exchanges. Had the rest of the trial gone as well as Wilde's celebrated defense of his novel, he would have walked off in triumph. As it was, however, on the second day of the trial, Carson scored heavily in questioning Wilde about a series of associations with newsboys, telegraph boys, and young men identified by the police as homosexual male prostitutes. When Carson produced and began questioning these witnesses about their relations with Wilde, the jig was up. Wilde's counsel, Sir Edward Clarke, conceded justification for the libel, thereby hoping to avoid criminal prosecution against his client. That action was not long in coming. However, a decent interval was allowed for Wilde to follow the example of Lord Arthur Somerset of Cleveland Street fame and leave the country. Everyone held his breath; but instead of "levanting," as it was called, Wilde stayed in a room at the Cadogen Hotel and awaited martyrdom in a nearly paralyzed state of indecision and apprehension. Two trials followed, the first ending in a hung jury, the second in conviction, which sent Wilde away for two years at hard labor.

The cost of the Queensbury trial ruined Wilde financially, and the conviction and imprisonment destroyed him socially and as a writer. Wilde's genius flourished in society but withered in prison and died during his continental exile, plagued as he was by poverty and ill health and haunted by the specter of his ruined life. And yet a sympathetic observer cannot help but conclude that Wilde had blindly reached toward a stage of self-development that would raise him above the sordidness of his own life, and he found it in suffering. He died in Paris as the century ended, in November 1900.

ST. JAMES'S GAZETTE

A Study in Puppydom
(June 24, 1890)†

Time was (it was in the '70's) when we talked about Mr Oscar Wilde; time came (it came in the '80's) when he tried to write poetry and, more adventurous, we tried to read it;[1] time is when we had forgotten him, or only remember him as the late editor of *The Woman's World*[2]—a part for which he was singularly unfitted, if we are to judge him by the work which he has been allowed to publish in *Lippincott's Magazine* and which Messrs Ward, Lock & Co. have not been ashamed to circulate in Great Britain. Not being curious in ordure, and not wishing to offend the nostrils of decent persons, we do not propose to analyse "The Picture of Dorian Gray": that would be to advertise the developments of an esoteric prurience. Whether the Treasury or the Vigilance Society will think it worth while to prosecute Mr Oscar Wilde or Messrs Ward, Lock & Co., we do not know; but on the whole we hope they will not.

The puzzle is that a young man of decent parts, who enjoyed (when he was at Oxford)[3] the opportunity of associating with gentlemen, should put his name (such as it is) to so stupid and vulgar a piece of work. Let nobody read it in the hope of finding witty paradox or racy wickedness. The writer airs his cheap research among the garbage of the French *Décadents* like any drivelling pedant, and he bores you unmercifully with his prosy rigmaroles about the beauty of the Body and the corruption of the Soul. The grammar is better than Ouida's; the erudition equal; but in every other respect we prefer the talented lady who broke off with "pious aposiopesis" when she touched upon "the horrors which

†From Stuart Mason (pseud. Christopher Sclater Millard, 1872–1927), *Oscar Wilde: Art and Morality* (1912; New York: Haskell House, 1971) 27–34. All notes are Mason's.
1. His "Poems," published by David Bogue in 1881 at 10s. 6d., went through five editions within a year.

2. Wilde edited this publication for Messrs Cassell from 1887–89.
3. Wilde was a demy of Magdalen College, 1874–78.

are described in the pages of Suetonius and Livy"—not to mention the yet worse infamies believed by many scholars to be accurately portrayed in the lost works of Plutarch, Venus, and Nicodemus, especially Nicodemus.

Let us take one peep at the young men in Mr Oscar Wilde's story. Puppy No. 1 is the painter of the picture of Dorian Gray; Puppy No. 2 is the critic (a courtesy lord, skilled in all the knowledge of the Egyptians and aweary of all the sins and pleasures of London); Puppy No. 3 is the original, cultivated by Puppy No. 1 with a "romantic friendship." The Puppies fall a-talking: Puppy No. 1 about his Art, Puppy No. 2 about his sins and pleasures and the pleasures of sin, and Puppy No. 3 about himself—always about himself, and generally about his face, which is "brainless and beautiful." The Puppies appear to fill up the intervals of talk by plucking daisies and playing with them, and sometimes by drinking "something with strawberry in it." The youngest Puppy is told that he is charming; but he mustn't sit in the sun for fear of spoiling his complexion. When he is rebuked for being a naughty, wilful boy, he makes a pretty *moue*—this man of twenty! This is how he is addressed by the Blasé Puppy at their first meeting:

"Yes, Mr. Gray, the gods have been good to you. But what the gods give they quickly take away. . . . When your youth goes, your beauty will go with it, and then you will suddenly discover that there are no triumphs left for you. . . . Time is jealous of you, and wars against your lilies and roses. You will become sallow, and hollow-cheeked, and dull-eyed. You will suffer horribly."

Why, bless our souls! haven't we read something of this kind somewhere in the classics? Yes, of course we have! But in what recondite author? Ah—yes—no—yes, it *was* in Horace! What an advantage it is to have received a classical education! And how it will astonish the Yankees! But we must not forget our Puppies, who have probably occupied their time in lapping "something with strawberry in it." Puppy No. 1 (the Art Puppy) has been telling Puppy No. 3 (the Doll Puppy) how much he admires him. What is the answer? "I am less to you than your ivory Hermes or your silver Faun. You will like them always. How long will you like me? Till I have my first wrinkle, I suppose. I know now that when one loses one's good looks, whatever they may be, one loses everything. . . . I am jealous of the portrait you have painted of me. Why should it keep what I must lose? . . . Oh, if it was only the other way! If the picture could only change, and I could be always what I am now!"

No sooner said than done! The picture *does* change: the original doesn't. Here's a situation for you! Théophile Gautier could have made it romantic, entrancing, beautiful. Mr Stevenson could have made it convincing, humorous, pathetic. Mr Anstey could have made it screamingly funny. It has been reserved for Mr Oscar Wilde to make it dull and nasty. The promising youth plunges into every kind of mean depravity, and ends in being "cut" by fast women and vicious men. He finishes with murder: the New Voluptuousness always leads up to blood-shedding—that is part of the cant. The gore and gashes wherein Mr Rider Haggard takes a chaste delight are the natural diet for a cultivated palate which is tired of mere licentiousness. And every wickedness or filthiness committed by Dorian Gray is faithfully registered upon his face in the picture; but his living features are undisturbed and unmarred by his inward vileness. This is the story which Mr Oscar Wilde has tried to tell; a very lame story it is, and very lamely it is told.

Why has he told it? There are two explanations; and, so far as we can see, not more than two. Not to give pleasure to his readers: the thing is too clumsy, too tedious, and—alas! that we should say it—too stupid. Perhaps it was to shock his readers, in order that they might cry Fie! upon him and talk about him, much as Mr Grant Allen recently tried in *The Universal Review* to arouse, by a licentious theory of the sexual relations, an attention which is refused to his popular chatter about other men's science. Are we then to suppose that Mr Oscar Wilde has yielded to the craving for a notoriety which he once earned by talking fiddle-faddle about other men's art, and sees his only chance of recalling it by making himself obvious at the cost of being obnoxious, and by attracting the notice which the olfactory sense cannot refuse to the presence of certain self-asserting organisms? That is an uncharitable hypothesis, and we would gladly abandon it. It may be suggested (but is it more charitable?) that he derives pleasure from treating a subject merely because it is disgusting. The phenomenon is not unknown in recent literature; and it takes two forms, in appearance widely separate—in fact, two branches from the same root, a root which draws its life from malodorous putrefaction. One development is found in the Puritan prurience which produced Tolstoy's "Kreutzer Sonata" and Mr Stead's famous outbursts.[4] That is odious enough and mischievous enough, and it is rightly execrated, because it is tainted with an hypocrisy not the less culpable because charitable persons may believe it to be unconscious. But is it more odious or more mischievous than the "frank Paganism" (that is the word, is it not?) which delights in dirtiness and confesses its delight? Still they are both chips from the same block—"The Maiden Tribute of Modern Babylon"[5] and "The Picture of Dorian Gray"—and both of them ought to be chucked into the fire. Not so much because they are dangerous and corrupt (they are corrupt but not dangerous) as because they are incurably silly, written by simpleton *poseurs* (whether they call themselves Puritan or Pagan) who know nothing about the life which they affect to have explored, and because they are mere catchpenny relevations of the non-existent, which, if they reveal anything at all, are revelations only of the singularly unpleasant minds from which they emerge.

---

4. In the *Pall Mall Gazette*.   5. *Pall Mall Gazette*, July 6–10, 1885.

OSCAR WILDE

To the Editor of the *St. James's Gazette* †

25 June [1890]   16 Tite Street

Sir, I have read your criticism of my story, *The Picture of Dorian Gray*, and I need hardly say that I do not propose to discuss its merits or demerits, its personalities or its lack of personality. England is a free country, and ordinary English criticism is perfectly free and easy. Besides, I must admit admit that, either from temperament or from taste, or from both, I am quite incapable of understanding how any work of art can be criticised from a moral standpoint. The sphere of art and the sphere of ethics are absolutely distinct and separate; and it is to the confusion between the two that we owe the appearance of Mrs Grundy, that amusing old lady who represents the only original form of humour that the middle classes of this country have been able to produce. What I do object to most strongly is that you should have placarded the town with posters on which was printed in large letters: MR OSCAR WILDE'S LATEST ADVERTISEMENT; A BAD CASE.

Whether the expression "A Bad Case" refers to my book or to the present position of the Government, I cannot tell. What was silly and unnecessary was the use of the term "advertisement."

I think I may say without vanity—though I do not wish to appear to run vanity down—that of all men in England I am the one who requires least advertisement. I am tired to death of being advertised. I feel no thrill when I see my name in a paper. The chronicler does not interest me any more. I wrote this book entirely for my own pleasure, and it gave me very great pleasure to write it. Whether it becomes popular or not is a matter of absolute indifference to me. I am afraid, sir, that the real advertisement is your cleverly written article. The English public, as a mass, takes no interest in a work of art until it is told that the work in question is immoral, and your *réclame* will, I have no doubt, largely increase the sale of the magazine; in which sale, I may mention with some regret, I have no pecuniary interest.

I remain, sir, your obedient servant   OSCAR WILDE

---

† [The text of this selection is printed in full from *The Letters of Oscar Wilde*, ed. Rupert Hart-Davis (London: Hart-Davis; New York: Harcourt, 1962) 257.] Sidney James Mark Low (1857–1932, knighted 1918) was editor of the *St James's Gazette* 1888–97. Wilde's only novel, *The Picture of Dorian Gray*, was first published on 20 June 1890, in the July number of *Lippincott's Monthly Magazine*, where it occupied pp. 3–100. It was extensively reviewed. The *St James's Gazette* printed a scurrilous notice on 24 June, under the heading "A Study in Puppydom." Its anonymous author was Samuel Henry Jeyes (1857–1911). The full text of all the important reviews of, and letters about, *Dorian Gray* is given in Stuart Mason's *Art and Morality* (1912). This letter of Wilde's was published on 26 June, under the heading MR OSCAR WILDE'S "BAD CASE."

ST. JAMES'S GAZETTE

Editorial Note
(June 25, 1890) †

In the preceding column will be found the best reply which Mr Oscar Wilde can make to our recent criticism of his mawkish and nauseous story, "The Picture of Dorian Gray." Mr Wilde tells us that he is constitutionally unable to understand how any work of art can be criticised from a moral standpoint. We were quite aware that ethics and æsthetics are different matters, and that is why the greater part of our criticism was devoted not so much to the nastiness of "The Picture of Dorian Gray," but to its dulness and stupidity. Mr Wilde pretends that we have advertised it. So we have, if any readers are attracted to a book which, we have warned them, will bore them insufferably.

That the story is corrupt cannot be denied; but we added, and assuredly believe, that it is not dangerous, because, as we said, it is tedious and stupid.

Mr Wilde tells us that he wrote the story for his own pleasure, and found great pleasure in writing it. We congratulate him; there is no triumph more precious to your "æsthete" than the discovery of a delight which outsiders cannot share or even understand. The author of "The Picture of Dorian Gray" is the only person likely to find pleasure in it.

OSCAR WILDE

To the Editor of the *St. James's Gazette* ‡

26 June [1890]   *16 Tite Street*

In your issue of today you state that my brief letter published in your columns is the "best reply" I can make to your article upon *Dorian Gray*. This is not so. I do not propose to fully discuss the matter here, but I feel bound to say that your article contains the most unjustifiable attack that has been made upon any man of letters for many years. The writer of it, who is quite incapable of concealing his personal malice, and so in some measure destroys the effect he wishes to produce, seems not to have the slightest idea of the temper in which a work of art should be approached. To say that such a book as mine should be "chucked

†From Stuart Mason, *Oscar Wilde: Art and Morality* (1912; New York: Haskell House, 1971) 37–38.

‡ [The text of this selection is printed in full from *The Letters of Oscar Wilde*, ed. Rupert Hart-Davis

(London: Hart Davis; New York: Harcourt, 1962) 258–59.] The editorial note which accompanied Wilde's letter of the 25th was so offensive that it called forth this further letter, which appeared on the 27th, under the heading MR OSCAR WILDE AGAIN.

into the fire" is silly. That is what one does with newspapers.

Of the value of pseudo-ethical criticism in dealing with artistic work I have spoken already. But as your writer has ventured into the perilous grounds of literacy criticism I ask you to allow me, in fairness not merely to myself but to all men to whom literature is a fine art, to say a few words about his critical method.

He begins by assailing me with much ridiculous virulence because the chief personages in my story are "puppies." They *are* puppies. Does he think that literature went to the dogs when Thackeray wrote about puppydom? I think that puppies are extremely interesting from an artistic as well as from a psychological point of view. They seem to me to be certainly far more interesting than prigs; and I am of opinion that Lord Henry Wotton is an excellent corrective of the tedious ideal shadowed forth in the semi-theological novels of our age.

He then makes vague and fearful insinuations about my grammar and my erudition. Now, as regards grammar, I hold that, in prose at any rate, correctness should always be subordinate to artistic effect and musical cadence; and any pecularities of syntax that may occur in *Dorian Gray* are deliberately intended, and are introduced to show the value of the artistic theory in question. Your writer gives no instance of any such peculiarity. This I regret, because I do not think that any such instances occur.

As regards crudition, it is always difficult, even for the most modest of us, to remember that other people do not know quite as much as one does oneself. I myself frankly admit I cannot imagine how a casual reference to Suetonius and Petronius Arbiter can be construed into evidence of a desire to impress an unoffending and ill-educated public by an assumption of superior knowledge. I should fancy that the most ordinary of scholars is perfectly well acquainted with the *Lives of the Caesars* and with the *Satyricon*. The *Lives of the Caesars*, at any rate, forms part of the curriculum at Oxford for those who take the Honour School of *Literæ Humaniores*; and as for the *Satyricon*, it is popular even among passmen, though I suppose they are obliged to read it in translations.

The writer of the article then suggests that I, in common with that great noble artist Count Tolstoi, take pleasure in a subject because it is dangerous. About such a suggestion there is this to be said. Romantic art deals with the exception and with the individual. Good people, belonging as they do to the normal, and so, commonplace, type, are artistically uninteresting. Bad people are, from the point of view of art, fascinating studies. They represent colour, variety and strangeness. Good people exasperate one's reason; bad people stir one's imagination. Your critic, if I must give him so honourable a title, states that the people in my story have no counterpart in life; that they are, to use his vigorous if somewhat vulgar phrase, "mere catchpenny revelations of the non-existent." Quite so. If they existed they would not be worth writing about. The function of the artist is to invent, not to chronicle. There are no such people. If there were I would not write about them. Life by its realism is always spoiling the subject-matter of art. The supreme pleasure in literature is to realise the non-existent.

And finally, let me say this. You have reproduced, in a journalistic form, the comedy of *Much Ado about Nothing*, and have, of course, spoilt it in your reproduction. The poor public, hearing, from an authority so high as your own, that this is a wicked book that should be coerced and suppressed by a Tory Government, will, no doubt, rush to it and read it. But, alas! they will find that it is a story with a moral. And the moral is this: All excess, as well as all renunciation, brings its own punishment. The painter, Basil Hallward, worshipping physical beauty far too much, as most painters do, dies by the hand of one in whose soul he has created a monstrous and absurd vanity. Dorian Gray, having led a life of mere sensation and pleasure, tries to kill conscience, and at that moment kills himself. Lord Henry Wotton seeks to be merely the spectator of life. He finds that those who reject the battle are more deeply wounded than those who take part in it. Yes; there is a terrible moral in *Dorian Gray*—a moral which the prurient will not be able to find in it, but which will be revealed to all whose minds are healthy. Is this an artistic error? I fear it is. It is the only error in the book. OSCAR WILDE

ST. JAMES'S GAZETTE

Editorial Note
(June 26, 1890)†

Mr Oscar Wilde may perhaps be excused for being angry at the remarks which we allowed ourselves to make concerning his "moral tale" of the Three Puppies and the Magic Picture; but he should not misrepresent us. He says we suggested that his novel was a "wicked book which should be coerced and suppressed by a Tory Government." We did nothing of the kind. The authors of books of much less questionable character have been proceeded against by the Treasury or the Vigilance Society; but we expressly said that we hope Mr Wilde's masterpiece would be left alone.

Then, Mr Wilde (like any young lady who has published her first novel "at the request of numerous friends") falls back on the theory of the critic's "personal malice." This is unworthy of so experienced a literary gentleman. We can assure Mr Wilde that the writer of that article had, and has, no "personal malice" or personal feeling towards him. We can surely censure a work which we believe to be silly, and know to be offensive, without the imputation of malice—especially when that book is written by one who is so clearly capable of better things.

† From Stuart Mason, *Oscar Wilde: Art and Morality* (1912; New York: Haskell House, 1971) 44–46.

As for the critical question, Mr Wilde is beating the air when he defends idealism and "romantic art" in literature. In the words of Mrs Harris to Mrs Gamp, "Who's a-deniging of it?"

Heaven forbid that we should refuse to an author the "supreme pleasure of realising the nonexistent"; or that we should judge the "æsthetic" from the purely "ethical" standpoint.

No; our criticism starts from lower ground. Mr Wilde says that his story is a moral tale, because the wicked persons in it come to a bad end. We will not be so rude as to quote a certain remark about morality which one Mr Charles Surface made to Mr Joseph Surface. We simply say that every critic has the right to point out that a work of art or literature is dull and incompetent in its treatment—as "The Picture of Dorian Gray" is; and that its dulness and incompetence are not redeemed because it constantly hints, not obscurely, at disgusting sins and abominable crimes— as "The Picture of Dorian Gray" does.

OSCAR WILDE

To the Editor of the *St. James's Gazette* †

27 June [1890]   16 Tite Street

Sir, As you still keep up, though in a somewhat milder form than before your attacks on me and my book, you not merely confer on me the right but you impose upon me the duty, of reply.

You state, in your issue of today, that I misrepresented you when I said that you suggested that a book so wicked as mine should be "suppressed and coerced by a Tory Government." Now you did not propose this, but you did suggest it. When you declare that you do not know whether or not the Government will take action about my book, and remark that the authors of books much less wicked have been proceeded against in law, the suggestion is quite obvious. In your complaint of misrepresentation you seem to me, sir, to have been not quite candid. However, as far as I am concerned, the suggestion is of no importance. What is of importance is that the editor of a paper like yours should appear to countenance the monstrous theory that the Government of a country should exercise a censorship over imaginative literature. This is a theory against which I, and all men of letters of my acquaintance, protest most strongly; and any critic who admits the reasonableness of such a theory shows at once that he is quite incapable of understanding what literature is, and what are the rights that literature possess. A Gov-

† [The text of this selection is printed in full from *The Letters of Oscar Wilde*, ed. Rupert Hart-Davis (London: Hart-Davis; New York: Harcourt, 1962) 259–61.] Once again the editor of the *St James's* *Gazette* had added an abusive note to Wilde's previous letter. This one appeared on 28 June, under the heading MR OSCAR WILDE'S DEFENCE.

ernment might just as well try to teach painters how to paint, or sculptors how to model, as attempt to interfere with the style, treatment and subject-matter of the literary artist; and no writer, however eminent or obscure, should ever give his sanction to a theory that would degrade literature far more than any didactic or so-called immoral book could possibly do.

You then express your surprise that "so experienced a literary gentleman" as myself should imagine that your critic was animated by any feeling of personal malice towards him. The phrase "literary gentleman" is a vile phrase; but let that pass. I accept quite readily your assurance that your critic was simply criticising a work of art in the best way that he could; but I feel that I was fully justified in forming the opinion of him that I did. He opened his article by a gross personal attack on myself. This, I need hardly say, was an absolutely unpardonable error of critical taste. There is no excuse for it, except personal malice; and you, sir, should not have sanctioned it. A critic should be taught to criticise a work of art without making any reference to the personality of the author. This, in fact, is the beginning of criticism. However, it was not merely his personal attack on me that made me imagine that he was actuated by malice. What really confirmed me in my first impression was his reiterated assertion that my book was tedious and dull. Now, if I were criticising my book, which I have some thoughts of doing, I think I would consider it my duty to point out that it is far too crowded with sensational incident, and far too paradoxical in style, as far, at any rate, as the dialogue goes. I feel that from a standpoint of art these are two defects in the book. But tedious and dull the book is not. Your critic has cleared himself of the charge of personal malice, his denial and yours being quite sufficient in the manner; but he has only done so by a tacit admission that he has really no critical instinct about literature and literary work, which, in one who writes about literature, is, I need hardly say, a much graver fault than malice of any kind.

Finally, sir, allow me to say this. Such an article as you have published really makes one despair of the possibility of any general culture in England. Were I a French author, and my book brought out in Paris, there is not a single literary critic in France, on any paper of higher standing, who would think for a moment of criticising it from an ethical standpoint. If he did so, he would stultify himself, not merely in the eyes of all men of letters, but in the eyes of the majority of the public. You have yourself often spoken against Puritanism. Believe me, sir, Puritanism is never so offensive and destructive as when it deals with art matters. It is there that its influence is radically wrong. It is this Puritanism, to which your critic has given expression, that is always marring the artistic instinct of the English. So far from encouraging it, you should set yourself against it, and should try to teach your critics to recognise the essential difference between art and life. The gentleman who criticised my book is in a perfectly hopeless confusion about it, and your attempt to help him out by proposing that the subject-matter of art should be limited does not mend matters. It is proper that limitations should be placed on action. It is not proper that limitations should be placed on art. To art belong all things that are and all things that are not, and even the editor of a London paper has no right to restrain the freedom of art in the selection of subject-matter.

I now trust, sir, that these attacks on me and on my book will cease. There are forms of advertisement that are unwarranted and unwarrantable.

I am, sir, your obedient servant.   OSCAR WILDE

ST. JAMES'S GAZETTE

Editorial Note
(September 24, 1890) †

Mr Oscar Wilde has explained. We know now how "Dorian Gray" came to be written. In 1887, about the genial season of Christmas, a Canadian lady artist[1] yearned to transfer to the glowing canvas the classic features of Mr Oscar Wilde. Mr Wilde gave her a sitting. When the sitting was over and Mr Wilde had looked at the portrait, it occurred to him that a thing of beauty, when it takes the form of a middle-aged gentleman, is unhappily not a joy for ever. "What a tragic thing it is," he exclaimed. "This portrait will never grow older, and I shall. If," he added, "if it was only the other way." Then the passion of his soul sought refuge in prose composition, and the result was "Dorian Gray." No wonder Mr Wilde didn't like it when we hinted that this great work was a study of puppydom, and its hero himself a puppy of an unpleasant kind.

DAILY CHRONICLE

Review
(June 30, 1890) †

Dulness and dirt are the chief features of *Lippincott's* this month. The element in it that is unclean, though undeniably amusing, is furnished by Mr Oscar Wilde's story of "The Picture of Dorian Gray." It is a tale

†From Stuart Mason, *Oscar Wilde: Art and Morality* (1912; New York: Haskell House, 1971) 63.
1. Miss Frances Richards, a pupil of Carolus Durand.

†From Stuart Mason, *Oscar Wilde: Art and Morality* (1912; New York: Haskell House, 1971) 65–69.

spawned from the leprous literature of the French *Décadents*—a poisonous book, the atmosphere of which is heavy with the mephitic odours of moral and spiritual putrefaction—a gloating study of the mental and physical corruption of a fresh, fair and golden youth, which might be horrible and fascinating but for its effeminate frivolity, its studied insincerity, its theatrical cynicism, its tawdry mysticism, its flippant philosophisings, and the contaminating trail of garish vulgarity which is over all Mr Wilde's elaborate Wardour Street æstheticism and obtrusively cheap scholarship.

Mr Wilde says his book has "a moral." The "moral," so far as we can collect it, is that man's chief end is to develop his nature to the fullest by "always searching for new sensations," that when the soul gets sick the way to cure it is to deny the senses nothing, for "nothing," says one of Mr Wilde's characters, Lord Henry Wotton, "can cure the soul but the senses, just as nothing can cure the senses but the soul." Man is half angel and half ape, and Mr Wilde's book has no real use if it be not to inculcate the "moral" that when you feel yourself becoming too angelic you cannot do better than to rush out and make a beast of yourself. There is not a single good and holy impulse of human nature, scarcely a fine feeling or instinct that civilisation, art, and religion have developed throughout the ages as part of the barriers between Humanity and Animalism that is not held up to ridicule and contempt in "Dorian Gray," if, indeed, such strong words can be fitly applied to the actual effect of Mr Wilde's airy levity and fluent impudence. His desperate effort to vamp up a "moral" for the book at the end is, artistically speaking, coarse and crude, because the whole incident of Dorian Gray's death is, as they say on the stage, "out of the picture." Dorian's only regret is that unbridled indulgence in every form of secret and unspeakable vice, every resource of luxury and art, and sometimes still more piquant to the jaded young man of fashion, whose lives "Dorian Gray" pretends to sketch, by every abomination of vulgarity and squalor is—what? Why, that it will leave traces of premature age and loathsome sensualness on his pretty facy, rosy with the loveliness that endeared youth of his odious type to the paralytic patricians of the Lower Empire.

Dorian Gray prays that a portrait of himself which an artist, who raves about him as young men do about the women they love not wisely but too well, has painted may grow old instead of the original. This is what happens by some supernatural agency, the introduction of which seems purely farcical, so that Dorian goes on enjoying unfading youth year after year, and might go on for ever using his senses with impunity "to cure his soul," defiling English society with the moral pestilence which is incarnate in him, but for one thing. That is his sudden impulse not merely to murder the painter—which might be artistically defended on the plea that it is only a fresh development of his scheme for realising every phase of life-experience—but to rip up the canvas in a rage, merely because, though he had permitted himself to do one good action, it had not made his portrait less hideous. But all this is inconsistent with Dorian Gray's cool, calculating, conscienceless character, evolved logically enough by Mr Wilde's "New Hedonism."

Then Mr Wilde finishes his story by saying that on hearing a heavy fall Dorian Gray's servants rushed in, found the portrait on the wall as youthful looking as ever, its senile ugliness being transferred to the foul profligate himself, who is lying on the floor stabbed to the heart. This is a sham moral, as indeed everything in the book is a sham, except the one element in the book which will taint every young mind that comes in contact with it. That element is shockingly real, and it is the plausibly insinuated defence of the creed that appeals to the senses "to cure the soul" whenever the spiritual nature of man suffers from too much purity and self-denial.

The rest of this number of *Lippincott* consists of articles of harmless padding.

OSCAR WILDE

To the Editor of the *Daily Chronicle* †

30 June [1890]   *16 Tite Street*

Sir, Will you allow me to correct some errors into which your critic has fallen in his review of my story, *The Picture of Dorian Gray*, published in today's issue of your paper?

Your critic states, to begin with, that I make desperate attempts to "vamp up" a moral in my story. Now, I must candidly confess that I do not know what "vamping" is. I see, from time to time, mysterious advertisements in the newspapers about "How to Vamp," but what vamping really means remains a mystery to me—a mystery that, like all other mysteries, I hope some day to explore.

However, I do not propose to discuss the absurd terms used by modern journalism. What I want to say is that, so far from wishing to emphasise any moral in my story, the real trouble I experienced in writing the story was that of keeping the extremely obvious moral subordinate to the artistic and dramatic effect.

When I first conceived the idea of a young man selling his soul in exchange for eternal youth—an idea that is old in the history of literature, but to which I have given new form—I felt that, from an aesthetic point of view, it would be difficult to keep the moral in its proper secondary place; and even now I do not feel quite sure that I have been able

† The text of this selection is printed in full from *The Letters of Oscar Wilde*, ed. Rupert Hart-Davis (London: Hart-Davis; New York: Harcourt, 1962) 265–67.

to do so. I think the moral too apparent. When the book is published in a volume I hope to correct this defect.

As for what the moral is, your critic states that it is this—that when a man feels himself becoming "too angelic" he should rush out and make a "beast of himself!" I cannot say that I consider this a moral. The real moral of the story is that all excess, as well as all renunciation, brings its punishment, and this moral is so far artistically and deliberately suppressed that it does not enunciate its law as a general principle, but realises itself purely in the lives of individuals, and so becomes simply a dramatic element in a work of art, and not the object of the work of art itself.

Your critic also falls into error when he says that Dorian Gray, having a "cool, calculating, conscienceless character," was inconsistent when he destroyed the picture of his own soul, on the ground that the picture did not become less hideous after he had done what, in his vanity, he had considered his first good action. Dorian Gray has not got a cool, calculating, conscienceless character at all. On the contrary, he is extremely impulsive, absurdly romantic, and is haunted all through his life by an exaggerated sense of conscience which mars his pleasures for him and warns him that youth and enjoyment are not everything in the world. It is finally to get rid of the conscience that had dogged his steps from year to year that he destroys the picture; and thus in his attempt to kill conscience Dorian Gray kills himself.

Your critic then talks about "obtrusively cheap scholarship." Now, whatever a scholar writes is sure to display scholarship in the distinction of style and the fine use of language; but my story contains no learned or pseudo-learned discussions, and the only literary books that it alludes to are books that any fairly educated reader may be supposed to be acquainted with, such as the *Satyricon* of Petronius Arbiter, or Gautier's *Émaux et Camées*. Such books as Alphonso's *Clericalis Disciplina* belong not to culture, but to curiosity. Anybody may be excused for not knowing them.

Finally, let me say this—the aesthetic movement produced certain colours, subtle in their loveliness and fascinating in their almost mystical tone. They were, and are, our reaction against the crude primaries of a doubtless more respectable but certainly less cultivated age. My story is an essay on decorative art. It reacts against the crude brutality of plain realism. It is poisonous if you like, but you cannot deny that it is also perfect, and perfection is what we artists aim at.

I remain, sir, your obedient servant   OSCAR WILDE

SCOTS OBSERVER

From "Reviews and Magazines"
(July 5, 1890) †

Why go grubbing in much heaps? The world is fair, and the proportion of healthy-minded men and honest women to those that are foul,
fallen, or unnatural is great. Mr Oscar Wilde has again been writing
stuff that were better unwritten; and while "The Picture of Dorian Gray,"
which he contributes to *Lippincott's*, is ingenious, interesting, full of
cleverness, and plainly the work of a man of letters, it is false art—for its
interest is medico-legal; it is false to human nature—for its hero is a
devil; it is false to morality—for it is not made sufficiently clear that the
writer does not prefer a course of unnatural iniquity to a life of cleanli-
ness, health, and sanity. The story—which deals with matters only fitted
for the Criminal Investigation Department or a hearing *in camera*—is
discreditable alike to author and editor. Mr Wilde has brains, and art,
and style; but if he can write for none but outlawed noblemen and perverted telegraph-boys, the sooner he takes to tailoring (or some other
decent trade) the better for his own reputation and the public morals.

OSCAR WILDE

To the Editor of the *Scots Observer* ‡

9 July 1890   *16 Tite Street, Chelsea*

Sir, You have published a review of my story, *The Picture of Dorian
Gray*. As this review is grossly unjust to me as an artist, I ask you to
allow me to exercise in your columns my right of reply.

                    *   *   *

Your reviewer, sir, while admitting that the story in question is "plainly
the work of a man of letters," the work of one who has "brains, and art,
and style," yet suggests, and apparently in all seriousness, that I have
written it in order that it should be read by the most depraved members
of the criminal and illiterate classes. Now, sir, I do not suppose that the

---

† From Stuart Mason, *Oscar Wilde: Art and
Morality* (1912; New York: Haskell House, 1971)
75–76.
‡ [The text of this selection is printed in full from
The Letters of Oscar Wilde, ed. Rupert Hart-Davis
(London: Hart-Davis); New York: Harcourt, 1962)
265–67.] The *Scots Observer's* anonymous notice
of *Dorian Gray* on 5 July was for long thought to

have been written by W. E. Henley, the paper's
editor; the author was in fact his henchman Charles
Whibley (1860–1930). The outlawed nobleman
and perverted telegraph-boys refer to Lord Arthur
Somerset and the Cleveland Street scandal of 1889.
This letter of Wilde's appeared on 12 July, under
the heading MR WILDE'S REJOINDER. It was reprinted
in *Miscellanies*.

criminal and illiterate classes ever read anything except newspapers. They are certainly not likely to be able to understand anything of mine. So let them pass, and on the broad question of why a man of letters writes at all let me say this. The pleasure that one has in creating a work of art is a purely personal pleasure, and it is for the sake of this pleasure that one creates. The artist works with his eye on the object. Nothing else interests him. What people are likely to say does not even occur to him. He is fascinated by what he has in hand. He is indifferent to others. I write because it gives me the greatest possible artistic pleasure to write. If my work pleases the few, I am gratified. If it does not, it causes me no pain. As for the mob, I have no desire to be a popular novelist. It is far too easy.

Your critic then, sir, commits the absolutely unpardonable crime of trying to confuse the artist with his subject-matter. For this, sir, there is no excuse at all. Of one who is the greatest figure in the world's literature since Greek days Keats remarked that he had as much pleasure in conceiving the evil as he had in conceiving the good.[1] Let your reviewer, sir, consider the bearings of Keats's fine criticism, for it is under these conditions that every artist works. One stands remote from one's subject-matter. One creates it, and one contemplates it. The further away the subject-matter is, the more freely can the artist work. Your reviewer suggests that I do not make it sufficiently clear whether I prefer virtue to wickedness or wickedness to virtue. An artist, sir, has no ethical sympathies at all. Virtue and wickedness are to him simply what the colours on his palette are to the painter. They are no more, and they are no less. He sees that by their means a certain artistic effect can be produced, and he produces it. Iago may be morally horrible and Imogen stainlessly pure. Shakespeare, as Keats said, had as much delight in creating the one as he had in creating the other.

It was necessary, sir, for the dramatic development of this story to surround Dorian Gray with an atmosphere of moral corruption. Otherwise the story would have had no meaning and the plot no issue. to keep this atmosphere vague and indeterminate and wonderful was the aim of the artist who wrote the story. I claim, sir, that he has succeeded. Each man sees his own sin in Dorian Gray. What Dorian Gray's sins are no one knows. He who finds them has brought them.

In conclusion, sir, let me say how really deeply I regret that you should have permitted such a notice as the one I feel constrained to write on to have appeared in your paper. That the editor of the *St James's Gazette* should have employed Caliban as his art-critic was possibly natural. The editor of the *Scots Observer* should not have allowed Thersites to make mows in his review. It is unworthy of so distinguished a man of letters. I am, etc.   OSCAR WILDE

1. "The poetical character . . . has as much delight in conceiving an Iago as an Imogen. What shocks the virtuous philosopher delights the cameleon poet." John Keats to Richard Woodhouse, 27 October 1818.

JULIAN HAWTHORNE

The Romance of the Impossible †

Fiction, which flies at all game, has latterly taken to the Impossible as its quarry. The pursuit is interesting and edifying, if one goes properly equipped, and with adequate skill. But if due care is not exercised, the Impossible turns upon the hunter and grinds him to powder. It is a very dangerous and treacherous kind of wild-fowl. The conditions of its existence—if existence can be predicted of that which does not exist—are so peculiar and abstruse that only genius is really capable of taming it and leading it captive. But the capture, when it is made, is so delightful and fascinating that every tyro would like to try. One is reminded of the princess of the fairy tale, who was to be won on certain preposterous terms, and if the terms were not met, the discomfited suitor lost his head. Many misguided or overweening youths perished; at last the One succeeded. Failure in a romance of the Impossible is apt to be a disastrous failure; on the other hand, success carries great rewards.

Of course, the idea is not a new one. The writings of the alchemists are stories of the Impossible. The fashion has never been entirely extinct. Balzac wrote the "Peau de Chagrin," and probably this tale is as good a one as was ever written of that kind. The possessor of the Skin may have everything he wishes for; but each wish causes the Skin to shrink, and when it is all gone the wisher is annihilated with it. By the art of the writer this impossible thing is made to appear quite feasible; by touching the chords of coincidence and fatality, the reader's common sense is soothed to sleep. We feel that all this might be, and yet no natural law be violated; and yet we know that such a thing never was and never will be. But the vitality of the story, as of all good stories of the sort, is due to the fact that it is the symbol of a spiritual verity: the life of indulgence, the selfish life, destroys the soul. This psychic truth is so deeply felt that its sensible embodiment is rendered plausible. In the case of another famous romance—"Frankenstein"—the technical art is entirely wanting: a worse story, from the literary point of view, has seldom been written. But the soul of it, so to speak, is so potent and obvious that, although no one actually reads the book nowadays, everybody knows the gist of the idea. "Frankenstein" has entered into the language, for it utters a perpetual truth of human nature.

At the present moment, the most conspicuous success in the line we are considering is Stevenson's "Dr Jekyll and Mr Hyde." The author's literary skill, in that awful little parable, is at its best, and makes the most of every point. To my thinking, it is an artistic mistake to describe

†From Stuart Mason, *Oscar Wilde: Art and Morality* (1912; New York: Haskell House, 1971) 175–85. This essay review of *Dorian Gray* by Julian Hawthorne (son of the American novelist Nathaniel Hawthorne) appeared in *Lippincott's Magazine* in September 1890.

Hyde's transformation as actually taking place in plain sight of the audience; the sense of spiritual mystery is thereby lost, and a mere brute miracle takes its place. But the tale is strong enough to carry this imperfection, and the moral significance of it is so catholic—it so comes home to every soul that considers it—that it has already made an ineffaceable impression on the public mind. Every man is his own Jekyll and Hyde, only without the magic powder. On the bookshelf of the Impossible, Mr Stevenson's book may take its place beside Balzac's.

Mr Oscar Wilde, the apostle of beauty, has in the July number of *Lippincott's Magazine* a novel or romance (it partakes of the qualities of both), which everybody will want to read. It is a story strange in conception, strong in interest, and fitted with a tragic and ghastly climax. Like many stories of its class, it is open to more than one interpretation; and there are, doubtless, critics who will deny that it has any meaning at all. It is, at all events, a salutary departure from the ordinary English novel, with the hero and heroine of different social stations, the predatory black sheep, the curate, the settlements, and Society. Mr Wilde, as we all know, is a gentleman of an original and audacious turn of mind, and the commonplace is scarcely possible to him. Besides, his advocacy of novel ideas in life, art, dress, and demeanour had led us to expect surprising things from him; and in this literary age it is agreed that a man may best show the best there is in him by writing a book. Those who read Mr Wilde's story in the hope of finding in it some compact and final statement of his theories of life and manners will be satisfied in some respects, and dissatisfied in others; but not many will deny that the book is a remarkable one, and would attract attention even had it appeared without the author's name on the title page.

"The Picture of Dorian Gray" begins to show its quality in the opening pages. Mr Wilde's writing has what is called "colour,"—the quality that forms the mainstay of many of Ouida's works,—and it appears in the sensuous descriptions of nature and of the decorations and environments of the artistic life. The general aspect of the characters and the tenor of their conversation remind one a little of "Vivian Gray" and a little of "Pelham," but the resemblance does not go far: Mr Wilde's objects and philosophy are different from those of either Disraeli or Bulwer. Meanwhile his talent for aphorisms and epigrams may fairly be compared with theirs: some of his clever sayings are more than clever,— they show real insight and a comprehensive grasp. Their wit is generally cynical; but they are put into the mouth of one of the characters, Lord Harry, and Mr Wilde himself refrains from definitely committing himself to them; though one cannot help suspecting that Mr Wilde regards Lord Harry as being an uncommonly able fellow. Be that as it may, Lord Harry plays the part of Old Harry in the story, and lives to witness the destruction of every other person in it. He may be taken as an imaginative type of all that is most evil and most refined in modern civilisation,—a charming, gentle, witty, euphemistic Mephistopheles, who depreciates the vulgarity of goodness, and muses aloud about "those renunciations that men have unwisely called virtue, and those natural rebellions that wise men still call sin." Upon the whole, Lord Harry is the most ably portrayed character in the book, though not the most original in conception. Dorian Gray himself is as nearly a new idea in fiction as one has nowadays a right to expect. If he had been adequately realised and worked out, Mr Wilde's first novel would have been remembered after more meritorious ones were forgotten. But, even as "nemo repente fuit turpissimus," so no one, or hardly any one, creates a thoroughly original figure at a first essay. Dorian never quite solidifies. In fact, his portrait is rather the more real thing of the two. But this needs explanation.

The story consists of a strong and marvelous central idea, illustrated by three characters, all men. There are a few women in the background, but they are only mentioned: they never appear to speak for themselves. There is, too, a valet who brings in his master's breakfasts, and a chemist who, by some scientific miracle, disposes of a human body: but, substantially, the book is taken up with the artist who paints the portrait, with his friend Lord Harry aforesaid, and with Dorian Gray, who might, so far as the story goes, stand alone. He and his portrait are one, and their union points the moral of the tale.

The situation is as follows: Dorian Gray is a youth of extraordinary physical beauty and grace, and pure and innocent of soul. An artist sees him and falls æsthetically in love with him, and finds in him a new inspiration in his art, both direct and general. In the lines of his form and features, and in his colouring and movement, are revealed fresh and profound laws: he paints him in all guises and combinations, and it is seen and admitted on all sides that he has never before painted so well. At length he concentrates all his knowledge and power in a final portrait, which has the vividness and grace of life itself, and, considering how much both of the sitter and of the painter is embodied in it, might almost be said to live. The portrait is declared by Lord Harry to be the greatest work of modern art; and the painter himself thinks so well of it that he resolves never to exhibit it, even as he would shrink from exposing to public gaze the privacies of his own nature.

On the day of the last sitting a singular incident occurs. Lord Harry, meeting on that occasion for the first time with Dorian, is no less impressed than was Hallward, the artist, with the youth's radiant beauty and freshness. But whereas Hallward would keep Dorian unspotted from the world, and would have him resist evil temptations and all the allurements of corruption, Lord Harry, on the contrary, with a truly Satanic ingenuity, discourses to the young man on the matchless delights and privileges of youth. Youth is the golden period of life: youth comes never again: in youth only are the senses endowed with divine potency; only then are joys exquisite and pleasures unalloyed. Let it therefore be indulged without stint. Let no harsh and cowardly restraints be placed upon its glorious impulses. Men are virtuous through fear and selfishness. They are too dull or too timid to take advantage of the godlike gifts that are showered upon them in the morning of existence; and before they can realise the folly of their self-denial, the morning has passed, and weary day is upon them, and the shadows of night are near. But let Dorian, who is matchless in the vigour and resources of his beauty, rise above the base shrinking from life that calls itself goodness. Let him accept and welcome every natural impulse of his nature. The tragedy of old age is not that one is old, but that one is young: let him so live that when old age comes he shall at least have the satisfaction of knowing that no opportunity of pleasure and indulgence has escaped untasted.

This seductive sermon profoundly affects the innocent Dorian, and he looks at life and himself with new eyes. He realises the value as well as the transitoriness of that youth and beauty which hitherto he had accepted as a matter of course and as a permanent possession. Gazing on his portrait, he laments that it possesses the immortality of liveliness and comeliness that is denied to him; and, in a sort of imaginative despair, he utters a wild prayer that to the portrait, and not to himself, may come the feebleness and hideousness of old age; that whatever sins he may commit, to whatever indulgences he may surrender himself, not upon him but upon the portrait may the penalties and disfigurements fall. Such is Dorian's prayer; and, though at first he suspects it not, his prayer is granted. From that hour the evil of his life is registered upon the face and form of his pictured presentment, while he himself goes unscathed. Day by day, each fresh sin that he commits stamps its mark of degradation upon the painted image. Cruelty, sensuality, treachery, all nameless crimes, corrupt and render hideous the effigy on the canvas; he sees in it the gradual pollution and ruin of his soul, while his own fleshy features preserve unstained all the freshness and virginity of his sinless youth. The contrast at first alarms and horrifies him; but at length he becomes accustomed to it, and finds a sinister delight in watching the progress of the awful change. He locks up the portrait in a secret chamber, and constantly retires thither to ponder over the ghastly miracle. No one but he knows or suspects the incredible truth; and he guards like a murder-secret this visible revelation of the difference between what he is and what he seems. This is a powerful situation; and the reader may be left to discover for himself how Mr Wilde works it out.

WALTER PATER

A Novel by Mr. Oscar Wilde †

There is always something of an excellent talker about the writing of Mr Oscar Wilde; and in his hands, as happens so rarely with those who practise it, the form of dialogue is justified by its being really alive. His genial, laughter-loving sense of life and its enjoyable intercourse, goes far to obviate any crudity there may be in the paradox, with which, as with the bright and shining truth which often underlies it, Mr Wilde, startling his "countrymen," carries on, more perhaps than any other writer, the brilliant critical work of Matthew Arnold. "The Decay of Lying," [1] for instance, is all but unique in its half-humorous, yet wholly convinced, presentment of certain valuable truths of criticism. Conversational ease, the fluidity of life, felicitous expression, are qualities which have a natural alliance to the successful writing of fiction; and side by side with Mr Wilde's "Intentions" (so he entitles his critical efforts) comes a novel, certainly original, and affording the reader a fair opportunity of comparing his practice as a creative artist with many a precept he has enounced as critic concerning it.

A wholesome dislike of the common place, rightly or wrongly identified by him with the *bourgeois*, with our middle-class—its habits and tastes—leads him to protest emphatically against so-called "realism" in art; life, as he argues, with much plausibility, as a matter of fact, when it is really awake, following art—the fashion an effective artist sets; while art, on the other hand, influential and effective art, has never taken its cue from actual life. In "Dorian Gray" he is true certainly, on the whole, to the æsthetic philosophy of his "Intentions"; yet not infallibly, even on this point: there is a certain amount of the intrusion of real life and its sordid aspects—the low theatre, the pleasures and griefs, the faces of some very unrefined people, managed, of course, cleverly enough. The interlude of Jim Vane, his half-sullen but wholly faithful care for his sister's honour, is as good as perhaps anything of the kind, marked by a homely but real pathos, sufficiently proving a versatility in the writer's talent, which should make his books popular. Clever always, this book, however, seems intended to set forth anything but a homely philosophy of life for the middle-class—a kind of dainty Epicurean theory, rather— yet fails, to some degree, in this; and one can see why. A true Epicureanism aims at a complete though harmonious development of man's entire organism. To lose the moral sense therefore, for instance, the sense of sin and righteousness, as Mr Wilde's hero—his heroes are bent

† From Stuart Mason, *Oscar Wilde: Art and Morality* (1912; New York: Haskell House, 1971) 188–95. This review of the revised edition of *Dorian Gray* appeared in the first number of *The Book-* man (October 1891).
1. Appeared first in *The Nineteenth Century*, January 1889, and was afterwards included in "Intentions" *[Mason's note]*.

on doing as speedily, as completely as they can, is to lose, or lower, organisation, to become less complex, to pass from a higher to a lower degree of development. As a story, however, a partly supernatural story, it is first-rate in artistic management; those Epicurean niceties only adding to the decorative colour of its central figure, like so many exotic flowers, like the charming scenery and the perpetual, epigrammatic, surprising, yet so natural, conversations, like an atmosphere all about it. All that pleasant accessory detail, taken straight from the culture, the intellectual and social interests, the conventionalities, of the moment, have, in fact, after all, the effect of the better sort of realism, throwing into relief the adroitly-devised supernatural element after the manner of Poe, but with a grace he never reached, which supersedes that earlier didactic purpose, and makes the quite sufficing interest of an excellent story.

We like the hero, and, spite of his, somewhat unsociable, devotion to his art, Hallward, better than Lord Henry Wotton. He has too much of a not very really refined world in and about him, and his somewhat cynic opinions, which seem sometimes to be those of the writer, who may, however, have intended Lord Henry as a satiric sketch. Mr Wilde can hardly have intended him, with his cynic amity of mind and temper, any more than the miserable end of Dorian himself, to figure the motive and tendency of a true Cyrenaic or Epicurean doctrine of life. In contrast with Hallward, the artist, whose sensibilities idealise the world around him, the personality of Dorian Gray, above all, into something magnificent and strange, we might say that Lord Henry, and even more the, from the first, suicidal hero, loses too much in life to be a true Epicurean—loses so much in the way of impressions, of pleasant memories, and subsequent hopes, which Hallward, by a really Epicurean economy, manages to secure. It should be said, however, in fairness, that the writer is impersonal: seems not to have identified himself entirely with any one of his characters: and Wotton's cynicism, or whatever it be, at least makes a very clever story possible. He becomes the spoiler of the fair young man, whose bodily form remains un-aged; while his picture, the *chef d'œuvre* of the artist Hallward, changes miraculously with the gradual corruption of his soul. How true, what a light on the artistic nature, is the following on actual personalities and their revealing influence in art. We quote it as an example of Mr Wilde's more serious style.

> I sometimes think that there are only two eras of any importance in the world's history. The first is the appearance of a new medium for art, and the second is the appearance of a new personality for art also. What the invention of oil-painting was to the Venetians, the face of Antinoüs was to late Greek sculpture, and the face of Dorian Gray will some day be to me. It is not merely that I paint from him, draw from him, sketch from him. Of course I have done all that. But he is much more to me than a model or a sitter. I

won't tell you that I am dissatisfied with what I have done of him, or that his beauty is such that Art cannot express it. There is nothing that Art cannot express, and I know that the work I have done, since I met Dorian Gray, is good work, is the best work of my life. But in some curious way . . . his personality has suggested to me an entirely new manner in art, an entirely new mode of style. I see things differently, I think of them differently. I can now recreate life in a way that was hidden from me before.

Dorian himself, though certainly a quite unsuccessful experiment in Epicureanism, in life as a fine art, is (till his inward spoiling takes visible effect suddenly, and in a moment, at the end of his story) a beautiful creation. But his story is also a vivid, though carefully considered, exposure of the corruption of a soul, with a very plain moral pushed home, to the effect that vice and crime make people coarse and ugly. General readers nevertheless, will probably care less for this moral, less for the fine, varied, largely appreciative culture of the writer, in evidence from page to page, than for the story itself, with its adroitly managed supernatural incidents, its almost equally wonderful applications of natural science; impossible, surely, in fact, but plausible enough in fiction. Its interest turns on that very old theme, old because based on some inherent experience or fancy of the human brain, of a double life: of Dŏppelgänger—not of two *persons*, in this case, but of the man and his portrait; the latter of which, as we hinted above, changes, decays, is spoiled, while the former, through a long course of corruption, remains, to the outward eye, unchanged, still in all the beauty of a seemingly immaculate youth—"the devil's bargain." But it would be a pity to spoil the reader's enjoyment by further detail. We need only emphasise once more, the skill, the real subtlety of art, the ease and fluidity withal of one telling a story by word of mouth, with which the consciousness of the supernatural is introduced into, and maintained amid, the elaborately conventional, sophisticated, disabused world Mr Wilde depicts so cleverly, so mercilessly. The special fascination of the piece is, of course, just there—at that point of contrast. Mr Wilde's work may fairly claim to go with that of Edgar Poe, and with some good French work of the same kind, done, probably, in more or less conscious imitation of it.

ART VERSUS MORALITY:
DORIAN GRAY ON TRIAL

The first trial was an action for libel brought by Wilde at the instigation of Lord Alfred Douglas against the latter's father, John Sholto Douglas, eighth marquess of Queensberry. The purpose of the suit was to punish and silence "The Scarlet Marquess," who had threatened both Wilde and his own son with scandal. Indeed, he had threatened in a letter to his son to shoot Wilde on sight if rumors of Wilde's homosexual activities should be proved publicly. To that end, perhaps, Queensberry left the now famous calling card with the words "For Oscar Wilde posing as a somdomite [sic]." Those were the fighting words that provoked Wilde to sue for criminal libel. During the trial, Queensberry's defense attorney, Edward Carson, confronted Wilde with *Dorian Gray* as evidence of his corrupting influence on Alfred Douglas.

From Edward Carson's Cross-Examination of Wilde (First Trial) †

*   *   *

After the criticisms that were passed on *Dorian Gray*, was it modified a good deal?—No. Additions were made. In one case it was pointed out to me—not in a newspaper or anything of that sort, but by the only critic of the century whose opinion I set high, Mr. Walter Pater—that a certain passage was liable to misconstruction, and I made an addition.[1]

This is in your introduction to *Dorian Gray:* "There is no such thing as a moral or an immoral book. Books are well written, or badly written." That expresses your view?—My view on art, yes.

Then, I take it, that no matter how immoral a book may be, if it is well written, it is, in your opinion, a good book?—Yes, if it were well written so as to produce a sense of beauty, which is the highest sense of which a human being can be capable. If it were badly written, it would produce a sense of disgust.

Then a well-written book putting forward perverted moral views may be a good book?—No work of art ever puts forward views. Views belong to people who are not artists.

A perverted novel might be a good book?—I don't know what you mean by a "perverted" novel.

Then I will suggest *Dorian Gray* as open to the interpretation of being such a novel?—That could only be to brutes and illiterates. The views of Philistines on art are incalculably stupid.

An illiterate person reading *Dorian Gray* might consider it such a novel?—The views of illiterates on art are unaccountable. I am concerned only with my view of art. I don't care twopence what other people think of it.

The majority of persons would come under your definition of Philistines and illiterates?—I have found wonderful exceptions.

Do you think that the majority of people live up to the position you are giving us?—I am afraid they are not cultivated enough.

Not cultivated enough to draw the distinction between a good book and a bad book?—Certainly not.

† From H. M. Hyde, *The Three Trials of Wilde* (New York: UP Books, 1956) 121–33.

The affection and love of the artist of *Dorian Gray* might lead an ordinary individual to believe that it might have a certain tendency?—I have no knowledge of the views of ordinary individuals.

You did not prevent the ordinary individual from buying your book?—I have never discouraged him.

[Mr. CARSON then read the following extracts from *The Picture of Dorian Gray*, in which the painter Basil Hallward tells Lord Henry Wooton of his first meetings with Dorian Gray. The quotations were from the original version of the work as it appeared in *Lippincott's Monthly Magazine* for July, 1890.]

". . . The story is simply this. Two months ago I went to a crush at Lady Brandon's. You know we poor painters have to show ourselves in society from time to time, just to remind the public that we are not savages. With an evening coat and a white tie, as you told me once, anybody, even a stockbroker, can gain a reputation for being civilized. Well, after I had been in the room about ten minutes, talking to huge over-dressed dowagers and tedious Academicians, I suddenly became conscious that some one was looking at me. I turned half-way round, and saw Dorian Gray for the first time. When our eyes met, I felt that I was growing pale. A curious instinct of terror came over me. I knew that I had come face to face with some one whose mere personality was so fascinating that, if I allowed it to do so, it would absorb my whole nature, my whole soul, my very art itself. I did not want any external influence in my life. You know yourself, Harry, how independent I am by nature. My father destined me for the army. I insisted on going to Oxford. Then he made me enter my name at the Middle Temple. Before I had eaten half a dozen dinners I gave up the Bar, and announced my intention of becoming a painter. I have always been my own master; had at least always been so, till I met Dorian Gray. Then—but I don't know how to explain it to you. Something seemed to tell me that I was on the verge of a terrible crisis in my life. I had a strange feeling that Fate had in store for me exquisite joys and exquisite sorrows. I knew that if I spoke to Dorian I would become absolutely devoted to him, and that I ought not to speak to him. I grew afraid, and turned to quit the room. It was not conscience that made me do so: it was cowardice. I take no credit to myself for trying to escape."

*   *   *

Cross-examination continued—Now I ask you, Mr. Wilde, do you consider that that description of the feeling of one man towards a youth just grown up was a proper or an improper feeling?—I think it is the most perfect description of what an artist would feel on meeting a beautiful personality that was in some way necessary to his art and life.

You think that is a feeling a young man should have towards another?—Yes, as an artist.

[Counsel began to read another extract from the book. Witness asked for a copy and was given one of the original version]

Mr. CARSON (in calling witness's attention to the place— *Lippincott's Monthly Magazine*, Vol. XLVI, at p. 56)—I believe it was left out in the purged edition.

WITNESS—I do not call it purged.

Mr. CARSON—Yes, I know that; but we will see.

"Let us sit down, Dorian," said Hallward, looking pale and pained. "Let us sit down. I will sit in the shadow, and you shall sit in the sunlight. Our lives are like that. Just answer me one question. Have you noticed in the picture something that you did not like?—something that probably at first did not strike you, but that revealed itself to you suddenly?"

"Basil!" cried the lad, clutching the arms of his chair with trembling hands, and gazing at him with wild, startled eyes.

"I see you did. Don't speak. Wait till you hear what I have to say. It is quite true that I have worshipped you with far more romance of feeling than a man usually gives to a friend. Somehow, I have never loved a woman. I suppose I never had time. Perhaps, as Harry says, a really 'grande passion' is the privilege of those who have nothing to do, and that is the use of the idle classes in a country. Well, from the moment I met you, your personality had the most extraordinary influence over me. I quite admit that I adored you madly, extravagantly, absurdly. I was jealous of every one to whom you spoke. I wanted to have you all to myself. I was only happy when I was with you. When I was away from you, you were still present in my art. It was all wrong and foolish. It is all wrong and foolish still. Of course I never let you know anything about this. It would have been impossible. You would not have understood it; I did not understand it myself. One day I determined to paint a wonderful portrait of you. It was to have been my masterpiece. It is my masterpiece. But, as I worked at it, every flake and film of colour seemed to me to reveal my secret. I grew afraid that the world would know of my idolatry. I felt, Dorian, that I had told too much. Then, it was that I resolved never to allow the picture to be exhibited. You were a little annoyed; but then you did not realize all that it meant to me. Harry, to whom I talked about it, laughed at me. But I did not mind that. When the picture was finished and I sat alone with it, I felt that I was right. Well, after a few days the portrait left my studio, and as soon as I had got rid of the intolerable fascination of its presence it seemed to me that I had been foolish in imagining that I had said anything in it, more than that you were extremely good-looking and that I could paint. Even now I cannot help feeling that it is a mistake to think that the passion one feels in creation is ever really shown in the work one creates. Art is more abstract than we fancy. Form and colour tell us of form and colour—that is all. It often seems to me that art conceals the artist far more completely than it ever reveals him. And so when I got this offer from Paris I determined to make your portrait the principal thing in my exhibition. It never occurred to me that you would refuse. I see now that you were right. The picture must not be shown. You must not be angry with me, Dorian, for what I have told you. As I said to Harry, once, you are made to be worshipped."

Cross-examination continued—Do you mean to say that that passage describes the natural feeling of one man towards another?—It would be the influence produced by a beautiful personality.

A beautiful person?—I said a "beautiful personality." You can describe it as you like. Dorian Gray's was a most remarkable personality.

May I take it that you, as an artist, have never known the feeling described here?—I have never allowed any personality to dominate my art.

Then you have never known the feeling you described?—No. It is a work of fiction.

So far as you are concerned you have no experience as to its being a natural feeling?—I think it is perfectly natural for any artist to admire intensely and love a young man. It is an incident in the life of almost every artist.

But let us go over it phrase by phrase. "I quite admit that I adored you madly." What do you say to that? Have you ever adored a young man madly?—No, not madly; I prefer love—that is a higher form.

Never mind about that. Let us keep down to the level we are at now?—I have never given adoration to anybody except myself. (Loud laughter.)

I suppose you think that a very smart thing?—Not at all.

Then you have never had that feeling?—No. The whole idea was borrowed from Shakespeare, I regret to say—yes, from Shakespeare's sonnets.

I believe you have written an article to show that Shakespeare's sonnets were suggestive of unnatural vice?—On the contrary I have written an article to show that they are not.[1] I objected to such a perversion being put upon Shakespeare.

---

1. "The Portrait of Mr. W. H.," which appeared in *Blackwood's Edinburgh Magazine*, Vol. cxlvi, No. 885 (July, 1889). A revised and enlarged version of this essay was later announced by Wilde's publishers, but the manuscript which had been returned to Wilde by the publishers on the day of his arrest, mysteriously disappeared, no doubt stolen during the sale of Wilde's effects of his bankruptcy. It turned up many years afterwards in New York, where the complete text was published in a limited edition in 1921 by Mr. Mitchell Kennerley, the collector who had acquired the manuscript.

"I have adored you extravagantly"?—Do you mean financially?

Oh, yes, financially! Do you think we are talking about finance?—I don't know what you are talking about.

Don't you? Well, I hope I shall make myself very plain before I have done. "I was jealous of every one to whom you spoke." Have you ever been jealous of a young man?—Never in my life.

"I wanted to have you all to myself." Did you ever have that feeling?—No; I should consider it an intense nuisance, an intense bore.

"I grew afraid that the world would know of my idolatry." Why should he grow afraid that the world should know of it?—Because there are people in the world who cannot understand the intense devotion, affection, and admiration that an artist can feel for a wonderful and beautiful personality. These are the conditions under which we live. I regret them.

These unfortunate people, that have not the high understanding that you have, might put it down to something wrong?—Undoubtedly; to any point they chose. I am not concerned with the ignorance of others.

In another passage Dorian Gray receives a book. Was the book to which you refer a moral book?—Not well written, but it gave me an idea.

Was not the book you have in mind of a certain tendency?—I decline to be cross-examined upon the work of another artist. It is an impertinence and a vulgarity.

[Witness admitted that the book in question was a French work, *A Rebours*, by J. K. Huysmans. Mr. CARSON persisted in his desire to elicit the witness's view as to the morality of this book, with the result that Sir EDWARD CLARKE appealed to Mr. JUSTICE COLLINS, who ruled against any further reference to it.[2]

MR. CARSON then read a further extract from *The Picture of Dorian Gray*, quoting the following conversation between the painter and Dorian Gray.]

". . . I think it right that you should know that the most dreadful things are being said about you in London—things that I could hardly repeat to you."

"I don't wish to know anything about them. I love scandals about other people, but scandals about myself don't interest me. They have not got the charm of novelty."

"They must interest you, Dorian. Every gentleman is interested in his good name. You don't want people to talk of you as something vile and degraded. Of course you have your position, and

2. *A Rebours* was first published in 1884. "It was a novel without a plot," wrote Wilde in the passage alluded to by Carson in *The Picture of Dorian Gray*, "and with only one character, being, indeed, simply a psychological study of a certain young Parisian, who spent his life trying to realize in the nineteenth century all the passions and modes of thought that belonged to every century except his own, and to sum up, as it were, in himself the various modes through which the world-spirit had ever passed, loving for their mere artificiality those renunciations that men have unwisely called virtue, as much as those natural rebellions that wise men still call sin."

your wealth, and all that kind of thing. But position and wealth are not everything. Mind you, I don't believe these rumours at all. At least, I can't believe them when I see you. Sin is a thing that writes itself across a man's face. It cannot be concealed. People talk of secret vices. There are no such things as secret vices. If a wretched man has a vice, it shows itself in the lines of his mouth, the droop of his eyelids, the moulding of his hands even. Somebody—I won't mention his name, but you know him—came to me last year to have his portrait done. I had never seen him before, and had never heard anything about him at the time, though I have heard a good deal since. He offered an extravagant price. I refused him. There was something in the shape of his fingers that I hated. I know now that I was quite right in what I fancied about him. His life is dreadful. But you, Dorian, with your pure, bright, innocent face, and your marvellous untroubled youth—I can't believe anything against you. And yet I see you very seldom, and you never come down to the studio now, and when I am away from you, and I hear all these hideous things that people are whispering about you, I don't know what to say. Why is it, Dorian, that a man like the Duke of Berwick leaves the room of a club when you enter it? Why is it that so many gentlemen in London will neither go to your house nor invite you to theirs? You used to be a friend of Lord Cawdor. I met him at dinner last week. Your name happened to come up in conversation, in connexion with the miniatures you have lent to the exhibition at the Dudley. Cawdor curled his lip, and said that you might have the most artistic tastes, but that you were a man whom no pure-minded girl should be allowed to know, and whom no chaste woman should sit in the same room with. I reminded him that I was a friend of yours, and asked him what he meant. He told me. He told me right out before everybody. It was horrible! Why is your friendship so fateful to young men? There was that wretched boy in the Guards who committed suicide. You were his great friend. There was Sir Henry Ashton, who had to leave England with a tarnished name. You and he were inseparable. What about Adrian Singleton, and his dreadful end? What about Lord Kent's only son, and his career? I met his father yesterday in St. James Street. He seemed broken with shame and sorrow. What about the young Duke of Perth? What sort of life has he got now? What gentleman would associate with him? Dorian, Dorian, your reputation is infamous. . . ."

Cross-examination continued—Does not this passage suggest a charge of unnatural vice?—It describes Dorian Gray as a man of very corrupt influence, though there is no statement as to the nature of the influence. But as a matter of fact I do not think that one person influences another, nor do I think there is any bad influence in the world.

A man never corrupts a youth?—I think not.

Nothing could corrupt him?—If you are talking of separate ages.

No, sir, I am talking common sense?—I do not think one person influences another.

You don't think that flattering a young man, making love to him, in fact, would be likely to corrupt him?—No.

Where was Lord Alfred Douglas staying when you wrote that letter to him?—At the Savoy; and I was at Babbacombe, near Torquay.

It was a letter in answer to something he had sent you?—Yes, a poem.

Why should a man of your age address a boy nearly twenty years younger as "My own boy"?—I was fond of him. I have always been fond of him.

Do you adore him?—No, but I have always liked him. I think it is a beautiful letter. It is a poem. I was not writing an ordinary letter. You might as well cross-examine me as to whether *King Lear* or a sonnet of Shakespeare was proper.

Apart from art, Mr. Wilde?—I cannot answer apart from art.

Suppose a man who was not an artist had written this letter, would you say it was a proper letter?—A man who was not an artist could not have written that letter.

Why?—Because nobody but an artist could write it. He certainly could not write the language unless he were a man of letters.

I can suggest, for the sake of your reputation, that there is nothing very wonderful in this "red rose-leaf lips of yours"?—A great deal depends on the way it is read.

"Your slim gilt soul walks between passion and poetry." Is that a beautiful phrase?—Not as you read it, Mr. Carson. You read it very badly.

I do not profess to be an artist; and when I hear you give evidence, I am glad I am not——

* * *

From Edward Carson's Opening Speech for the Defense (First Trial) †

* * *

Let us contrast the position which Mr. Wilde took up in cross-examination as to his books, which are for the select and not for the ordinary individual, with the position he assumed as to the young men to whom he was introduced and those he picked up for himself. His books were written by an artist for artists; his words were not for Philistines or illiterates. Contrast that with the way in which Mr. Wilde chose his com-

†From H. M. Hyde, *The Three Trials of Wilde* (New York: UP Books, 1956) 166–67.

panions! He took up with Charles Parker, a gentleman's servant, whose brother was a gentleman's servant; with young Alphonse Conway, who sold papers on the pier at Worthing; and with Scarfe, also a gentlemen's servant. Then his excuse was no longer that he was dwelling in regions of art but that he had such a noble, such a democratic soul (Laughter.), that he drew no social distinctions, and that it was quite as much pleasure to have the sweeping boy from the streets to lunch or dine with him as the greatest *littérateur* or artist.

In my judgment, if the case had rested on Mr. Wilde's literature alone, Lord Queensberry would have been absolutely justified in the course he has taken. Lord Queensberry has undertaken to prove that Mr. Wilde has been "posing" as guilty of certain vices. Mr. Wilde never complained of the immorality of the story "The Priest and the Acolyte" which appeared in *The Chameleon*. He knows no distinction, in fact, between a moral and an immoral book. Nor does he care whether the article is in its very terms blasphemous. All that Mr. Wilde says is that he did not approve of the story from a literary point of view. What is that story? It is a story of the love of a priest for the acolyte who attended him at Mass. Exactly the same idea that runs through the two letters to Lord Alfred Douglas runs through that story, and also through *The Picture of Dorian Gray*. When the boy was discovered in the priest's bed, the priest made exactly the same defence as Mr. Wilde has made—that the world does not understand the beauty of this love. The same idea runs through these two letters which Mr. Wilde has called beautiful, but which I call an abominable piece of disgusting immorality.

Moreover, there is in this same *Chameleon* a poem which shows some justification for the frightful anticipations which Lord Queensberry entertained for his son. The poem was written by Lord Alfred Douglas and was seen by Mr. Wilde before its publication. Is it not a terrible thing that a young man on the threshold of life, who has for several years been dominated by Oscar Wilde and has been "adored and loved" by Oscar Wilde, as the two letters prove, should thus show the tendency of his mind upon this frightful subject? What would be the horror of any man whose son wrote such a poem?

Passing now to *The Picture of Dorian Gray*, it is the tale of a beautiful young man who, by the conversation of one who has great literary power and ability to speak in epigrams—just as Mr. Wilde has—and who, by reading of exactly the same kind as that in "Phrases and Philosophies for the Use of the Young," has his eyes opened to what they are pleased to call the "delights of the world." If *Dorian Gray* is a book which it can be conclusively proved advocates the vice imputed to Mr. Wilde, what answer, then, is there to Lord Queensberry's plea of justification?

※   ※   ※

CRITICISM

The history of critical opinion on *The Picture of Dorian Gray* is an index of the past century's changing self-image. For convenience, critical opinion on *Dorian Gray* may be divided into five phases. The first is the contemporary reaction illustrated in Reviews and Reactions above and indirectly in Max Nordau's reactionary *Degeneration* (1895). Stuart Mason's *Oscar Wilde: Art and Morality* and the later bibliography laid the foundation for all later scholarship in this area. The second phase was "post-mortem criticism," dominated as it was by continued polemics over Wilde's character and influence and by usually ambivalent personal reminiscence. The critical milestones of this period were R. H. Sherard's biographies and defensive pamphlets and Arthur Ransome's *Oscar Wilde: A Critical Study* (1912), in which it was publicly revealed that *De Profundis* had been written to Alfred Douglas. Douglas sued for libel and lost in a trial reminiscent of Wilde's 1895 libel action. Douglas retaliated with the intemperate *Oscar Wilde and Myself* (1914), which he later repudiated. This phase ends with Frank Harris's personal biography, *Oscar Wilde: His Life and Confessions* (1916).

The third phase, "late post-mortem," remained dominated by biographical criticism, ranging from anecdotal to popular, during the twenties and thirties; but during this time, several more critical studies appeared that foreshadowed the next development. Milestones of this era were Yeats's "The Trembling of the Veil" (1922) and Mario Praz's *The Romantic Agony* (1933), in which Wilde plays a prominent part; Lloyd Lewis and Henry Justin Smith's *Oscar Wilde Discovers America* (1936); and Boris Brasol's *Oscar Wilde: The Man, the Artist, the Martyr* (1938).

The fourth, "post-war" phase, begins clearly with Roditi's study of Oscar Wilde for New Directions (1947) and is reinforced in Graham Hough's *The Last Romantics* (1947). The emphasis begins to shift during this era to the psychological, symbolic, and literary aspects of Wilde as a writer. Another milestone is Hesketh Pearson's *Life* (1946), a summing up of all the best anecdotes and stories related to Wilde's life. The fifth and most recent phase is the "post-modern," in which we find the emergence of authoritative bibliographical scholarship and a criticism that adds to its psychological interests an emphasis on existential and moral ideas and on the place of Dorian Gray in both literary history and the history of ideas. Dominating this phase has been the work of H. Montgomery Hyde, Sir Rupert Hart-Davis and Richard Ellmann, with important contributions by the other critics whose work is represented in this section and by a new generation of critics whose work begins with the assumption that Wilde is a central figure in the literary, intellectual, and even moral life of the 1890's and of the modern world.

In terms of *The Picture of Dorian Gray*, the main critical problems of the past hundred years are more easily summarized than explained, but they follow roughly the historical division above. The bibliographical problems first explored by Mason have only recently been carried forward and resolved in the work of Isobel Murray, Donald Lawler, Ian Fletcher, and E. H. Mikhail. The art and morality issue that dominated contemporary criticism has become a chapter in literary and cultural history. The charges of hasty, careless composition are being laid to rest by the evidence of the manuscript revisions. The old charges of plagiarism and insincere derivation may never be entirely exorcised thanks to Wilde's own use of handy reference sources for some of his decorative touches, but at least critics are beginning to see that the practice had a long-standing place in literary Aestheticism, from Gautier to the present. Although the source and analogue industry shows no signs of shutting down, some critics realize that the quest for a definitive source for *Dorian Gray* has established rather the power of the archetype of which *Dorian Gray* is an especially inspired expression. A great deal remains to be attempted in studying the formal and genre problems raised by *Dorian Gray* as an amalgamated fiction constructed out of several modes and types of literature, just as to date relatively little has been done with the questions raised by its position as one of the popular culture icons of the past century. The strength of post-war and post-modern criticism has been with approaches to the novel that stress its psychological and autobiographical elements. Study of its literary, intellectual, and moral relation to its times have been materially aided by the invaluable edition of Wilde's *Letters* published and edited by Sir Rupert Hart-Davis (1962) and *More Letters of Oscar Wilde* (Vanguard, 1985) and by the accumulation of biographical evidence of a more objective type produced by Rupert Croft-Cooke in *Feasting with Panthers* (1967) and *The Unrecorded Life of Oscar Wilde* (1972), and by H. Montgomery Hyde in *Oscar Wilde* (1975). As the result of this and other scholarship on *Dorian Gray* and on Wilde as its author, the novel has taken its place as a key work of art that both expresses its time while it redefines the moral norms by which the times are to be judged by later generations.

EDOUARD RODITI

From "Fiction as Allegory" †

*   *   *

From the eighteenth-century vogue of Ann Radcliffe and Horace Walpole to the success, in the early decades of the nineteenth century, of the novels of "Monk" Lewis, a whole literary genre had culminated, in 1820, in the publication of *Melmoth the Wanderer*. Its author, Charles Robert Maturin, was, by marriage, a uncle of Wilde's mother, the poetess Speranza. Wilde knew *Melmoth* well, and was proud of this relationship. When the old novel was reprinted in 1892 with a long biographical introduction, the editors expressed their thanks, in a preface, "to Mr. Oscar Wilde and Lady Wilde (Speranza) for details with regard to Maturin's life." And when Wilde retired to France after his release from Reading Gaol, he lived there under the name of Sebastian Melmoth which he used as a pseudonym until his death. From Reading Gaol, in a letter to Robert Ross dated April 6th, 1897, Wilde wrote, of Rossetti's letters which he had just read and considered forgeries, that he had been interested, "to see how my grand-uncle's *Melmoth* and my mother's *Sidonia* have been two books that fascinated his youth." Though

† From *Oscar Wilde* (Norfolk: New Directions, 1947) 113–24.

certainly ignorant of Lautréamont's passion for the Satanic wanderer, Wilde surely knew that Baudelaire had praised *Melmoth* in *De l'Essence du Rire*; and he was proud of the high esteem in which two of his favorite authors, Byron and Balzac, had held his mother's uncle.

Of Maturin's influence on Wilde we have ample proof. Maturin's biographers state that "he always showed an extravagant taste for dressing up" and that "throughout his life a love of masquerade and theatrical display never deserted him." His eccentricities of dress were noted, besides, by many contemporaries: Byron described him, in a letter, as "a bit of a coxcomb." Speranza likewise attracted much attention, in Dublin society and later in London by her none too tasteful splendors, recorded by several contemporaries. Wild's own sartorial extravagances thus seem to have been inspired to some extent by a family weakness, though a well-established tradition of dandyism, from the age of Byron and Maturin, through that of Bulwer Lytton and Disraeli, still encouraged the affectations of a Brummel among artists of Wilde's generation.

Much as Wilde may have been influenced, in his art and his life, by the more dandified Romanticism of such novels as Bulwer Lytton's *Pelham* or Disraeli's *Vivian Grey* and *Lothair*, with their epigrammatic brilliance and foppish haughtiness inherited from the Regency bucks, there is also, in *The Picture of Dorian Gray*, distinct evidence of direct borrowings from *Melmoth*. In the opening chapter of Maturin's novel, when Melmoth, the young student, comes to his miserly uncle's death-bed, he is sent to fetch some wine from a closet "which no foot but that of old Melmoth had entered for nearly sixty years." There, amidst "a great deal of decayed and useless lumber" such as that which later furnished the locked and abandoned school-room where Dorian Gray concealed his compromising portrait, young Melmoth's eyes were "in a moment, and as if by magic, rivetted on a portrait" whose eyes "were such as one feels they wish they had never seen, and feels they can never forget." This portrait represents an evil ancestor, a third Melmoth who, by a pact with the devil, has been permitted to live one hundred and fifty years without showing any signs of aging, much as Dorian Gray was mysteriously permitted to retain the appearance of his youth in spite of his crimes and debauchery. And this ancestor, Melmoth the Wanderer, is still alive: fear of him has even caused the old miser's death.

Maturin's whole romance then unfolds as a tangled series of episodes from the Wanderer's legendary life. And when, in the last pages, the evil ancestor returns to the place of his birth because "the clock of eternity is about to strike," in his last moments of life he suddenly ages: "the lines of extreme age were visible in every feature. His hairs were as white as snow, his mouth had fallen in, the muscles of his face were relaxed and withered—he was the very image of hoary decrepit debility."

The magic formula of Dorian Gray's sinister youth was thus an heirloom in Wilde's family, handed down like some choice recipe from old Maturin, from one of the sources of the Dracula myth in novels and movies to the author of *The Picture of Dorian Gray* which, when it was finally filmed, was acclaimed by the poet Parker Tyler as "the last of the movie Draculas." And Dorian Gray himself, whose mere presence, as his lasting youth became more and more sinister, would "make a man like the Duke of Berwick leave the room," whose friendship "was so fatal to young men," is a half-brother of Lautréamont's Maldoror. The arch-fiend of Surrealist satanism is indeed but another scion of the same Melmoth who boasts: "It has been reported of me, that I obtained from the enemy of souls a range of existence beyond the period allotted to mortality—a power to pass over space without disturbance or delay, and visit remote regions with the swiftness of thought—to encounter tempests without the *hope* of their blasting me, and penetrate dungeons whose bolts were as flax and tow at my touch."

From Melmoth, Dorian Gray thus inherited his lasting youth, and Maldoror his gift of ubiquity, of travel without disturbance or delay, and "that singular expression of the features, (the eyes particularly), which no human glance could meet unappalled." But both of these Draculas outdid, in one respect, their ghoulish sire. The Reverend Maturin, a worthy Anglican minister with what even a snob in a Somerset Maugham novel calls "a good old Irish name," was apparently unwilling to permit his monster to lead any victims to damnation. And as he is about to die, the Wanderer exclaims: "No one has ever exchanged destinies with Melmoth the Wanderer. *I have traversed the world in the search, and no one, to gain that world, would lose his own soul.*" Maldoror and Dorian Gray, however, were both more successful as tempters, and each of them left a trail of blasted lives behind him.

The portrait concealed in Melmoth's closet is bound to the ghoulish wanderer by no such ties of sympathetic magic as those which bind Dorian Gray to his portrait; it occupies no such central position in Maturin's story and remains a mere accessory which is destroyed, without dire consequences, shortly after it is discovered, so that one barely remembers it as one reads the rest of the romance. Between its literary avatars in *Melmoth* and in *Dorian Gray*, this portrait had indeed undergone a strange metamorphosis, under the influence of the magical portrait, as Richard Aldington has pointed out, of Max Rodenstein in Benjamin Disraeli's *Vivian Grey*, published in 1826, and also of the magical skin in *La Peau de Chagrin*, written by Balzac in the period in which he was most deeply affected by his readings of Maturin, only a couple of years before he wrote his sequel to the Wanderer's tale, *Melmoth Reconcilié à l'Eglise*. Dorian Gray's portrait is thus born of the Wanderer's, but by Disraeli's miraculous portrait of an incidental character in *Vivian Grey*; and it inherited its central position in Wilde's novel from Balzac's magical skin, together with analogous qualities which reveal themselves just as accidentally and prove just as dire a source of temptation.

As a macabre novel, in spite of this noble ancestry, *The Picture of Dorian Gray* is not entirely successful. The thread of its narrative is too frequently interrupted by Wilde's esthetic preaching, by useless displays of esthetic erudition, by unnecessary descriptions of works of art and by paradoxical table-talk which have little bearing on the plot, except where Lord Henry dazzles and convinces Dorian. The conversation, at times, even distorts the plot. It allows a vague number of duchesses and other characters, doomed to vanish almost immediately after their first appearance, to wander into Wilde's novel, straight from the pages of *Vivian Grey* or of *Pelham*, in a frenzy of brilliant repartee and shrill laughter like the extras who suddenly give life to a court-scene in an old-fashioned light-opera. Between these pauses, where the atmosphere has been slapped on so thick that it clogs the machinery of plot, Wilde's plot itself reveals several curious weaknesses; had not the book been so hastily written that it is almost unjust to analyze it as if it were a carefully devised work of art, these weaknesses would suggest an unexpected mixture, in the author, of amateurishness and prudish guilt-feelings.

Wilde's naïvely romantic descriptions of low life, for instance, are full of pathetic echoes of the melodrama of earlier decades, of De Quincey's years of misery in the London slums where he met Ann, of the drug-addict poet James Thomson's *The City of Dreadful Night* and even of Charles Dickens; and they contrast oddly with Wilde's infinitely more sophisticated and knowing descriptions of high society. When Wilde's young men with perfect profiles stop flinging themselves petulantly upon the divans of their extravagantly furnished bachelor quarters or dining out with duchesses in a haze of epigrams, they stalk forth, as Vivian Grey or Lothair had done some decades earlier in their moments of tension or despair, into the vast wilderness of London. And there, in the night, Wilde's dandies discover another world, whence they return, at dawn, with "a dim memory of wandering through a labyrinth of sordid houses, of being lost in a giant web of sombre streets" or of "narrow shameful alleys."

Victor Hugo's *Les Misérables* and Eugène Sue's *Les Mystères de Paris* had contributed much to Wilde's romantic vision of London's nocturnal underworld, with its grisly prostitutes, its drunken brawls before the doors of degraded dock-land taverns, its foul opium-dens and its sinister Jewish theater-owner like De Quincey's money-lenders or the hideous Jews of Rowlandson's cartoons. All the props, save the sewers, of Victor Hugo's Paris had been imported to England in such popular melodramas of the Seventies as *The Streets of London* or *London by Gaslight*; and it is from this naïve panorama of the sinful city that Wilde's young men at last emerge in Covent Garden, among the vegetables glistening in the dawn light and the rustics who, "rude as they were, with their heavy, hob-nailed shoes, and their awkward gait . . . brought a little of Arcady with them."

Between these two worlds, no decent or comfortable middle class, no quiet family life, no dormitory sections in Wilde's vision of the big city. From the brilliantly lit society with which the author seems so well acquainted, we step straight into a dim slum-land of which he seems ignorant, scared or ashamed, whose denizens are all stock characters from almost "gothic" melodrama, like Sybil Vane's mother in *Dorian Gray*, living in a poverty almost too proverbial to be convincing. And it is perhaps significant that Marcel Proust, who translated Ruskin into French and was influenced by his thought even more than Wilde, likewise neglected, in general, to describe, except his own family, a mean of people who live and work decently, between the maximum of the idle Guermantes world, with its dependent servants and its less brilliant gate-crashers such as the Verdurin set and Madame Cottard, and the minimum of Jupien's den of prostitution.

In his handling of crime too, Wilde seems just as ill at ease and inhibited as in his descriptions of the surroundings of crime and poverty. The Reverend Maturin, in *Melmoth the Wanderer*, had never been able to bring himself to write the exact terms of the pact that his satanic character offered to his prospective victims: "Every night he besets me, and few like me could have resisted his seductions. He has offered, and proved to me, that it is in his power to bestow all that human cupidity could thirst for, on the condition that—I cannot utter! It is one so full of horror and impiety that, even to listen to it, is scarce less a crime than to comply with it!" In *Dorian Gray*, Wilde likewise refrains from ever revealing the exact nature of Dorian's evil influence on the many friends, such as Adrian Singleton or Alan Campbell, whose lives his friendship has irremediably seared; and even when Dorian blackmails Alan into helping him dispose of the murdered painter's corpse, he writes "something" on a paper and hands it to Alan, "something" that makes Alan shudder and comply, but that is never revealed to the reader. Such a curious blockage, in both Maturin and Wilde, can suggest, to the psychoanalytically inclined reader, only a crime which is terribly repressed by the prejudices of the age, perhaps what Lord Alfred Douglas called "the Love that dare not speak its name." And Wilde's unwillingness to name this sin in *Dorian Gray* makes one all the more sceptical of his authorship of *The Priest and the Acolyte*, a strangely sacrilegious and outspoken story which is sometimes attributed to Wilde and, though it handles Wilde's favorite theme of "each man kills the thing he loves," contains none of his ubiquitous paradoxes and epigrams. At the time of Wilde's trial, it was moreover proved conclusively that he had not written *The Priest and the Acolyte*, nor ever met its author, an obscure Oxford undergraduate.

Wilde's unwillingness to handle the details of vice, crime and the underworld as firmly and realistically as he does those of the world of fashion is indeed more than a mere concession to Victorian prudery. He shrinks from it, in his art if not in his life, with the neurotic's resistance, as if from a confession or from the discovery of a maëlstrom of experience into which, as in the tempting visions of *The Sphinx*, he fears being irretrievably drawn. And this squeamishness imposes, on the plot of his novel, some odd distortions which the more objective author of an ordinary mystery-novel would easily have avoided. When Dorian Gray, for instance, seeks "to cure the soul by means of the senses, and the senses by means of the soul," he presses a spring in a cabinet in his home and thus releases a secret drawer where he keeps a box of an unnamed "green paste waxy in lustre, the odour curiously heavy and persistent." This paste is opium; but Dorian Gray, unlike all addicts who always have their pipes at home even if they occasionally run out of "junk," has the opium, it seems, but no pipes. Putting his good opium back in the secret drawer, he therefore rushes out into the night, takes a cab and goes far into London's dock-land, to a low den frequented by sailors and derelicts where the "junk" is surely inferior to what he left at home.

Why this unlikely twist in the novel's plot? The habits of opium-addicts were probably little known to Wilde, and Dorian Gray had to be brought somehow to dock-land in order to be recognized there by dead Sybil Vane's avenging sailor-brother. But James Vane is then so clumsy in shadowing Dorian that he follows him onto a moor, in the midst of a shooting-party, and gets killed accidentally, as he hides behind a bush, by a shot aimed at a hare! This whole episode of frustrated revenge is thus introduced by means of one unlikely scene and resolved in another; and the awkward lack of verisimilitude of its beginning and end reveals Wilde's ignorance and fear of a world of crime with which, in real life, he was doomed to become all too familiar.

In spite of its many weaknesses, *The Picture of Dorian Gray* yet remains, in many respects, a great novel. Though hastily written and clumsily constructed, it manages to haunt many readers with vivid memories of its visionary descriptions. As a masterpiece of the macabre, it is infinitely less diffuse or rhetorical, and told with more economy and fewer tangles and snappings of the thread of narrative, than *Melmoth the Wanderer*. Wilde had indeed profited by the art of Balzac and Flaubert; and when he revived the obsolete genre of the "gothic" or sartorial novel, he avoided much of the formlessness of *Malmoth*, *The Monk* or *Vivian Grey*, so that Wilde's tale now reads better than most of its literary ancestors and conforms more exactly to our stricter and more sober standards of plot, of atmosphere and of probability for the improbable.

But the true greatness of *The Picture of Dorian Gray* resides in the philosophical doctrine which the novel is intended, as a myth, to illustrate. The *Erziehungsroman* of dandyism pretended to instruct the nineteenth-century reader much as Lord Chesterfield had once taught his son, but in a more fictional form, better suited to the tastes of an age which had outgrown even the eighteenth-century taste for the epistolary novel. As a genre, it produced, in England, four resounding successes: *Tremaine*, by Robert Plumer Ward in 1825, Disraeli's *Vivian Grey* in 1826, Bulwer Lytton's *Pelham* in 1828 and, half a century later, *The Picture of Dorian Gray* in 1890. For all its success, *Tremaine* has little doctrine beyond a pious conformism or conservatism and is of no interest today; both *Vivian Grey* and *Pelham* refer to it sarcastically as a favorite among fashionable women. The doctrine of Disraeli's youthful work, for all its refined tastes in Romantic art and scenery, was one of brashly unscrupulous ambition. In his machiavellian intrigues, Vivian was guided by immediately practical considerations; as a more businesslike and less foolish Beau Brummel, he failed to achieve his ends, though he accepted all the corrupt standards of his society, only because he found himself pitted against Mrs. Felix Lorraine, an even more unscrupulous enemy. Bulwer Lytton's novel portrays a "man of fashion" who is saved, by his intellect and his more fastidious moral judgment, from being corrupted by the fashionable society in which he is so successful; *Pelham* portrays Brummel, in Russelton, as a man who came to grief not so much because he failed to manage his affairs according to the principles of the world of fashion as because he lacked the sound sense of values which only a more intellectual or prudential attitude toward life can provide.

The ethical message of *The Picture of Dorian Gray*, though rarely understood because rarely sought, is no less clear than that which Bulwer Lytton explained in his preface. Lord Henry, Wilde's perfect dandy, expounds to Dorian a paradoxical philosophy of dandyism which shocks Basil Halward [*sic*] but appeals to the young narcissist. In the passion of his self-love, Dorian Gray distorts this doctrine and becomes a fallen dandy, corrupting all those who accompany him along his path and murdering his conscience, Basil Halward [*sic*]; finally, in self-inflicted death, Dorian meets the punishment of excessive self-love. But Lord Henry's true doctrine, more spiritually and less prudentially intellectual that Pelham's, was a philosophy of inaction: beyond good and evil, for all his evil-sounding paradoxes which only illustrate the Taoist identity of contraries where both conscience and temptation are placed on the same footing but then transcended, Lord Henry never acts and never falls.

MORSE PECKHAM

From "Identity and Personality" †

In some ways the objectist artists were in the position of Stendhal and Byron and other men of their stage in the development of the nineteenth-century vision. Both groups were reduced to the naked confrontation of self and world. It is, for example, probably one of the consequences of the objectist orientation that Byron's *Don Juan* began, at last, to receive the admiration it deserved, and that this later Byron was seen as far greater than the Byron of *Harold* and *Manfred*. The

---

† From *Beyond the Tragic Vision* (New York: George Braziller, Inc., 1962) 307–25.

morale of both groups, likewise, depended upon the capacity of the self to endure the vision of what it saw.

But there was also a profound difference, and the later groups was in a more perilous and disturbing situation. Both Byron and Stendhal retained enough of the ancient way of thinking to be able to support that endurance with a vision of the self as paradise. Indeed, to individuals who had with great difficulty escaped from valueless negation, it is not surprising, indeed, it is inevitable, that the recovery of selfhood should be felt as an entry into paradise. But the successive attempts to find a metaphysical or divine ground for that paradise—the symmetrical stage and the asymmetrical or transcendental stage—had both failed. When the world was turned inside out, and when value, meaning, and order were derived from the self, a metaphysical ground for that self had to be created; that was the activity of the imagination, whether artistic, metaphysical, or moral. But with the failure of transcendentalism, there was no ground for the self. Consequently, the function of the imagination had to be carried on from without, by imposing upon the self an order not derived from the self. Thus the self could create value by gazing fixedly upon the hell, or meaninglessness, of society and personality. I have compared this imposed order to armor; it would be—or it came to be—better to compare it to stocks, in which the self was rigidly fixed.

In that very act, however, of imposing an external order lay the solution; for if the order was imposed from without, it was the artist who went out and looked for it. If he was in stocks, he was there by his own choice, decision, and moral responsibility. If the imagination chose, from without, a structure to sustain its fixed vision, the decision to choose and the choice itself were acts of the imagination. This realization united all of the formal activities of the objectist imagination; and it was perceived that each of the external controls was a symbolization of the self's orientation, of its creation of value by opposing self to object. It followed, therefore, that all of the various styles used by the objectist were united by the fact that reach was an aspect of style.

In the terms of this book, the function of the orientative drive was seen in a new way. If it was no longer possible to validate the orientative drive and hence the sense of identity or selfhood by appealing to a transcendental source, it first appeared, in the objectist stage, that the orientative drive could be justified only by deriving an orientation from the empirical world. Now it could be seen that the act of derivation was itself the justification for the orientative drive; and that the validity of the orientative drive lay in its very power to seek an orientation for the purpose of engaging with reality. The artistic task, therefore, was no longer to find an external controlling form but to symbolize the orientative drive itself, the power of the individual to maintain his identity by creating an order which would maintain his gaze at the world as it is, at things as they are. In short, the orientative drive became an instrument.

But this was a far different instrumentalism from that evolved by Carlyle and Balzac. With them the instrumental symbol worked to embody, to incarnate the divine, to make the Word into flesh. This new instrumentalism was not a transcendental tool but an orientative tool. The order which style could create was not, then, a divine order which justified man in creating order out of the chaos of a world without value, but a purely human instrumental order which would symbolize man's power to create a subjective order which could fix his gaze upon that valueless world. Further, it was an impersonal order, and for this reason. In distinguishing between self and role, the first two major stages, through transcendentalism, had marked off a preserve within the personality from which redemption could flow. The task was to redeem the rest of the personality (the task of transcendental love) and from that redemption to move on to the redemption of the world. But the objectists had shown that personality is but an aspect of nature and society, and that therefore the personality was also hell. It followed that no area of the personality could be fenced off and designated as paradisiacal, as inherently structured, ordered, valuable, and meaningful.

Therefore, for the old distinction between self and role a new distinction was made, between self and personality. Style, consequently, could not be derived from an internal, accidental randomness which was no different from, which was indeed identical and continuous with, the accidental randomness of society and nature. Hence the new style, which symbolized the distinction between self and personality, could not be extravagant in the transcendental fashion. It could not symbolize the individual's power to maintain orientation in the face of that experienced world of personality, society, and nature. It was, then, the artist's task not to create and symbolize an orientation but to symbolize the orientative power itself. An orientation must necessarily be derived from the personality or, in the objectist mode, from outside the personality, from science, or history, or natural language, and so on. The capacity to find an orientation was, consequently, an impersonal potential. Stylism is marked by a peculiar impersonality.

But it is not marked by non-individuality. The self, even though it was now distinguished from the personality, could be experienced only by the orienting individual. Selfhood, though it was impersonal, was not objective; it remained and necessarily had to remain subjective. As Parsifal revealed, the hell of personality cannot be redeemed by concealing dependence upon the mother under the mask of transcendental eroticism. Personality, as he discovered in his wanderings between Act II and Act III, cannot be redeemed; only selfhood can be redeemed. The individual, therefore, cannot redeem others, for that would be to attempt to redeem their personalities; he can only demonstrate that he has redeemed his selfhood. He can only be a model to others, by exhibiting the power of self-redemption. Parsifal does not return from his wandering a conquering hero; that would mean a redemption of his personality. He returns exhausted, his personality reduced to valuelessness. Nevertheless, he remains Parsifal. He does not become "man" or "Christ" or anything of the sort. Nor, when he has touched Amfortas' wound and thus healed with the spear of selfhood the bleeding and torturing horror of personality, does he vanish from the earth or ascend into heaven. Quite the contrary, he becomes king of the Grail knights. The achievement of selfhood makes it possible for him to use personality as an instrument to empathize with other men's experience of the hell of personality, and his own sufferings enable them to empathize with his. He does not become Christ or a symbol of Christ. He uses Christ's suffering in the hell of personality and world as a model which gives him the power to perceive that world and personality are hell, are valueless. Thus he remains Parsifal, a unique individual; only the self-redeemed is truly redeemed. His individuality has value, though his personality does not.

For this reason, the new style was at once impersonal and individual, and the art of the past was neither a tradition to be triumphantly exploited by the personality nor the source of styles and forms to be arbitrarily imposed from without. Rather, it became a model; and the artist's task was not to imitate it but to grasp its essence. A tradition gave the artist impersonality; to make a unique use of the tradition gave him individuality or selfhood. Thus Wagner used, in *Parsifal*, the Christian tradition; but he used it in a unique way, in a manner that was uniquely his own, with style. Further, the essence of any orientative tradition is, of course, not what it says, not the orientation its presents, but its power to order and thus to symbolize value. This was what distinguished art from all other orientative activities; its power to symbolize individuality and selfhood as opposed to personality and lack of identity meant that it was the opposite of hell—personality and the objective world. Art, therefore, was not symbolic of paradise; it was paradise. In itself it was order, meaning, and value.

The men who came after the objectists, therefore, applied to the essence of art the word which had been traditionally applied to paradise: beauty. The religion of beauty, "aestheticism," was thus born; for the word "aesthetic" was traditionally applied both to "that which is characteristic of works of art" and "that which is beautiful." The relation between religion and art was conceived as symbolic; but the symbolism went in the opposite direction. Art was not symbolic of the divine; rather, the fiction or illusion of the divine was man's way of symbolizing the essence of art. As in *Parsifal*, religion did not redeem art; art redeemed religion. Indeed, it also redeemed science; and the vitality of this tradition appears today when the scientist attempts to demonstrate that his also is an aesthetic activity and worthy to rank beside the artist's. Beauty, then, is the union of the impersonal and of the individual's experience of selfhood; and beauty is immanent in the work of art. The task of the artist is to create that beauty.

Nevertheless, the position was not arrived at in one leap; two stages may be discerned. In the first there is a continuity of the objectist confrontation of self with the valuelessness of the world; but the function of the external and arbitrary control is assumed by the impersonal and individual style derived from artistic tradition. To the ugliness of personality and reality is opposed the beauty of selfhood. We have already seen that shift in *Parsifal*, in which expressiveness is subordinated to a stylistic continuity of aesthetic surface, to beauty. In the work of the English poet, Algernon Charles Swinburne, born in 1837, we see the poetic analogy to *Parsifal*, but the subordination of expression to beauty is even more striking than in Wagner's last work, even though Swinburne formed his style in the 1860's, when Wagner, still an objectist, was composing *The Meistersinger* and had still to complete *The Ring of the Nibelungs*. Swinburne's achievement may be brought out by contrasting *Atlanta in Calydon*, published in 1865, with Wagner's *Tristan and Isolde*, completed in 1859, when Swinburne, like Siegfried, was just beginning to forge his style out of the shattered fragments of the tradition.

That Swinburne belonged to a new generation, with an orientation profoundly different from that of his objectist predecessors, comes out in the way he trained himself to be a poet. No English poet before him had so thoroughly mastered the styles which tradition had already created. The traditional ballad style of the Scotch border (he grew up in Northumbria, the northernmost shire of England), the Chaucerian style, the various Elizabethan and seventeenth-century baroque styles, the styles of Dryden and Pope, and of the nineteenth-century poets, particularly those friends and immediate predecessors, Rossetti and William Morris—he not only experimented with all of them, he mastered them so completely that he could write in each with the ease of the original poets who created and used them. He became a poetic chameleon, able to use any of the major styles of the tradition with stylistic mastery and expressiveness. From these he forged his own style, which began to emerge in the early 1860's.

The peculiar character of Swinburne's poetry, which is in general the character of the first stage of the stylistic era, is the contrast between the beauty of the aesthetic surface and the material from the world of experience which is the subject matter. In this he goes, as already suggested, beyond Wagner, for the aesthetic surface is far more non-expressive than it is even in *Parsifal*. In the ordinary, non-metaphysical and non-evaluative use of the word "beauty" it is a quality most commonly ascribed to sets of sensory data to which we can relate ourselves with the least loss of energy. It offers the maximum opportunities for orientation. Each discriminable element or entity within the situation offers of itself a minimum of emotional disturbance, to the point of being emotionally negative, and at the same time permits the observer to perceive readily a large number of relationships between it and the other elements or entities present. In short, it presents the maximum degree of structure which the artist can manage to create. Or the mathematician. The claim, cor stantly encountered in both the Platonic tradition and any form of the aesthetic or stylistic tradition, that there is an affinity between art and mathematics, and the continuous, though mistaken, efforts to solve the problem of artistic judgment by asserting that a work of art is beautiful to the degree its formal relationships may be mathematically described, are both instances of identifying art with structure. The offer by the work of art of a rich opportunity to experience a high degree of structure is precisely the character of Swinburne's style. In the ordinary sense, non-metaphysical and non-evaluative, it is as "beautiful" as Swinburne could make it. His study of traditional styles and the innumerable poetic exercises he wrote in them had but one aim: to discover the essence of their art, that is, by stylistic standards, the peculiar structural devices to be found in each. By abstracting these structural devices and coordinating them in his own poetry—poems, that is, which were not exercises—he created his own style. It was, then, at once traditional and individual, highly disciplined and unmistakably Swinburne's.

There is no device of poetic form which he does not master and incorporate: sound relations, that is, rhyme, alliteration (consonantal repetition), assonance (vowel repetition and similarity); stress relations, that is, rhythmical patterns and an extraordinary rapidity of rhythmical movement which makes the patterns of rhythm leap out at the reader so that he grasps them immediately; and syntax relations, long sentences of great syntactical complexity which are, however, given continuity and repetition of pattern by exploiting the possibilities of parallel syntactical structure.

This beauty of surface is responsible for very positive reactions from the reader. One reader finds it ravishing and enchanting, utterly irresistible; another, perceiving only the continuity of the aesthetic surface but incapable of responding to the variety within the patterning, to the subtle and constant play of discontinuity, finds it monotonous and excessively lengthy; a third, more perceptive, objects violently to the disparity between the extreme beauty of the surface and the highly disturbing content of the poems. It is notable that each of these objections has been made to *Parsifal*, and in general is constantly made to all of the work of this first stage in the development of stylism. Both of the first two responses are equally imperceptive; the one, carried away by the beauty, and the other, bored by it, experience the surface so powerfully that they are unable to get beyond it into what the poem is saying. To the one the poem is meaningless but beautiful; to the other the poem is merely beautiful but makes no sense. The third, however, sees what is there, but objects to Swinburne's work on the ground that the aesthetic surface is nonfunctional, that is, it is inexpressive of the emotions presented by the structure of the poem's meanings. Such critics are, of course, perfectly correct; but they miss the point.

To Swinburne, as a stylist, the emotion of situations is inseparable both from society and personality, while the self if not part of the personality but antithetical to it. The capacity of the self to create a world of order, meaning, and value, that is, beauty, is symbolized by the style, the consistency of aesthetic surface. Everything that the self experiences, however, is meaningless, chaotic, and without value. What the poem refers to outside of itself, therefore, is highly disturbing and intensely emotional. In the stylistic stage of nineteenth-century culture, the self functions both as gratifying cave and as observatory tower. The highly structured style, with its maximum opportunities for ready orientation and formal and sensuous gratification, offers a position or a stance from which one may safely observe and experience the chaos and ugliness of reality, whether that reality is within the personality or outside of it or lies in the relation between the personal and the non-personal. Thus the drive toward orientation is satisfied and simultaneously the drive toward reality is released. The chaos of reality can be permitted to invade the utmost recesses of the personality. Consequently Swinburne and his fellows and their successors have an extraordinary psychological penetration and a power to admit the existence within the personality, in society, and in the natural world, of horrors which even Baudelaire and the objectists had not quite been able to encounter. The first stage of stylism, therefore, involves the reconsideration of everything the objectists had looked at, but with a structured self, symbolized in aesthetic surface or style, rather than with an enduring self, the presence of which is only implicit.

The subject matter of Swinburne's poetry moves outward in steadily expanding circles; he begins with the horrors of personality, proceeds to the horrors of the family, goes on to the horrors of society, and ends with the horrors of nature, its indifference, its amused and equivocal juggling of creation and destruction. His early poetry, most of which was written before *Atalanta in Calydon*, though it was published in 1866, in *Poems and Ballads*, a year after *Atalanta*, is mostly concerned with one theme, the eroticism of submission and domination, with sadism and masochism, in this resembling *Parsifal* and *Venus in Furs*, published, it will be remembered, in 1870. Swinburne himself was a masochist; he knew what he was talking about, whereas Baudelaire, who inspired Swinburne to these themes, probably was less familiar than he with the actual practices, such as achieving erotic gratification by being whipped. It is an instance of how the stylists can go farther even than the objectists and can admit in themselves horrors which one is supposed to conceal, even from oneself, if possible.

It is not surprising, therefore, that Swinburne should also, in several poems, have written about Lesbianism, homo-eroticism among women. It is interesting, though anything that can be called evidence is wholly lacking, that a persistent rumor in the English literary world affirms that Swinburne himself was homosexual or at least, like Byron, bisexual. Were the poems about Sappho and her maidens a Proustian reversal of the actual state of affairs within Swinburne's own personality? Certainly, in his letters he vehemently denies such imputations and excoriates contemporaries, such as John Addington Symonds, who were homo-erotic. Perhaps the tendencies were there, but repressed, Swinburne permitting them to reveal themselves only in reversal, in the Lesbos poems.

Whatever the biographical facts, it is not difficult to see the place of the Sappho poems in the psychological structure of *Poems and Ballads*; for both homo-eroticism and hetero-eroticism are seen as equally characterized by sadism and masochism, by violation of others and by submitting to others so that one may suffer violation. Further, this exposure of the true nature of eroticism as an excuse for violation and self-violation is no mere expression of tendencies in Swinburne's own personality. If they were that, the poems would be a defense or rationalization of sadism and masochism. On the contrary, they are an exposure of the failure of eroticism, which from its very nature produces a frustration which can be gratified only with destruction or self-destruction, torture and murder, or self-laceration and suicide. Eroticism is revealed as something inseparable from emotional and physical suffering and torture.

Swinburne's experience in publishing these poems was much like Baudelaire's with *The Flowers of Evil*. The outcry against them was so great that though no legal steps were taken, Swinburne's publisher refused to continue and the poet had to find another publisher, one with a rather unsavory reputation for publishing and dealing in pornography and semi-pornography. His fury against the Philistines is quite understandable. He was condemned for attempting a serious and poetic treatment of themes the existence of which the critics, those Cerberus guardians of the public morality, would scarcely even admit, ascribing everything in Swinburne's book to his own diseased imagination; yet while Swinburne was being attacked and an attempt was being made to drive his book out of the literary market, two streets in London were entirely devoted to selling pornographic literature, art, and objects which were not always *objets d'art*.

A similar attempt was made for the rest of the century to discredit the followers of Swinburne in this stage of his development, the decadents, who likewise created works of art characterized by great beauty or surface and style with an exploration of the most profoundly concealed and erotically sinister aspects of the personality. Their style was exquisite; their subject was sexual transgression and what the Philistine called perversion. The strategy of the attacks on the decadents was, of course, always to ascribe the creation of such works to the depravity of their personalities. The truth of the matter is that sometimes the transgressions of the decadents were imaginative and sometimes they themselves were transgressors. In either case their explorations into the horrors of personality were sustained by style. In art they were aesthetes or, to use the term of this book, stylists; in life they were dandies.

In considering this matter it is wise to remember that the market for true pornography, the purveying of pornography unredeemed by style, of pornography for its own sake, is primarily the well-to do middle class. The respectable citizen buys the vast majority of pornographic publications. The high prices for such books are and always have been the proof; only the economically self-disciplined can afford them. As Wagner said in the opening of *The Rhinegold*, the lust for economic power is the consequence of frustrated eroticism. There is even some reason to believe that economic lust can be more easily controlled in a country in which little or no legal control is extended over pornography. There is certainly every reason to believe that pornography serves an important social function of some kind or other, and that it best serves that function when enough legal barriers are put up to make procuring it not really dangerous but truly venturesome, at least when, as in middle-class society, it functions in part as a reward for economic self-discipline.

The difference between pornography and the literature and art of the decadents lies precisely here. In pornography eroticism is not presented as a horror, as an illusion, as necessarily frustrating all true gratification. In the part of the Swinburnian decadents it is. The Philistine hates the decadents because they spoil his favorite reading matter, whether found forthrightly in pornography or concealed in sentimental novels, plays, magazine stories, movies, and television. The Philistine lives and loves under the illusion that eroticism is gratifying; that it is an illusion the active practice of psychiatrists—not to speak of those cassocked men in confession booths who serve the same function—demonstrates only too amply. The literature of the decadents reveals that illusion for what it is, something that invariably leads to domination or submission, or both, and thus invariably to violation of another human being. Pornography, however, not only does not reveal violation as violation; it positively approves it. It is a morality of immediate and total gratification consequent upon the erotic invasion of another personality. Pornography, then, finds its great market among the Philistine middle classes not because it is immoral but precisely because it thoroughly embodies the Philistine morality. The literature of the decadents is morally responsible; it reveals the horror of eroticism.

The interpretation of Oscar Wilde's *The Picture of Dorian Gray* (1891) is a case in point. Dorian remains forever young and beautiful, but his picture reflects the progressive effects upon his personality of his exploration of vice, which seems all the more vicious because it is so inadequately specified. But it was not Wilde's purpose to write a pornographic novel, nor yet a cautionary tale. Dorian is the dandy, the man of style. The point of the story is that such a man can maintain his identity while he investigates the most terrible pits of London's erotic and economic sub-world. The elegance of London civilization and the horror of the world on which it is built and on the existence of which its own economic and emotional existence depends are sharply juxtaposed. Dorian is the artist, the dandy, the stylist whose identity is presented as antithetical to his personality. True, he is destroyed by what he experiences, but not until he is an old man. And after all, who is not destroyed by the hell of the personality and the society which his identity exists in? If the novel were a mere middle-class morality tale, when he dies the beautiful Dorian should become as ugly, as depraved, as misshapen as his picture. But actually, as he becomes what his picture is, his picture regains all the beauty of Dorian as a young man, a beauty which he had kept throughout his long life. The end products of his life are a ruined body which is continuous with his personality and his society, and a work of art which will symbolize forever his power to explore the hell of reality.

Wilde's mistake was to attempt to live his novel, to use, as he said, his genius in his life and his mere talent in his art. He was condemned to prison and driven into exile and poverty because he had sexually cohabited with a few of the large class of London homosexual prostitutes. These male prostitutes would not have existed—and would not exist today, and not just in London—had there not been an economic demand for them. Like pornography, and for the same reason and in the same way, they were supported—in modest splendor—by the economic discipline of the middle classes, and had been for decades; and before them, so far as we can tell, by the aristocracy. Perhaps, after all, Wilde was not condemned for immorality but for poaching.

* * *

BARBARA CHARLESWORTH

Oscar Wilde †

In *A Vision* Yeats used Oscar Wilde as one of his examples of those who live in the nineteenth phase of the lunar cycle, the phase which marks the beginning of "the artificial, the abstract, the fragmentary, and the dramatic." The man of this phase is forced "to live in a fragment of himself and to dramatise that fragment."[1] Others have had the same sense of Wilde's fragmentation. Arthur Symons describes him as one who made for himself many souls "of intricate pattern and elaborate colour, webbed into infinite tiny cells."[2] Then he modified the image: Wilde is not only a craftsman but also a skilled juggler who amuses people by whirling his separate "souls" before them. Later he uses yet another metaphor, clearing the theatre and making Wilde the only spec-

† From *Dark Passages: The Decadent Consciousness in Victorian Literature* (Madison: U of Wisconsin P, 1965) 53–80.
1. W. B. Yeats, *A Vision* (New York, 1938), p. 148.

2. Arthur Symons, *A Study of Oscar Wilde* (London, 1930), p. 50.

tator of his own performance: "One sees that to him everything was drama, all the rest of the world and himself as well; himself indeed always at once the protagonist and the lonely king watching the play in the theatre emptied for his pleasure."[3]

On the basis of a somewhat similar theory about Wilde, Arthur Nethercot made a study of *The Picture of Dorian Gray* and of Wilde's plays in which he suggested that "he [Wilde] split himself into two parts, into two types of self-representative."[4] The later discovery of a letter from Wilde to an otherwise unknown admirer, Ralph Payne, helped to prove that both his theory and Symons' were correct: that is to say, that Wilde, even more consciously than most writers, split himself into various characters and saw in all of them some portion of his actual or potential self: "I am so glad you like that strange many coloured book of mine *[The Picture of Dorian Gray]*: it contains much of me in it. Basil Hallward is what I think I am: Lord Henry, what the world thinks me: Dorian what I would like to be—in other ages, perhaps."[5] This letter suggests the way in which it might best be possible to understand Oscar Wilde: by separating him, as he separated himself, into several selves (each, however, watching the other selves and offering comments upon or even engaging in dialogues with the self at stage-center), remembering always that the man and his work are inextricable, though the work too is a mask.

I   The Mask of Dorian Gray

In the opening scene of *The Picture of Dorian Gray* Basil Hallward and Lord Henry Wotton discuss Dorian Gray's physical beauty and his innocence: these are his given characteristics, but when he himself appears, the qualities in him that seem more striking are his quickness and docility—he is a good student. When Lord Henry "with that graceful wave of the hand that was always so characteristic of him" (and of Wilde) tells him that "the aim of life is self-development," Dorian understands immediately, just as a good student in the humanities might, the relevance of the doctrine to actual experience. And Oscar Wilde, like Dorian Gray, was also in this sense a good student. In his first term at Oxford in 1874, Wilde attended Ruskin's lectures on the "Aesthetic and Mathematic Schools of Art in Florence"; he became such an enthusiastic follower of Ruskin's teaching that he was one of the group which helped to build—or attempted to build—a road between Upper and Lower Hinksey. "Art and the Handicraftsman," one of Wilde's American lectures, gives his version of the story; in it he becomes one of the students with whom Ruskin first discussed the project. And, after all, he made it a good story, although the road-work had already begun when Wilde

3. *Ibid.*, pp. 84–85.
4. Arthur Nethercot, "Oscar Wilde and the Devil's Advocate," *PMLA*, LIX (September, 1944), 843.
5. Oscar Wilde, *The Letters of Oscar Wilde*, ed.

Rupert Hart-Davis (New York, Harcourt, Brace, 1962), p. 352. Future references to this work will be cited in the text under the title *Letters*.

arrived in Oxford. Wilde's telling of it is only a slight elaboration, nothing to compare to the splendid lie with which he begins his account: "Well, let me tell you how it first came to me at all to create an artistic movement in England, a movement to show the rich what beautiful things they might enjoy and the poor what beautiful things they might create."[6]

While he was still a student Wilde wrote an essay on the Grosvenor Gallery exhibition of 1877 that showed a truer sense of intellectual history. There he mentioned "that revival of culture and love of beauty which in great part owes it birth to Mr. Ruskin, and which Mr. Swinburne, and Mr. Pater, and Mr. Symonds, and Mr. Morris, and many others, are fostering and keeping alive, each in his own particular fashion."[7] The review itself is written wholly under the influence of Ruskin: Wilde praises all the pictures done in the Pre-Raphaelite manner and gives Whistler only a slighting mention; moreover, his criticism itself tends, like Ruskin's, to be anecdotal. For instance, Wilde praises a painting called "Afterglow in Egypt" for its coloring, but, he says, "It is difficult to feel a human interest in this Egyptian peasant."[8]

It was partly as a result of this essay that Wilde began to move from the orbit of Ruskin towards that of Walter Pater: Wilde sent Pater a copy of his essay and received a cordial reply in which Pater suggested that they meet to discuss certain points about which they were not in agreement, "though," he continued, "on the whole I think your criticisms very just, and they are certainly very pleasantly expressed" (*Letters*, p. 47).

In *De Profundis* Wilde says that it was in his first term at Oxford, the term in which he trundled stones for Ruskin's road, that he read Pater's *The Renaissance*, "that book which was to have such strange influence over my life"[9] (*Letters*, p. 471). Of course, it may be an oversimplification—more than that, an affectation—to say that the course of one's life has been changed by a book; nevertheless, it is possible that, like many of Wilde's dramatic simplicities, this "explanation" is true in essentials.[1] A single book could change the whole course of a man's life if it expressed all the things that he was already prepared to believe. And Pater's uncanny ability to catch and hold the drift of intellectual experience in his time gave his work extraordinary power. Arthur Symons, for instance, also

6. Oscar Wilde, "Art and the Handicraftsman," *Miscellanies*, Vol. XIV of Robert Ross's edition of Wilde's collected works (14 vols.; Boston, [1910]), p. 307. This edition of Wilde's works will be referred to hereafter as *Collected Works*.
7. Oscar Wilde, "The Grovesnor Gallery," *Miscellanies* (*Collected Works*, Vol. XIV), p. 23.
8. *Ibid.*, p. 11.
9. Yeats remembers hearing Wilde say of *The Renaissance*: "It is my golden book; I never travel anywhere without it; but it is the very flower of decadence: the last trumpet should have sounded the moment it was written."—W. B. Yeats, *The Autobiography of William Butler Yeats* (New York, 1938), p. 114.
1. Robert Sherard, discussing the statement, "For years Dorian Gray could not free himself from the influence of this book [*A Rebours*]," says sharply, "This is, of course, silliness. Yet Oscar Wilde used to make the same silly self-deceiving statements about himself, and attributed to some 'poisonous book' which he had once read [*The Renaissance*?] many of the abnormalities of his conduct."—Sherard, *The Life of Oscar Wilde* (New York, 1928), p. 66.

writes about *The Renaissance* as a book which "opened a new world to me, or rather, gave me the secret of the world in which I was living," and with a single detail he gives his comment the ring of truth: he says that he read *The Renaissance* in its first edition on ribbed paper—"I have the feel of it still in my fingers."[2]

In the world of art, in any event, such things are possible, and Lord Henry Wotton changes Dorian Gray's life within the space of an afternoon by preaching a sermon based on the "Conclusion" to *The Renaissance*, beginning with the horror of time's passing, the loss of youth, the short time in which strong sensation is possible, and ending with the exhortation: "Live! Live the wonderful life that is in you! Let nothing be lost upon you. Be always searching for new sensations." As he preaches, Lord Henry notices the strong effect of his words, and his memories make it clear that he is not meant to represent Pater; he is the older Wilde remembering what he himself had once learned: "He [Lord Henry] was amazed at the sudden impression that his words had produced, and, remembering a book that he had read when he was sixteen, a book that had revealed to him much that he had not known before, he wondered whether Dorian was passing through a similar experience." The point is an important one because of the changes which Lord Henry makes in the message of *The Renaissance*; the words he uses may almost paraphrase Pater's, but the doctrine is Wilde's.

A scene from *The Ambassadors* shows the difference. The situation is very like that in *The Picture of Dorian Gray*: an older man, Lambert Strether, is giving a younger one, Little Bilham, the philosophy taught him by his own experience. The very words echo Lord Wotton's: "Live all you can; it's a mistake not to. It doesn't matter what you do in particular, so long as you have your life."[3] But the difference between Lord Wotton and Lambert Strether lies in Strether's belief that he must desire nothing, save his impressions, for himself. In his selflessness he is a Paterean saint, while Lord Wotton, whose search is not for "impressions" but for "sensations," is among the damned. Strether finds his pleasure in his vision of others; Lord Wotton is interested in the effects of external stimuli upon his own consciousness. His gaze is fixed upon himself. Pater had written, "We may well grasp at any exquisite passion, or contribution to knowledge that seems by a lifted horizon to set the spirit free for a moment."[4] The moment of great intensity, whether sensual, emotional, or intellectual, serves as an escape from imprisoning self-consciousness. Dorian Gray, under the tutelage of Lord Wotton, takes pleasure not so much in enjoyment of the moment as in watching the effect of the moment upon himself.

Gray makes another important modification of Pater's doctrine when

2. Arthur Symons, "Introduction," *The Renaissance* (Modern Library Edition, New York, [1919]), p. xv.
3. Henry James, *The Ambassadors* (2 vols.; New York, 1909), I, 217.
4. Walter Pater, "Conclusion," *Studies in the History of the Renaissance* (London, 1873), p. 211.

he uses evil acts as a means of achieving "sensations." His hope as he does so is to come to ever deeper self-knowledge, ever wider self-expression. And so it fascinates him to think that he can watch the gradual process of his own corruption in the portrait: "He would be able to follow his mind into its most secret places. This portrait would be to him the most magical of mirrors. As it revealed to him his own body, so it would reveal his own soul."

But the portrait really gives only a partial revelation; it presents no vision of the "best self," and by taking its partial revelation for the whole truth, Dorian Gray narrows his consciousness. Pater in his review of the book makes that point and protests at the same time against the interpretation put upon his theory—if so strong a word as "protest" may be used for his blandly remote comment: "A true Epicureanism aims at a complete though harmonious development of man's entire organism. To lose the moral sense, therefore, for instance, the sense of sin and righteousness, as Mr. Wilde's hero—his heroes seem bent on doing as speedily, as completely as they can, is to lose, or lower, organization, to become less complex, to pass from a higher to a lower degree of development."[5] And indeed, although his first letter to Wilde was flatteringly cordial, Pater came in time to find his young student just as distressing as he later found the fictitious Dorian Gray.[6]

André Gide's account of one of the stories Wilde often told (though from behind the Lord Henry mask) makes Pater's distrust understandable. Wilde had noticed that Gide listened with intensity to all that was said: "You listen with your eyes," Wilde commented, and he went on to tell of the flowers which had asked the river for water that they might weep for Narcissus, who had just died. The river refused, saying that all the drops of water it contained were not enough for his own tears, so much had he loved Narcissus:

> " 'Oh!' replied the flowers of the field, 'how could you not have loved Narcissus? He was beautiful.' 'Was he beautiful?' said the river. 'And who could know better than you? Each day, leaning over your banks, he beheld his beauty in your water . . .' "
>
> Wilde paused for a moment . . .
> " 'If I loved him,' replied the river, 'it was because, when he leaned over my water, I saw the reflection of my waters in his eyes.' "
>
> Then Wilde, swelling up with a strange burst of laughter, added, "That's called *The Disciple*."[7]

5. Walter Pater, "A Novel by Mr. Oscar Wilde," *Uncollected Essays* (Portland, Maine, 1903), p. 127.
6. In the Introduction to his edition of Wilde's reviews Robert Ross comments: "The great men of the previous generation, Wilde's intellectual peers, with whom he was in artistic sympathy, looked on him askance. Ruskin was disappointed with his former pupil, and Pater did not hesitate to express disapprobation to private friends; while he accepted incense from a disciple, he distrusted the thurifer."—*Reviews* (*Collected Works*, Vol. XII), p. xii. Ross is not reliable in his interpretation or even his presentation of facts—it seems unlikely, for instance, that Ruskin thought about Wilde one way or another—but here he may be giving at least a partial truth.
7. André Gide, *Oscar Wilde*, tr. Bernard Frechtman (New York, 1949), pp. 3–4.

This, however, is the attitude of a different Oscar Wilde; his youthful change from following Ruskin to following Pater was much less conscious and not at all cynical. By the time he wrote another criticism of a Grosvenor Gallery exhibition, that of 1879, he showed a difference in his views by the praise he gave to Whistler;[8] in "L'Envoi," written in 1882 while he was in America, Wilde formally avowed his withdrawal from Ruskin's sphere of influence and made his presence in Pater's apparent by his generous (though unacknowledged) quotation from the master.

Although Wilde says that "we of the younger school have made a departure from the teaching of Ruskin,—a departure definite, and different and decisive," he realizes at least partially the effect Ruskin's teaching had had upon Oxford. Wilde's opinion of the nature of his achievement is interesting in that, with some justice, it relates Ruskin's work more closely to Pater's than either man might have liked; he writes that Ruskin "taught us at Oxford that enthusiasm for beauty which is the secret of Hellenism." But Ruskin cannot be an acceptable master, "for the keystone of his aesthetic system is ethical always."[9]

Wilde posed in "L'Envoi" as the acknowledged leader of his generation. Indeed, his high-handedness offended Rennell Rodd, the author of *Rose Leaf and Apple Leaf* for which this essay served as preface, because Wilde, as self-appointed editor, cut out of the book two poems Rodd had intended to publish and then wrote himself a fulsome dedication in Rodd's name.[1] But Wilde's lofty tone and loftier actions show that he would have liked to be what later he attempted to make of Dorian Gray: "Indeed there were many . . . who saw, or fancied that they saw, in Dorian Gray the true realization of a type of which they had often dreamed in Eton or Oxford days—a type that was to combine something of the real culture of the scholar with all the grace and distinction and perfect manner of a citizen of the world." It may have been Wilde's desire to be the man of this new Renaissance—a Renaissance patterned by Pater—that moved him in 1881 to issue his *Poems*. It is hard otherwise to explain how a man who wrote so fine a critical essay as "The Critic as Artist" would not recognize his own poems as bad art.

A good many of the *Poems* are simply schoolboy exercises in which Wilde wrote patriotic, hortatory sonnets in the manner of Milton and Wordsworth; wistful, Catholic sonnets in the manner of Rossetti; lush,

8. Wilde, *Miscellanies* (*Collected Works*, Vol. XIV), p. 27.
9. Oscar Wilde, "L'Envoi, an Introduction to *Rose Leaf and Apple Leaf*," *Miscellanies* (*Collected Works*, Vol. XIV), pp. 31–32. In the Widener Collection there is a copy of *The Happy Prince and Other Tales* (London, 1888) which bears the autograph inscription: "To John Ruskin in all love and loyalty from Oscar Wilde. June '88."

1. A manuscript letter in Houghton Library from Walter E. Ledger to Thomas B. Mosher, written from Wimbledon, England, on February 12, 1906, says that "Sir Rennell Rodd quarrelled with Wilde when the latter published Rose Leaf and Apple Leaf, for it was without Rodd's permission. The original title of the work was 'Songs in the South' and it was dedicated to Rodd's father. Two of the poems in it were omitted in the American edition."

pagan effusions in the manner of Swinburne.[2] Nevertheless, the general
pattern of the book parallels Wilde's account of Dorian Gray's "search
for sensations." In the section of *Dorian Gray* modelled mainly upon
Huysmans' *A Rebours* Wilde says that Dorian, desiring experience "that
would be at once new and delightful, and possess that element of
strangeness so essential to romance . . . would often adopt certain modes
of thought that he knew to be really alien to his nature." He was, for
instance, attracted for a while to the Roman Catholic ritual, as well as
to mysticism ("and the subtle antinomianism that seems to accompany
it") and to the materialism of the *Darwinismus* movement in Germany.
"Yet as has been said before, no theory of life seemed to him to be of
any importance compared with life itself."

Now as it happened there seemed also the possibility around the year
1877 that Wilde might become a Catholic,[3] and several of the earlier
poems in the book describe the Church's fascination for him: "Rome
Unvisited," "Urbs Sacra Æterna," and "Sonnet on hearing the Dies Irae
sung in the Sistine Chapel." Following the section of the book which
contains these poems comes "The Burden of Itys," which rejects Catholicism and celebrates the return of a splendid new Hellenism:

> Poor Fra Giovanni bawling at the mass
> Were out of tune now, for a small brown bird
> Sings overhead, and through the long cool grass
> I see that throbbing throat which once I heard
> On starlit hills of flower-starred Arcady.[4]

A later poem, "Panthea," takes the position that human happiness lies
in the recognition that we shall "through all æons mix and mingle with
the Kosmic Soul!" (*Poems*, p. 191)—while further on "Humanitad" asserts
that "That which is purely human, that is Godlike, that is God" (*Poems*,
p. 228). Of course, it is possible to argue that Dryden's *Collected Works*
would show just as many changes of opinion: the opinion itself is poeti-
cally not of importance so much as the truth of its expression, its truth,
so to speak, to itself. But this is precisely where Wilde fails: he is not true
even to his changing opinions; he is much more conscious of himself as
Wilde the Catholic, Wilde the pagan, Wilde the humanist, than he is
of the Catholicism, paganism, or humanism he professes. Knowing that
such an objection is possible, he gives this justification for the "insincerity" of Dorian Gray:

2. *The Athenaeum* reviewed the poem, listing the
imitations from Shakespeare, Milton, Tennyson,
and Swinburne, and concluding that "there is
scarcely a poet of high mark in this century who'se
influence is not perceptible."—*The Athenaeum*,
No. 2804 (July 23, 1881), p. 103.
3. A letter from Wilde to Reginald Harding, sent
from Merrion Square, Dublin, in July, 1877, shows

that Wilde's "Romish leanings" moved a wealthy
cousin virtually to strike him from his will.—
Vyvyan Holland, *Son of Oscar Wilde* (London,
1954), p. 243.
4. Oscar Wilde, "The Burden of Itys," *Poems*
(*Collected Works*, Vol. I), p. 83. Future references
will be made in the text under the title *Poems*.

Is insincerity such a terrible thing? I think not. It is merely a method by which we can multiply our personalities.

Such at any rate was Dorian Gray's opinion. He used to wonder at the shallow psychology of those who conceive the Ego in man as a thing simple, permanent, reliable, and of one essence. To him, man was a being with myriad lives and myriad sensations, a complex multiform creature that bore within himself strange legacies of thought and passion, and whose very flesh was tainted with the monstrous maladies of the dead.

As the passage continues, it becomes obvious that the adoption of a new idea or belief serves only as the opportunity for acting a different role, for Wilde moves from a discussion of Dorian Gray's changing opinions to a description of his imaginative identification with different personalities, first those of his historical ancestors and then those of his "ancestors in literature." It is worth noting that he is drawn only to depravity, but what is really more important is that his imagination shows a reverse, a Decadent 'negative capability." Instead of losing himself in other people or ideas, he brings them into himself until indeed only his own ego exists: "There were times when it appeared to Dorian Gray that the whole of history was merely the record of his own life, not as he had lived it in act and circumstance, but as his imagination had created it for him, as it had been in his brain and in his passions."

Wilde's poem "The Sphinx" and the play *Salomé* are both marred by qualities which resemble those of Dorian Gray's reveries. Both are sexual fantasies which dwell on the morbid and even the depraved, but although the subject matter itself can partially account for the atmosphere of decay which pervades them, it is its manner of presentation which throws around these works an even more lurid, phosphorescent light. The meditations on the strange half-bestial lovers of the Sphinx or on Salomé's passion for John the Baptist are auto-eroticism, not negative capability. There is no question of Wilde thinking himself into the soul of Salomé, understanding her motivation, suffering her passion; he is simply using Salomé imaginatively in order to experience a new *frisson*. And, when Herod turns at the end of the play and gives orders, "Tuez cette femme,"[5] the act itself means nothing save that the reverie is over: Salomé has fulfilled her function.

When Dorian Gray, frightened by the near success of Jim Vane's vengeful attempt to kill him, decides that he will reform his life, his first act of virtue is to spare the honor of a country maiden—an act which

5. Oscar Wilde, *Salomé* (*Collected Works*, Vol VI), p. 67. Sometimes Wilde's inability to efface himself in a poetic reverie has very amusing consequences. In "The Burden of Itys," for instance, he adopts Baudelaire's lines on Michelangelo's "Night":

Ou bien toi, grande Nuit, fille de Michel-Ange,
Qui tords paisiblement dans une pose étrange
Tes appas façonnés aux bouches des Titans!

(Charles Baudelaire, "L'Idéal," *Les Fleurs du Mal*)
and makes them:
"O . . . that I could charm
The Dawn at Florence from its dumb despair
Mix with those mighty limbs and make that giant breast my lair!" (*Poems*, p. 92.)

shows Gray's lack of originality in virtue as well as in sin. But Lord Henry Wotton makes him realize that even goodness is now only another form of self-consciousness for him, still another *frisson* for one to whom every sort of vice has now become monotonous. Dorian begins to wonder: "Had it been merely vanity that had made him do his one good deed? Or the desire of a new sensation, as Lord Henry had hinted with his mocking laugh? Or that passion to act a part that sometimes makes us do things finer than we are ourselves? Or perhaps all of these?" At last he concludes that it was, indeed, all of these, and utterly trapped, he stabs the portrait and kills himself.

One of the reasons that *De Profundis* makes such painful reading is that Wilde there shows himself equally trapped within the mask of Dorian Gray. Though he may wish and intend repentance, he cannot keep himself from dramatizing the wish at the same time, so that it becomes unreal, perhaps even to himself. Repentance itself becomes a new and different kind of "moment":

> I remember that as I was sitting in the dock on the occasion of my last trial listening to Lockwood's appalling denunciation of me . . . and being sickened with horror at what I heard, suddenly it occurred to me. *How splendid it would be, if I was saying all this about myself.* I saw then at once that what is said of a man is nothing. The point is, who says it. A man's very highest moment is, I have no doubt at all, when he kneels in the dust, and beats his breast, and tells all the sins of his life (*Letters*, p. 502).

But Lord Henry Wotton, watching such a performance, would have given his mocking laugh.

II The Mask of Lord Henry Wotton

Throughout the trials, but especially in the first, Wilde retained the mask by which he was at the time best known: that of the dandy—calm, intellectually acute, remote and almost cynical (for even outright cynicism would imply too much emotion)—in the tradition described by Barbey d'Aurévilly. He was the aphorist, the creator of paradoxes which, however light-hearted and even light-minded they might seem, showed the ability to detect and expose affectation in a moment. Moreover, he could expose evil or weakness without professing to be either good or strong—only indifferent. This was the mask of Lord Henry Wotton, which Wilde said was "what the world thinks me."

Wilde put on the mask of Lord Henry very early; at least it is possible to catch glimpses of him wearing it even on his trip to America, when his part was more often that of a young man living for the sake of intense experience, a Dorian Gray. Lord Henry's attitude toward experience, though it possesses similarities, is really quite different: " 'I have known

everything,' said Lord Henry, with a tired look in his eyes, 'but I am
always ready for a new emotion. I am afraid, however, that, for me at
any rate there is no such thing.' " George Woodberry, who met Wilde
in Lincoln, Nebraska, wrote a long letter to Charles Eliot Norton
describing him; in it he mentions a very similar pose of world-weary
remoteness from vital experience, a self-conscious abstention from life
instead of a self-conscious desire to enjoy it: "He [Wilde] told every[thing]
of his early life to show that he had developed, and he may keep on; but
I am sorry for the man who loves Ruskin and says that 'like Christ he
bears the sins of the world,' and who straightway speaks of himself as
'always, like Pilate, washing his hands of all responsibility.' The contrast
is unfortunate."[6]

It is possible to think of all the essays in *Intentions*, including "The
Soul of Man under Socialism," as spoken through the mask of Lord
Henry Wotton, not so much for the ideas expressed in them as for the
way in which they are expressed: the pose of the writer, or of the main
speaker in the dialogues, is in all of them that of the detached ironist,
the aristocratic observer. The necessary separation between art and nature
is the first premise of Wilde's mature criticism: it was an old doctrine,
but it had been given a new interpretation, its truth revealed in a new
way by Baudelaire when he insisted that "la première affaire d'un artiste
est de substituer l'homme à la nature et de protester contre elle"[7] and
that "Tout ce qui est beau et noble est le résultat de la raison et du
calcul."[8] Even as early as 1882, Wilde with his enormous capacity for
the fruitful combination of ideas, if not for their creation, had brought
this theory into harmony with the doctrine of Rossetti and Pater on art's
capturing of the "moment":

> For him [the poet] there is but one time, the artistic moment; but
> one law, the law of form; but one land, the land of Beauty—a land
> removed indeed from the real world yet more sensuous because
> more enduring; calm, yet with that calm which dwells in the faces
> of Greek statues, the calm which comes not from the rejection but
> the absorption of passion.[9]

Wilde wrote whimsically in "The Decay of Lying" and "The Critic as
Artist," but his theory is the same: out of the flux of experience art must
create form, for raw experience is meaningless—the only pattern possible is that made within the human mind. Wilde also takes the next
logical step to a position which superficially resembles Arnold's on the

6. Manuscript letter from George E. Woodberry
to Charles Eliot Norton, written from Lincoln,
Nebraska, April 25, 1882. Charles Eliot Norton
Collection, Houghton Library, Harvard University.
7. Charles Baudelaire, "De L'Eclectisme et du
Doute: Salon de 1846," *Curiosités Esthétiques*

(*Oeuvres Complètes de Charles Baudelaire* [Paris,
1858–73], Vol. II), p. 165.
8. Charles Baudelaire, "Elogue du Maquillage: Le
Peintre de la Vie Moderne," *L'Art Romantique*
(*Oeuvres Complètes*, Vol. III), p. 100.
9. Oscar Wilde, "The English Renaissance,"
Miscellanies (*Collected Works*, Vol. XIV), p. 258.

poet's role as "myth-maker" in the society of the future[1] but actually stands Arnold on his head—Arnold intended that poetry serve as a bridge between man and the world surrounding him; Wilde makes it a defense, a drawbridge: "I am certain that, as civilization progresses and we become more highly organized, the elect spirits of each age, the critical and cultured spirits, will grow less and less interested in actual life, and will seek to gain their impressions almost entirely from what Art has touched. For Life is terribly deficient in form."[2]

One of Wilde's most interesting paradoxes allows for a relationship between art and nature but reverses their usual order of precedence, saying that, if the truth of the matter is properly understood, it is obvious that nature does her fumbling best to imitate art. The Impressionists created "those wonderful brown fogs that came creeping down our streets"; Rossetti and Swinburne have made "the long throat, the strange square-cut jaw, the loosened shadowy hair" common attributes in women;[3] that is to say, the artist by making us aware of objects, brings them into existence for us. Along with this rather simple psychological point, however, goes a more mysterious interpretation of art's function:

> The Greeks, with their quick artistic instinct, understood this [art's influence on life], and set in the bride's chamber the statue of Hermes or Apollo, that she might bear children as lovely as the work of art she looked at in her rapture or her pain. They knew that Life gains from Art not merely spirituality, depth of thought and feeling, soul-turmoil or soul-peace, but that she can form herself on the very lines and colours of art, and can reproduce the dignity of Pheidias as well as the grace of Praxiteles.[4]

Yeats read that sentence while "The Decay of Lying" was still on galley sheets,[5] and although he may also have found the doctrine elsewhere, especially in the work of the Symbolists, it is interesting to see it appear, relatively unchanged, even in his very late poems. In "The Statues" he refers to it—and mentions Phidias—in the lines:

> when Phidias
> Gave women dreams and dreams their looking-glass.[6]

His final poem, "Under Ben Bulben," has this stanza:

> Poet and sculptor, do the work,
> Nor let the modish painter shirk
> What his great forefathers did,

1. Matthew Arnold, "The Study of Poetry," *Essays in Criticism*, Second Series (London, 1898), p. 1.
2. Wilde, "Critic as Artist," *Intentions and The Soul of Man (Collected Works*, Vol. III), pp. 164–65.
3. Wilde, "Decay of Lying," *Intentions (Collected Works*, Vol. III), p. 33.

4. *Ibid.*, p. 34.
5. This was at the first meeting of Yeats and Wilde, just after the latter had written a review praising *The Wanderings of Usheen.*—Yeats, *Autobiography*, p. 118.
6. W. B. Yeats, *The Collected Poems of W. B. Yeats* (New York, Macmillan, 1956), p. 322.

Bring the soul of man to God.
Make him fill the cradles right.[7]

Wilde, at least in his character of Lord Henry, would not have liked to see the matter put so strongly. He always insisted on art's inutility; and yet his interest in art as the mirror of the creator's personality led him to give much less importance to form and style than, say, Gautier would have given, even when he seems to be repeating Gautier's ideas. For instance, in a review of George Sand's letters Wilde writes that "art for art's sake is not meant to express the final causes of art but is merely a formula of creation." The review continues: "She [George Sand] thought Flaubert too much preoccupied with the sense of form and makes these excellent observations to him—perhaps her best piece of literary criticism. 'You consider the form as the aim, whereas it is but the effect. Happy expressions are only the outcome of emotion and emotion itself proceeds from a conviction.' "[8] George Woodberry even questioned the real strength of Wilde's feeling for form: "He speaks of form; it seems to me he has more sense of color. He spoke of prose style, but he cared for its iridescence, as in Pater."[9] And it is true that Wilde's interpretation of "art for art's sake" carries none of the overtones of an almost grim dedication to the careful chiseling of a lien, the arduous polishing of a phrase. Wilde's doctrine is really "art for the artist's sake": "A *work of art is the unique result of a unique temperament. Its beauty comes from the fact that the author is what he is. It has nothing to do with the fact that other people want what they want.*"[1]

As early as 1882 Wilde's eclectic talent had established a relationship between the ideas of "art for art's sake" and of "self-realization":

> For it is not enough that a work of art should conform to the aesthetic demands of its age: there must be also about it, if it is to affect us with any permanent delight, the impress of a distinct individuality, an individuality remote from that of ordinary men.
>
> *La personalité*, said one of the greatest of modern French critics, *voilà ce qui nous sauvera.*[2]

Admittedly, Baudelaire had already done much of Wilde's work for him when he established two principles: first that the thought of the artist dominates his model, and second that an artist must work with enor-

7. *Ibid.*, p. 342. Yeats also echoed Wilde's idea in his prose when he wrote in 1937: "Somebody saw a woman of exuberant beauty coming from a public-house with a pot of beer and commended her to Rossetti; twenty years later Mrs. Langtry called upon Watts and delighted him with her simplicity. . . . Two painters created their public; two types of beauty decided what strains of blood would most prevail."—W. B. Yeats, "Introduction," *Essays and Introductions* (New York, 1961), p. xi.
8. Oscar Wilde, "The Letters of a Great Woman," *Reviews* (*Collected Works*, Vol. XII), pp. 49–50.

9. The discussion between Wilde and Woodberry on form touched upon the Grand Canyon: "He spoke of Colorado Canyons; 'but are they beautiful in form,' I said, and he said 'Oh yes!' and gave a description to convince me, that was pure color without one line in it."—Woodberry, manuscript letter to C. E. Norton, Charles Eliot Norton Collection, Houghton Library, Harvard University.
1. Wilde, "The Soul of Man," *Intentions* (*Collected Works*, Vol. III), p. 300.
2. Wilde, "The English Renaissance," *Miscellanies* (*Collected Works*, Vol. XIV), p. 251.

mous fidelity to his craft.[3] However, Wilde makes an extremely important change in the theory by linking it with his own interpretation of
Pater's impressionism. When Baudelaire writes of an artist's "naïveté"—
his ability to express his essential nature—he makes that nature a constant, perhaps the only constant in the artist's work. Wilde, however,
like Anthony Beavis in Aldous Huxley's *Eyeless in Gaza*, thought the
permanence of personality "a very subtle metaphysical problem";[4] the
"chameleon poet" thus has his counterpart in a Wildean "chameleon
critic," but just as Wilde reversed the direction of negative capability,
bringing all outside experience into himself, so he makes the process of
appreciation "the record of one's own soul" and criticism "the only civilized form of autobiography," one which deals with "the spiritual moods
and imaginative passions of the mind."[5]

Nevertheless, any change Wilde makes in Baudelaire's theory is the
result of a difference in emphasis and not in theory—the outcome of
Wilde's tendency to link critic and artist more closely than Baudelaire
would have done, for Wilde' impressionism is very closely related to
Baudelaire's belief that "la meilleure critique est celle qui est amusante
et poétique . . . un beau tableau étant la nature réfléchie par un artiste,—
celle qui sera ce tableau réfléchi par un esprit intelligent et sensible.
Ainsi, le meilleur compte rendu d'un tableau pourra être un sonnet ou
une élégie."[6] Wilde entirely agreed—as had his aesthetic masters Pater,
Rossetti, and Swinburne—though when he himself attempted such critical set pieces (as he did, for instance, when describing *A Rebours* in *The
Picture of Dorian Gray*), he was not really successful at all: his very self-
consciousness, his desire to do a piece of "fine writing" came between
the art work and his "esprit intelligent et sensible." When he reached
for less, as he did in the essays of *Intentions*, he achieved more real
insight, and if he was not poetic, he was very amusing. Moreover, he
was, willy-nilly, instructive; his two sentences on Wordsworth are the
equal of several paragraphs on the "egotistical sublime": "Wordsworth
went to the lakes but he was never a lake poet. He found in stones the
sermons he had already hidden there."[7]

Of the names which have appeared so far as influences upon Wilde,
only one might cause a slight start of surprise—Matthew Arnold—and
yet his is, one might say, the guest of honor in Wilde's criticism. In
"The Critic as Artist" Wilde (or rather, Gilbert, the Wildean character
in the dialogue) speaks of Arnold as one "whose gracious memory we all
revere" but adds that Arnold's definition of the aim of criticism—"to see
the object as in itself it really is"—is "a very serious error, and takes no
cognizance of Criticism's most perfect form, which is in its essence purely

3. Charles Baudelaire, "Eugène Delacroix: Salon
de 1846," *Curiosités Esthétiques (Oeuvres Complètes*, Vol. II), p. 102.
4. Wilde, "Pen, Pencil, and Poison," *Intentions*
(*Collected Works*, Vol. III), pp. 88–89).
5. Wilde, "The Critic as Artist," *Intentions*, (*Col-

lected Works*, Vol. III), p. 144.
6. Charles Baudelaire, "A Quoi Bon la Critique?:
Salon de 1846," *Curiosités Esthétiques (Oeuvres
Complètes*, Vol. II), p. 82.
7. Wilde, "Decay of Lying," *Intentions* (*Collected
Works*, Vol. III), p. 21.

subjective, and seeks to reveal its own secret and not the secret of another."[8]
But although Wilde and Arnold may begin by describing their ideal
critic in opposite terms, their concepts of his role within society are
surprisingly similar. Wilde's individualistic critic, like Arnold's man of
culture, is not active but contemplative. He is devoted to the principle
of beauty, just as the Arnoldian perfect man is devoted to "sweetness and
light," and as a result of his disciplined devotion he has a similar order,
harmony, and breadth of mind: "The true critic will, indeed, always be
sincere in his devotion to the principle of beauty, but he will seek for
beauty in every age and in each school, and will never suffer himself to
be limited to any settled custom of thought, or stereotyped mode of
looking at things."[9] Wilde, like Arnold, must defend the contemplative
vision of the individualist's "good life" from those who would charge
that in remaining aloof from all philanthropic and humanitarian activity, in refusing to be socially useful, the critic is not only unsocial but
anti-social. He makes a very telling point: philanthropic activity, if carried on unthinkingly, only serves to increase social injustice because it
glosses over and sentimentalizes but does not eradicate social evil:

> *The proper aim is to try to reconstruct society on such a basis that
> poverty will be impossible.* And the altruistic virtues have really pre-
> vented the carrying out of this aim. Just as the worst salve-owners
> were those who were kind to their slaves, and so prevented the
> horror of the system being realized by those who suffered from it,
> and understood by those who contemplated it, so, in the present
> state of things in England, the people who do most harm are the
> people who try to do most good.[1]

Summing up the world in a phrase, Wilde concludes: "There is also this
to be said: It is immoral to use private property in order to alleviate the
horrible evils that result from the institution of private property. It is both
immoral and unfair." Philanthropic endeavor is individually as well as
socially harmful in Wilde's opinion: its necessary activity and emotion
have the bad effect of beclouding what might otherwise have been a
clear mind: "The sure way of knowing nothing about life is to try to
make oneself useful."[2]
    Gilbert says, "But perhaps you think that in beholding for the mere
joy of beholding, and contemplating for the sake of contemplation, there
is something that is egotistic. If you think so, do not say so."[3] And
Wilde's analysis, through Gilbert, has been so intelligent that the reader,
like Ernest, is silent—but is he convinced? The difficulty is that Wilde,
when he writes of the good life for the individual and for society, is
writing in the spirit of Lord Henry Wotton: that is to say, his intellectual

8. Wilde, "The Critic as Artist," *Intentions (Col-*
lected Works, Vol. III), p. 145.
9. *Ibid.,* p. 197.
1. Wilde, "The Soul of Man," *Intentions (Col-*

lected Works, Vol. III), pp. 274–75.
2. Wilde, "The Critic as Artist," *Intentions (Col-*
lected Works, Vol. III), p. 184.
3. *Ibid.,* p. 185.

understanding of society's problems carries with it no desire "to make reason and the will of God prevail." Sometimes one senses even in the Arnold of *Culture and Anarchy* a latent wish to remove himself from society, a latent fear of Victorian society's violent growth and change: Wilde makes both the wish and the fear overt by transforming the Arnoldian man of culture into a Baudelairean dandy: "Calm and self-centered and complete, the aesthetic critic contemplates life, and no arrow drawn at a venture can pierce between the joints of his harness. He at least is safe, he has discovered how to live."[4] The dark side of that statement finds its expression in Lord Henry's comment: "I can sympathize with everything except suffering. . . . It is too ugly, too horrible, too distressing. There is something terribly morbid in the modern sympathy with pain."

To the Romantics' sense of isolation from society and Arnold's distrust of "the masses," Wilde added the contempt of Gautier and of Baudelaire for "la marée montante de la démocratie" which is one of the most important elements in both *Dandyisme* and Parnassianism.[5] Or, it would be more truthful to say, Wilde seems at times to have wished that he could be capable of a dandy's lofty contempt. Time and again, however, his desire to win approval, his extraordinary dependence on the good opinion of the whole society, shows through the mask of Lord Henry. When he writes privately, as in this note to Lord Alfred Douglas, it is obvious: "Please *always* let me see *anything* that appears about myself in the Paris papers—good or bad, but especially the *bad*. It is a matter of vital import to me to know the attitude of the community" (*Letters*, p. 591).

Although Wilde's desire for others' good opinion may seem a "happy fault," no matter how ridiculous it might occasionally make him appear, it is necessary to remember that, in part of his nature at least, he himself regarded it as a terrible weakness; though he could not always preserve the mask of Lord Henry, he would have like to do so, as he confessed to André Gide: "It is not through excessive individualism that I have sinned. My great mistake, the error I cannot forgive myself, is having, one day, ceased to believe in it in order to listen to others, ceased to believe that

---

4. *Ibid.*, p. 183.
5. Baudelaire's dandy is the last representative of an old aristocratic order: "Le dandysme est un soleil couchant; comme l'astre qui décline, il est superbe, sans chaleur et plein de mélancolie. Mais, hélas! la marée montante de la démocratie, qui envahit tout et qui nivelle tout, noie jour à jour ses derniers représentants de l'orgueil humain et verse des flots d'oubli sur les traces de ces prodigieux mirmidons."—"Le Dandy: Le Peintre de la Vie Moderne," *L'Art Romantique* (*Oeuvres Complètes*, Vol. III), p. 95.

The link between aristocracy and dedication to poetic form had been made by Alexis de Tocqueville: "Prise dans son ensemble, la littérature des siècles démocratiques ne saurait présenter, ainsi que

dans les temps d'aristocratie, l'image de l'ordre, de la régularité, de la science et de l'art: la forme s'y trouvera, d'ordinaire, négligée et parfois méprisée."—*De la Démocratie en Amérique* (2 Vols.; Paris, 1951), II, 83.

In De Tocqueville's opinion, however, there was to be a gain as well as a loss. The Parnassians saw only the loss and set themselves to proving De Tocqueville false. The fear of democracy that they felt in doing so is obvious in the violence with which Théophile Gautier "explains" his principles: "Non, imbéciles, non, crétins et goîtreux que vous êtes, un livre ne fait pas de la soupe à la gélatine."—"Preface," *Mademoiselle de Maupin* (Paris, 1873), p. 18.

I was right to live as I did, doubted myself." [6] Nevertheless a part of Wilde's nature always doubted the "self" of Lord Henry; the spokesman for that part is Basil Hallward.

III   Basil Hallward

Basil Hallward is, on the surface at least, a much less interesting character than either Lord Henry or Dorian Gray. Yet it is of him that the flamboyant Wilde writes, "Basil Hallward is what I think I am." His comment adds greatly to the significance of Basil's murder, which otherwise has the air of a plot device that is both awkward and ineffective, and it also gives yet another possible explanation for Wilde's decision to remain in England and face trial for homosexuality. It is now almost a tradition for those who write on Wilde to offer an explanation for his refusal to flee the country when flight was still possible: Frank Harris says that Wilde's cowardice made it impossible for him to face a decision, so that, in a lethargy of fear, he stayed; Yeats believes that Wilde showed his greatest courage in remaining and makes his doing so a proof of the theory that Wilde really was a man of action; Hesketh Pearson thinks Wilde's resolution the result of his incurable love of self-dramatization, itself caused by his emotional immaturity; Robert Sherard believes that Wilde was caught in the grip of megalomania. [7] What is interesting about every one of these theories is that each is a reflection of the particular biographer's ordering vision of Wilde's character. And although every one of them might be partially true in the case of a personality as fragmented as Wilde's, none offers the explanation hidden in the character of Basil Hallward: that there was in Wilde an "ordinary man" who felt terrible guilt for the sins of that part of him represented by Dorian Gray and who could never really be convinced, as Lord Henry Wotton was convinced, that sin is merely another form of self-realization.

Conversations between Lord Henry, Basil Hallward, and Dorian Gray become very interesting, then, if one thinks of them as an internal dialogue. [8] First Dorian Gray, the student, the one given over to influences, asks:

> "What do you mean by good, Harry?"
> "To be good is to be in harmony with oneself," he replied, touching the thin stem of his glass with his pale, fine pointed fingers. "Discord is to be forced to be in harmony with others."

6. André Gide, *The Journals of André Gide*, tr. Justin O'Brien (4 vols.; New York, 1947–51), II, 400.

7. Frank Harris, *Oscar Wilde: His Life and Confessions* (2 vols.; New York, 1918), I, 299; Yeats, *Autobiography*, p. 245; Hesketh Pearson, *Oscar Wilde: His Life and Wit* (New York, 1946), p. 271; Sherard, *Life of Oscar Wilde*, pp. 354–57.

8. Arthur Nethercot's study "Oscar Wilde and the Devil's Advocate" uses a similar method in analysing *The Picture of Dorian Gray* and Wilde's plays, though he insists too much perhaps on the truth of the "moral" Wilde, saying, "He [Wilde] knew that the truth about the man Oscar Wilde was preserved in his writings" (p. 850). Is it really clear, however, that Wilde ever came to so good an understanding of himself?

Lord Henry continues with an exposition of the philosophy of individualism, and in the course of it makes a telling point: the dandy, by making himself the center of his morality, is at least without illusions. He is not acting from a pretended belief in a code no longer in existence: "Modern morality consists in accepting the standards of one's age. I consider that for any man of culture to accept the standard of his age is a form of the grossest immorality." Lord Henry had adjusted to a world without absolute values by making himself his own absolute. But Basil Hallward still believes in objective absolutes of right and wrong and even gives society the right to punish those who transgress them, not because society really understands either the sin or the sinner but because society's vengeance is the sinner's purification:

> "But surely, if one lives merely for one's self, Harry, one pays a terrible price for doing so?" suggested the painter.
> "Yes, we are overcharged for everything nowadays . . . Beautiful sins, like beautiful things, are the privilege of the rich."
> "One has to pay in other ways but money."
> "What sort of ways, Basil?"
> "Oh! I should fancy in remorse, in suffering, in . . . well, in the consciousness of degradation."

There is another conversation which gives the impression of interior dialogue: it is held between Basil Hallward and Dorian Gray not long before Basil's murder: " 'I owe a great deal to Harry, Basil,' he [Dorian Gray] said at last—'More than I owe to you. You only taught me to be vain.' 'Well, I am punished for that Dorian—or shall be some day.' " And later Dorian says: "I am changed, but you must always be my friend. Of course, I am very fond of Harry. But I know you are better than he is. You are not stronger—you are too much afraid of life—but you are better." Basil seems weaker than Lord Henry only because his conscience makes him vulnerable as Lord Henry is not.

Still another point is illuminated by thinking of Hallward as a reflection of Wilde. The sins with which Dorian Gray experiments are left vague, though the suggestion that homosexuality is the chief of them is clear enough, and Lord Henry talks much about self-realization through sin but never seems to commit any (with the single, but terrible, exception of Hawthorne's unforgivable sin[9]): as the book was originally writ-

9. When describing Lord Henry, Wilde writes: "And so he had begun by vivisecting himself as he had ended by vivisecting others"; this is the sin of Roger Chillingworth and of Ethan Brand. Julian Hawthorne reviewed *The Picture of Dorian Gray* for *Lippincott's Magazine*; there he compares it with Balzac's story "La Peau de Chagrin" and with Stevenson's *Dr. Jekyl and Mr. Hyde*, but, disappointingly, he makes no parallels between his father's stories and *Dorian Gray*; yet there are enough similarities in thought and even in method to make such a comparison very interesting.—Julian Hawthorne, "The Romance of the Impossible," *Lippincott's Magazine*, XLVI (September, 1890), 412–15.

Vincent O'Sullivan says that Wilde did not take American literature seriously except for the works of Poe, Whitman, and Hawthorne, "not really liking any of them, I think, but Hawthorne—the Hawthorne of *The Scarlet Letter*."—*Aspects of Wilde* (New York, 1936), p. 133.

ten, however, it is Basil who openly confesses to homosexuality and regards it as a sin that he must expiate. At the the suggestion of Walter Pater, the whole passage was much toned down in the book's final version, with the result that Basil's central explanation falls a little flat; he explains only the obvious. In the earlier version, this was not so; Basil there says to Dorian Gray:

> It is quite true that I have worshipped you with far more romance of feeling than a man usually gives to a friend. Somehow, I have never loved a woman. I suppose I never had time. Perhaps, as Harry says, a really "grande passion" is the privilege of those who have nothing to do, and that is the use of the idle classes in a country. Well, from the moment I met you, your personality had the most extraordinary influence over me. I quite admit that I adored you madly, extravagantly, absurdly. I was jealous of every man to whom you spoke. I wanted to have you all to myself. I was only happy when I was with you. When I was away from you, you were still present in my art. It was all very wrong and foolish. It is all wrong and foolish still.[1]

André Gide is of the opinion that, although Wilde always "insisted on the mask" in his work, yet "always he managed in such a way that the informed reader could raise the mask and glimpse, under it, the true visage (which Wilde had such good reasons to hide)."[2] His description of a reading of Wilde's work is unfortunate, however, if not unfair; it creates such an ugly picture of the knowing, rather prurient reader who, with an insinuating leer, can enjoy a special peep show of the soul—whereas in actuality, Wilde is like an elegant Ancient Mariner who fixes his readers with a glittering eye and demands that they hear his confession over and over again.

Gide's interpretation of the reasons behind Wilde's use of the mask is also open to question. In his opinion "this artistic hypocrisy was imposed on him by respect, which was very keen in him, for the proprieties, and by the need of self-protection."[3] Gide does not take into account the possibility that Wilde's respect for propriety may have had its basis in a respect for morality. Wilde can repeat as much as he pleases that "the artistic critic, like the mystic, is an antinomian always";[4] he remained in his heart a Manichean, nonetheless. His Manicheanism sometimes turns up unexpectedly, in fact, to contradict points he has carefully made about the complete separation between aesthetics and ethics; for example, it does so in his letter to the *St. James Gazette* about *Dorian Gray*. In defending his book he describes the sin committed by each of the

1. H. Montgomery Hyde, ed., *The Trials of Oscar Wilde* (London, 1948) p. 128. This is also the version printed in *Lippincott's Magazine*, XLVI (July, 1890), 1–100, but its repetition at the trial is cited here because in the course of the questioning the point was made that through Pater's influence this passage was changed.

2. Gide, *The Journals of André Gide*, II, 409.

3. *Ibid.*, pp. 409–10.

4. Wilde, "The Critic as Artist," *Intentions* (*Collected Works*, Vol. III), p. 221.

main characters and the inevitable punishment it brings. He concludes: "Yes, there is a terrible moral in *Dorian Gray*—a moral which the prurient will not be able to find in it, but it will be revealed to all those whose minds are healthy." Then, catching himself up in the realization that all this talk of morality is beneath his dignity as an artist, he adds: "Is this an artistic error? I fear it is. It is the only error in the book."[5]

The stories told in *The House of Pomegranates* offer further evidence that Wilde was disturbed by a sense of guilt which he attempted to soothe by this partial, hidden confession. Each one of the stories, except "The Birthday of the Infanta," tells of a sin and a resulting fragmentation of personality, of repentance and ultimate healing—though sometimes the last is won only by death. The only mask Wilde uses in telling these stories is that of the style itself: it is a mingling of the ornate "jewelled" style (a mixture of Swinburne, perhaps, and Gautier) which he often uses in *Dorian Gray* and the carefully simple phrasing of Rossetti's *Hand and Soul*, heavily seasoned with the Bible and the *Arabian Nights*.[6] The result is exotic but not really unpalatable, perhaps because, in spite of their artifice, the stories have the quality of parables and carry a genuine human emotion.

"The Young King" describes the dreams by which a young "lover of the beautiful" is made aware of the human suffering necessary to provide him with beautiful robes and jewels; "The Star Child" concerns the long repentance of a beautiful child who in his pride repudiated his mother. But the most interesting of these tales is "The Fisherman and his Soul," which tells of a young fisherman's love for a mermaid. She promises to carry him with her to the caverns of the sea if he first will separate himself from his soul. The fisherman goes to the priest for help in sending his soul away and explains the reason, concluding:

> "And as for my soul, what doth my soul profit me, if it stand between me and the thing I love?"
> "The love of the body is vile," cried the Priest, knitting his brows, "and vile and evil are the pagan things God suffers to wander through His world. Accursed be the Fauns of the woodland, and accursed be the singers of the sea!"[7]

The fisherman finally gets his wish in spite of the priest, though he must use the powers of black magic to do it. He cuts off his soul and sends it away, refusing it the heart it pleads for; then he dives into the sea. Each year the soul attempts to lure him away from his mermaid, once with the promise of wisdom, next with the promise of wealth; each time the

5. Wilde, *Miscellanies* (*Collected Works*, Vol. XIV), pp. 139–40.
6. Aubrey Beardsley drew a delightful cartoon which serves as frontispiece for Stuart Mason's *Bibliography of Oscar Wilde* (London, 1914). The picture is entitled "Oscar Wilde at Work '(Il ne faut pas le regarder)' "; it shows Wilde at his desk surrounded by those works on which he is particularly dependent: books by Gautier, Flaubert and Swinburne, a copy of *French Verbs at a Glance*, and, largest of all, a well-thumbed family Bible.
7. Oscar Wilde, *A House of Pomegranates* (*Collected Works*, Vol. II), p. 74.

fisherman refuses, saying that love is stronger than either, but at the last temptation, which is really only that of physical desire—the promise that he shall see the white feet of a dancer nearby—the fisherman leaves the sea. Then he discovers not only that he cannot return but that his soul, which is heartless, leads him into acts of evil: violence, robbery, and finally murder.

Repentant and horrified, the fisherman binds himself so that his soul may not influence him further and returns to the shore (though always dogged by his soul) to search for the mermaid. Only after her death does he find her; at the sight of her body his heart breaks, and his soul, now purified, can again be united with him. The story has a coda: the priest's vision of the world is changed by the discovery of flowers growing from the grave in which the mermaid and the fisherman are buried:

> And in the morning, while it was still dawn, he went forth with the monks and the musicians, and the candle-bearers and the swingers of censers, and a great company, and came to the shore of the sea, and blessed the sea, and all the wild things that are in it. The Fauns also he blessed, and the little things that dance in the woodland, and the bright-eyed things that peer through the leaves. All the things in God's world he blessed, and the people were filled with joy and wonder.[8]

Both Basil Hallward and Lord Wotton have as their ideal the union of heart, soul, and body that "The Fisherman and his Soul" describes. Lord Henry believes that he has found the secret in his new hedonism: "to cure the soul by means of the senses, and the senses by means of the soul," but Basil, while he too says, "The harmony of soul and body— how much that is!" does not feel that such a harmony can be achieved by going against conscience. It is on the question of conscience that he and Lord Henry disagree: " 'Conscience and cowardice are really the same thing, Basil. Conscience is the trade-name of the firm. That is all.' 'I don't believe that, Harry, and I don't believe you do either'." The conflict in Basil between his conscience and his love for Dorian Gray is not resolved intellectually at all, though it finds an emotional resolution in his death. Through the more complex character of Sir Robert Chiltern, however, Wilde continues the discussion, the weighing and considering of the validity of conscience.

Sir Robert is the protagonist of Wilde's play, *An Ideal Husband*.[9] When the play opens Sir Robert is presented as a wealthy and very suc-

---

8. *Ibid.*, pp. 128–29.
9. Frank Harris gave Wilde the central idea for the plot when he told him of an event in the life of Benjamin Disraeli that had been described to him while he was in Cairo: there a Mr. Cope Whitehouse told Harris that Disraeli had made money by entrusting the Rothschilds with the purchase of Suez Canal shares. The story is substan-

tially true, though Frank Harris was not himself convinced. "It seemed to me strange that this statement, if true, had never been set forth authoritatively; but the story was peculiarly modern and had possibilities in it. Oscar admitted afterwards that he had taken the idea and used it in 'An Ideal Husband.' "—*Oscar Wilde: His Life and Confessions*, I, 182.

cessful, highly respected undersecretary for foreign affairs. The mask he attempts to wear—and until the opening of the play he has been successful—is nothing less than perfection: he appears to be an incorruptible servant of the state, a supremely happily married man, an omniscient financier. However impossible it is to relate the mask to reality (and one of Wilde's points is that it is indeed impossible), the wearing of it proves how conventional Sir Robert is, how much he is bound by the code of society. Very early in the play Mrs. Chevely, an intelligent woman even though the villainess, points out society's hypocrisy:

> In old days nobody pretended to be a bit better than his neighbours. In fact to be a bit better than one's neighbour was considered excessively vulgar and middle class. Nowadays, with our modern mania for morality, every one has to pose as a paragon of purity, incorruptibility, and all the other seven deadly virtues—and what is the result? You all go over like ninepins. . . . Not a year passes in England without somebody disappearing. Scandals used to lend charm, or at least interest, to a man—now they crush him.[1]

The whole play turns on Sir Robert's fear of unmasking, his imaginative picture of "the loathsome joy" with which the newspapers would describe his fall and of the hypocritical dismay which would be expressed by his colleagues who "every day do something of the kind themselves. Men who, each one of them have worse secrets in their own lives" (p. 76). The secret of Sir Robert's life is that at the beginning of his career he had given state information to a Baron Arnheim about the British Government's intention to buy Suez Canal shares; on the strength of that knowledge the Baron had brought into the company when its stock was still very low and had made a fortune; in "gratitude" he gave Sir Robert £110,000.

Sir Robert is described in the stage directions as a man whose very features suggest "an almost complete separation of passion and intellect, as though thought and emotion were each isolated in its own sphere through some violence of will-power" (p. 11). The division becomes clear in his attitude toward the swindle: one side of his nature thinks it perfectly justifiable—more than that, courageous. He describes Baron Arnheim, who rather resembles Lord Henry Wotton and has "a strange smile on his pale, curved lips,"[2] as a man of splendid intellect, and he holds, with the Baron, that to wield power is the one pleasure of which one never tires. When his friend Lord Goring says that he was weak in yielding to Baron Arnheim's temptation, Sir Robert is almost indignant: "Weak? Do you really think, Arthur, that it is weakness that yields to temptation? I tell you that there are terrible temptations that it requires

1. Oscar Wilde, *An Ideal Husband* (*Collected Works*, Vol. IX), p. 46.
2. André Gide recalls Wilde's saying to him: "I don't like your lips; they're straight, like those of someone who has never lied. I want to teach you to lie, so that your lips may become beautiful and twisted like those of an antique mask."—*Oscar Wilde*, p. 6.

strength, strength and courage to yield to. To stake all one's life on a single moment, to risk everything on one throw, whether the stake be power or pleasure, I care not—there is no weakness in that. There is a horrible, a terrible courage" (pp. 82–83). When Lord Goring only answers that he is sorry for him, Sir Robert says immediately, "I don't say that I suffered any remorse. I didn't. Not remorse in the ordinary, rather silly sense of the word." Nevertheless, the remorse he goes on to describe bears all the characteristics of the ordinary variety, including the use-lessness—silliness, one might say—of remorse without repentance: "But I have paid conscience money many times. I had a wild hope that I might disarm destiny. The sum Baron Arnheim gave me I have distrib-uted twice over in public charities since then." (Lord Goring, speaking as one part of Wilde to another, cannot let that pass: "In public charities? Dear me, what a lot of harm you must have done, Robert!" [p. 85].) And later the purely emotional side of Sir Robert cries out, "I would to God that I had been able to tell the truth . . . to live the truth. Ah! that is the great thing in life, to live the truth" (p. 96).

Through the good offices of Lord Goring, who, like the Scarlet Pim-pernel, is a dandy with a heart, Sir Robert is finally able to tell the truth, at least to his wife, and to win forgiveness; at the same time he preserves and even increases his position in the world. All this is done, though, in such a whirl of attempted blackmail, intercepted letters, and mutual misunderstandings and reassurances that the central conflict in the prin-cipal character is left unresolved—or rather, its resolution is practical, not psychological. Lord Goring is able to convince the puritanical Lady Chiltern that "life cannot be understood without much charity" (p. 101), and he says of Sir Robert: "What you know about him is not his real character. It is an act of folly done in his youth, dishonourable, I admit, shameful, I admit, unworthy of him, I admit, and therefore . . . not his real character" (p. 177). Even granted that this is so, there is nothing in the play to suggest that Sir Robert himself comes to know his own "real character," or that there is any final union between his intellectual amo-rality and his emotional sense of sin. By the end of the play the relation of the mask to the reality is as great a mystery as ever.

Indeed, *The Importance of Being Earnest* is the only one of Wilde's successful plays in which mask and reality prove to be one; it is possible to think of it (as it is of Mark Twain's *The Adventures of Huckleberry Finn*) as the author's evocation of a never-never land in which the indi-vidual, though part of society, is in his essence free of its rule.[3] In their self-centeredness Jack Worthing and Algernon Moncrieff have mastered life; they live remote from any real evil, any scarring emotion, any intel-lectual problem. But they can only do so in a world specially patterned for them and by them: one in which a broken engagement or a buttered

3. "Never speak disrespectfully of Society, Alger-non," says Lady Bracknell. "Only people who can't get into it do that."—Oscar Wilde, *The Impor-* *tance of Being Earnest* (*Collected Works*, Vol. VII), p. 163.

muffin is of equal moment because all the members of it know both engagement and muffin to be at once all-important and unimportant. This knowledge gives all the freedom that life on the Mississippi gave to Huck.

The Importance of Being Earnest has one sort of sincerity; "The Ballad of Reading Gaol" has another. Certainly the poem has any number of artistic faults: it is repetitive, has abrupt and unnecessary changes of style and imagery, and moves equally abruptly from realism to melodrama. Yet in spite of all this the poem works because the emotion behind it is a genuine, not a constructed one, and because in the writing of it Wilde seems more conscious of the situation than of himself describing the situation. The letters Wilde sent to Robert Ross while he was writing the "Ballad" make a delightful collection, because in them too Wilde seems almost self-forgetful. Moreover, his tone is that of a genuine artist-critic: he gives his achievement its proper value. Once he writes whimsically, "I think bits of the poem very good now—but I will never again out-Kipling Henley' (Letters, p. 649). He is amusing again when he insists on putting in a few melodramatic stanzas in the style he enjoyed:

> I have just sent Smithers four more stanzas for insertion—one of them very good, in the romantic vein you don't quite approve of; but one the whole it will, I think, make a balance in the poem. I can't be always "banging the tins." Here it is:

> > It is sweet to dance to violins
> > When Life and Love are fair:
> > To dance to flutes, to dance to lutes,
> > Is delicate and rare:
> > But it is not sweet with nimble feet
> > To dance upon the air.

> On the whole, I like the poem now, except the second and third stanzas of Part III. I can't get that part right (*Letters*, pp. 652–53).[4]

"The Ballad of Reading Gaol" also has a significance beyond itself as the last communication, so to speak, between Wilde and the world outside him, before he became completely enclosed in the prison of him-

---

4. In another letter Wilde also has a very sensible technical discussion on the difficulty there is in describing a prison within the objective, impersonal ballad form: "With regard to the adjectives, I admit there are far too many 'dreadfuls' and 'fearfuls'; the difficulty is that the objects in prison have no shape or form. To take an example: the shed in which people are hanged is a little shed with a glass roof, like a photographer's studio on the sands at the Margate: for eighteen months I thought it *was* a studio for photographing prisoners. There is no adjective to describe it. I call it 'hideous' because it became so to me after I knew its use. In itself it is a wooden, oblong, narrow shed with a glass roof.

"A cell may be described psychologically with reference to its effect on the soul: in itself it can only be described as 'whitewashed' or 'dimly lit.' It has no shape, no contents; it does not exist from the point of view of form or colour.

"In point of fact, describing a prison is as difficult artistically as describing a water-closet would be. If one had to describe the latter in literature, prose or verse, one could say merely that it was well or badly papered; or clean or the reverse. The horror of prison is that everything is so simple and commonplace in itself, and so degrading and hideous and revolting in its effect" (*Letters*, pp. 654–55).

self. While he was still in Reading, Wilde wrote to Robert Ross: "Of course from one point of view I know that I shall be merely passing from one prison to another, and there are times when the whole world seems to me no larger than my cell and as full of terrors for me. Still I believe that at the beginning God made a world for each separate man, and in that world which is within us we should seek to live" (*Letters*, p. 512). When he was released from one prison and found himself indeed in another, he struggled for escape and failed. Then he fell back without hope, resigned to living in "that world which is within us," the world of Walter Pater's "Conclusion" to *The Renaissance*, which now, however, bore a great resemblance to Reading Gaol, where there are "crowds of people, walking round in a ring": "I must reconsider my position as I cannot go on living here as I am doing, though I know there is no such thing as changing one's life—one merely wanders round and round within the circle of one's own personality" (*Letters*, p. 671).

Wilde took the name "Sebastian Melmoth" when he left prison, the first name after the martyred Saint Sebastian, whom Wilde had once identified with Keats: "Fair as Sebastian, and as early slain,"[5] and the second after Melmoth, the outcast of Maturin's novel, doomed to wander eternally through the world. Thus the name itself is a sort of analogue for the title of Yeats' story, "The Crucifixion of the Outcast"; at their last meeting, just before his downfall, Wilde told Yeats that the story was "sublime, wonderful, wonderful."[6] Wilde took a family pride in the fact that Charles Maturin was his great-great-uncle[7]—and indeed the terrible, living portrait of Melmoth may have been in Wilde's mind when he wrote *Dorian Gray*—but in his choice of the name Melmoth he was undoubtedly influenced as well by Baudelaire's comments on "la grande création satanique du reverend Maturin": "Il [Melmoth's laughter] est, qu'on me comprenne bien, la résultante nécessaire de sa double nature contradictoire, qui est infiniment grande relativement á l'homme, infiniment vile et basse relativement au Vrai et au Juste absolus. Melmoth est une contradiction vivante."[8] And although it suited Wilde's melodramatic nature to wrap himself in the great cloak of such a name, playing the part of a "last Romantic," still there is this justice in his using it: his too was a nature of contradictions from which he could find no escape, and in which he finally walked solitary, utterly isolated.

With the intelligence to understand all the conflicts of his age, yet without the ability or the will to resolve them, Wilde was finally broken by them. Arnold had made Empedocles complain because the mirror of his soul caught only glimpses of reality, but at least the mirror itself was whole; in Wilde it was as if the glass were shattered and he set dancing and posturing before its pieces like the dwarf in his own story, "The

5. Oscar Wilde, "The Grave of Keats," *Poems*, p. 157.
6. Yeats, *Autobiography*, p. 244.
7. Sherard, *Life of Oscar Wilde*, p. 40.

8. Charles Baudelaire, "De L'Essence du Rire," *Curiosités Esthétiques* (*Oeuvres Complètes*, Vol. II), p. 369.

Birthday of the Infanta"—seeing himself as an aesthete, a member of
the Oxford Movement, an artist like Balzac wrapped in a white gown, a
disciple of Renan, an aristocratic dandy. All these were, he believed,
ways of expressing himself, of multiplying his personality, and all the
time his real personality remained as much a puzzle to him as it was to
those who described him. The bewilderment that one senses beneath all
the posing, and the strange quality that could only be called sincerity—
or at least the desire to be sincere, could he only find a basis for sincerity—these and his very real humor give Wilde charm almost in spite of
himself. Even George Woodberry, who saw through all the poses, said
of him: "I have seen no one whose charm stole on me so secretly, so
rapidly, and with such entire sweetness. His poems are better than his
theories, and he better than his poems."[9] His charm would not have to
be very impressive to be better than his poems, it is true; however,
Woodberry's statement might be made broad enough to include all of
Wilde's works. His writings, like the costume of a court jester, were a
fantastic patchwork of other men's ideas in which he walked proudly as
a king, thinking himself splendidly attired. And, like a court jester, he
made it his business to amuse his age—by his wit, if possible; by his
antics, if necessary. But it may well be that at times he caught sight of
himself in his own shattered mirror and stopped short.

PHILIPPE JULLIAN

Dorian Gray [†]

The teeming, mysterious city, where danger was so near to pleasure,
provided Wilde with the background for his most celebrated works. On
the other hand *Lord Arthur Savile's Crime* and *Mr. W.H.* prepared the
way for *Dorian Gray*. Was the model on whom he based this story taken
from one of Oscar's disciples? Certainly the habitual young visitors to
Tite Street had well-cut suits and plenty of intelligence, but they lacked
the glamour of luxury and birth, therefore none of these 'dear boys'
could boast of personifying the hero in full.

As well as the poets, there were artists too among the disciples. John
Sargent was a little too much linked to 'the establishment' to be of interest to his neighbour. But, still in Chelsea, Wilde was constantly in the
company of two painters who worked together: Ricketts and Shannon.
The former, half French, wore a pointed beard, while Shannon was fair,
with a snub nose; they strove to simplify the figures in the pictures of
Burne-Jones and William Morris ever since they had visited the studio

---

9. George Woodberry, manuscript letter to C. E.
Norton, Charles Eliot Norton Collection, Houghton Library, Harvard University.

† From *Oscar Wilde*, trans. Violet Wyndham
(London: Constable, 1969) 213–23.

of Puvis de Chavannes. They were young, they had taste—their studio was furnished with greco-florentine bric-á-brac enlivened by chinoiserie in the best romantic tradition. Oscar amused himself by suggesting marvellous subjects for pictures which no one would ever paint, and in trying to see again the colours he had so much admired in Gustave Moreau's studio, 'divinely false, this green', 'pistachio dressed as emerald'. He would decipher an inscription on a Greek vase that the two painters had just unearthed. He brought them clients, made the models laugh by taking off Whistler's mannerisms, and left prodigiously late for some grand dinner party. There, one evening, stretched out on a cushioned divan, watching the spirals made by the smoke of his cigarette, he told them his original idea of *The Picture of Dorian Gray*; what he later wrote was but one episode in the much more complex story, which was to have taken place in the eighteenth century and would have comprised some of his favourite tales; there was one about an actress who lost her talent when she fell in love, which inspired the character of Sibyl Vane. Other episodes were to have included the story of a crucifix invented by the Inquisition, which suffocated in its iron arms the sinner who, repenting too late, embraced it. Religion was to play a large part in this curious 'legend of the centuries', at the end of which the body of Christ was to be found in a grotto at the foot of Golgotha. Laziness caused Oscar to abandon this medley, but he used the décor of Ricketts' studio for the setting of the first chapter of *Dorian Gray*.

The Picture of Dorian Gray was published in June 1890. About six years previously, Oscar had visited the studio of a painter called Basil Ward, for whom a very handsome young man was sitting; Oscar often dropped in after this first visit and kept the sitter entertained. When the portrait was finished, Wilde happened to say, 'What a pity that such a glorious creature should ever grow old'. The artist agreed, adding, 'How delightful it would be if he could remain exactly as he is, while the portrait aged and withered in his stead.' It was this experience that inspired the story of Dorian Gray and the character of Lord Henry Wotton was based on Oscar himself, with, perhaps, the addition of Lord Ronald Gower's complete cynicism. Wilde expressed his obligation by calling the painter in the story Basil Hallward.

Lord Henry Wotton talks in maxims, as do the characters in Oscar's plays, yet, in spite of the care with which he cultivates artificiality, he is the only consistent person in the novel. Perhaps the melancholy of this ageing seducer represented the feelings of Oscar Wilde, who at thirty-five was already surrounded by much younger men.

The person of that time most like Dorian Gray in his tastes, his neckties and his good looks, alas, so soon to pass, was Robert de Montesquiou who * * * took good care never to meet Oscar. As to the portrait itself, one can imagine it to be like Sargent's challenging portrait of Graham Robertson.

Much was borrowed in this story, but what is original is that it is a real romance of London, in the same way that Zola's *Nana* and Daudet's *L'Immortel* are novels of Paris. The reader is led from the Park to Whitechapel, from an artist's studio to a Duchess's drawing-room; Wilde is very much at home and opens all the doors, displays the treasures and the floral decorations, and from time to time actually allows the reader a glimpse behind the scenes. One of the reasons for the success of this book is that it is redolent of great luxury, a real luxury not that of Ouida's novels. Lord Henry and Dorian have their suits cut at Pooles, scent their baths with Floris bath salts, Fortnum and Mason deliver to their houses the rarest teas, the most exquisite jams; one knows that they belong to exclusive clubs and invite their friends to shoot, they have hot-houses, and yachts. They were the demi-gods watched by the crowds in Hyde Park as they rode their horses worth several hundred guineas each, whom the new-rich pointed out in the Duchess of Sutherland's box at the Opera. Like *Le Côté de Guermantes*, *The Picture of Dorian Gray* glorifies the aristocracy, even as far as its vices and its ridiculousness. It is also one of the last pictures of that world by a great writer because from the moment the nobility dismounted from their horses to get into motorcars, when they received at the Ritz rather than in their own houses, when they preferred night-clubs to the Opera, their aesthetic glamour vanished. The scene and the style was that of the Society in which for the last ten years Oscar had been entertained in the evenings, but he wanted to give his heroes one more luxury—his wit. It is Oscar who often speaks through Dorian, and always through Lord Henry. That life of walks and conversations is a little reminiscent of Oxford, but an Oxford where the college is a great house in Belgrave Square or Park Lane, where the gentlemen cultivate 'exquisite passions'. In this world, as at Oxford, women had very little place; they come, as it were, from the outside. It is conversation that plays the chief part, and which is idealised as the supreme art.

The Picture of Dorian Gray has been said to be a succession of parodies, almost a compilation: material borrowed from Balzac *(Le Peau de Chagrin, Splendeurs et misères)*, from Gautier *(Mademoiselle de Maupin)*, from Stevenson *(The Strange Case of Dr. Jekyll and Mr. Hyde)*. And from *William Wilson* in which Edgar Allan Poe tells the story of a young criminal haunted by a man who looks exactly like him; he finishes by killing him and he sees in a mirror 'his own image, but with features all pale and dabbled in blood', but it was his antagonist whom he saw and who said, 'You have conquered and I yield. Yet, henceforth art thou also dead—dead to the World, to Heaven and to Hope. In me didst thou exist—and, in my death, see by this image, which is thine own, how utterly thou hast murdered thyself.' There is also to be found something of the terrifying stories of Sheridan Le Fanu which had made such an impression on Oscar in his youth in Dublin; also an affinity with Conan Doyle (Sherlock Holmes and Dorian Gray might easily have met in a London fog on one of their respective searches for crime and pleasure). When Doyle travelled to London from Southampton one day for a luncheon given him by *Lippincott's* magazine, Oscar was one of the fellow guests. They were both commissioned to write tales of mystery for the magazine and a few months later there arrived *The Picture of Dorian Gray* and the *Sign of Four* in which Sherlock Holmes made his second appearance. Oscar's debt to Pater was immense, Dorian and Sibyl are like the young lovers in *Imaginary Portraits*—and often the style is melancholy in the same way, despite the purple passages threaded with gold.

It is obvious that many of the jewels and perfumes in *Dorian Gray* are taken straight out of *A Rebours*, 'the poisonous book' in a yellow cover that Lord Henry makes Dorian read. Wilde himself recognised this debt: 'The book in Dorian Gray is one of the many books I have never written, but it is partly suggested by Huysmans' *A Rebours*, which you will get at any French booksellers. It is a fantastic variation on Huysmans' over-realistic study of the artistic temperament in our inartistic age.' The Duc Floressas des Esseintes is really the father of Dorian Gray, but one can find many cousins in Byzantium and decadent Paris. The taste for trinkets and low company was very *fin de siècle* and had been exploited since 1885 by Jean Lorrain. This love of low life was very French, so much so that the French expression '*nostalgie de la boue*' has become almost colloquial in the English language, but it was Oscar who introduced it into the aesthetic domain. 'Ugliness was the one reality. The coarse brawl, the loathsome den, the crude violence of disordered life, the very vileness of thief and outcast, were more vivid in their intense actuality of impression than all the gracious shapes of Art, the dreamy shadows of Song.' Like Huysmans and Lorrain, Wilde leads his heroes to hovels, but, like a child given the run of a pastry-cook's shop, he then proceeds to gorge himself with rare words, and with quotations drawn from *The Cabala* and little-known Elizabethan authors.

Part of the novel is in dialogue, which anticipates the comedies. The dinner at Lady Narborough's after the crime is a completely theatrical scene, and the contrast between the social event and the murder is typically Wildean. The idea of a novel in dialogue originated in France; in 1885 the first works of Gyp appeared in *La Vie Parisienne* in this form; another Frenchwoman from whom Wilde had borrowed, very different from the author of *Le Mariage de Chiffon* was Rachilde,[1] author of *Monsieur Vénus*. This novel was a catalogue of different forms of elegance and perversity. With the same appetite as he showed for curiosities, Oscar also filled his pages with peeresses; there is a Duchess in every two chapters, this iridescence of rare words and great names was necessary to encourage so indolent an author to write his novel. But with what simplicity of style he tells of the metamorphosis and discovery of Dorian

1. A young girl who wrote, very badly, scandalous novels and who married the editor-in-chief of the *Mercure de France*.

Gray's body! There is not one word too many, and no emotion—just the bare facts.

This book could only have been written by Wilde; impressions graven on his heart since the gardens of Oxford are to be found in it: '. . . Dorian Gray burying his face in the great cool lilac-blossoms, feverishly drinking in their perfume as if it had been wine.' Oscar reveals himself as an admirable florist and an expert jeweller. The descriptions should be read in the insinuating and at the same time precise voice of a tempter who displays his treasures, and transforms flowers into precious stones. 'In a month there will be purple stars on the clematis, and year after year the green night of its leaves will hold its purple stars.' As to ivy? . . . its leaves are like green lacquer', and at Covent Garden there are '. . . the huge jade-green piles of vegetables', and as he is equally himself in the amusing passages, his laughter can be imagined in the following description of a woman 'looking like a bird of paradise that had been out all night in the rain, she flitted out of the room, leaving a faint odour of frangipani'. All Lord Henry's ridicule of marriage is Wilde himself venting his irritation at his own mistakes. In Proust's *Sodome et Gomorrhe*, there is the same combination of vice and comedy—one strengthens the other. But as Wilde was good-hearted he was malicious without going as far as Proust's ferocity. For him 'sin' alone was awful, for Marcel the awfulness was in human beings.

Like his creator, Dorian knew the attractions of Catholicism: 'The daily sacrifice, more awful really than all the sacrifices of the antique world, stirred him as much by its superb rejection of the evidence of the senses as by the primitive simplicity of its elements and the eternal pathos of the human tragedy that it sought to symbolise. . . . The fuming censers, that the grave boys, in their lace and scarlet, tossed into the air like great gilt flowers, had their subtle fascination for him.' Oscar's two great friends, Gray and Ross, both yielded to this charm, but his reply to them was that: '. . . he never fell into the error of arresting his intellectual development by any formal acceptance of creed or system, or of mistaking, for a house in which to live, an inn that is but suitable for the sojourn of a night, or for a few hours of a night in which there are no stars and the moon is in travail'. Wilde was never more superficial than when he took himself seriously. He could be excessively pretentious in the rôles of Plato or of Christ, as in the commandments which serve as a preface to the novel and which appear to have been dictated from the top of a would-be aesthetic Sinai.

Also typical of him is the narcissism which is the real subject of the novel; Wilde worshipped the superhuman proportions of his body and of his intelligence. If it is easy, with hindsight, to analyse the extraneous elements used by Wilde in this book which of all his works has been reissued the most, the Victorian public and critics were well able to recognise Oscar himself in every page when *Dorian Gray* appeared as a serial in *Lippincott's* magazine in June 1890 and in book-form in April of the following year. The novel, when examined in detail by prosecuting counsel at his trials, was to be used in evidence against him.

The bitter philosophy of these delightful pages is also Wildean, but this is not to be found so much in the paradoxes or in the elaborate reflections as in the melancholy which emerges from the story. A life dedicated to Beauty, so much luxury and so many works of Art, only hide deception and decomposition, and here again one is reminded of Charlus. It seems as if Oscar had had a premonition of his own ruin, inevitable although delayed by success, in the way he shows Dorian's beauty suddenly crumbling into decay. The clash between the life he led, his material pleasures, and the life he dreamed of, could only lead to catastrophe.

The critics could have recognised extracts from Flaubert's correspondence in the aphorisms of the preface, and indeed his work is one of the many sources of the novel itself. Had they done so, it would have been less serious than to bring Wilde's own nature into the limelight, as they did. After Oscar, the Prince of Elegance, the public was now being treated to Oscar, the arbiter of vice. Chauvinism ran riot, thus the *Daily Chronicle*: 'It is a tale spawned from the leprous literature of the French decadent'; the critic of *Punch* was very insulting, and the adjectives 'morbid' and 'unhealthy' came from every pen. They said that Dorian had all the vices, an expression which, in reality, designated only one. For the first time the question of the law was brought up, by the *Scots Observer*: 'The story—which deals with matters only fitted for the Criminal Investigation Department or a hearing *in camera*—is discreditable alike to author and editor. Mr. Wilde has brains, and art, and style; but if he can write for none but outlawed noblemen and perverted telegraph-boys, the sooner he takes to tailoring (or some other decent trade) the better for his own reputation and the public morals.' For once Oscar became anxious; had he gone too far? No, it was the journalists who understood nothing and he took the trouble to reply to them at length. He compared himself to Flaubert. In a letter to the editor of the *Scots Observer* of 13th August 1890: 'You may ask me, sir, why I should care to have the ethical beauty of my story recognised. I answer, simply because it exists, because the thing is there. The chief merit of *Madame Bovary* is not the moral lesson that can be found in it, any more than the chief merit of *Salambô* is its archaeology, but Flaubert was perfectly right in exposing the ignorance of those who called the one immoral and the other inaccurate . . . the critic has to educate the public, the artist has to educate the critic.'

No one was convinced, and the Victorians were horrified because *Dorian Gray* was the first overt pederastic novel written since the *Satyricon*. The painter frankly admits his love for Dorian; Lord Henry lures him away: the intimate relationships between Dorian and the young men, all of whom come to a bad end, can be guessed. Women are deliberately sacrificed, like Sibyl Vane, flouted, like Lord Henry's wife, reduced to the status of dolls, like the young Duchess who appears in the last chapters; not once is it suggested that Dorian feels for them any more than a certain curiosity which soon turns to contempt.

Mr. Robert Merle has rightly compared Wilde to Byron (who also occasionally practised homosexuality): 'The poet saw very clearly the artistic potential of this sin which is never named, or this perversion symbolised by a continual paradox. By instinct he recognised the attitude of Byron, who allows the shadow of a terrible sin to hover over Manfred without specifying its nature.' Dorian is the Don Juan of the decadence, and not for twenty years, with *Death in Venice* by Thomas Mann, was a good book which is as completely homosexual, to be written. Even Gide was more discreet. Proust, much more indiscreet in some ways, repudiated his characters by caricaturing them. In Julian Green's *Journal* he underlines the divergence between the qualities and the faults of *Dorian Gray* by saying that, 'the story itself is admirable, as rich, as profound as a Greek myth but the action is of the most feeble, in the hands of those brilliant talkers who are the characters. All is false, but to such a degree that this falsity ends by attaining to a sort of bitter and cruel truth.' Wilde has put all homosexual literature under a tragic sign, perhaps because he looked upon his pleasures if not as sins then at least as offences against society. The verve of the *Satyricon* and the caricatures by Proust are much nearer to the reality.

Walter Pater, who saw in Dorian Gray the brother of his heroes, was the only one of all the critics to like the book and to mitigate the scandal: In the *Bookman* he pointed out that the gay and natural taste for life and the charming meetings between people did much to diminish anything in the paradox that might shock. But Pater was near to death, and did not want to see bad in anything. He is a Presbyterian Verlaine, said Oscar. Friends were no more consoling than the Press, and many of them looked upon *Dorian Gray* with disgust, as did the young and brilliant American art historian Bernard Berenson, who wrote in his book *Sunset and Twilight*: 'On the morning of its publication, Oscar came to my room in North Street, Westminster and handed me a copy, saying it was the first from the Press. I took it with appreciation of the gift. The next day Oscar came to lunch, and I did not hesitate to tell him how loathsome, how horrible the book seemed to me. He did not make the slightest attempt to defend it, but explained that he being hard up, the publisher had given him a hundred pounds for a story. . . .' In contrast, Mallarmé's letter was a fine consolation: 'I have finished the book, one of the few which can move one. Its deep fantasy and very strange atmosphere took me by storm. To make it so poignant and human with such astonishing intellectual refinement, and at the same time to keep the perverse beauty is a miracle that you have worked through the use of all the arts of the writer. . . . This disturbing, full-length portrait of a Dorian Gray will haunt me, as writing, having become the book itself.'

After *Dorian Gray* the name of Wilde became a synonym for all that
was most unhealthy. Oscar realised this but instead of becoming prudent
he became provocative, parading a cynicism which was more dangerous
than the lack of deference to public opinion that he had displayed in his
youth. He had provoked public opinion after having scoffed at it, and
he was already dedicated to courting disaster. For example, having dined
one evening with Robert Ross at the Hogarth Club, once they had
adjourned to the smoking-room, a member ostentatiously left the room.
Other members rose to follow, but Oscar sized up the situation quickly,
strode over to one of those about to leave and haughtily addressed him:
'How dare you insult a member of your own club! I am Mr. Ross's guest.
An insult to me is an insult to him. I insist on your apologising to Mr.
Ross.' The member was driven to pretend that no insult had been
intended, and they all returned to their seats.

RICHARD ELLMANN

From "Overtures to Salome" †

*   *   *

The tutelary presences of Pater and Ruskin survived in Wilde's more
mature writings. In *The Picture of Dorian Gray*, for example, Pater is
enclosed (like an unhappy dryad caught in a tree trunk) in Lord Henry
Wotton. Lord Henry's chief sin is quoting without acknowledgement
from *The Renaissance*. He tells Dorian, as Pater told Mona Lisa, 'You
have drunk deeply of everything . . . and it has all been to you no more
than the sound of music.' He predicts, against the 'curious revival of
Puritanism' (a cut at Ruskin) a new hedonism, the aim of which will be
'experience itself, and not the fruits of experience.' It will 'teach man to
concentrate himself upon the moments of a life that is but a moment.'
These are obvious tags from the Conclusion to *The Renaissance*. Lord
Henry's advice to Dorian, 'Let nothing be lost upon you. Be always
searching for new sensations,' was so closely borrowed from the same
essay that Pater, who wrote a review of the book, was at great pains to
distinguish Lord Henry's philosophy from his own. Wilde seems to have
intended not to distinguish them, however, and to offer (through the
disastrous effects of Lord Henry's influence upon Dorian) a criticism of
Pater.

As for Ruskin, his presence in the book is more tangential. The painter
Hallward has little of Ruskin at the beginning, but gradually he moves

† From *Oscar Wilde: A Collection of Critical Essays*, ed. Richard Ellmann (Englewood Cliffs: Prentice-
Hall, 1969) 87–91.

closer to that pillar of aesthetic taste and moral judgment upon which Wilde leaned, and after Hallward is safely murdered, Dorian with sudden fondness recollects a trip they had made to Venice together, when his friend was captivated by Tintoretto's art. Ruskin was of course the English discoverer and champion of Tintoretto, so that the allusion is specific. The ending of *Dorian Gray* executes a Ruskinesque repudiation of a Pateresque career of self-gratifying sensations. Wilde defined the moral in so witty a way as to content neither of his mentors: in letters to newspapers he said *Dorian Gray* showed that 'all excess, as well as all renunciation, brings its own punishment.' Not only are Hallward and Dorian punished by death, but, Wilde asserted, Lord Henry is punished too. Lord Henry's offence was in seeking 'to be merely the spectator in life. He finds that those who reject the battle are more deeply wounded than those who take part in it.' The phrase 'spectator of life' was one that Wilde used in objecting to Pater's *Marius the Epicurean*. However incongruous his conception of himself as activist, with it he lorded it over his too donnish friend. For Pater, while he touted (sporadically at least) the life of pleasure, was careful not to be caught living it. He idealized touch until it became contemplation. He allowed only his eye to participate in the high passions about which he loved to expatiate. Dorian at least had the courage to risk himself.

In *Dorian Gray* the Pater side of Wilde's thought is routed, though not deprived of fascination. Yet Hallward, when his ethical insistence brings him close to Ruskin, is killed too. In 'The Soul of Man under Socialism', also written in 1891, Wilde superimposes Ruskin's social ethic upon Pater's 'full expression of personality', fusing instead of destroying them. In *Salome*, to which we are led at last, the formulation is close to *Dorian Gray*, with both opposites executed. Behind the figure of Iokanaan lurks the image of that perversely untouching, untouchable prophet John whom Wilde knew at Oxford. When Iokanaan, up from his cistern for a moment, cries to Salome, '*Arrière, fille de Sodome! Ne me touchez pas. Il ne faut pas profaner le temple du Seigneur Dieu*,' a thought of Ruskin, by now sunk down into madness, can scarcely have failed to cross Wilde's mind. By this time Wilde would also have recognized in the prophet's behaviour (as in Ruskin's) something of his own, for after his first three years of marriage he had discontinued sexual relations with his wife. Iokanaan is not Ruskin, but he is Ruskinism as Wilde understood that pole of his character. Then when Salome evinces her appetite for strange experiences, her eagerness to kiss a literally disembodied lover in a relation at once totally sensual and totally 'mystical' (Wilde's own term for her), she shows something of that diseased contemplation for which Wilde had reprehended Pater. Her adaptation, or perversion, of the Song of Songs to describe a man's rather than a woman's beauty also is reminiscent of Pater's *Renaissance* as well as of Wilde's predisposition. It is Salome, and not Pater, who dances the dance of the seven veils, but her virginal yet perverse sensuality is related to Paterism.

*   *   *

From "The Critic as Artist as Wilde" †

*   *   *

* * * Wilde summarizes his state or rather his flow of mind in a letter:

> Sometime you will find, even as I have found, that there is no such thing as a romantic experience; there are romantic memories, and there is the desire of romance—that is all. Our most fiery moments of ecstasy are merely shadows of what somewhere else we have felt, or of what we long some day to feel. So at least it seems to me. And, strangely enough, what comes of all this is a curious mixture of ardour and of indifference. I myself would sacrifice everything for a new experience, and I know there is no such thing as a new experience at all. I think I would more readily die for what I do not believe in than for what I hold to be true. I would go to the stake for a sensation and be a sceptic to the last! Only one thing remains infinitely fascinating to me, the mystery of moods. To be master of the these moods is exquisite, to be mastered by them more exquisite still. Sometimes I think that the artistic life is a long and lovely suicide, and am not sorry that it is so.

Life then is a willed deliquescence, or more exactly, a progressive surrender of the self to all the temptations appropriate to it.

What Wilde needed was not to avoid the precious occasions of evil in 'Hélas!' but to approach more enterprising ones. Yet after his Poems appeared in 1881 he was at check for almost six years. He kept busy; he went on a lecture tour for a whole year to America; he returned to England and went lecturing on; he tried unsuccessfully for a post as schools inspector such as Matthew Arnold had; erratically still, he married in 1884 and took up husbanding, begetting two children born in 1885 and 1886. Then in 1887 Wilde began the publications by which he is known. He wrote a volume of stories, and one of fairy tales, then one of criticism, then five plays, besides editing from 1887 to 1889 a magazine, Woman's World—a patrician ladies' magazine. It would seem that something roused him from the pseudo-consolidation of marriage and lectures, which were dilettantism for him, to genuine consolidation which seemed dilettantism to others.

This something appears in the original version of The Picture of Dorian

† From Golden Codgers (New York: Oxford UP, 1973) 68–80.

Gray, published in *Lippincott's Magazine* (July 1890). Wilde emphasizes more there than in the final version the murder of the painter Basil Hallward by Dorian; it is the turning-point in Dorian's experience, a plunge from insinuations of criminal tendency to crime itself. The murder at once protects the secret of his double life and vents his revulsion against the man who wants him innocent still. In *Lippincott's* Wilde specifies: 'It was on the 7th of November, the eve of his own thirty-second birthday, as he often remembered afterwards. . . .' Then when the novel was published as a book, Wilde altered this date: 'It was on the ninth of November, the eve of his own thirty-eighth birthday, as he often remembered afterwards.'

Altering Dorian's age would be gratuitous if Wilde had not attached significance to his own thirty-second year which began in 1886. The passage must have been autobiographical, and such a conjecture receives support from Robert Ross, who boasted that it was he, at the age of seventeen, who in 1886 first seduced Wilde to homosexual practices.[1] (Dorian's Sibyl Vane was also seventeen.) Wilde evidently considered this sudden alteration of his life a pivotal matter, to be recast as Dorian's murder of Hallward. He himself moved from pasteboard marriage to the expression of long latent proclivities, at some remove from the 'ancient wisdom' and 'austere control' to which he had earlier laid claim as his basic nature. Respectability, always an enemy, was destroyed in his own house. The first work which came out of the new Wilde was, appropriately. 'Lord Arthur Savile's Crime', in which murder is comically enacted and successfully concealed.

From late in the year 1886, then, Wilde was able to think of himself, if he wanted to, as criminal. Up to that time he could always consider himself an innocent misunderstood; now he lived in such a way as to confirm suspicions. Instead of challenging Victorian society only by words, he acted in such a way as to create scandal. Indiscreet by nature, he was indiscreet also by conviction, and he waged his war somewhat openly. He sensed that his new life was a source of literary effect. As he wrote later of Thomas Wainewright: 'His crimes seem to have had an important effect upon his art. They gave a strong personality to his style, a quality that his early work certainly lacked.' He returned to this idea: 'One can fancy an intense personality being created out of sin,' and in 'The Soul of Man Under Socialism,' he thought that 'Crime . . . under certain conditions, may seem to have created individualism.' In 'The Portrait of Mr. W. H.' (1889), he made Shakespeare's sonnets depend upon a similarly forbidden love affair, with an actor the same age as Ross. Thomas Mann's Tonio Kröger speaks of a banker who discovers his literary talent by committing a serious crime for which he is put in prison. The artist-criminal is implicit in romantic and symbolistic theories of art, but Wilde anticipates the explicitness on this subject of both

---

1. Wilde also regarded Ross as his first lover, as unpublished evidence confirms.

Mann and Gide, as he does that of Cavafy in 'Their Beginning' or of
Auden in *About the House*:

> Time has taught you
>   how much inspiration
> your vices brought you. . . .

Wilde might have discounted the sinfulness of his conduct and applied
to himself his own epigram: 'Wickedness is a myth invented by good
people to account for the curious attractiveness of others.' But he was
quite content to think of himself as sinful.

He now succeeded in relating his new discoveries about himself to
aesthetic theory. His only formal book of criticism, *Intentions*, has the
same secret spring as his later plays and stories. Ostensibly he is accustomed to say that the spheres of art and of ethics are absolutely distinct
and separate. But occasionally, overtly or covertly, he states that for the
artist crime does pay, by instilling itself in his content and affecting his
form. Each of the four essays that make up *Intentions* is to some degree
subversive, as if to demonstrate that the intentions of the artist are not
strictly honourable. The first and the last, 'The Decay of Lying' and
'The Truth of Masks', celebrate art for rejecting truths, faces, and all
that paraphernalia in favour of lies and masks. Wilde doesn't do this in
the romantic way of extolling the imagination, for while he uses that
word he is a little chary of it; the imagination is itself too natural, too
involuntary, for his view of art. He prefers lying because it sounds more
wilful, because it is no outpouring of the self, but a conscious effort to
mislead. 'All fine imaginative work', Wilde affirms, 'is self-conscious
and deliberate. A great poet sings because he chooses to sing.' On the
other hand, 'if one tells the truth, one is sure, sooner or later, to be
found out!' 'All bad poetry springs from genuine feeling.' Wilde celebrates art not in the name of Ariel, as the Romantics would, but in the
name of Ananias.

He finds art to have two basic energies, both of them subversive. One
asserts its magnificent isolation from experience, its unreality, its sterility. He would concur with Nabokov that art is a kind of trick played on
nature, an *illicit* creation by man. 'All art is entirely useless,' Wilde
declares. 'Art never expresses anything but itself.' 'Nothing that actually
occurs is of the smallest importance.' Form determines content, not
content form, a point which Auden also sometimes affirms and which
is often assumed by symbolists. With this theory Wilde turns Taine upon
his head; the age does not determine what its art should be, rather it is
art which gives the age its character. So far from responding to questions
posed by the epoch, art offers answers before questions have been asked.
'It is the ages that are her symbols.' Life, straggling after art, seizes upon
forms in art to express itself, so that life imitates art rather than art life.
'. . . This unfortunate aphorism about Art holding the mirror up to
nature, is', according to Wilde, 'deliberately said by Hamlet in order to

convince the bystanders of his absolute insanity in all art-matters.' If art be a mirror, we look into it to see—a mask. But more precisely, art is no mirror; it is a 'mist of words', 'a veil'.

Sometimes the veil is pierced. This indifferent conferral of forms upon life by art may have unexpected consequences which implicate art instead of isolating it. In 'The Decay of Lying' Wilde speaks of 'silly boys who, after reading the adventures of Jack Sheppard or Dick Turpin, pillage the stalls of unfortunate applewomen, break into sweetshops at night, and alarm old gentlemen who are returning home from the city by leaping out on them in suburban lanes, with black masks and unloaded revolvers.' In *Dorian Gray* the effect is more sinister; Dorian declares he has been poisoned by a book, and while Lord Henry assures him that art is too aloof to influence anybody, Dorian is felt to be right. Art may then transmit criminal impulses to its audience. Like Whitman, Wilde could and did say, 'Nor will my poems do good only, they will do just as much evil, perhaps more.'

The artist may be criminal and instil his work with criminality. Wilde's second essay in *Intentions* is 'Pen, Pencil and Poison'. He uses Thomas Wainewright as the type of the artist. We need not expect to find a beautiful soul; Wainewright was instead 'a forger of no mean or ordinary capabilities, and . . . a subtle and secret poisoner almost without rival in this or any age.' Among his interesting tastes, Wainewright had 'that curious love of green, which in individuals is always the sign of a subtle artistic temperament, and in nations is said to denote a laxity, if not a decadence of morals.' When a friend reproached him with a murder, he shrugged his shoulders and gave an answer that used to be identified as camp: 'Yes; it was a dreadful thing to do, but she had very thick ankles.' Wilde concludes that 'the fact of a man being a poisoner is nothing against his prose,' and 'there is no essential incongruity between crime and culture.' Wainewright's criminal career turns out to be strictly relevant to his art, fortifying it and giving it character. The quality of that art it is too early to judge, Wilde says, but he clearly believes that Wainewright's personality achieves sufficient criminality to have great artistic promise.

'The Critic as Artist' is the most ambitious of the essays in *Intentions*. It too conveys the notion that art undermines things as they are. The critic is the artist's accomplice in crime, or even masterminds the plot in which they are mutually engaged. Criticism overcomes the tendency of creation to repeat itself; it helps the artist discover unused possibilities. For at bottom, Wilde says, criticism is self-consciousness; it enables us to put our most recent phase at the distance and so go on to another. It disengages us so we may re-engage ourselves in a new way.

From this argument Wilde proceeds to find criticism and self-consciousness to be as necessary as sin. 'What is termed Sin is an essential element of progress'; without it, he holds, the world would stagnate or grow old or become colourless.

> By its curiosity [there is Arnold's word with Wilde's meaning], Sin
> increases the experience of the race. Through its intensified asser-
> tion of individualism it saves us from monotony of type. In its rejec-
> tion of the current notions about morality, it is one with the higher
> ethics.

By a dexterous transvaluation of words, Wilde makes good and evil
exchange places. Even socially sin is far more useful than martyrdom,
he says, since it is self-expressive rather than self-repressive. The goal of
man is the liberation of personality; when the day of true culture comes,
sin will be impossible because the soul will be able to transform.

> into elements of a richer experience, or a finer susceptibility, or a
> newer mode of thought, acts or passions that with the common
> would be commonplace, or with the uneducated ignoble, or with
> the shameful vile. Is this dangerous? Yes; it is dangerous—all ideas,
> as I told you, are so.

What muddies this point of view in Wilde is his looking back to conventional meanings like sin, ignoble, and shameful. He is not so ready as
Nietzsche to transvaluate these, though he does reshuffle them. His private equation is that sin is the perception of new and dangerous possibilities in action as self-consciousness is in thought and criticism is in
art. He espouses individualism, and he encourages society to make individualism more complete than it can be now, and for this reason he
sponsors socialism as a communal egotism, like the society made up of
separate but equal works of art.

   Meantime, before socialism, what should be thought of the criminal
impulses of the artist? Increasingly in his later writings, Wilde spreads
the guilt from the artist to all men. If we are all insincere, masked, and
lying, then the artist is prototype rather than exception. If all the sheep
are black, then the artist cannot be blamed for not being white. Such an
exculpation is implied in three of Wilde's plays after *Salome*—*Lady
Windermere's Fan*, *A Woman of No Importance*, *An Ideal Husband*.
Wilde allows his characters to be found guilty, but not guiltier than
others, and more courageous in their wrongdoing.

   Even as he defends them, he allows them to be mildly punished.
Half-consciously, Wilde was preparing himself for another abrupt shift
in his experience, such as he had made in 1886. It would be false to say
that Wilde wanted to go to prison, yet the notion had frequently crossed
his mind. He had always associated himself with the *poètes maudits*,
always considered obloquy a certificate of literary merit. In 'The Soul of
Man under Socialism' he had opposed suffering, yet acknowledged that
the Russian novelists had rediscovered a great medieval theme, the realization of man through suffering. More particularly, in a review of a
new book of poems by Wilfrid Scawen Blunt in 1889, he began: 'Prison
has had an admirable effect on Mr. Wilfrid Blunt as a poet.' It was like

the effect of crime on Wainewright. Blunt had been merely witty and affected earlier, now his work had more depth. Mr. Balfour must be praised, Wilde says jestingly, since 'by sending Mr. Blunt to gaol . . . [he] has converted a clever rhymer into an earnest and deep-thinking poet.' Six years later, just before his own disgrace, Wilde wrote in 'The Soul of Man under Socialism,' 'After all, even in prison a man can be quite free.' These hints indicate that Wilde was prepared, or thought he was, for trial and prison, and expected he would derive artistic profit from them. He had no idea of running away, even on a boyish holiday, whatever his friends might say. Instead he accepted imperial authority as readily as Christ had done—a precedent he discovered for himself, though hardly the first or last in hot water to do so. Blunt's poems written in prison were called *In Vinculis*, and Wilde's letter to Douglas from prison, which we know by Ross's title as *De Profundis*, was originally entitled by Wilde *Epistola: In Carcere et Vinculis*.

Hélas! Wilde's literary career was not transmogrified by prison as he hoped, but his experiences there, which were so much worse than he anticipated, gave him his final theme. '*La prison m'a complètement changé,*' he said to Gide at Berneval: '*je comptais sur elle pour cela.*' As before, he made no effort to exonerate himself by saying that his sins were venial or not sins at all. Defences of homosexual or 'Uranian' love were common enough at this period; except once at his trial, he did not make them. But he reached for the main implication of his disgrace through a double negative; though men thought he was unlike them, he was *not*. He was a genuine scapegoat.

This ultimate conception of himself was never put into an essay, but it is involved in his *De Profundis* letter to Douglas, and in *The Ballad of Reading Gaol*. Both are predictably full of imagery of Christ. Before this Wilde had depreciated pity as a motive in art; now he embraced it. The hero of his poem is a man who has murdered his mistress and is about to be hanged for his crime. Wilde identifies himself closely with this prisoner. The poem's tenor is that the prisoners are humanity, all of whom are felons:

> Yet each man kills the thing he loves,
>   By each let this be heard,
> Some do it with a bitter look,
>   Some with a flattering word,
> The coward does it with a kiss,
>   The brave man with a sword! . . .
>
> Some love too little, some too long,
>   Some sell, and others buy;
> Some do the deed with many tears,
>   And some without a sigh:
> For each man kills the thing he loves,
>   Yet each man does not die.

This poem was chosen for the *Oxford Book of Modern Verse* by Yeats, but he removed what he regarded as the commentary, including these stanzas. His effort to improve the poem evokes sympathy; it must be said, however, that whatever the quality of the bare narrative that Yeats prints, for Wilde—as for D. H. Lawrence and most readers—the commentary was the excessive and yet determining part of the poem. During the six years before his imprisonment he had demonstrated first that the artist was basically and usefully criminal, and second that criminality was not confined to artists, but was to be found as commonly among members of the Cabinet. Where most men pretend to a virtue they don't have, the artist, fully aware of his own sins, takes on those they don't acknowledge. The purpose of sin has subtly shifted in Wilde's mind—it is no longer a means for the artist of extending the boundaries of action, it is a means for him to focus and enshrine guilt. He has the courage, exceptional among men, of looking into the heart of things and finding there not brotherly love so much as murder, not self-love so much as suicide. In recognizing the universality of guilt he is like Christ; in revealing his own culpability he plays the role of his own Judas. Wilde, who had written in one of his poems ('Humanidad') that we are ourselves 'the lips betraying and the life betrayed,' had in fact brought about his own conviction. The result was that he was remarried to the society from which he had divorced himself; he was no outcast, for he accepted and even sought the punishment which other men, equally guilty, would only submit to vicariously through him, just as all the prisoners suffer with the doomed murderer. By means of submission and suffering he gives his life a new purpose, and writes over the palimpsest once again.

In this concern with social role Wilde has clearly moved away from Pater, and perhaps we can conceive of him as moving towards another writer, Jean Genet. Genet is of course ferocious and remorseless in a way that Wilde was not, and makes much less concession to the world. But the two men share in insistence on their own criminality and on a possible sanction for it. The comparison with Christ has been irresistible for both. As Genet says in *The Thief's Journal*:

> Let us ignore the theologians. 'Taking upon Himself the sins of the world' means exactly this: experiencing potentially and in their effects all sins: it means having subscribed to evil. Every creator must thus shoulder—the expression seems feeble—must make his own, to the point of knowing it to be his substance, circulating in his arteries, the evil given by him, which his heroes choose freely.

Wilde in *De Profundis* remembered having remarked to Gide that 'there was nothing that . . . Christ had said that could not be transferred immediately into the sphere of Art, and there find its complete fulfilment.' And again, Genet speaks like Wilde of the courage required to do wrong, saying: 'If he has courage, the guilty man decides to be what crime has made him.' He wishes to obtain 'the recognition of evil.' Both writers envisage a regeneration which can come only from total assumption of their proclivities and their lot; as Genet puts it:

> I shall destroy appearances, the casings will burn away and one evening I shall appear there, in the palm of your hand, quiet and pure, like a glass statuette. You will see me. Round about me there will be nothing left.

Wilde summons for this sacred moment a red rose growing from the hanged man's mouth, a white one from his heart. He had terrified André Gide by trying to persuade that strictly reared young man to authorize evil, as to some extent in the *acte gratuit* Gide did, and it is just such authorization that Genet asserts with more fierceness than Wilde.

In his criticism and in his work generally, Wilde balanced two ideas which, we have observed, look contradictory. One is that art is disengaged from actual life, the other that it is deeply incriminated with it. The first point of view is sometimes taken by Yeats, though only to qualify it, the second without qualification by Genet. That art is sterile, and that it is infectious, are attitudes not beyond reconciliation. Wilde never formulated their union, but he implied something like this: by its creation of beauty art reproaches the world, calling attention to the world's faults through their very omission; so the sterility of art is an affront or a parable. Art may also outrage the world by flouting its laws or by picturing indulgently their violation. Or art may seduce the world by making it follow an example which seems bad but is discovered to be better than it seems. In these various ways the artist forces the world towards self-recognition, with at least a tinge of self-redemption.

Yet this ethical or almost ethical view of art co-exists in Wilde with its own cancellation. He could write *Salome* with one hand, dwelling upon incest and necrophilia, and show them as self-defeated, punished by execution and remorse. With the other hand, he could dissolve by the critical intellect all notions of sin and guilt. He does so in *The Importance of Being Earnest*, which is all insouciance where *Salome* is all incrimination. In *The Importance of Being Earnest* sins which are presented as accursed in *Salome* and unnameable in *Dorian Gray* are translated into a different key, and appear as Algernon's inordinate and selfish craving for—cucumber sandwiches. The substitution of mild gluttony for fearsome lechery renders all vice harmless. There *is* a wicked brother, but he is just our old friend Algernon. The double life which is so serious a matter for Dorian or for The Ideal Husband, becomes a harmless Bunburying, or playing Jack in the country and Ernest in town. In the earlier, four-act version of the play, Wilde even parodied punishment, by having a bailiff come to take Jack to Holloway Prison (as Wilde himself was soon to be taken) not for homosexuality, but for running up food bills at the Savoy. Jack is disinclined, he says, to be imprisoned in the suburbs for dining in town, and makes out a cheque. The notion of expiation is also mocked; as Cecily observes: 'They have been eating

muffins. That looks like repentance.' Finally, the theme of regeneration
is parodied in the efforts of Ernest and Jack to be baptized. (By the way,
in the earlier version Prism is also about to be baptized, and someone
comments, 'To be born again would be of considerable advantage to
her.') The ceremonial unmasking at the play's end, which had meant
death for Dorian Gray, leaves everyone barefaced for a new puppet show,
that of matrimony. Yet amusing as it all is, much of the comedy derives
from Wilde's own sense of the realities of what are being mocked. He
was in only momentary refuge from his more usual cycle which ran
from scapegrace to scapegoat.

During his stay in prison Wilde took up the regeneration theme in *De
Profundis* and after being freed he resumed it in *The Ballad of Reading
Gaol*. But he was too self-critical not to find the notion of rebirth a little
preposterous. When his friends complained of his resuming old habits,
he said, 'A patriot put in prison for loving his country loves his country,
and a poet in prison for loving boys loves boys,' But to write about himself as unredeemed, unpunished, unreborn, to claim that his sins were
nothing, that his form of love was more noble than most other people's,
that what had happened to him was the result merely of legal obtuseness,
was impossible for Wilde. So long as he had been a scapegrace the door
to comedy was still open; once having accepted the role of scapegoat the
door was closed. He conceived of a new play, but it was in his earlier
mode and he could not write it. Cramped to one myth, and that sombre
and depleted, Wilde could not extricate himself. There was nothing to
do but die, which accordingly he did. But not without one final assertion
of a past enthusiasm: he allowed himself to be converted to Catholicism
the night before his death.

JOYCE CAROL OATES

The Picture of Dorian Gray:
Wilde's Parable of the Fall †

Its parable-like simplicity and the rather painful remorselessness of its
concluding chapters have made it possible for readers to underestimate
the subtlety of *The Picture of Dorian Gray*. So clearly does its famous
plot move to its ineludible climax—so explicitly are its major "points"
articulated (the poisonously charming Lord Henry is told: "You cut life
to pieces with your epigrams")—that the complexity of Oscar Wilde's
imagination is likely to be minimized. While in one sense *The Picture
of Dorian Gray* is as transparent as a medieval allegory, and its structure
as workman-like as that of Marlowe's *Dr. Faustus*, to which it bears an

† From *Contraries* (New York: Oxford UP, 1981) 3–16.

obvious family resemblance, in another sense it remains a puzzle: knotted, convoluted, brilliantly enigmatic: and if one might be "poisoned by
a book" (as poor Dorian charges he has been, by Huysmans's rather silly
novel), *The Picture of Dorian Gray* might very well be that book.

Joyce saw in Wilde not only a fellow-artist but a betrayed artist and a
"dishonored exile"—a kind of Christ—though his initial response to *The
Picture of Dorian Gray* was qualified: the book was "crowded with lies
and epigrams" and its spirit muted by the fact that Wilde felt obliged to
"veil" the homosexual implications.[1] That Joyce was insensitive to Wilde's
deeper theme is suggested by his frequent echoing of Wilde ("My art is
not a mirror held up to nature," Joyce boasts. "Nature mirrors my art"),
which develops only the explicit, daylight side of Wilde's aesthetics and
makes no allusion to the cautionary and even elegiac tone of much of
The Picture of Dorian Gray. It is not, certainly, the homosexual nature
of Dorian's behavior—or, for that matter, his allegedly promiscuous het-
erosexual behavior—that constitutes Dorian's sin, but the fact that he
involves others in his life's drama "simply as a method of procuring
extraordinary sensations," and without emotion. Joyce's imagination was
earthbound, even domestic, and if Stephan Dedalus with his ashplant
and his pose of languid weariness brings to mind the adolescent defiance
of Wilde's infamous "The Decay of Lying" of 1889, it is the case nonetheless that Joyce's artist was hardly likely to drift into satanism, let alone
murder. Nighttown, in fact, will make a victim of *him*.

Beyond the defiance of the young iconoclast—Wilde himself, of
course—and the rather perfunctory curve of *Dorian* to that gothic final
sight (beautiful Dorian dead with a knife in his heart, "withered, wrinkled, and loathsome of visage") there is another, possibly less strident,
but more central theme. That one is damned for selling one's soul to
the devil (for whatever prize—"eternal youth" is a trivial enough one) is
a commonplace in legend; what arrests our attention more, perhaps, is
Wilde's claim or boast or worry or warning that one might indeed be
poisoned by a book—and that the artist, even the presumably "good"
Basil Hallward, is the diabolical agent. Wilde's novel must be seen as a
highly serious meditation upon the moral role of the artist—an interior
challenge, in fact, to the insouciance of the famous pronouncements
that would assure us that there is no such thing as a moral or an immoral
book ("Books are well written, or badly written. That is all"), or that all
art is "quite useless." Wilde's genius was disfigured by his talent: he
always sounds much more flippant, far more superficial, than he really
is. So one is always saying about *Dorian*, with an air of surprise, that the
novel is exceptionally good after all—and anyone who has read it recently
replies, with the same air of faint incredulity, yes, it *is* exceptionally
good—one of the strongest and most haunting of English novels, in fact.
Yet its reputation remains questionable. Gerald Weales virtually dis-

1. See Richard Ellmann, *James Joyce* (New York, 1959), p. 283 and p. 241.

misses it as "terribly *fin de siècle*" in his rather flippant introduction to the Signet paperback edition, and it would be difficult to find a critic who would choose to discuss it in terms other than the familiar ones of Decadence, Art-for-Art's-Sake, Art as "the telling of beautiful untrue things."

Beneath the entertaining and often distracting glitter of Wilde's verbal surfaces, however, one does discover another work; or if not precisely another *work*, then another tone, and another Wilde. Suddenly life is not a matter of dialogue, of drawing-room repartee; it takes on the nostalgia of "unutterable longing" which Pater found in Shakespeare (see Pater's *Appreciations* of 1889), and that ceremonial, elegiac rhythm one senses in the great plays: as if Shakespeare had had in mind some "inverted rite" by which human justice executes its sentences. Just as Pater translated Shakespeare's drama into other, more static forms—the tapestry, the religious rite, sculpture, pictorial art—so Wilde translates, or transmutes, what might be in another era a tragedy of the violent warring of consciousness with itself into a reassuringly old-fashioned morality play. The ceremonially correct punishment of Dorian Gray seems to complete the novel; but it merely ends the novel. The preoccupation with the questionable morality of the artist's interference with life—Basil Hallward's appropriation of Dorian's image, for instance, for his uncanny portrait—is never satisfactorily resolved, and even the final appearance of the aging and somewhat attenuated Lord Henry hints at another level of human concern which Wilde has no space to investigate. What the strangely moved reader is likely to carry away from *Dorian* is precisely this sense of something riddling and incomplete. One feels about it as one feels about the most profoundly haunting works of art—that it has not been fully understood.

The murder of Basil Hallward by Dorian Gray is usually seen as one of the more demonic of Dorian's acts. Yet the murder is symbolically appropriate, and appropriate too is the fact that, for Dorian, this former idolator ("I worshipped you too much") becomes a loathsome "thing" after his death and must be eradicated by crude scientific means. (Cut up, presumably, and dissolved with nitric acid in a sleight-of-hand Wilde feels no need to make plausible.) Basil functions as a "good" character, one of Lord Henry's straight men, but his role in Dorian's damnation is hardly an ambiguous one, and his sudden death answers to an internal logic.

"Actual life was chaos," Dorian thinks, as his moral disintegration allows him insight, "but there was something terribly logical in the imagination": by which Wilde suggests the limits of Lord Henry's (and his own) faith in the power of the individual will. To become a spectator of one's own life, as Henry has boasted, not only fails to save one from suffering—it makes suffering inevitable, although the "suffering" of course will come in unanticipated forms, as ennui, paralysis, the "shallow moods and sickly thoughts" of protracted adolescence. Dorian's wickedness appears to be involuntary; he would not have exchanged his soul for eternal youth and beauty had not an artist, Basil Hallward, presented him with an image of himself utterly new, unrequested, and irresistible—if, that is, the terrible logic of the imagination had not set into play a tragic sequence of events of which "Dorian Gray" happens to be the central figure.

There is no doubt but that Basil Hallward initiates the tragedy, for it is his worshipping of the young man's physical beauty and his appropriation of his image (as "art") that calls Dorian's attention to himself—and stimulates Lord Henry's undisguised homoerotic interest. (To Henry, Dorian is a young Adonis who looks as if he were made of "ivory and rose-leaves." He is a Narcissus, a brainless beautiful creature "who should always be here in winter when we have no flowers to look at.") Basil, however, is deeply troubled by his painting. He understands instinctively—despite his friend's gibes—that he must not exhibit it in public because it reveals too much of himself. *Why* he has painted Dorian Gray's picture is not clear, given his ambivalent feelings about Dorian's beauty and the fatality he believes attends all human beings of distinction. He says, in words that must echo Wilde's own thoughts on the subject, and on the very creation, in prose, of Dorian: "Every portrait that is painted with feeling is a portrait of the artist, not of the sitter. The sitter is merely the accident, the occasion." Though Basil cannot know that his dream-image will destroy him, quite literally, he has experienced, at their first meeting, one of those violent and inexplicable spasms of emotion that attend a "fatal" attraction. The role of the artist, so extravagantly proclaimed by Wilde as self-determined, and superior to mere life, sounds here as if it were a matter of involuntary fate. Basil felt terror in Dorian's presence: "I knew that I had come face to face with someone whose mere personality was so fascinating that, if I allowed it to do so, it would absorb my whole nature, my whole soul, my very art itself." But Basil's resistance is, of course, futile. He does give away his soul, he does fall in love with a boy who symbolizes the harmony of soul and body, and soon comes to feel that he could not live as an artist without Dorian.

Then again he says, quite bluntly, that Dorian is "simply a motive in art," and that his likeness on canvas might bear little resemblance to the young man himself. He reduces, in Basil's aesthetic imagination—overheated as it is—to a manner of painting, to "the curves of certain lines" and the loveliness and subtlety of "certain colors." Dorian has no soul or worth of his own; he functions as the artist's Muse or Anima, and his value lies in his unconsciousness (and feminine) stimulation of the male artist's energy. Basil Hallward is not in love with Dorian Gray but with his own image of Dorian, which is to say his own "motive" in art. Wilde knows that the artist oscillates between the frenzy of inspiration and the lucidity of an almost impersonal wisdom when he has Basil speak in this way, and to allude to a godly or supra-human destiny that will involve both the artist and his mesmerizing subject. Basil is fated to single out Dorian for his art and by means of his art to force Dorian into a tragic self-consciousness: by appropriating the boy's image in answer to an artistic motive he begins the boy's destruction, and it is altogether fitting that Dorian should murder him some years later. (As, it might be argued, Oscar Wilde's "artfulness" came close to destroying him, and did expel him forever from the society of presumably normal people.)

In a far less graceful fashion Hawthorne explored the problematic relationship between an artist of sorts and his subject, in the cautionary allegory "The Birthmark." Here, a scientist of genius attempts to remove the defect of a birthmark on his beautiful wife's cheek, with the inevitable result that the woman dies. In this ponderous tale there is no doubt that the scientist is the villain. He interferes with beauty, his "fatal hand" dares to grapple with "the mystery of life," and so an angelic spirit is loosed from its mortal frame. Hawthorne's Aylmer is an awkward Yankee cousin of Faust whose experience is more blundering than wicked; Hawthorne ends, somewhat obscurely, with the remark that had Aylmer reached a more profound wisdom "he need not thus have flung away the happiness which would have woven his mortal life of the selfsame texture with the celestial."

By contrast the fateful union of Basil and Dorian is predetermined by the gods. Basil, as the artist, *must* succumb to his motive; he *must* be seduced by the Adam-like Dorian, whose erotic powers are of course entirely unconscious. (Before meeting Lord Henry, and his own likeness, Dorian is indeed a brainless beautiful creature. He is somewhat spoiled, but spoiled in a child-like way; he is good-natured, spontaneous, and generous, an absolute innocent.) But the artist takes his image from him and exhibits it to him as art, as an object for contemplation. Dorian *objectifies* his own physical being, and his corruption begins at once: "When he saw [the portrait] he drew back, and his cheeks flushed for a moment with pleasure. A look of joy came into his eyes, as if he had recognized himself for the first time. . . . The sense of his own beauty came on him like a revelation." And immediately the boy begins to think, in language not unlike that of Lord Henry's, that his predicament is a very unhappy one. The surprise of the scene is that he *thinks* at all, still less in such a manner:

> "I shall grow old, and horrible, and dreadful. But this picture will remain always young. It will never be older than this particular day of June. . . . If it were only the other way! If it were I who was to be always young, and the picture that was to grow old! For that— for that—I would give everything! . . . I am jealous of everything whose beauty does not die. I am jealous of the portrait you have painted of me. Why should it keep what I must lose? . . . Why did you paint it? It will mock me some day—mock me horribly!"

Dorian's background, revealed later to Lord Henry, is suitably romantic: his mother was a beautiful young woman who ran away with a penniless subaltern, and who died shortly after his birth. The boy's misfortune
charms Lord Henry, for beyond every exquisite thing there must be
something tragic, "worlds had to be in travail, that the meanest flower
might blow." The charm of Dorian is precisely his awakening from
innocence to a realization of his own power. Talking to such a person,
Henry thinks, is like playing upon an exquisite violin—and it strikes him
as highly desirable that *he* should seek to dominate Dorian as Dorian,
without knowing it, dominates Basil. There is something enthralling to
Henry in the exercise of influence: "To project one's soul into some
gracious form . . . ; to hear one's own intellectual views echoed back to
one . . . ; to convey one's temperament into another. . . ." So Basil's
"subject" becomes Henry's.

The Picture of Dorian Gray is a curious hybrid. Certainly it possesses
a "supernatural" dimension, and its central image is gothic; yet in other
respects it is Restoration comedy, energetically sustained for more than
two hundred pages. It approximates the novel Lord Henry would write
if he had the ambition—a book as lovely as a Persian carpet, and as
unreal. The supernatural element, however, is never active except in
terms of the portrait. It would be quite ludicrous if introduced to Lord
Henry's drawing-room society, and it is really inexplicable given the
secular nature of Dorian's personality. Evidently diabolical powers are
stirred by Basil's art but Basil himself has no awareness of them, apart
from a certain uneasiness regarding the morality of his relationship with
Dorian. Is the Devil responsible? But does the Devil exist? Hell is hardly
more than theoretical to Wilde, and Heaven is equally notional; when
Dorian is attracted to the Catholic Church it is primarily for the sake of
exotic ritual, ecclesiastical vestments, and other somewhat ludicrous
treasures of the Church, which Wilde delights in cataloguing. The *consequences* of a Faustian pact with the Devil are dramatized, but the Devil
himself is absent, which suggests that the novel is an elaborate fantasy
locating the Fall within the human psyche alone. Basil, Lord Henry,
and Dorian are all artists, aspects of their creator. Basil is conventional
artist, apart from his attraction to Dorian; Lord Henry and Dorian are
aesthetes—artists of their own lives—whose hope is to generate a New
Hedonism. Wilde echoes Pater, of course, but with a unique intensity,
and it is significant that there is nothing remotely supernatural about
such passages as the following, which are clearly at the very heart of the
novel:

> There are few of us who have not sometimes wakened before dawn,
> either after one of those dreamless nights that makes us almost ena-
> moured of death, or one of those nights of horror and misshapen
> joy, when through the chambers of the brain sweep phantoms more
> terrible than reality itself, and instinct with that vivid life that lurks

in all grotesques, and that lends to Gothic art its enduring vitality. . . . Veil after veil of thin dusky gauze is lifted, and by degrees the forms and colors of things are restored to them, and we watch the dawn remaking the world in its antique pattern. The wan mirrors get back their mimic life. . . . Nothing seems to us changed. Out of the unreal shadows of the night comes back the real life that we had known. We have to resume it where we had left off, and there steals over us a terrible sense of the necessity for the continuance of energy in the same wearisome round of stereotyped habits, or a wild longing, it may be, that our eyelids might open some morning upon a world that had been refashioned anew in the darkness . . . a world in which the past would have little or no place, or survive, at any rate, in no conscious form of obligation or regret. . . . It was the creation of such worlds as these that seemed to Dorian Gray to be the true object . . . of life.

Certainly it will not do to dismiss such sentiments as "romantic"—they strike a very deep chord, and underlie all creations of alternate worlds in art. If it is the case that the hedonist, unrestrained by morality, customs, or the surveillance of his neighbors, always drifts to the most extreme experiences, then it might be hypothesized that the hedonist is an archetype of man, not perverse but representational. His quest for new sensations in order to give vitality to his flickering life is nothing more than an exaggeration of any quest for meaning.

Wilde's contempt for the "shallow psychology" that defines man in terms of his social and familial position is as savage as D. H. Lawrence's. How is it possible, Dorian wonders, to conceive of man's ego as "a thing simple, permanent, reliable, and of one essence"? Wilde, like Lawrence, sees man as "a being with myriad lives and myriad sensations, a complex multiform creature that bore within itself strange legacies of thought and passion, and whose very flesh was tainted with the monstrous maladies of the dead." Insincerity, Wilde wittily observes, is merely a method by which we multiply our personalities. Where in Wilde the experimentation with alternative lives is a desperate means of escaping that *taedium vitae* that "comes upon those to whom life denies nothing," in Lawrence it is clearly quite different. Lawrence, who believed that "nothing that comes from the deep, passional soul is bad, or can be bad,"[2] was repulsed by the kind of hedonism Wilde preached, and he created the gnomish Loerke of *Women in Love* as a spokesman for *fin de siècle* aesthetics—with something of Italian Futurism thrown in. To the bat-like but highly articulate Loerke, art is purely self-referential: it is "a picture of nothing, of absolutely nothing," with no relationship to the everyday world, which exists on a separate and distinct plane of existence. Loerke is the "rock-bottom" of all life, the perfect stoic who is also the perfect epicure, troubled about nothing, connected to no one,

2. See the Introduction to *Women in Love*, written in 1919.

a parody of Decadent aesthetics as it shades into European Fascism. That Loerke crouched in Lawrence's soul and fascinated him as he does Gudrun goes without saying. Even Lawrence's hatreds sprang out of sympathy.

Yet it would be wrong to assume that Lawrence's insights are inevitably deeper than Wilde's, or that his vicious portrait of Loerke ("I expect he is a Jew—or part Jew," Birkin mutters) is a more critical portrait than that of Dorian himself. Wilde's great theme is the Fall—the Fall of innocence and its consequences, the corruption of "natural" life by a sudden irrevocable consciousness (symbolized by Dorian's infatuation with himself)—but this falling from grace is available only to those who have attained a certain degree of economic and intellectual freedom. Restlessness, ennui, the inability to apply one's strength to anything— these are not merely symptoms of Dorian's perverse nature, but symptoms of a highly advanced and sophisticated civilization. So Dorian is a victim—not unlike Dostoyevsky's similarly emblematic Stavrogin, who drifts into a life of unimaginative vice because he is "freed" of the earth and of the necessity to labor as ordinary men do. Stavrogin is accursed by boredom: "As to my political views," he says in his confession, "I just felt I'd have liked to put gunpowder under the four corners of the world and blow the whole thing sky-high—if it had only been worth the trouble."[3] Stavrogin's role in the death of a young girl is more convincing than Dorian's role in the death of Sybil Vane, just as Stavrogin's predicament, generally, is more convincing in realistic terms than Dorian's: but both young men, handsome as they are, with the power to move others deeply while remaining unmoved themselves, are allegorical figures whose fates are meant to symbolize the sterility of an "advanced" civilization. How, Stavrogin asks, is one to apply one's strength, one's "limitless" strength, to anything that is not an illusion?

Dostoyevsky, no less than Wilde, is enamoured of his creation, but quite serious about the "strength" that might be applied to sheer labor, peasant labor. Stavrogin might have been redeemed had he knelt down to kiss the earth he had defiled, as Raskolnikov does; he might have saved himself had he followed Shatov's advice to "find God through labor." But Wilde would have none of this. He can be as sentimental as Dostoyevsky, and as unreasonably pious, but his "lower classes" are never anything but lower. They appear, in fact, to belong to a level of consciousness distinctly different from that of their elegant masters—tiptoeing about with their "masks of servility," lapsing into unwelcome "garrulousness" about tiresome household matters when their masters are eager to begin a night of vice. Two kinds of human beings, two species—those who are "free" and those who are not.

Dorian's freedom, however, as we know, is a consequence primarily of his loss of humanity. His soul is no longer his own: it has been appro-

3. Dostoyevsky,. *The Possessed*, trans. Andrew R. MacAndrew (New York, Signet edition, 1962), p. 418.

priated by art. His response to Sybil Vane's melodramatic death is one of surprise and alarm at his own failure to feel grief: "Why cannot I feel this tragedy as much as I want to?" he complains to Lord Henry. "Real life" is eclipsed by art, and by the emotional responses we commonly give to works of art, rejoicing in their artificiality. The girl's death has for Dorian "all the terrible beauty of a Greek tragedy, a tragedy in which I took a great part, but by which I have not been wounded." In the end Henry explains Dorian's egotism to him, and assures him that Sybil Vane never lived—not for *him*—apart from the phantom in his imagination.

After the girl's death Dorian becomes increasingly detached from what might be called normal human emotions. It is interesting to note that the Shavian ideal—the man of disinterested sensibility who looks unmoved upon the melodrama of life—does not greatly differ from the precious, rather infantile, and supremely confident model of the dehumanized personality Wilde offers. Dorian is a golem, a parody of Lord Henry, assuring Basil Hallward that it is only shallow people who require years to get rid of an emotion: "A man who is master of himself can end a sorrow as easily as he can invent a pleasure. I don't want to be at the mercy of my emotions. I want to use them, to enjoy them, to dominate them."

Is it inevitable that a doctrine of Art-for-Art's Sake reduces to the sort of sickly, simpering aestheticism of a Des Esseintes? Is there something doomed in the very notion of a purely self-referential art that, at the very most, *uses* materials from the "real world"? One encounters repeatedly in literary history the belligerent claim that art has nothing to do with anything beyond itself, and that writing that aspires to the loveliness of, let us say, a Persian carpet must necessarily be "unreal." The stylist is encouraged to cultivate his own sensibility, for where actual life is surrendered to chaos one might nevertheless forge a certain logic of the imagination. In *Dorian*, Wilde surely believes in his aesthetics and at the same time offers, by way of Dorian and his fate, and Basil Hallward and *his* fate, a disturbingly prescient commentary on his beliefs: the artist who succumbs to the spell of Beauty will be destroyed, and so savagely that nothing of him will survive. The novel's power lies in the interstices of its parable—in those passages in which the author appears to be confessing doubts of both a personal and an impersonal nature.

It might be hypothesized that the airless and claustrophobic world of self-referential art, when it is not primarily a reaction against prevailing norms of "social realism" in its various guises, is actually a paradigm of the infant's world. Everything in that world is self-referential: everything refers inward: words, as they are grasped one by one, appear to be *created* by the child (just as the mother and other adults, mobilized by cries of hunger or alarm, certainly appear to be controlled by the child). The illusion of possessing and controlling everything is a powerful one, and its charms are not readily surrendered even in adulthood. So we encounter the theoreticians of self-referential art both the puzzling contempt for "real" worlds and the sentimental hope for a forcible remaking of the universe as if there were not already a universe to be acknowledged. The impulse for such creation—Faustian in its aspirations—must spring from a sense of insignificance; for even the infant's delusion of omnipotence is compensatory to its actual helplessness. *It is the spectator, and not life, that art really mirrors.*

The value of Wilde's allegory lies in the questions it asks rather than in the experience it transcribes. For *Dorian* gives us hardly any experience at all—it is surface and symbol, and too tidily constructed. Dorian, Lord Henry, and Basil Hallward fade, but their voices remain, asking certain unanswerable questions that are as appropriate for our time as they were for Wilde's: Is the Fall from innocence inevitable? Is the loss of illusion tragic, or comic, or merely farcical? Is the artist by his very nature inclined to manipulate and pervert his subject?—and is his doom bound up with the fact of his artistry, his autonomy? Lord Henry declares that if a man treats life artistically, his brain is his heart, but Wilde's novel—and Wilde's experience—suggests otherwise.

DONALD L. LAWLER

Keys to the Upstairs Room: A Centennial Essay on Allegorical Performance in *Dorian Gray* †

The centenary of Oscar Wilde's *The Picture of Dorian Gray*, which first appeared in the July 1890 number of *Lippincott's Monthly Magazine*, will offer critics a good excuse for revaluation of this popular classic. As a preliminary step, this essay takes another look at some of the traditional approaches to *Dorian Gray*, especially at those allegorical structures eclipsed, partially or totally, by the prominence of the well-known moral. Besides the literal, or narrative, level, I propose to look at the other major levels of allegorization, beginning with the social and historical and advancing through the autobiographical, psychological, moral, and aesthetic. In the course of identifying and illustrating the various allegorical modes, we must look also at some other intentions of the narrative that either branch from allegory as it develops or modify the allegory in ways both subtle and interesting—I refer especially to Wilde's applications of the gothic, social comedy, aestheticism, and social criticism.

This essay has been written especially for this text, and my approach relies heavily on preceding editorial work done for this critical edition. There are two sorts of critical movement in this study. One is within the

† First published in this Norton edition.

vertical space of the narrative, moving along an imaginary axis that takes us from caricature to moral and aesthetic philosophy. The second vector follows the transmission of the text from the MSS to the final, revised version (1891). In successive revisions, at least four of them prior to the bound version of *Dorian Gray*, Wilde worked to encourage a more complex response in the reader by suggesting more than one possible interpretation of the main action and its related themes. Naturally enough, we are most interested in Wilde's final and most extensive revision. The argument that follows, therefore, interprets and in some cases re-interprets already established primary and secondary historical records together with the evidence of the various states of the text. The purpose is not so much to produce a revisionist interpretation as to enrich our traditional reading of a critically underserved masterpiece.

As a test case of this approach, I propose addressing a question of design that remained constant through all the revisions but whose significance or meaning was modified in varying degrees as each layer of allegory was applied and enhanced. It is the question implied in the title of this essay, namely, why did Dorian store his magic portrait in the abandoned, upstairs nursery and schoolroom of his youth? [1]

I

The foundations of Wilde's allegory in *Dorian Gray* are located in contemporary history and in as lively a sense of place as that of A. C. Doyle. Even with a contemporary map of London in hand, one can follow Dorian's movement around town, with Wilde as our unfailing guide to late Victorian interiors. The novel opens in Basil Hallward's studio, whose decor as described by Wilde was probably patterned on the studio of Charles Ricketts (1866–1931), an artist friend who designed several of Wilde's books, including *Dorian Gray*. Ricketts lived with his friend and fellow artist Charles Shannon in a Chelsea cul-de-sac called the Vale. The house had formerly belonged to James Abbott McNeill Whistler, and Wilde had often been a guest there under both encumbancies. This is our first clue that *Dorian Gray* is a romance of place as well as of personality.

Supporting the allegories of *Dorian Gray*, Wilde served up an elaborately allusive narrative, rooted in contemporary life with a vivid a sense of place and time. Starting at this level, we will find ourselves moving from allusion, through the galleries of a roman à clef into the allegori-

1. One common-sense answer readily comes to mind, in that the design of Victorian townhouses, such as the one Wilde lived in with his family on Tite Street, typically had nurseries and servants' rooms on the top floor. In Dorian's case, a nursery would have been empty for some time. Given this option, the old nursery was a convenient, out-of-the-way hiding place for an explicitly self-critical portrait, the living emblem of Dorian's guilty conscience. A disadvantage was that it was near the servants' quarters, and in MS the narrator makes frequent references to Dorian's anxiety on that score, changing servants regularly.

cal. The transitions are so deftly managed that the reader is seldom conscious of moving from one plane to another. Although there is no way to translate into a critical idiom the way in which these effects are orchestrated in the novel, we may look at some representative examples of this vertical movement in the narrative.

Hallward's account of Lady Brandon's party, where he first met Dorian, introduces a gallery of fashionable London. Wilde as lion of the dinner table knew this world well. Notable among the cameos is Lady Brandon herself—"a peacock in everything but beauty" was Lord Henry's quip—reputed by two of Wilde's close friends and early biographers, R. H. Sherard and Frank Harris, to be based in part on Lady Jane Wilde, Oscar's mother. If that is so, and it seems likely enough, this none-too-flattering sketch is of Lady Wilde well past her prime. Perhaps if she had remained with her salon long enough in Dublin, she would have made an appearance in James Joyce's fiction instead of modeling for her son's gazette caricatures in *Dorian Gray*. Indeed it seems that Lady Wilde did extra duty as the basis for two more portraits in the revised version of 1891. The first is the blowzy mother of Sibyl Vane, a crone without a redeeming feature. The second is Lady Narborough, hostess of a London dinner party later attended by Dorian and Lord Henry, who may represent a younger Speranza when she was queen of Dublin society and her salon was sure to be attended by artists and intellectuals both in residence in and in transit through Dublin.[2] Hallward's review of the party in the *Lippincott's* version was filled with references to actual personalities of the day from William Gladstone to the Russian ambassador Count Peter Schuvaloff.[3]

Later in the story, we hear of an ancestor of Dorian Gray, one Sir Anthony Sherard, the "lover of Giovanna of Naples," (1371–1455), a queen notorious for immorality. Sir Anthony bequeathed an "inheritance of sin and shame" to Dorian. When Wilde's friend and later biographer R. H. Sherard protested the geneology, Wilde assured him that

2. Here and elsewhere, we should be wary of drawing conclusions about Wilde's use of models for his characters, although *Dorian Gray* is a book of portraits. No doubt it would be naïve to argue that details, sketches, caricatures, or impersonations are value-neutral in this novel, but the fact is that nearly every identifiable character in *Dorian Gray* was a relation or a friend of the author.
3. Count Peter Schuvaloff served as ambassador to England from 1873 to 1879. He died in 1889. This suggests a setting for the *Lippincott's* version between 1873 and 1879, most likely the last season of Schuvaloff's embassy, since everyone that year was talking of his diplomatic coup in settling the Russo-Turkish war on terms highly favorable to Russian claims. If this inference is correct, then the period covered in the *Lippincott's* version from Basil's first encounter with Dorian to his murder is about eight years, or from 1878 to 1886.

The murder date is based on Ellmann's speculations in "The Critic as Artist as Wilde" (*Golden Codgers* 33) (see above, p. 415). In the revised version of 1891, Wilde dropped reference to Schuvaloff, a change that supports Ellmann's view that the alterations Wilde made in the date of Basil's murder had autobiographical meaning. The original date was "the 7th of November, the eve of his own thirty-second birthday," which Wilde altered to the "ninth of November, the eve of his own thirty-eighth birthday." Ellmann suggests that the original reference had a specific significance for Wilde, whose life as a homosexual began during his thirty-second year, according to Robert Ross. Changing the date and eve is entirely consistent with the revisions Wilde made in the book version, obliterating all traces of the homoeroticism in the magazine edition.

he would reduce the charges in the revised 1891 version.[4] Putting Sherard into Dorian's gallery of naughty ancestors was a joke whose implications, like many other things about Wilde's personality, Sherard never quite understood. Sherard was one of those young men whose good looks corresponded to Wilde's obsessive image of idealized youth as described in "The Portrait of Mr. W. H." and in the novel. Sherard could easily have been a physical model for Dorian's portrait, but he possessed the temperament of a loyal if rather naïve friend, instead of the corruptible Dorian we are given in the novel. Sherard would never believe that Wilde was a practicing homosexual until an exasperated Wilde finally told him so. Thereafter, Sherard insisted that Wilde's carnal appetites were the effect of a case of syphilis he had contracted as a student at Oxford. Although he considered Sherard at times a great bore, Wilde never interfered with either the man or his illusions, perhaps rewarding Sherard's staunch heterosexualism with the imagined charms of the disreputable Giovanna II of Naples. This is but one instance among many of Wilde's Puckish humor in assigning names and identities to his characters.[5]

Sibyl Vane is a far more important character. She is an actress and Dorian's first love. There is good reason for believing that she is modeled after two women. One is Constance Wilde, Oscar's wife. Once he described her in a letter to Lily Langtry in terms that he later applied to Sibyl:

> I am going to be married to a beautiful girl called Constance Lloyd, a grave, slight, violet-eyed little Artemis, with great coils of heavy brown hair which make her flower-like head droop like a blossom, and wonderful ivory hands. . . . (*Letters* 154)

There is strong evidence from the manuscripts, however, suggesting another possible source for her personality. In the holograph MS at the Morgan Library, Wilde had miswritten "Sybil Fane" more than a dozen times in addition to the familiar Vane, as it now stands. He corrected the variants in revision, and later, J. M. Stoddart, Wilde's *Lippincott's* editor, changed the spelling of the first name to its present form. However the mistakes suggest another possible key to Sibyl's character. Wilde knew socially and corresponded with Mary Montgomerie Lamb, who wrote under the name "Violet Fane." He sent her an inscribed copy of

4. Sherard's reference to the incident is in *Bernard Shaw, Frank Harris and Oscar Wilde*: "I had to get him to take out the 'Lord Anthony Sherard' from *The Picture of Dorian Gray* because there was an estimable Baron Sherard then in being. However, Oscar did not let me escape completely, but reduced me to the rank of a baronet, as which I now figure in the novel as having sold my soul for a great pearl or something of the kind" (137). Since Wilde did not make the changes Sherard writes about, perhaps we should assume the changes were promised by Wilde but either forgotten or ignored.

5. Here is another of a different kind. When Wilde received the galleys of the revised 1891 version from Coulson Kernahan, his editor, Wilde wired immediately: "Terrible blunder in book. Coming back specially. Stop all proofs—Wilde" (Kernahan 212–13). The blunder proved to be a hoax. Wilde explained: " 'Ashton is a gentleman's name' he spoke brokenly, and wrung his hands as if in anguish, 'and I have given it—God forgive me—to a tradesman! It must be changed to Hubbard. Hubbard positively smells of the tradesman.' "

his poems in 1881. At Wilde's invitation, she later contributed to *Woman's World* when he was editor. Thus, they had been friends for more than a decade prior to the appearance of *Dorian Gray*. Coincidentally, Mary Lamb had taken her pen name from the heroine of Benjamin Disraeli's popular novel *Vivian Gray* (5 vols., 1826–27), a novel that has been suggested as a possible source for *Dorian Gray* by contemporary reviewers and later critics.[6]

If Lady Jane Wilde is suspected of inspiring more than one character in *Dorian Gray* so is Constance, Oscar's wife. Several of Wilde's close friends have mentioned that Constance was the original of Victoria Wotton. Henry's wife, who appears once, and only in the revised, 1891 version, when Dorian visits Lord Henry's Mayfair residence. Whatever qualities there may be of Constance Wilde in Victoria Wotton, they are not her best features, for Victoria is given a shrill voice, a nervous laugh, and a tendency to talk rather aimlessly in order to make conversation.[7] The last we hear of Victoria is at the end of the novel when Lord Henry reports to Dorian that she had run off with a concert pianist. Whatever resemblance there may have been to Victoria, Constance was too well-bred for such behavior or for the worse fate that life had in store for her.

In the revised, 1891 text, Wilde added several scenes, indeed entire chapters, devoted to what Walter Pater described in his review as the "elaborately conventional, sophisticated, disabused world Mr. Wilde depicts so cleverly, so mercilessly."[8] In his social gazette, such as he might have given in reports to his mother at her London home, Wilde introduces numerous cameos, many hardly more than names on the page, and yet most contain in those names or in a detail of appearance, a gesture, or a phrase, at least a gene from someone Wilde knew. Like Browning's Fra Lippo, he worked into his pictures and scenes the faces he saw in the street, at the theater, or at a dinner party. Some of these cameos are later given fuller development in other works, such as Mrs. Erlynne, a guest of Lady Narborough, who returns as the mother with a past in *Lady Windermere's Fan* (1892).[9]

Another minor character, Alan Campbell, the former associate of

---

6. The best case was made by Charles G. Nickerson in *TLS* (August 14 and 21, also October 9, 1969), and the evidence of the MSS, which were not available to Nickerson, strengthens his case. The description of Disraeli's doomed beauty, Violet Fane, also agrees in every particular with Wilde's account of Sibyl. Of course, each is an example of a familiar type of nineteenth-century heroine, but still the resemblance is highly specific. Moreover, following Violet's premature demise of consumption in the novel, Vivian Gray, the hero, forms another attachment, indeed, his grand passion for none other than Baroness Sybilla. So it would seem that consciously or otherwise Disraeli's novel made its contribution to Wilde's novel and its ingenue.

7. The narrator depicts her in the following terms:

She was a curious woman, whose dresses always looked as if they had been designed in a rage and put on in a tempest. She was usually in love with somebody, and as her passion was never returned, she had kept her illusions. She tried to look picturesque, but only succeeded in being untidy. Her name was Victoria, and she had a perfect mania for going to church. (195)

8. See above, p. 354.
9. In *Dorian Gray* there is the merest hint of scandal about her; but in the play, the parallels to the once-adored Lillie Langtry were clear enough to have caused some notice in society and a permanent estrangement between Wilde and the woman he had once called the "new Helen."

Dorian blackmailed into disposing of Basil's corpse, was claimed by Sir Peter Chalmers Mitchell and duly reported by Hesketh Pearson in his biography (318–19). Mitchell once performed a social work of mercy by sitting with the author at a cafe in Fountainebleau when Wilde was being cut by every English tourist who recognized him. At that meeting, Mitchell reminded Wilde that they had once been introduced at the Café Royale in Regent Street, a favorite haunt of Wilde and the art world of the early nineties. Wilde was supposed to have responded: "Of course, I remember you. We talked and talked, and I asked you how to get rid of a body. I used you in *Dorian Gray*, but I don't think you would be so easy to blackmail." [1]

Some keys to the social allegory were lost in revision or through editorial intervention, as I have noted in the preface at the beginning of this volume. The most celebrated instances are the suppressed allusions to the famous "yellow book" given Dorian by Lord Henry, which is credited with finishing the job of Dorian's corruption. Wilde himself confessed that the book was "partly suggested by Huysmans's A *Rebours*, which will be found at any French booksellers. It is a fantastic variation on Huysmans's over-realistic study of the artistic temperament in our inartistic age" (*Letters* 313). As is often the case with similar Wildean pronouncements, this one reveals much while it conceals even more. The yellow book was originally given the title "The Secret of Raoul by Catulle Sarrazin." The brief references to it and its contents suggest that it was far less influenced by Huysmans's novel than has been supposed. All traces of the imaginary author and title were penciled out of the copy-text typescript by J. M. Stoddart, who much preferred an unnamed, mysterious "yellow book" to the leering original, with its echoes of the scandalous French novel of 1889, *Monsieur Venus* by "Rachilde" (Marguerite Eymery Vallette), one of whose principals was named Raoul. [2]

Wilde's allusions to the fictitious "Secrets" were probably intended as an inside joke for some of his companions for whom Rachilde's novel would have had a private significance. One of the insiders was Robert Ross, to whom Wilde confided in a letter after completing "The Portrait of Mr. W. H.": ". . . the story is half yours, and but for you would not have been written. . . . Now that Willie Hughes has been revealed to the world, we must have another secret" (247). Willie Hughes was the boy actor Wilde invented as the "onlie begetter" of Shakespeare's son-

1. Reported in Sir Peter Chalmers Mitchell, *My Fill of Days* (183–84). Although this anecdote has the familiar ring of memoir writer in search of notoriety, it also suggests that the author did not wish to place himself and his reputation in parallel with the blackmailed Alan Campbell. But the story, whatever its provenance, reinforces for us the anecdotal and allusive richness of *Dorian Gray*.

2. We may wonder whether Stoddart knew *Monsieur Venus*, but the context of *Dorian Gray* was sufficient to make such titillations as "The Secret of Raoul" too strong for Stoddart's taste. There is

little doubt that Wilde knew Rachilde's book, and he is reported by the rather vindictive Andre Rafflovich to have been enthusiastic about the story and its handling of sexual inversion and the romance between the aristocratic Raoule de Venerande and the commoner Jacques Silvert, with its implication of déclassé scandal. Both themes were becoming obsessive in Wilde's writing. Jacques was the name given Dorian's original valet, dismissed from his service after the painting was moved to the upstairs nursery and from the text in one of the early revisions before its first publication.

nets. The underlying analogy of Shakespeare-Willie Hughes and Wilde-Ross allegorizes one part of the letter. Perhaps the promised secret inspired "The Secret of Raoul," preserved now in the typescript and in the limbo of editorial notes.[3]

"The Secret of Raoul," with all its parallels to *Monsieur Venus*, undoubtedly would have pushed Wilde over the brink of disclosure, and the critical howling over "Raoul" surely would have been much louder than it proved to be after Stoddart's discrete intervention to pension off "Raoul," secret and all, together with "Catulle Sarrazin" and all subsequent references and allusions. For the most part, Wilde accepted Stoddart's deletions and emendations, and "Raoul" and Catulle remained an inside joke, known only to Wilde, Ross and possibly one or two others.[4]

Thus far we have looked into some of the historical and biographical allusions that serve as keys to the allegory of *The Picture of Dorian Gray*. Although it is richly allusive, it is not so transparent as either W. H. Mallock's satire of Paterian aestheticism, *The New Republic* (1877) or Hichens's later satire of Wildean decadence in *The Green Carnation* (1894); but, then, Wilde was playing a different game.

II

One of the games Wilde played was in writing a roman à clef. The spirit with which this level of the story is told belongs as much to good-natured social caricature and private gossip as it does to allegory. However, the technique is allegorized elsewhere and on several levels. The major keys here are the three principals: Basil Hallward, the artist; Lord Henry Wooton, the dandy, and Dorian Gray, the protégé.

Basil and Henry are introduced immediately while Dorian waits in the wings. Speculations of possible originals for the two began at the publication of the *Lippincott's* version and continues still. Ernest Dowson believed that the original of Basil was Charles Shannon, the artist and companion of Charles Ricketts, who was, in fact, just as likely a nominee.[5] The *St. James's Gazette*, for which Wilde had done regular

---

3. As for the imaginary author, Catulle Sarrazin, he bears the names of two contemporary French authors of the period whom Wilde knew. One was Gabriel Sarrazin, French critic and man of letters who reported on the English literary scene and served as a French counterpart of Arthur Symons, interpreting movements of modern English poetry to his countrymen. At Wilde's invitation, Sarrazin contributed to *Woman's World*, and the two knew each other socially (*Letters* 241).

The second of "Catulle Sarrazin's" potential literary godfathers was very probably Catulle Mendes (1841–1909), the French Parnassian poet-novelist, who married Judith, the younger daughter of Théophile Gautier.

4. Wilde did review carefully the text of the magazine version as he revised the novel for the last

time. Indeed, there were a number of cases in which he returned to his original language. But he kept the "yellow book" in favor of "The Secret of Raoul."

For discussions of Stoddart's editorial interventions, see Murray (*Dorian Gray* 230) and Espey (27–35). My own views are presented in the preface to the two versions of the novel, above.

5. Dowson's remark is mentioned in Rupert Croft-Cooke, *Unrecorded Life* (26). Taken together, Shannon and Ricketts would have provided Wilde with everything he would have needed for Basil, including the studio and garden in which the first scenes of the novel are set.

The character of Basil eventually became the subject of apocryphal histories of the novel's origination. For example, in 1904, an edition of *Dorian Gray* surfaced with an "Artist's Preface," over the

reviews of the literary scene, reported what it said was Wilde's explanation of the novel's origin (September 24, 1890). The artist involved was
Frances Richards, a Canadian whom Wilde met on his 1882 lecture
tour in Ottawa. The claim was that she later did a portrait of Wilde at
her London studio in 1887. Following a sitting, Wilde is reputed to have
uttered the prophetic words: "What a tragic thing it is. This portrait will
never grow older, and I shall. If it was only the other way."[6]

Competition for the original inspiration of Lord Henry has been less
apocryphal but no less varied. The most obvious choice is the author
himself, and that claim will be examined below. There are other candidates, among whom Lord Ronald Sutherland-Gower, younger son of
the duke of Sutherland and several years Wilde's senior, seems a possibility.[7]

Interesting as these candidates may be, both real and imaginary, there
is bigger and better game afoot. In an inspiring piece of literary detec-
tion, Richard Ellmann disclosed an allegorical dimension to the char-
acterizations of Basil and Henry involving the two great schooling figures
of Wilde's Oxford years. In his "Overtures to Salome" (*Oscar Wilde* 83–
90), Ellmann proposed that Basil and Henry are types of John Ruskin

signature of "Basil Hallward," who explained that
it was in his very studio that Wilde had met the
youth he later portrayed as Dorian. "Basil" oblig-
ingly records for posterity the following exchange
as the painting session concluded: " 'What a pity
such a glorious creature should ever grow old,'
sighed Wilde. 'Yes, it is indeed,' said I. 'How
delightful it would be if "Dorian" could remain
exactly as he is, while the portrait aged and withered in his stead. I wish it might be so!' " (see Mason
298). The publisher described his artist-author, Basil
Hallward, as "an artist famous the world over."

A variant story later grew up around one "Basil
Ward," another fictitious painter of international
renown. In a way, the apocryphal Basils are as much
a tribute to the power of Wilde's novel as to the
ingenious dishonesty of the publishers. Wilde would
have been delighted by such disreputable imitations of art by life.

The legends of the many Basils were first exposed
by Mason in *Art and Morality* and later by Charles
Nickerson (*TLS*, August 14, 1969) and Rupert
Croft-Cooke (*Unrecorded Life* 26–27). Croft-Cooke
is mistaken in his claim that the story of "Basil
Ward" was fathered by Pearson, who was not above
such activity. The Basil Ward variant had been
bouncing around in prefaces since the turn of the
century. In the United States someone even lectured as "Basil Ward" on the origins of the novel,
and the story was recorded by Brasol (216–17) eight
years before Pearson repeated it. All this may be
taken as an affecting testimony of human faith in
narrative realism.

6. Mason 63. Kevin O'Brien, in "Oscar Wilde and
Canadian Artists," makes the case for the Richards

claim. The portrait has never been heard of since.
If, indeed, Richards was midwife to the germinal
idea of *Dorian Gray*, perhaps Basil's effeminatism
needs reassessment as the expression of a more
androgynous than inverted nature.

7. André Gide was perhaps the first to suggest Lord
Ronald, and the cause has been supported by Philippe Jullian and Rupert Croft-Cooke. St. John
Ervine, in *Oscar Wilde: A Present Time Appraisal*,
thinks that Robert Ross might have been the model.

Lord Ronald was a well-known wit and master
of paradox whose style of speaking and living seemed
to have provided Wilde with an ideal. The case for
Sutherland-Gower is supported further by the following description of Lord Henry in the *Dorian
Gray* MS, deleted by Wilde before publication:
"Lord Henry pulled his little straw coloured moustache and stroked his Henri Deux beard." This
description fits Lord Ronald's appearance at the time
very well, as we may judge from photographs.
Unfortunately for the theory, the description also
appears to fit the features of William More Adey,
a close friend of Robert Ross and a friend of Wilde
also. The More Adey case is supported a little by
the derivation of Lord Henry's surname from Wotton-under-Edge in Gloucestershire near Adey's
family residence. Wilde thought the place name
droll. The derivation illustrates a practice of Wilde,
who frequently converted place names into names
of characters and also derived imaginary place
names from the names of people. Lady Bracknell
of *The Importance of Being Earnest* derived her
name from the residence of Lord Alfred Douglas's
mother, a fact that has suggested that the character
is a caricature of the marchioness of Queensberry.

and Walter Pater in their relation to Wilde. The rivalry between Basil and Henry for influence over Dorian thereby takes on new resonances. Since the morality of influence is one of the serious ethical speculations of the novel (and also of key essays written at the time), there are grounds for suspecting that Wilde felt it was one of the crucial dialectics of his own personal development.[8] Looked at from this perspective, parallels between Basil and Ruskin, on the one hand, and Lord Henry and Pater, on the other, are remarkably specific.

As we know, Ruskin was an amateur painter as well as the most influential art critic of his era. Basil is portrayed as awakening in Dorian a vanity and a strong but inchoate desire for beauty. However, for Basil as for Ruskin, morality depended on the authority of supernatural forces that transcended art, so that in the end the love of art must serve love of a higher truth. We recall that Basil's moralizing drove Dorian, goaded also by a bad conscience, to homicide. After the murder, from time to time, Dorian suffered nostalgic longings for Basil's good influence on his soul. The parallel to Wilde's own psychic life is too exact here to be coincidental. Ruskin represented to Wilde a moral idealism he wished to live up to but knew he could not. Indeed, it was an idealism that none could live up to, including Ruskin. Trying half drove Ruskin mad. While it may elevate the spirit, it eventually destroys the self, and Wilde had Ruskin's own tragic example to illustrate that lesson. *De Profundis* aside, Wilde's last major essay was "The Soul of Man under Socialism," his transformation of and final homage to the John Ruskin of Oxford.

Basil's effect on Dorian was to arouse vanity in him over his youth and good looks and to inspire a longing for beauty. Unintentionally, Basil prepared Dorian for Lord Henry's cynical and pernicious influence. Henry's doctrine of sensation, egoism, and hedonism is a somewhat extreme derivation of Pater's more disengaged aestheticism of *The Renaissance*. Much closer to home are Lord Henry's reflections on making a work of art out of one's life, especially out of one's most intense and fully realized sensations. These meditations also include speculations on the ethical and moral implications of Darwinism, particularly, on the connection between heredity and personality, evolution and will-directed action.

If Henry is a Mephistopheles, he is a devil well-versed in contemporary evolutionary theory, especially as it applied to the psychology of human development. In this interest, Wilde's debt to Pater seems to have been at least as great as it was in the realm of aesthetics. Instructed by Henry, Dorian rationalizes his own pursuit of sensation by calling it a method of multiplying personality. This Paterean view is given further apparent legitimacy by an invocation of the Darwinist psychological

8. The essays are "The Decay of Lying" and "The Critic as Artist," both collected in *Intentions* (1891), and "The Soul of Man under Socialism," pub- lished in the *Fortnightly Review* the same year as the *Lippincott's* version of *Dorian Gray* appeared (1890).

speculations of Herbert Spencer and Ernst H. Haeckel, stressing bioge-
netic origins of human behavior.[9] We must conclude that Wilde was
familiar with these speculations and the theories on which they depended.
Speculations of possible connections between racial and individual genetic
programming recall Pater's synthesis of evolutionary psychology and aesthetics in *The Renaissance*, but they suggest further that Wilde had continued his interest in the development of new, scientific thinking in
these areas.[1] The special importance of these ideas is not only for Dorian
and Lord Henry but also for the narrator, who frames the incidents of
Dorian's life on which such theories of heredity impinge and who comments upon and interprets the behavior as well as the theory. The
importance of heredity to Wilde and to his own dramatization of self
finds expression in the reflections of the narrator upon the theories of
Lord Henry and the trespasses of Dorian Gray. Henry's ideal seems to
make of evolutionary forces in the psychological life of the individual
the rationale of a new art form, which in practice he is content to observe.
Dorian, on the other hand, appears determined to make those same
necessary forces self-conscious by experiencing all the sensations, passions, and emotions through which soul and imagination have passed in
their long evolution up the chain of being from preconscious life in
Cenozoic muck to the aesthetic life of the dandy at the end of the nineteenth century.

In these and other terms, the echoes, analogues, allusions, and at
times even paraphrases of Pater's work have been well-documented in
Ernst Bendz, Isobel Murray, and Ellmann; indeed, it should be clear
that Wilde fully expected readers to be aware of a least some of the
borrowings here in *Dorian Gray* as elsewhere.[2] Wilde's confrontation of

9. Haeckel was the most influential and popular
disciple of Darwin in the "Darwinismus Movement," mentioned by that name in *Dorian Gray*.
One of the key ideas of this school was the analogy
between the biological evolution of a species and
its individual, embryonic development. Hence the
developmental process of a fetus was believed to
repeat the acquisition of inherited characteristics
over the course of its ancestry. Haeckel's famous
formulation of that idea, "ontogeny recapitulates
phylogeny," was soon extended by Spencer into
the realm of psychological and then social development.

1. Less attention has been given than should be to
Wilde's interest in scientific thought and methodology. His father was, after all, a medical scientist
of renown. When Oscar Wilde wrote for the
Chancellor's Prize and a fellowship, his hopes took
the form of an essay called the "Rise of Historical
Criticism," which has as much to do with the
origins of scientific thinking in historical method
as it does with literary or cultural criticism. This
interest continues throughout his life and shows
itself especially in essays and stories written about
the time this novel was being produced; see especially "The Portrait of Mr. W. H." and "The Soul

of Man under Socialism."
2. Wilde was often accused of plagiarism by
detractors. His attitude toward appropriation of
materials taken from other authors was consistent,
if misunderstood, and anticipates the practice if not
the philosophy of modern writers. Wilde stressed
that the artist is responsible for originality of treatment not of subject: "It is only the unimaginative
who ever invents. The true artist is known by the
use he makes of what he annexes, and he annexes
everything (*Reviews* 29).

Most of Wilde's annexations are ornamental, and
there are specific relations between the decorative
and the allegorical in the art and literature of the
period. Angus Fletcher argues that the "decorative
and daemonic are visual partners" (109n). Wilde's
use of decoration is best understood in terms of its
allegorical associations. The effect is often to produce a sense of surrealist isolation, or what Fletcher's study of allegory describes as "encapsulation."
Instead of contemptible plagiarisms, the spawn of
artistic insincerity, the contagious magic of allegory suggests an alternate view. First, Wilde
expected readers of different cultural attainments
to recognize and identify some of the allusions,
borrowings, and paraphrases in *Dorian Gray*, drawn

ethical with aesthetic values in a context of post-Darwinist psychology is his own derivation of Pater's Oxford influence and the persistence of that influence in his essays and fiction. But if the philosophy derives from Pater, the tone does not; and if we are to locate another tutor who had a shaping influence on Wilde at this time, we need look no further than James Abbott McNeill Whistler. Although he and Wilde ended in public recrimination just before *Dorian Gray* was written, there can be no doubt that Whistler's influence strongly confirmed Wilde's tendencies toward dandyism cultivated earlier at Oxford.

Although neither portrait is especially flattering, Basil is a far more sympathetic figure than Lord Henry. If Basil has a weakness for Victorian moralizing, Lord Henry ends a disillusioned egoist whose cynicism conceals a progressively empty and sterile existence. This sounds more like the judgment due a Whistler than a Pater.

The third member of Wilde's troika is Dorian Gray, who makes his debut at the beginning of the second chapter, after the stage has been carefully dressed. Basil and Henry discover Dorian at the piano, looking over Schumann's "Forest Scenes," a piece suggesting Dorian's natural innocence. The action that begins is primarily psychological and moral. Dorian's sense of sin is awakened, first, by Hallward's worshipful and inadvertent appeal to the youth's vanity and, second, by Henry's deliberately experimental evocation of Dorian's own egoism. The finished portrait is placed before Dorian as an icon whose worship transforms Dorian into a Narcissus, abetted by the art of Basil and confirmed in the philosophy of Henry. The scene before the portrait is the primal scene of the story and is echoed with some important variants later when Dorian plays Chopin for Lord Henry on the night of his own death twenty years removed.[3]

Dorian is himself an idealization of youthful beauty, one that appears with obsessive iteration in such stories as "Lord Arthur Savile's Crime" (1887), "The Young King" (1888), and "The Portrait of Mr. W. H." (1889). There are a few keys in old photographs of youths "with perfect profiles," as Wilde liked to call them, with whom he surrounded himself whenever he could.

Incredible as it may seem to those who have seen photographs of Wilde from youth onward, there are strong linkages between Dorian Gray and Wilde himself. One of the links becomes apparent if we continue the allegorical progression from Basil to Ruskin and Lord Henry

as they were out of a very wide cultural spectrum from the Bible to contemporary museum catalogues. Second, in his use of decorative flourishes, Wilde offers simultaneously a protest against, a critique of, and a proposed cure for cultural boredom in psychosensual stimuli. As Wilde wrote in "Pen, Pencil and Poison": "In a very ugly and sensible age, the arts borrow, not from life, but from each other" (*Intentions* 78).

3. Wilde more than doubled the elapsed time between the scenes in the two published versions of the novel, partly because he hoped to establish a more evolved process and to leave himself enough room to expand the aesthetic and psychological dimensions of the gothic. These effects were two means to the end of suppressing the too prominent moral of the 1890 version and helped support the contrary movement of aesthetic allegory that Wilde elaborated in the revised, 1891 version.

to Pater, leaving Dorian as Wilde. This delusion will seem a bit more reasonable if we regard Dorian as a projection of an obsessive ideal that had haunted Wilde for several years in both life and fiction before writing *Dorian Gray*. Wilde once spoke of himself in one of his early letters as "burying his face in the great cool lilac blossoms, feverishly drinking their perfume," a description later applied to Dorian as he walks in Basil's garden in chapter 2. Another key is Dorian's residence on Grosvenor Square. Wilde once lived on Charles Street, Grosvenor Square, during his bachelor days, and lilke Dorian, his at-home day was Wednesday. Although in themselves these details are trivial enough, they support the following revelation vouchsafed to an admirer in early 1894:

> I am so glad you like that strange colored book of mine; it contains much of me in it. Basil Hallward is what I think I am; Lord Henry what the world thinks me; Dorian what I would like to be—in other ages perhaps. (*Letters* 352)

This familiar statement suggests three divisions of Wilde's personality that both define his self-perceived relation to the novel and provide us with another key to his artistic method.[4]

Wilde's letter reveals that the three main characters represent different aspects of himself, or perhaps even different selves, and this in turn implies that no one is intended to be more authentic than any other. Whatever we may think of Wilde as Dorian, the identification suggests a motive to his personal quest for the living embodiment of his fictionalized self, which ended with Lord Alfred Douglas, who proved himself a Dorian in everything, including temperament.

Dorian seems to be prophetic in another way as well, because despite the differences between creator and character, the letter symbolizes a personal variant of the powerful myth of the fall of the race from original innocence.[5] In the novel, Dorian acts out Lord Henry's philosophy of hedonism after experiencing that fall from innocence of the awakened conscience; and just as Wilde himself had been touched by Pater and provoked by Whistler, Dorian was inspired to pursue the vision of making life into art, first by Basil's portrait—a false ideal as it turns out—and then by Lord Henry's sermon on multiplying personality through varied sensations in a manner that both recalls and anticipates Wilde's own pursuit of epiphanic sensations. Seen as a man of action, Dorian dramatizes the side of Wilde's personality that might be termed the *experiencing self*. It was by that very aspect that Yeats chose to define Wilde as the man of action who pursues a necessarily destructive vision of self-

4. Cf. Charlesworth above, pp. 382–392.

5. I say "personal" because the archetype appears so frequently in Wilde's fiction and essays and because the variant we find in *Dorian Gray* is clearly specific to Wilde's life. The myth of the fall itself depends upon the prior archetype of original inno-

cence, one to which Wilde was especially devoted. Indeed, that archetype makes meaningful everything else both in so much of what he wrote and in how he lived the last ten to twelve years of his life.

realization through a life of sensation and appetite (148–51).[6]

Lord Henry, as many have observed, represents the reflective and paradoxical side of Wilde's personality, what we may term the *rationalizing self*. Here we have the dandy philosopher and wit who became the lion of the dinner table and the theater. Wotton was a more sophisticated version of the aesthetic Bunthorne who lectured American audiences about the house beautiful and later English audiences on American manners, mores, and the livery of silver miners. Wotton is both a self-projection and a reflection, as Wilde said, of how the world perceived him. In this mask, there is obviously much of the maker, for we encounter the wit and the voicing again and again in the essays and the plays— the dandy in Mayfair. What is more, Henry's speech is said by many like André Gide, Bosie Douglas, Frank Harris, and Coulson Kernahan, who knew Wilde intimately and later wrote about him, to be a faithful reproduction of the author's public manner. And the Mephistophelean touches remind us of Wilde's ambivalent treatment of the theme of influence in the novel and his own equally ambivalent behavior. In one forum, he preached that "all imitation in morals and life is wrong" ("The Soul of Man under Socialism"), whereas in his private life, he would dominate his younger acquaintances with the force of his personality, as he liked to put it. Of course, we should not assume that Wilde approved of his own conduct.

If Dorian is inspired to play the would-be artist of his own life, Lord Henry is another *artiste manqué*, who matures into the impotent and slightly fatuous presence listening to Dorian play Chopin and congratulating his protégé with unintended irony on the success that he has made of his life. Lord Henry ends more deceived than anyone about Dorian and what he has become. He neither understands nor knows anything of Dorian's criminal pathology or of his walk on the wild side. Whenever Dorian broaches the subject, the solipsistic Henry interrupts him with conversation-closing platitudes that only reinforce his original self-deception. At this point in the story, Lord Henry and Dorian are speaking from two different worlds. For Wotton, the world of fashion is stable, dominated by the deflating irony and polite iconoclasm of the dandy. Dorian speaks from the gothic world of compulsive desire and fear. One wonders, are we hearing echoes here of bygone interviews between Wilde and Pater?

Basil Hallward was what Wilde thought himself, according to the let-

---

6. If we look into Wilde's writing, it is clear that the Oxford debate between the active (Ruskin) and contemplative (Pater) sides of his nature was still going on as he wrote this novel and after. In a review for *The Speaker* (February 8, 1890) written while he was at work on *Dorian Gray*, he writes eloquently of the great creed of inaction and of the wisdom of the teaching of Lao Tzu. In "The Critic as Artist," Gilbert warns that to become involved in action is to become predestined and controlled by mechanical and hereditary forces. In the same essay, Gilbert argues that "It is very much more difficult to talk about a thing than to do it" (*Intentions* 132). These lessons from philosophy and biology Dorian fails to understand or to learn, a failure he shared with his maker.

ter, and in autobiographical terms that characterization was both confessional and prophetic. As a young man, Wilde was an amateur painter himself, although not, as far as we know, *of* himself. And it is in Basil's voice that Wilde flirted with public disclosure of his homosexualism in a manner that prompted Queensberry's defense attorney, Edward Carson, to cite the *Lippincott's* version of the novel as evidence of Wilde's personal immorality and corrupting influence.

What a sad irony that one always thinks of Basil as "poor" Basil. His mistake was, unlike Henry, unintended; but to the author, his chief sin was to betray his art in the service of his emotions. In the guise of Basil, Wilde represents his *artistic self*, revealing his own mixture of aestheticism and sentimentalism. Clearly, Basil and Henry represent different strains of the aesthetic movement, both of which were expressed, perhaps even summed up, in Wilde's personality and life. Basil is the self-effacing lover of Dorian who never approached his protégé with his feelings. Instead, he put them into a portrait and committed the artistic mistake of making it a living one. At first, though, neither Basil nor Dorian understands how to interpret the text of that picture: only Lord Henry guesses. Later, when Basil refuses to believe the rumors circulating about Dorian's immoral life, it is because he again misinterprets his text: what he sees before him is the Dorian he had painted, not the one who then seethed upon his canvas. Dorian's appearance of perpetual innocence enchants as it deceives all who do not know him. Basil is as self-deceived as Lord Henry, and his way is to be self-deceived by the magical projection of his own emotions. How difficult for Basil to know them as they were.

Basil's relationship with Dorian is prophetic of Wilde's own disastrous affair with Alfred Douglas, and the parallels were later not to be lost on Wilde. That friendship drove Wilde to financial and artistic ruin, imprisonment, and exile. Of course, compulsion like character is predictive, but rarely has literary history seen anything as prophetic as the symbolism of this novel for the future life of its author: almost as though the fiction were a rehearsal for the life. And it was at this same time in his life that Wilde was writing with such exquisite paradox in "The Decay of Lying" and "The Critic as Artist" about life imitating art.

When Basil is confronted by his own work that Dorian, the experiencing self, has grotesquely transformed, he has nothing to offer but platitudes and prayer; and he is murdered for his lack of originality. Basil's artistic gesture had been transformed by Dorian (the experiencing self) into a hideous self-parody through the influence of Henry (the rationalizing self). Even as we trace it, Wilde's allegory changes its forms. In a transformation of transformations, his characters become not one but many, speaking with different and sometimes contradictory voices. Basil is Ruskin, Ricketts or Shannon or both, and also Wilde. Lord Henry is Pater, Whistler, Lord Ronald Sutherland-Gower, Wilde again, and, together with Basil, who knows how many others as the voices of the century echo through them. But Dorian is always Wilde—the obsessive ideal never realized, always lost, betraying itself. Dorian is the projected self both acknowledged and denied, as contradictory as the portrait concealed in the upstairs nursery and the model posing in his Grosvenor Square library. And the knife that killed Basil is the knife that cuts the tangled knots of identity, becoming a magic blade that restores art to its proper sphere and experience to its ruined estate: "As it had killed the painter, so it would kill the painter's work, and all that that meant."

III

It is time we looked to the moral allegory that so dominated the *Lippincott's* version of the novel. Wilde was determined to suppress the moral to the point that it "realizes itself purely in the lives of individuals, and so becomes simply a dramatic element in a work of art, and not the object of a work of art itself" (*Letters* 263). Had he been working with what he described as "the real moral" of the story: "that all excess as well as all renunciation brings its punishment" (*Letters* 263), the revision would have been a piece of cake. However, the archetypal devil's bargain, when combined with the power of the magical portrait, proved to be another matter entirely.

What gave Wilde so much trouble was the mythic archetype that is the source of the novel's power and its long popularity with the public.[7] Wilde never altered the novel's archetypal core because he discovered there was no way to make any major surgical changes there without destroying the story. The archetypal core of the novel and its original inspiration express the force that Carl G. Jung, in "On the Relation of Analytic Psychology to Poetry," termed an "autonomous complex," a primitive inspiration outside conscious design that is not susceptible of fundamental alteration (*Collected Works* 78).[8]

Wilde developed several strategies for dealing with the "too obvious" moral in the last revision; chiefly, they involved adding and emphasizing the decorative, melodramatic, comic, gothic, and aesthetic aspects of the original.[9] Despite what he was later to claim at the trials, Wilde did continue purging homoerotic allusions and overtones (a process begun as early as the first surviving MS). We recall that he had some help with that from J. M. Stoddart, the *Lippincott's* editor. Paradoxical as always,

---

7. Apparently Wilde's initial prospect for doing a final revision for the volume edition was much simpler than the task proved. Writing to an "unidentified publisher" even before the *Lippincott's* version appeared, Wilde promised: "After three months the copyright reverts to me, and I propose to publish it, with two new chapters, as a novel" (*More Letters* 87–88). The two chapters grew to five, and Wilde made extensive deletions, alterations, and additions to the existing text of the magazine version.

8. Wilde, writing as Gilbert in "The Critic as Art-

ist," proposes a literary perspective on this issue: "I myself am inclined to think that creation is doomed. It springs from too primitive, too natural an impulse."

9. The revisions have been examined by Isobel Murray in "Some Elements in the Composition of *The Picture of Dorian Gray*" and are considered in her edition of *Dorian Gray*. For a more complete account of the revisions from the manuscripts through the final revision, see Donald Lawler, "The Revisions of *Dorian Gray*" and "Oscar Wilde's First Manuscript of *The Picture of Dorian Gray*."

Wilde was making his story more moral, in one sense, while doing his best to conceal the moral archetype, thus making the story less moral, in another sense. Although the addition of catalogs of aesthetic ornament, the James Vane revenge subplot, the interludes of social comedy, and a more gothic psychology for Dorian distract reader attention from the moral, the ethical force of the original argument still burns through. This truth has never been lost on those who have adapted the novel to stage, radio, movie, and television as a gothic cautionary tale.[1]

There appears to be a fundamental contradiction between the impression most of us have of Wilde's public life as an aesthetic dandy and the positions he takes in his writing, especially in the essays. Perhaps it is no more than another contradiction in a personality that was distinguished by its complexity. Then again, it may be that even a century removed from Wilde's lifetime our judgment continues to be influenced by the *Punch* caricatures, the Bunthorne burlesque, and the mask Wilde more or less successfully paraded until the debacle of 1895.

The most subtle of the strategies in the final revision for muffling the force of the moral allegory was the introduction of a counter-allegory. We may think of this aesthetic allegory as designed either to neutralize the moral or to create a movement in the action away from the ethical and didactic toward the aesthetic and speculative. If we accept the view that Wilde tried to neutralize the moral, then we must conclude that he failed. If, however, we think of the aesthetic as a counter-allegory that serves as a translation (or a decoding/recording program), changing or threatening to change the meaning of the moral allegory into an aesthetic system of reference, then we will take a different, more appreciative view of the ways allegory works in this novel. Since the aesthetic is another level of allegory superimposed by Wilde upon an earlier and more elemental level, it functions not as a replacement but as a supplement. In terms of exegetical allegory, the aesthetic allegory becomes Wilde's equivalent of an anagogical level among his systems, but perhaps this is too fanciful, even in an era of critical permissiveness, because the aesthetic argument is nothing like an equivalent for the supernatural order of a true anagogical level. Anyway, assurance of supernatural orders is necessarily limited by the ambiguities of magic itself. However, I believe that Wilde had something like an anagogical overtone in mind when he launched his counter-allegory.

The aesthetic allegory is set up by the opening scene, and the main

1. Wilde was so anxious to have the revised version reviewed from "the proper point of view," that is from the artistic point of view, that he wrote to W. L. Courtney asking him for such a notice in his paper, *The Daily Telegraph:* "The reason I ask is this: when it first appeared it was very grossly and foolishly assailed as an immoral book, and I am anxious to have it treated purely from the art-standpoint: from the standpoint of style, plot, construction, psychology, and the like" (*More Letters* 97).

Another part of Wilde's scheme to defuse the archetype in the final revision was to emphasize other mythic parallels. The most important of these is the elaborately worked-out analogy to the Genesis story of the Fall. Two other myths, drawn from classical mythology, Narcissus and Adonis, are elaborated, each carrying its own rich allusiveness of language and reference. Each of these myths also helps dramatize aesthetic dimensions of the central myth.

theme is announced in the dialogue between Basil and Henry. Basil's confession of adoration for Dorian as a new artistic ideal contrasts with his decision to pose Dorian as he was in life rather than in a stylized manner.[2] Basil lost his aesthetic distance, which led him into the fatal error of painting a confessional portrait. Instead of the artistic ideal he spoke about in theory, Basil created a personal icon. Seeing the finished portrait, Dorian intuitively felt the emotion that inspired the painting, but lacking perception, internalized that revelation of ideal beauty. Henry then taught him to personalize that feeling and make it the basis of a new pattern for the age, to make living itself an art. Dorian gives his soul and his own artistic self as hostages to mortality in order to free his experiencing self from the price of aging and ugliness. Given the transforming power of the magic portrait, the effect of the new hedonism Dorian practices is to gothicize both his social and aesthetic life—not only the portrait but also all he turns to in pursuit of new sensations becomes transformed into an extension of the gothic world. The infamous chapter 11 (1891) is therefore not only Decadent but also gothic, and in that combination it proved a type of its age.

We can see now that the aesthetic allegory in *Dorian Gray* interacts with both the moral allegory and the gothic mode in which the novel is written. The dynamo that powers the movement among these and various other modes is the portrait. The allegory of aesthetic life is not limited to London's fashionable society and the protected world of its artists, but it infiltrates the London underworld, symbolizing the realm of the unconscious from which reason and civilizing culture have been displaced. Such back and forth movement between the over- and underworlds of London finds its parallels in the contrasting moods of social comedy and the revenge melodrama, in the related movements in and out of the gothic world of the magic portrait with its dynamic interactions of fear and desire, and in the tensions set up between the moral and aesthetic allegories.

The magical portrait Dorian wishes to be a talisman to the endless spring of unlimited possibilities soon becomes the most uncompromising of schooling figures, and Dorian hides it away in the upstairs nursery to brood upon the effects of vanity and sin and time upon the ambitions and delusions of the one who chooses to live beyond limits. In becoming the piper of the portrait. Dorian must also dance to his own music. If Basil's masterpiece was the brilliant portrait and Lord Henry's was the production of a puppet Dorian and a living illusion, then Dorian's masterpiece is his self-portrait, reinscribed upon the original. The Decadent ideal of artistic control over life and its laws merges with the scientific dream of a similar control, dramatized in such nineteenth-century gothic science fiction as *Frankenstein* and *The Strange Case of Dr. Jekyll and*

2. Wilde once wrote of Lillie Langtry: "this single face [gives] fresh life and inspiration in the form of a new artistic ideal" (*The New York World* [November 7, 1882]). See *Miscellanies* (*First Collected Edition* 9. 44).

Mr. Hyde. Dorian pursues sensation not as Pater's sensuous ideal of art but as the extension of his ego. As the self-made *artiste manqué,* Dorian repudiates self-control, in which lies the true power of the artist (as this tale teaches on all its levels of meaning), following no law but the impulses of the will and appetites, which exist outside the governance of art.[3]

In uttering his famous wish, Dorian gothicized both himself and art: the painting becomes the gateway to the gothic world of fear and desire in which part of Dorian lives from that moment on. It is a world none shares with Dorian but his divided self, and in that ghastly attraction and repulsion, we have a classic case of the fate of the gothic hero who in doubling himself becomes both hero and antihero. Dorian is trapped in the gothic world even as he appears to control it. For Dorian, there is no redeeming power. Basil tries to rescue him but fails because the platitudes he offers have no power to dissolve the gothic world in which Dorian lives. Only Dorian can defeat that world, but he has lost his potential for reforming his life as the portrait proves to him. Despite its hideous disfigurement, the portrait represents authentic life, passions and their effects, whereas Dorian has become a puppet. He has founded his strange double life on both sin and misperception. The root of the sin is obvious; the misperception lies in Dorian's inability to see that the spheres of art and action are both separate and mutually exclusive.

Dorian's attempt to escape the gothic world of the portrait is the climactic action of the story. He acts to be free of the law of art as well as morality. But to free himself from the life of the picture and from the life of conscience is impossible, and his attempt is suicidal. Once again, Dorian is caught in the art of the portrait, with his original youth and beauty restored as the rightful attributes of art. The painting becomes,

---

3. The considerable weight of Henry's and the narrator's Darwinist speculations on free will and biological necessity give them an unexpected resonance in the novel. The theme is touched upon several times and prominently in the novel and the essays, especially "The Critic as Artist," in which Gilbert seems to speak in the same tones as Lord Henry: "By revealing to us the absolute mechanism of all action and so freeing us from the self-imposed and tramelling burden of moral responsibility, the scientific principle of Heredity has become, as it were, the warrant for the contemplative life. It has shown us that we are never less free than when we try to act" (*Intentions* 182).

In terms of aesthetic allegory, then, art becomes the captive of not only time and change but also those unconscious forces directing human biology and behavior. Even imagination, the transforming power of romanticism, is "the result of heredity. It is simply concentrated race experience" ("The Critic as Artist," *Intentions* 181). The lesson is obvious: Dorian's experimental life never had a chance of success. Once art had been placed in the service of life, both were doomed.

The importance for psychological allegory is emphasized by Angus Fletcher: "the author shows over and over that men suffer from a primary illusion when they imagine they are in control of their own actions" (64). Indeed, the idea of allegorical control of narrative itself violates Wilde's most cherished idea of freedom of both will and self-expression. It is another example of the ambivalences that inform this work that is both so deceptively simple on its surface and so deceptively complex below.

Thus for Dorian the intentions of self-creation embrace those of self-discovery in sensations and experience. It is one of the keys to the neurosis of the modern mind. Dorian finds fascinating clues to his own unconscious in myth (Narcissus, for instance) and in his inherited traits (discovered in his genetic ancestry), leading him to the conviction that he is not one but many. These self-encounters lead to an allegorization of the self as directed by the impulses inherent in the traits of all one's ancestors back to the apes and perhaps beyond. Dorian thus finds in action the recovery of resistless archetypal patterns, which Dorian neurotically and superstitiously believes he must live out. This is a pattern of thinking very close to Wilde's at the time.

finally, art rather than life. And the will, trapped in its artifact, the ruined flesh, dies with the corpse. The self that is returned to Dorian out of the gothic world rests at last beneath the feet of the idealized self raised up for worship by art. It makes a stirring tableau, even today.

The aesthetic lesson, then, for the artist or would-be artist is that life can be art only in art, never in life. But if Dorian's failure is inevitable, Wilde allows no clear victory for conventional morality either, as has been assumed so often. This much at least Wilde accomplished by adding his aesthetic counter movement to the undertext. Because Dorian is a gothic figure, he is not sympathetic. He is instead an unbalanced personality, and his purpose of multiplying personality through a controlled series of aesthetic experiments transforms him into an aesthetic Dr. Jekyll. Worse, perhaps, is the effect of his experimental pursuit of sensation in gothicized art, which leads to final madness.[4]

IV

As the pattern for his age, Dorian cuts against what Pater called the disabused world of fashion, over which he ruled, and therefore by extension against the upper and leisured classes. Wilde's comedy of manners, augmented so emphatically in the revised version of 1891, when matched with the gothic, also has its allegorical implications. The wittiest dialogue since Congreve is the foil for Dorian's rising tide of anxiety and, later, hysteria. More than that, it is also the vehicle for irony. There is a social analysis implied in the hidden portrait and in Wilde's solid evocation of contemporary London. One effect of this overlay of the weird upon the contemporary is to transform the solid world of London in which the story has been steeped. In this way, it seems, the novel allegorizes itself. By the power of contagious magic, the witness of the portrait implies that what lies behind the dignified façades of the townhouses of Mayfair and Belgravia may be equally horrible—is equally horrible. Festering and hidden vices are the more hideous for their secrets than the visible evils of the East End, with its poverty and sordid ugliness. Was the prostitute that Dorian meets in the opium den of Blue Gate Fields in London's Chinatown worse than the ruined self-image he encounters in the nursery?

His realistic locations permit Wilde to intensify Dorian's increasing realization of dislocation. The gothic portrait creates a true sense of the weird in otherwise fashionable surroundings, suggesting an implied clash of values that subtly displaces the reader. Dorian's sense of dislocation is effective because the agency is concealed, hidden, admitted to none, while at the same time it remains central, persistent, uncompromising,

4. Gothicized art is a legacy of nineteenth-century decadence, foreshadowed in the hallucinated visions of Coleridge and De Quincey, and symbolized in Tennyson's neurotic allegories ("The Lady of Shalott" and "The Palace of Art"), in D. G. Rossetti, and, of course, in Swinburne. The idea of art as both entrapment and escape has a history in English, French (Gautier, Baudelaire), and American (Poe, Hawthorne) literature, which prepares us for Wilde's treatment of the idea.

and destructive of both conventional order and morality.

The portrait that Dorian hides away in the upstairs room is itself, as Henry said of its subject, the type of an age. From the perspective of social criticism, especially from Marxist literary applications, Dorian's portrait stands for the corrupt values of exploitation, the bogus idealism, and the hegemony of a self-assured ruling class. It allegorizes public as well as private vices—the crimes and sins concealed beneath rich brocades.

London's world of fashion is portrayed mercilessly, in Pater's words, as a collection of the shallow and dull who have enjoyed wealth, privilege, and power without having formed an appreciation of their possible benefits. What would society be, after all, without the leavening wit of Lord Henry, the youthful recklessness of Dorian, and Basil's appreciation of beauty and his power to create it? What would that society have been without Oscar Wilde, or he without it?

We watch as the paneled doors of Mayfair drawing rooms slowly open and Mr. Oscar Wilde invites us to guess the secret vices and nameless terrors of hidden selves. The *Punch* cartoon showing Wilde as the "Fad Boy" holding out a copy of *Dorian Gray* to a shrinking Mrs. Grundy over the caption "I want to make your flesh creep" was far more accurate than its creator probably guessed. For the most part, his contemporaries ignored Wilde's invitation. Pater had some idea of what Wilde was up to because he had been made privy to some of the plans for revision by the author. Characteristically, Victorians looked only to the Christian moral allegory, as though that were the extent of allegorical indexing. It hardly occurred to them that the allegory was also unlocking the doors to their own houses, disclosing the workings of their secret vices, pointing the way to their hidden upstairs rooms where conscience was revising portraits that none but the artist would be permitted to see.[5]

Since this is a novel of symbolic disclosure and concealment, readers of this essay may be already far ahead of me in seeing its prophetic relevance for the author's future life.[6] It is prophetic in three senses. First, it anticipates future events in Wilde's life. Second, and for that reason, the novel appears to be self-actualizing. Third, it traces the moral outlines of social actions.

---

5. The words of Osbert Burdett on Beardsley may be applied as fittingly to Wilde: "If we admit the sincerity of the age's intentions and contrast this with the ugliness and misery and degradation of the period, the growing disillusion is comprehensible. It was the one reality left, and on its insistence, therefore, the art of Beardsley and the period was concentrated. The corruption of the soul that he depicted was no nightmare of a disordered imagination. The pretension of health was the fantastic dream. To give outline and definition to the sense of corruption, to recover the vision of evil, was a sign of healthy vitality in his work. The forces that make for corruption are no less living than their opposites" (118–19).

6. Prophetic allegory is a rare and exotic study, and yet it is impossible to read *Dorian Gray* in the light of the novel's intentions and Wilde's later biography without being impressed by the ways his later life seems to have imitated his art. This has not gone unnoticed by Wilde's biographers and critics, most of whom have sense enough not to speculate further on the phenomenon. Those who have speculated, however, seem to prefer the romance of prophetic magic in which, fittingly enough, the novel becomes a kind of magic portrait not only foreshadowing but also participating in events future to its composition. I attempt here a more rational but no less speculative explanation, which fits the overall shape of this study.

In a way, Wilde has already given us his clue to the compulsive pattern of behavior he wrote into *Dorian Gray* and was living out in London. Biographical evidence is scarce, but what there is suggests that Wilde's personal obsession anticipated its literary appearance in "The Portrait of Mr. W. H." and the novel. The public Wilde finds expression in the social allegory, in aspects of the roman à clef, and in the settings and the tone of much of the narrative. The private Wilde is represented in the personal dimensions of the allegory, especially the parallels to Ruskin, Pater, Whistler, and himself—to which we should add the private allusions to friends and the theme of homoeroticism. The artistic Wilde is ably represented in the plan of his final revision and his use of decoration, the gothic transformations, and the aesthetic allegory. Yet another Wilde remains to be brought to the surface, the unconscious self, related to the moral allegory, the often reiterated theme of heredity, and the prophetic mode.

It is to the prophetic mode that I now turn in order to examine the linkage between Wilde's compulsive patterns of action and the foreshadowing of that behavior in the fiction. Perhaps the pattern we are looking for is nothing more than Wilde's struggle as an artist against the dualism or simple ambivalence of the moral allegory anticipating similar life struggles. That is, the author, like his eponymous hero, felt the compulsive need for both masking and unmasking. Moreover, Wilde's quest for an ideal represented in Dorian carried with it a psychological need for punishment, most likely through exposure. We must remind ourselves that Wilde chose to live as he did *because* it was criminal and, he believed, sinful: the "feasting with panthers" he later mentioned in *De Profundis* was the excitement he craved.

Whatever prophetic features *Dorian Gray* appears to have are related to Wilde's performance of concealment/disclosure symbolized by Dorian's other self hidden in the nursery room. Carl Jung throws some light on the prophetic force of the *Dorian Gray* archetype for us in the first chapter of his *Memories, Dreams, Reflections*, where he recounts an incident from childhood with uncanny relevance for interpreting Wilde's novel and its author as well. As a child, Jung carved a dreamlike figure, placed it in a box together with a painted stone, and hid them in the attic. Although his action remained mysterious to him for years, he regarded the hidden figure as highly significant: "I contented myself with the feeling of newly won security, and was satisfied to possess something that no one knew and no one could get at. It was an inviolable secret which must never be betrayed, for the safety of my life depended on it. Why this was so I did not ask myself. It simply was so" (22).

Only much later as an adult did Jung find analogies for his own experience in the soul stones of divergent cultures in Australia and Germany, which convinced him for the first time that "there are archaic psychic components which have entered the individual psyche without any direct line of tradition" (23). "If things became too bad I would think of my secret treasure in the attic, and that helped me regain my poise. For in my forlorn state I remembered that I was also the 'Other,' the person who possessed that inviolable secret, the black stone and the little man in the frock coat and top hat" (26). Still later, Jung associated his "manakin" figure with the " 'breath of life,' the creative impulse."

In this experience of Jung lies a clue, I believe, to Wilde's performance as a writer producing a kind of prophetic text. First, the archetype originates, according to Jung's theory, not in the individual unconscious but as an "archaic psychic component" of the collective unconscious. If so, this would account for the powerful appeal this archetype has had for the modern imagination as both a touchstone of popular culture and a subject of critical inquiry, especially as the focus for so many studies of its possible origins and literary analogues.

The second point is that the specific form of the myth does represent Wilde's unconscious, whose content expresses itself in the symbolism of the story. We have noted earlier that Jung refers to a kind of inspiration that gave rise to the moral allegory of the story as an "autonomous complex," that is a spontaneous idea or image that arises complete from the unconscious and that does not admit alteration. In the moral archetype of *Dorian Gray*, there was encoded a clear warning from Wilde's subconscious that the life principle of Wilde's creative powers would be destroyed if he persisted in living out the scenario of that archetype. Of all the consequences of Wilde's ruin and imprisonment, his loss of creative power was most deeply felt. The experiencing self destroyed the artistic self just as Dorian killed Basil.

Dorian Gray is indeed a prophetic book, but we are not limited to mystical explanations of this aspect. We may instead look upon the prophetic features as extensions of the psychological allegory of the novel with both private as well as literary references. The novel appears to predict Wilde's meeting with Lord Alfred Douglas because it contains an obsessive ideal that Wilde had been reiterating in both his fiction and the essays of the period as well as in his private life. The novel appears to predict the consequences of that relationship because it also contains the pattern of compulsive, self-destructive behavior that was seeking an outlet in Wilde's life. Wilde's increasingly risky social indiscretions that led to the debacle of the 1895 trials are foreshadowed once again in the patterns of concealment and disclosure we have turned up in *Dorian Gray*. Therefore, the assumption that there operates in the novel some sort of artistic prescience, however appealing it may feel and appropriate it may seem, need not be made. That view is but an extension of the magical thinking indulged in by Dorian Gray and his author and adopted by sympathetic biographers.

There is one last key to be considered to the allegories of *Dorian Gray*, and that is the key of allegory itself. Since Angus Fletcher's study (1979), there has been renewed interest shown in allegory, and poststructuralism has opened new perspectives on allegory from which we may profit.

When Paul de Man wrote in "Pascal's Allegory of Persuasion" that in the "wavering status of the allegorical sign, the system of which the allegorical is a constitutive component is being itself unsettled" (2), he might have cited *Dorian Gray* as an illustration. (He didn't.) When de Man later pointed to the paradox that allegory "pretends to order sequentially, in a narrative, what is actually the destruction of all sequence," he confirms for us what we have observed in Wilde's doing and undoing of allegory in his novel. In the pattern of its allegories, *The Picture of Dorian Gray* is a deconstructed novel.[7]

In this context, let us look back one more time upon the execution of Wilde's final revision of the novel and his attempt to establish the integrity of an aesthetic counter argument that art is superior to life because it is or should be self-referential. Jonathan Culler's *The Pursuit of Signs* can help us here. Paraphrasing J. Hillis Miller's methodology of deconstructive analysis, Culler writes: ". . . the text does not just contain or perform a self-deconstruction but is *about* self-deconstruction, so that a deconstructive reading is an interpretation of the text, an analysis of what it says or means" (15). Clearly this is the case with *Dorian Gray*: the self-deconstructive nature of the allegories and of the movement produced in the final revision has just been demonstrated, and the evidence for this in the manuscripts, the letters, essays, and stories is conclusive and overwhelming. Although Wilde did not begin his revisions in manuscript with a process in mind that we would call today self-deconstruction, he developed that process as the principle of the final version of *Dorian Gray* because he sought the effect of a dynamic indeterminacy of meaning.

Wilde discovered the way to self-deconstruction in his final revision of *Dorian Gray*. It was a development fully consistent with positions he had been establishing on the critical margins of his day in the reviews and essays he had been writing in the later eighties and with his experimental work in the short story, in particular in the fairy story for adults and the prose poem. To the man who wrote "all work criticizes itself" (*Reviews*: Vol. 13 in *First Collected Edition*, 360) and "A truth in art is that whose contradictory is also true" ("The Decay of Lying"), self-

---

7. I want to claim something different for *Dorian Gray* from that implied in the usual attribution of the term "deconstructed." Here's why: deconstruction is a critical dialectic, as I understand it, through which the critic anatomizes and controls the work of art or the text. Perhaps this is the very reason that one of the most obviously deconstructed works in English literature has to date received no formal attention from poststructuralists.

In *Dorian Gray*, Oscar Wilde turned from being the critic who had just written one of the earliest and still the best illustrations of deconstructionism, in "The Portrait of Mr. W. H.," and who had written one of the most subtle statements of deconstructionist philosophy, in "The Critic as Artist," to being a novelist. The result should not have surprised us. Wilde turned the dialectical tables upon his own critical position and that of criticism itself in writing (and rewriting) a narrative that may be deconstruction-proof because there is a deconstructive methodology built into the text already. This may be the only way an author can retain control of a work against the dialectic of the deconstructionally minded critic—that is, to use the deconstructive process as the principle of narrative. Wilde does nothing less than use what is clearly, explicitly, and deliberately what we would term a deconstructive strategy in organizing and balancing his novel between two conflicting allegorical schemes, each of which denies and thereby deconstructs the other, while neither is permitted to defeat the legitimacy of the other.

deconstruction came as naturally as dandyism. That is to say they were strategies or, as the Victorians liked to put it, poses.[8] In the case of *Dorian Gray*, Wilde's litotic design was developed so that the novel would never resolve itself as a moral or an immoral book; more appropriately for art, it would be neither. The counter-allegory resists the closure of the original moral allegory. Or to put it in other terms, "the discrepancy between sign and meaning (significant and signifie)" (de Man 12) is another key to an appreciation of Wilde's method in revising *Dorian Gray*. In the end, perhaps his attempts at modifying the dualism of the moral allegory are as revealing as the allegory itself. It seems that Wilde personalized allegory, as he later boasted in *De Profundis* he had personalized drama.

V

He also wrote in *De Profundis* that he stood in symbolic relations to the culture of his times. Even more could be said of his novel. It stands in symbolic relations not only to the times but also to its author in some rather special ways. At the switching point of Wilde's public and private selves, between the dandy and the social critic, the aesthetic imposter and the poet, the narratist and the dramatist, the novel sums up interests and tendencies of Wilde's earlier life and work while foreshadowing the emergence of its final phase.

We have looked into some of these relations as they relate to the allegories at work in the story and found them to be both more complex and subtler than criticism has heretofore suggested. More than that, a new critical foundation has been uncovered for the continued vitality of the text in the very indeterminacy of its meaning and the complementarity of its allegorical systems.

It is a fitting conclusion to a centenary essay to see how well the allegorical keys work in the lock of Dorian's upstairs room. Given the narrator's speculations on biological necessitarianism versus the illusion of free will, Dorian's selection of his nursery as the hiding place for the magic portrait invites attention. Indeed, as the argument develops, the nursery and its contents become the focus for the reader's growing sense of apprehension and moral revulsion. The nursery is the theater for the moral revelations of Dorian's conscience, representing true history through the painting's degeneration. Also, the nursery becomes the site for most of the sensational incidents of the novel: Basil's murder, Alan Camp-

---

8. In a review of George Sand's letters for *Pall Mall Gazette* (March 6, 1886) Wilde wrote: ". . . art for art's sake is not meant to express the final cause of art but is merely a formula of creation" (*Reviews* 49).

If Wilde is not the first deconstructionist critic, he should be recognized as both a forerunner and an influence. "The Portrait of Mr. W. H." and *Intentions* alone qualify him for that distinction, but there are hints of deconstructionist tendencies nearly everywhere in the prose, from "The Rise of Historical Criticism" to *De Profundis*. It was after all Wilde, writing in the tradition of Arnold and Pater, who argued in "The Critic as Artist" that criticism was higher than creation and that criticism was essentially a self-referential system.

bell's gothic postmortem, and Dorian's suicide. Without doubt, the nursery is the most dramatic location in the story.

Instead of being the repository of happy childhood memories, Dorian's nursery is the reliquary of the dusty books and forgotten playthings of a childhood that was unhappy and lonely, haunted by the ghosts of the boy's dead parents. It is haunted also, Dorian imagines, by a heredity that has predestined him to recapitulate the past and revive the maladies of the dead world. It is a room dominated by Dorian's authentic, hidden self and destined to be associated with the ghosts of Basil and Sibyl. There is a specific symbolic connection between Dorian's nursery and the fact that he chooses it as the hiding place for his magic portrait. It gives him a sense of power, control, safety—as Jung reported of his own case—that prove both as real and as illusory as the gothic world itself. The circumstances of his ancestry and birth, interpreted by the narrator in an idiom of gothic Darwinism, together with the conditions of his growing up and his education are thereby related to the role of the portrait as teacher and judge. As it stands in place of Dorian's pitiless grandfather and his former tutors, other eminences move from behind the portrait in Dorian's nursery to assume their full allegorical dimensions for the life and mind of the author.

The upstairs room is associated with the exorcism of schooling figures of both Dorian and Oscar Wilde also. They are among the avatars from whom Dorian wishes to free himself. Indeed, it is those allegorical presences that make the choice of an upstairs room such an exquisitely right one. When Dorian brings the portrait there, he places it in relation to other forces that have controlled his life and shaped his fate. From dead parents and ancestral avatars to schooling figures, they anticipate and modify the action of the portrait. It is difficult to avoid the conclusion that in the symbolism of gothicized art, the author escaped the dominant influences of his Oxford and post-Oxford development through an allegorical transaction.

The linkage of conscience with both childhood and heredity is consistent with Wilde's idealized treatment of childhood innocence and at the same time echoes his assertion that the very existence of conscience represents a social avatar. Dorian's identifications of the portrait with his soul and the changes with his conscience define the terms of his obsessive attraction and at the same time repulsion. The portrait as the emblem of both conscience and the gothic world is denied by neither Dorian nor the narrator. In fact, Wilde places his chief symbol in the same relation to the modern world and its ruling class as he related gothic to the themes of childhood and heredity.

Another answer to our question about the choice of the upstairs room lies in its symbolism as supported by the allegory. The painting is not merely a piece of incriminating evidence to be suppressed. If it were, it should have been walled up or buried in the basement, where suppressed or repudiated things symbolically reside. Its authority is rather

456   DONALD L. LAWLER

exalted than denied, and therefore it must be hidden away where it chal-
lenges the higher faculties of conscience, mind, and imagination because
its struggle is against will. How fitting that the nursery links the portrait
to Dorian's lost childhood, representing lost innocence, and to his ancestry,
for it was in heredity, as the new biology prophesied, that the futility of
action and the paradox of free will are dramatized for the contemporary
reader at the very juncture of moral and aesthetic allegory. Both higher
and lower faculties are incorporated into the picture's text: conscious and
unconscious life being one continuous process. Allegorically, Dorian's
painting is in its proper place as Wilde's emblem of the gothic world.

Surely it is Wilde's own ambivalence that is expressed in the allegories
of *Dorian Gray*. Allegory is a form whose very nature has been identified
recently by two of its most subtle critics, Fletcher and de Man, with
ambivalence, paradox, self-contradiction; and form in *Dorian Gray* is
an integer of its meanings. Although it has been traditional to trace the
special power of *Dorian Gray* to the archetype embedded in the moral
allegory, what Pater called the "special fascination" of the story relies as
well on the artistry with which Wilde combined elements taken from
the gothic, social comedy, melodrama, and the rest of his layered allegory.

This study of Wilde's uses of allegory puts us in a position to form an
appreciation of the rich substructures of *Dorian Gray* concealed beneath
its apparent simplicity of plotting and character presentation. We recognize that Wilde did much in his revisions to contest and modify the
original moral allegory that directed what Fletcher calls an "authoritative, thematic, 'correct' reading" of his text (305). Wilde revised his novel
to deny such closure and to encourage a more complex response by
suggesting potential variants of the main allegory and its related modes.
When he finished, he had made a work "mined with a motion," to use
Hopkins's phrase, rather than one at rest. It is a novel whose various and
sometimes contradictory modes and features have been a legacy that has
enriched our culture and employed its critics for the past century and
promises to do so for as long as people are fascinated by the story of
Dorian Gray and the secrets of his upstairs room.

Works Cited

Brasol, Boris. *Oscar Wilde: The Man, the Artist, the Martyr*. New York: Scribner's, 1938.
Burdett, Osbert. *The Beardsley Period*. New York: Boni & Liveright, 1925.
Croft-Cooke, Rupert. *The Unrecorded Life of Oscar Wilde*. London: Allen, 1972.
Culler, Jonathan. *The Pursuit of Signs*. Ithaca: Cornell UP, 1981.
de Man, Paul. *Blindness and Insight*. 2nd ed. Minneapolis: U of Minnesota P, 1983.
Ellmann, Richard. *Golden Codgers*. New York: Oxford UP, 1973.
———. *Oscar Wilde: A Collection of Critical Essays*. Englewood Cliffs: Prentice-Hall, 1969.
Ervine, St. John. *Oscar Wilde: A Present-Time Appraisal*. New York: Morrow, 1925.
Espey, John. "Resources for Wilde Studies at the Clark Library." *Oscar Wilde: Two Approaches*.
    Ed. Richard Ellmann and John Espey. Los Angeles: William Andrews Clark Memorial Library,
    1977.
Fletcher, Angus. *Allegory: The Theory of a Symbolic Mode*. Ithaca: Cornell UP, 1964.

Gide, André. *Oscar Wilde*. 1905; London: Oxford UP, 1951.

Jullian, Phillipe. *Oscar Wilde*. London: Constable, 1969.

Jung, Karl G. *Collected Works* 15. Ed. William McGuire, et al. New York: Pantheon, 1966. 19 Vols.

————. *Memories, Dreams, Reflections*. New York: Pantheon, 1963.

Kernahan, Coulson. *In Good Company*. London: Lane, 1917.

Mason, Stuart [pseud. Christopher S. Millard]. *Oscar Wilde: Art and Morality*. London: Jacobs, 1908; rpt. New York: Haskell House, 1971.

Lawler, Donald L. "Oscar Wilde's First Manuscript of *The Picture of Dorian Gray*." *SB* 25 (1972): 125–35.

————. "The Revisions of Dorian Gray." *VIJ* 3 (1974): 21–36.

Mitchell, Sir Peter Chalmers. *My Fill of Days*. London: Faber, 1937.

Murray, Isobel, ed. *The Picture of Dorian Gray*. By Oscar Wilde. London: Oxford UP, 1974.

————. "Some Elements in the Composition of *The Picture of Dorian Gray*." *Durham University Journal* 64 (June 1972): 220–31.

O'Brien, Kevin. "Oscar Wilde and Canadian Artists." *Antagonish Review* 1 (Winter 1971): 11–28.

Pearson, Hesketh. *Oscar Wilde*. New York: Harper, 1946.

Sherard, Robert H. *The Life of Oscar Wilde*. London: Laurie, 1906; New York: Kennerley, 1907.

————. *Bernard Shaw, Frank Harris and Oscar Wilde*. New York: T. Werner Laurie, 1937.

Oscar Wilde. *The Complete Works of Oscar Wilde*. Rev. ed. Ed. Vyvyan Holland. London: Collins, 1966.

————. *First Collected Edition of the Works of Oscar Wilde*. Ed. Robert Ross. Vols. 1–11, 13–24. London: Methuen, 1908; Boston: Luce, 1910. Vol. 12. Paris: Carrington, 1908.

————. *Intentions*. London: Osgood, McIlvaine; New York: Dodd, Mead, 1891.

————. *The Letters of Oscar Wilde*. Ed. Rupert Hart-Davis. London: Hart-Davis; New York: Harcourt, 1962.

————. *More Letters of Oscar Wilde*. Ed. Rupert Hart-Davis. New York: Vanguard, 1985.

Yeats, William Butler. *A Vision*. New York: Macmillan, 1961.

Oscar Wilde:
A Chronology

1854   Born October 16, 1854. Second son of Dr. (later Sir) William Wills and Jane Francesca Elgee Wilde. Sir William was a famous surgeon and author of both medical books and studies of Irish folklore and custom. Before her marriage, Lady Wilde became famous throughout Ireland under the name "Speranza," for writing passionate editorials calling for Irish independence. She later collected and wrote on folktales and sponsored literary salons in Dublin and London. Oscar Wilde's older brother, Willie, a journalist, died an alcoholic in London the year before Oscar died in Paris. A sister, Iseult, died in 1867, her eleventh year.

1864–74   Wilde attended Portora Royal School, Enniskillen (until 1871), and then Trinity College, Dublin, where he won the Berkeley Gold Medal for Greek and a scholarship to Magdalen College, Oxford.

1874–78   While at Oxford, Wilde traveled twice to Italy, the second time to Greece also, with J. P. Mahaffy, his tutor at Trinity College. These trips confirmed Wilde's devotion to Greek art and culture and his fascination with the culture of the Italian Renaissance. While a student at Oxford, Wilde was influenced first by the social and moral earnestness of John Ruskin and then, later, by the aesthetic impressionism of Walter Pater. Wilde's career at Oxford ended triumphantly. In 1876, he took a first in Moderations in the Honors School and completed his double first in 1878 with a first in Classical Moderations. He also won the Newdigate Poetry Prize that same year for "Ravenna."

1879   Wilde's hopes for an academic career were dashed when his essay "The Rise of Historical Criticism" failed to win the Chancellor's Prize, which was not awarded that year, and when he failed to be elected a fellow. He then turned to the literary and cultural world of London, determined to become if not famous then notorious. He became both.

1880–81   Wilde established himself as the leading aesthete in London, took to wearing outlandish costumes, worshipped sun-flowers and Lillie Langtry (calling her the "New Helen"), and indulged the pleasures of being lampooned in *Punch*. In 1880, he published his first play, *Vera, or The Nihilists*.

1881–82   *Poems* appeared in June 1881 to generally unfavorable review. Wilde agreed to undertake a lecture tour in the United States, sponsored by D' Oyly Carte, who intended to use Wilde to promote trade for the latest Gilbert and Sullivan operetta, *Patience*, which burlesqued British Aestheticism. Wilde's tour was an unexpected success, lasting a full year and taking him around the country and into Canada.

1883   A year divided among Paris, New York (to attend production of his play *Vera*, which proved a failure), and London. He also began an English lecture tour on his impressions of America.

1884–87   Wilde married Constance Lloyd on May 29, 1884, and undertook domestic life at 16 Tite Street, Chelsea. Two sons were born of the marriage: Cyril in 1885 and Vyvyan in 1886. Wilde wrote reviews and literary columns for the London quarterlies. In 1887, he became editor of *Woman's World*. In 1886, he met Robert Ross, who later claimed to have introduced Wilde to homosexuality.

1887–89   Wilde turns from a man of letters to the author of short stories and critical essays, gradually relinquishing his editorship and his active reviewing. *The Happy Prince and Other Tales* appeared in May 1888; "Pen, Pencil and Poison," in the *Fortnightly Review*, and "The Decay of Lying," in the *Nineteenth Century*, both appeared in January 1889; and "The Portrait of Mr. W. H." was published in *Blackwood's* in July 1889.

1890–91   Eighteen-ninety opened with Wilde's public quarrel with Whistler over the latter's charge of plagiarism. *The Picture of Dorian Gray* appeared in *Lippincott's*, creating public debate in the press on the subject of art and morality. In rapid succession, Wilde published "The True Function and Value of Criticism" in two parts, later retitled "The Critic as Artist" when collected in *Intentions* (1891); "The Soul of Man under Socialism" and "The Preface to *Dorian Gray*" in the *Fortnightly Review* (February and March 1891); the revised, bound version of *The Picture of Dorian Gray* (April); *Lord Arthur Savile's Crime and Other Stories* (July); *A House of Pomegranates* (November). Also, in January 1891, *The Duchess of Padua*, a play, was anonymously produced in New York under the title *Guido Ferranti*.

1892–94   Writes *Salomé* in French; later denied license for English production. *Lady Windermere's Fan* produced (February

1892), his first theatrical success. A *Woman of No Importance* (1893), another successful production. *The Sphinx* (1894). *Salomé* translated by Lord Alfred Douglas (1894). "Poems in Prose" in the *Fortnightly Review* (July 1894). "Phrases and Philosophies for the Use of the Young" in *The Chameleon* (December 1894). In 1893 Wilde took rooms at the Savoy Hotel and lived away from his Tite Street home regularly thereafter, moving from place to place in London and abroad, frequently in the company of Lord Alfred Douglas, whom he more or less supported.

1895–97   Wilde and Douglas in Algiers. *An Ideal Husband* opens in January 1895 and *The Importance of Being Earnest* in February in London to rave reviews. In March Wilde brings libel action against the marquess of Queensberry. On the trial's third day, Wilde withdraws; Queensberry acquitted with costs. Wilde arrested that evening (April 5). Wilde's possessions sold at auction (April 24). Twice tried at the Old Bailey: first trial ends in hung jury, the second in conviction and sentence of two-year imprisonment at hard labor. Wilde transferred to Wandsworth and later Reading Gaol to serve his sentence in solitary confinement. Mother dies (February 1896). Wilde completes letter to Alfred Douglas, later titled *De Profundis*. Wilde released from prison May 19, 1897. Leaves England for Berneval, France, under pseudonym Sebastian Melmoth.

1898–   *The Ballad of Reading Gaol* published (February 1898).
1900   Constance Wilde dies in Genoa (April 1898). Wilde travels in Europe. Willie Wilde dies (March 1899). Wilde received into Roman Catholic church on deathbed and dies November 30, 1900. Burial in Bagneaux, Paris. Remains removed to Pére Lachaise, Paris, by his executor, Robert Ross, in 1909.

Selected Bibliography

Except for Wilde's own publications and editions, books from which selections have been taken for this volume and essays that are reprinted in this volume are not listed here.

WORKS

Poems. London: Bogue; Boston: Roberts, 1881.

"L'Envoi." [Introduction.] *Rose Leaf and Apple Leaf.* By Rennell Rodd. Philadelphia: Stoddart, 1882.

The Happy Prince and Other Tales. London: Nutt; Boston: Roberts, 1888.

"The Portrait of Mr. W. H." *Blackwood's Edinburgh Magazine* 146 (July 1889): 1–21. Enl. ed. New York: Kennerley, 1921. Later ed. London: Methuen, 1958.

"The Soul of Man under Socialism." *The Fortnightly Review* 49 (February 1891). Rpt. Arthur L. Humphreys, 1895, 1907, as *The Soul of Man*; and in 1912 intro. Robert Ross as *The Soul of Man Under Socialism.*

The Picture of Dorian Gray. Lippincott's Monthly Magazine 46 (July 1890): 3–100; London: Ward, Lock and Company, 1891.

The Picture of Dorian Gray. Ed. Wilfried Edener. Nurnburg: Carl, 1964.

The Picture of Dorian Gray. Ed. Isobel Murray. London: Oxford UP, 1974.

Intentions. London: Osgood, McIlvaine; New York: Dodd, Mead, 1891.

Lord Arthur Savile's Crime and Other Stories. London: Osgood, McIlvaine; New York: Dodd, Mead, 1891.

A House of Pomegranates. London: Osgood, McIlvaine, 1891; New York: Dodd, Mead, 1892.

Lady Windermere's Fan. London: Mathews and Lane, Bodley Head, 1893. Opened at St. James Theatre in February, 1892.

Salomé: drame en un acte. Paris: Librarie de l'Art Independent, 1893. Trans. Alfred Douglas. London: Mathews and Lane, Bodley Head, 1893. London: Mathews and Lane; Boston: Copeland and Day, 1894. Produced at Théâtre de L'oeuvre, Paris in February, 1896.

The Sphinx. London: Mathews and Lane, Bodley Head; Boston: Copeland and Day, 1894.

A Woman of No Importance. London: Mathews and Lane, Bodley Head, 1894. Opened at Haymarket Theatre, London in April, 1893.

The Ballad of Reading Gaol [pseud. C.3.3.]. London: Smithers, 1898.

The Importance of Being Earnest. London: Smithers, 1899. Opened at the St. James Theatre, London, in February 1895.

An Ideal Husband. London: Smithers, 1898. Opened at the Haymarket Theatre, London, in January 1895.

De Profundis. London: Methuen; New York: Putnam, 1905. The first of numerous incomplete texts of Wilde's famous letter from prison. The complete, authoritative text appears in *Letters* (1962).

COLLECTED EDITIONS

First Collected Edition of the Works of Oscar Wilde. Ed. Robert Ross. Vols. 1–11, 13–24. London: Methuen, 1908; Boston: Luce, 1910. Vol. 12. Paris: Carrington, 1908. The *Second Collected Edition* appeared in 1909 (vols. 1–12), 1910 (vol. 13), and 1912 (vol. 14).

The Complete Works of Oscar Wilde. Rev. ed. Ed. Vyvyan Holland. London: Collins, 1966.

The Annotated Oscar Wilde. Ed. H. Montgomery Hyde. New York: Potter, 1982.

LETTERS

The Letters of Oscar Wilde. Ed. Rupert Hart-Davis. London: Hart-Davis; New York: Harcourt, 1962.

More Letters of Oscar Wilde. Ed. Rupert Hart-Davis. New York: Vanguard, 1985.

BIBLIOGRAPHIES

Fletcher, Ian, and John Stokes. "Oscar Wilde." *Recent Research on Anglo-Irish Writers*. Ed. Richard Finneran. New York: Modern Language Association, 1983.
Mason, Stuart [pseud. Christopher S. Millard]. *Bibliography of Oscar Wilde*. London: Laurie, 1914; rpt. London: Rota, 1967.
Mikhail, E. H. *Oscar Wilde: An Annotated Bibliography of Criticism*. Totowa: Roman, 1978.

BIOGRAPHIES

Byrne, Patrick. *The Wildes of Merrion Square*. London: Staples, 1953.
Croft-Cooke, Rupert. *The Unrecorded Life of Oscar Wilde*. London: Allen, 1972.
Douglas, Lord Alfred. *My Friendship with Oscar Wilde*. New York: Coventry, 1932. First pub. as *The Autobiography of Lord Alfred Douglas*. London: Martin Secker, 1929.
———. *Oscar Wilde and Myself*. London: Long; New York: Duffield, 1914.
———. *A Summing Up*. London: Duckworth, 1940.
———. *Without Apology*. London: Richards, 1938.
Harris, Frank. *The Life and Confessions of Oscar Wilde*. New York: Dell, 1960.
Hyde, H. Montgomery. *Oscar Wilde*. New York: Farrar, 1975.
Pearson, Hesketh. *Oscar Wilde*. New York: Harper, 1946.
Ricketts, Charles. *Recollections of Oscar Wilde*. London: Nonesuch, 1932.
Sherard, Robert H. *The Life of Oscar Wilde*. London: Laurie, 1906; New York: Kennerley, 1907.

CRITICISM

Beckson, Karl. *Oscar Wilde: The Critical Heritage*. New York: Barnes and Noble, 1970.
Bloom, Harold, ed. *Oscar Wilde*. New York: Chelsea, 1985.
Brasol, Boris. *Oscar Wilde: The Man, the Artist, the Martyr*. New York: Scribner's, 1938.
Braybrook, Patrick. *Oscar Wilde: A Study*. London: Braithwaite, 1930.
Broad, Lewis. *The Friendships and Follies of Oscar Wilde*. New York: Crowell, 1955.
Chamberlin, J. E. *Ripe Was the Drowsy Hour: The Age of Oscar Wilde*. New York: Seabury, 1977.
Cohen, Philip. *The Moral Vision of Oscar Wilde*. Rutherford: Fairleigh Dickinson UP, 1978.
Ellmann, Richard. *The Artist as Critic: Critical Writings of Oscar Wilde*. Englewood Cliffs: Prentice-Hall, 1969.
———, and John Espey. *Oscar Wilde: Two Approaches*. Los Angeles: Clark Library, 1977.
Holland, Vyvyan. *Son of Oscar Wilde*. London: Hart-Davis, 1954.
Hyde, H. Montgomery. *The Cleveland Street Scandal*. New York: Coward, 1976.
———. *Their Good Names*. London: Hamilton, 1970.
———. *The Trials of Wilde*. London: Hodge, 1948; Enl. ed. pub. as *The Three Trials of Oscar Wilde*. New York: NYU Press, 1956.
Jones, John B. "In Search of Archibald Grosvenor: A New Look at Gilbert's *Patience*." *Victorian Studies* 3 (1965): 45–53.
Kernahan, Coulson. *In Good Company*. London: Lane, 1917.
Kronenberg, Louis. *Oscar Wilde*. Boston: Little, Brown, 1976.
Lawler, Donald L. "Oscar Wilde's First Manuscript of *The Picture of Dorian Gray*." *SB* 25 (1972): 125–35.
———. "Oscar Wilde in the *New Cambridge Bibliography of English Literature*." *PBSA* 67 (1973): 172–88.
———. "The Revisions of *Dorian Gray*." *Victorian Institute Journal* 3 (1974): 21–36.
Lawler, Donald L., and Charles E. Knott. "The Context of Invention: Suggested Origins of *Dorian Gray*." *Modern Philology* 73 (1976): 389–98.
Lloyd, Lewis, and Henry Justin Smith. *Oscar Wilde Discovers America*. New York: Harcourt, 1936.
Nassaar, Christopher S. *Into the Demon Universe: A Literary Exploration of Oscar Wilde*. New Haven: Yale UP, 1974.
Ojala, Aatos. *Aestheticism and Oscar Wilde*. 2 vols. Helsinki: 1954.
Ransome, Arthur. *Oscar Wilde: A Critical Study*. London: Secker, 1912.
San Juan, Epifanio Jr. *The Art of Oscar Wilde*. Princeton: Princeton UP, 1967.
Shewan, Rodney. *Oscar Wilde: Art and Egoism*. New York: Barnes and Noble, 1977.
Simpson, Colin, et al. *The Cleveland Street Affair*. Boston: Little, Brown, 1976.
Symons, Arthur. *A Study of Oscar Wilde*. London: Sawyer, 1930.
Winwar, Francis. *Oscar Wilde and the Yellow Nineties*. New York: Harper, 1940.

ANDERSON Winesburg, Ohio edited by Charles E. Modlin and Ray Lewis White
AQUINAS St. Thomas Aquinas on Politics and Ethics translated and edited by
Paul E. Sigmund
AUSTEN Emma edited by Stephen M. Parrish Second Edition
AUSTEN Persuasion edited by Patricia Meyer Spacks
AUSTEN Pride and Prejudice edited by Donald Gray Second Edition
BEHN Oroonoko edited by Joanna Lipking
Beowulf (the Donaldson translation) edited by Joseph F. Tuso
BLAKE Blake's Poetry and Designs selected and edited by Mary Lynn Johnson and
John E. Grant
BOCCACCIO The Decameron selected, translated, and edited by Mark Musa and
Peter E. Bondanella
BRONTË CHARLOTTE Jane Eyre edited by Richard J. Dunn Second Edition
BRONTË EMILY Wuthering Heights edited by William M. Sale, Jr., and Richard Dunn
Third Edition
BROWNING Aurora Leigh edited by Margaret Reynolds
BROWNING, ROBERT Browning's Poetry selected and edited by James F. Loucks
BYRON Byron's Poetry selected and edited by Frank D. McConnell
CARROLL Alice in Wonderland edited by Donald J. Gray Second Edition
CERVANTES Don Quixote (the Ormsby translation, revised) edited by Joseph R. Jones and
Kenneth Douglas
CHAUCER The Canterbury Tales: Nine Tales and the General Prologue edited by
V. A. Kolve and Glending Olson
CHEKHOV Anton Chekhov's Plays translated and edited by Eugene K. Bristow
CHEKHOV Anton Chekhov's Short Stories selected and edited by Ralph E. Matlaw
CHOPIN The Awakening edited by Margo Culley Second Edition
CLEMENS Adventures of Huckleberry Finn edited by Sculley Bradley,
Richmond Croom Beatty, E. Hudson Long, and Thomas Cooley Second Edition
CLEMENS A Connecticut Yankee in King Arthur's Court edited by Allison R. Ensor
CLEMENS Pudd'nhead Wilson and Those Extraordinary Twins edited by Sidney E. Berger
CONRAD Heart of Darkness edited by Robert Kimbrough Third Edition
CONRAD Lord Jim edited by Thomas C. Moser Second Edition
CONRAD The Nigger of the "Narcissus" edited by Robert Kimbrough
CRANE Maggie: A Girl of the Streets edited by Thomas A. Gullason
CRANE The Red Badge of Courage edited by Donald Pizer Third Edition
DARWIN Darwin selected and edited by Philip Appleman Second Edition
DEFOE A Journal of the Plague Year edited by Paula R. Backscheider
DEFOE Moll Flanders edited by Edward Kelly
DEFOE Robinson Crusoe edited by Michael Shinagel Second Edition
DE PIZAN The Selected Writings of Christine de Pizan translated by Renate
Blumenfeld-Kosinski and Kevin Brownlee edited by Renate Blumenfeld-Kosinski
DICKENS Bleak House edited by George Ford and Sylvère Monod
DICKENS David Copperfield edited by Jerome H. Buckley
DICKENS Hard Times edited by George Ford and Sylvère Monod Second Edition
DICKENS Oliver Twist edited by Fred Kaplan
DONNE John Donne's Poetry selected and edited by Arthur L. Clements Second Edition
DOSTOEVSKY The Brothers Karamazov (the Garnett translation) edited by Ralph E. Matlaw
DOSTOEVSKY Crime and Punishment (the Coulson translation) edited by George Gibian
Third Edition
DOSTOEVSKY Notes from Underground translated and edited by Michael R. Katz
DOUGLASS Narrative of the Life of Frederick Douglass, an American Slave, Written by Himself
edited by William L. Andrews and William S. McFeely

DREISER Sister Carrie edited by Donald Pizer Second Edition
Eight Modern Plays edited by Anthony Caputi
ELIOT Middlemarch edited by Bert G. Hornback
ELIOT The Mill on the Floss edited by Carol T. Christ
ERASMUS The Praise of Folly and Other Writings translated and edited by Robert M. Adams
FAULKNER The Sound and the Fury edited by David Minter Second Edition
FIELDING Joseph Andrews with Shamela and Related Writings edited by Homer Goldberg
FIELDING Tom Jones edited by Sheridan Baker Second Edition
FLAUBERT Madame Bovary edited with a substantially new translation by Paul de Man
FORD The Good Soldier edited by Martin Stannard
FRANKLIN Benjamin Franklin's Autobiography edited by J. A. Leo Lemay and P. M. Zall
GOETHE Faust translated by Walter Arndt, edited by Cyrus Hamlin
GOGOL Dead Souls (the Reavey translation) edited by George Gibian
HARDY Far from the Madding Crowd edited by Robert C. Schweik
HARDY Jude the Obscure edited by Norman Page
HARDY The Mayor of Casterbridge edited by James K. Robinson
HARDY The Return of the Native edited by James Gindin
HARDY Tess of the d'Urbervilles edited by Scott Elledge Third Edition
HAWTHORNE The Blithedale Romance edited by Seymour Gross and Rosalie Murphy
HAWTHORNE The House of the Seven Gables edited by Seymour Gross
HAWTHORNE Nathaniel Hawthorne's Tales edited by James McIntosh
HAWTHORNE The Scarlet Letter edited by Seymour Gross, Sculley Bradley,
Richmond Croom Beatty, and E. Hudson Long Third Edition
HERBERT George Herbert and the Seventeenth-Century Religious Poets selected and edited by
Mario A. DiCesare
HERODOTUS The Histories translated and selected by Walter E. Blanco, edited by
Walter E. Blanco and Jennifer Roberts
HOBBES Leviathan edited by Richard E. Flathman and David Johnston
HOMER The Odyssey translated and edited by Albert Cook Second Edition
HOWELLS The Rise of Silas Lapham edited by Don L. Cook
IBSEN The Wild Duck translated and edited by Dounia B. Christiani
JAMES The Ambassadors edited by S. P. Rosenbaum Second Edition
JAMES The American edited by James W. Tuttleton
JAMES The Portrait of a Lady edited by Robert D. Bamberg Second Edition
JAMES Tales of Henry James edited by Christof Wegelin
JAMES The Turn of the Screw edited by Robert Kimbrough
JAMES The Wings of the Dove edited by J. Donald Crowley and Richard A. Hocks
JONSON Ben Jonson and the Cavalier Poets selected and edited by Hugh Maclean
JONSON Ben Jonson's Plays and Masques selected and edited by Robert M. Adams
KAFKA The Metamorphosis translated and edited by Stanley Corngold
LAFAYETTE The Princess of Clèves edited and with a revised translation by John D. Lyons
MACHIAVELLI The Prince translated and edited by Robert M. Adams Second Edition
MALTHUS An Essay on the Principle of Population edited by Philip Appleman
MANN Death in Venice translated and edited by Clayton Koelb
MARX The Communist Manifesto edited by Frederic L. Bender
MELVILLE The Confidence-Man edited by Hershel Parker
MELVILLE Moby-Dick edited by Harrison Hayford and Hershel Parker
MEREDITH The Egoist edited by Robert M. Adams
Middle English Lyrics selected and edited by Maxwell S. Luria and Richard L. Hoffman
Middle English Romances selected and edited by Stephen H. A. Shepherd
MILL Mill selected and edited by Alan Ryan